Oceans

Oceans

Trevor Day

Facts On File, Inc.

Oceans

Facts On File, Inc.
11 Penn Plaza
New York NY 10001

Library of Congress Cataloging-in-Publication Data

Day, Trevor.
    Oceans / Trevor Day.
        p.   cm.—(Ecosystem)
    Includes bibliographical references and index.
    ISBN 0-8160-3647-0 (alk. paper)
    1. Oceanography. I. Title. II. Series.
GC11.2.D39 1999
551.46—dc21   98-18110

Facts On File books are available at special discounts when purchased in bulk quantities for businesses, associations, institutions or sales promotions. Please call our Special Sales Department in New York at (212) 967-8800 or (800) 322-8755.

You can find Facts On File on the World Wide Web at http://www.factsonfile.com

Text design by Cathy Rincon and Sandra Watanabe
Cover design by Cathy Rincon
Illustrations by Richard Garratt

Printed in Hong Kong

Creative FOF 10 9 8 7 6 5 4 3 2 1

Contents

Acknowledgments

The author would particularly like to thank the following people and organizations:

Wendy Perry, educationalist; Emanuela Molinaroli of the University of Venice; and Len Hockley, shipping analyst, for reviewing sections of the manuscript.

The staff of Southampton Oceanography Center, National Oceanographic Library, and Somerset Library Services for their great efforts in obtaining material on my behalf.

Students: on my courses at the University of Bath, for their constructive and inspirational comments.

Hilary Poole, for her attentive, enthusiastic, and good-humored editorial management of this book, and Eleanora von Dehsen, at Facts On File, for her guiding hand on the project.

Richard Garratt, for supplying the illustrations, and Sarah Pagliasotti, Gerry Ellis, and the photographers of ENP Images.

Finally, to my partner, Christina Malkowska, who never fails to be a source of encouragement and support.

In the history of planet Earth life has existed on land only one-tenth of the time it has flourished in the oceans. Several authors of books about the oceans argue that Earth should be called Oceanus or some such name. From our modern perspective, they are right. It is our land-based focus—the importance we attach to the ground beneath our feet—that makes us name the planet after the soil we walk on. Centuries ago, it was also our ignorance of the size and importance of the oceans that made us call our planet *Earth*.

This book is one of a series about different ecosystems on Earth. The other titles address ecosystems that are land-based. Even lakes and rivers are really small depressions on the land surface. Oceans are different.

Consider the land surface of the planet. Deserts cover about 23 percent of its surface (or 7 percent of the planet) and agricultural land for crops and grazing about 30 percent (9 percent), while truly "natural" environments cover perhaps 30–40 percent (9–12 percent); a proportion of that is ice. Contrast this with the oceans. About 8 percent of ocean area (about 6 percent of the planet's surface) is occupied by shallow waters of continental shelves, where much of the ocean's biological and economic productivity is concentrated. This is where the bulk of fishing and oil and mineral exploration takes place; it is also where marine pollution is concentrated. The remaining 92 percent of the ocean surface (about 64 percent of the planet) overlies water greater than 200 meters (about 650 feet) deep. By comparison to coastal waters, these waters are barely exploited, although to do so requires overcoming formidable technical challenges.

The oceans, in comparison to land-based habitats, are a much more three-dimensional environment. We can put aside the air as a habitat—which, in any case, extends above the sea as well as above the land. If we do so, on land the thin veneer that teems with life extends a few meters below the surface (in the soil) and a few tens of meters above the land surface (to the tree canopy). There are some exceptions to this, such as cave systems, which penetrate hundreds of meters underground, but these are rare. The

Waves breaking off Cape Kiranda, along the northern Oregon coast (D.C. Lowe/ENP Images)

oceans, on the other hand, are kilometers deep over much of Earth's surface, and although life-forms are sparse over much of their depth, the oceans teem with life in the surface waters and over much of the seafloor. Seen in this way, the oceans make up about 98 percent (by volume) of the biosphere. Whichever way you look at it, this book has a lot of ground—or rather, water—to cover.

Thinking about the world under the sea does take a leap of the imagination. Compared to our everyday experience on land, the seas are an upside-down world. On land, we stand and look upward to the tops of the trees. In the sea, we start at the water surface and look down toward the seafloor. In a sense, this is akin to floating above the treetops and looking down through the branches to the ground below. As we shall see in Part 5, this comparison is not as strange as it sounds.

Studying the Oceans

Oceanography is a relatively new science. It is only since the mid-18th century, when longitude could be reliably determined, that the oceans have been charted with accuracy. Oceanography as an interdisciplinary science—one that drew together the findings from biology, chemistry, physics, and geology—began to emerge in the late 19th century. It is only in the 20th century that we have really begun to appreciate the interrelatedness of natural processes on land, in the sea, and in the air.

Part 1 explores the geography of the oceans. It explains prevailing scientific ideas about how planet Earth came to be formed and how the oceans were born. For convenience, we describe ocean environments as separate provinces, but in reality they form one continuous superocean. Oceans and major seas are considered individually, including their geology, water circulation, the human populations associated with them, their living and nonliving resources, and the environmental issues of particular importance. Part 1 concludes by considering the oceans' boundaries that link the seas to the land.

Part 2 reveals how Earth's geology accounts for the nature and shape of the oceans. Since the 1950s, with the gradual acceptance of plate tectonics and the movement of continents, marine geology has undergone a revolutionary change. We now know that the world's ocean basins—the depressions that contain the world's oceans—are changing and have, in fact, done so since they were created. Even within the span of a person's lifetime, the Atlantic Ocean is becoming measurably narrower and the Red Sea broader. Part 2 picks up the story from Part 1, considers the geological structure of the planet in more detail, and reveals the relationship between oceans and continents. Sections explain where water is found and how it is cycled between land, sea, and air. The sections plot the evolution of the oceans and describe the structure of a "typical" ocean basin. Sections on sediments and shoreline processes lead to a consideration of how geological forces and climatic changes—including global warming—are altering today's sea levels. Part 2 finishes with an overview of recent developments in marine geology, from satellite remote sensing, sonar, and submersibles to the use of computers in running models to describe (and hopefully predict) the effects of global warming on sea-level change.

In Part 3, the physical and chemical nature of the oceans is explored. Water's unusual physical and chemical properties have left their mark on the planet. Water determines climatic conditions, shapes the landscape, and determines where life is to be found. In the ocean, water's physical properties—its transparency, its ability to transmit sound, and its capacity to absorb, store, and transmit heat—create demands and opportunities that organisms must conquer or exploit in order to survive. Growing awareness about how chemicals in the water column and at the bottom of the sea are cycled between land, sea, and air is making scientists appreciate the intimate connection between diverse environments. This understanding is vital if we are to avoid (or to help counter) some of humanity's worst impacts on the global ecosystem.

Part 4 concerns the interactions between ocean and atmosphere. Meteorologists (those who study weather and climate) and oceanographers often talk of the ocean-atmosphere system, so intimately do the two environments interact. It is differential heating by the Sun—in other words, Earth is warmer at the equator than at the poles—and the way that this heating pattern changes with the seasons that both determine the planet's weather and climate and power Earth's wind systems and ocean currents. The oceans represent huge heat stores that carry heat from the tropics toward the poles and thus moderate the world's climate. Air pollution that enhances the greenhouse effect seems to be giving rise to global warming—arguably the planet's most serious environmental problem as we enter the 21st century.

Part 5 surveys the rich biology of the oceans. Beginning with the evolution and diversity of life-forms, the chapter goes on to consider the many different habitats—across the ocean's surface and down into its depths—that are parts of the ocean domain. Notable aspects of animal behavior, particularly vertical and horizontal migrations, are considered. Fishes, reptiles, birds, and mammals are explored in some detail, as are some of the most diverse and threatened biological communities: mangrove swamps, coral reefs, seagrass meadows, and kelp forests. Part 5 concludes with intriguing new developments in marine biology. Discoveries on the ocean floor are rapidly changing the way we view oceanic ecosystems, both in terms of their biogeochemical cycles and the biochemical resources that are found there. Technological developments—from computer modeling to satellite remote sensing—mean that scientists can now track biological phenomena over vast areas and test the predictions of their ecosystem models. Such developments are crucial if we are to maintain healthy and productive oceanic systems.

In Part 6, the spotlight shifts to the oceans as a backdrop for historical events. Many of the world's epoch-making battles have occurred at sea, and in peacetime or war, the bulk of global trade is still transported by ships across oceans. The history of humankind—from prehistoric times to the present day—is inextricably tied to a population's capacity to cross the oceans. Human migrations across seas have determined the nature and distribution of most human cultures today, and much of our archaeological heritage has still to be wrestled from the ocean floor.

Part 7 plots the progression of humankind's exploration of the oceans from ancient times to the present day. For much of human history, travel across the sea has been accomplished in relatively frail craft propelled by oarsmen, driven by winds, or drifting on ocean currents. The last 200 years,

however, have seen oceangoing vessels progress from sailing ships to nuclear-powered submarines. Artificial satellites now monitor the oceans from space, and underwater vehicles—whether piloted or remote controlled—can reach the deeper parts of the sea. Computer technology that retrieves and manipulates remotely sensed data is generating "virtual" ocean panoramas. Navigational technology has similarly undergone transformation. A small "black box" on board ship, communicating with satellites overhead, now fixes a vessel's position to within a few tens of meters.

The last 30 years have seen the realizable economic value of the oceans increase at an astonishing rate, although this increase is now plateauing. During that time, the annual catch of marine fish has increased fivefold, and marine oil and gas exploration has increased from almost nothing to an annual revenue worth hundreds of billions of dollars. The future, as Part 8 explains, opens up possibilities for abundant mineral supplies from the ocean floor and clean, renewable energy from the moving sea, plus medicinal drugs and other useful chemicals extracted from the vast biological wealth of the oceans.

The exploitation of the oceans has its costs, as Part 9 makes clear. We treat the oceans as dumping grounds, destroying or damaging many coastal habitats and removing many of the ocean's inhabitants at a rate that cannot be sustained. Many populations of sea creatures—from gigantic whales to tiny corals, snails, and clams—have been decimated by hunting, fishing, or collecting. Some species have been driven to extinction. We are in danger of destroying some of the oceans' biological riches before we have even had the chance to study them. The negative impacts of human activities on the world's oceans have important repercussions for us all—whether it is the impact on global climate, the inability to provide much-needed food, or the loss of much of the world's natural beauty.

As Part 10 explains, maintaining the health of the oceans requires management of its resources. The issue of ownership—who owns which parts of the oceans and who has access to its resources—has seen significant progress in the last 20 years. The growth of international legislation together with greater scientific understanding is reaching the point where we now have the opportunity to mitigate the worst effects of human impact on the oceans—providing we act. We need the political will to do so.

I hope this book, above all else, will go some way toward showing the interconnectedness of all environments and living creatures on planet Earth. On a global scale, what happens on land and in the sky affects the oceans. What happens in the oceans—one way or another—affects us all.

Oceans

Land and Sea

Seen from space, planet Earth is blue, or, rather, it is mostly blue. As the weather systems swirl across Earth's surface, they tantalizingly lift the veil and reveal that about two-thirds of the planet's surface is blue—the blue of oceans and seas. The dirty browns of the planet's landmasses and the stark whiteness of the polar regions are, in comparison, almost drops in the ocean. From our perspective as air-breathing, land dwellers most of us lose sight—literally—of the fact that Earth is largely water covered.

Almost 71 percent of the planet's surface is submerged beneath seawater. The average depth of this water is an astonishing 2.3 miles (3.7 km). Indeed, were the contours of the planet's surface to be leveled, the seawater would cover Earth to a uniform depth of 1.6 miles (2.7 km). The abundance of seawater is well conveyed by this statistic: for each person on the planet, there are more than 60 billion gallons (about 230 bil l) of seawater.

When we stop to consider our planet and its surface, questions spring to mind. Where did the oceans come from? Or the landmasses for that matter? Or, indeed, planet Earth itself?

The Formation of the Oceans

Earth and the rest of the solar system are believed to have originated about 4.5 billion years ago from clouds of debris. These were remnants of a huge cosmic explosion—the big bang. Astrophysicists estimate that this universe-creating explosion took place some 15 billion years ago. In the resultant shockwaves traveling across space and time, some of the debris gradually merged to form larger and yet larger particles that collided and accumulated, time after time, to eventually form the Sun and its orbiting planets.

Planet Earth, like the other newly formed planets, became violently hot as the impacting particles of debris collapsed in on themselves under the force of gravity. Augmented by the radioactive decay of unstable elements, the heat melted the rocks of the young planet. The constituents of the molten planet were now free to move and arrange themselves according to density, with the most-dense material toward the center of Earth (later to form the core), the least dense at the surface (to form the crust), and layers of intermediate density in between (the mantle).

On the planet's surface, the rocks cooled to form a solid crust overlying the semisolid rock of the mantle below. The rocks of the crust were not of uniform density. The denser regions contained largely basalt rock and these formed relatively thin, low-lying areas of crust. The less-dense regions were largely granite and floated higher on the mantle, forming a thicker crust. The low-lying regions were to form the basins that contain the oceans; the thicker, raised regions were to form the continents. The crust under the oceans (oceanic crust) is thus denser than that comprising the continents (continental crust).

Most scientists believe the water that fills the ocean basins was released from Earth's crust and mantle as vapor and then fell from the sky as a deluge of precipitation (rain, hail, and snow). Water accounts for about 5 percent of the mass of rock, and when molten rock flows to the surface and cools, some of the water in it vaporizes. This probably happened when the planet's crust cooled some four billion years ago. This would have been supplemented by volcanic activity from then and to this day that erupts molten rock onto Earth's surface.

Others, among them top space scientist Louis Frank, have suggested that Earth's water arrived, after the crust had partly solidified, as comets collided with the planet. Comets are like "dirty snowballs" made from mixtures of rock particles and ice. Although today large comets reside in the further reaches of the solar system and make only occasional visits to us, had they been more numerous in our region of space they could have contributed large amounts of water. In any case, small cometlike balls of ice may be impacting on Earth's atmosphere even now, and some calculations show that had this been happening over a period of four billion years, it would have been sufficient to provide the water for our oceans.

Although all the planets were formed by similar processes, whether a planet retains water—and in what form—depends on factors such as the distance from the Sun and the strength of the gravitational field. Mars, a smaller, cooler planet than ours with a relatively thin atmosphere, has lost most of its water, and what remains is mainly in the form of ice. Venus, closer to the Sun than Earth, has lost virtually all of its water by evaporation. Planet Earth was in a fortuitous position: The combination of a suitably strong gravitational field and moderate temperatures resulted in planet Earth developing a rich atmospheric layer combined with the availability of liquid water. Both conditions are prerequisites if organic life as we know it is to evolve.

The Formation of the Ocean Basins

The ocean basins have not always had their present-day form. Indeed, the ocean basins are—and always have been—changing, but at a pace that is not immediately obvious until we start to think in terms of geological time—in millions of years rather than in days, months, or years.

Earth's crust and the topmost part of Earth's mantle comprise seven major plates of rocky material that float on the rest of the upper mantle. Currents within the upper mantle create slow, swirling movements that cause the plates to move slowly across Earth's surface—a phenomenon described by the theory of plate tectonics (page 32). One of the consequences of the plates moving is that the continents shift and that the oceans change shape, too.

Plenty of geological and biological evidence suggests that about 250 million years ago the present-day continents formed a single landmass—a supercontinent that geologists call Pangaea. This

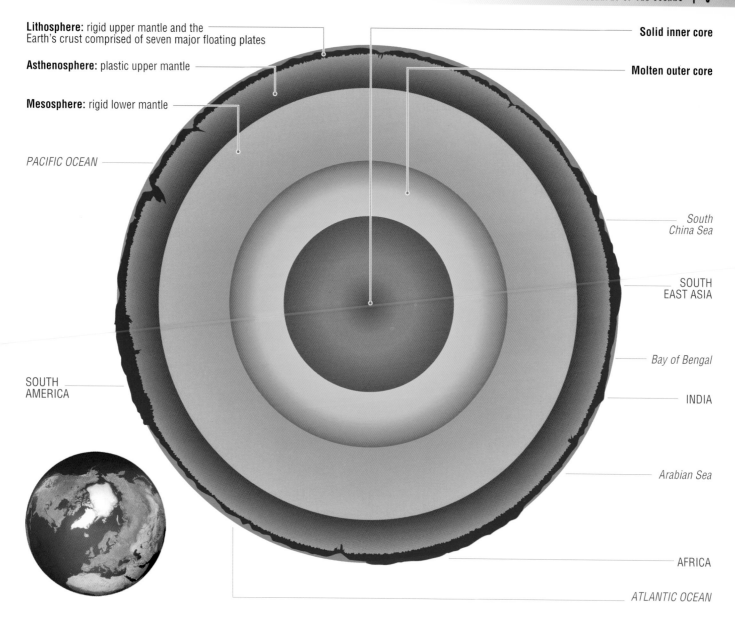

Lithosphere: rigid upper mantle and the Earth's crust comprised of seven major floating plates

Asthenosphere: plastic upper mantle

Mesosphere: rigid lower mantle

PACIFIC OCEAN

SOUTH AMERICA

Solid inner core

Molten outer core

South China Sea

SOUTH EAST ASIA

Bay of Bengal

INDIA

Arabian Sea

AFRICA

ATLANTIC OCEAN

A slice through Earth—simplified

huge landmass was surrounded by a superocean, Panthalassa—the precursor of the Pacific Ocean today. Geologists believe that Pangaea broke up some 140–180 million years ago and that during the Jurassic period—the age of the dinosaurs—it formed two supercontinents: Laurasia, which comprised present-day North America, Europe, and Asia, to the north; and Gondwanaland, containing present-day South America, Africa, India, Australia, and Antarctica, to the south. The shallow Sea of Tethys was formed between the two supercontinents. Within the next 100 million years or so, the two supercontinents fragmented to form the present-day continents, and these landmasses moved in easterly and westerly directions, in some cases colliding with one another. For example, Africa moved north and collided with the Eurasian landmass, so closing the Sea of Tethys; later, India moved north and collided with Asia, so creating the Himalayas. In geological terms, the present-day ocean basins are quite young, less than 80 million years old, and they are constantly changing; for example, the Pacific Ocean is gradually shrinking and the Atlantic Ocean is enlarging. Given another 150 million years, the arrangement of the oceans will be quite different from the way they are today.

Oceans and Seas

The waves gently lapping a tropical shore; the dark, gray skies and heaving seas of an Atlantic swell; Arctic temperatures that freeze a sailor's hand to the rigging: these are three facets of the ever-changing oceans that cover our planet. From the equator to the poles, our oceans offer a complex and diverse environment. But how many oceans are there? And where are they?

Four main bodies of seawater are true oceans: the Pacific, the Atlantic, the Indian, and the Arctic oceans. The Pacific Ocean is by far the largest both in area and volume. A fifth body of water, the Antarctic Ocean, is not strictly a true ocean but is a southern extension of the Pacific, Atlantic, and Indian Oceans. Nevertheless, because of its distinctive features, the Antarctic Ocean is often considered as a separate body of water.

The oceans are all interconnected and so, in fact, form one continuous body of water—in a sense, a superocean with many branches. The oceans and the smaller regions within or attached to them—seas, bays, and gulfs—differ not only in size, shape, and depth, but also in the physical and chemical characteristics of the water they contain. These differences create various environments inhabited by different communities of organisms.

Seas and Gulfs

A sea is part of an ocean, as in the case of the Sargasso Sea, or is a large partly or fully enclosed body of salt water, as in the case of the Black Sea. A marginal sea is simply a single body of water connected to the ocean, as in the case of the Red Sea. The word *gulf* is used to refer to some marginal seas, as in the case of the Gulf of Mexico and the Persian Gulf. Because seas and gulfs tend to be semi- or fully enclosed bodies of water, they are often strongly influenced by local factors, such as runoff from adjacent land and the climate of surrounding landmasses. Thus seas and gulfs often have their own special characteristics that are distinct from those of the ocean to which they are connected.

Profile of an Ocean

If the physical features of Earth's surface are dramatic on land, they are even more so under the ocean. To begin with, the oceans are much deeper than the land is high: the average depth of the oceans is about 12,470 feet (3,800 m), whereas the average height of the land above sea level is 2,760 feet (840 m). The tallest mountain emerging from the sea is Mauna Kea in Hawaii at about 33,450 feet (10,200 m) above the ocean floor; on land, Mount Everest reaches 29,020 feet (8,848 m) above sea level. The Grand Canyon in the United States, one of the deepest canyons on land at 5,300 feet (1,615 m) deep almost pales into insignificance against the Mariana Trench, which is 36,163 feet (11,022 m) below sea level and about 16,400 feet (5,000 m) below the level of its flanking seafloor.

The physical features of the ocean floor are dominated by the workings of plate tectonics and

Oceans of the World

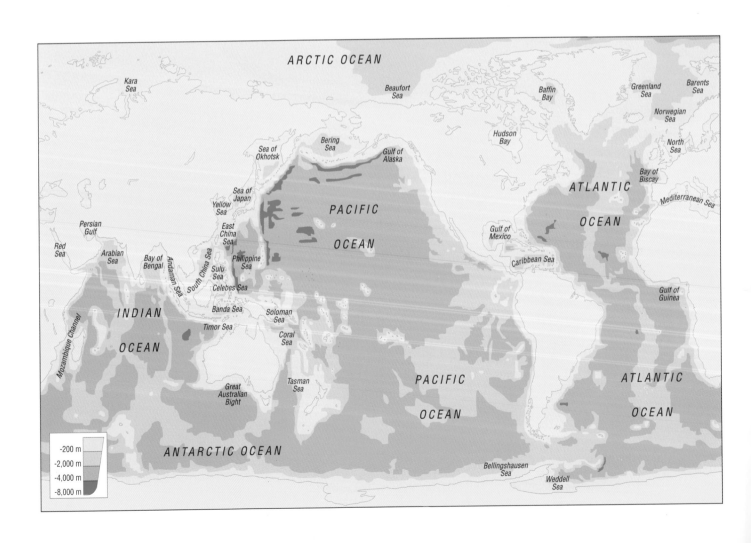

OCEANS

Ocean[+]	Surface Area (million square kilometers)	Average Depth (meters)	Volume (million cubic kilometers)
Pacific[*]	166	4,188	696
Atlantic[*]	84	3,844	323
Indian[*]	73	3,872	284
Arctic	12	1,117	14

[+] *Excluding adjacent seas*

[*] *The Antarctic Ocean is included within the Pacific, Atlantic, and Indian Oceans.*

SOME MAJOR SEAS: DATA FILE

Sea or Gulf	Surface Area (million square kilometers)	Average Depth (meters)	Volume (million cubic kilometers)
Atlantic Ocean			
Caribbean Sea (including adjacent seas and the Gulf of Mexico)	4.4	2,164	9.4
Mediterranean Sea (including Black Sea)	3.0	1,450	4.4
North Sea	0.6	93	0.05
Baltic Sea	0.4	55	0.02
Pacific Ocean			
Sea of Okhotsk	1.4	971	1.4
East China Sea	1.2	275	0.3
Sea of Japan	1.0	1,673	1.7
Indian Ocean			
Red Sea	0.5	538	0.2
Persian Gulf	0.2	25	0.01
Arctic Ocean			
Bering Sea	2.3	1,491	3.4
Hudson Bay	1.2	128	0.2

seafloor spreading (page 30); broadly speaking, there are similarities in the physical features of the ocean floor across the world. The seafloor is divided into three regions: the continental margins, the ocean-basin floor, and the mid-oceanic ridge.

Continental Margins

The shallow waters at the edge of continents are called continental margins. They usually consist of three parts: a shallow, gently sloping continental shelf at the edge of the landmass, a steeper continental slope beyond that, and beyond that a more gently sloping continental rise. The continental slope beyond the shelf is the closest thing to the exact edge of the continent—the boundary between continental crust and oceanic crust.

Continental shelves comprise less than 8 percent of the surface of the seafloor, but they are vital for many reasons. Continental shelves support some of the world's most important fishing grounds and are sufficiently accessible for the oil, gas, and coal reserves beneath them to be exploited commercially in many locations. It is the continental shelves that have been investigated by oceanographers more than any other part of the ocean system. Shelves are sufficiently shallow to be explored by scuba divers as well as research vessels and manned submersibles. It is the continental shelves that contain many of the sea's most fragile and threatened ecosystems—coral reefs and mangroves, for example—and it is shelves that are commonly most at risk from marine pollution (page 180).

Ocean Basin Floor

The flat part of the deep-sea ocean floor at the base of the continental rise is called the abyssal plain. It is typically 11,500–18,200 feet (3,500–5,500 m) deep and rises very gently toward the mid-ocean ridge. The seafloor covering is usually derived from the shells of microscopic plankton and is called ooze (page 36).

Scattered on the abyssal plain may be significant features: shallow abyssal hills, submarine volcanoes called seamounts, volcanic islands, and flat-topped seamounts called guyots.

Mid-Ocean Ridges

A mid-ocean ridge is a line of geological activity where material from the underlying mantle wells up and pushes up the overlying crust and lays down new plate material. Along the center line of the ridge, the plates are pulling apart, and these leave a great gap or depression known as the central rift valley. Crevices and fractures riddle the floor and sides of this valley. Seawater seeps into these cracks, is heated to high temperatures, and is forced back out, taking dissolved minerals with it. These emissions emerge through hydrothermal vents (page 43), and the combination of raised water temperature and rich mineral supplies provides the energy source for fascinating communities of organisms first discovered in the 1970s.

The mid-ocean ridges are the birthplaces of the ocean floor. Conversely, the deep-ocean trenches are where the seafloor is being destroyed. These are the oldest parts of the abyssal plain, and here the ocean plate is drawn back down to the mantle below Earth's surface and is recycled. The Mariana Trench in the western Pacific is the deepest and one of the oldest parts of the ocean floor. Here, the plate material is up to 36,163 feet (11,022 m) below the sea surface and is about 135 million years old before it disappears below Earth's surface.

The Pacific Ocean

Perhaps best known for its romantic, tropical islands, the Pacific Ocean is a huge expanse of water that, like the Atlantic Ocean, extends from the subpolar waters of one hemisphere to the subpolars waters of the other hemisphere.

The Pacific Ocean covers more than a third of the surface of the globe and is by far the world's largest ocean. A satellite view from above the center of the Pacific shows that hemisphere almost covered in ocean, such is the size of the Pacific. It is also the deepest ocean, and the Mariana Trench of the Northwest Pacific is the deepest place on Earth, at about 7 miles (11 km) below sea level. Distances across the Pacific are equally daunting: from the equatorial west coast of South America to the easternmost islands of Indonesia is about 10,000 miles (16,000 km).

Geology

Geologically, the Pacific Ocean basin is very active. It comprises one of Earth's largest crustal plates, and its mid-ocean ridges are constantly producing new oceanic crust; indeed, the East Pacific Ridge is one of the world's fastest spreading plate boundaries. The oceanic crust on either side of the ridge is moving apart at the rate of around 15 centimeters (6.5 inches) per year. The edges of the plate submerge below surrounding plates so that the whole of the Pacific basin is encircled by destructive plate margins. This results in a ring of volcanoes, both active and dormant, that are a testament to the geological stresses generated at these boundaries. This arc of earthquake and volcanic activity is often called the Ring of Fire and stretches from New Zealand, north of Indonesia, around Japan, then south of the Aleutian Islands along the east coast of North America (the earthquake-prone regions of California), and down the east coast of Mexico and South America. These destructive plate margins are gradually encroaching on the oceanic plate so that the Pacific Ocean is shrinking.

Almost all the oceanic islands of the Pacific are of volcanic origin and run along ridges in an approximately northwest-southeast direction. Along the ridges, the oldest islands are to the northwest and the youngest and most volcanically active (and those yet to emerge from the sea) are to the southeast. In some of the older established islands chains, such as the Society Islands, all stages in the development of coral reefs are shown and relate to the age of the islands (page 113). The older islands to the northwest are coral atolls (a continuous or broken ring

of reef surrounding a lagoon) or are enclosed by barrier reefs; those of intermediate age are enclosed by fringing reefs, and the youngest island Mehetia to the southeast has yet to develop a reef system.

Oceanic Circulation and Currents

As with the Atlantic Ocean, the circulation of water in the Northern Hemisphere is in a clockwise direction and that in the Southern Hemisphere is counterclockwise, as generated by winds deflected by the Coriolis effect (page 63). A complex system of currents and countercurrents separates the two circulations. Variations in these currents, from year to year, have significant effect on fisheries; the most notable deviation from normal patterns is the El Niño event (page 68).

Human Population

Bordering the Pacific Ocean are some of the world's most populous countries, including China, Japan, and Russia to the west and the United States and Brazil to the east. These five alone make up more than one-third of the world's population. Based on the United Nations Human Development Index (a measure that takes into account a population's average years of schooling, income, literacy, and life expectancy) most of the countries bordering the Pacific Ocean are among the most highly developed, with some notable exceptions such as Guatemala to the east and Vietnam, Cambodia, and Papua New Guinea to the west. The islands of the South Pacific are not the idyll so commonly depicted, and levels of development are often low in these areas.

Living Resources

In terms of fisheries, the northern, southern, and eastern regions are the most productive parts of

the Pacific. In places, cold, nutrient-rich waters rise up to the surface and—in the presence of sunlight—fuel phytoplankton (plant plankton) photosynthesis. The high turnover of phytoplankton forms the basis of food chains (page 84) with humans, cropping fish, shellfish, and crustaceans such as crabs toward the top of these chains. In the central and western regions, nutrient levels in the crystal-clear surface waters are often low and so is productivity. In the Central, South, and West Pacific, many of the fisheries are concentrated around island shelves and coral reefs and are cropped on little more than a subsistence basis. However, there is great economic interest in the diverse species of coral-reef fish, less for their edible qualities and more for their visual spectacle and their often extraordinary behavior, as a draw for tourists and divers.

According to the Food and Agriculture Organization of the United Nations (FAO), in the period 1991–93 more than 60 percent of the world's marine-fish catch came from the Pacific Ocean, with the bulk of this from the northwest and southeast regions. A sizable part of this catch is composed of herringlike fishes, such as the Japanese sardine, the South American sardine, and the Peruvian anchovy. These are often processed into fish oil or fish meal, which, among other uses, serve as a food source in fish farming.

Mid-water tuna form a high-value catch in many parts of the Pacific. In the eastern Pacific they are caught using purse seines; in the west and central regions, long lines are used. Drift nets that are many kilometers long are set up by long-distance fishing fleets from some East Asian countries. These nets, the so-called walls of death, are a real cause for concern among environmentalists and for smaller Pacific nations whose tuna represent their sole exportable resource. In the oceanic islands of the central Pacific, fisheries tend to be small-scale artisanal operations that harvest the wide diversity of fish and other species associated with coral reefs. A U.N. regional convention sought to ban the use of massive drift nets in 1992; many are still loose in the Pacific.

PACIFIC OCEAN: DATA FILE	
Area	64 million square miles (166 million km²)
Mean depth	13,741 feet (4,188 m)
Maximum depth	36,161 feet (11,022 m)—Mariana Trench
Volume of water	167 million cubic miles (696 mil km³)

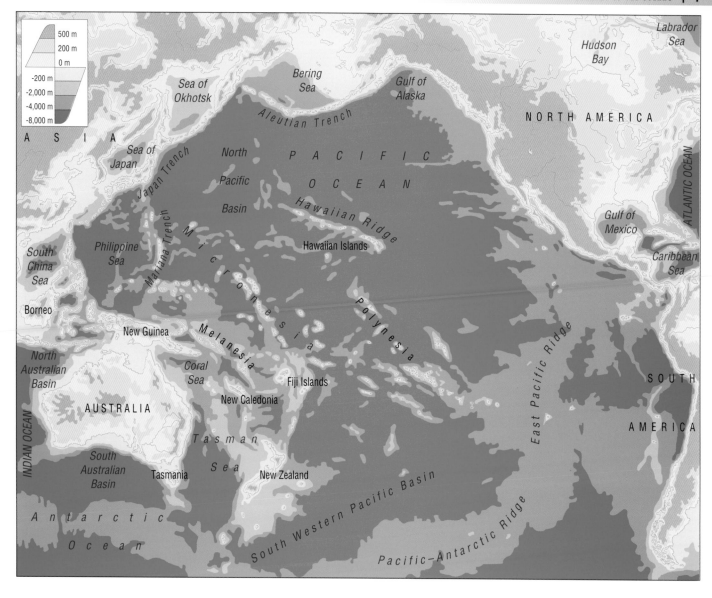

The Pacific Ocean

Nonliving Resources

On the continental shelves surrounding the Pacific basin, placer deposits (minerals eroded from the continental landmass) are being exploited. Gold is mined from Alaska beaches, tin is extracted in the Southeast Asia region, and in the western Pacific, extensive offshore deposits of iron ore are mined by the Japanese. Polymetallic (mixed-metal) nodules (page 37) are widely distributed throughout the deep Pacific, particularly between Hawaii and Mexico, but as yet it remains uneconomic to harvest them.

Pollution and Conservation

More than half of the world's surface area of coral reef is associated with the Pacific Ocean and its connected seas to the west. Many of the coral reefs of the Central and Southwest Pacific are stable, and some of the world's first marine parks, such as the Great Barrier Reef, Australia, are established there. However, most of the coral reefs in the Northwest Pacific, in a belt stretching from the Philippines to Japan, are in a critical state because of overexploitation and pollution of the coral-reef ecosystem (page 113). Some of the coral reefs associated with South Pacific islands that form Melanesia, Micronesia, and Polynesia are also threatened by similar problems. In the Northwest Pacific and South Pacific, mangrove swamps are cleared to make room for urban expansion, agriculture, and fish farming. This destruction of mangrove communities removes nursery grounds for fish, shrimp, prawn, and shellfish. This may affect the numbers of juveniles that are recruited to replace exploited stocks of adults over a wide area. The commercial impact of mangrove removal may be much greater than is generally recognized (pages 25 and 111).

The Atlantic Ocean

Oceanography—the scientific study of the oceans—began in the North Atlantic Ocean, and historically more is known about this region of the world's oceans than any other.

The Atlantic, the second largest ocean, contains about one-quarter of the world's oceanic water and is about one-half the volume of the Pacific Ocean. Its most prominent underwater feature is the Mid-Atlantic Ridge—the longest mountain range in the world—that curves through the basin roughly halfway between North and South America to the west and the coasts of Europe and Africa to the east. The Puerto Rico trench, close to the West Indies, is the deepest part of the Atlantic, at more than 5.6 miles (9 km) below sea level.

Geology

Geologically, the Atlantic Ocean basin is less obviously active than the Pacific. Along the zigzag middle line of the Atlantic basin, the Mid-Atlantic Ridge produces seafloor spreading at the rate of 0.4–0.8 inches (1–2 cm) per year. There are only minor destructive plate boundaries, and these are found where continents are moving past one another, as in Atlantic-connected seas of the Caribbean and the Mediterranean. Thus, the Atlantic Ocean is gradually expanding. The island of Surtsey, to the south of Iceland, is a new arrival and was formed by volcanic action in 1963. The British Isles are continental islands, still linked by the continental shelf to the European continent.

Oceanic Circulation and Currents

The elongated zigzag shape of the Atlantic is much more open to the south than to the north, and there is far greater exchange of water between the Atlantic and the Antarctic, Indian, and Pacific Oceans than there is between the Atlantic and the Arctic Ocean.

In the North Atlantic, the clockwise gyre (a circular or spiral movement of water) picks up water warmed in the Gulf of Mexico and carries it northwestward to western Europe as the Gulf Stream and then on to the Arctic as the North Atlantic Drift. The warm water of the Gulf Stream dominates the western North Atlantic. Warm saline water emerging from the Mediterranean (page 16) moderates the temperatures of water in the eastern North Atlantic.

In the South Atlantic, water circulation is a classic counterclockwise gyre that is determined

ATLANTIC OCEAN: DATA FILE	
Area	32 million square miles (84 mil km²)
Mean depth	12,612 feet (3,844 m)
Maximum depth	30,248 feet (9,219 m)—Puerto Rico Trench
Volume of water	77 million cubic miles (323 mil km³)

by winds and currents deflected by the Coriolis effect (page 62).

Human Population

Bordering the Atlantic Ocean are many of the world's most economically developed countries, particularly those of North America and Northwest Europe. This has placed considerable fishing and pollution pressure on the North Atlantic. Three of the world's largest cities—Buenos Aires, Rio de Janeiro, and São Paulo—are located along the east coast of South America and border the South Atlantic. Along the West Africa coast, most communities are still relatively poorly developed, and much of the activity in this region is at subsistence level; development hotspots include Ghana and Nigeria.

Living Resources

According to the Food and Agriculture Organization of the United Nations (FAO), during the period 1991–93 just more than 26 percent of the world's marine fish catch came from the Atlantic Ocean; two-thirds of this came from the northeast and east-central regions—in other words, off the coasts of Canada, Northwest Europe, and North Africa. The North Atlantic is the world's most heavily fished ocean area, and numerous fish stocks are suffering from overfishing. For example, annual North Atlantic cod catches in the early 1990s were one-quarter of their size in the late 1960s. The cod fishery of the Canadian Grand Banks, once one of the world's most-prolific fisheries, is now commercially exhausted and may never recover (page 190).

Small, free-swimming fish species, such as sardine, anchovy, and herring, make up the bulk of the North Atlantic catch by weight but not by value. Higher-valued demersal (bottom-dwelling) fish are important, particularly cod, flounder, and plaice in the northeast and northwest, and hake from southern Europe and northern Africa. The

Atlantic tuna fishery is also significant but is not as large as the Pacific operations. Fisheries for crustaceans such as lobsters, prawns, shrimps, and crabs are widespread in shallow waters across the North Atlantic, and mariculture has rapidly expanded, with salmon and trout being farmed in Canada, Scandinavia, and western Scotland. France, Spain, and the United States each culture hundreds of thousands of metric tons of clams and other shellfish each year.

The rich fisheries off the West African coast are the consequence of the upwelling of cold, nutrient-rich waters that fuel high phytoplankton productivity often close to mangrove areas. Further nutrient input is provided by the outflows of the Congo and Zaïre Rivers. Off the Namibian and Angolan coasts, about 1.7 million tons (about 1.5 mil t) of mostly pelagic fish, particularly pilchards, are caught annually. Throughout the West African region, about 3.9 million tons (about 3.5 mil t) of fish and shellfish are taken annually. Many fishery operations are small scale and artisanal but are becoming increasingly mechanized. They are vital to local economies, even in countries such as Nigeria where much of the catch is exported.

Fleets from the former Soviet Union, Spain, Japan, and Norway—sometimes with 15 catcher ships servicing one giant processing vessel—trawl off the continental shelf, and one fleet can catch, process, and freeze up to 1,000 metric tons (1,100 tons) of fish a day. Often the fish are reduced to fishmeal, which will be fed to livestock. Most tuna taken in West African waters are caught by these foreign "process" fleets without any benefit to local countries.

Nonliving Resources

Oil and gas are the main mineral resources that are exploited, and these are primarily extracted from continental shelf regions off the West African coast and in deposits in Atlantic-associated seas, namely the Caribbean Sea and the North Sea. Of the hard minerals that are exploited, a greater value of sand and gravel is extracted than all other hard minerals combined. Most of this activity occurs in the North Sea off the coast of Northwest Europe (page 168), but aragonite sands rich in calcium carbonate are dredged from the Great Bahamas Bank. The calcium carbonate is used in the manufacture of cement, glass, and animal feed supplements. Gem-quality diamonds are obtained off the southwest coast of Africa.

Pollution and Conservation

The destruction of marine habitats, as in other parts of the world, is most serious in coastal zones. Pollution hotspots include high-population cities close to the sea, such as Rio de Janeiro, Brazil. In the Atlantic, barges dump sewage sludge hauled from coastal cities, although thankfully places such as New York banned such dumping in the 1980s. The shipping routes between North America and Northwest Europe are among the most seriously polluted in the world: ballast-tank emissions discharge a cocktail of harmful chemicals, and in regular shipboard operations, oil tankers discharge much larger quantities of oil than they do in well-publicized spills (page 184). The oil is dispersed over a much larger area, causing chronic low-level pollution.

Along the West African coast, tropical rain forests are being cut down and mangroves cleared, which increases freshwater runoff into coastal waters. Coastal erosion is perhaps the worst of many problems in this region. Countries with newly industrialized economies, such as Nigeria, see pollution control as a low priority, and most urban and industrial wastes enter the sea without any kind of treatment. With increasing intensification of agriculture, runoff now carries toxic residues from pesticides and fertilizers into coastal waters (pages 181–182).

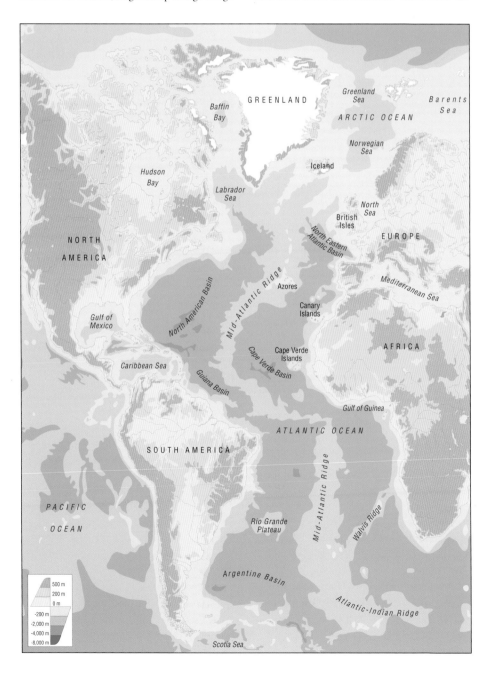

The Atlantic Ocean

The Indian Ocean

The Indian Ocean, the third largest ocean, occupies about one-fifth of the world's surface area of oceanic water. The surface conditions of the northern Indian Ocean—the Arabian Sea and the Bay of Bengal—are dominated by monsoon winds that reverse direction seasonally. Far south of the equator, the Indian Ocean basin opens out into the Antarctic Ocean and South Atlantic. Swells generated by storms in these southerly regions are transmitted northward right up into the western Indian Ocean, causing periodic flooding in island countries as far north as the Maldives and Sri Lanka.

The Indus and the Ganges-Brahmaputra, two of the world's largest river systems, empty into the Indian Ocean. They have created enormous fans of sediment brought down from erosion of the Himalayas, which in turn has created large areas of shallow water off the Indian coast.

One of the features of the Indian Ocean, like the Pacific, is the presence of coral atolls—ringlike structures of living reef. The Maldives and the Seychelles are major atoll island groups of the Indian Ocean. Between the Indian and the Pacific basins lies the Indo-West Pacific, a region that has the highest biodiversity for any shallow marine ecosystem. It has received colonizing species from both the Central Pacific to the east and the Indian Ocean to the west.

Geology

The seafloor of the Indian Ocean is dominated by the mid-ocean ridge, which forms an inverted Y-shape: the western arm runs roughly parallel with the East African coast, and the eastern arm runs south of Australia toward New Zealand. In contrast to the Pacific and Atlantic Oceans, the geological history of the Indian Ocean is quite complex. The ocean's beginnings are traced back to the breakup of Gondwanaland, some 130–140 million years ago. The African continent broke away from what is now Antarctica, and during the next 70 million years or so, northeasterly and northwesterly movements resulted in what is now India breaking free from Africa and moving north to collide with Asia, the resultant impact creating the Himalayas. When India broke free of Africa, it tore other fragments off the African continent and scattered them behind it across the ocean floor. The islands of Madagascar and the Seychelles were formed in this way: they contain continental granite, not the volcanic material associated with most Pacific and Atlantic islands. Australia separated from Antarctica about 50 mil-

INDIAN OCEAN: DATA FILE	
Area	28 million square miles (73 mil km^2)
Mean depth	12,704 feet (3,872 m)
Maximum depth	24,460 feet (7,455 m)—Sunda Trench
Volume of water	68 million cubic miles (284 mil km^3)

lion years ago, and the Indian Ocean basin in its present form is a mere 36 million years old.

Oceanic Circulation and Currents

The North Indian Ocean circulation is unique in that its surface currents reverse twice a year under the influence of the monsoon winds. In the Northern Hemisphere's spring and summer, southwest monsoon winds generate a north-flowing current off the Somali coast of Africa, which helps power a clockwise gyre in the North Indian Ocean. At this time, coastal upwellings occur off Somalia and the Arabian Peninsula, where warm surface water is replaced by nutrient-rich upwelling colder water. From November to April, the northeast monsoon winds blow from the Asian subcontinent and cause the northern gyre to reverse direction and to break down into a series of minigyres, with resultant stoppage of upwellings. Throughout the year, the gyre south of the equator is counterclockwise.

Human Population

Countries bordering the north coast of the Indian Ocean—Pakistan, India, Bangladesh—are among the poorest in the world. This is the most congested part of the planet, and the highest population densities are often found in low-lying areas. When natural disasters strike—such as flooding in Bangladesh—the loss of life may be enormous. The countries of the North Indian Ocean contrast strongly with the relatively affluent countries within Indonesia and Australasia to the east. Some oil-rich states, such as Oman and Iran, lie to the northwest. Five of the world's largest cities—Bangkok, Bombay, Calcutta, Karachi, and Jakarta—lie on or near Indian Ocean coasts.

Along the West Africa coast, most countries—with the conspicuous exception of South Africa—are still relatively underdeveloped, and much of the activity in this region is at a subsistence level.

Living Resources

According to the FAO statistics, during the period 1991–93 just under 9 percent of the world's marine-fish catch came from the Indian Ocean; yet this ocean occupies about 20 percent of the world's ocean surface. Why is the catch so low? Two natural factors are at least partly responsible. First, much of the continental shelf around the Indian Ocean, particularly along the East African coast, is very narrow, thereby limiting opportunities for fishing in shallow waters. Second, the reversal of the surface currents in the North Indian Ocean and the closing down of the upwelling along the western margins of the ocean basin during the northwest monsoon season probably reduce nutrient availability in the surface waters and contribute to relatively low biological productivity. While gross overfishing occurs in coastal waters—particularly those of India, Pakistan, Bangladesh, Sri Lanka, and the Maldives—it is quite likely that some midwater and deep-water oceanic fisheries are underutilized.

Subsistence fisheries around oceanic islands and off the East Africa coast are associated with coral reef areas and are valuable sources of protein for coastal populations in developing countries. On the east side of the Indian Ocean, particularly in Indonesia, low productivity is compensated for by the development of mariculture for finfish, shellfish, and seaweed for both local use and export.

Larger-scale commercial fisheries are based on capture of high-value fish such as tuna, sailfish, and marlin or by trawling for penaeid shrimp from offshore areas. The latter are associated with large mangrove stands that support the juvenile shrimp. The Maldives specialize in the capture of tuna using dolphin-friendly pole-and-line methods. Expansion of the deep-swimming tuna catch, using long-line and purse seines, is viable. Currently, such tuna fisheries are operating in the western Indian Ocean based in Mauritius and the Seychelles.

For many of the smaller island nations, tuna fishing and tourism that capitalizes on the beautiful sandy beaches and clear, coral-rich waters are the sole sources of foreign currency.

Nonliving Resources

Large mineral reserves have been discovered but have yet to be exploited. Among these are considerable areas of the deep seafloor, particularly in the southern basins, that are scattered with manganese nodules. Phosphate nodules, for potential use in fertilizers, are found on the Argulhas Plateau to the southwest.

Placer deposits (minerals eroded from the continent) have been actively exploited around the margins of the Indian Ocean since the 1920s. Of these deposits, tin in the form of cassiterite is perhaps the most significant. The ore-containing sediment is dredged from shallow seabeds and transferred to plants on land, where the tin is extracted. This occurs off the coast of Indonesia, Myanmar (Burma), and Thailand, and in the 1970s these deposits accounted for about one-quarter of the world's tin production. Semiprecious minerals such as zircon are mined from beaches in southern India and northern Sri Lanka. In eastern South Africa, glauconite, a rock mineral rich in potash, is mined for use in fertilizers.

Oil and gas production from offshore reserves is, of course, prevalent in the northern Arabian Sea. Significant offshore reserves are also being exploited in the Indonesian region.

Pollution and Conservation

Two of the world's most precious marine ecosystems—coral reefs and mangrove swamps—are prevalent in the Indian Ocean and are severely threatened or already eradicated in many areas. Dozens of Madagascan, Indonesian, Malaysian, and Sri Lankan coral systems are severely threatened. Many mangrove areas in Indonesia have been cleared to provide fuelwood or land for rice cultivation or have been converted to mariculture ponds for shrimp and fish.

Major oil-tanker routes emerge from the northwest Indian Ocean—the Persian Gulf and Arabian basin. The tankers carry oil eastward to Japan and other East Asian countries, and westward to Africa, South America, and northern Europe. Apart from the occasional major spill (usually in coastal waters), routine shipping operations discharge much more oil in total than the occasional major spillage incident. The chronic pollution adversely effects both coral reefs and mangrove stands.

The smaller islands of the Indian Ocean depend on their coral reefs and white sandy beaches to attract tourists. In many cases, these same tourists are damaging the environment that they have traveled to see. When large numbers of

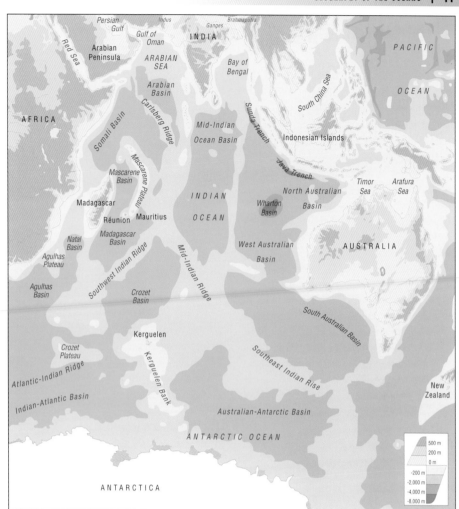

The Indian Ocean

people swim, dive, and pillage from coral reefs, environmental degradation is inevitable and gradually destroys the resource on which the industry depends. Sewage discharge from increased numbers of tourists may also cause local overproduction of marine algae that smoother reefs. Many countries are making moves to develop more responsible tourism that minimizes damage to reef ecosystems (page 200).

The Polar Oceans

The Arctic Ocean

The Arctic Ocean around the North Pole is the world's smallest and shallowest ocean. Unlike other oceans, it is virtually surrounded by land: It is almost enclosed by Russia, Eurasia, Greenland, and North America and is contained by four major basins separated by three oceanic ridges: the Alpha Ridge, the Lomonosov Ridge, and the Nansen Cordillera. The latter ridge is continuous with the Mid-Atlantic Ridge further south. The Canadian Abyssal Plain is by far the largest of the Arctic sub-basins. As an ocean, the Arctic is particularly unusual in having vast areas of continental shelf—up to 1,000 miles (1,600 km) wide off the Eurasian landmass—forming extensive shallows areas, such as the Chukchi, Kara, Laptev, and East Siberian Seas.

Much of the Arctic Ocean is covered by a skin of floating ice to a depth of 10 feet (3 m) or so. During the winter, the sea ice extends over most of the Arctic Ocean; in summer, when temperatures rise well above freezing, the sea ice shrinks to about half that of the winter coverage.

ARCTIC OCEAN: DATA FILE

Area	4.7 million square miles (12.2 mil km²)
Mean depth	3,665 feet (1,117 m)
Maximum depth	17,878 feet (5,449 m)—Eurasian Basin
Volume of water	3.3 million cubic miles (13.7 mil km³)

ANTARCTIC OCEAN: DATA FILE

Total area	13.5 million square miles (35 mil km²)
Area of permanent sea ice	1.2 million square miles (3 mil km²)
Total area of sea ice in winter	3.9 million square miles (10 mil km²)
Maximum depth	17,878 feet (5,449 m)

The bulk of water movement into and out of the Arctic is through the Greenland Sea and into the Atlantic Ocean next to Scandinavia; the remainder occurs through the shallow Bering Straits into the Pacific Ocean. The warm water from the North Atlantic Drift enters the Greenland Sea and keeps the Norwegian coast free of ice throughout the year, even well north of the Arctic Circle. This becomes a cold current that sweeps southward past eastern Greenland so that the eastern coastline is icebound and innaccessible to all but ice-breaking vessels, except for a brief period in summer.

Icebergs are shed, or calved, from the Greenland icecap and drift southward. They can be a great danger to shipping—most are 5–80 meters (15–260 feet) above water level and 200–370 meters (650–1,200 feet) below, and they may reach up to a kilometer or more long. One such iceberg was shed by Arctic polar ice and traveled through the Labrador Sea to the Atlantic Ocean off Newfoundland: it was responsible for the tragic sinking of the RMS *Titanic* in 1912 (page 137). Icing of a ship's superstructure (those parts at or above deck level) is an even greater hazard. Freezing ice can make a ship top-heavy and may raise the craft's center of gravity to the point where it is in danger of capsizing.

LIVING RESOURCES

The Arctic region is, understandably, sparsely populated, although indigenous peoples of North America, Siberia, and Greenland continue to

The Arctic Ocean

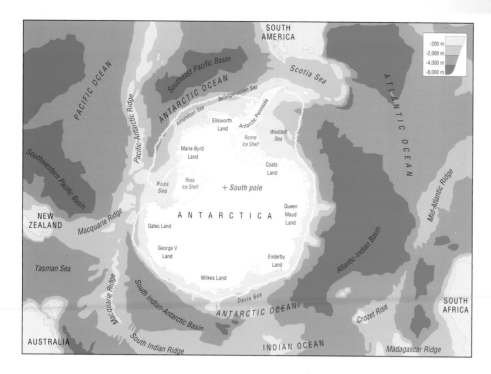

The Antarctic Ocean

make a living there, including hunting marine birds and mammals on a subsistence basis. Commercial hunting of marine mammals has, more or less, stopped. The culling of young harp seals for the fur trade declined in the 1980s after a campaign by environmental pressure groups to raise public awareness. The European Community banned sealskin imports, which effectively removed the main market for this product.

The Arctic ecosystem depends on a system of primary production that is highly seasonal. In deep winter, there is continual darkness; sufficient light and temperature for phytoplankton photosynthesis is only present between about February and September. Nevertheless, the continental shelves of the Arctic support some of the world's richest fishing grounds: the region now produces about one-tenth of the global fish catch. Arctic cod is taken from the Arctic subbasins, and in winter the shallow continental shelves yield Arctic char and capelin. In the warmer waters of the west Spitzbergen and North Cape currents, cod, haddock, and plaice are the main commercial prize.

NONLIVING RESOURCES

The sedimentary basins of the Arctic Ocean are suitable geological formations for oil and gas deposits. Large oil deposits have been discovered in the Beaufort Sea off Northern Canada and in 1977 a trans-Arctic pipeline was installed to carry oil south from the Alaskan coast. Alaska now meets a quarter of the United States's oil requirements. Rich gas reserves are found near some of the North Canadian islands. Within the Arctic Circle on the Russian side, known oil and gas reserves are extensive but have yet to be exploited. The Arctic holds some of the world's largest deposits of metals, including iron, copper, lead, and the radioactive element uranium. Given the inhospitable conditions in this region—the extreme cold, high winds, and shifting sea ice—the extraction of mineral solids, liquids, and gases still remains at a relatively low level.

The Antarctic Ocean

The Antarctic Ocean is, like the Arctic, extremely cold and substantially frozen. In most other respects, however, it is quite unlike the Arctic. It is an open ocean that surrounds a continent, rather than an ocean enclosed by continents. Antarctica itself comprises an ice-covered landmass about twice the size of western Europe and straddling the South Pole. The region contains about 90 percent of the planet's permanent ice: the South Polar icecap averages more than 5,750 feet (1,600 m) deep, compared to the few dozen meters at the North Pole. Water-poor and oil-rich countries of the Middle East have even considered towing giant icebergs from Antarctica, although they have rejected the possibility for technical and economic reasons.

The Antarctic Ocean is normally taken as being the area of ocean south of the Antarctic convergence zone, a band between about 50° and 55°S. This convergence zone represents the invisible boundary where the cold waters of the Antarctic Ocean—at surface *and* deep levels—interact with the warmer midlevel waters of the sub-Antarctic. The resulting turbulence raises nutrient-rich water to the surface, supports growth of phytoplankton, and thus makes the area very productive biologically.

The Antarctic continental shelf is much narrower and deeper than that of most other continents and lies at a depth of between 1,200 and 1,600 feet (370 and 490 m). It is depressed by the mass of ice that overlies the continental landmass. Beyond the continental shelf, the deep ocean basin is bounded to the north by the mid-ocean ridge system and is subdivided into the Southeast Pacific, South Indian, and Atlantic-Indian basins.

Antarctica and its coastal areas are the coldest parts of the planet. Coastal areas average only -22°F (30°C) and rise above freezing only during the Antarctic summer (December to March).

LIVING RESOURCES

The Antarctic Ocean ecosystem, like that of the Arctic, is dependent on phytoplankton production, which is highly seasonal. The long daylight hours of the Antarctic summer result in high phytoplankton productivity: an estimated 660 million tons (600 mil t) or so per year. This vast phytoplankton community is cropped by zooplankton such as krill, which in turn are eaten by fish, squid, seals, whales, and some seabirds such as penguins (page 202).

The deep waters and extreme conditions of the Antarctic Ocean make commercial fishing a difficult proposition. Although krill is the major harvestable resource, its commercial value is not very high, and much is used as animal feed. In the early 1990s, catch levels averaged 330,600–440,000 tons (300,000–400,000 t) a year (less than 0.5 percent of the world's total marine catch), taken mostly by the former U.S.S.R. and Japan. Of the 100 or so fish species in the region, only a few have been extensively trawled, and average annual fish catches in the period 1991–93 were low, only about 62,814 tons (57,000 t).

A moratorium on commercial whaling in Antarctic waters came into force in 1986, but Japan still hunts for minke whales for "scientific research."

NONLIVING RESOURCES

Geologists believe that there are many major mineral deposits under the South Polar icecap, and U.S. scientists believe that there are large oil reserves under parts of the continental shelf.

Antarctica's pristine environment holds vital interest for scientists who study Earth's atmospheric and climatic record. In October 1991, nations with an interest in Antarctica signed the Madrid Environmental Protocol to ban mineral exploitation in Antarctica for at least 50 years (page 203). In 1996 there were more than 40 permanently occupied scientific stations operated by a total of 18 nations.

The Caribbean Sea

The Caribbean is a place of contrasts: poverty and wealth, isolation and population, clear waters and polluted beaches.

The wider Caribbean, sometimes called the American Mediterranean, is a southwest extension of the North Atlantic Ocean and consists of two large areas—the Caribbean Sea itself to the south and the Gulf of Mexico to the north. Between the two lies the Yucatán basin. In the following account, we consider the wider Caribbean, not just the Caribbean Sea itself.

Geology

The wider Caribbean is separated from the North Atlantic by three island belts: the Bahamas, the Greater Antilles, and the Lesser Antilles. Geologically, the ocean area is fairly young, having been formed by the closure of the Isthmus of Panama, Central America, some 3 million years ago. Unlike the Mediterranean Sea of Europe, the wider Caribbean is much more like an ocean basin, or rather four ocean basins: the Gulf of Mexico to the north, the Yucatán basin in the center, and the Columbian and Venezuelan basins to the south. The last two, together with the Grenada Trough to the east, form the Caribbean Sea.

The lesser Caribbean—the Caribbean Sea itself—lies on a small tectonic plate bordered to the east and west by zones where major plates dip beneath the Caribbean basin. Because of this tectonic activity, both to the east (Central America) and to the west (Lesser Antilles) are regions of sometimes violent earthquakes and volcanoes. For example, the volcanic Mount Pelée on Martinique erupted on the May 8, 1902, causing the death of some 30,000 nearby inhabitants. The northern boundary of the Caribbean plate is a fault line (a boundary where two plates are moving past one another); in February 1976, a shift along this fault caused the Guatemala City earthquake, which claimed 12,000 lives.

Oceanic Circulation and Currents

Surface water flows into the Caribbean Sea itself from the Atlantic Ocean and exits through the Yucatán Channel and into the Gulf of Mexico. There, large eddies are created so that some water stays in the Gulf of Mexico for relatively long periods where it is warmed, supplying the Gulf Stream with heated water. The Gulf Stream (page 64) originates in the Caribbean region and sweeps across the North Atlantic, where it moderates the climate of Northwest Europe.

Eight major river systems, from the Mississippi of the United States to the Orinoco of Venezuela, empty into the wider Caribbean and discharge copious amounts of freshwater, silt, and pollutants that affect coastal waters for many hundreds of miles.

The Caribbean Sea itself and the southern half of the Gulf of Mexico have a tropical climate. Surface seawater temperatures are high and fluctuate little. As a result, through much of the wider Caribbean there is a permanent thermocline (a steep temperature gradient) at a depth of about 330 feet (100 m). This serves to prevent deep nutrient-rich water from rising to the surface of much of the area. As a result, any upwellings that raise biological productivity tend to be very localized.

Human Population

The populations that border the wider Caribbean are extremely diverse. The 12 mainland nations encompass parts of North America, South America, and the whole of Central America; in addition, there are 24 island territories and states. Many of the island inhabitats are of West African or central African origin. There is a rich mix of languages—most communities are Hispanic, some are Dutch- English-, or French-speaking. There are dramatic economic inequalities in the region: the oil-rich United States and Venezuela on the one hand, and the poor Central American and densely populated island states on the other. A few islands, such as Costa Rica, are rich from tourism; many are not.

Living Resources

Much of the wider Caribbean is relatively deep, and because of this—as well as the lack of major upwellings—much of the region is naturally nutrient deficient. However, in the past few decades, rivers that discharge into the Gulf of Mexico and the Caribbean Sea have added heavy loads of nitrates and other nutrients from agricultural land.

The most significant fisheries are associated with mangroves, seagrasses, and coral reefs in shallows off the Mexican and United States coasts. Penaeid prawns, fish, lobster, blue crabs, and oysters account for much of the catch, with artisanal and small-scale commercial operations taking the bulk of the harvest. In the mid-1990s, the U.S. commercial fishery in the Gulf of Mexico was worth about $500 million. The income from recreational fishing—especially for tuna and billfish, such as marlin—was at least this size.

The wider Caribbean is second only to the European Mediterranean Sea in its popularity as a holiday destination. Fourteen percent of the world's coral reefs are found there, and vacationers come from both hemispheres to sample the region's sandy beaches and relatively dry tropical climate.

Nonliving Resources

The Caribbean yields very large quantities of oil and natural gas. The four major oil-producing countries—the United States, Colombia, Mexico, and Venezuela—between them extract several million barrels of oil a day, and throughout the wider Caribbean, 5 million barrels are transported each day. The economies of Barbados and Trinidad and Tobago have benefited enormously from the presence of local oil. Across the wider Caribbean, some 70 or so refineries operate to process locally drilled oil.

Volcanic and sedimentary processes have produced a range of useful mineral deposits in the Gulf of Mexico. Volcanic magma in contact with seawater has yielded precipitates containing potash, magnesium, and calcium sulfate (in the form of anhydrite). Evaporation of seawater over geological time has produced extensive salt deposits, particularly on the northern and western margins of the Gulf of Mexico. Placer

WIDER CARIBBEAN: DATA FILE	
Area	1.7 million square miles (4.4 mil km²)
Mean depth	7,100 feet (2,164 m)
Maximum depth	25,200 feet (7,680 m)—Cayman Trench
Volume of water	2.3 million cubic miles (9.4 mil km³)

deposits (useful minerals eroded from landmasses and accumulating on the sea floor) are quite widespread but have yet to be exploited commercially on any large scale.

Pollution and Conservation

As in many other tropical and subtropical regions of the world, coral reefs and mangrove stands are subject to the deleterious effects of pollution, urban and industrial development, and tourism.

Pollution from oil-extraction and transport operations continues to have widespread environmental impact. One of the world's biggest oil spills occurred in the Ixtoc I field off the Mexican coast in the Bay of Campeche between June 1979 and March 1980 (page 181). Prevailing winds drove crude oil away from the nearby Mexican coastline and onto Texas shores some 500 miles (800 km) away. The cleanup operation cost $4 million, while other costs—lost oil revenue, containing the environmental damage, capping the well, and so on—cost nearly $220 million. Luckily, the long-term environmental effects were comparatively small. Spillage or discharge of oil from oil tankers not following operating procedures closely is still an insidious and continuing threat. Coral reefs, mangrove stands, and seagrass meadows have been locally devastated by chronic oil pollution. Windward-exposed beaches from Florida down to Barbados are patchily contaminated by tar balls and oily residues.

Pesticides and other chemicals enter the Gulf of Mexico from the Mississippi River; this massive river system drains about 40 percent of the land area of the United States. Added to this is a cocktail of pesticides, many banned in the United States, that are discharged by rivers from the 16 South and Central American states that border the wider Caribbean. The likely long-term effects of these pesticides on the Caribbean flora and fauna have yet to be established.

Tourism in the wider Caribbean, as in some parts of the Pacific and Indian Oceans, is a localized threat to many coastal habitats. Tourists, drawn by the white sands and clear waters, visit at the rate of about 100 million a year. There is increasing environmental awareness among hotel owners, but some of the older established hotels do not have proper sewage-treatment facilities, and discharges massively reduce local water quality. Also, coastal developments remove seagrass beds and mangroves that would otherwise have a filtering effect on coastal waters. The loss of these habitats may increase water turbidity locally. In the early 1990s, around the Caribbean basin itself, fewer than 10 percent of the population was being provided with any form of sewage-treatment facility.

Two major environmental initiatives operate within the greater Caribbean. The Environmental Protection Agency (EPA) of the United States began its Gulf of Mexico Program in mid-1988. Among the environmental issues being tackled are habitat loss in coastal ecosystems, pesticide and heavy metal contamination in runoff from land, and shoreline erosion. The Caribbean Environment Program (CEP), under the auspices of the United Nations Environment Program (UNEP), was begun 1981. Although hampered by lack of sizable funding, there is a commitment within the region to manage coastal and marine resources in a sustainable manner and with regard for the environment. For this to become a priority for Central and South American countries, it needs not just political and institutional support, but also a grassroots commitment from individuals in local communities. Environmental education is likely to be a major factor in making this commitment become a practical reality.

The Greater Caribbean

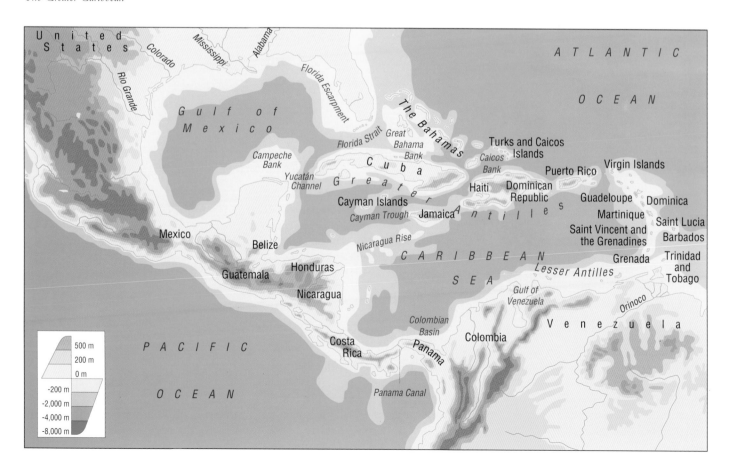

The Mediterranean Sea

The central role of the Mediterranean Sea in Western history is captured in its name, which is derived from the Latin for "middle of the Earth." The sea is enclosed by three continents, Europe, Africa, and Asia. The countries bordering the sea include those that gave birth to civilizations of classical antiquity and huge cultural influence, among them Egypt, Greece, and Rome. Today, the shores of the Mediterranean Sea are the temporary home of more than 100 million sun-seeking tourists each year.

The Mediterranean Sea is in reality a complex of several seas. During recent ice ages, the region comprised several giant lakes, but in today's postglacial period, these are engulfed by water to form a series of connected basins. The Mediterranean is connected to the Atlantic Ocean by the narrow Strait of Gibraltar, the sea's only natural connection to an ocean. At the eastern end, the Mediterranean is linked via the Bosporus and Dardanelles to the Black Sea. The Suez Canal, completed in 1869, connects the Mediterranean to the Red Sea and thus to the Indian Ocean. Several hundred Red Sea species have colonized the Mediterranean since the canal was opened.

The Mediterranean Sea is itself usually recognized as containing several semienclosed smaller seas: the Tyrrhenian Sea; the Adriatic, Ionian, and Aegean Seas; and the small Sea of Marmara that forms the connection to the Black Sea.

Four major rivers—the Ebro, the Nile, the Rhône, and the Po—discharge into the Mediterranean and in so doing form deltas that deposit sediments and influence the salinity and productivity of coastal waters for hundreds of kilometers.

Geology

The Mediterranean is probably a remnant of the Tethys Sea, the body of water that separated the landmasses of Laurasia and Gondwanaland in Jurassic times, 140–180 million years ago. It is thus an old sea, much older than the adjacent Atlantic Ocean. The present-day Mediterranean occupies several deep basins that were formed when the African continent moved northward into Eurasia, buckling the crust into folds, and forming the Alpine and Atlas mountain systems. Comparatively recent geological movements of Europe and Asia away from one another have caused land between Greece and Turkey to subside and water to flow in, so creating the Aegean Sea and opening a connection to the Black Sea.

MEDITERRANEAN SEA: DATA FILE	
Area	1.2 million square miles (3.0 mil km²)
Mean depth	4,760 feet (1,450 m)
Maximum depth	16,700 feet (5,090 m)—eastern Mediterranean basin
Volume of water	1.1 million cubic miles (4.4 mil km³)

Circulation and Currents

The Mediterranean is moderately deep by the standards of most enclosed seas; about 30 percent of the seafloor is 6,550 feet (2,000 m) or more below the surface. In the Mediterranean, sea-surface evaporation is about three times greater than the water that replaces it by precipitation and runoff. The difference is largely made good by inflow of water from the Atlantic Ocean. Prevailing surface currents tend to flow eastward, being warmed and losing water by evaporation as they travel so that surface waters in the eastern Mediterranean tend to be warmer and slightly more saline than those in the western Mediterranean.

The surface current in the Strait of Gibraltar may flow eastward, but below this, at a depth of about 900 feet (275 m) or so, there is a reverse flow of dense, saline water from the Mediterranean into the Atlantic. This deep current was used by submarine commanders in World War II to pass through the strait with engines off, in silent mode, and so be less detectable to surface craft.

Human Population

Coastal populations are much denser on the northern side of the Mediterranean; particularly along the French, Italian, and Spanish coasts, the numbers swell massively during the summer tourist season. The southern side of the Mediterranean—the coast of North Africa—is, by contrast, mostly arid, with few coastal cities and industrial centers.

Living Resources

The surface waters of the Mediterranean are, except in localized areas, relatively nutrient deficient. In many areas, as water evaporates from surface layers, the now more saline water sinks, carrying nutrients with it. This means that the surface waters are fairly unproductive and that fisheries productivity is only moderate. Edible fish are at a premium in many parts of the Mediterranean and command much higher prices than they do elsewhere. The shortfall in supply is largely met by imports from the Atlantic.

According to FAO catch statistics, the annual weight of Mediterranean-caught fish has dropped by about 25 percent between the early 1980s and the early 1990s, largely because of overfishing from ports in southern Europe. Stocks of hake, red mullet, and sole are severely depleted.

In some localities, untreated sewage discharge—although unpleasant and unhealthy locally—does provide a nutrient input that raises productivity. This occurs, for example, in some of the brackish-water lagoons of the Nile Delta, where production of algae-eating tilapia—a small, edible fish—can be very high, approaching levels found in intensive mariculture. On the other hand, damming of the Nile at Aswan has had the reverse effect, reducing the nutrient load over the wider area of the Nile Delta. This may well be the primary cause of the demise of the sardine fishery in this region, with catches dropping by 70 percent after construction of the Aswan Dam.

The potential for mariculture in the Mediterranean is considerable. Shellfish culture, particularly of mussels, is important along the north coast, with sea bream being grown experimentally in cages within the Adriatic. Lagoons border north and south Mediterranean coasts, and fish such as mullet and sea bass have been grown in enclosures in Italy, Israel, and Egypt using methods that date back 2,000 years or more.

Recent estimates suggest that about two-thirds of the world's tourists—many from Europe—visit the Mediterranean region each year.

Nonliving Resources

The Mediterranean has extensive gas and oil reserves, but these are currently exploited only in the most accessible areas—shallow geological features that extend from the shore. The deep-sea

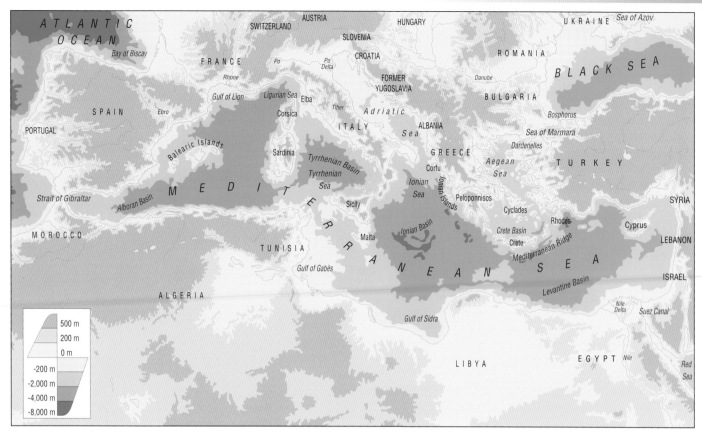

The Mediterranean Sea

drilling ship *Glomar Challenger* in 1972 discovered extensive deposits of anhydrite (rich in calcium sulfate), which is formed where near-surface saline groundwater evaporates. Such findings not only suggest that the Mediterranean Sea was empty of water within the last 5 million years, but also that extensive deposits of such evaporites as anhydrite, potash, and rock salt are available for extraction. Currently these deposits are only exploited where they outcrop on such Mediterranean islands as Sicily.

Pollution and Conservation

Oil tankers regularly enter and cross the Mediterranean from both the Atlantic and the Red Sea, and small discharges from seaboard operations are commonplace. Oil refineries and oil-handling ports are scattered along Libyan, Tunisian, Israeli, and Lebanese coasts to the south and along French, Italian, and Spanish coasts to the north. Not surprisingly, the Mediterranean is an oil-pollution hotspot; tar balls and oily deposits are a relatively common occurrence on many beaches.

A more harmful pollutant, from a human perspective, is untreated sewage. Since the 1970s, great improvements have been made across the Mediterranean in the treatment of sewage before it is discharged into the sea. In 1972, of those areas that were monitored, the worst affected were in parts of the French, Italian, and Spanish Rivieras, and in Israel. Since then, France, and Israel have tackled the treatment problem on a large scale, Italy and Spain on a smaller scale; thus in some regions of the latter two countries, problems still persist. Discharge of untreated sewage is an offense to both the eye and the nose and is a potential threat to public health: gastric disorders still remain a problem for those who visit some parts of the Mediterranean.

The United Nations Environment Program (UNEP) in 1975 provided the catalyst for convincing Mediterranean countries to meet to address the environmental problems facing their sea. The Barcelona Convention brought together representatives from 17 countries to consider ways to reduce or eliminate the discharge of pollutants of various kinds: sewage, industrial waste such as heavy metals, and agricultural pesticides.

A protocol in 1982 began to address the issue of protecting specific areas, and in Genoa in 1985, signatory countries agreed on an action plan, the Mediterranean Action Plan (MAP). This encompassed measures to reduce solid-waste disposal and industrial pollution; the construction of large-scale sewage treatment plants in all major Mediterranean cities; and protection for certain endangered species, such as the Mediterranean sea turtle. In similar situations—where coastal states are diverse in their level of development and have very different views as to the priority afforded to environmental matters—progress has been patchy and intermittent. Also, there are territorial clashes in the region, for example, the dispute between Greece and Turkey over Cyprus. Despite such difficulties, the existence of more than 80 marine laboratories across the Mediterranean, all monitoring environmental parameters, provides a strong scientific baseline to argue the case for preventative action. A new MAP was adopted in 1995. This was influenced by Agenda 21, a plan of action that emerged from the Rio Earth Summit in 1992 (page 197). Agenda 21 seeks to halt futher global environmental degradation while improving the quality of life of the world's poor.

The North Sea

The North Sea, scene of many of the most pivotal events of World War II, is a northeasterly extension of the Atlantic Ocean. It is a shallow expanse bordered by seven of the countries of Northwest Europe. The North Sea is delineated by the Straits of Dover to the south, forming a connection through the English Channel to the North Atlantic; its northerly extent is normally taken to be the west–east line between the Shetland Islands and the Norwegian coast just north of Bergen. The North Sea's easterly limit is commonly taken as a north–south line between the south coast of Norway and most northerly point of Denmark. The narrow Strait of Dover is arguably the busiest shipping lane in the world; at any one time, there may be 500 ships negotiating this 25-mile (40-km)-wide corridor. The North Sea itself is scene of as great a variety of activities as any body of seawater in the world.

Geology

Only 18,000 years ago, the North Sea did not exist: its southern half was covered in scrub and woodland, its northern half was buried below an ice sheet. Since this last ice age, the North Sea has been formed in a region of the continental crust that has subsided and become covered with rising seawater as conditions have warmed and glaciers have melted. Today, the North Sea receives freshwater input from nine major river systems—the Rhine, the Elbe, the Weser, the Schelde, the Ems, the Thames, the Trent, the Tees, and the Tyne—that deposit their sediments in a thick layer over the seafloor.

Circulation and Currents

The prevailing circulation is countercyclonic (in a counterclockwise direction), which means that currents tend to flow southward down the east coast of Britain, then eastward along the French, Belgium, Netherlands, and German shorelines, and northward along Danish and Norwegian coasts. Much of the pollutant-laden runoff from land thus tends to be carried from the U.K. and other countries toward Denmark and Norway. Warm water from the North Atlantic enters the North Sea via the English Channel and keeps the North Sea free of ice throughout the year.

Human Population

On and around North Sea coasts and estuaries live more than 30 million people, most inhabiting

cities and industrialized centers. This population is supplemented by an influx of tourists in summer months, most visiting the cleaner, sandy beaches.

Living Resources

The shallow waters, combined with high nutrient input from rivers and moderate temperatures, make biological productivity high. The North Sea contains some of the most heavily exploited fisheries in the world. The total fish catch has remained nearly level (in the region of 8–10 million metric tons) since the 1960s, but the composition of the catch has markedly altered. Formerly, herring and mackerel predominated, but now such small fish as sandeels, sprats, and Norway pout (all converted into fishmeal) and such larger fish as cod and haddock make up a much more sizable proportion of the catch. A victim of overfishing, the herring fishery had collapsed by the late 1970s.

Although European quota systems serve to regulate the total catch, the value of the catch is declining in real terms. What remains is more-intensively harvested than ever before, using heavy trawl techniques that are particularly damaging to the seafloor and its inhabitants. The maximum sustainable yield to be expected from a region such as the North Sea is not a simple statistic: seas and their inhabitants are dynamic systems and respond to numerous environmental factors—and not just those imposed by humans (page 198).

Nonliving Resources

The discovery and exploitation of gas and oil reserves in the central and northern North Sea is a success story, particularly for the economies of the British Isles and the Netherlands. The environmental costs, however, are often invisible: chronic low-level pollution around oil rigs reduces the diversity of seafloor life. Highly visible oil spills, though devastating to bird life locally, are relatively uncommon.

Gravel and sand for the construction industry is extracted from the North Sea in greater amounts than anywhere else in the world. The deposits are of high, uniform quality with little processing necessary before use. Nearshore, shallow-water dredging operations may be a cause of nearby coastal erosion (page 39). Scientists do not know whether sand and gravel extraction from the floor of the North Sea is having a significant effect on fisheries. Herring use gravel beds as their spawning grounds, and sand eels, an important food source for larger fish, live permanently on gravel beds. Dredging sand releases clouds of silt that can smother bottom-living organisms and may also release toxic materials previously trapped in sediments. One recent study has shown poor recovery of seafloor life following such dredging operations.

Pollution and Conservation

Much of the sewage produced by populations bordering the North Sea was, until recently, discharged into the sea with minimal treatment or none at all. This is changing, and, increasingly, seaside towns are building advanced treatment works. The practice of discharging sewage sludge from coasts or dumping it at sea was discontinued by the mid-1990s. Germany and the Netherlands have now stopped the dumping at sea of heavy metal-contaminated dredgings from Hamburg and Rotterdam harbors.

The environmental health of the North Sea appeared on the political agenda in the 1970s when the German government acknowledged that the health of its coastal waters was an international matter, not a national one. Germany's coastal waters were among the most polluted of any North Sea state. They received river Rhine water that had come not just from Germany itself, but from Switzerland, France, Luxemburg, and Holland as well. The river Elbe discharged into German coastal waters, yet carried wastes from the former Czechoslovakia; and the coastal currents in the southern part of the North Sea

NORTH SEA: DATA FILE	
Area	220,000 square miles (580,000 square km²)
Mean depth	305 feet (93 m)
Maximum depth	2,380 feet (725 m)—Skagerrak Area
Volume of water	12,000 cubic miles (50,000 km³)

The North Sea

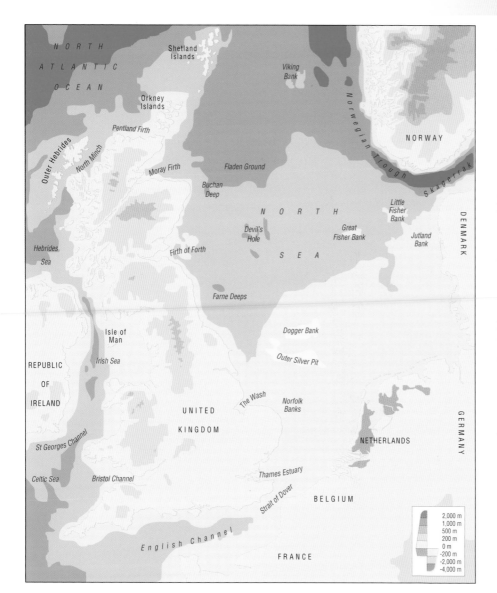

carried wastes from the U.K., France, Belgium, and the Netherlands and dumped them on Germany's "doorstep." Germany, in turn, was adding to this pollution load, and the sum total was then swept away toward the coastal waters of Denmark. Along the German coastline, blooms of phytoplankton were becoming so dense that they were producing unsightly foam; in some cases, they were depleting the bottom waters of oxygen. High nutrient inputs from discharging rivers were suspected of being a contributing factor.

In 1984, the first Conference on the North Sea was held to begin to formulate an international plan for reducing marine pollution. By the late 1980s, the North Sea Task Force—a coordinating group of scientists from all North Sea states—was set up to outline the scientific facts on which to base policy. The North Sea Conference meets every three years and is seeking to develop a strategic plan for the sustainable development of the natural resources of the North Sea while maintaining the quality of the environment. Halving the nutrient load on the North Sea by limiting nutrient-rich runoff from agricultural land is one of their long-term commitments. The North Sea Conference claims to adopt the "precautionary principle." If there is scientific uncertainty about the effect an action may have on the environment, the "benefit of doubt" is given in favor of the environment. It remains to be seen how this will work in practice.

The Red Sea and the Persian Gulf

The Red Sea

The Red Sea is an ocean in the making. Chemical deposits below the seafloor show that 5 million years ago the sea was but a shallow basin with high rates of evaporation. Today, the Red Sea is widening at the rate of about 0.5 inches (1.25 cm) a year. If seafloor spreading continues at this same rate, in 200 million years the Red Sea will be the breadth of the present-day Atlantic Ocean.

The Red Sea is a northward extension of the Indian Ocean and an important shipping corridor for shallow-draft vessels. By taking the Suez Canal route, cargo vessels and small tankers can travel from the Indian Ocean to the Mediterranean and North Atlantic and so avoid the much longer and more hazardous trip around the tip of Africa. Since the canal was opened in 1869, more than 40 species of Red Sea fish that were able to make the journey through the low-salinity reaches of the canal have colonized the Mediterranean. The colonizers have even been accorded a unique name—Lessepsian migrants, after Ferdinand de Lesseps, the French engineer who oversaw the building of the canal.

LIVING RESOURCES

The underwater environment is dominated by a well-established coral reef system that fringes the Red Sea. The waters are comparable to those of the Indo-Pacific region in their rich biodiversity. More than 350 species of Red Sea coral have been recorded, and of these, about 20 species are reported nowhere else. Some of the coral reef fish are also unique to the area.

Human settlements on the shores of the Red Sea are mostly small except for the few larger urban centers such as Al Ghurdaqah and Suez in the north and Port Sudan and Jidda in the south. Much of the fishing is done on a small scale. The few more commercial fisheries include some trawling for bottom-living species near Al Ghurdaqah, Egypt, and sardine fishing in and around the Gulf of Suez. Sardines are caught by lowering large circular nets below the sea surface at night and then attracting sardines by using banks of lights. When shoals gather below the lights, the nets are raised, catching the fish.

Tourism is gradually increasing in the Red Sea area, particularly in the Sinai region. More than 15 dive centers are now established, the majority in Egypt, where enthusiasts come from all over the world to view the underwater splendors of the coral reefs. With the lack of urbaniza-

RED SEA: DATA FILE	
Area	170,000 square miles (450,000 km²)
Mean depth	1,765 feet (538 m)
Maximum depth	8,545 feet (2,604 m)
Volume of water	60,000 cubic miles (240,000 km³)

PERSIAN GULF: DATA FILE	
Total area	90,000 square miles (240,000 km²)
Mean depth	82 feet (25 m)
Maximum depth	560 feet (170 m)
Volume of water	2,000 cubic miles (10,000 km³)

tion and industrialization in the region, the sea has remained relatively free of pollution. Exceptions are the petrochemicals released from offshore oil fields in the Gulf of Suez and untreated sewage discharged close to some major towns and cities.

NONLIVING RESOURCES

The main reasons for the lack of development on the shores of the Red Sea are the desert conditions and the acute lack of water. Seawater itself is a valuable resource. Desalination plants in Saudi Arabia use seawater as a source of drinking and municipal water.

In 1963, metallic residues were discovered in the deeper parts of the Red Sea between Saudi Arabia and Sudan. Metals such as copper, zinc, silver, and gold precipitate from hotwater springs that discharge onto the seafloor. Although these deposits are valuable, it is not yet commercially viable to extract them. Sophisticated technology is required to harvest them from muds at depths of 6,562 feet (2,000 m) or more.

A Red Sea Action Plan was devised by six of the coastal states in 1981. Since the early 1980s, environmental conditions in key parts of the Red Sea have been monitored, and baseline studies have been made to establish the living resources of the sea and the potential pollution hazards. The scientific work and policy making that has developed since then aims to spare the Red Sea the pollution and environmental degradation problems that have beset other enclosed seas, such as the Caribbean, the Mediterranean, and the Persian Gulf.

The Persian Gulf

In comparison to the Red Sea, the Persian Gulf is so shallow (over much of its area it is less than 300 feet [or 100 m] deep) that it is more like a giant lake than a sea. It is about 620 miles (1,000 km) long and varies in width from 45 to 215 miles (75 to 350 km).

Oil, sandy desert, and the Persian Gulf itself are three obvious features that link the eight Gulf states—Bahrain, Kuwait, Iran, Iraq, Oman, Qatar, Saudi Arabia, and the United Arab Emirates. More than 10 million people live on or close to the Gulf shores. Within the region are fierce economic, political, and religious rivalries that, in the last two decades, have erupted in military conflict—the Iran-Iraq war of 1980–88 and the Gulf War of 1991.

Despite the relative affluence of the Gulf states, discord within and between states tends to hamper the development of coordinated strategies for managing the Persian Gulf as a marine ecosystem. Priorities tend to lie with development of the petrochemical resource (oil and gas) rather than the natural environment.

The Persian Gulf, despite its shallowness and landlocked nature, is subject to strong tidal currents that flush waterborne pollutants out of the Persian Gulf and into the larger and deeper Arabian Gulf. This fortunate circumstance, coupled with the high temperatures that prevail in the region, means that agricultural, domestic, and industrial pollution that enters the Persian Gulf is often removed or degraded relatively quickly.

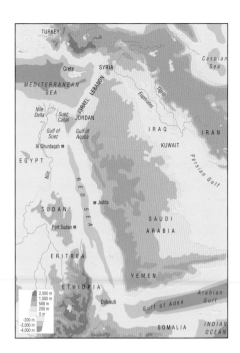

The Red Sea

LIVING RESOURCES

Because Persian Gulf water is shallow and well circulated and receives nutrient input from coastal runoff and discharges, production of phytoplankton is high—much higher than in the Red Sea. Species diversity is much lower, however, and the coral-reef systems are less well developed. Small-scale artisanal fisheries catch a wide range of bottom-living fish species, often by using fish traps; commercial fisheries are largely based on catching surface-water or midwater species such as anchovy, barracuda, mackerel, and sardine. Green turtles are culled from seagrass meadows off the coast of Oman. Kuwaiti and Saudi fisherman trawl for penaeid shrimp. Most Gulf states regulate the fishing through fishermen's associations, which limit quotas. Kuwait and some other Gulf states are developing large-scale fish-farming operations for grouper, sea bream, and tilapia.

NONLIVING RESOURCES

Land-based and offshore oil fields in Iran form one of the world's largest oil-producing industries. Although the Gulf states have given a high priority to sewage treatment, and domestic discharges into the Persian Gulf do not form a severe environmental problem, the same cannot be said for the region's past attitude to industrial pollution. Kuwait is leading the way, however, having constructed a massive industrial wastewater-treatment plant in the early 1990s near Al Fuhayhil. There is a strong impetus to maintain the relative health of Persian Gulf waters, if only to ensure that supplies to desalination plants are relatively untainted: freshwater is a scarce commodity in the Gulf and volume-for-volume is more valuable than oil. Most drinkable water is obtained from desalination plants that use Gulf seawater, and the intake valves at desalination plants are closely monitored for the presence of harmful pollutants.

More than 700 offshore oil and gas platforms operate in the Persian Gulf and more than half of all world oil carried by ships is exported from 25 major oil terminals scattered throughout the Gulf region. Much of the oil is transported by large tankers that have capacities of much more than 220,400 tons (200,000 t). Chronic oil pollution results in detectable, if not harmful, levels of hydrocarbon residues (from petrochemicals) being found in the tissues of many marine organisms, particularly those near shipping lanes and offshore oil rigs.

During the Gulf War of 1991 and the Iran-Iraq War of 1980–88, several million barrels of oil were released into the sea from damaged installations and tankers. In January 1991, Iraqi forces deliberately released oil from a Kuwaiti oil terminal and opened several land-based well heads. An estimated 550 billion tons (500 billion t) of oil were released into the Persian Gulf, making this the world's biggest combined oil spill. What is surprising is how quickly shallow-water biological communities, including coral reefs, have recovered from what seemed like catastrophic swamping by heavy oil fractions. Nevertheless, countless thousands of birds and larger sea creatures have been killed, and some beaches and shallow-water areas are still covered by dense, tarry deposits that have destroyed most of the local flora and fauna. An encouraging sign is that oil-degrading bacteria and a few photosynthetic forms—among them some diatoms and cyanobacteria (page 88)—seem able to survive such inhospitable conditions and are in the process of breaking down some deposits.

The Regional Organization for the Protection of the Marine Environment (ROPME) was established in 1982 and is the only truly Gulf-wide forum for dealing with environmental issues. It is currently supported by all the Gulf states and is focusing on the issues of oil pollution and fisheries management. Its activities have been hampered by armed hostilities in the region.

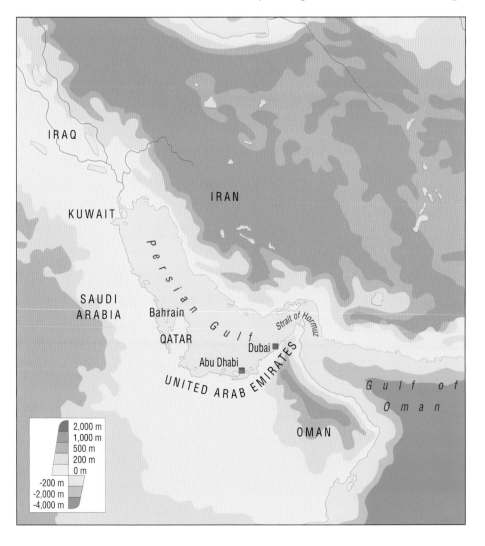

The Persian Gulf

Shores and Estuaries

Shores

Shores are the places where land and sea meet. They are the places where discoverers first set foot on distant lands. They are places of solace, where we go for quiet walks, to listen to the rhythmic crashing of waves, and to lose ourselves in thought. Shores are dynamic places: in some locations waves tear and gouge at cliffs; in others the sea deposits a bountiful load of sand or mud on flat, expansive beaches. Shores are demanding places: creatures that live there have to withstand alternate immersion in seawater and exposure to air as the tides rise and fall.

Strictly, the shore is that zone that lies between extreme low tide (page 86) and the highest regions of the coastline that are affected by storm waves. The coast itself extends inland from the shore to encompass the strip of land that is obviously affected by marine processes. Shorelines are shaped by the action of wind, waves (page 72), tides (page 70), and currents (page 7). Whether a shoreline is rocky or sandy depends on local circumstances: the height of the land relative to the sea; the nature of the underlying rock, and whether the local waves, tides, and currents deposit material on the shore or tend to remove it.

ROCKY SHORES

Rocky shores, often characterized by cliffs and dramatic scenery, are the scenes of geological events where high, rocky landforms are brought into direct contact with sea on an exposed coastline. One way in which this can happen is the rise of the sea level relative to the land to create a submergent coastline (page 38). Low-lying river valleys become flooded with seawater to form deep inlets from the sea. Headlands between the flooded valleys are then exposed to wave action and are gradually worn away to form cliffs.

Erosion of a rocky shore is caused, in part, by suspended particles in seawater being driven against the rock and so wearing away the surface by abrasion. For animals and plants to survive, they need to be able to resist strong turbulence and battering as waves crash against them, or else they need to stay secure in fissures and crevices. Where the underlying rock is soft and easily eroded, the community of seashore organisms tend to be sparse because there is a lack of a secure and long-term footing. Where the rock is hard and erosion resistant, communities of organisms tend to better establish themselves; where the surface is pitted and creviced, it offers opportunities for organisms to survive in damp, protected environments higher up the shore.

Well-established vertical or steeply angled rocky shores develop what is called a vertical zonation of plants and animals (page 86): Those better able to withstand wave action and competition from other marine creatures exist toward the bottom of the shore, and those better able to withstand desiccation (drying out) are found toward the top of the shore.

SANDY SHORES

Sandy or muddy shores are found in sheltered parts of the coastline where particles—from erosion of other parts of the coast and sediments emptying into the sea from rivers—settle and accumulate. The particles are carried along by currents that move parallel to the shore, a process called longshore drift. Wooden, stone, or cement barriers called groins are commonly set up across the beach at right angles to the shoreline to help counteract beach drifting. Sand accumulates on the up-current side of the barrier and is swept away from the down-current side.

As particles are washed to and fro by waves and currents, they rub against each other and gradually become reduced in size by mechanical abrasion. At the same time, water movement sorts the material into particles of different size: Larger particles fall out of the water column much more readily and tend to be deposited on the highest parts of the beach; smaller particles tend to remain suspended in water; the finest sediments—mud, which is composed of small particles of silt and clay—are found below the tidal range of the shore or below slow-moving coastal waters such as the mudflats of estuaries.

Most of the animals on sandy shores live below the surface. The sand offers protection and trapped moisture; the surface, however, is an exposed, hostile, ever-changing environment. Most animals on sandy shores are burrowers, many remaining for most of their lives below the surface. In many cases, worms and clams stay in their protective burrows and simply extend their feeding apparatus into the suspended larder of food—planktonic organisms and particles of decaying matter—above the surface of the sand. So, although a sandy beach or a tidal mudflat may appear lifeless when exposed at low tide, in reality there is a seething mass of life below the surface, and when the seawater covers the sand or mud, the inhabitants spring into action.

TAMING THE COASTLINE

Humans spend much time and money constructing coastal defenses in attempts to combat the erosional effects of the sea. This is not necessarily time and money well spent. Protecting one part of the coastline by constructing storm defenses or tidal barriers often serves simply to shift the problem to another part of the coast, and resulting changes in currents have unpredictable effects. Recent findings suggest that sea levels have risen by 4 inches (10 cm) in the last century and are probably continuing to rise (page 41). A much more systematic and long-term approach to coastal defense is required, rather than the piecemeal approaches commonly employed today. By understanding how coastal processes work, we may well be able to harness them for our benefit rather than striving ineffectually to keep them at bay.

Estuaries

To many people, estuaries are forbidding, inhospitable places, sometimes seemingly little more than large expanses of mud with creeks cutting through them. But to those who understand the role of estuaries in the rhythm of tides and seasons, estuaries are a storehouse of treasures for us and other creatures. Despite appearances, estuaries are among the most productive environments on Earth.

Estuaries are places where rivers meet the sea. They are the meeting place of freshwater and seawater. Estuaries provide natural harbors, and many of the world's great cities—Bombay, Buenos Aires, New York, São Paulo, Shanghai, and Tokyo—have grown up beside them. Humans try to tame estuaries and their mudflats. They dredge them, drain them, fill them, and build on them. They also use the edges of estuaries as landfills to dispose of garbage.

There are four main kinds of estuary. As sea-levels rose after the last ice age, lowland areas and river mouths became engulfed by seawater, forming drowned river valleys (or coastal plain estuaries). The bar-built estuary is a shallow estuary separated from the open ocean by sandbars. Tectonic estuaries, such as part of the San Francisco Bay in California, were created not because sea levels rose, but because the land has dropped (subsided) or become folded as a result of geological movements, and river water has entered the low-lying area. The fourth type of estuary—a fjord—is created by glaciers that have cut deep, steep-sided, U-shaped valleys along the coast.

A DIFFICULT LIFE

Living in an estuary is not easy, but for those organisms that have adapted successfully, the

Windward cliffs, Galápagos Islands, Equador (Gerry Ellis/ENP Images)

rewards are enormous. Beneath the surface of the mud, microorganisms and burrowing animals occur in immense numbers. Between the mud particles is a microscopic world of grazers, scavengers, and predators all more-or-less dependent on the energy obtained from a rainfall of detritus (dead organic matter and the microscopic organisms that coat its surface) that is carried to the estuary by rivers and the photosynthesis of single-celled plants that live in the top few millimeters of the mud. Buried in the mud but feeding above it are clams that use inhalent siphons (tubelike structures) to vacuum the surface of the mud. Burrowing worms and shrimp too feed largely on deposits settling on the mud's surface, but some are suspension feeders and trap particles while they are still suspended in the water column and before they settle.

Some of the larger animals associated with estuarine mud move onto and off the mudflats at different states of the tide. When the tide rises and seawater covers the mudflats, fish move in to feed on animals that move about on the mud's surface

or that protrude parts of their bodies above the surface. Often, the fish do not eat their entire prey but simply nip off the most accessible part of the creature, for example, the siphon of a clam. When the tide falls and the mudflats are uncovered, wading shorebirds assemble in their thousands to feed on the animals in the mud. Estuaries are a lifeline for migrating birds—ducks, geese, and more exotic birds such as flamingos, as well as waders. Estuaries also have an unseen and unusual role to play: They recycle nutrients between the sea and the land. Nutrients that are brought down by rivers and that accumulate in the estuarine mud pass through food chains and, in many cases, are eventually consumed by birds. The birds' droppings, falling on the land, return lost nutrients to the soil.

THE HUMAN IMPACT

Estuaries have suffered greater human impact—intentional and unintentional—than any other part of the marine environment. Because many people seem to regard estuaries as a waste of good land—land that could be developed for human use—estuaries are under constant threat from developers. Unintentional impact includes many forms of pollution. The freshwater runoff that carries nutrients to the estuaries and makes them

so productive also carries pollution—heavy metals, fertilizers, and pesticides. Untreated sewage is discharged into estuaries on the assumption that tides and currents will sweep the waste away, but this assumption is misguided. Also, the close proximity of industrial complexes, oil refineries, docks, and marinas ensure that a rich mix of chemicals and garbage enters the estuary directly from human activities.

In North America and northern Europe, many estuarine shellfish beds have now been closed due to bacterial contamination from human sewage. The exploitation of estuarine fisheries has, in some cases, been halted because of heavy metal and pesticide accumulation in fish. At least three-quarters of all fished marine species in the eastern United States spend part of their life in estuaries. Anadramous fish (those, such as salmon, that travel from the sea to spawn in freshwater) and catadramous fish (those, such as freshwater eels, that travel from freshwater to sea to spawn) must run the gauntlet of estuaries in order to breed. We cannot go on removing or degrading the estuarine environment at the present rate without creating long-term problems for the health of our coastal waters and our seaside towns and cities and, ultimately, harming the wider oceans, too.

Coastal Wetlands

Coastal wetlands are commonly found in the hinterland between inland areas and partly enclosed coastal areas such as estuaries. These low-lying coastal strips are intermittently covered by new supplies of seawater on the rising tide and during ocean swells. The substrate underfoot is oxygen-poor mud and peat (partly decayed organic material associated with oxygen-deficient conditions). Worldwide, biologists generally recognize two main types of coastal wetland: salt marshes and mangrove swamps.

Salt Marshes

Salt marshes are known to occur from the equator to latitudes as high as 65°, although in tropical and subtropical latitudes, the marshes tend to give way to mangrove communities. In North America, salt marshes are particularly extensive along the Atlantic and Gulf of Mexico coasts because of the optimal conditions provided by relatively sheltered shorelines and low-lying coastal strips.

Like the mudflats of estuaries, the salt marsh is a severe environment, fluctuating widely in temperature and salinity. In temperate latitudes, salt marshes are dominated by marshgrasses. On the seaward edge of North American saltmarshes, these tend to be cord grasses of the genus *Spartina* that grow as much as 6 feet (2 m) tall. The landward edges often give way to rushes (*Juncus*) and other grasses such as glasswort (*Salicornia*). Throughout much of the salt marsh, the roots of plants bind the mud together, so the substrate becomes stabilized. In this community—a transitional area between land and sea—land-living animals enter, among them insects, snakes, birds, and mammals such as rats and, in North America, raccoons. However, the vegetation itself is relatively indigestible and comparatively little is actually consumed by larger plant-eating animals. Most is decomposed by microscopic bacteria and fungi. The detritus and inhabitants of the water of the salt marsh provide food for many birds, while the vegetation itself provides concealed (and often predator-inaccessible) nesting sites. Salt marshes often provide vital stop-off points for birds on migratory routes; others use them as their main overwintering grounds or summer feeding areas. So, throughout the year there is plenty of birdlife of one form on another on salt marshes.

Unhampered, salt marshes have a surprisingly high—but by and large unrecognized—economic value. In the southeastern United States alone, salt marshes serve as nursery grounds for more than half the species of commercially important marine fish, among them menhaden and mullet. Within the marshes are located fisheries for crab, eel, and smelt, together with shellfish resources such as clams, oysters, and scallops.

Red mangroves at sea edge, south Florida to northern South America (Gerry Ellis/ENP Images)

Mangroves

Mangrove communities are restricted to tropical and subtropical regions at latitudes 30° or less, where they are found on the upper tidal range of many coastlines. The mangrove trees themselves, of which there are about 60 species, range in size from the diminuitive shrubs less than 3 feet (1 m) high, to the high-rise black mangroves and red mangroves of equatorial South America that reach 130 feet (40 m) tall. Mangroves are tolerant of a wide range of salinities and are able to live in oxygen-poor mud by having both shallow and aerial (aboveground) roots through which they can absorb oxygen. Mangroves are probably found scattered along two-thirds of tropical and subtropical coastlines but are most extensive in the Indian Ocean–West Pacific region. In places such as the Ganges delta in the Bay of Bengal, they protect the coastal zone from damage that would otherwise be wrought by floods, storms, and cyclones (page 76). Removal of mangroves thus has a profound effect on the stability of a coastline.

Although mangroves are not among the most biodiverse marine communities, their major aboveground component, the mangrove trees themselves, provide food and shelter for many insects, reptiles, birds, and mammals that may also feed on animals and plants associated with the water and mud below. The vertical roots of the mangroves—sometimes exposed, sometimes covered by seawater—provide a firm place of attachment for various molluscs, including barnacles and oysters, and snails roam on their surfaces. The aquatic component of the mangrove community is extremely important because it provides nursery grounds for a range of commercially important marine animals: fish, crustaceans (crabs, prawn, and shrimp), and shellfish (clams, mussels, and oysters). Mangrove swamps are also extremely productive, being in high light-intensity regions of the world and in a nutrient-rich swampy environment, although salinity stress (coping with the demands of a strongly saline environment) may limit productivity.

In many parts of the world, indigenous peoples have lived in harmony with mangrove swamps for thousands of years. The trees themselves provide durable building material and fuel for fires, and the wood and leaves are used to construct fish traps. The leaves are also used as fodder for goats and cattle, and the tannin extracted from mangroves is used as a preservative for netting and cloth. As in other wetland and coastal environments, problems arise where mangroves are systematically cleared. Where this renewable resource is removed to make way for intensive agriculture, as in the rice paddies of India and Indonesia, the short-term gain of a few may be made at the expense of the long-term benefit of many. In Ecuador, the removal of stands of mangroves has drastically reduced the supply of juvenile shrimp for stocking growing-on ponds. By the early 1990s, many of these ponds lay empty.

Coastal Lagoons

On the landward side of saltmarshes and other coastal features are sometimes found shallow bodies of water called coastal lagoons. These are complex, dynamic environments, often offering a freshwater environment on the landward side, where rivers of streams flow into them. On the seaward side, they may afford hypersaline (above the salinity of seawater) environments where evaporation concentrates the salt water. Between the hypersaline and freshwater environments is brackish water: the precise boundaries between one region and the other shift with tide, degree of freshwater runoff, season of the year, and other factors. The intensively fished Lake Manzala in the Nile Delta of northern Egypt is a lagoon of this type.

Some lagoons have relatively little freshwater input, and their connections to the sea are also marginal. As water evaporates in the lagoon, hypersaline conditions are produced. Such a challenging environment is survived by few animals and plants. The Laguna Madre—a long, narrow strip of water on the Texas coast between Corpus Christi and the mouth of the Rio Grande—is one such lagoon.

Prime Real Estate

More than half of United States mainland's total wetlands (including freshwater ones) have been lost; about 90 million acres (36 mil ha) remain from an estimated original of 215 million acres (87 mil ha). In 1986, the Environmental Protection Agency established the Office of Wetlands Protection (OWP) to help stem the continued loss. This agency helps identify the most valuable wetlands for protection, those worthy of restoration, and takes action against polluters and developers who violate federal regulations.

Coastal wetlands play an unseen but vitally important role in cleaning groundwater. Agricultural runoff is often rich in nitrates and other chemicals that might cause overenrichment (eutrophication) of coastal waters. Salt marshes and mangroves can "cleanse" this runoff by a combination of living and nonliving activities that take place in the mud. The chemicals are trapped by mud particles, and bacteria recycle them into innocuous or less potent chemical forms. Harmful heavy metals from industrial discharges are also adsorbed onto mud particles and are temporarily removed from circulation. Nitrates and other macronutrients (major growth-promoting chemicals) are absorbed by plants—grasses or mangroves—and contribute to wetlands being some of the world's most productive communities. When the plants die, they are either partially decomposed and form part of the peat, or they are broken down still further and their fragments form detritus that is consumed by all manner of larger animals, including some birds, finfish, and shellfish. Organic material is finally broken down into inorganic material by microscopic bacteria and fungi.

The Structure of Earth

Geology is the scientific study of the structure and functioning of Earth. Today, geology, like the other sciences, has become an interdisciplinary subject, overlapping with other sciences to spawn subdisciplines such as geophysics (the study of geology using methods derived from the physical sciences) and biogeochemistry (how biological and chemical processes are involved in geological phenomena).

In our scientific exploration of the oceans, geology is an appropriate starting place. The study of geology tells us how oceans were first formed and how they are continuing to evolve. But first we need to know more about how Earth itself is formed.

The structure of Earth reflects the planet's early history (page 2). When Earth was entirely molten, more than 4 billion years ago, high-density material (rich in iron and nickel) gravitated toward the center of the planet and less-dense material (rich in silicates) rose toward its outer edge. Now that Earth has cooled, the planetary material occupies several distinct layers.

Earth's inner region, appropriately called the core, is solid at its center and is less dense, partially molten rock toward its outer edge. The swirling motions of the iron-rich material in this layer are like a dynamo generating Earth's changing magnetic field. Temperatures and pressures within the core are so high that conventional laws of physics may not apply; the center of the core is probably at a temperature of 8,672°F (4,800°C) and a pressure of 3.5 million atmospheres.

Surrounding the molten outer core is a layer of moderately hot, moderately dense rocks called the mantle. This comprises more than 80 percent of Earth's bulk and more than two-thirds of its mass. It consists of stony material, rich in magnesium and iron silicates. The inner part of the mantle tends to be solid (the mesosphere), and the outer part tends toward being a slow-moving liquid (the asthenosphere).

Outside the asthenosphere is the lithosphere—a relatively thin, solid outer layer of mantle material

PLANET EARTH: DATA FILE	
Diameter at the equator	7,926 miles (12,756 km)
Diameter at the poles	7,900 miles (12,714 km)
Circumference at the equator	24,901 miles (40,075 km)
Circumference at the poles	24,860 miles (40,008 km)
Earth's total surface area	197 million square miles (510 mil km²)
Total land area (flattened)	57 million square miles (148 mil km²)
Total ocean area	140 million square miles (362 mil km²)
Mean land elevation	0.52 miles (0.84 km)
Mean ocean depth	2.32 miles (3.73 km)

COMPARISON OF OCEANIC AND CONTINENTAL CRUST

	Oceanic crust (basaltic)	Continental crust (granitic)
Density (grams per cubic centimeter)	3.0	2.7
Average thickness (kilometers)	5	20–50
Geological age (in millions of years)	0–180	0–3,800
Characteristic color	Dark	Light
Typical chemical composition	Rich in iron and magnesium	Rich in aluminum, calcium, sodium, and potassium

covered by Earth's crust. The crust is the material we recognize as making up Earth's surface. The lithosphere comprises seven major plates of material that float on the liquid part of the upper mantle. Convection currents (caused by differential heating) create slow, swirling movements in the upper mantle, and these cause the plates to move slowly across Earth's surface—a phenomenon described by the theory of plate tectonics (page 32).

The lithospheric plates floating on Earth's mantle comprise either continental crust or oceanic crust or a mixture of both. The crust under the oceans (oceanic crust) is denser than that comprising the continents (continental crust):

Oceanic crust is composed mainly of silica (Si) and magnesium (Mg) ores that form dark-colored rocks commonly classified as basaltic (made of basalt). Continental crust comprises massive chunks of twisted and contorted rocks, most containing silica (Si) and aluminum (Al) ores and that are lighter in color and usually termed as granitic (made of granite). In effect, the oceanic crust and the continental crust float on the semiliquid mantle; because the continental crust is lighter (less dense), it floats higher and thus forms land. The oceanic crust being heavier (more dense), it occupies low-lying areas that have since become filled with salt water to form seas and oceans.

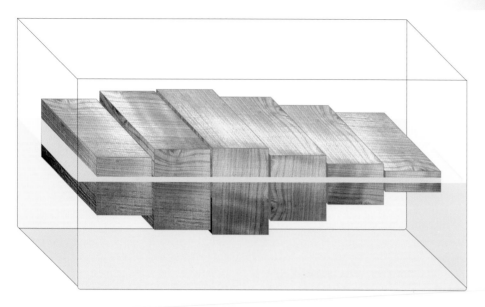

Demonstration of isostasy

named after the Croatian seismologist Andrija Mohorovičić (1857–1936), who first suggested its presence in 1909. The Moho discontinuity marks the boundary between the lithosphere and the asthenosphere.

Isostasy: Earth's Crust in Balance

The explanation offered earlier—the continental crust and oceanic crust floating on the upper mantle—is essentially correct but is simpler than the real situation. In fact, granitic continental crust lies above a layer of deeper continental crust that is basaltic and is similar in character to oceanic crust. Granitic crust floats higher than basaltic crust; both are supported by the more-dense upper mantle. The different heights of continental regions (and therefore different masses of rock) are supported and balanced from below, in a similar manner to blocks floating in water. High mountains require more support than lowland areas and so have a greater depth of "submerged" crust. The process of "keeping a state of balance" in Earth's crust is termed isostasy. Realizing the implications of this process is important in understanding certain geological phenomena. On land, when mountains are eroded, the rocks below them gradually rise as the overlying weight is removed: This is equivalent to cutting the top off a wooden block—the lower part of the block will now be less submerged than before. Conversely, in the sea, the buildup of sediment in shallow water may cause the underlying crust to sink, so lowering the seabed and keeping it submerged. More sediment can then be accommodated.

So the oceans are not just places where seawater happens to cover the land. The seafloor is geologically distinct from the continental crust: it has a different appearance, physical properties, and chemical composition (see table on page 26). Also, oceanic crust is quite young by geological standards: The oldest rocks are probably about 180 million years old. Rocks on continental landmasses, on the other hand, can be as old as 3.8 billion years. As we shall see later, the relative youth of the seafloor is due to the process of seafloor spreading (page 30), which continuously creates new oceanic crust while old oceanic crust is continually destroyed.

Earthquakes occur when masses of rock are fractured and moved by gigantic forces within Earth's crust or mantle. The nearest point on Earth's surface directly above the earthquake site is called the epicenter. Shock waves from the earthquake are felt most strongly at this point, but they spread outward in all directions, including down into Earth's depths. The shockwaves can be detected and their form and intensity measured using a seismograph. Commonly, three types of shockwaves are detected, and each yields different kinds of information. By analyzing the reflections and refractions of the different kinds of waves, it is possible to estimate the nature and thickness of the different layers within Earth. One of the major features detected in this way is the Mohorovičić (*Moho* for short) discontinuity

Investigating Earth's Structure

Information about the deep structure of Earth has to be gathered indirectly. Even the deepest drilling operations barely scratch Earth's surface. The deepest borehole is found in the Kola Peninsula of Arctic Russia and although more than 7.5 miles (12 km) deep, it is barely one-eighth of the distance through Earth's lithosphere. However, useful information can be gathered even at this depth. The measured temperature rise over this distance, if extrapolated to 1,865 miles (3,000 km) below Earth's surface, gives some indication of the likely temperature at the edge of the core—about 7,050°F (about 3,900°C). The lava that erupts from volcanoes provides information about the chemical composition of Earth's crust and mantle. However, earthquakes provide geophysicists with the bulk of their knowledge about Earth's deep structure.

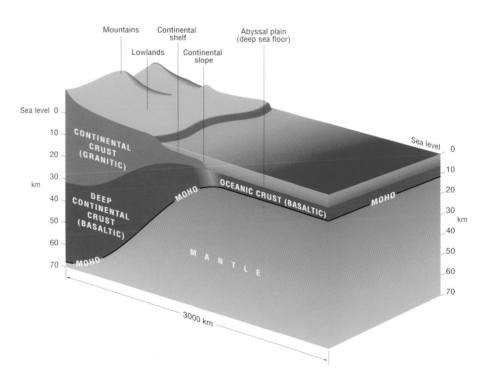

Continental and oceanic crust

Earth's Water

Water is vitally important to life on Earth; it is the presence of liquid water that makes life possible and distinguishes Earth from apparently "dead" planets such as Venus and Mars. Water has the remarkable property of partially or completely dissolving many different kinds of substances; hence, it is dubbed the universal solvent. The distribution of water on the planet largely governs the location and abundance of life. Organisms of all kinds—from microscopic bacteria to large plants and animals—are, themselves, composed of at least two-thirds water.

Water is the planet's most potent chemical and heat transporter, taking substances between land and sea and acting as a massive heat sink that distributes tropical heat to the subtropical, temperate and polar regions. The presence of water in the atmosphere determines the nature of our climate. Clouds of condensed water droplets reduce sunlight penetration, release rain, and form an insulating layer that shrouds Earth. Water is also one of the most powerful erosive agents, literally shaping the land whether as moving liquid or ice.

Of the available water on the planet, seawater comprises about 97.2 percent; the remaining 2.8 percent is freshwater. About three-quarters of the freshwater fraction (2.1 percent of total water) is frozen in icecaps and glaciers; the remainder is contained in rivers, lakes, and groundwater (0.7 percent of total), with the amount within clouds and the water vapor in the atmosphere a minute fraction of the whole (0.001 percent), and the amount within living organisms an even tinier fraction (0.00004 percent). Such statistics fly in the face of many people's everyday experience, and it puts the volume of space occupied by living organisms in proper relation to the vastness of the nonliving world.

The planet's available water is transported between the land, atmosphere, and oceans through the continuous water cycle, called the hydrological cycle. Water leaves the oceans, freshwater, and land through evaporation and enters the atmosphere as water vapor. There it cools, condenses, and then falls as precipitation (rain, hail, or snow). Although the volume of water in the atmosphere is comparatively small, it moves rapidly through this part of the cycle and stays in the air, on average, for about 10 days—although in that time it may have traveled across Earth's surface by 620 miles (1,000 km) or more. It is the relative distributions of evaporation and precipitation, coupled with ambient temperatures, that determine which parts of the landmasses are luxuriant with plant growth and which are arid. Once a rich biological system is formed, it strongly influences the environment and may alter the local climate: tropical rain forests, for example, seed their own clouds.

About 90 percent of the water that evaporates from the oceans returns directly to the oceans as rainfall; the remaining 10 percent is carried over landmasses, where it falls as precipitation. Most seeps into sediments and into porous or fractured rock where it forms groundwater; relatively little stays on soil or rock surfaces and evaporates into the air. The bulk of water is then returned to the oceans via rivers and groundwater seepage. Within the hydrological cycle, the total water extracted from the sea and returned to it remains about the same; otherwise the oceans would fluctuate considerably in volume, and mean sea levels would change. Climatic changes do, however, alter sea levels over thousands of years, and recent evidence suggests that sea levels are now changing quite rapidly (page 41).

The hydrological cycle depicted here simplifies the real situation. (Figures in parentheses refer to stores of water in different environments [in million cubic centimeters]. Figures alongside arrows refer to movements of water [in million cubic kilometers per year].) At each stage of the cycle, there are many possible routes for the water: water precipitating on land may become locked in a frozen glacier for thousands of years, may immediately evaporate back into the atmosphere, may enter the groundwater and be

The hydrological cycle

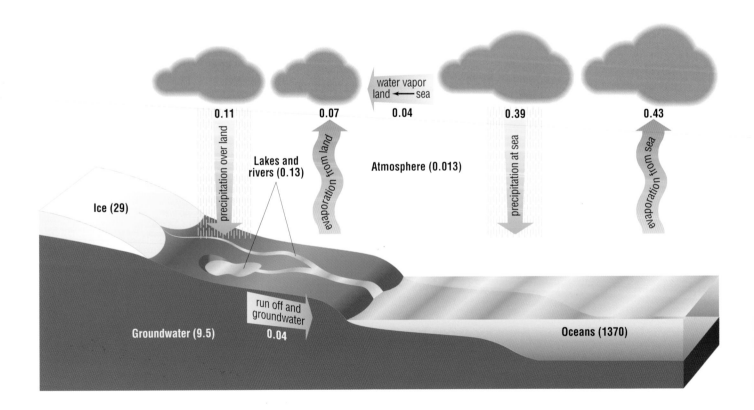

water vapor
land ← sea

0.11   0.07   0.04   0.39   0.43

precipitation over land

Lakes and rivers (0.13)

evaporation from land

Atmosphere (0.013)

precipitation at sea

evaporation from sea

Ice (29)

run off and groundwater
0.04

Groundwater (9.5)

Oceans (1370)

absorbed by the roots of a plant, or may take one of numerous other routes through this part of the water cycle. The time water spends in any one part of the cycle thus varies considerably. A water molecule spends typically just a few days in the lower atmosphere before precipitating, but in the upper atmosphere it may remain a year or more. Traveling down a river to the sea may take a water molecule just a few days; alternatively it could be stored in groundwater for 10,000 years or locked up in an ice sheet for 100,000 years. Geologists calculate that it takes 38,000 years for

the average molecule of water to make the round trip from the oceans, via the atmosphere, through the groundwater, and back into the oceans. Calculations by oceanographers suggest that a molecule of water takes 1,000 years to travel through the planet's oceans and return to near its starting point.

However vast the amounts of surface water, they probably comprise only about 10 percent of the planet's total reservoir: The bulk is chemically locked into mineral matter below Earth's surface. During volcanic activity, the water is released as

Rivers empty into the Gulf of Papua, east of Port Moresby, Papua New Guinea (Gerry Ellis / ENP Images)

superheated steam, and it is this water, falling as precipitation, that probably gave rise to the oceans during the planet's evolution (page 2). The existence of large areas of sedimentary rock laid down about 3.8 billion years ago suggests that oceans have been on planet Earth since at least that time.

How Oceans Are Created

As recently as the early 1960s, many geologists believed that the continents were relatively fixed in their positions on the planet's surface. They also rejected suggestions from physicists that the oceans were much younger than the continents. Discoveries since then have overturned these views. Since that time our understanding of how the oceans and continents were created and how they have evolved has been transformed. The textbooks of geology have been rewritten.

It was not until the 16th and 17th centuries that maps were sufficiently detailed and accurate to begin to make out the true shapes of continents. English philosopher Sir Francis Bacon (1561–1626) was reputedly the first person to note that the coasts on opposite sides of the Atlantic appeared to fit together rather like the pieces of a jigsaw puzzle. It remained until the late 19th century before someone, in this case Eduard Suess (1831–1914), professor of geology at the University of Vienna, pieced together the outlines of southern continents. He brought them together in a manner that suggested that they had all formed part of a supercontinent, which he named Gondwanaland. Further evidence in support of this view began to accumulate as strata and fossils in eastern South America and western Africa—now separated by the South Atlantic—were found to correspond closely. Also, strata and fossils found in present-day cold climates were found to be associated with previously tropical conditions and vice versa. Geologists were hard pressed to explain these observations in terms of traditional theories. Suess also suggested that the present-day northern continents were once joined together in a supercontinent called Laurasia, which was separated from Gondwanaland by the Tethys Sea.

Continental Drift

Nevertheless, by the beginning of the 20th century, the prevailing view was that continents were fixed in their present positions and had been since their formation. However, Alfred Wegener (1880–1930), a German meteorologist, gathered together the evidence available at the time and in 1912 published a German-language book entitled *The Origin of Continents and Oceans*. This text contained the first well-formulated hypothesis regarding continental drift—that the continents gradually moved long distances over Earth's surface. Wegener went further than Suess and suggested that Northern and Southern Hemisphere continents had all been joined in a single supercontinent, which he called Pangaea. He believed that Pangaea began to break up into continents about 180 million years ago, and since

that time they have been drifting into their present-day positions. The climate of scientific opinion at the time was hostile to Wegener's ideas, and no one was able to suggest a plausible mechanism as to what might cause continents to drift. Wegener himself suggested tidal or gravitational forces that operate at different points on the globe. In a special meeting of the Royal Geographical Society in London in January 1923, the following sentiment was recorded: No one who "valued his reputation for scientific sanity" would propose a hypothesis about drifting continents. It was not until the 1950s, some 20 years after Wegener's death, that his ideas about continental drift could begin to be tested rigorously.

After World War II, surplus naval vessels became available to U.S. oceanographers. In the early 1950s, scientists began to map the ocean floor in some detail using sonar equipment. Later expeditions analyzed ocean-floor samples to determine age and magnetic polarity of underlying rock. By the late 1950s, the sonar surveys had established the existence of mid-ocean ridges. These are raised areas of the mid-ocean floor that form a continuous chain of undersea mountains that encircle the globe and connect between one major ocean and another. In places, the submarine mountains rise above the surface of the sea as volcanic islands. Under the sea, the ridge system is crossed at fairly regular intervals by large splits called transform faults. Some distance away from the ridges—often long distances away—are found deep depressions in the seafloor called trenches.

Seafloor Spreading

By the early 1960s, it was apparent that volcanic and earthquake activity was associated with the system of trenches and ridges. Deep-focus earthquakes and surface or submerged volcanoes were often found near trenches; shallow-focus earthquakes and volcanoes were commonly associated with mid-ocean ridges. In 1960, Robert S. Dietz working with the U.S. Coast and Geodetic Survey and Harry Hess at Princeton University independently came to the conclusion that oceanic crust was continuously spreading from the oceanic ridges. They suggested that convection currents in the underlying mantle were responsible for this movement. By the mid-1960s, evidence was building that new crustal material was being formed at the mid-ocean ridges and was being taken down into Earth (subducted) at trenches. Close to a mid-ocean ridge, the oceanic crust is young; farther away, it is older.

This is confirmed by the fact that close to the ridge, the layer of sediment (loose material that settles on the ocean floor) is thin but becomes thicker as one moves away from the crest of the ridge. Radiometric dating techniques (using the radioactive decay of rock-embedded isotopes for accurate dating) provide additional confirmation.

Some of the strongest evidence in support of the seafloor-spreading concept came from measuring magnetic anomalies on either side of mid-ocean ridges. Earth's magnetic field undergoes a reversal every few hundred thousand years, and newly established crustal material retains an imprint of the prevailing magnetic field at the time of its creation. The pattern of magnetic anomalies in the crust on either side of the ridge were found to form a mirror-image pattern of one another, suggesting that the anomalies had been formed at the same time and were moving away from the ridge in opposite directions and at the same rate. By using the radiometric dating and magnetic anomaly data, it is found that seafloor spreading from mid-ocean ridges is taking place at the rate of between 2 and 20 centimeters a year, depending on location. Growth at the Mid-Atlantic Ridge is about 2.5 centimeters a year, which means that in the 500 years or so since Christopher Columbus sailed across the Atlantic from Europe to the American continent, the Atlantic Ocean has increased in width by 12 meters or so—he would now have 12 meters further to sail. In fact, the Atlantic is growing in width at the same rate as your fingernails. Next time you cut your nails, the trimmings will indicate how far the Atlantic has widened since you last cut your nails.

In the period 1968–1975, an extraordinarily successful series of expeditions by the U.S. deep-sea drilling ship *Glomar Challenger* was able to confirm predictions made for the seafloor-spreading theory. Seafloor spreading was to provide the framework to explain how continents moved in relation to one another and how the oceans were created and are changing.

The Wilson Cycle

If we accept that oceanic crust is being formed at mid-ocean ridges, is spreading outwards, and is then being subducted into ocean trenches, how is an ocean (or rather the basin that contains the ocean) formed in the first place? Canadian geophysicist Tuzo Wilson suggested in the 1960s that an ocean basin progresses through a number of stages in its creation and maturation. These stages form what is what is now termed the Wilson cycle. The creation of an ocean basin explains, in fact, how a continent might break up, as happened when Pangaea fragmented to form the present day continents.

The first stage in the cycle occurs when tension in a weak part of Earth's crust causes continental crust to be uplifted and to move apart, so forming a rift valley (stage 1); the East African Rift Valley provides an example. If the valley is sufficiently deep and creates a major weakness in Earth's crust, and if the valley has a connection with an already existing ocean, then seawater will enter the rift valley and a new ocean will be in the making. As magma (molten rock originating from the lower crust or mantle) rises up into the flooded valley, seafloor spreading takes place, and the landmasses on either side of the valley move apart (stage 2). The Red Sea between Africa and Arabia is just such an example. It is only about 20 million years old, but given another hundred million years or so, it will be a mature ocean (stage 3). The Atlantic Ocean, at nearly 200 million years old, is currently in this mature phase and is still growing. The mature ocean does not expand indefinitely, but material is subducted into trenches and under continental landmasses and the ocean begins to shrink (the declining stage of an ocean). This is happening in the case of the Pacific Ocean, and where oceanic crust is sliding under continental crust, there is a high incidence of volcanic and earthquake activity. As this process continues and the ocean becomes substantially smaller, the ocean shrinks to a narrow sea (the terminal stage of an ocean); on land, young mountains are uplifted. This has happened in the case of the Mediterranean Sea, which is probably the remnant of the much larger Tethys Sea that once separated Gondwanaland and Laurasia. The European Alps are the result of nearby uplifting on the continental landmass. Eventually, the sea may disappear entirely, and the two continents on either side may collide: for example, India collided with the Eurasian continent some 35 million years ago; the Himalayas are the result.

Stages 1–3 of the Wilson Cycle describing the evolution of an ocean basin

❶ The embryonic stage of an ocean (e.g., East African Rift Valley)

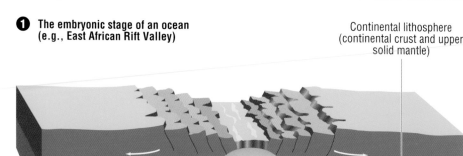

❷ The juvenile stage of an ocean (e.g., Red Sea)

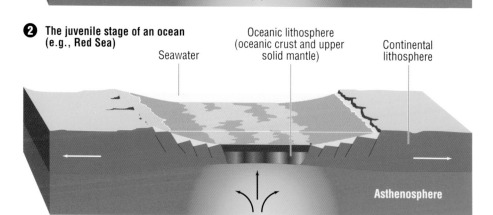

❸ The mature stage of an ocean (e.g., Atlantic Ocean)

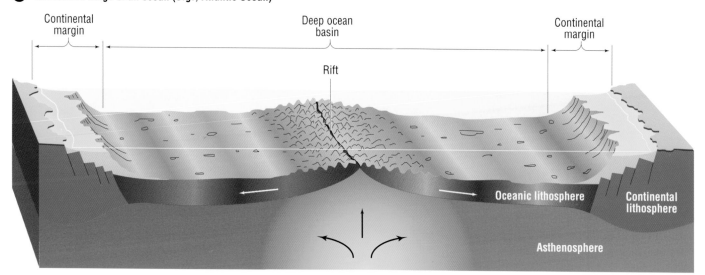

Plate Tectonics (How Oceans Evolve)

The theory of plate tectonics is concerned with the giant lithospheric plates that incorporate Earth's crust. *Tectonic* refers to how the plates are involved in building processes within Earth's crust. The modern theory of plate tectonics has come to encompass earlier ideas about continental drift (page 30).

Earth's outer layer is constructed of seven major, and several smaller, slabs of rocky material called plates. More correctly, they are termed lithospheric plates because they are composed of lithosphere (crust plus the uppermost part of the mantle [page 26]). Each plate is some 50–75 miles (80–120 km) thick and moves about Earth's surface at the rate of a few centimeters per year. The movement of plates is probably driven by slow convection currents within the semiliquid part of the mantle. Across the world, belts of high geological activity are situated along the edges, or boundaries, of the moving plates. The plates themselves are composed of either continental lithosphere or oceanic lithosphere or a combination of the two. The lithospheric composition of plates is important in determining what happens when two plates collide.

Plate Boundaries

Mid-ocean ridges are found at many of the plate boundaries. Here, adjacent lithospheric plates *move apart* as lava erupts from the ridge and cools to form new seafloor material (oceanic crust) on either side of the ridge. As this happens, the plate on either side moves away from the ridge. This is the process of seafloor spreading (page 30).

As new seafloor material is being created at mid-ocean ridges, so old seafloor material is being destroyed at other locations. These are the deep trenches. Trenches are formed at plate margins were two plates collide and one plate slides below the other. As the plate descends, it is subjected to intense heat and pressure and begins to fragment, giving rise to local earthquakes. The plate material, as it sinks, begins to melt, and some of this material escapes back onto Earth's surface as erupting lava, which forms volcanoes. The bulk of the descending plate, however, continues to melt and moves downwards into the mantle. Some of this material may well be recycled, rising at a mid-ocean ridge perhaps hundreds of millions of years later. The process of material being taken into the mantle and melted at depth is called subduction. It follows that if oceanic crust is being created at mid-ocean ridges and is being

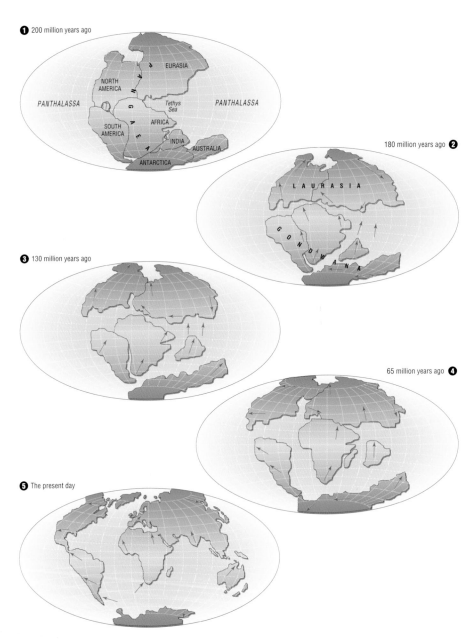

❶ 200 million years ago

❷ 180 million years ago

❸ 130 million years ago

❹ 65 million years ago

❺ The present day

Continental drift and the formation of the present-day oceans

destroyed at trenches, other things being equal, the two processes must balance out if Earth's surface is not to keep changing in size. Whereas this is indeed the case overall, the balance between seafloor spreading and subduction varies from ocean to ocean so that some oceans are growing and some are shrinking (page 31).

Returning to trenches, where one plate contains oceanic crust at the boundary and the other contains continental crust, it is the oceanic crust that slips below the continental crust because oceanic crust is more dense—the less-dense continental crust rides on top. This occurs, for example, where the Nazca Plate of the eastern Pacific (oceanic crust) slides under the South American Plate (continental crust). As the Nazca Plate sinks

and fragments, local earthquakes are produced. As the plate melts at depth, so lighter material finds its way back to the surface through the South American Plate. This volcanic activity on the continental landmass is associated with the Andes mountain range.

At trenches where two oceanic plates collide, both plates are of similar density, but one nevertheless descends below the other. Such trenches also are associated with volcanic and earthquake activity. Volcanoes may form on the overlying plate and may be sufficiently large to rise all the way to the sea surface. Whether they do or not, chains of volcanoes are associated with the trench.

Where two continental plates collide (in other words, two continents collide), because of the relatively low density of continental crust, neither plate is subducted and a trench is not formed. Instead, the two continents continue to push together, so causing the continental crust to buckle and fold like an accordion. The eastern European Alps, for example, were formed when Africa collided with Eurasia within the last 65 million years.

Sometimes two plates neither collide nor move away from each other but slide past each other with neither creation nor destruction of lithosphere. This type of plate boundary is called a transform fault, or a shear boundary. Perhaps the best-known example is California's San Andreas Fault, formed where the North American Plate comes into contact with the spreading ridge of the East Pacific Rise. Friction prevents the plate edges from sliding smoothly past one another; instead, they tend to lock. Stresses build up, and suddenly the plates slide past one another, the sudden release of energy creating an earthquake. As a result, San Francisco, close to the San Andreas Fault, is one of the most earthquake-prone cities in the world. Meanwhile, nearby Los Angeles and the California peninsula on the Pacific Plate to the southwest, are moving toward Alaska at the rate of about 2 inches (5 cm) a year.

Plate Tectonics and the Changing Oceans

Alfred Wegener's idea (page 30) that the present-day continents were originally joined together and have since separated and moved has, in the last 30–40 years, been vindicated. For example, the southern continents and subcontinents—South America, Africa, India, Antarctica, and Australia—can be "backtracked" to earlier locations and shown to fit together to reconstruct the supercontinent Gondwanaland. Rock strata, fossils, and palaeomagnetic and climatological data support the view that these continents were joined together at the predicted location. Even before this, the world's continents appear to have been joined together in one huge supercontinent, Pangaea. Based on available evidence, the sequence for the drifting of continents into their current positions and the accompanying formation of present-day ocean is summarized below and is shown in the figure on page 32.

1. Some 200 million years ago, all of today's continents were within a single giant landmass, the supercontinent Pangaea. Antarctica was in a broadly similar but more northerly location than its present-day position. The other "continents-to-be" were in rather different positions to their current ones. There was just a single giant ocean—Panthalassa, the precursor of today's Pacific Ocean. Two shallow seas were evident: the Sinus Borealis, later to become the Arctic Ocean, and the much larger Tethys Sea, the ancestor of today's much smaller Mediterranean Sea. The Atlantic and Indian Oceans were yet to be born.

2. By 180 million years ago Pangaea had begun to break apart to form two supercontinents—Laurasia to the north and Gondwanaland to the south. The splitting of Pangaea took place along a rift between what is now North America and Eurasia to the north and South America and Africa to the south. The Tethys Sea flowed into the rift which was to become the Mid-Atlantic Ridge. The formation of the rift marked the birth of the northern Atlantic Ocean.

3. By 130 million years ago, a rift had appeared between Africa and Antarctica, so initiating the breakup of Gondwanaland, followed by the release of India and the formation of the young Indian Ocean from what was once part of the giant ocean Panthalassa.

4. By 65 million years ago, the southern Atlantic Ocean had been born from the rift between South America and Africa. The Pacific Ocean—the descendent of Panthalassa—began to shrink and continues to do so until this day. Australia was still attached to Antarctica, and North America and Europe were still joined in the north.

5. The present day. Some 60 million years ago, the rift in the Indian Ocean extended between Antarctica and Australia and separated the two continents. Since that time, the Atlantic Ocean has widened, North America and Europe have separated, and India has collided with Eurasia to form the Himalayas. Within the last 20 million years, the Red Sea has formed from the extension of the mid-ocean ridge from the northern Indian Ocean. The Red Sea represents the birth of a new ocean that is being formed as Africa and Arabia gradually move apart. North and South America have become fully connected by the Isthmus of Panama only within the last 5 million years.

The stages above are part of a continuing cycle of ocean formation and disappearance, continental fragmentation and merging. The location of oceans and continents today is but a snapshot in geological time.

The Ocean Floor

With our knowledge of plate tectonics and seafloor spreading, we can now return to consider the structure of the ocean floor

Mid-Ocean Ridges

The mid-ocean ridges form the largest continuous geological network on the planet's surface. They form a narrow continuous belt of submarine mountains stretching almost entirely the length of each ocean and connecting one ocean with another.

The mid-ocean ridge marks the boundary where one lithospheric plate is moving away from another and new oceanic crust is being formed. The crest towards the center of the ridge is formed where the plates are moving apart and magma (molten rock) derived from the asthenosphere wells up. Being relatively light (low density), the magma pushes up the crust to create the crest of the ridge. Some rising magma slowly crystallizes in the lower crust, some reaches the middle of the crust and solidifies in fissures, and some may be extruded as lava onto the ocean floor, thereby forming new seafloor material. As seafloor spreading progresses, new oceanic crust moves away from the ridge crest. It cools, becomes denser and more viscous, and gradually solidifies. It subsides, and thus the seafloor is lower farther away from the ridge.

The highest parts of a mid-ocean ridge usually lie at a depth of 1.5–2 miles (2–3 km), but sometimes they rise to the sea surface to form volcanic islands, as in the case of Iceland, the Azores, and Tristan da Cunha—all emergent parts of the Mid-Atlantic Ridge.

The ridge itself does not form along a straight line but is usually broken at intervals by fractures, called transform faults, that cause the ridge crest to be offset. Thus, the ridge is divided into a series of distinct spreading units separated by transform faults.

At the center of a mid-ocean ridge, the "wound in the Earth's crust" where magma emerges is called the central rift valley. Dotted around the edges of this valley may be found hydrothermal vents—places where water, superheated by hot material from the mantle and lower crust, belches out a cloud of mineral-rich water. These vents and their associated mineral deposits are some of the most exciting geological discoveries of recent years (page 43)

Trenches

Old oceanic crust is continually being taken back down (subducted) into the mantle at ocean trenches. While mid-ocean ridges are creating new oceanic crust, trenches are "digesting" old crust, and so the status quo of global oceanic crust is maintained.

During subduction, the upper layer of oceanic crust is partially melted and absorbed into the mantle at depths of more than 60 miles (100 km). Melting occurs because of the effects of friction and rising temperatures. Some of the magmas that formed as a product of the melting process rise up toward the surface and commonly form a series of volcanic islands in a roughly straight line following the line of the trench. Because of the curvature of the earth, when such island chains are depicted on maps they appear as arcs, appropriately called island arcs. The Aleutian Islands of the North Pacific and the Mariana Islands of the Southwest Pacific are of this type.

Subduction does not only occur at deep ocean trenches where one oceanic plate meets another. It may occur at the edge of an ocean between an oceanic plate and a continental plate, in which case the oceanic crust is subducted below the continental crust. This is happening along the west coast of South America where the Nazca Plate is being subducted below the South American Plate. Marine sediments on the continental shelf and slope are scraped off the subducting plate and are compressed to deform and rise, so creating fold mountains. The South

The profile of an ocean

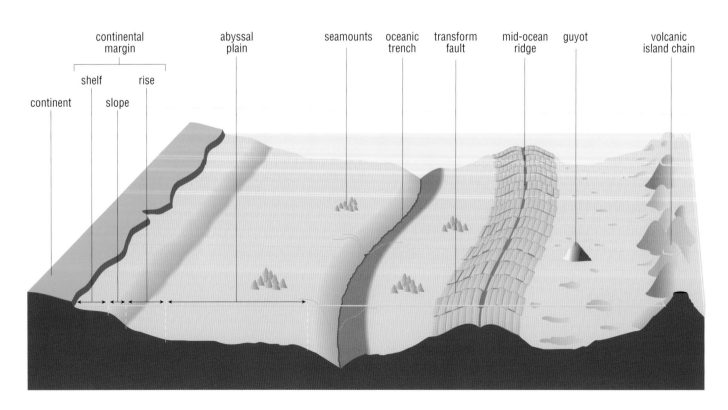

continent — continental margin (shelf, slope, rise) — abyssal plain — seamounts — oceanic trench — transform fault — mid-ocean ridge — guyot — volcanic island chain

American Andes show good evidence of their marine origin: On the highest peaks, marine fossils are found that conform to the marine sediments present before the mountains were constructed. The compression forces acting from east to west have created deep folds with axes running from north to south. Where subduction zones are found alongside a coast, the more familiar oceanic topography—wide continental shelf, gentle slope, and continental rise (see below)—is not found. Instead, the continental shelf is narrow or absent, the slope is steep, and the rise is absent; in its place is a deep trench. This topography is found off the west coast of South America.

The Abyssal Plain and Other Ocean Floor Features

Much of the seafloor is relatively flat, is typically 2.2–3.4 miles (3.5–5.5 km) below the sea surface, and extends from mid-ocean ridges to oceanic trenches and continental margins. This is the abyssal plain. It is covered in a layer of sediment that is usually thinner on newer parts of oceanic crust and thicker on older parts. Most of the sediments consist of loose material that is eroded and then washed or blown off the land (terrigenous) or of skeletal remains of planktonic organisms (biogenous) (page 36).

Where features are found on the abyssal plain, these are typically formed by volcanic activity. Small volcanic features less than 0.62 miles (1 km) above the ocean floor are called abyssal hills. The Pacific Ocean floor is particularly rich in volcanic features: more than 20,000 are found there. Submerged volcanic peaks that extend more than 0.62 miles (1 km) above the abyssal plain are called seamounts. When the peaks of seamounts become flattened by erosion, they form guyots. Commonly, volcanic islands and submerged volcanoes are associated with cracks at the edges of mid-ocean ridge crests. However, in a few spectacular cases, chains of volcanoes are associated with "hot spots" in Earth's mantle. When a lithospheric plate passes over the top of a hot spot, magma finds its way up through the seafloor and erupts as a volcano. As the plate moves, a string of volcanoes may be formed. The Hawaiian Islands and the associated Emperor Seamount chain to the northwest are probably the best example of a volcanic chain formed in this way. The island of Hawaii, the youngest of the Hawaiian Islands, is presently close to the hot spot. While moving northwest, the islands become progressively older and then are replaced by seamounts; in seamounts, the lithospheric plate has subsided so that what were once volcanic islands have now submerged.

The Continental Margins

Between the abyssal plain and the continental landmasses themselves are found continental margins. These usually comprise a wide continental shelf, a steep continental slope, and then a continental rise that slopes gently down to the ocean floor. However, a much-steeper topography is found where a trench is found alongside a continent, as occurs on the west coast of South America.

The continental shelf is where the continental crust extends beyond the shore to form a shallow slope that is covered in seawater. Its gradient is typically about 0.1° to the horizontal, and it usually extends to a depth of no more than 820 feet (250 m). The width of a continental shelf varies considerably, being up to 620 miles (1,000 km) across near the southeastern tip of South America, but less than 31 miles (50 km) wide along much of South America's west coast. The North Sea off the coast of Northwest Europe is entirely continental shelf.

Continental shelves are often covered in a thick layer of sedimentary material that washed off the land and into the sea. Where currents are strong, sandy bottoms often form, whereas in quieter offshore areas, fine silts and muds may be deposited. Where the supplies of sand or mud are meager, and the water is clear, warm, and shallow, limestone tends to be deposited, often in the form of the chalky skeletons from once-living microscopic plankton.

Because continental shelves are next to landmasses and are accessible to human exploration, and because they tend to be biologically productive as well as geologically significant, their importance far outweighs their size. Economically, they are the most important part of the ocean, as well as that part most susceptible to pollution damage.

The continental slope beyond the shelf is the closest thing to the real edge of the continent—the boundary between continental crust and oceanic crust. Compared to the shelf, it is steeply sloping with a gradient of about 4° to the horizontal (up to 20° near trenches) and extends to a depth anywhere in the range 4,920–13,120 feet (1,500–4,000 m). The size and type of sediment that reaches the continental slope depends on the width of the shelf and the prevailing currents: On narrow shelves, sand may be carried out as far as the slope; on wider shelves, only finer clays tend to reach so far from the continental landmass.

Occasionally, the continental slope is cut by deep V-shaped valleys called submarine canyons. Most of these were formed by glaciers or rivers during geological periods when sea levels were much lower. Since then, they have become submerged and are like undersea rivers, carrying sediments from the continental shelf to the deep ocean floor. Within these canyons and along the slope itself, deposits may become unstable and slide or slump toward deeper areas. Large-scale movements are triggered by shock waves from seabed earthquakes. These disturbances trigger undersea avalanches called turbidity currents that carry thousands of metric tons of sediment in an unstoppable cloud that sweeps aside or covers everything in its path. Such currents are responsible for the destruction of seafloor installations and the snapping of transoceanic telephone cables.

The continental rise is a shallower slope, with a gradient of about 0.1° to 1°, formed by the accumulation of sediments at the base of the continental slope. Deep-sea alluvial fans, not dissimilar to river deltas, are formed by the accumulation of sediments at the base of submarine canyons. These deposits are spread along the edge of the continental slope by currents and join other sediments that accumulate on the continental rise.

Seafloor Sediments

Sediment refers to the loose material that settles on the seafloor. Throughout much of the oceans, the topography of the seafloor is moderated by a blanket of sediment that forms from particles that descend to the ocean depths day after day, millennium after millennium, eon after eon. This snowfall of material, in time, may form layers several kilometers thick. The deep ocean sediments form a historical record of activities on land, sea, and air. Sediments that are relatively undisturbed retain an imprint of local and global events that stretch back for millions of years. They are a resting place (albeit in geological terms, a temporary one) for all manner of pollutants—from the land, air, and sea.

Types of Sediment

Sediments are added to the seafloor from four major sources. There is a continuous snowfall of material from once-living organisms, mostly in the form of skeletal remains. These sediments of biological origin are termed biogenous. Sediments are also commonly derived from rocks that were weathered on continental landmasses and then deposited in the sea. Added to this are sediments formed by volcanic activity on land or on the seafloor. Such sediments—derived more or less directly from rock—are called lithogenous. Some sediments are formed from chemicals that are dissolved in seawater but precipitate out under certain conditions. Perhaps the best known of these deposits, which are termed hydrogenous, are manganese nodules (see below). Lastly, a few sediments have an extraterrestrial origin: They originate from beyond Earth's atmosphere and fall to Earth where they form cosmogenous sediments.

Sediments of Biological Origin

Many of the world's tiniest planktonic forms are remarkably innovative in constructing highly intricate outer skeletons (exoskeletons) that support and protect their cell contents. When these planktonic forms die (usually by being consumed by other organisms), their indigestible skeletons find their way into fecal pellets—the solid waste egested by a grazer or predator. These fecal pellets form the bulk of the "marine snowfall" that settles on the ocean floor. They form biogenous deposits that accumulate typically at the rate of about 1 centimeter (0.39 inches) every thousand years. During millions of years, this snowfall may accumulate to form massive deposits several hundred meters thick. If the ocean floor sediment contains 30 percent or more of skeletal remains, it is called ooze. Such calcareous and siliceous oozes form where this snowfall of skeletal material outstrips rates of deposition from other sources.

Calcareous deposits (from the chalky exoskeletons of foraminiferans and coccolithophores) are commonly found in subtropical and temperate waters of moderate depth where there is relatively high productivity of appropriate phytoplankton and zooplankton forms. Calcareous deposits do not accumulate in water of more than about 14,750–16,400 feet (4,500–5,000 m) depth because the high pressure and low temperature readily dissolves chalk. This phenomenon—combined with differences in plankton productivity—helps explain why the Atlantic Ocean, the shallowest ocean, has calcareous deposits covering about two-thirds of its floor, whereas the deepest ocean, the Pacific, has about one-third coverage. Siliceous deposits (from the siliceous exoskeletons of diatoms and radiolarians) form where silica is dissolved in the water in reasonably large quantities, where productivity of appropriate phytoplankton forms is high, and where productivity of calcareous deposit-forming planktonic forms is low, or at depths where calcium carbonate readily dissolves. In practice, this means that siliceous deposits form in preference to calcareous ones in polar waters (which are too cold for carbonate-producing forms) and in the deeper parts of equatorial and certain tropical and subtropical waters.

The thick limestone sediments formed from the chalky skeletons of long-dead plankton represent a huge store of fixed carbon. This carbon was once present in the atmosphere within the greenhouse gas, carbon dioxide. The plankton, by absorbing carbon dioxide for photosynthesis, play a vital role in regulating the greenhouse effect and in reducing global warming (page 78).

Sediments from Land

Much of the sediment on continental margins and also on the ocean floor originates from continental crust (called terrigenous sediments). Sizable regions of the major ocean depths contain sediments called red mud that accumulate at rates of about 1 millimeter every 1,000 years. These deposits comprise mud particles that have been carried by winds and currents and have settled in areas where other forms of sedimentation are slow. Closer to continental landmasses, the larger particles discharged from rivers settle out to form bottom sediments in estuaries, on continental shelves, and at the base of continental slopes. Deeper-water submarine fans are formed by some major tropical rivers and, in some cases, such as the Ganges, these fans have been formed for millions of years. The huge Ganges fan in the Bay of Bengal, for example, extends well beyond the continental shelf for a distance of about 1,500 miles (2,500 km). Often, such sediments contain accumulated toxins derived from industrial and agricultural processes (page 182).

Much of the particulate material carried in river water to the sea is derived from the weathering of continental rocks and is, in fact, of sedi-

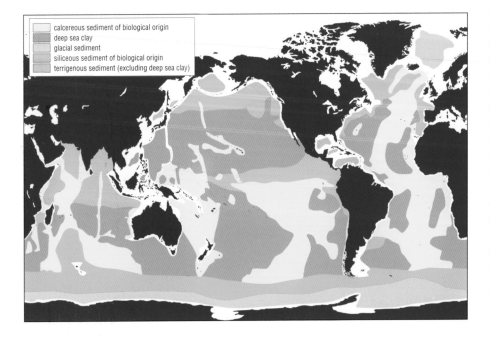

calcereous sediment of biological origin
deep sea clay
glacial sediment
siliceous sediment of biological origin
terrigenous sediment (excluding deep sea clay)

The distribution of sediments in the oceans

THE K-T EXTINCTION

In 1980, a scientific paper reported the discovery in northern Italy of a layer of iridium-enriched sediment in the boundary layer associated with the end of the Cretaceous period and the beginning of the Tertiary period 65 million years ago. This boundary layer is of particular interest to scientists because it coincides with the date when land-living dinosaurs and many marine organisms—almost overnight in geological terms—became extinct. The demise of dinosaurs created the opportunity for the group we call mammals to diversify and achieve the range and abundance we observe today. Where did the iridium come from, and what does it have to do with the disappearance of dinosaurs?

The metallic element iridium (Ir) is found in greater concentrations within meteors than in rock of Earth origin. Iridium-rich layers of sediment are usually accepted as evidence of meteoric impact unless there is evidence that certain types of volcanic events might have produced them. If a very large meteorite (say, 6 miles, or 10 kilometers, across) had impacted with Earth 65 million years ago, then the impact itself and the resulting debris thrown into the atmosphere could cause sufficient planetary disruption to account for the dinosaur extinction. In the early 1980s, this proposal was regarded with much skepticism. In the following decade, however, supporting evidence began to accumulate from around the world. By 1990 the likely impact site for such a large meteor had been pinpointed. Seismic surveying carried out by an oil company in the Gulf of Mexico in 1980 had shown the existence of a 112-mile (180-km) diameter crater along the north coast of the Yucatán Peninsula. This information was not made public until 1990. In the locality, rocks of the appropriate age showed the characteristics of meteor impact, and the distribution pattern of iridium-rich debris suggested that the region was, indeed, the location of the impact. Larger particles of debris were found close to the site, and smaller particles further away. Also, deposits found bordering the Gulf of Mexico and the Caribbean basin showed evidence of giant waves (tsunamis page 73) impacting on coastlines 65 million years ago. Such waves would be expected from a large meteor impact at sea.

Once the evidence for the meteor impact is more firmly established, the next step will be to determine more precisely how this event might have affected life on Earth. Did ejected debris enter the atmosphere and shield sunlight, thereby having a devastating impact on plant growth and, in turn, on the animals that directly or indirectly depended on them? Did released gases cause global warming or acid rain? The unraveling of this detective story is still in its early stages.

mentary origin; in other words, it is rock sediments that have been formed in ancient seas, uplifted onto land by geological processes, and then eroded and returned to the oceans.

Sediments from Seawater

Chemical reactions in seawater produce some seafloor deposits that are both commercially and scientifically significant. Undersea volcanic activity and associated hydrothermal vents (page 43) discharge into seawater high concentrations of metals such as manganese, iron, cobalt, copper, and nickel. Under high temperature and pressure, oxides of these metals precipitate out onto the local seafloor. Some geologists see these deposits as a potentially valuable resource.

Of more promising economic potential are manganese (polymetallic) nodules, which, as their name suggests, contain mostly manganese but also other, economically more-valuable metals, such as copper, nickel, and cobalt. Nodules form on the deep ocean floor where rates of deposition by other forms of sediment are low. Often about the size of a potato (4 inches or 10 cm, across), nodules form incredibly slowly, adding layers at the rate of between 1 and 200 millimeters every million years.

Commercially important evaporites, such as common salt, are formed when seawater in shallow waters is concentrated by evaporation, which makes salts crystallize out.

Sediments from Space

Tiny particles derived from colliding asteroids in the asteroid belt, together with meteorites that enter Earth's atmosphere, form a light shower that sprinkles extraterrestrial material onto the seabed. Most of these particles are a fraction of a millimeter across in the range 0.004–0.25 inches (10–640µm) and are composed of nickel-iron and silica. However, every few tens of millions of years, one or more large meteors impact with Earth. They have a devastating effect at the site of impact and may have a global effect on Earth's climate. A wave of animal and plant extinctions appears to follow such events; the so-called K-T event, believed to have led to the demise of the dinosaurs, is the one that has captured the public's imagination.

Shifting Ocean Sediments

The thickness of ocean sediments depends on several factors that influence the rate at which sediment is being added and the rate at which it is being carried away or displaced. Physical, chemical, geological, and biological activities contribute to both processes. For example, newly formed crust close to mid-ocean ridges will, other things being equal, have a thinner layer of sediment than crust that is older and farther away from the ridge. Other tectonic events—earthquakes and volcanoes, for example—may cause sudden additions or displacements of material on the seafloor. Deep-water currents may shift fine sediments: Crescent-shaped sand waves, reminiscent of those found in deserts on land, have been observed moving across the deep ocean floor. Also, taking one biological example, thousands of walruses, and gray whales each year dive to the floor of the Bering Sea and feed by scooping up bottom sediments. The particles become suspended in the water column and are then carried away by bottom currents.

Human activities have greatly accelerated or altered sedimentation patterns in many parts of the world. Activities on land—in particular, deforestation and agriculture—are creating a heavy burden of soil particles that are carried into the sea by rivers. In other locations, damming of rivers has stopped the deposit of land-based particles, so creating relict sediments; coastlines that were once depositional have become erosional. Sewage discharge, drilling activities, and dumping of waste at sea have locally altered the sediment profile of parts of the seafloor, particularly on continental shelves.

The link may not be immediately obvious, but the industrialized economies of the world are sustained by marine sedimentary deposits. Petroleum products such as oil and natural gas are created by the rapid burial of microscopic marine plankton. In the high-pressure, high-temperature environment deep below shallow seas, oil and gas are squeezed into existence from the planktonic remains (page 170).

Shoreline Processes

Coastlines and their vicinities are seen as attractive, healthy places to live. This, coupled with the historical use of the sea as a highway for transport, has culminated in about two-thirds of the world's population living within about 60 miles (100 km) of the nearest coast. Humans have a long history of interfering with coastal processes, often with disastrous results.

The features of a coastline are influenced by many factors—not least, the tectonic processes that operate locally. For example, on the western side of North America, much of the coastline is closely associated with subduction zones or transform faults (page 34). Above the waterline, cliffs may rise steeply overhead. Below the waterline, there is often a narrow continental shelf with a relatively steep drop to thousands of meters. The eastern side of North America is far removed from a boundary between two moving plates: The coastline topography here is much gentler, with broad beaches and sandy offshore islands associated with a wide continental shelf.

Once a coastal geology is established by tectonic forces, the coastline is modified by natural erosional and depositional processes, principally the actions of waves, currents, and tides. On rocky shores (page 22), crashing waves split and loosen rocks, particularly those already cracked. Water driven into cracks compresses air that, in turn, widens the cracks. Occasional storm waves move rocks, boulders, or concrete blocks that weigh many hundreds of tons. When salt crystallizes inside crevices, it expands, thereby tending to split the surrounding rock; sand and gravel particles suspended in waves form highly abrasive tools of erosion. Waves also erode by dissolving chemicals in rock: Limestone, with its calcium carbonate, is particularly susceptible (no wonder that chalky cliffs can be cut back by a meter or more on a stormy night!).

Waves attack headlands more actively than they do intervening bays because wave energy is concentrated on headlands by wave refraction (bending). As a wave front nears a promontory, that part closest to the promontory, where water is shallower, touches bottom first and is slowed. Those parts of the wave front on either side of the headland, however, proceed at normal rate and are refracted until they are parallel to the shore. Wave refraction, therefore, concentrates erosion on the headlands, while sediment tends to be deposited in the bays in between. This partially accounts for jagged shorelines becoming straightened in time.

Rising and falling tides are of geological importance because they allow waves to attack different levels on the shore. Tidal currents can, in themselves, have a strong erosional effect, particularly in narrow bays and inlets.

Landforms of Marine Erosion

The most obvious feature likely to be found on an eroded shoreline is a sea cliff. Its height depends on the slope and elevation of the land surface, the energy of the attacking waves, and the composition of the cliff rock. Wave erosion and landslides give the cliff its characteristic shape. Sea caves may be formed where there are recesses or softer rock in low-lying parts of the cliff. If caves are on opposite sides of a headland, they may meet to form sea arches which, if they collapse, form stacks—isolated rocky pinnacles or small islands. Dramatic stacks and arches are a prominent feature of the Oregon coastline of North America.

As a sea cliff gradually retreats following prolonged bombardment by attacking waves, a wave-cut platform develops at the cliff's base. Sometimes the platform is exposed at low tide where it is seen to be bare, abraded rock that is interrupted perhaps by tide (rock) pools. Sand, gravel, shingle, or even boulders may be deposited toward the landward end of the platform to form a relatively narrow beach. The wave-cut platform extends until it reaches a critical width when it is able to absorb most of the wave energy, and cliff erosion by wave action becomes much reduced.

Where there is a prominent drop in sea level or an uplift of coastal land, wave-cut platforms are left high and dry and form marine terraces. An ascending series of steplike terraces may form where tectonic uplift is occasional but substantial. This has occurred in the Palos Verdes hills of southern California, where the highest marine terrace is found at about 1,300 feet (400 m) above sea level.

Landforms of Marine Deposition

While exposed coastlines are subjected to heavy erosion, sheltered coastlines tend to be depositional—they receive deposits from eroded parts of the coastline, together with any sediment discharged from nearby rivers. They may also receive particles blown onto the beach from inland. Such shorelines are common along the United States

Wave refraction at a headland

Atlantic and Gulf coasts. Strictly, the beach is the gently sloping surface on the shoreline that is washed over by waves and is covered by sediment. Particles of different sizes—from mud, through sand and gravel, to shingle—are usually deposited on the shore according to the strength of wave action and local currents.

Sandy beaches have been called rivers of sand because longshore drift almost invariably causes the particles to be transported gradually in one direction along the beach parallel to the sea. Longshore drift and longshore currents give rise to several characteristic coastal features, particularly where the coastline is irregular and the water is comparatively shallow. On the down-current side of a promontory, an extension or spit may form where sand is deposited roughly parallel to the main body of the coast. Where a spit grows sufficiently large to almost close off a bay or a harbor, it becomes a bar. Where sand is deposited between a near-shore island and the mainland to form a causeway, the connection is called a tombolo.

The beach is usually an effective line of defense, even in the case of storm waves. Much of the energy of the incoming water is expended as it breaks upon the gradual slope of the beach. Even where much of the sand or shingle is removed from a beach during violent seas, it will often be replaced by deposition in calmer weather, providing the shape of the coastline has not been too drastically altered or the source of sediment removed. At La Jolla, California, the beach is sandy in summer and fall when seas are relatively quiet, but it reverts to being gravel in winter and spring when sand is removed by stormy seas.

Barrier islands are a prominent feature of United States Atlantic and Gulf coasts, from Long Island, New York, to southern Texas. They are low, elongate islands running parallel to the coast but somewhat offshore from it. They are suspected of being formed through the action of longshore currents that redistribute sands deposited by river deltas. Sea-level changes may also be implicated. They are popular coastal areas for development, but they are very liable to flooding and tend to retreat landward under the onslaught of high-energy waves on their seaward side. In the face of globally rising sea levels, the likelihood of such islands being inundated will only increase.

Learning to Live with Shoreline Processes

The loss of sandy beaches due to erosion is becoming increasingly common. Some of this loss is entirely natural and part of the continuing geological process. However, rising global sea level (page 40) is claiming some beaches, and more direct human activities are claiming others. In order to protect local beaches, private individuals and local organizations build groins on shores and jetties at harbour entrances. Both types of structure are built at right angles to the shore and are designed to trap sand and other sediments on the up-current side. Although this may retain sediment locally, it usually has a detrimental effect down-current where deposition is now reduced and the effects of erosion are consequently increased.

Concrete seawalls seem like a good way of protecting coastal communities from storm damage and flooding. However, this bold approach is expensive and may not be effective for long. Instead of dissipating the sea's energy gradually, as a naturally sloping beach would, an otherwise unprotected vertical barrier is subject to the full force of the sea and erodes severely as a result. Water turbulence also creates little opportunity for a natural beach to form below the flood defense.

More-fruitful approaches often take account of the way that natural shore processes work. For example, in some locations sand is imported and spread on the shore to create an artificial beach. If this is done with some sensitivity and awareness of how local shore processes work, then such a barrier can dissipate the sea's energy and direct it toward sediment transport rather than shore erosion. Such beaches, however, need to be regularly replenished—at a cost. Research is needed to ensure that enough sediment of the right particle size is placed in the right location. It is very costly when things go wrong: Local inhabitants footed a bill of $5.2 million to replenish the beach at Ocean City in New Jersey in 1982, but the new beach lasted just 12 weeks.

Experience shows that two general principles apply to shoreline engineering. First, it permanently alters the characteristics of a shoreline; sec-

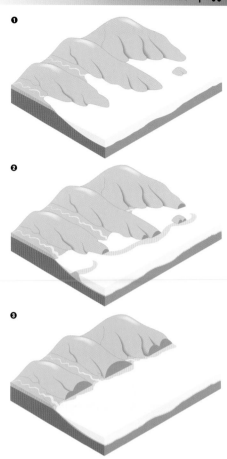

❶

❷

❸

Idealized evolution of a submerged shoreline. Shoreline processes gradually erode headlands and deposit sediments in bays, so creating a straighter coastline. The process rarely occurs without interruption caused by the sea level rising or falling or by the coastline uplifting or subsiding.

ond, once begun, it must be maintained and adapted if shoreline structures and beaches are not eventually to be abandoned and left to their fate at the hands of the sea. Gradually rising sea levels are a key factor in the repeated failure of shoreline-stabilization efforts. The high-energy coastal environment does not just present a difficult engineering problem in itself, but it is a continually changing problem. As water levels rise, the impact of wave action on existing shoreline structures is that much greater; if these structures are breached, the problems then extend inland.

Changing Sea Levels

Sea level relative to the land is never constant. If you lived on a tidal coastline, you would notice the sea level rise and fall twice a day with the ebb and flow of the tide. This change can be phenomenal. In the Bay of Fundy on Canada's Atlantic coast, the vertical difference between high water and low water on the highest tides is 40 feet (12 m), and more when storm surges occur. Weather conditions affect local sea level, raising the sea when there are onshore winds and lowering it when the winds are offshore. Weather conditions and tidal events can combine to produce dramatic—and destructive—rises in sea level. When a spring high tide (page 70) and onshore winds coincide, seawater may be driven much farther inland than usual to inundate land normally well beyond the reach of the sea.

Longer-term changes in sea level, and those occurring in the open sea, are much less obvious. Within a period of weeks or months, major shifts in ocean currents can raise sea levels by several centimeters (inches) in some areas and depress them in others. For example, during an El Niño event (page 69), during which upwelling is suppressed, the sea level in the western Pacific drops by as much as 6 inches (15 cm). A world sea-level rise averaging $\frac{1}{16}$ inch (1.5 mm) a year has occurred during the last hundred years—probably the result of global warming (see below and page 78), and massive changes in sea level have occurred within the last 100,000 years. When Earth's climate becomes substantially colder, as during an ice age, much of the precipitation freezes and stays on landmasses rather than returning to the sea. The sea level drops markedly

as a result. During the last ice age, sea levels fell by some 560 feet (170 m). Since the beginning of the thaw some 18,000 years ago, melting glaciers and shrinking ice sheets have raised the global sea level by about 395 feet (120 m). Were all the ice remaining in the planet's icecaps and glaciers to melt—a rather unlikely scenario—then the global sea level would rise by another 215–230 feet (65–70 m).

Local Changes in Sea Level

Sea level is a relative measurement. The land as well as the oceans can rise and fall, and we must

Point Reyes National Seashore, California (D. C. Lowe/ENP Images)

establish some absolute baseline of measurement. The level of the land changes with time because forces in Earth's crust and mantle—tectonic forces—cause large-scale uplift or subsidence of portions of continents. Other uplifts and subsidence can be the result of isostasy (page 27). This occurs where heavy loads of ice, sediment, or lava accumulate or are removed and where the change in weight of overlying material causes a readjustment of the underlying crust to reach a new equilibrium, or isostasy. This readjustment is quite slow and takes place in thousands of years.

Some of the most widespread changes occurring today are due to post-glacial rebound (PGR)—isostatic readjustment of Earth's crust since the retreat of glaciers from the last ice age. The weight of a glacier or ice sheet will depress Earth's crust, and when the ice melts, the land underneath gradually rises. Elsewhere on the continent, the land may sink, causing a seesaw effect. This is happening in the British Isles, where Scotland is gradually rising as a result of postglacial rebound. As Scotland rises, southern England sinks. During the last ice age, the glacial ice sheet of northern Canada was up to 3 kilometers (2 miles) thick, and some geologists believe that by the time the postglacial rebound is finished, the floor of Hudson Bay, currently about 492 feet (150 m) below sea level, will form part of the land.

Evidence of dramatically shifting land and sea levels are prevalent if we look. The shale band that forms a difficult hurdle for climbers who approach the top of Mount Everest is formed from marine sedimentary rock; this shows that Mount Everest was once part of a continental shelf covered in sea. Areas of uplift exhibit raised beaches (page 38) left high and dry, whereas areas of subsidence exhibit features such as rias—drowned valleys that have been inundated by rising sea.

Natural events alone do not account for all major shifts in land levels; human intervention plays a hand, too. In Venice, Italy, parts of the historic city began to experience floods following 30 years or so of extracting groundwater to provide local water supplies. By 1970, some locations had subsided by 6 inches (15 cm), at which point it was decided to stop pumping water. In the first half of the 20th century, oil extraction in the vicinity of Long Beach, California, caused local subsidence.

Currently, the best data for rises or falls in global sea level is derived by using tide-gauge readings and making corrections for rises or falls in landmasses due to isostasy and other tectonic events. Where these factors have been taken into account, tide-gauge readings are included in the analysis; where these factors have not been taken into account, tide-gauge readings are excluded. New technologies such as satellite altimetry (page 42) are providing global measurements that will complement those made using more traditional approaches.

Global Changes in Sea Level

Based on tide-gauge measurements, the global mean sea level has risen by 4 inches (10 cm) between 1880 and 1980. When the effect of isostatic recovery (the land rising or falling as a result of postglacial recovery) is taken into account as well, the mean sea level rise for the last 50 years alone is about 0.08 inches (2 mm) a year (equivalent to 8 inches or 20 cm, in a 100-year period). The Intergovernmental Panel on Climate Change (IPCC), reporting in 1995, reached the conclusion that much of this rise came from both the thermal expansion of ocean water and the partial melting of glaciers and icesheets. Although there is a lack of consensus among scientists as to whether global warming would initially cause the polar icecaps to melt or grow even thicker (atmospheric warming might well increase precipitation in polar regions and so cause accumulation on the icecaps), there is a consensus that global warming is raising sea levels.

During the period 1880–1980, there was an apparent global warming of about 32.9°F (18°C). The temperature rise may well be due, in part if not predominantly, to the increase in levels of the greenhouse-gas carbon dioxide within the atmosphere (page 78). IPCC's best estimate for the predicted temperature rise for the 21st century is 3.6°F (2°C) with estimates in the range 1.6°F to 6.3°F (0.9° to 3.5°C). A sea level of rise of about 20 inches (50 cm) between 1990 and the year 2100 is predicted (estimates lie within the broad range 5–38 inches or, 13–94 cm). This being the case, on the United States Atlantic coast alone, some low-lying coastal and estuarine environments would be flooded and many islands would become partially or totally submerged. Hugely increased costs for flood defense would, in any case, be only a temporary expedient in the face of a rising sea level. Many coastal areas slope very gently or are nearly flat, so even a small rise in sea level results in a very considerable inland intrusion of water.

A sea-level rise of 20 inches (50 cm) in the next century would result in a landward intrusion of several hundred meters along stretches of the Florida coastline and would completely submerge many existing beaches. Worldwide, the effects in the Tropics are likely to be worse than elsewhere: Because of the centripetal effect of Earth's rotation, the water bulges outward slightly around the equator. Thus many of the Pacific islands and some of the Maldive Islands in the Indian Ocean might become threatened. Globally, apart from flooding of low-lying areas, raised sea levels would cause much greater coastal erosion and an intrusion of seawater into groundwater, thus affecting potential water supplies for agricultural, industrial, and domestic use. With the possibility of parts of the Antarctic icesheet slipping into the sea, this raises the specter of giant waves (tsunami) being generated, which would be highly destructive to both newly established and traditional coastal areas.

Although the precise effects of global warming are uncertain, we cannot afford to be complacent. The repercussions for the survival of life on Earth—and human life in particular—are too important to ignore. What can we do to slow the pace of global warming and so lower the rate of sea-level rise? (see page 79).

New Developments in Marine Geology

Remarkable advances have taken place within marine geology in the last 40 to 50 years. In the early 1950s, geology was still a discrete science, very little of the deep ocean floor had been mapped, and seafloor spreading was a concept yet to be developed. Today, on the verge of the 21st century, geology has spawned numerous subdisciplines, topographic maps exist for all the deep oceans, and the evolution of our ocean basins is beginning to be closely mapped in space and time.

Of Satellites and Seafloors

Satellites, with their vast array of transmitting and sensing equipment, can provide us with false-color images of the ocean's surface that yield remarkable insights into the behavior of surface waters (page 156). Some satellites can also reveal what is happening on the ocean floor. Sonar imaging (see below) is used to plot the morphology of the seabed in detail, but doing this for the world's entire ocean floor will take many decades. In the meantime, remotely sensed data obtained by satellite provides a very useful overview. One of the methodologies of greatest interest to geologists is radar altimetry (measuring heights using radio waves). The satellite sends a short pulse of microwave energy to the sea surface that is reflected and picked up by the satellite's sensor. The time taken for the round trip, multiplied by the speed of travel and divided by 2, gives the distance between satellite and sea surface, and many such readings can be compiled to give a three-dimensional representation of the sea surface. The lumps and bumps on the surface of the sea reflect the contours below: Where there are trenches, the sea surface is very slightly depressed; where there are submerged mountain ranges, the sea surface is very slightly raised.

Satellite altimetry, with the satellite's location in space, established moment to moment by a laser tracking system, and sea conditions and weather conditions compensated for, can measure sea level to an accuracy of ± 2 inches (5 cm) or better.

The first satellite altimetry readings were from Seasat–A, a craft launched by the U.S. Navy. Although it operated for only three months (it malfunctioned due to an electrical failure), its usefulness in mapping the contours of the ocean floor was demonstrated beyond doubt. In 1985 the U.S. Navy completed the mapping of the deep ocean floor using a second satellite to finish the job Seasat–A had begun. The new data was kept secret and used for military purposes only until the launching of a European satellite in 1992. This satellite was to provide publicly available data of a similar nature and quality, and in the face of this, the U.S. Navy declassified its material. Remote sensing by satellite has revolutionized the speed with which deep-sea topographic investigations can be carried out. Using satellite data, we now know that there are far more volcanoes under the sea than there are on land, and many of these are associated with the 75,000 kilometer mid-ocean ridge system.

Mapping the Seafloor with Sound

In water, sound travels much further than light, so it is not surprising that "seeing underwater" has involved the development of sophisticated sound-emitting and -receiving equipment. Sonar (SOund Navigation And Ranging) was developed by allied forces during World War I to enable detection of submarines, underwater obstacles, and icebergs. Today's sonars are far more sophisticated than the basic "pingers" and cathode-ray screen displays of old. Modern sonars can be used to survey the topography of the ocean floor and even determine the nature of sediments below the seafloor (page 36).

Most types of sonar work in a way similar to radar. In sonar a pulse of sound is transmitted, and the time taken for the echo to return is used to compute the distance between the ship and the sound-reflecting object. In mapping the seafloor using sonar, the sound-transmitting/detecting device is usually towed behind the ship at a specified depth. A wide sonar beam is used to scan a strip of seafloor on either side of the vessel—a so-called side-scan configuration. By scanning adjacent strips of seafloor as the vessel moves forward, a three-dimensional representation of the seafloor can be constructed. One deep-towed side-scan sonar system called TOBI (Towed Ocean Bottom Instrument), operated by Southampton Oceanography Center in the U.K., can locate natural formations the size of a truck when they are 3.7 miles (6 km) below the sea surface. Another system called GLORIA (Geological Long Range Inclined Asdic), also operated by the Southampton team, is towed at a shallow depth: It can scan an area of seafloor the size of Massachusetts (about 7,700 square miles or 20,000 square kilometers), in a single day. An early version of GLORIA was used in the international collaborative effort that led to the pinpointing of the hydrothermal vents in the eastern Pacific in the mid-1970s. Such devices are providing the fill-in detail to the large-scale topographic maps generated from satellite data.

Underwater Vehicles

A submersible is essentially a diving vessel that is pressure resistant and contains air at or near sea-level pressure. Today's manned-submersibles include the Alvin, which can descend to 13,120 feet (4,000 m). In 1977, an early form of this vessel discovered the remarkable hydrothermal vent communities associated with the Galápagos ridge (see page 43), while a later version was used in exploring the wreck of RMS Titanic in 1985–86. The deepest-diving manned submersible is the Japanese vessel Shinkai 6500, which is designed to descend to 21,239 feet (6,500 m) with three occupants. Since starting operations in 1991, it has dived to more than 20,886 feet (6,365 m), discovered several unsuspected deep fissures off the Japanese east coast, located the world's deepest known community of clams, and examined a series of hydrothermal vent communities.

Although manned submersibles are exciting—they have captured the imagination of both the scientific and the wider community—much of the day-to-day scientific work on the ocean floor is done by unmanned vehicles. These are not only safer but they can stay submerged for much longer periods without the need for an oxygen supply. Among unmanned craft, perhaps most useful are the remotely operated vehicles (ROVs); they are robotic and can be controlled from a surface ship or a submersible. Increasingly, several undersea vessels, working closely with a parent ship, coordinate their activities in carrying out investigations on the seafloor. Perhaps the most successful system of this type is the Seabeam/Argo-Jason system operated by Woods Hole Oceanographic Institution. Elements of this system were involved in locating and exploring the wreck of the RMS Titanic in 1985.

The Seabeam/Argo-Jason system uses a complex sonar system (Seabeam) to map the seafloor and to produce an electronic grid of the area that is displayed on a screen in the parent ship. Argo, a ROV, is towed behind the parent ship and carries an array of sonar and television equipment to scan the terrain in detail within the grid system established by Seabeam. Jason, the third major element of the system, is an ROV that is often launched from Argo and stays connected to it. It is used for detailed sonar surveying and for gathering samples. The parent ship is in satellite communication with the mainland base at Woods Hole, and sonar and television images from the Seabeam/Argo-Jason system are viewed simultaneously on board ship and back at base.

land and their delivery into the sea was regarded as the most convincing explanation for the sea's salinity. No current explanation for the sea's saltiness is entirely satisfactory, however, and the mineral salts spewed out of the deep-sea vents may provide more of the picture. The hydrothermal vents do explain why the seawater concentration of the element magnesium (Mg) remains constant, even though magnesium is constantly being eroded from dry land and finding its way into the oceans. Hydrothermal vents seem to strip seawater of its magnesium. As the seawater passes through the hot rock, the magnesium is removed. All the world's seawater is probably cycled through cracks in the mid-ocean ridge system once every 10 million years—as magnesium is added from the land, so it is removed from the deep ocean. The relative constancy of oceanic levels of other chemical elements may be explained in similar ways.

The Future

Monitoring geological activities will most likely involve even greater international cooperation in the future. Data gathered by remote sensing—from above and below the sea surface—will be closely coupled to that generated by more conventional approaches. Computers will play a much greater role, not only in recording and analyzing data, but also in the construction of models to simulate geophysical events and model global changes. Take the monitoring of global sea-level change as an example. At present, the Global Sea Level Observing System (GLOSS) consists of a worldwide network of about 300 tide gauges, many of which use latest technology to generate real-time data (moment by moment measurements) that are relayed to a computer network via satellite or telephone systems. These measurements are being precisely located within a global system of coordinates established by a body called the International Terrestrial Reference Frame (ITRF), which uses data from various sources including Satellite Laser Ranging (SLR) and Global Positioning System (GPS) observations. Vertical movements of the land close to tide gauges can be established to within the nearest 0.2 inches (5 mm) by precisely measuring changes in gravity. At the same time, satellite altimetry is providing sea-level data every 10 days with a precision of within a few centimeters. All these sources of data, coupled with measurements of ocean temperatures using techniques such as acoustic-pulse travel times, form baseline information that describes changes in global sea level and helps us determine likely causes. The data will form the basis for more-sophisticated computer models to predict global-warming and sea-level rise as we enter the 21st century.

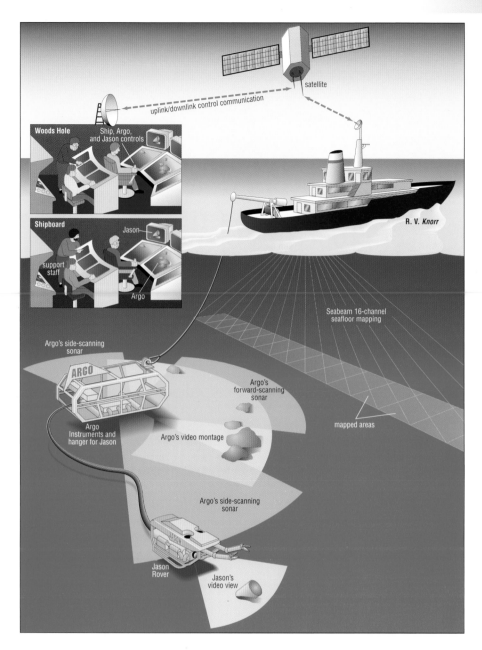

The Seabeam/Argo–Jason system. The Seabeam complex sonar system mounted on board ship scans the seafloor and enables a three-dimensional model of the ocean floor to be completed. Argo, an ROV, is then towed across the mapped region, and sonar and television camera systems make more detailed observations. Jason, another ROV, can be released from Argo to collect specimens and to make detailed observations using its stereo color TV cameras. The ROVs are controlled by a shipboard operator, and TV images are transmitted simultaneously to a shore base that is in constant communication with the ship.

Hydrothermal Vents

The first hydrothermal vents were seen directly by the human eye in 1977. Geophysicists from Woods Hole Oceanographic Institution were traveling in the *Alvin* submersible toward a mid-ocean ridge system—part of the Galápagos ridge in the eastern Pacific—when they were confronted with chimneylike structures rising from the ocean floor and belching inky clouds of water. A thermometer placed in the outflow of one of these vents promptly melted.

The vents are associated with the influx of seawater into cracks close to the central rift valley. The water, superheated and rich in minerals, is belched out through holes that eventually form long chimneys of deposited minerals where the hot water meets the cold-water surroundings. The heat comes from the new seafloor material rising up from the lower crust and mantle. One of these chimneys—they are called "black smokers"—is about 148 feet (45 m) tall and is nicknamed Godzilla.

Hydrothermal vents may be an important piece in the jigsaw that explains why the sea is so salty. Until recently, the erosion of salts from the

The Physical and Chemical Properties of Water

It will come as no surprise that the liquid we see in the ocean is mostly water—about 96.5 percent water, in fact. The remaining 3.5 percent is composed of chemical substances dissolved in the water. In terms of its abundance, water is remarkably common; in terms of its physical and chemical properties, it is remarkably uncommon. It is water's special properties that determine the conditions that exist on our planet, that have shaped the surface of the planet, and that govern the distribution of life. Before we can appreciate how water exerts such a profound influence on our planet in general, and our oceans in particular, we need to explore water's remarkable properties.

The Water Molecule

A water molecule is the smallest amount of water that can still be truly called water. In a drop of water are found at least one billion billion water molecules. It is the properties of these water molecules and how they act in concert that determine the properties of water as a whole.

Each water molecule is made up of three atoms: two hydrogen (H) atoms and one oxygen (O) atom. The structure of a water molecule has two unusual features. First, the three atoms are not arranged in a straight line, as is the case for many three-atom molecules; instead, the two hydrogen atoms are separated by an angle of 105° with the oxygen atom between them. Second, although a water molecule is electrically balanced overall, there is an unequal distribution of charge over the surface of the molecule. The hydrogen atoms are slightly positively charged, and the oxygen atom is slightly negatively charged. These two effects—the bent molecule and the unequal charge distribution on its surface—are the root causes of most of water's unusual properties.

Because water has slightly positive *ends* to the molecule (where the hydrogens are) and has a slightly negative end (where the oxygen is), it is called polar. *Polar* refers to the separation of opposite electrical charges on the surface of the molecule. Because opposite charges (+ and −) attract one another, the slightly positive parts of one water molecule will be attracted to the slightly negative part of another water molecule. As a result, water molecules tend to be attracted to one another. Witness this when you next drop some water on a polished surface: the water molecules form a raised drop. They don't soak into the surface, nor do they spread out to form a large moist patch. They stay together and form a coherent drop.

The force of attraction between water molecules is an electrostatic attraction (attraction between opposite electrical charges). Between water molecules, these forces of attraction are called hydrogen bonds because hydrogen is involved. Hydrogen bonds momentarily form and then break as water molecules tumble past each other within the liquid. These bonds *between* water molecules are relatively weak compared to the strong bonds *within* water molecules that hold the molecule together. Despite their relative weakness, hydrogen bonds nevertheless exert a profound influence on the way water behaves, both physically and chemically.

The Physical States of Water

Among substances on our planet, water is unique in being found in all three physical states—solid, liquid and gas—under normal atmospheric conditions. In polar regions and high up in the atmosphere, water exists habitually as solid ice. On much of the planet, water, of course, is present in its liquid form: in oceans, seas, lakes and rivers, and as groundwater. The air around us also contains water molecules in the form of water vapor—water as a gas. In desert regions, water in the atmosphere is almost entirely absent; in tropical rainforests the air may be saturated with it.

In its liquid state, water molecules move relatively freely. As they pass one another, they are attracted and form hydrogen bonds, but these bonds are quickly made and broken. The overall result is that the molecules stay together but can move past one another. Under the force of gravity, they settle and occupy the bottom of any container into which they are placed. They adopt the inner shape of the container, but the liquid flows if the container is tilted.

At one atmosphere pressure (standard sea-level pressure), water freezes at 32°F (0°C); indeed, the Celsius (centigrade) temperature scale was designed around the properties of water. When water freezes, the molecules no longer move freely. In the solid state, water molecules are held together in a rigid structure called a lattice. Interestingly, in ice, the water molecules are held together by hydrogen bonds but at distances that are slightly longer than those found in cold water. Water is most dense at 4°C, and at temperatures between 4° and 0°C, water expands slightly as it nears freezing point. The effect is that ice is less dense than cold water, which is why it floats. The situation is more complicated for seawater because of the presence of dissolved salts, but the effect is the same: Ice floats. Were it not for this property of water (liquids usually sink as they cool and crystallize), lakes and shallow seas would freeze solid. As it is, surface layers tend to freeze, while below the ice, organisms carve out their existence in the cold but unfrozen waters.

At one atmosphere pressure, liquid water boils at 212°F (100°C). In the change from the liquid to the gaseous state, the water molecules are now able to move very freely and will tend to distribute themselves randomly throughout any container into which they are placed. The molecules are so far apart and move so rapidly that any hydrogen bonding is negligible.

Of course, the transition from one physical state to another is governed by temperature—by the input or removal of heat energy. The hydrogen bonding between water molecules has an impressive influence on water's thermal (heat) properties:

- **Water has a high specific heat (or high heat capacity).** Put simply, this means that liquid water requires a lot of heat energy to raise its temperature, and, conversely, it needs to lose a considerable amount of heat energy before its temperature becomes lowered. This is a consequence of hydrogen bonding. Considerable energy is needed to overcome hydrogen bonding and make water molecules move faster and more freely. Water's high heat capacity means that large volumes of the ocean rarely change by more than 1.8°F (1°C) in a 24-hour period; meanwhile the soil, rocks, and vegetation of nearby landmasses may be rising and falling over a daily range of 27°F (15°C). Water has a massive buffering effect on temperature change in coastal regions and accounts for the moderate climates usually found there. For organisms living in the sea, water provides a thermally stable environment.

- **Water has a relatively high boiling point.** It takes considerable amounts of heat energy for the hydrogen bonds between water molecules to be broken to the extent that water molecules are released from one another's clutches and can enter the gaseous state. Thus, water has a high boiling point compared to other liquids of similar molecular size. Only in natural regions where there is geothermal activity does water tend to reach anywhere near its boiling point.

- **Water has relatively high freezing and melting points.** The hydrogen bonding between water molecules encourages lattice formation at a comparatively high temperature; once ice is formed, it requires a high input of energy to provide enough kinetic energy to overcome the hydrogen bonding in the lattice and so melt the solid.

- **Ice is less dense than liquid water.** As we have seen earlier, ice floats.

- **Water has a high thermal conductivity.** Heat applied to one part of a body of water tends to spread to other parts, thereby reducing the build up of local hot spots. This is not to say, however, that water cannot stratify into layers of different temperature. Indeed, temperature stratification of seawater in hot climates plays a major role in reducing biological productivity (page 85).

- **Water has a high latent heat of evaporation (vaporization).** It takes a considerable input of heat energy to change water from its liquid to its gaseous state. This energy is needed to make water molecules move sufficiently quickly to break free of hydrogen bonding to other water molecules and thereby leave the surface of the liquid. This explains why evaporation has a cooling effect—for example, when perspiration evaporates on the surface of your skin. Conversely, when water condenses—changes from its gaseous state to a liquid form—a considerable amount of heat energy is released.

Water's high latent heat of evaporation has major implications for our weather systems and for Earth's climate. The heat released when water vapor condenses in the atmosphere to form clouds is sufficient to power thunderstorms and hurricanes. In the tropics and subtropics, evaporation of water from the sea's surface cools the oceans. This water vapor then travels on winds in the upper atmosphere and condenses in temperate, polar, and subpolar regions. Every gram of water that evaporates in low latitudes, travels to high latitudes, and then condenses represents a "package" of heat energy that has been transferred from the heat-rich low latitudes to the heat-deficient high latitudes. It is the thermal properties of water that moderate Earth's climate—that ensure that tropical regions do not become too hot and polar regions too cold. Indeed, the conditions for the life on Earth to exist would never have occurred but for the presence of water.

In this brief introduction to the properties of water, we have barely dipped our toes into the mysteries of this substance. Water's other important properties include its high surface tension (liquid water behaves as though it has a "skin") and its remarkable properties as a solvent. In this section we have treated water as a pure substance. Seawater, of course, is not a pure substance: the chemicals dissolved in seawater modify its behavior, as we shall see later.

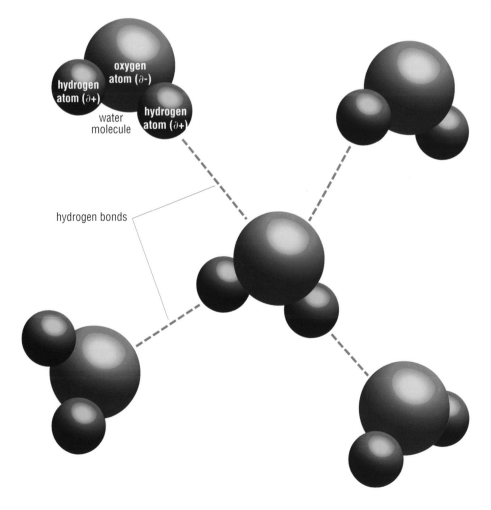

hydrogen bonds

oxygen atom (∂-)

hydrogen atom (∂+)

water molecule

hydrogen atom (∂+)

The water molecule and hydrogen bonding. Water molecules are attracted to one another by hydrogen bonds, the electrostatic attraction between slightly positive hydrogen atoms and slightly negative oxygen atoms.

Light and Sound in the Sea

Light in the Sea

Before we consider how light penetrates the sea, let us refresh our understanding of light itself. The light we see (visible light) is but a narrow range of wavelengths within the electromagnetic spectrum as a whole. Electromagnetic energy has electrical and magnetic properties, travels at the speed of light, and behaves as particles or waves. Spectrum refers to a range of these energies with different wavelengths. Sunlight itself is a balanced range of wavelengths that includes the whole color spectrum. Even though the Sun itself appears golden in the sky, the light we receive from it is white light.

When sunlight strikes the surface waters of the sea, the various wavelengths of light within it are selectively absorbed. Longer wavelengths of light are blocked much more readily than shorter wavelengths. Red wavelengths have been largely removed within 31 feet (10 m) of the sea's surface, but blue, green, and violet wavelengths penetrate much further: it is this blue light, for example, reflected back to the surface in clear water, that gives the ocean its blue color.

On land, the colors we see are due to the amount and quality of prevailing light. In bright sunlight (and assuming we are not color blind), we can see all colors. In very dull light, we can only see blacks, whites, and shades of gray. Assuming that there is sufficient light to see colors, an object's color is due to the wavelengths of light being reflected from it. In sunlight, sand appears yellow because predominantly yellow wavelengths of light are reflected from it; other wavelengths of visible light are absorbed. Similarly, grass appears green because it reflects green wavelengths of light and absorbs others. In bright sunlight, objects appear white because they reflect all visible wavelengths; they appear black because they absorb all visible wavelengths and so none are reflected. This situation is complicated when the prevailing light is no longer sunlight—or "white" light—but is light with some of the wavelengths already removed. This is the situation occurring in the sea at depth.

At 3,280 feet (1,000 m) depth, there is little light remaining from that which penetrated the sea's surface. The residual light is mostly of blue and green wavelengths. At this depth, what color would a red prawn appear to be? Without any red wavelengths in the ambient light, the prawn will appear black: there are no red wavelengths of light to be reflected from it. Being red is a useful camouflage strategy for a prawn because it cannot be readily seen against a background of dim bluey

green light. Of course, were a manned submersible to penetrate to this depth and its occupants to catch a glimpse of the prawn in the craft's "white" beam of light, the prawn would be revealed for the color it really is. This phenomenon of differential light absorption in water explains why coral reefs look so spectacular at shallow depths (less than 33 feet or 10 meters) but become more drab as a subaqua diver descends to 98 feet or 30 meters or so. The red and orange wavelengths of light are filtered out by the water, and at depths the coral reef takes on a bluey green cast, without the vivid reds, oranges and yellows.

It is not just the properties of water that affect the penetration of light. The angle with which light strikes the surface of the water—and any particles or organisms suspended in water—has a big influence, too. In tropical and equatorial seas, the water tends to appear indigo blue because the water is relatively clear and contains few suspended particles or drifting organisms (plankton). This contrasts markedly with the yellow-green color often found in coastal waters at temperate latitudes. Here, the availability of nutrients in shallow water—where sunlight penetrates—means that plant plankton (phytoplankton) are able to photosynthesize and multiply to form dense clouds of individuals. Within the phytoplankton, the light-trapping pigment, chlorophyll, gives the surface waters their characteristic greeny color. Suspended nonliving particles, too, absorb light and affect the apparent color of the seawater, often appearing yellowy green where suspended sand is found or greeny brown where there is drifting mud or silt.

How does light affect the distribution and abundance of life within the sea? Profoundly. It is in the sunlit surface waters down to a depth of about 3,300 feet (1,000 m) that most marine organisms are found because it is here that sunlight trapped by phytoplankton fuels photosynthesis. Also it is phytoplankton that form the basis of many marine food chains (page 84). Sunlight, too, warms the surface waters and provides suitable temperatures for active animal life. The heating effect of sunlight—largely by wavelengths within the infrared range—drives the ocean currents and Earth's weather systems.

Sound in the Sea

In exploring the oceans, light is of limited usefulness because the depth of penetration of natural light is about 1,000 meters (about 3,300 feet) at most. Although artificial light sources can be attached to underwater vehicles and used for

exploring the ocean depths, such investigations are very expensive and time consuming and cannot be used for mapping large areas of the ocean floor. Here, sound waves come into their own.

Sound is transmitted faster and farther through water than through air. This has made it possible to develop sound systems for all manner of marine applications: for obtaining large-scale "sound pictures" of the ocean floor, for determining the thickness and nature of layers underlying the seafloor, for locating shoals of fish, and for locating or communicating with underwater scientific instruments. Sonar (SOund Navigation And Ranging) is the main technique that uses sound to detect the locations of objects underwater. Sonar equipment utilizes a transponder (to send a sound signal) and a receiver (to detect the reflected signal). Once the velocity or speed of sound has been determined for local conditions, the distance to an object is equal to the speed times one-half the time required for the sound signal to reach the object and return.

Sound waves travel through seawater, on average, at about 4,750 feet per second (1,450 m per second), more than four times faster than the speed of sound in air. Furthermore, the speed of sound in the ocean is slightly greater at increased temperatures, salinities (salt concentrations), and pressures. These factors vary with season of the year, depth in the water, and so on, so if the speed of sound is to be used for measuring distances, these variables need to be taken into account. Also, any sharp differences in these variables may produce an underwater "boundary" that causes sound waves to be refracted (bent) or even reflected (bounced back).

One such boundary is a layer associated with the thermocline (steep temperature gradient) found in many oceans. Where it occurs, it is usually found at a depth of between 980 and 3,280 feet (300 and 1,000 m) the precise depth depending on locality and season of the year. Sound waves originating above the thermocline may travel to the layer and then become refracted, or bent, into the layer. In effect, the sound waves become trapped in the layer. The layer is called the sound channel or the Sofar channel (SOund Fixing And Ranging); sound waves, once trapped in it, can travel thousands of kilometers across the oceans. The Sofar channel is used by scientists for transmitting data over long distances and for measuring horizontal distances underwater. It is likely that marine mammals, especially whales (page 107), utilize the properties of this channel for communicating by sound over long distances. The sound channel also has military significance. Submarines can hide by floating just below the

Visible light within the electromagnetic spectrum and its penetration in seawater.

Sofar channel, with the crew safe in the knowledge that any noise they and the vessel make may be refracted away horizontally when it enters the sound channel and that little, if any, will reach the ocean surface where vessels searching for them might be. Also, any sonar echo from the submarine may be confused with that produced by the Sofar channel itself—although with the increased sensitivities of today's Sonars, such "cat-and-mouse" tactics are less likely to be successful.

In 1991, Walter Monk and his team at the Scripps Institution of Oceanography, California, sent acoustic signals from the southern Indian Ocean through the Sofar channel that were picked up as far as the east and west coasts of North America, some 9,940 miles (16,000 km) away. This technique may provide a means of monitoring wholesale temperature rise in the open ocean. A rise in temperature increases the speed of sound in water, and acoustic signals thus take less time to travel the same distance. If such measurements are taken every year, they may provide a widespread and cost-effective means of measuring the impact of global warming on the oceans. Further trials, under the acronym ATOC (Acoustic Thermometry of Ocean Climate), have continued in the Pacific Ocean since 1994, with sound transmitters based off Hawaii and California and an array of receivers dotted about the Pacific rim. This acoustic technique is expected to be sufficiently sensitive to measure a year-on-year temperature rise in the Pacific of as little as four-thousandths of a centigrade (0.004°C).

With suitable microphones to pick up the sounds, the undersea world is far from quiet. In tropical and subtropical coastal waters, local aggregations of millions of shrimp produce sounds not unlike the sizzle of frying fat or the crackle of burning twigs. Some fish produce clicks by rubbing together parts of their skeletons; other fish produce grunts or whistles using their gas-bladders (page 102). The range of noise-producing structures in fishes and their use in communication is remarkable in itself. However, the sound communicators *par excellence* are dolphins and whales (page 107). Dolphins produce high-frequency clicks that are used for echolocation (locating objects by reflected sound) and for communication. It is theoretically possible for them to use focused bursts of high-frequency sound to stun prey, although this has yet to be confirmed by observation.

Humpback whales produce melodic low-frequency patterns of sound—"songs"—that vary with locality and change in time. They consist of moans, squeaks, and whistles and are sung by breeding males to attract females; the songs can travel hundreds of kilometers under water. Toothed whales, such as the sperm whale and the orca (killer whale), also have a wide repertoire of sounds, used for both communication and echolocation. The echolocation systems of dolphins and toothed whales can pinpoint single fish and precisely judge their prey's movement, distance, and size. It is clear that human attempts to develop underwater sound systems have yet to reach even close to the sophistication already employed in the natural world.

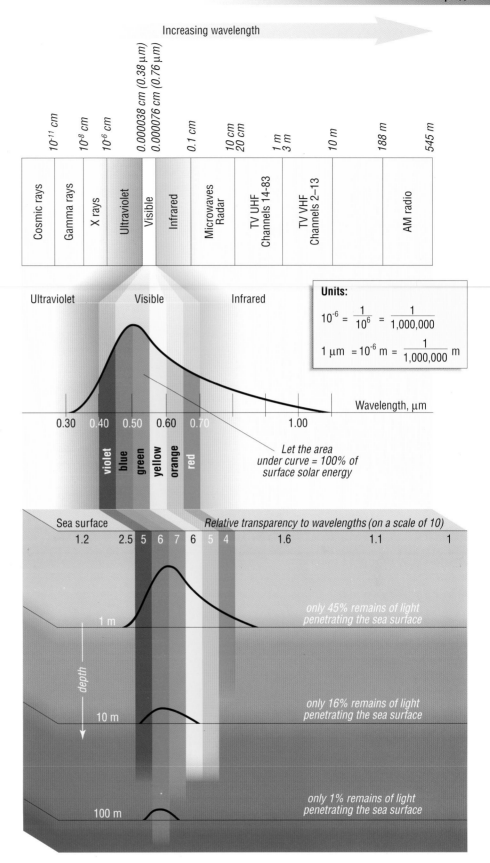

Sea Temperatures

Temperature has a profound influence on the other physical properties of water. For example, temperature in combination with salinity (salt concentration) determines the density of seawater (page 50), and the relative density of seawater determines how and when water moves: When cold (and therefore dense) water sinks from the surface, water moves across from the surroundings to replace it. Elsewhere in the oceanic system water must, ultimately, rise to replace the water that has sunk. It is such movements of water up and down and across the oceans from polar to tropical regions at different levels that produce the major ocean currents that, in turn, influence the global weather system (page 74).

Biological productivity (page 85) in the marine environment is largely determined by the availability of nutrients in the surface waters. Often, these nutrients arrive by upward movement of water (upwelling) from deep in the water column. Conversely, the downward movement of water (downwelling) may deliver oxygen-rich surface water to depth. Water temperature also affects the ability of gases to dissolve, including

gases such as oxygen and carbon dioxide that are intimately associated with biological processes. Temperature also has a direct effect on the rate of chemical processes—within and outside living organisms—and so temperature is a key factor determining the geographic distribution of different forms of marine life (page 82)

Sea-Surface Temperatures

Surface temperatures in the world's oceans lie between the freezing point of seawater (-28.6°F or 1.9°C) in icy polar and subpolar regions and about +86°F (30°C) in tropical and equatorial waters. The buffering effect produced by water's high specific-heat capacity means that this temperature range is much narrower than that found on land, where temperatures range from -89°C on the Antarctic continent in winter to +58°C in parts of North Africa in the summer. The sea thus represents a relatively stable thermal environment, although temperatures can reach +40°C in small bodies of water such as shallow tropical

Pancake ice formations at the edge of the pack ice, Weddell Sea, Antarctica (Konrad Wothe/ENP Images).

lagoons or tide pools, and there may be marked fluctuations during the course of a day. In the open ocean, the surface temperature normally fluctuates less than 0.6°F (0.3°C) over a 24-hour period, and at 10 meters (33 feet) depth the fluctuation is barely measurable if at all.

The surface water of an ocean warms as it absorbs the infrared wavelengths of light found in solar radiation (sunlight). This warming effect takes place largely within the first meter or so of the surface. Not only does it take large amounts of heat energy to raise the temperature of water, but evaporation at the surface of water tends to maintain a stable water temperature as heat energy is used to convert liquid water into water vapor. In this way, great quantities of heat energy can be transferred from the sea to overlying air, thereby powering weather systems (page 74).

During the course of a year, open-ocean surface temperatures in tropical and polar regions fluctuate remarkably little—a range of 4–9°F (2–5°C) in Arctic and tropical seas and even less in Antarctic waters. In temperate and subtropical regions, the temperature variation is significant, and enough to affect biological processes markedly. At latitudes of 30–40° (warm temperate) the annual variation is about 11–13°F (6–7°C) and in western areas of the North Atlantic and North Pacific, where continental airstreams deliver warm air in summer and cold air in winter, the annual variation may reach as high as 32°F (18°C). Biological productivity in temperate seas tends to be markedly seasonal; it is dependent, in part, on water temperature and the availability of nutrients that are brought to the surface after winter storms. The complex interplay between surface temperatures, weather systems, and biological productivity is well demonstrated by study of the El Niño event that happens every 2–10 years (page 69). On a wider scale, the effect on marine ecosystems of previous climatic change is written in the historical records of marine sediments and suggests that dramatic changes have happened in the past and will no doubt happen again in the future (page 40).

So although temperature variations in the sea are markedly less than those on land, their influence is considerable, both on the unfolding drama of life in the sea and—via their influence on the world's weather patterns—on events on land.

Vertical Temperature Gradients

In most open oceans for all or most of the year, there are characteristically three different layers delineated by their temperatures. There is a topmost warm layer, typically reaching a depth of 330–985 feet (100–300 m) that is kept mixed by wind action at the surface. Below this layer and extending vertically over perhaps 660–985 feet (200–300 m) is a steep temperature gradient called the permanent thermocline. Across this layer, the temperature difference may be as much as 68°F (20°C). Because warm water is generally lighter (less dense) than cooler water, the gradient is not just one of temperature but is a density gradient as well. The density of the water changes markedly between the top and bottom of the thermocline, being less dense at the top and more dense at the bottom. The thermocline, in effect, forms a physical barrier. Water—and the nutrients dissolved or suspended in water—have difficulty crossing from one side of the thermocline to the other, and organisms may be unable to pass (page 90).

Below the thermocline lie the cool, relatively constant temperatures of the deep ocean. This deep water makes up more than 75 percent of the volume of the world's oceans and has a temperature in the range -1 to +5°C, with the deepest water being at the lower end of that range. Only in localities where there is geothermal activity is deep water warmer than +5°C (page 43). Most of the world's oceanic water is, by our standards, cold.

Because the bulk of seawater—that below several hundred meters—is remarkably constant in temperature, oceanographers attach great significance to even minor temperature changes, and the accurate monitoring of water temperatures and salinity (page 51) is an important means of tracing the origins of water and tracking its movement.

Sea Ice

Ice in the sea occurs in two main forms: icebergs, which are calved (broken off) from glaciers and land-based ice sheets, and pack ice, which is formed when seawater freezes.

Icebergs, because of their origins on land, are formed from freshwater and contain no salt. Arctic and Antarctic icebergs differ from each other in both size and shape. Antarctic icebergs tend to be larger than Arctic ones and are calved from the iceshelf that fringes the Antarctic continent. The Antarctic iceshelf moves forward some 330 feet (100 m) each year, and as it does so, some of the ice breaks off to form bergs. Several thousand are formed each year, and most are in the region of 5 miles (8 km) long and project 130 feet (40 m) or more out of the water. They are broad rather than deep with a flattened tabular form. As much as 165 feet (50 m) above the waterline and 490 feet (150 m) below it, they can be huge—as long and broad as 185 by 60 miles (300 by 100 km). Such bergs may drift thousands of miles northward before finally melting in warm temperate waters.

Around the Arctic Sea, more than 10,000 icebergs each year are produced by calving from glaciers. When a glacier meets the sea, its leading edge breaks into large pieces to form floating blocks of ice. Sometimes the ice blocks arise from below the waterline and bob up to the surface; they may be colored green from the algae growing on their previously submerged surfaces. Arctic icebergs tend to be deeper but less broad than those found in the Antarctic; as much as 330 feet (100 m) above the waterline and 1,300 feet (400 m) below it. Most weigh 1–2 million metric tons (1.1–2.2 million tons). Often they are streaked green, brown, or black from the sediment they contain. They become locked in pack ice or drift freely in open water, often making their way

down the western side of the North Atlantic Ocean even as far south as Newfoundland. Icebergs lose most of their bulk before they even enter the Atlantic.

Seawater freezes at a lower temperature than the freezing point of pure water (at -1.9°C, or 28.6°F, rather than 0°C, or 32°F) because the salt that is dissolved in seawater (page 54) depresses the freezing point. The freezing process is gradual and takes place in a series of recognizable stages. The first ice crystals to form are approximately spherical and merge with one another to create thin discs or plates known as frazil ice. The plates gradually merge, and the sea takes on a translucent appearance and a soupy texture known as grease ice. In calm seas, this freezes to form a smooth, solid, semitransparent surface layer called nilas. In disturbed water, the smooth layer may break up into separate plates, which become buckled at their edges by collisions with one another. As the frozen layer thickens to form an ice floe, the freezing process slows as the overlying ice insulates the water below the ice from the surface cold above.

Pack ice contains varying amounts of salt, depending on its age, thickness, and how it was formed, but always its overall salt concentration is less than that of the ocean water below. Ice crystals are almost pure water, and they exclude salt, which becomes localized in pockets of salty liquid within the ice (each pocket is less than a tenth of millimeter, or 0.004 inch across). As the ice ages, the pockets (called brine cells) coalesce and form a system of tiny channels through which the salty water can escape into the seawater below the ice.

In the Arctic, first-year pack ice reaches about 6.5 feet (2 m) thick in the Arctic and 10 feet (3 m) thick in the Antarctic. If this ice survives the following summer, it may in time form multiyear ice that becomes increasingly thick. The surface layers of this ice may melt and refreeze every year to form smooth blue ice. Multiyear ice, such as that found in the central Arctic, can be many meters thick and is impassable even to ice-breaking vessels.

Ice floes drift with the prevailing winds and currents. In the Arctic, two major drift patterns predominate. A gyre in the Beaufort Sea causes bergs and ice floes to circulate for as many as 20 years. A drift stream crosses the North Pole from Siberia to the east coast of Greenland, taking the ice with it. In the Antarctic, winds blowing from the west generate northeast-flowing currents that carry floating ice into subpolar waters.

Using sonar to detect the thickness and conformation of ice, submarines can travel below even the thickest pack ice of the central Arctic. Submarines can break surface through thin pack ice.

Pressure, Density, and Depth

Snorkeling on a coral reef, a dive to 10 meters (33 feet) brings us into a very different watery world. The quality of light alters and the temperature drops, but one thing above all changes—the pressure.

Pressure

On land, each part of our body is subjected to the weight of the column of air above it, something we take entirely for granted and only notice when we climb to high altitudes and the air thins and becomes more difficult to breathe. At sea level, the column of air exerts a pressure of 1 atmosphere. As soon as we descend below the surface of the sea, it is not just a column of air weighing down on us; there is a column of water as well, and, of course, water is much denser than air. We do not have to descend far for the weight of water above us to exert a very noticeable effect. Simply diving 10 meters below the surface doubles the pressure on our bodies. At the surface, the pressure is 1 atmosphere; 10 meters down it is 2 atmospheres. For each 10 meters we descend, so the pressure increased by 1 atmosphere.

There are many different units used to measure pressure: 1 atmosphere is equivalent to 1 bar, or 1,000 millibars (mb); or 14.7 pounds per square inch (14.7 psi); or, in metric units, 10,000 newtons per square meter.

The increase in pressure with depth has a profound effect on us and on other creatures in the sea. If we are swimming on the sea surface and then dive to 10 meters (33 feet), the effect of pressure is immediate and obvious. If we are wearing a diving mask, it will be pressed into our face with greater force. We may experience discomfort as our middle ears adjust to the increased pressure of their new surroundings. Although we are probably unaware of it, our lungs will have deflated to 50 percent of their normal volume as the external pressure exerts its effect. When we return to the surface, so the pressure is relieved, and conditions return to normal.

Gases are readily compressed by high pressures; liquids are not. Any gases contained in a thin-walled container will be compressed as the container descends through the water column. A gas will halve its volume when the pressure on it is doubled. At 10 meters depth, the pressure is 2 atmospheres, and the volume of gas will be half that at the surface. At 30 meters (99 feet) depth, the pressure is 4 atmospheres, and the volume of gas will be one-quarter that at the surface. The container, unless it

can resist the drop in pressure, will collapse. So, any gas-filled structure inside an organism—the swim bladder of a fish or the lungs of a mammal—will shrink or collapse as the organism dives deeper. Conversely, as a creature rises in the water column, any gas-filled structures it contains will expand, perhaps with disastrous consequences. The swim bladder of a fish will inflate like a balloon if the fish is brought to the surface too quickly (page 102). Scuba divers breathing air at depth must be careful to expel the air from their lungs as they rise. If not, the lungs may overinflate and effectively burst, causing an air embolism (a bubble of air) in the bloodstream; death may result unless corrective action is taken rapidly.

Pressure changes with depth limit the vertical movements of organisms (page 90), and they pose major problems for humans who wish to explore the ocean depths. In the deepest ocean trenches, the ambient pressure is 1,000 atmospheres, equivalent to more than 6.5 tons per square inch or about 1 metric ton per square centimeter. Submarines, submersibles, and technical equipment (page 154) must be engineered to withstand very high pressures.

With increasing depth, there are other problems for humans. Nitrogen comprises about 78 percent of the volume of normal air; at a depth of about 50 meters (165 feet), the pressure is sufficient to cause inhaled nitrogen gas to dissolve in the blood. This causes problems if the diver ascends too rapidly. Nitrogen gas forms bubbles in the blood, and these may impede blood flow and collect in narrow blood vessels, causing damage; for example, where blood vessels pass through joints or in nervous tissue. The result is excruciating pain called the bends. To avoid the problem, the diver has to slow his ascent, or undergo decompression (sit in a pressurized enclosure while the pressure is gradually reduced to sea-level pressure). At depths of about 40 meters (131 feet) or more, there is also the possibility of nitrogen narcosis, which can impair thinking. In commercial diving operations, if divers are operating regularly at depths of 60 meters (about 195 feet), mixtures of oxygen and helium (in place of normal air) are supplied to circumvent the problems of nitrogen narcosis and the bends (page 153).

High pressures have surprising effects on the chemistry and physiology of organisms. Mutation rates (the rate at which spontaneous changes occur in the genetic material) are greater at higher pressures, and various aspects of cell functioning—including how substances are transported within the cell and the cell's electrical activity—are mod-

ified under pressure. High-pressure biology is still a very new field of inquiry.

Density

Density is a form of measurement that incorporates two variables: mass and volume. Density is the mass per unit volume of a substance. One gram of Styrofoam has the same mass as 1 gram of lead, but lead, of course, is much denser. One gram of lead will occupy much less space than 1 gram of Styrofoam. The denser a substance, the greater its mass for a given volume.

In the open ocean, the relative densities of bodies of water are extremely important. They determine the positions of waters in the water column (the column of water between the sea surface and the seafloor) and how these waters will rise and fall. These shifts, in turn, determine the movement of currents across the oceans, which, in turn, influence the world's weather systems.

The two factors that are most influential in changing the density of seawater are temperature and salinity. As salinity (the concentration of dissolved salt) increases, density increases. Your body floats lower in freshwater than it does in seawater. In the highly saline Dead Sea, you will float even higher, such is the buoyancy of the salty water.

In most cases, as water temperature increases, the water expands and its density therefore decreases. The relationship between temperature and density helps explain why much of the ocean system is effectively three layered: there is a warm, mixed, low-density surface layer and a cold, deep, high-density layer, between which is sandwiched a layer of intermediate temperature and density—the permanent thermocline (page 49). Thus, the ocean is usually layered or stratified, with the densest water at the bottom and the least-dense at the surface. This stratification is maintained, and the water column is regarded as stable, unless some major input of energy—an intrusion of warm water, or mixing by winds or storm waves—disturbs this arrangement.

Water of uniform temperature and salinity has a specific density and acts as a discrete body of water in the open ocean. As this water comes into contact with another body of water that has a higher density—perhaps one that is more saline and/or lower in temperature—the first water mass will ride above the second. In this way, it may well remain at the surface for long periods, unless it cools significantly by evaporation and/or becomes more saline, in which case it becomes more dense and may sink.

When surface water becomes more dense than the water below, the arrangement is unstable, and it is only a matter of time before the surface layer sinks. This occurs in polar regions in winter when surface water cools. The implications of this instability are significant. Oxygen-rich surface water descends through the water column, and nutrient-rich deep water ascends; this overturn (reversal in position between surface and deep water) is beneficial because it raises the productivity of the surface waters and enriches the deeps with oxygen.

The distinctive characteristics of a body of water—its temperature and salinity—are usually generated at the top of the water column because it is here that its defining temperature and salinity regime is established in contact with the atmosphere. Once this water mass is formed and leaves the surface, insulation by surrounding water masses means that its characteristics will change only slowly. Such water masses—defined by their specific combination of salinity and temperature—can then be tracked vertically and horizontally across the oceans of the world. When two water masses mix together, a new water mass with its own defining characteristics may be created—its "signature" reflecting the degree of mixing between the two original water masses.

The density of oceanic water is difficult to measure directly, particularly at depth, and oceanographers do this indirectly by measuring the water's temperature and salinity and then making a slight adjustment to take into account pressure. Under increasing pressure a liquid is very slightly compressed and so its density increases very slightly. In the deepest ocean trenches, the bottom water is subjected to 1,000 atmospheres pressure, which is sufficient to compress water by 5 percent (or put another way, the bottom water occupies 95 percent of the volume that water of the same temperature and salinity would occupy on the surface). The compressive effect of pressure on water, though small, is nevertheless significant. Oceanographers calculate that the water column in ocean trenches is compressed by about 30 meters (100 feet) under its own weight. If water were incompressible, then the world's sea levels would probably be 10 meters (33 feet) or so higher than they are.

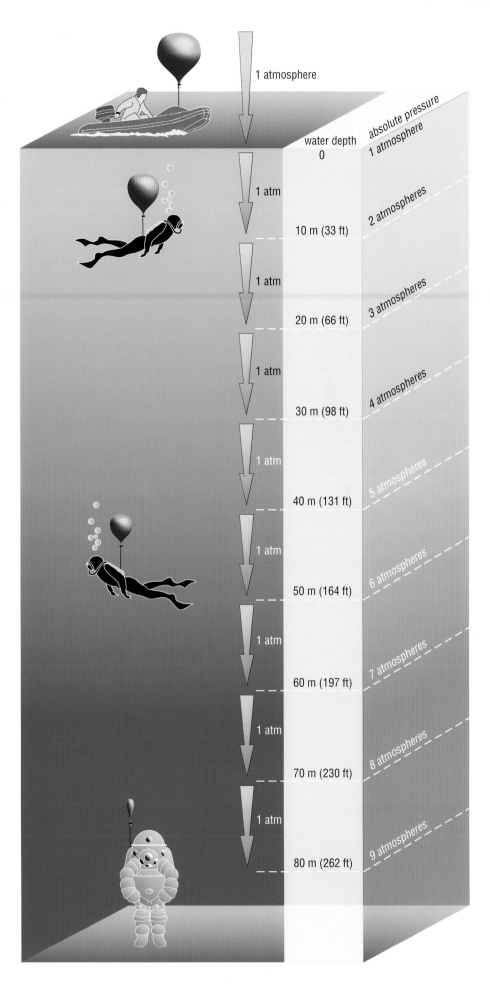

The rise in pressure with depth and its effect. Pressure rises by 1 atmosphere for each 32.8 feet (10 meters) of depth. Gas-filled structures decrease in volume with rise in pressure, becoming compressed during a dive. Various factors limit breathing of normal air during scuba diving to a depth of about 50 meters (164 feet) or so.

The Chemistry of Seawater

Studying the traffic of energy and material among Earth's crust, atmosphere, and ocean is central to our understanding of Earth as a place in which to live. The uptake and release of gases from the world's oceans play a major role in determining the chemical composition of Earth's atmosphere. The moisture content of the air, for example, affects various features of the global climate, such as local temperatures and rainfall patterns, which, in their turn, determine which land-living organisms can survive where.

Exchanges of various substances between land and sea influence the distribution of marine life. Biological productivity, for example, tends to be rich where high nutrient loads are emptied into the sea via runoff from land. Marine mineral resources—from gold and diamonds to oil and gas—are the domain of marine chemists, and most forms of pollution are *chemical* pollution. So, the study of marine chemistry has great practical significance. It gives us insight into both the biological and mineral world of the oceans and can teach us lessons about how these invaluable resources can be conserved.

Water as a Solvent

One of the most remarkable properties of water is its ability to dissolve a huge range of chemical substances; for this ability, it is termed the universal solvent. If the epithet is perhaps overstated, it is nonetheless likely that a small amount of almost every substance on the planet is present in a dissolved form somewhere in the ocean. Substances in solution, with particles that are mobile and yet not too widely dispersed, are usually more likely to react than they are in their gaseous or solid phases. But why is water such a good solvent?

Solubility depends, among other things, on the particle size of the substance to be dissolved (the solute) and the degree of attraction between these solute particles and the liquid into which they are placed (the solvent). Other things being equal, the smaller the solute particle size, the better its solubility in a suitable solvent. At a molecular level, small molecules or ions tend to dissolve more readily than larger ones. Regarding attraction between solvent and solute, the general rule is that "like dissolves in like"—nonpolar substances tend to dissolve nonpolar solvents; polar or ionic substances tend to dissolve in polar solvents. Water, to some extent, exhibits the best of the both worlds: It behaves partly as a nonpolar solvent, and to a small extent it dissolves nonpolar substances such as hydrocarbon oils (page 170). It behaves better as a polar solvent and dissolves polar and ionic substances particularly well (ionic substances are made of charged atoms or groups of atoms called ions). Sodium chloride, or common salt, that gives seawater its salinity, is an ionic solid.

When an ionic substance is in its solid state, the ions are attracted to one another to form a crystalline lattice—to outward appearances, a crystal. Inside the crystal, the ions are arranged in such a way that any positively charged ions (called cations) are surrounded by negatively charged ions (called anions). In seawater, the most abundant ionic substance is sodium chloride; in its solid crystalline form (common salt), its sodium ions (positively charged) are surrounded by chloride ions (negatively charged) in a crystal lattice. The ions are held together by strong electrical attraction between the oppositely charged ions. These attractions are called ionic bonds. When the crystal is placed in water, water molecules disrupt these bonds and cause the ions to separate, and so the substance dissolves. The sodium ions become surrounded by water molecules with the slightly negative end of each molecule toward the ion. The chloride ions too become enclosed by water molecules but with the slightly positive ends of each molecule toward the ion. In this form, loosely attached to water molecules, the ions are termed hydrated.

The Chemical Composition of Seawater

Most of the physical properties of ocean water are, by and large, the properties of water; after all, water accounts for about 96.5 percent of it. However, the chemicals making up the remaining 3.5 percent also have an important chemical role to play. These dissolved solids are simply called salts, of which common salt (sodium chloride) is by far the most abundant. Of course, it is these salts—and sodium chloride in particular—that give seawater its salty taste.

In the late 18th century, French chemist Antoine-Laurent Lavoisier (1743–94) was the first to attempt to analyze systematically the chemical constituents in seawater. He did this by fractional crystallization—heating and then cooling the water, through a series of gradually rising temperatures. Slightly changing the experimental conditions markedly changed the mass and composition of the crystals he collected. This is, in part, accounted for by the fact that many of the salts in seawater are crystallized to form

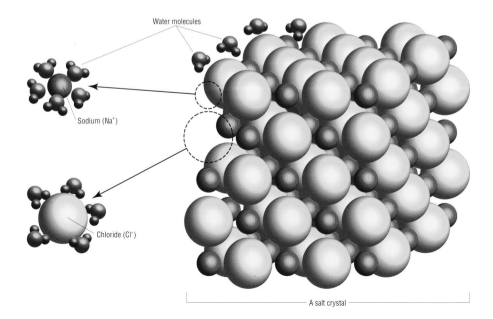

Water molecules

Sodium (Na⁺)

Chloride (Cl⁻)

A salt crystal

Water as a solvent. Water is particularly good at dissolving ionic substances such as sodium chloride (common salt). Common salt comprises positively charged sodium ions and negatively charged chloride ions. When a crystal of salt dissolves in water, the slightly positive parts of the water molecules (the H atoms) are attracted to chloride ions, and the slightly negative part of a water molecule is attracted to sodium ions. The overall effect is for water molecules to "pull" sodium and chloride ions out of the crystal lattice and into solution.

CONSTITUENTS OF SEAWATER

The top seven chemical constituents of seawater (excluding the hydrogen and oxygen in water itself) based on seawater of average salinity, that is, 35°/00 (35 parts salt per thousands parts of seawater)

Constituent (grams per kilogram of seawater)	Concentration % by weight of total salts in seawater
Chloride ion (Cl⁻)	18.98	55.04
Sodium ion (Na⁺)	10.56	30.61
Sulphate ion (SO₄²⁻)	2.65	7.68
Magnesium ion (Mg²⁺)	1.27	3.69
Calcium ion (Ca²⁺)	0.40	1.16
Potassium ion (K⁺)	0.38	1.10
Bicarbonate ion (HCO₃⁻)	0.14	0.41

hydrates—their constituent ions in association with water molecules. Also, the important chemical constituents in seawater—apart from more-complex organic compounds—are the ions themselves, rather than the compounds in which they may crystallize. Analysis of the chemical composition of seawater is more an analysis of individual ions, rather than the compounds in which they might be found.

In the 1880s, British chemist Wilhelm Dittmar analyzed samples of seawater that were collected during the famous HMS *Challenger* cruise. He was able to detect eight elements in seawater and showed that samples from different seas and oceans were remarkably constant in composition. Today, we are able to detect more than 80 elements in seawater with some at staggeringly low concentrations. Other than the hydrogen (H) and oxygen (O) in the water component of seawater, the six elements most abundant in the sea are: chlorine (Cl), sodium (Na), sulfur (S), magnesium (Mg), calcium (Ca) and potassium (K). All these are present in the form of ions (see table).

Concentrations of the major constituents are little affected by biological and chemical processes. It is only where freshwater runoff from the land enters the sea—and where this runoff has a balance of major ions that is noticeably different from that in the sea—that the percentage occurrence of the different chemical constituents will vary markedly from those shown.

Of the 80 or so other chemical elements in the sea, many are present in very low concentrations, but because the oceans are so large, on a global scale they represent enormous reserves. For

example, there is probably about 11 million tons (10 t) of gold in the sea but its concentration is infinitesimal—only about one part gold to each thousand billion parts water.

Those elements strongly associated with biological processes (e.g., nitrogen [N] in the form of the nitrate [NO_3^-] ion and phosphorus [P] as the phosphate [PO_4^-] ion) vary considerably in abundance, in part because they are added or removed by the activities of animals and plants. The role of nitrate and phosphate as nutrients (page 85) is very important in the biological economy of the sea, but their chemical concentrations remain very low compared to the major ions.

Residence Times

The constituent chemical elements in seawater are constantly being added and removed via the atmosphere, Earth's crust, and runoff from the land. The composition of the oceans seems to be relatively stable both from one ocean to another, and over time. Because of this, marine chemists consider the world's oceans to be well mixed and in a steady state—the rate at which elements are being added to and removed from the oceans must be about equal. However, some elements are being added and removed at much higher rates than others. This leads us to the concept of residence times.

Residence time refers to how long a particular element can be expected to stay in the ocean system. The more reactive chemical species will have much shorter residence times than the less reactive ones. Sodium ions (Na⁺), as

opposed to sodium atoms (Na), are highly stable in solution and can be expected to stay in the ocean for millions of years. Aluminum ions (Al^{3+}), on the other hand, are highly reactive in the marine environment and tend to combine with other chemical species to precipitate out as particulate matter. The average residence time of aluminum is about 100 years. Residence time is calculated as:

$$\text{Residence time} = \frac{\text{Amount of chemical constituent in the oceans}}{\text{Rate at which the constituent is added to or removed from the oceans}}$$

Dissolved Gases

There are gases as well as solids that are dissolved in seawater. The two most important gases from the point of view of marine life are oxygen (O_2) and carbon dioxide (CO_2). Nitrogen (N_2), although relatively inert, is present at quite high concentrations and poses potential difficulties for diving organisms (page 51). All three gases are major constituents of Earth's atmosphere and enter or leave seawater at the air-sea surface boundary, with wave or current turbulence enhancing this exchange of gases. A given gas will diffuse (there will be a overall movement) from a region of high concentration to one of lower concentration.

High pressure and raised salinities both tend to raise water's ability to dissolve gases. A rise in temperature, however, makes water less soluble to gases (this is in contrast to solids, which tend to dissolve *more* readily in warm water). So in the cool, high-pressure depths of the ocean, gases dissolve readily, whereas in warm, shallow seas, water becomes saturated with gas at much lower concentrations.

Oxygen, a gas that is essential for respiration in most organisms, enters the surface waters from the atmosphere and is also produced and released by the photosynthetic activities of marine plants and phytoplankton. It is consumed by most animals, plants, and bacteria in the process of respiration (page 81). Carbon dioxide, on the other hand, is produced by respiratory activities and is an essential reactant required in photosynthesis. It is present in much higher concentrations in seawater than in the atmosphere, and its concentration in polar regions at certain times of the year helps fuel massive phytoplankton blooms (page 88).

The Salty Sea

Seawater is obviously salty. Its salty taste is its most distinguishing characteristic. But why is the sea so salty? Where, exactly, does the salt come from?

According to an old Norse legend, the sea is salty because somewhere in the depths of the ocean, a salt mill is grinding away, day after day, year after year. Oceanographers have been searching for this salt mill—or rather, its geochemical equivalent—for many decades. We are closer to finding a convincing explanation, but the answer is much more complex than we expected, and our searchings have raised many new questions. But first things first.

What Is Salt?

In everyday usage, the word *salt* refers to common salt or sodium chloride (NaCl), and it is this, apart from water itself, that is the most abundant constituent of seawater. To chemists, however, the word *salt* has a broader meaning and refers to many substances. In chemical terms, the word *salt* refers to a chemical compound (a substance made of two or more elements that are chemically combined) that is formed when an acid reacts with a base. An acid is a substance which, when measured on the pH scale (a measure of a chemical's tendency to give or receive hydrogen ions) has a pH value below 7.0. A base, of which alkalis such as sodium hydroxide (NaOH) are examples, have pH values above 7.0. Pure water has a pH value of 7.0. It is regarded as neutral; in fact, water provides the standard against which acids and bases are measured. Salts are formed when acids and bases react together, and common salt or sodium chloride (NaCl) is just one kind of salt, albeit the most common one.

Salinity and Its Measurement

The saltiness of seawater is measured in terms of salinity, which refers to the amount of dissolved solid (in grams) in one kilogram of ocean water. Because there are 1,000 grams in one kilogram, salinity is often quoted as parts per thousand ($^{o}/oo$ in shorthand). Throughout the world's oceans, seawater's average salinity is 34.7$^{o}/oo$ (34.7 parts salt in every 1000 parts of seawater); put another way, there are, on average, 34.7 grams of salt in every 1,000 grams of seawater.

During the famous HMS *Challenger* expedition of the 1870s (page 150), seawater samples were taken from more than 70 locations in the Atlantic and Pacific Oceans. When these samples were analyzed by British chemist Wilhelm Dittmar in 1884, two features soon became apparent. First, salinities in the surface waters of the open ocean across the world vary relatively little. Second, in terms of its main chemical constituents, seawater from the surface waters of the open ocean is remarkably constant in its composition. The proportions of the main chemical constituents—Na^+, Mg^{2+}, Ca^{2+}, K^+, Cl^- and SO_4^{2-}—were remarkably uniform. This constancy makes measuring salinity much easier. If the proportions of the different chemical constituents remain relatively constant, then measuring the concentration of one constituent enables you to compute the rest and therefore determine the overall concentration of salts. Measuring just one chemical constituent enables you to determine salinity. In practice, because the chloride ion is the most abundant constituent dissolved in seawater and is easy to determine chemically, salinity used to be computed by measuring the chloride con-

---

SEAWATER VS. FRESHWATER

The table below shows the top seven chemical constituents of typical seawater (excluding the hydrogen and oxygen in water itself) compared with the equivalent constituents in freshwater. Notice that the constituents of freshwater are present in much smaller concentrations and in differing proportions to those in seawater. For example, the chloride-ion concentration in seawater is more than 200 times greater than that in freshwater; the seawater bicarbonate concentration is only about 2 1/2 times that in freshwater. Silicate (SiO_3^{2-})—not shown in the table—is one of the major constituents of freshwater (0.013 grams per kilogram) but is one of the least abundant major ions in seawater (0.007 grams per kilogram).

Constituent	Concentration (grams per kilogram of seawater)	
	Seawater	Freshwater
Chloride ion (Cl^-)	19.0	0.008
Sodium ion (Na^+)	10.6	0.006
Sulfate ion (SO_4^{2-})	2.7	0.011
Magnesium ion (Mg^{2+})	1.3	0.004
Calcium ion (Ca^{2+})	0.40	0.015
Potassium ion (K^+)	0.38	0.002
Bicarbonate ion (HCO_3^-)	0.14	0.058

MARINE ENVIRONMENTS CLASSIFIED BY SALINITY

Environment	Salinity range ($^{o}/oo$)
Open ocean	32–37 (average, 35)
Shallow coastal areas	27–30
Semienclosed seas (e.g. Baltic Sea)	25 or less (termed brackish or hyposaline)
Estuaries	0–30 (brackish or hyposaline)
Regions with high water loss by evaporation and low fresh water input (e.g. tidal pools, tropical lagoons, the Red Sea)	40 or more (termed hypersaline)

centration by chemical means. Today, salinities are measured much more quickly and easily by measuring the electrical conductivity of seawater with a device called a salinometer.

Variations in Salinity

Salinities in the surface waters of the open ocean lie within a surprisingly narrow range (32–37°/00), with readings commonly close to 35°/00. The addition or removal of pure water— or nearly pure water—is the main factor that alters open-ocean salinities, and most commonly this balance is established by the prevailing climatic regime in the locality. Evaporation under hot conditions or the formation of sea ice under cold ones tend to remove water from the sea but leave salts behind; these processes tend to concentrate the seawater and so make it more saline. High rates of precipitation and the melting of ice both add water to the sea and thereby tend to reduce salinities. The overall balance of water addition and water extraction processes determines the overall salinity in a particular region.

In the open ocean, the highest salinities tend to occur where evaporation is high and precipitation is low. Typically, this is between latitudes 20° and 30° north and south of the equator—in other words, in tropical and subtropical regions. In equatorial waters, although evaporation rates may be high, these are commonly countered by high precipitation rates that lower salinity. In polar and subpolar regions, salinities tend to be low because of water melting from the icecaps, which themselves are added to by precipitation. In temperate regions, precipitation and evaporation vary considerably with the seasons, although overall there is a fairly equal balance between the two.

The deep ocean is much less affected by climatic conditions locally. Salinities at depths of 3,280 feet (1,000 m) or more are remarkably uniform throughout the world, with most readings in the 34.5–35°/00 range. Where marked differences occur, these are usually associated with the discharge of mineral-rich water associated with volcanic activity, such as occurs along mid-ocean ridges, or cold-water seeps of hypersaline water (page 117).

Based on evidence from ancient evaporite deposits, the salinity of the open oceans has remained remarkably constant for long periods of geological time. Evaporites are salts that have been deposited naturally when seawater evaporates to dryness in regions cut off—wholly or partially—from the open ocean. The makeup of such deposits provides good evidence for the composition of the seawater that formed them. This evidence, from deposits around the world, suggests that the average salinity of seawater has declined, in stops and starts, from 45°/00 to 35°/00 during a period of 570 million years (since Cambrian times, page 81).

Returning to the present day, wide salinity variations do occur in smaller bodies of water and in near-shore regions that are subject to high rates of evaporation or to the input of relatively large volumes of freshwater. In landlocked seas where evaporation greatly exceeds freshwater input, salinities may reach 41°/00, as in the Red Sea. Animals and plants that exploit the demanding environment of intertidal rock pools (page 86) must cope with hypersaline conditions (salinities well above 40°/00) produced by high temperatures and high evaporation rates in summer, and at the other extreme, must deal with hyposaline conditions (salinities well below 30°/00) created by high precipitation rates in winter.

In estuaries, salinities vary both spatially (vertically and horizontally within the estuarine ecosystem) and with time (changing with state of the tide, weather conditions affecting freshwater runoff, and so on). Within estuaries, salinities lie within the range 0.5°/00 at the riverward end and 35°/00 at the seaward end, with intermediate values at locations in between. Salinity fluctuations within the estuarine ecosystem place great demands on the organisms living there.

Salinity and Deepwater Currents

The relationship between salinity, temperature, and density is instrumental in generating deep ocean currents. Other things being equal, water's density *increases* with a rise in salinity but (for temperatures well above freezing point) *decreases* with a rise in temperature. The evaporation of surface water in the tropics raises salinity, thereby tending to increase the density of seawater, but this is compensated for by the fact that the water becomes warmer, which has the tendency to lower its density. However, as this saline surface water moves away from the tropics to cooler latitudes and therefore cools, it grows more dense. Eventually it sinks to produce the cold, dense masses of bottom water that travel from high latitudes toward the equator (page 67).

The Biological Significance of Salinity

Most organisms on planet Earth are in a constant battle to maintain the amount of water and salts in their bodies within narrow limits. Maintaining a suitable salt/water balance often involves expending considerable amounts of energy, whether in utilizing special active mechanisms or in manufacturing an impervious covering that prevents water and salts from entering or leaving.

Living organisms probably first evolved in the sea or in tidal pools associated with the sea, and most marine invertebrates (animals without backbones) and cartilaginous fish (sharks, skates, and rays, page 100) still have body fluids that have a similar salt/water balance to that of their seawater surroundings. Bony fish (teleosts, page 102), however, have body fluids with a salt concentration only 30–50 percent that of the surrounding seawater. Because of this salt/water imbalance between the fish and its surroundings, water tends to diffuse out of the fish, and salts tend to diffuse in. To counteract these tendencies, the fish constantly pumps out salts across its gills, and it drinks seawater but produces very little urine (liquid waste), thereby conserving seawater's water component while actively removing its salt component.

Vertebrates (animals with backbones) that have a terrestrial origin and have since returned to the sea include marine reptiles (page 104) and marine birds (page 105). They too have body fluids that are less concentrated than their seawater surroundings, but they have evolved the capacity to drink seawater while getting rid of excess salts through special salt glands. In the case of turtles, the salt glands discharge close to the eyes, producing the turtle's legendary salty tears.

The problems of maintaining the body's salt/water balance are most demanding for those organisms living in an environment where salinities rapidly fluctuate. The most challenging of such environments include estuaries and rock pools. The ability to cope with such demanding salinity fluctuations can be remarkably simple—as in the case of clams that simply "shut up shop" and close their shells when the salinity of their surroundings becomes too high or low for comfort. Even here, however, clams have highly adapted physiological mechanisms that enable them to survive long periods with their shells closed, and they also have highly acute sensory abilities to detect changing salinities, plus the ability to regulate their shell opening and closure according to the state of the tide. Sophisticated mechanisms for coping with salinity difference are found in catadramous fish (such as American and European freshwater eels) and anadramous fish (salmon, shad, and sturgeon) that spend part of their lives in the sea and part in freshwater. The water/salt balance problems they experience in the sea are precisely the opposite of those they experience in freshwater. These fish reverse the direction of their salt-regulatory mechanisms when moving from one environment to the other (page 108).

Cycling of Chemicals in the Sea

We have already seen (page 52) how remarkably constant the chemical constitution of seawater is. Seawater's main chemical constituents—its major ions—are remarkably constant in their proportions no matter which ocean system is sampled. Chemicals are constantly being washed off the land and into the sea; yet the salinity of the world's oceans appears to have remained remarkably constant for many millions of years. The oceans do not appear to be growing saltier. Why not? The answers to these questions lie in our understanding of how chemicals are cycled among the land, the sea, and the air. Despite superficial appearances, chemicals are not simply washed into the sea, never to return, but are restored to the land often via surprising chemical forms and through unusually circuitous routes. Many of these chemical cycles are only just beginning to be understood. The unraveling of these cycles is beginning to show us just how tightly connected are biological, chemical, and geological processes in nature.

Chemicals Are Added to, and Removed from, the Sea

The major ions that contribute to the ocean's salinity are continually added from several natural sources. The most obvious source of major ions is from chemicals weathered from rocks and leached from soils on land. These find their way, via rivers or glaciers, to the sea. Volcanic activity on land discharges chemicals into the atmosphere—either as gases or particulate material—and these may eventually dissolve in, or in other ways enter, the surface waters of the sea. Hydrothermal activity at mid-ocean ridges (page 58) adds ions to the deep ocean. The significance of this source is in the process of being evaluated. Finally, some chemicals entering the sea have a cosmic origin—they arrive from outside Earth's atmosphere. By and large, their influence is small, although when a large meteorite impact is involved, the significance may temporarily be very great (page 37). The activities of humans have relatively little effect on the major ions in the oceans as a whole, with the possible exception of sulfate (SO_4^{2-}) and bicarbonate (HCO_3^-), but human activities certainly have a massive impact in specific localities (page 184), and of great concern is our introduction of harmful exotic chemical substances into the world's oceans as though these waters were a chemical dumping ground of unlimited capacity.

Just as chemicals are added to the world's oceans, so they are removed. If they were not, then chemicals levels would gradually increase, which, in most cases, they do not appear to do. One of the most important routes for the removal of chemicals from seawater is via authigenesis—chemical reactions in seawater that are inorganic (not associated with living organisms) and that cause chemicals to settle out of the water column or be removed in other ways. Authigenesis can happen in several ways. For example, water can become temporarily trapped in sediments and in major ions such as sodium (Na^+), sulfate (SO_4^{2-}) and magnesium (Mg^{2+}) that are removed by reacting with rocks, such as basalt, within the ocean floor. Some of the less common chemicals, such as nickel, copper, manganese, cobalt, and iron, are incorporated in natural formations called nodules that accumulate and grow on the seafloor (page 37), but of greatest importance is the sinking of particles of sediment, notably mud, onto the ocean floor. As the particles descend, they attract major ions that are adsorbed onto their surfaces and are completely removed from the water column when the particles settle.

Biological processes also play a major role in removing major chemical ions from the oceans, in a process called biogenesis (the extraction of chemicals by biochemical reactions). Marine phytoplankton and zooplankton (page 88) extract silicate (SiO_3^{2-}), calcium (Ca^{2+}), and bicarbonate (HCO_3^-) ions from seawater to construct their exoskeletons (outer skeletons). When these organisms die, the chemicals in the form of calcium carbonate ($CaCO_3$) and calcium silicate ($CaSiO_3$) are deposited on the seafloor. Such biogenous sediments cover many parts of the ocean floor (page 36), and they represent huge stores of carbon (C) and oxygen (O) that were previously found in the atmosphere in the form of the greenhouse gas carbon dioxide (CO_2) (page 78).

The feces (solid waste) produced by marine animals form a constant rain of particles that fall to the ocean floor. On the journey down, the fecal material is typically eaten, digested, and egested (released as solid waste) by several different animals. The resulting fecal particles, in a similar manner to clay particles, tend to attract major ions that are adsorbed onto their surfaces and then become part of the sediment when the particles settle.

A final route by which chemicals are removed from the oceans is by windborne sea spray. When waves break at sea, small droplets of seawater become airborne (forming an aerosol spray) and may travel on the wind before settling on land. Once there, the salts may eventually find their way back to the sea via freshwater runoff or through the groundwater.

The chemicals locked in sediments on the ocean floors of the world do not stay there indefinitely. Through tectonic processes, they may become withdrawn (subducted) into Earth's mantle (page 34) or uplifted onto land (page 41).

The Major Chemical Cycles

Several cycles are particularly important in understanding the chemical economy of the oceans. These cycles are called biogeochemical cycles in recognition of the fact that biological, chemical, and geological processes are involved in the transfer of material within different parts of the cycle. The nitrogen (N) and phosphorus (P) cycles (page 85) are of particular interest because these elements are essential nutrients that fuel biological productivity. Where these elements are abundant—and providing water quality is good and the physical conditions are appropriate—then phytoplankton growth is high, and the resultant food chains based on them are highly productive. The carbon (C) cycle is of great interest because living organisms are carbon based and the extraction of carbon dioxide (CO_2) by plants helps regulate the atmospheric level of this gas—carbon dioxide is a major greenhouse gas that is strongly implicated in global warming (page 78). The sulfur (S) cycle is one of the chemical cycles most profoundly influenced by human activities. Until recently, the exact way that sulfur found its way back from the sea onto land remained something of a mystery. Several breakthroughs in recent years suggest that a remarkable interplay between biological and chemical phenomena is involved in the process.

The Sulfur Cycle

The sulfur cycle has, for several decades, remained something of an enigma. The element sulfur (S) in the form of the sulfate ion (SO_4^{2-}) is an important nutrient for plant growth on land and in the sea. Sulfate ions are continually being weathered from rocks and leached from soils, and they find their way via rivers to the sea. Volcanoes release sulfur in the form of noxious sulfur dioxide

(SO_2), and human activities such as burning fossil fuels also release this gas, but scientists failed to find a sufficiently abundant renewable source of sulfur on land. In the absence of this source, scientists speculated that sulfur must somehow find its way from the sea to the land. But how?

Scientific speculation up until the 1970s predominantly rested with hydrogen sulfide (H_2S), a noxious gas smelling of rotten eggs, being the sulfur carrier between sea and land. Presumably produced by biological processes in the ocean, it would find its way through the atmosphere and back onto land. However, hydrogen sulfide is very strong-smelling and is highly reactive in oxygenated water; for both these reasons, it is a less than convincing suspect. In the early 1970s, English scientist James Lovelock, proponent of the Gaia hypothesis (page 60), sought other sulfurous gases that might play the role. He found dimethyl sulfide (DMS for short)—a gas produced by many marine organisms, including algae and phytoplankton—to be a prime suspect. In 1972, during a voyage on the RV *Shackleton* from the U.K. to Antarctica, his suspicions were confirmed when he regularly found DMS in ocean water samples.

Further work by other researchers in the early 1980s confirmed that DMS was produced by phytoplankton in the open ocean in sufficient quantities to justify its role as being the primary sulfur carrier from sea to land. DMS leaves the surface waters and enters the atmosphere, where it reacts with oxygen to form tiny sulfuric acid droplets that can be carried overland and fall in precipitation. The tiny sulfuric acid droplets also have a remarkable property—they are highly efficient at seeding the formation of clouds.

This has led to some very interesting speculation that by triggering the formation of clouds, marine phytoplankton can regulate the environment for their own benefit. Lovelock has suggested that the formation of DMS in some phytoplankton might have evolved as a biproduct of the formation of dimethylsulfonio propionate (DMSP), a salt that would help maintain the organism's salt/water balance using a readily available chemical element—sulfur. Once DMS was formed, it could then confer advantages on the organism. By producing cloud cover, which partially blocks transmission of certain wavelengths of light, the DMS could reduce the amount of harmful ultraviolet radiation that penetrates the surface waters. Cloud formation could also have other benefits, such as encouraging surface winds that might stir the surface waters, thereby helping bring nutrients to the surface. Also, water disturbance might encourage micro-scopic algae to become airborne. Updrafts then take them into clouds, where they can be dispersed over long distances and return to Earth in rainfall. All this is rather speculative, but the role of DMS as a sulfur carrier is now well established.

The Activity of Chemicals

In our description of the chemical constituents of seawater, we have taken for granted than the chemical ions are free in solution and are available to react with other chemicals in a straightforward manner. This is, in fact, often far from the truth. Chemicals interact with one another in the water column—for example, becoming hydrated as water molecules cluster around them or becoming attracted to tiny sediment particles. These interactions are important, and their precise nature changes under different physical conditions—altered temperature, pressure, and so on—so the interactions at one level in the water column may be quite different to those at another level. Marine chemists now appreciate that recognizing and studying such differences—and how they are affected by biological processes—is of great importance in understanding biogeochemical cycles.

Chemistry of the Seafloor

The chemistry of the seafloor is dominated by the accumulation of sediments (page 36) derived from biological and nonbiological activities, the formation of globular deposits such as manganese nodules, and the deposition of products of underwater volcanic activity, as occurs at hydrothermal vents. When rich organic sediments become buried below the seafloor, they achieve great importance when they are transformed into valuable resources such as oil and gas.

Here we consider chemical events involved in two quite different but influential features of the ocean floor: hydrothermal activity and the formation of petroleum deposits.

Hydrothermal Activity at Mid-Ocean Ridges

One of the most exciting developments in the history of oceanography was the discovery, in the mid-1970s, of hydrothermal vents associated with mid-ocean ridges. To marine geochemists, these vents were perceived as a novel route for chemicals entering the ocean system, perhaps of comparable significance to the input of chemicals from rivers flowing off the land. The role of these vents in the chemical economy of the oceans is still in the process of being investigated.

Hydrothermal vents are fed by water that percolates down through fractured oceanic crust. As the water descends through the crust and comes in contact with hot rocks close to molten magma associated with the mid-ocean ridge, the water may become superheated to temperatures as high as 662–752°F (350–400°C) but does not boil because of the high pressures (200–400 atmospheres) at these depths (6,500–13,000 feet or 2,000–4,000 m). The water expands and finds its way rapidly back to the surface of the crust, through routes of least resistance, which often culminate in natural channels emerging as vents on the seafloor. During the water's journey through the crust, it loses magnesium (Mg^{2+}) and sulfate (SO_4^{2-}) ions and picks up metals such as manganese (Mn), iron (Fe), cobalt (Co), copper (Cu), and nickel (Ni), together with silica (SiO_3^{2-}) and sulfide (S^-). This exchange of chemicals occurs rapidly, so although vent systems may seem very localized in the ocean system as a whole, their influence in regulating levels of the major ions throughout the oceans may nevertheless be substantial.

When the metal-rich, sulfide-bearing, superheated water is discharged through a vent, the metals immediately react with oxygen within the ocean's cool bottom water, and metal oxides and sulfides precipitate to form a dense back cloud, so giving hot vents their colloquial name, black smokers. The metal oxides and sulfides deposit themselves around the vent, forming a chimney that grows over months and years.

In some cases, the water cools to 330°C or less before being discharged through a vent; many of the metal-rich precipitates have deposited themselves within channels in the crust; the water that emerges from the vent does not produce black smoke but instead a white cloud, thereby giving this slightly cooler type of vent the name white smoker. The water being discharged through such vents is rich in silica, as well as sulfates and oxides of metals.

Remarkable bacterial and animal communities are found in the vicinity of these vents (page 116). They depend not on solar energy trapped by plants, but on chemical energy locked within hydrogen sulfide and other reduced (oxygen-free or oxygen-deficient) chemicals such as methane. In these strikingly unusual communities, plants do not form the base level of food webs; instead bacteria are the food source on which all other organisms directly or indirectly depend.

Since the mid-1980s, cold-water seeps that discharge hypersaline water have been discovered in deep water. They too support communities that are based on bacteria that extract chemical energy from reduced substances (page 117).

Petroleum Deposits

Fossil fuels—including oil, natural gas, and coal—are the main energy source used to sustain our highly industrialized societies. In the United States alone, petroleum products and natural gas account for more than two-thirds of energy consumption. Both these fossil fuels are formed most abundantly in the sediments below biologically productive inshore waters. In a geological sense, at least some of the plankton populations of continental waters today will form the fossil fuels of tomorrow.

Oil, or petroleum, is not a single chemical compound, but a complex mixture of many. Petroleum is a variable mixture containing mostly hydrocarbons (compounds made up of different proportions of the elements carbon and hydrogen). Natural gas, a product of some petroleum deposits, comprises the smallest hydrocarbon molecules, most notably methane (CH_4), but also ethane (C_2H_6), propane (C_3H_8), and butane (C_4H_{10}).

The conditions under which oil and gas are formed are reasonably well known, even if the details about how the conversion actually occurs have yet to understood fully by scientists. To produce a large fossil-fuel deposit, a rich accumulation of organic matter (once-living material) is required that is rich in hydrogen and carbon. This organic material needs to be buried quickly and air excluded if biological decay and reactions with oxygen are not to degrade the material. Biologically productive inshore waters often fulfill both these criteria: they are rich sources of planktonic forms, which, when they die, settle to the bottom of the sea and may be rapidly covered by sediment, where oxygen is excluded.

Once burial occurs, increased pressure and temperature cause chemical changes. Under the weight of overlying material, and with the increased temperatures deeper in Earth, the large hydrocarbon molecules in the organic material begin to break down into simpler, smaller hydrocarbon molecules. In the early stages of oil formation, the solid organic material gradually changes into a thick, near-solid consistency—like asphalt—when it comprises hydrocarbons of moderately large size. As the process continues and further breakdown of the hydrocarbon molecules occurs, successively "lighter" hydrocarbons are produced. The consistency of the developing petroleum deposit changes to thick liquid and then gradually to thinner liquid as the constituent hydrocarbon molecules become smaller. As the petroleum matures, all or most of the oil may eventually be converted to natural gas. The temperature range over which these changes occur is about 120–210°F (50–120°C).

The best petroleum deposits, from a commercial point of view, not only fulfill the above criteria, but also have the oil or gas in a location where extraction is both feasible and profitable. Many petroleum deposits are in fine-grained sedimentary rock of low permeability. Extraction from such rocks is difficult and prohibitively expensive. However, during hundreds of thousands of years, oil and gas can migrate out of their source rocks and collect in reservoirs of more permeable rock. The most valuable deposits are found where oil and gas have accumulated in porous rocks but have been prevented from rising and dispersing by a covering layer of impermeable rock. This combination of factors—petroleum migrating from source deposits and into porous rock overlaid by impermeable strata—is not very common and, in part, explains why the search for suitable oil and gas deposits is such an intensive one.

A given petroleum deposit produces its own distinctive crude oil, which has a characteristic mix of hydrocarbons that results from the specific organic source material and unique history of the deposit. After drilling (page 171), the recovered crude oil is refined to separate its constituent hydrocarbons into different fractions with specific properties and uses. Some of the heavier hydrocarbons can also be converted to lighter and more useful ones through the process of cracking. The heaviest oils are used as fuel oils in ships, power plants, and industrial boilers. Medium oils are also used in power plants and in domestic as well as industrial boilers, but they also provide kerosene, diesel fuels, and aviation (jet) fuel. Light oils provide benzene, gasoline, and light aviation fuels. Thus, crude oil is an immensely valuable resource that is able to provide a wide range of products after processing.

Virtually no petroleum is found in rocks less than 1–2 million years old, so the formation of extractable oil or gas is hardly a rapid process. It is very clear that we are consuming existing reserves at a rate several thousand times faster than that at which they can be replaced. Oil and natural gas are truly nonrenewable energy sources.

New Developments in Marine Chemistry

Extraordinary progress is being made in marine chemistry. Our increased understanding of the complexity and sophistication of chemical cycles means that scientists are now looking at ways of "turning up the volume" of parts of a biogeochemical cycle in order to counter the most disturbing effects of environmental pollution. Iron-seeding experiments are making a significant contribution to this approach. Detailed analysis of the chemical constituents of the water column—as pioneered in the GEOSECS program, below—is an important aspect of such work.

Increasingly, marine organisms are being seen as a source of all manner of chemical products, including medicinal drugs. With our increased awareness of the chemical complexity of the marine environment comes a realization that the world is at once more elegant, more finely tuned, than we expected. One expression of this view, albeit a controversial one, is that the biological, chemical, and geological components of the environment are integrated in a self-regulating system that behaves, superficially at least, like a superorganism. This is the view promoted in the Gaia hypothesis.

Gaia

In the late 1960s, former NASA scientist James Lovelock proposed a hypothesis that sought to explain why atmospheric and oceanic conditions on planet Earth had remained relatively stable for millions or even billions of years. He poetically entitled the proposal the Gaia hypothesis, after the Greek word for the Earth goddess. Lovelock suggested that Earth is a self-regulating system that is able to maintain its environmental components—the atmosphere, climate, soil, and oceans—in a balance favorable to life. He suggested that this was achieved through the activities of the organisms themselves that influence chemical and geological processes in their surroundings. Environmental conditions are kept relatively stable by an intricate system of checks and balances that operates through feedback mechanisms.

In a sense, Earth's system of living organisms and physical and chemical components operate in a manner similar to a single living organism. An organism, a human being for example, regulates its internal environment through homeostatic mechanisms (mechanisms that maintain the constancy of the internal environment). Take temperature, for example. When the temperature of the human body rises—perhaps during exercise or on a particularly hot day—various responses are triggered. Sweating increases and the skin becomes flushed with diverted blood. These responses serve to increase heat loss through the skin and thereby help cool the blood so that body temperature returns to within the normal range—close to 98.4°F (36.9°C). These responses form part of a negative feedback mechanism— a mechanism that corrects deviations from "normal."

Lovelock likens the way planet Earth responds to change to the self-regulating mechanisms of the human body. The surface temperature of Earth has remained relatively constant for approaching 4 billion years—in fact, since about the time that life-forms arose. This constancy has existed in the face of rising heat output from the Sun—the Sun's heat has increased by about a quarter. So why has planet Earth not warmed too? Lovelock and his colleagues point to the fact that atmospheric carbon dioxide levels have (until recently) dropped, thereby reducing the heat-retaining properties of the atmosphere. This is but one way that temperature gain could be countered. Another possibility is that Earth's albedo (its reflectiveness) could be altered so that less heat energy is absorbed and more is reflected. Organisms—through photosynthesis and respiration—are prime regulators of Earth's atmosphere, and they could be involved in altering the planet's albedo, perhaps by triggering the selective formation of certain types of cloud or by changing the settling pattern of highly reflective snow.

Aspects of the Gaia hypothesis can be tested by computer modeling and by detailed investigation of the workings of biogeochemical cycles through time. Whether the hypothesis proves to be a workable explanation for planetary processes or not, it has certainly served to focus attention on the interactivity of the living and nonliving parts of the world ecosystem.

GEOSECS

The Geochemical Ocean Sections (GEOSECS) program, begun in 1972, is an international approach to monitor systematically physical and chemical parameters in the water column at hundreds of locations throughout the world's oceans. Electronic probes, lowered to the ocean depths from research vessels of many countries, provide direct readings of temperature, pressure, salinity, dissolved oxygen, and so on. The results are relayed via telephone linkages to a display console aboard ship. For further investigation, rosettes (circular arrangements) of a dozen or more sampling bottles are lowered to a precise depth. Collected water is then routinely analyzed for 20 or more chemical constituents, and the amount and type of particulate matter assessed. The GEOSECS program, by measuring many parameters concurrently, is gradually providing marine scientists with a much better understanding of physical, chemical, and biological processes and how they interact.

Seeding the Oceans

The metal iron (Fe) is a chemical in short supply in the surface waters of the open ocean. It is an important micronutrient required by phytoplankton for various biochemical activities, including photosynthesis and respiration. In some ocean regions—notably the Antarctic Ocean and the equatorial and northeast Pacific—the nutrients nitrate and phosphate are in good supply in surface waters, but the productivity of phytoplankton is nevertheless low. Scientists have speculated that the reason for this low productivity is the absence of iron.

In the late 1980s, this idea was tested in laboratory experiments, and the results supported the notion that phytoplankton growth can be limited, where other nutrients are in good supply, by lack of iron. In 1993 and 1995, scientists from the U.K. and the United States collaborated in very large-scale experiments near the Galápagos Islands in the Pacific. A large patch of seawater was seeded with iron, and the biological and chemical activities within this patch were monitored for a period of 10 days. Very sophisticated techniques were used, including aircraft overflights, marking the patch with a radio-emitting buoy, and special chemical tracers to monitor activity within the patch. The results were startling and rather conclusive: seeding the surface waters with iron raised the standing biomass of phytoplankton (the weight of phytoplankton) and primary production (the photosynthetic activity of the phytoplankton) by more than threefold in the top 20 meters (66 feet) of the ocean.

Scientists involved in the project, called IronEx, believe that adding suitable amounts of soluble iron to nutrient-rich but iron-depleted parts of the ocean could, in theory, raise primary productivity. In turn this could, through increased carbon dioxide uptake for photosynthesis, help to counter the global rise in atmospheric carbon dioxide levels that are leading to global warming (page 78). The net effect of this action would be to help remove carbon dioxide from the atmosphere, which would then be incorporated into marine organisms. Ultimately, this carbon dioxide would rain down onto the ocean floor in the form of the calcium carbon-ate exoskeletons of recently deceased phytoplank-ton. Although this idea is appealing, we still know far too little about complex biogeochemical cycles such as the carbon cycle (page 79) to be able to pre-dict reliably the outcomes of tinkering with the system in this manner.

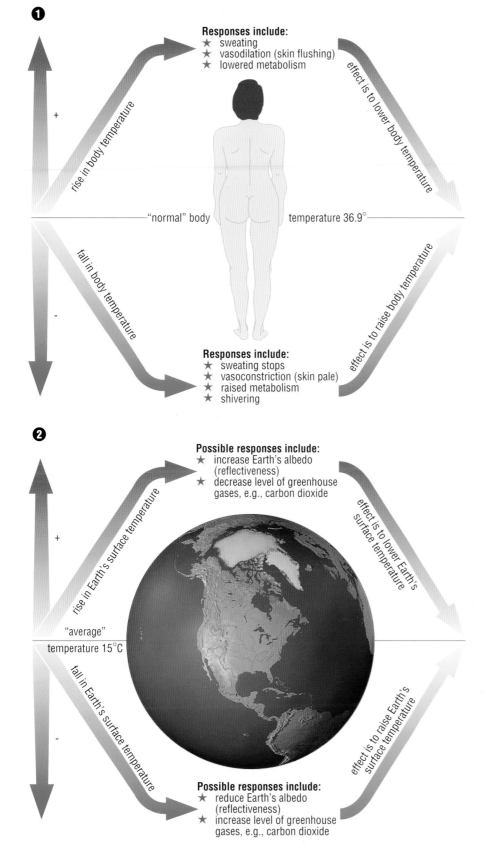

Possible ways of regulating the temperature of planet Earth. The precise mechanisms for doing this are not shown.

Useful Chemicals from Living Organisms

Because marine organisms often live in novel environments—and ones that are very different to those, as terrestrial creatures, we normally have access to—they yield some chemicals that are quite unlike those found on land. For example, many midwater species produce bioluminescent compounds (page 94), and these are beginning to be exploited for medical and scientific applica-tions. Some act as useful labels for attachment to other chemicals, such as when studying bio-chemical activities within a cell, and they can be detected at extremely low levels, well below one part in a thousand billion.

Attention is turning to marine-derived chemicals for use as medicinal drugs. With the extensive time required for screening, formulat-ing and testing possible substances—an expensive 10-year process—new products are coming on line relatively slowly. Nevertheless, there are a dozen or so drugs of marine origin that are in widespread use. Some of these drugs are useful as antibiotics, others for stimulating or depressing the activity of the immune system, and yet oth-ers are painkillers or anticlotting agents for treat-ing blood.

Marine organisms have yielded a wide range of other useful products, and although some of these have been used for thousands of years, the search is, in many ways, only just beginning. Products from marine organisms are being sought as environ-ment-friendly agents to replace toxic substances with well-established uses. For example, antifouling paints (used to protect boat hulls and submerged structures from fouling by settling organisms) often contain heavy metal-based products such as tributyl tin (TBT). The Marine Biotechnology Institute in Japan is currently testing a range of substances pro-duced by settling organisms, among them bry-ozoans, which produce chemicals to deter other settlers. If such substances can be isolated and then manufactured in large quantities, they may provide effective replacements for the current generation of toxic antifouling agents.

The production of useful marine-derived chemicals is likely to blossom in the next decade or so when the technologies associated with genetic engineering are turned to explore the potential of marine organisms. The range of possible applica-tions is large, from genetically engineered bacteria used to clear up oil spills to fast-growing, disease-resistant strains of fish and shellfish.

Global Winds

The atmosphere blanketing Earth is essential to the living planet's integrity. It contains the oxygen supply for living organisms, it carries water between sea and land, and its circulation creates our climate and weather. *Weather* refers to local day-to-day variations in atmospheric conditions, while *climate* applies to the long-term weather patterns prevailing in a particular area for years and decades.

The atmosphere shields us from the most damaging effects of the Sun's rays and protects us from the devastating impact of all but the largest meteors. The atmosphere is a protective blanket, retaining heat that ensures the survival of life on the planet while helping maintain a balance between solar energy reaching the planet's surface and heat energy that is reemitted back into space. Shifts in atmospheric composition caused by carbon dioxide pollution are altering this balance and are the most likely explanation for global warming (page 78).

The Atmosphere

The atmosphere is a remarkably thin layer. Were planet Earth to be represented by an inflated party balloon, the atmosphere itself would be no thicker than the rubber wall of the balloon. It extends about 430 miles (700 km) or so above Earth's surface. The bottom layer of the atmosphere, the troposphere, is 33,000–52,000 feet (10–16 km) thick—thicker at the equator than at the poles. It contains 80 percent of the atmosphere's mass and the vast bulk of the atmosphere's water. The troposphere is the part we are particularly concerned with because it is here that most of the phenomena we associate with climate and weather are found, and it is in or below this level that living organisms are found.

The next layer of the atmosphere, the stratosphere—at 36,000–164,000 feet (11–50 km)—is traversed by humans flying high-altitude aircraft. In the stratosphere lies the ozone layer, where oxygen (O_2) molecules are converted to ozone

(O_3) molecules by the action of sunlight. This conversion traps much of the potentially harmful ultraviolet radiation from the Sun that would otherwise reach Earth's surface.

The boundary between the troposphere and the stratosphere is called the tropopause. It is cooler than the lower stratosphere above it because the ozone layer is warmed by the solar energy it absorbs. The tropopause, being a cool layer, thus forms an important boundary that prevents rising warm air from Earth's surface from ascending any further (air will rise if it is warmer than the air above it).

Global Circulation

It is the unequal heating of Earth's surface by the Sun that powers the circulation of the atmosphere. The equator and the Tropics (between the tropic of Cancer and the tropic of Capricorn) receive a much higher intensity of solar radiation than the poles. This is a consequence of several factors. First, the Sun is overhead, or nearly overhead, at the equator and the Tropics, so the Sun's rays are angled almost directly downward. At the poles, however, the Sun's rays strike Earth's surface much more obliquely (at an angle) and have traveled further—through space and through the atmosphere—to reach Earth's surface. This means that at the poles the light is more likely to be reflected (bounced back) both before and after it reaches Earth's surface, and also that each spot on the polar surface receives more diffuse light than an equivalent area at the equator. Added to this is an effect called albedo (the reflectiveness of a surface based on its whiteness or color). At the poles, the pale ice and snow are very effective reflectors, thereby tending to reduce light absorption and heat buildup. In equatorial regions, in contrast, the green or yellow landscape and the clear oceans reflect less light. The sum total of all these effects is that the equator and Tropics heat up more than the poles. But

why don't the equatorial regions simply get hotter and hotter?

The answer is that both the atmosphere and the oceans carry heat from the equator and the tropics toward the poles. As tropical air warms, it rises, creating a low-pressure zone beneath. Low-level cool air moves in from higher latitudes to replace the warm air that has risen. The warm air travels across the upper troposphere toward the poles, and as it cools it becomes denser and gradually sinks. So, at its simplest, there is an equatorial-to-polar movement of warm air at high altitudes in the troposphere and a polar-to-equatorial movement of cool air at low altitudes.

This simple model for air movement was put forward by Englishman George Hadley (1686–1768) in the 1750s. His name is still associated with certain forms of air circulation—the Hadley cells (see page 63). His simple model, while a good starting point, did not take into account a number of complicating factors, most notable of which is Earth's rotation.

The Coriolis Effect

Although there is a continual heat transfer between the Tropics and the poles, winds do not blow directly north-south. Instead, they are deflected by Earth's rotation.

Seen from directly above the North Pole, Earth is rotating counterclockwise. The speed of rotation depends on which particular point on Earth is chosen. At the equator, the speed of rotation is fastest—about 1,000 miles an hour (1,600 km per hour)—but this decreases toward the poles, eventually being zero at the exact point of the pole. You can see this for yourself by spinning a globe. For one rotation of the globe, a point on the equator moves a much farther distance than a point near the North Pole. The effect of this is such that an object—or the wind or an ocean current—moving northward from the equator is subject to a slower rotational speed. Taking a northward-moving wind as our example, Earth's rotation deflects the wind eastward (creating a westerly wind because it blows from the west). Conversely, a wind moving southward in the Northern Hemisphere tends to be deflected to the west, as it is being subjected to a higher rotational speed, thereby creating an easterly wind. Another way of looking at this is that winds in the Northern Hemisphere are always deflected to the right of their direction of movement. In the Northern Hemisphere, winds moving northward are deflected to the right to form westerly winds (blowing from the west), while winds moving southward are deflected to the right to form easterly winds (blowing from the east). An important point: winds are always described in terms of the direction from which they come; ocean currents are described in terms of the direction in which they are going.

In the Southern Hemisphere, traveling toward the pole is a southward movement rather than a northward one. A southward-moving wind is deflected eastward to form westerlies; a northward-moving wind is deflected westward to form easterlies. Winds in the Southern Hemisphere are always deflected to the left of their direction of movement. The effect of Earth's rotation on south–north air movements is to generate reliable westerly and easterly winds that sailing ships rely on as they traverse the oceans.

The deflecting effect of Earth's rotation is called the Coriolis effect, after Gustave-Gaspard de Coriolis (1792–1843), who first investigated it in the 1830s. One of the charming demonstrations of the Coriolis effect is the vortex formed when bathwater disappears down a plughole. In the Northern Hemisphere, the water forms a clockwise vortex; in the Southern Hemisphere, the vortex is counterclockwise. Check this out next time you have a bath.

It is not just wind system and bathwater that are deflected by Earth's rotation; major ocean currents are too (page 64). The Coriolis effect generates major clockwise currents in the Northern Hemisphere and counterclockwise currents south of the equator—circular currents called gyres.

In some parts of the world, particularly where there is open water that is uninterrupted by land, the combination of Hadley's model and the Coriolis effect provides a reasonable explanation for the prevailing winds and climatic conditions. At the equator, warm, humid air rises, creating a belt of low pressure. Associated with this belt are clouds and heavy rainfall. The ascending air stops rising at the tropopause—the boundary between troposphere and stratosphere—and then travels poleward, cooling as it does so. It sinks back down to Earth's surface at about 30° north and south—the horse latitudes—producing a high-pressure region associated with warm, dry conditions.

Many sailing ships used to become becalmed at these latitudes and, short of water, sailors sometimes used to throw dying horses overboard—hence the name, horse latitudes, a term still used today. Air moving from the high-pressure regions to the equator and deflected by the Coriolis effect form the trade winds—northeasterlies in the Northern Hemisphere and southeasterlies in the Southern. In the open ocean, these form the steadiest and most reliable of Earth's winds. Where the trade winds die out near the equator is a region that sailors used to call the doldrums (from an old English word meaning dull). Early mariners feared being stranded there in windless conditions. The air circulations that climb in the Tropics, descend at 30° north and south, and then flow back to the equator are called Hadley cells, after George Hadley.

Not all the air that descends at 30° north and south returns to the equator; some of it continues poleward until it meets cold polar air at about 60° north or south. The warmer air from the Tropics rises above the polar air and then moves back to 30° north or south, descending as it does so and completing a second type of circulation called the Ferrel cell—named after William Ferrel (1817–1891), who identified them in 1856. These cells give rise to the westerlies found between 30° and 60° in Northern and Southern Hemispheres.

Finally, between 60° and 90° north and south are found a third type of cell—smaller Hadley cells or polar cells. These cells contain warm, poleward moving air at high altitude, and cold air moving to lower latitudes at low altitude. The latter winds, deflected by the Coriolis effect, form the polar easterlies.

The foregoing explanation does not take into account seasonal changes (due to Earth's axis being tilted) nor relative differences in the rate of heating between land and sea. Such effects produce seasonal climatic regimes and more localized wind systems, such as the monsoon winds of southwest Asia (page 10).

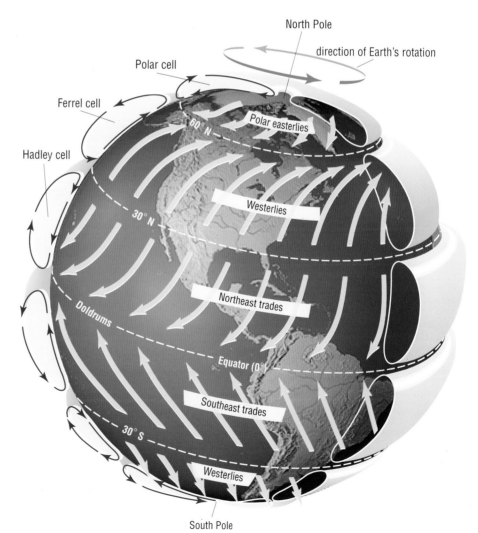

The global wind systems. The wind systems are shown as they would appear on an Earth entirely covered by water. In reality, the systems are modified by the presence of continental landmasses.

Major Ocean Currents

The ocean's major surface currents are created and driven by the wind systems on Earth's surface. As we have seen (page 62), the wind systems themselves are generated by temperature differences between the Tropics and the poles. The circulation of the air is then modified by Earth's rotation, which produces the so-called Coriolis effect (page 62). As we shall see, ocean currents are also influenced by this effect.

In the open ocean, about 40 named ocean currents dominate the movement of surface water. The great ocean currents are almost like rivers in the sea but carry a much greater loading of water than any freshwater river. The mighty Gulf Stream transports about 30 billion gallons (135 billion l) of water every second, many times that of all the rivers in the world.

The Major Surface Currents

Water, of course, is a much denser medium than air, and for this and other reasons, surface currents move much more slowly than the prevailing winds that create them. The fastest surface currents are found in the western part of oceans in the Northern Hemisphere—the Gulf Stream of the North Atlantic and the Kuroshio Current of the North Pacific, for example. These currents typically travel at about 2.5–4.5 miles per hour (4–7 km per hour). Much slower flows are found in the eastern part of oceans in the Southern Hemisphere: the Benguela Current of the South Atlantic and the Humboldt Current of the South Pacific typically move at about 1 kilometer per hour (0.6 miles an hour). Ocean currents do not move in quite the same direction as the winds; indeed, they usually move at an angle of 45° to the direction of the wind, because of the deflection of moving water by the influence of the Coriolis effect. Landmasses and continental shelves also constrain and deflect currents.

The generation of surface currents by the prevailing winds and their subsequent deflection by the Coriolis effect and landmasses results in circular patterns of water movement in the major oceans that straddle the equator. These spiral patterns of water movement are called gyres; in the Northern Hemisphere, they flow in a clockwise direction (the northern Indian Ocean is a partial exception to this), and in the Southern Hemisphere counterclockwise. In general, gyres in the Southern Hemisphere have weaker currents than those in the Northern Hemisphere, in part a result of the connection to the open system of the Antarctic Ocean. Taking the Atlantic Ocean as our example, the North Atlantic gyre comprises three major currents—the Gulf Stream, the Canary Current, and the North Equatorial Current. The South Atlantic gyre contains the Brazil Current, the Benguela Current, and the South Equatorial Current.

The circulation in the northern Indian Ocean is the exception to the clockwise-and-counterclockwise rule for gyres. In the summer, the prevailing winds blow from the African continent to the Indian subcontinent, producing a clockwise gyre in the northern Indian Ocean, the expected pattern, but in winter, the prevailing

The world's major surface currents. The distribution of these currents represents averages over time. The currents shift with season of the year and with changing weather conditions.

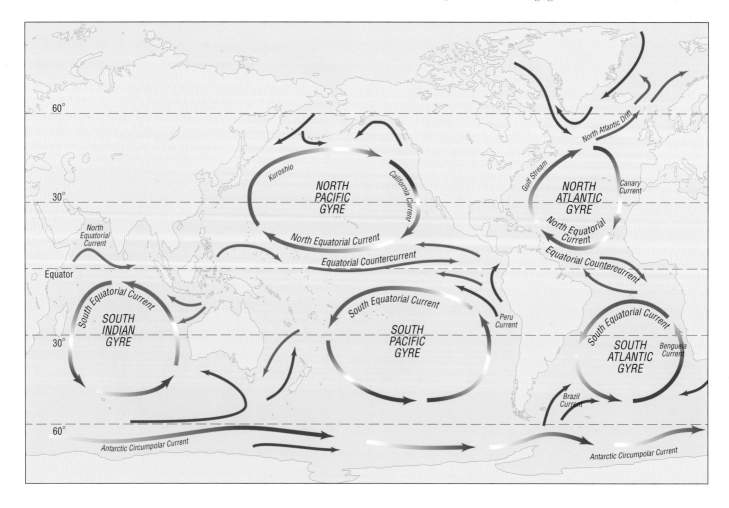

winds reverse direction and set up a counterclockwise gyre. The winds are the monsoon winds, and the influence on the gyre is called, not surprisingly, the Monsoon effect.

The currents on the western sides of gyres—for example, the Gulf Stream in the North Atlantic and the Brazil Current in the South Atlantic—carry warm water away from the equator. They often have a profound influence on the climate of neighboring landmasses. The Gulf Stream and the North Atlantic Drift, for example, make Iceland and northern Europe habitable at latitudes which, in the center of the Eurasian continent, would be inhospitably cold. The water that returns to the equator on the eastern sides of gyres—for example, the Canary and Benguela currents of the North and South Atlantic respectively—is cool and may have a chilling effect on neighboring landmasses. In the eastern North Pacific, onshore winds from the cool California Current moderate summer temperatures on the west coast of the United States. Ocean currents thus have a profound effect in moderating continental climates—cooling hot regions and warming cold ones—as well as influencing the geographic distribution of organisms on land as well as in the sea.

The spiral movement of water in a gyre results in water being piled up toward the center, where there is barely any water movement. The centers of gyres are strange places where floating weeds collect and remain, forming floating communities that harbor unique communities of animals and plants. The Sargasso Sea in the North Atlantic is perhaps the best example: its floor provides the mysterious spawning grounds for the Atlantic eel (page 108).

There is a unique current that flows all the way around the world—the Antarctic Circumpolar Current. Just north of the Antarctic landmass, a belt of open ocean encircles Earth. Here, the westerlies can drive the current eastward without being impeded by landmasses.

Near the equator, where the winds slacken and northern and southern gyres form westward-flowing equatorial currents, there is a narrow weak current separating the equatorial currents and flowing in the opposite direction—the Equatorial Countercurrent.

Coastal Currents

Unlike the major ocean currents, which are influenced by long-term meteorological conditions over wide geographic areas, the pattern of currents in coastal waters is much more influenced by short-term, local conditions. Runoff from rivers, tidal forces, and the topography of the continental shelf and the shape of the coastline all help determine the force and direction of coastal currents.

Sailing Ships and Surface Currents

Historically, the ocean-surface currents were some of the most important factors that influenced the ability of vessels to cross the oceans. In classical antiquity, the major ocean currents were essentially the same as those of today, and knowledge—or ignorance—of their existence has been the deciding factor in the success or failure of many a voyage. Portuguese sailors of the 15th century, under the guidance of Prince Henry ("The Navigator"), made careful observations of the currents along the west coast of Africa. Using this knowledge, later trading voyages were able to utilize the North and South Atlantic gyres to good effect. On the outward voyage from Portugal to West Africa, traders sailed down the Canary Current—the eastern part of the North Atlantic gyre—picked up a westward-flowing Equatorial Current, sailed with the Brazil Current down the western part of the South Atlantic gyre, and then crossed over to the African coast. On the return leg, they sailed up the Benguela Current in the Southern Hemisphere and avoided the Canary Current in the Northern Hemisphere. The overall figure-of-eight path for the round-trip voyage was longer than conventional routes, but nevertheless faster.

In the mid-18th century, Benjamin Franklin (1706–90), working as a colonial postmaster, noticed that mail ships typically took two weeks less time to reach Europe than they did to return. By questioning sea captains, especially his own nephew Timothy Folger, a Nantucket whaler, he realized that sailing against the flow of the Gulf Stream was a major impediment to ships returning from Europe. By publishing the first chart of the Gulf Stream and issuing instructions on how to avoid the current on the westward journey from Europe, Franklin provided an enormous service to transatlantic traders.

Surface and Subsurface Currents

The major ocean currents (page 64) are surface currents. These surface flows, however, account for probably only 10 percent of the total volume of ocean water; the other 90 percent is distributed by subsurface currents—termed intermediate, deep, and bottom water currents, in order of their increasing depth in the water column.

Unlike the major surface currents, which are driven primarily by wind systems that are themselves generated by rising air in the Tropics, deeper ocean currents are driven by differences in water density and are powered primarily by the formation of ice in polar waters. When ice forms, the water itself freezes, but the bulk of its salt content is not retained within the ice; it separates out and finds its way into the water below the ice, which as a result becomes more saline. Water becomes denser as its salinity increases, and when it is further chilled by cold polar winds, it becomes denser still. This cold, saline water sinks to the bottom of the sea and moves toward the equator. This process occurs throughout the year wherever polar ice is present but is most pronounced in winter.

The water that sinks at the poles to form bottom water is replaced by relatively deep water moving poleward from lower latitudes. This water is forced to rise to the surface in Antarctic waters when it encounters the cold, saline water that is sinking to form bottom water. The newly arrived surface water is now, in turn, chilled, is made more saline by the ice-making process, and then sinks to form bottom water. So there is a poleward flow of deep water and a return flow—toward the equator—of cold, saline bottom water. The three main sources of this bottom water are from around Antarctica in the Southern Hemisphere and from around Greenland and Iceland in the Northern Hemisphere.

The Antarctic itself is fed by deep water from the North Atlantic, which may take several hundred years to arrive. The destinations for Antarctic bottom water are the Atlantic Ocean, the Indian Ocean, and the North Pacific. The water takes several thousand years to reach this far and then make the return journey via the North Atlantic as deep water. When it does return, the water is rich in nutrients accumulating from the "snowfall" (page 90) of particulate matter from higher in the water column.

Only part of the arriving deep water forms bottom water when it reaches the Antarctic Ocean. Some forms moderately cold water that rides under the warm surface water from lower latitudes. After some mixing with the warm water, this moderately cold water forms a layer that is sandwiched between the surface water and the deep water and moves toward the equator. This layer is the Antarctic intermediate water located at a depth of around 1 kilometer (3,300 feet). The circulation of water at an intermediate level does not extend such distances as do the bottom water currents, and circulation takes place over years or decades rather than hundreds or thousands of years.

Current flows in the open ocean are complex: when we examine the three-dimensional nature of the water column, we discover that surface flows are often counterbalanced by water that flows in the opposite direction below the surface, appropriately called countercurrents. The Gulf Stream is one of the major exceptions, as its flow can penetrate almost to the seafloor, hence the enormously large volume of water it transports. Another surface current that extends deeply is the Florida Current of the North Atlantic gyre, which has been detected flowing strongly at 6,500 feet (2 km) below the surface.

The direction of flow of subsurface currents is partly explained by the polar ice-making process. But that is far from the whole story.

The Ekman Spiral

During the historic voyage of the research vessel the *Fram,* pioneering oceanographer Fridtjof Nansen (1861–1930) established that the Arctic sea ice was moving at 20–40° to the right of the wind blowing across its surface. Nansen passed this information on to Swedish physicist Vagn Walfrid Ekman (1874–1954), who determined the mathematical relationship between wind direction and surface flow. He also established a model to describe the likely movement occurring below the water surface. This model has since been dubbed the Ekman spiral.

In an idealized situation, when wind blows across the still surface of the ocean, a surface current is generated that is at 45° to the direction of the wind. This is generated, in part, by the friction between wind and sea surface and by the Coriolis effect. In the Northern Hemisphere, the Coriolis effect turns the water to the right of the wind; in the Southern Hemisphere the turn is to the left. Because water is so much denser than air, the movement imparted to the water is much slower than that in the air. Theoretically, surface water flows at 2–3 percent of the wind's speed. The movement of water at the surface is transmitted to successive layers of water descending through the water column. The movement is imparted from one layer to the next by friction, and because the movement becomes slower and slower descending through the water column, the Coriolis effect has greater opportunity to act; therefore, the turning effect on the direction of movement is greater. The result is that, by a depth of about 100 meters (330 feet), the subsurface flow is only about 4 percent of that at the surface, and the water is flowing in the opposite direction to that at the surface.

Although these idealized conditions rarely apply in the open ocean, this model does inform oceanographers about the forces acting on subsurface water that are induced by wind-generated surface currents. In general, surface currents are within 45° of the direction of wind travel. The overall direction of water flow within the top 330 feet (100 m) is within 90° of the direction of the wind. In shallow coastal waters, the direction of travel of water is often predominantly in the direction of the wind.

Eddies in the Sea

The oceanic gyres are circular or spiral currents thousands of miles across. On a much smaller scale, but nevertheless large as an oceanic feature, are circular or spiral currents—eddies—that are 60–300 miles (100–500 km) in diameter. A newly identified phenomenon, eddies are now being found in all major oceans. They are shed when a major current system becomes locally unstable and forms a meander that pinches off from the main current to form an eddy. Taking the Gulf Stream as an example, large eddies of water are pinched off close to where the cold southward-flowing Labrador Current meets the warm northeastward-flowing Gulf Stream. Those pinched off on the north side of the Gulf Stream rotate clockwise and enclose warm water from the Sargasso Sea. Those pinched off on the south side rotate counterclockwise and contain cold water from the Labrador Current.

Interestingly, the warm-water eddies tend to be quite temporary and rejoin the main body of the Gulf Stream within a matter of days or weeks. The cold-water eddies, however, tend to be larger and can remain as distinct circulations for several years, easily long enough to affect phytoplankton productivity in the locality. In fact, cold-water eddies tend to draw nutrient-rich water from the depths so that productivity tends to be higher

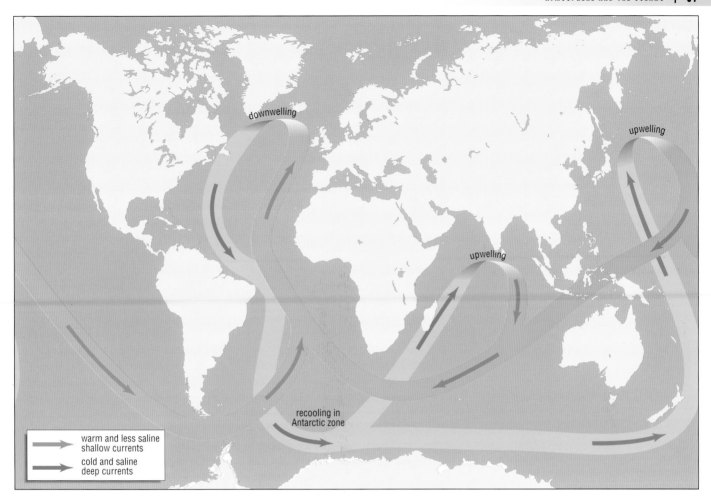

warm and less saline
shallow currents

cold and saline
deep currents

Global deep-water circulation. This highly simplified representation shows the "oceanic conveyor belt" that carries warm water to the poles and delivers cold water to tropical and subtropical regions.

within such eddies. Warm-water eddies do not have this effect. With the use of satellite technology (page 156) to map surface temperatures and phytoplankton activity on a day-to-day basis, the significance of such eddies is gradually becoming apparent.

The Deep-Water Climate Regulator

Because more than 80 percent of water in the open ocean is below the thermocline—at deep and bottom levels—the influence of the world's deeper subsurface currents may be much more profound, though less obvious, than that of sur-face currents. The deeper waters are isolated from surface waters, except at places where they are formed from downwellings or where they rejoin the surface at upwellings (page 68).

Paradoxically, sea ice forming in polar waters is a source of global warming. The arriving deep water is warmer than the polar air and transfers heat to the atmosphere. Also, when water freezes, it releases energy (the latent energy of freezing). One effect of global warming, as a result of raised atmospheric carbon dioxide levels (page 78), is that North Polar sea ice might melt away almost entirely in the summer. A resulting interruption in the formation of Atlantic bottom water would probably alter the entire circulation in the North Atlantic. One effect might be to reduce effectively the size of the North Atlantic gyre so that the Gulf Stream and the North Atlantic Drift would no longer reach Northwest Europe. Although the world as a whole might be growing warmer, northern Europe would lose its warm current. The British Isles, for example, would be plunged into near-glacial conditions. The disruption of deepwater circulation may not only have a profound influence on climate for large parts of the globe, but it will probably cut off the supply of upwelled water in some locations. How sensitive such upwellings are to changes in oceanic circulation patterns is demonstrated by the El Niño phenomenon (page 69).

The oceans play a dominant role in the workings of the world's climate machine. More than two-thirds of the planet's surface is covered by seawater, and because water is a better store of solar energy than is the land, the oceans provide the main source of heat energy that causes air to rise and thereby powers Earth's major wind systems. The major ocean currents are driven by the wind, and they too help distribute heat around the globe. Increasingly, the oceans and atmosphere are considered together as an interacting system that determines weather in the short term and climate in the long term.

Vertical Movements of Water

Vast areas of the oceans are, in effect, three layered. There is a warm surface layer extending to several hundred meters, a layer below this several hundred meters thick that has a steep temperature gradient (the thermocline), and a layer below this that is uniformly cold and includes the deep water and bottom water (page 66). This thermal stratification (layering by temperature) creates a relatively stable column of water in the sea, with the coldest (and densest) water at the bottom and the warmest (and least dense) water at the top. Vertical movements of water are limited, but where they do occur, they are often of great significance.

Upwellings

An upwelling is a rise of water from deep in the water column. In Antarctic waters, deep-level water is brought to the surface near the continental landmass and returns to lower latitudes as cold bottom water and warm intermediate water (page 67). In the Antarctic Ocean, this upwelling of nutrient-rich deep water nourishes the growth of phytoplankton in the sunlit surface waters and fuels high productivity in the spring and summer months, making the Antarctic Ocean potentially one of the most productive fisheries in the world.

Other economically significant upwellings occur on the western sides of the continents (the eastern sides of ocean basins). Here oceanic gyres bring water close to the continental landmasses, and offshore winds drive this surface water away from the coast. As a result, deep water rises up to occupy the vacated space, and an upwelling is created. The nutrients brought up to the sunlit surface waters again fuel a highly productive system, and many of the world's significant fisheries are centered on such upwellings. Such fisheries are associated with the Peru Current off the coasts of Peru and Chile, South America; the California current off Oregon shores (U.S.); the Canaries Current near Portugal; and the Benguela Current off Mauritania and Namibia (West Africa). Contrary to expectations, there is no comparable upwelling-based fishery off the west coast of Australia. The upwelling in this region is partially suppressed by a flow of warm surface water from the north. A similar situation occurs, with increasing regularity, in the eastern Pacific Ocean, when a spur of warm water partially suppresses the upwelling off the coast of Peru. This is the infamous El Niño event (see below).

There is also an upwelling associated with the Somali Current off the Arabian coast. Elsewhere in the oceans, upwellings arise where surface currents diverge. The most extensive occurrences are along the equator in the Pacific and Atlantic Oceans where trade winds cause surface waters in the Northern and Southern Hemispheres to move away from each other. Again, the resultant upwelling of nutrient-rich water fuels high phytoplankton productivity.

A variety of other phenomena also cause upwellings. In temperate latitudes, winter storms stir the surface waters and commonly erode the thermocline, thereby causing the mixing of waters to depths of several hundred meters. When the intensity and duration of sunlight increases in

The locations of major areas of upwelling, and the distributions of major coral reefs, often associated with downwellings

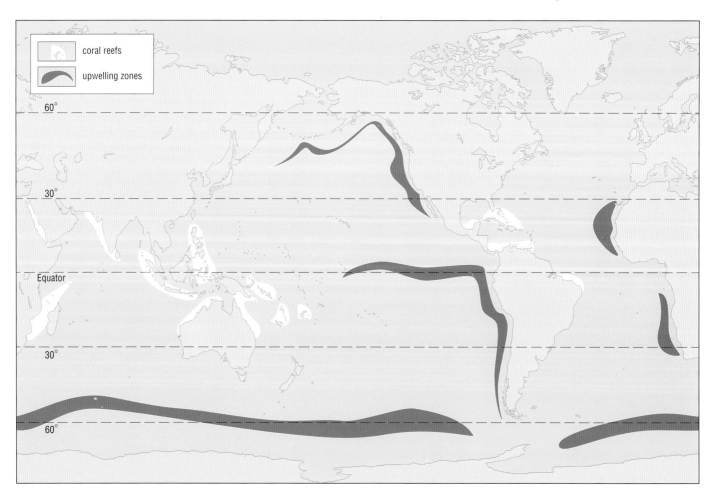

| | coral reefs |
| | upwelling zones |

60°

30°

Equator

30°

60°

spring, the availability of nutrients from storm-induced upwellings fuels a massive bloom of phytoplankton in spring—a very characteristic feature of North Atlantic waters.

Where two currents of markedly different properties come together, strong vertical mixing may occur, leading to highly productive conditions. The cold, nutrient-rich Oyashio Current off the northern coast of Japan meets the warm Kurashio Current of the western Pacific, and where they merge, they form the productive North Pacific Current, which supports a large fishery. Similarly, productive waters are associated with the North Atlantic Drift, formed by the merging of the cold Labrador Current and the warm Gulf Stream off the southeastern coast of the United States.

Other forms of upwelling operate on a smaller scale. Where oceanic water or a rising tide meets a continental slope or a bank on a continental shelf, the rising seafloor induces vertical mixing, enhances productivity locally, and can create neighboring phytoplankton blooms. Where a river enters the sea, the low-density freshwater moving away from the land may encourage the upwelling of water from offshore. If this water is nutrient rich, it may enhance the fertilizing effect of the river water and yield a long-lasting, offshore phytoplankton bloom fueled by the mixing of river water and upwelled seawater. Strong vertical mixing can also occur downstream from offshore islands or headlands.

By and large, upwellings increase nutrient availability in the surface waters and determine the distribution of the densest concentrations of phytoplankton (page 88). For those planktonic individuals that are denser than their surroundings and cannot swim, upwelling brings them into the sunlit surface waters and aids the ascent of other planktonic forms, too. In the case of phytoplankton, reaching the sunlit waters enables them to photosynthesize; in the case of zooplankton, this brings them into a rich zone for feeding.

El Niño

The complex interplay between wind, weather, currents, and upwelling is strikingly illustrated by the El Niño phenomenon. *El Niño* is a Spanish term meaning "the [male] child." In South America, it originally referred to an oceanic event that occurs around Christmastime—hence the reference to the male child. The event is a slackening in trade winds that occurs in December and causes a reduction in the upwelling off the coast of Peru. This upwelling, and the high phytoplankton productivity associated with it, forms the basis for the rich Peruvian anchovy fishery.

When the trade winds slacken and the upwelling declines, the coastal waters return to being warm and nutrient deficient, so the El Niño is associated with a decline in the productivity of the fishery: it marks the end of the peak fishing season.

In some years, the El Niño is much more pronounced—the upwelling is suppressed for months on end—and the high phytoplankton productivity is lost for that year. The explosion of fish numbers fails to occur, and the predators that depend on them, both fishermen and seabirds, are left with little or no catch. The effect on fishing communities along the Peru-Chile coast is devastating. The collapse of the fishery in the 1982–83 season saw the anchovy catch drop to a paltry one-six-hundredth of normal. Following the failure of the 1957–58 fishing season, the estimated numbers of seabirds—predominantly cormorants, boobies, and pelicans—fell from earlier estimates of around 28 million to a mere 6 million. In such years, the catastrophe is called an El Niño event, and the year is an El Niño year.

But how does an El Niño event arise? The answer—or at least part of the answer—lies many thousands of miles away.

The El Niño event is part of a wider phenomenon called the El Niño–Southern Oscillation (ENSO). The *Southern Oscillation* refers to a linkage between two atmospheric regions—one above the Southeast Pacific and the other above the eastern Indian Ocean and Indonesia. It is apparent that when atmospheric pressure is high above one region, it is low above the other. The shift in atmospheric pressure—from one to the other—occurs over months or years. During an El Niño event there is a weakening in the westerly winds that drive the southern arm of the South Pacific gyre. When this happens, not only is the speed of the Humboldt Current in the eastern Pacific slightly reduced, but the winds that produce the upwelling along the Peruvian coast are reduced too.

Just how widespread and devastating an El Niño event can be is evidenced from the experience of the 1982–83 El Niño—the most extreme event of this kind in the last hundred years. The following events were all attributed to the El Niño: the failure of Peru-Chile fisheries in that year; inland flooding in Ecuador, northern Peru, Paraguay, southern Brazil, and northern Argentina; and droughts in Bolivia, southern Peru, and northeastern Brazil. Further afield, Tahiti and Hawaii in the middle Pacific were hit by cyclones, and heavy rainfall resulted in floods on western Pacific islands. Meanwhile, there were droughts in central and Northwest Africa, northern India, and parts of Indonesia and Australia.

Less extreme El Niño events occurred in 1986–87 and in most years between 1991 and 1996. The concern over the effects of an El Niño is due largely to its disruption of normal events. The knock-on effects of an El Niño have a negative impact on many but are beneficial to a few. For example, in 1982–83 the eastern United States experienced an unusually mild winter, with great reductions in heating bills, and despite the failure of the South American anchovy fishery, high-value, warm-water species such as skipjack and yellowfin tuna appeared in record numbers in coastal waters, and the scallop fishery flourished.

Meteorologists can now predict the unfolding pattern in the ENSO (El Niño–Southern Oscillation) that leads to an El Niño event. If the episode cannot be prevented, it can at least be planned for. For that season, farmers can be encouraged to plant different crops and fishermen to harvest different species so that some of the worst effects of the event are mitigated.

There is concern that the frequency of El Niño events is increasing, perhaps due to subtle changes associated with global warming (page 78). The 1997–98 El Niño was anticipated to be the worst one since 1982–83. The ENSO phenomenon is being closely monitored by the international Tropical Ocean Global Atmosphere program (TOGA) and the World Ocean Circulation Experiment (WOCE) with a view to providing longer-range predictive models of an El Niño event and to determine what global factors, if any, are changing to make such an event more likely.

Downwellings

On the eastern sides of continents (the western sides of ocean basins) onshore winds drive surface water toward the coast and encourage downwelling, the descent of water. Downwelling does not raise nutrients to the surface waters, nor does it increase productivity in the surface waters, but it may carry oxygen-rich water and planktonic organisms to lower levels of the water column, which may be beneficial for organisms living there. Whereas upwellings occur where currents diverge, downwellings are found where currents converge; for example, downwelling, as well as upwelling, occurs in polar waters (page 66).

Major coral reefs are commonly found in tropical and subtropical regions of downwelling. Here, the warm, clear surface waters descend, bringing their meager but continuous supply of planktonic organisms to the feeding coral polyps (page 112). The reefs of the Caribbean, those around Madagascar, and the Great Barrier Reef off eastern Australia are all associated with downwellings on the eastern sides of continents.

Tides and Surges

The sea rises and falls in a rhythmic pattern in the period of a day. This phenomenon, called tides, is familiar to anyone who has visited a seashore for any length of time. The rise and fall of the tides exerts a strong influence on life on the seashore and in coastal waters. It alternately exposes and submerges seashore organisms (page 86) and powers circulation patterns in bays and estuaries. In more subtle ways, it exerts an influence on countless species inhabiting the oceans in general and continental shelf waters in particular.

Tides represent a very broad pulse or wave of water (page 72). A tide is almost imperceptible in the open ocean—it causes a rise and fall of up to 20 inches (50 cm)—but along a coastline, the rise and fall is often greatly amplified. The biggest tides in the world occur in the long, narrow Bay of Fundy between Nova Scotia and New Brunswick, Canada. Here, the difference between the maximum elevation of the tide (high tide) and the minimum elevation (low tide) may reach across 60 feet (18 m); this difference is called the maximum tidal range. Elsewhere the tidal range is much less: in the Mediterranean Sea, for example, it is a matter of only a few centimeters. An incoming tide is often referred to as a flood tide, and an outgoing tide, an ebb tide.

What Causes Tides?

The tides are caused by the gravitational attraction of the Moon, and to a lesser extent, the Sun. The Moon, being much closer than the Sun, exerts a relatively powerful gravitational force on the surface of Earth. This pulls the surface waters toward the Moon so that the waters in that part of the world closest to the Moon bulge out slightly. Rather strangely, the waters on the opposite side of the world bulge out a corresponding amount at the same time. This is a result of centrifugal force or, more correctly, centripetal force—an equal and opposite force that counterbalances a force applied to a fast-rotating body. If Earth were completely covered in water, the oceans would bulge slightly directly toward and away from the Moon, and they would be shallower at locations 90° to the direction of the Moon. As we shall see, because of the presence of landmasses and because ocean basins vary in shape and depth, the actual pattern of tides is more complex than this.

Planet Earth is spinning on its axis, and it rotates once in every 24 hours. Within this time, a given point on Earth will be closest to the Moon and then 12 hours later will be at its far-thest. Because either of these positions creates a tidal bulge, a given point on Earth experiences two tidal bulges, or two high tides, in every 24-hour period.

Then things start to become more complicated. While Earth is spinning, the Moon itself is not stationary. It advances slightly in its own orbit around Earth. The Moon orbits Earth about once every 29.5 days—a lunar month. So each day it takes a given point on Earth about 24 hours and 50 minutes—not 24 hours—to catch up and come to its closest position relative to the Moon again. A full tidal cycle therefore takes 24 hours, 50 minutes.

Spring and Neap Tides

What role does the Sun play in generating tides? The gravitational attraction of the Sun is superimposed on the tides generated by the Moon. When the gravitational attraction of the Sun and the Moon are in alignment, the gravitational effect of the Moon is enhanced, and the tides are particularly large. These are the spring tides. This alignment of the Sun, Earth, and the Moon occurs at the time of the full Moon or the new Moon, and the high tides are extra-high and the low tides extra-low. About one week later, when the Sun and the Moon are orientated at 90° to one another, their gravitational attractions have opposing effects on the tidal bulge, and the tidal range is particularly low. These are the neap tides, and they occur when the Moon is at one-quarter and three-quarters. In a lunar month, there are two sets of spring tides and two sets of neaps. They occur at about 14-day intervals. In between the spring and neap tides are tides of intermediate size.

The explanation provides the general framework for understanding how tides are generated. But there are further complications. For example, the Moon is closest to Earth at certain times of the year (perigee) and furthest away at other times (apogee). Similarly, the Sun's influence is greatest at certain times of the year when the Sun is directly over the equator, which means that there are extra-big and extra-small spring tides and neap tides superimposed on the overall pattern. This is where spring tides originally got their name, because the largest spring tides (those with the largest tidal ranges) occur in spring, when a spring tide, a perigee, and an equinox occur at or about the same time. On these occasions, the spring tides are about 20 percent higher than normal.

Types of Tide

So far we have not taken into account the effect of landmasses. Doing this helps to account for the fact that there are, in fact, at least three main types of tidal pattern, not just the straightforward twice-a-day type.

When it is viewed from above the North Pole, Earth spins counterclockwise: the tidal bulge progresses westward around the world. Continental landmasses impede the movement of the tidal pulse, and the deflection of water is influenced by the Coriolis effect—itself a phenomenon associated with Earth's rotation. These interactions create complex tidal patterns within each ocean basin; as a result, tides may vary widely even within a few kilometers.

The most familiar tidal pattern is of the twice-a-day form, with both tides of similar size and separated by about 12 hours 25 minutes, producing two tidal cycles within a lunar day (24 hours 50 minutes). This pattern is termed semidiurnal (semidaily). Such tides are characteristic of most North and South Atlantic coasts, the southern Mediterranean, the Red Sea, the Persian Gulf, and most of the western coast of Africa and Australia.

A single tide once a day, termed diurnal (daily), is characteristic of the Gulf of Mexico and the extreme North Pacific. Such tides are also found in parts of Southeast Asia, eastern Australia, and Antarctica.

The third tidal pattern is quite common. It is a twice-a-day tide, but the two tides are of different sizes—one is significantly larger than the other. This pattern is called mixed semdiurnal and is common in the northern and eastern Indian Ocean, Indonesia, and much of the eastern Pacific. It is also characteristic of the Caribbean Sea and the northern Mediterranean.

Tide Tables

The tidal pattern, including heights and timings, at a particular location on a specific day can be readily computed; after all, the phenomenon is determined by cyclical lunar and solar events and relatively fixed oceanic topography. Also, there are tide records stretching back over hundreds of years that can be correlated with the celestial interactions. Tide tables that summarize tidal predictions are available for most coasts of the world. The National Ocean Survey of the United States Department of Commerce, for example, publishes annual data for tidal predictions for the

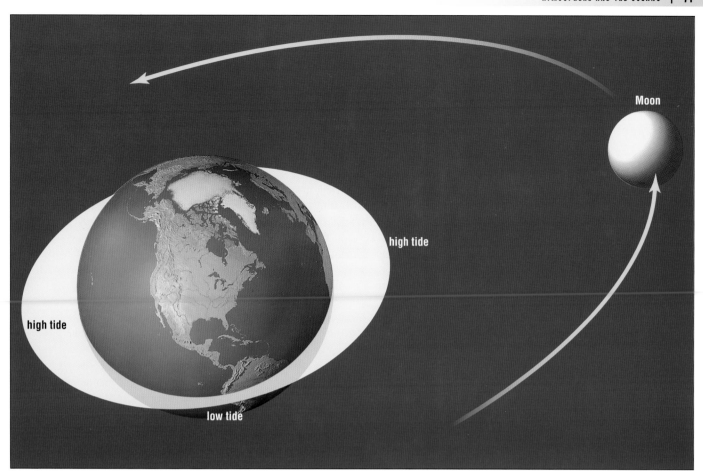

The generation of tides by the gravitational attraction of the Moon. Earth rotates on its axis once every 24 hours. The Moon completes an orbit of Earth about once every 29.5 days

world's principal ports. Predictions usually correspond extremely well with observations, although weather patterns can, of course, influence tides. Onshore winds can hasten and exaggerate a high tide, while offshore winds may have the opposite effect. The most damaging interactions between weather and tides occur when low-pressure storms coincide with the highest spring tides of the year, producing surges. On January 26–28, 1983, storm waves from the Russian east coast that had traveled across the North Pacific combined with unusually high tides to produce surges that hit the west coast of the United States. They caused $100 million of damage to homes, commercial properties, and municipal structures and led to the loss of at least a dozen lives.

Surges, Bores and Currents

When a shoreward-moving mass of water is constrained by a bay or estuary, the water at the leading edge is slowed but the water behind it is traveling at normal speed, and so the water piles up. This builds to form a wall of water moving rapidly towards the shore or up the mouth of a river. This surge of water is called a tidal bore and most commonly occurs during the biggest spring tides. Probably the world's largest bore takes place in the Chientang River estuary in northern China. There the tidal bore reaches a height of nearly 25 feet (7.5 m). In the Amazon estuary, the bore is called the *pororoca* and reaches up to 16.5 feet (5 m) in height, and travels several hundred miles inland at speeds of up to 13.5 miles an hour (22 km an hour).

The dynamics of tidal patterns create tidal currents that flow along coastlines, between islands, and through straits and channels. Tidal currents are most powerful in deep coastal water, but even in shallow water they pose a considerable hazard to swimmers and small craft. Currents of 7 miles an hour (11 km an hour) are quite typical, while in the Straits of Georgia between Vancouver Island and British Columbia flows may reach 11 miles an hour (18 km an hour).

The rise and fall of the tide represents a potentially bountiful source of available energy to generate electricity (page 172). Tides are also instrumental in determining the patterns of erosion and deposition on shorelines (page 38).

Waves, Swells, and Tsunamis

Winds blowing across the surface of the oceans set up surface currents (page 64) and waves. Whereas currents represent movement of water from one place to another, waves are vertical disturbances at or near the water surface. A wave is a vertical circular motion of water that causes an undulation on the water surface. When a wave travels across the ocean, it is the disturbance that is traveling, rather than the water itself. The wave possesses a considerable amount of kinetic energy (energy of movement), and when it travels across the ocean, it conserves much of this energy, which is dissipated when it crashes on a shore.

Ocean Waves

Most waves are created by winds, and, in such cases, the size and energy of waves are determined by the wind's speed, duration, and fetch (the distance over which the wind blows in contact with the sea). In general, the faster and longer the wind blows, the larger the waves become. The highest part of a wave is the crest, the lowest part the trough. Because waves usually travel in a repeating series of alternating crests and troughs, the characteristic features of ocean waves can be described by terms that apply to their repeating wave form. Typically, waves are characterized by their height (from crest to trough), by their wavelength (the distance from one crest to the next), and by their period (the time taken for two adjacent wave crests to pass a fixed point).

Most ocean waves have a height of 1.5–10 feet (0.5–3 m), although small waves or ripples only a few millimeters high are common, and giant storm waves more than 98 feet (30 m) tall are very occasionally encountered.

Once a wave is generated, it moves away from the place of formation and advances, transmitting its energy forward. The water itself moves up and down as the wave passes, but the water barely moves horizontally, so there is no overall flow of water horizontally as occurs in an ocean current.

Inside a wave, the water approximates a vertical circular path, with larger circles near the water surface and smaller ones farther down in the water column. The vertical mixing action of waves is important in distributing gases and nutrients in the surface waters. The vertical reach of a wave is about one-half its wavelength, so wind-driven ocean waves rarely mix the surface waters to a depth greater than 165 feet (50 m).

Waves on the Shore

When a wave enters shallow water, it behaves differently. The vertical circular motion becomes interrupted, and the wave curls over and breaks into surf. When the water depth is less than one-half the wavelength, friction with the seafloor begins to slow the forward progress of the wave. The wave heightens and steepens. At the point where the ratio of wave height/wavelength is greater than 1:7, the top of the wave is moving faster than the bottom, and the wave crest pitches forward, topples over, and breaks. Waves break on the shore when the water depth is about 1.3 times the height of the wave: a 10-foot (3-m) wave breaks in about 13 feet (4 m) of water. Surfers seek gently sloping shores where they can ride the "tube" of a wave that is breaking gradually; they avoid steeply shelving shores where waves crash abruptly.

When waves break, the force they apply to shorelines and to the organisms living there can be tremendous and is a key factor in shaping the seashore environment. Waves, together with tidal

Coastal waves, north coast, Puerto Rico
(Gerry Ellis/ENP Images)

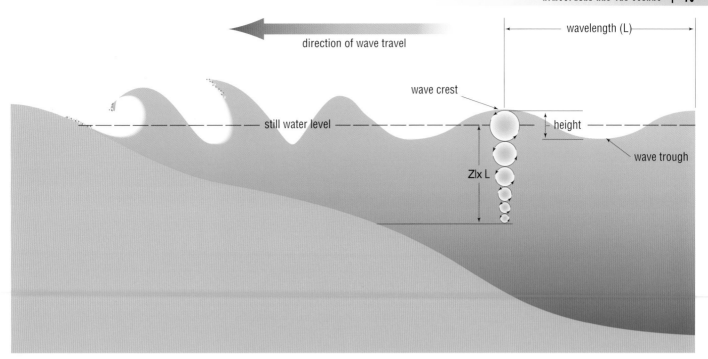

direction of wave travel

wavelength (L)

wave crest

still water level

height

wave trough

Zⅼx L

The characteristic features of waves. Where the water depth becomes less than half the wavelength, the wave breaks and becomes surf.

movements, are instrumental in moving sand and shingle up and down and along a shore. Often, waves are diffracted by promontories extending from coasts, and this influences the pattern of erosion on shorelines (page 38).

Seas, Swell, and Rogue Waves

Out at sea, when the winds are creating waves, the waves are often blown into sharp peaks, and the troughs are lengthened. This wave-generating area is often called simply sea. Away from the wind, the ragged sea surface settles down to a more nearly typical wave pattern described earlier and is often called a swell.

Of course, this simple description does not do justice to the choppy waters you often encounter at sea. The sea surface is often a confused jumble of waves arriving from different places. Where two waves merge and their wave crests coincide, a rogue wave is temporarily formed, with a crest much higher than normal. This is wave reinforcement, and it disappears when the contributing waves no longer coincide, such as when one is moving slightly faster than the other. Rogue waves, though rare, can appear seemingly from nowhere and, according to eyewitness accounts, may be large enough to endanger ships. Rogue waves off the southeastern coast of Africa have been implicated in the loss or damage of several oil tankers.

Conversely, when two waves meet—and the crest of one coincides with the trough of the

other—the two waves momentarily cancel out one another. Such interactions—between waves of different heights, wavelengths, speeds, and directions—produce highly complex interference patterns. During storms (page 76), the gusty, swirling winds create very choppy seas, and resulting waves move in all directions and are of different heights, periods, and wavelengths.

Tsunamis

The most destructive waves of all are tsunamis, after the Japanese term for "harbor wave." Tsunamis are often misleadingly called tidal waves. They are generated neither by tidal forces nor wind action but are born from tectonic events such as underwater earthquakes, volcanic eruptions above or below the sea surface, or landslides that enter the sea. Shifts in the seafloor displace large volumes of seawater, which disturb the ocean surface. A wave sequence is set in motion that travels outward from the source of disruption.

Unlike wind-driven waves, tsunamis travel extremely fast—up to about 500 miles an hour (800 km per hour), or the speed of a jet airplane. Their long wavelengths mean that their crests are often 100 miles (160 km) or more apart, with a crest passing only every 10–20 minutes. In the open ocean the wave height is small—only perhaps 40 inches (1 m)—and tsunamis usually pass unnoticed. Their character totally changes when they enter shallow water. On reaching the coastline, the water may build to 75–100 feet (23–30 m) high, sweeping boats and seashore structures inland. The backwash can then carry people and buildings out to sea. A tsunami may consist of a single crashing wave or several, depending on the

nature of the seismic activity. A few minutes before a tsunami makes landfall, there is a telltale withdrawal of water from the shoreline as the tsunami trough precedes the wave itself.

In 1883, the displacement of water caused by the volcanic eruption of the island of Krakatoa in the Indian Ocean caused some of the most devastating tsunamis in recorded history. Waves higher than 115 feet (35 m) smashed into the nearby islands, and the tsunamis reached halfway round the world. The resulting disruption claimed the lives of an estimated 36,000 people.

The shores of the Pacific have been ravaged by more tsunamis than other oceans because volcanic eruptions and earthquakes occur frequently around the Pacific Rim—the so-called Ring of Fire. Earthquake activity is particularly common in the western Pacific in and around Japan. One tsunami that struck Honshu Island, Japan, in June 1896 drowned an estimated 26,000 people. Hawaii's coastal town Hilo has been hit by tsunamis on several occasions this century. In 1946, 159 residents were lost in a major tsunami, while in 1960, the Chile earthquake caused tsunamis that took the lives of 61 Hilo inhabitants.

Today, seismic monitoring stations throughout the world screen earthquake and other seismic activity and give warnings of impending tsunamis via the International Tsunami Warning System (ITWS). In the case of seismic activity in the deep ocean, there is usually a delay of several hours between the seismic event itself and the resulting tsunamis making landfall on the nearest coasts and islands. In that time, evacuation plans can be put into action, thereby minimizing loss of life, but little can be done to prevent damage to property and disruption of services in coastal areas.

Weather Patterns

Some of nature's most terrifying and destructive phenomena are generated in the skies above the oceans, but the oceans are not only implicated in the more extreme meteorological phenomena, such as hurricanes and tornadoes, they are also instrumental in generating many day-to-day weather patterns.

The differential heating of land and sea—the sea takes longer to heat up and cool down—generates many weather phenomena at various scales of magnitude. The traffic of heat energy between ocean and atmosphere is much faster in an upward direction than it is downward. The sea rapidly affects the temperature of overlying air, but the air only slowly alters sea surface temperatures.

Directly and indirectly, the Sun's energy is the prime mover of the weather systems we experience. By causing differential heating, the Sun generates convection currents (warm air rising and being replaced by cooler air from below). This circulates the air in the atmosphere, generates wind, and stimulates cloud formation. Many familiar weather phenomena arise from this process. The rise and fall of air in the atmosphere, due to convection, creates subtle changes in air pressure: where air is rising, an area of low pressure forms below; where air is sinking, a region of high pressure forms near ground. Air moves from regions of high pressure to regions of low pressure, thereby

generating winds. Wide pressure differentials over short distances produce strong winds.

Often, as air rises, its water-vapor load condenses to form clouds. In middle latitudes, clouds and the precipitation that falls from them are commonly associated with low pressure. At these same latitudes, high pressure is normally associated with clear skies and sunny conditions in summer or with fogs and sharp, frosty spells in winter.

Frontal Systems

As winds shift air masses around the globe, they create weather. An air mass arriving in a particular locality may rise above the existing air mass or may displace it. The boundary between two interacting air masses is called a front. A warm front refers to warm air moving into a region occupied by cool air. The arriving warm air rises above the cold air and cools. Its water load condenses to form clouds, which may disperse over quite a large area and produce unsettled rainy weather for a day or two.

When a cold front enters a region of warm air, the warm air is displaced upward, creating low pressure near ground level. The severity and speed of the uplift may cause instability, triggering storms and high winds associated with the front. Showers may then follow.

Sunset through sea fog, Weddell Sea, Antarctica (Konrad Wothe/ENP Images)

Interactions between four main types of air mass are responsible for much of the world's weather. These are the maritime and continental air masses associated with tropical and polar regions. The fronts where these air masses interact determine the weather for much of the globe, particularly in the temperate regions.

Low-pressure systems, also called depressions or cyclones, form where cold air slides below warm air and they interact to generate a rotating weather system. This is common in middle latitudes along the boundary between cold polar air and tropical air that is warmed by oceanic currents. When the cold air arrives, the cold front creates an area of low pressure as it forces the warmer air upward. Winds are drawn into the region of low pressure, and in the Northern Hemisphere, these winds flow counterclockwise as they are deflected by the Coriolis effect (page 62); in the Southern Hemisphere they blow clockwise. Changeable, windy, rainy weather results. Usually, the supply of rising warm air diminishes after a day or so, and the stormy weather settles. However, if the warm-air upthrust is rapid and sustained, violent storms may result (page 76).

High-pressure systems, or anticyclones, result from air descending close to ground level (most strongly associated with latitudes 30° north and south, (page 63). As the air descends, winds blow outward from the high pressure zone. The winds, deflected by the Coriolis effect, turn clockwise in the Northern Hemisphere and counterclockwise in the Southern. In middle latitudes, high-pressure systems tend to produce clear skies and settled weather in summer and cold spells with frost and fogs in winter.

Coastal Breezes

The effect of surface waters on short-term weather events is well illustrated by the daily pattern of onshore and offshore breezes in coastal areas in many parts of the world. Water has a much higher heat capacity than air, so it warms up and cools down more slowly and also forms a large reservoir of heat. During the day in warm weather, land temperatures rise more rapidly than sea temperatures. As a result, the air above the land rises and is replaced by air moving from sea to land. This produces cool onshore breezes that help to moderate the heat of the day. At night, however, the land cools rapidly. Cold air now flows from the land toward the relatively warmer sea. The wind direction reverses, and gentle offshore breezes develop.

Water vapor, as well as heat, is transferred from ocean to atmosphere. Winds blowing over warm ocean water take up moisture. When the air currents subsequently encounter colder ocean water, their water load may condense to form thick ocean fog. At certain times of the year in the North Atlantic, heavy sea fogs are produced where the warm Gulf Stream and the cold Labrador Current converge. In the Northwest Pacific during summer months, southerly winds blowing over the warm Kuroshio Current create dense fog when they encounter the cold Oyashio Current.

Forecasting

The benefits of weather forecasting to mariners, farmers, and the public at large far outweigh the economic costs of providing a comprehensive meteorological service. Effective weather prediction demands international cooperation because the local weather two or three days hence is determined by atmospheric events hundreds of miles away. Next week's weather may be influenced by activities thousands of miles away. International recognition of the importance of weather prediction is exemplified by the fact that at the height of the cold war in 1961, 150 countries (including the U.S.S.R.) responded to President John F. Kennedy's suggestion to establish an international weather-prediction program. In reply to this, by 1963 the World Meteorological Organization (WMO) formulated a World Weather Watch

(WWW) program. Today, the WWW system collects data from some 12,000 land-based stations, more than 7,000 oceangoing vessels and oil rigs, many commercial airliners, and 700 upper-atmosphere weather balloons. This data is relayed to three global forecasting stations—one in the United States and two in the United Kingdom—for analysis. The data is fed into supercomputers that use highly sophisticated mathematical models to predict the weather for various timescales—from a few hours to several weeks. Global weather maps and accompanying forecasts are compiled every six hours and disseminated to countries worldwide.

The reliability of the forecast is highest at short time intervals (typically with an accuracy of about 85 percent for the forthcoming 24-hour period in most parts of the United States) but declines rapidly over the longer-term. Short-range forecasts (1–2 days) contain much detail, but medium-range (3–10-day) and longer-range (11–90-day) forecasts contain progressively less information. The complexity of land-sea-air interactions means that the predictability of weather systems is limited. Weather systems—and oceanic circulatory systems for that matter—show elements of predictable behavior interspersed with highly unpredictable phases. During phases of uncertainty, very small changes in ambient conditions can result in widely differing weather effects. This is a classic feature of chaotic

behavior (see "Chaos Theory," below). This means that both weather patterns and oceanic circulations are predictable only up to a point, and some unpredictability is an inherent feature of the system. Nevertheless, improved mathematical modeling and the gradual accumulation of millions of atmospheric data sets are gradually improving the ability of meteorologists to predict the weather several days hence. Accurate forecasting for the "window" 7–10 days ahead may become routine within the United States, Europe, and some other parts of the world during the next decade.

Studying the Air-Ocean Interface

The behavior of Earth's atmosphere cannot be understood without knowledge of oceanic circulation patterns. The costs of establishing comprehensive international programs to study ocean circulation and air-sea interactions pale into insignificance against the socioeconomic costs of failing to make meteorological and longer-term climatic predictions (page 69). Time, effort, and money funneled into investigating air-sea interactions is money well spent if the programs are well coordinated and on an international scale. The Global Ocean Observing System (GOOS) is such a response.

CHAOS THEORY

In the early 1960s U.S. meteorologist Edward Lorenz (1917–) explored simulated weather systems with mathematical models. Using computers to run various scenarios, he discovered that very small differences in starting conditions sometimes resulted in very different outcomes. This phenomenon became encapsulated in the metaphor called the butterfly effect: It is theoretically possible for a butterfly's wingbeat in Brazil to have repercussions that will determine whether the California coast of the United States will have fine weather or storms a month later.

Chaos theory attempts to describe mathematical principles underlying the chaotic behavior of unpredictable systems, such as long-term atmospheric phenomena. In the mid-1970s U.S. mathematician Mitchell Feigenbaum (1945–) examined the chaotic behavior of nonlinear systems—systems in which the elements are not linked in a linear or proportional manner. In such systems, doubling the magnitude of one component will not simply double the magnitude of another. Also, the

inputs of such a system are not directly proportional to the outputs. He discovered that when some of these systems break down from orderly behavior into seemingly unpredictable behavior, there is, nevertheless, an underlying pattern to the chaotic behavior.

Since that time, chaos theory has become a burgeoning area of scientific and mathematical enquiry. According to chaos theory, long-range forecasting of atmospheric, or even oceanic, phenomena is likely to be problematic because such systems are highly complex and often exhibit nonlinear and chaotic behavior. An example of this is the shedding of eddies by the Gulf Stream (page 66). Although general statements can be made as to what type of eddy is likely to form where, the details of this phenomenon are inherently unpredictable. It is not possible to predict exactly where and when an eddy will form, and what will happen to that eddy once created. Similarly, in the air above the sea, it is difficult to predict the precise path of a hurricane (page 77).

Catastrophic Weather Conditions

Storms, arising from severe depressions or low-pressure systems (page 63), can occur at any time. Calculations made by insurance companies and other vested interests suggest that the more severe storms probably account for about 20 percent of the huge annual cost of damage inflicted by natural disasters worldwide.

The storm waves generated at specific times of the year play a significant role in shaping coastlines. Often, sandy beaches are swept away or resculptured during autumn or winter storms, and erosion on rocky shores is often greatest during severe winter storms (page 22).

Thunderstorms

Thunderstorms are the most common form of violent storm and are notable for the loud and visually dramatic discharges of electrical energy associated with them. Satellite imagery shows us that about 40,000 or so thunderstorms arise across the world every day. From the satellite's view, the storms appear like giant flashbulbs backlighting the clouds below.

Most thunderstorms brew in tropical and subtropical regions in spring and summer. To form, they require three main ingredients: moisture, instability, and lift. These are found where warm, moist air rises rapidly to the top of the troposphere, forming dense clouds as it does so and then spreading out along the tropopause to form an anvil-shaped system. In the more extreme cases, the rising clouds punch through the tropopause—generally an indication of a severe thunderstorm or even a hurricane or tornado (see below).

As the rising air cools around the level of the tropopause, cool downdrafts descend and cause turbulence. The electrical nature of a thunderstorm seems to be enhanced by opposing air currents. Positively charged ice crystals accumulate toward the top of the cloud system, and negatively charged water droplets near the bottom. This charge separation is unstable, and given the opportunity, the accumulated charges will discharge themselves. The opposite charges are attracted to one another; in most cases, the negative charge toward the base of the cloud discharges into the positive charge near the top of the cloud or discharges into an adjacent cloud or into the air itself. Only about one lightning bolt in five is discharged into the ground. The passage of negative charges follows an invisible jagged path. But once the negative charge meets a positive charge, a massive electrical current is triggered and flows along the original path but in the opposite direction. It is this positively charged return stroke that is visible as a lighting bolt. The flow of electrical energy, first in one direction then the other, gives the lightning bolt its flickering effect. When the lighting bolt is visible, we talk of fork lightning; when the lightning bolt is shielded by clouds and we see only a flash, we talk of sheet lightning. Amazingly, about 100 lightning strikes occur somewhere on Earth every second.

The speed of positive charge transmission is very rapid—about 60,000 miles (96,000 km) per second. The temperature of a lightning bolt exceeds 40,000°F (22,000°C), and the current flowing is typically some 10,000 amps or more. The noise we call thunder is created by the air becoming superheated and then rapidly cooling and contracting. The resulting implosion of air is noisy. Because sound travels much more slowly than light, the flash of the thunder bolt is seen before the associated rumble of thunder is heard. The time delay between the flash and the rumble is a good indicator of the distance the viewer is from the electrical activity; a three-second delay is equivalent to one kilometer, a five-second delay, one mile. If there is no delay, the lightning is directly overhead.

The electrical activity itself enhances coalescence of ice or water droplets within the clouds, encouraging precipitation. The latent heat released by condensation has a warming effect that may continue to fuel the updraft of warm air that maintains the storm. Depending on the precise nature of the thunderstorm, the winds, rainfall, thunder, and lightning can last from a few minutes to several hours.

An electrical phenomenon associated with undischarged storm clouds is St. Elmo's fire. This refers to the greenish or white flashes seen in the rigging of sailing ships when passing through low storm clouds. St. Elmo is the patron saint of sailors. In stormy conditions the phenomenon is sometimes seen around flying aircraft and high-elevation structures on land.

Hurricanes

Hurricanes are among the most destructive forces in nature. The name, probably of Spanish-Portuguese origin and associated with the Caribbean, means "big wind"—appropriate because winds within a hurricane reach in excess of 100 miles an hour (160 km an hour). Hurricanes, called tropical cyclones in the Indian Ocean or typhoons in the West Pacific, are intense, circular low-pressure systems. They always develop at sea and generally within a region 350–1,000 miles (550–1,600 km) from the equator, although they typically move outward from that region.

To form, hurricanes require sea surface temperatures of about 82°F (27°C) or more, coupled with a disturbance in the atmosphere that creates a strong updraft of warm, moist air. As the water-vapor load condenses, the released latent energy promotes further convection and fuels the developing storm. There is a cumulative effect, with condensing warm air promoting further updraft. Moist winds begin to circulate rapidly around the central eye of the storm and rise swiftly to form spiraling belts of cumulus-type clouds, which, seen by satellite or aircraft from above, resemble a whirlpool. When sea-level winds increase to 39 miles (62 km) an hour, the system is classed as a tropical storm; when winds reach 74 miles (119 km) an hour, the storm is classed as a hurricane. Hurricanes are recognizable on radar screens and are tracked by satellites, but it is still inherently problematic plotting their precise path, which is why hurricane warnings may miss their mark.

The hurricanes that almost annually strike the shores of the Gulf of Mexico or the eastern U.S. coastline are generated in the Caribbean region or in the South Atlantic off the coast of Africa. Hurricanes—whether emerging in the Northern or Southern Hemispheres—generally drift westward. When they strike land, the winds and accompanying torrential rain can wreak havoc. The path of damage may be 200–500 miles (320–800 km) across, and accompanying downpours of 12–24 inches (30–60 cm) of rain have been recorded. However, once a hurricane begins to travel over land, it is deprived of its source of moisture and gradually dies out as updrafts of air become drier. Some hurricanes form tornadoes when they reach land (see following page).

The storm surge that accompanies a hurricane often poses the greatest danger to life. The low-pressure zone at the center of a hurricane causes a mound of water to form in the sea below. Barely noticeable in the open ocean, the mound may form a storm surge as it enters shallow, restricted water (page 71). In the worst hurricanes, this surge may reach a height of 18 feet (5 m) or more.

The United States's costliest storm, Hurricane Andrew, struck the states of Florida and Louisiana in August 1992. It caused devastation

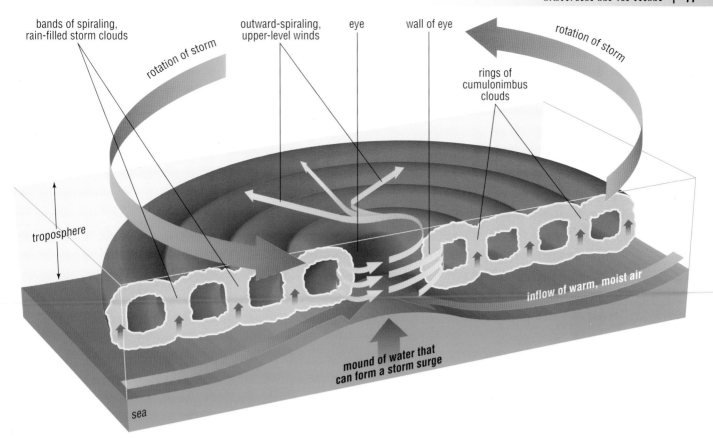

bands of spiraling,
rain-filled storm clouds

rotation of storm

outward-spiraling,
upper-level winds

eye

wall of eye

rotation of storm

rings of
cumulonimbus
clouds

troposphere

inflow of warm, moist air

mound of water that
can form a storm surge

sea

A hurricane in cross section

that cost billions of dollars in restitutions and was responsible for 23 deaths.

Tornadoes

Smaller than hurricanes, tornadoes are even more violent—but on a more local scale. Tornadoes are essentially whirlwinds that are anything from a few feet to 1,625 feet (500 m) or more across. They contain winds that probably reach a frightening 200–300 miles (320–480 km) per hour, and their destructive power is more than the stuff of legends. In 1931, a Texan tornado lifted an 80-ton railroad car and its 117 occupants from a railway track and deposited the entire assembly in a ditch. The Tri-State Tornado of 1925 swept through Missouri, Illinois, and Indiana; its 217-mile (350-km) journey was responsible for the deaths of 695 people.

Tornadoes are normally associated with the United States, and that is where they are most abundant and of greatest ferocity. They are common in tornado alley, a corridor in the Midwest running from Texas to Illinois. Here the warm, moist air from the Gulf of Mexico underlies cold dry air from the north and seems to provide a prime breeding area for tornadoes.

Tornadoes seem to arise from a rotating funnel of air that projects down from a turbulent cumulus thundercloud and is fueled by violently rotating updrafts that reach to the ground. The familiar cone shape of a tornado is formed from debris and condensing moisture drawn upward by the spiraling updraught. Tornadoes can move quite erratically across the landscape, stopping and starting, changing direction, and occasionally lifting off the ground. Their progress and impact strength is thus difficult to predict. They have been recorded moving horizontally at more than 100 kilometers (62 miles) an hour. They survive for a few minutes or for as long as an hour.

The destructive power of a tornado is attributed to several factors. The high winds, of course, cause much devastation, and their rotation is able to uproot trees and buildings and strip the branches from trees. The updraught of a tornado may be sufficient to lift large objects high into the air and deposit them elsewhere. There are several well-documented cases of tornadoes plucking people from the ground and safely returning them to the ground some distance away. Such a reassuring outcome is, however, quite uncommon. Numerous documented cases of animals "raining" from the sky—fish, frogs, and so on—are probably the result of updraughts carrying these creatures into the sky and then depositing them when the winds slacken. A tornado's suction effect has other impacts. When a tornado surrounds a building, the sudden drop in local pressure, sometimes as low as half the normal atmospheric pressure, causes a huge pressure differential between the inside and the outside of a building. Unless the building is well-ventilated and has plenty of open windows, the pressure differential is sufficient for the high pressure inside to make the building burst outward and effectively explode. This is why householders in tornado-torn areas are encouraged to keep doors and windows open at times of high risk.

Tornadoes at sea form a waterspout—a column of water dragged up from the sea surface that combines with condensed water in moist air. Not all waterspouts are formed from tornadoes, and those that are, while less violent than their land cousins, are nevertheless a danger to small vessels. One of the greatest hazards is from the deluge of water that accompanies the unloading of a waterspout as it starts to subside.

Global Warming

Many people, including numerous scientists, believe that global warming is the most pressing environmental issue of the early 21st century.

Is Global Warming Taking Place?

There is no simple answer. Between the early 1940s and mid-1960s, Earth appeared to be cooling slightly. Some scientists attributed this cooling trend to the presence of soot and other particles in the atmosphere, the result of air pollution from human activities. The particles reflect sunlight, and less solar radiation reaches Earth's surface to cause warming. Indeed, in some newly developing cities, this process is still happening, but in many industrialized countries, the enforcement of air pollution legislation has curbed this effect.

There are at least two key difficulties in pinpointing global warming: First, the global climate fluctuates naturally anyway, and any trend of artificially induced global warming needs to be disentangled from natural cycles of climate change. Data from many sources suggests that variations of up to 42.8°F (6°C) in average annual temperatures have occurred within the last 10,000 years, entirely independently of any human action. At present, we do not know enough about natural variations in solar activity to explain and predict background trends.

Second, global climate is the sum total of numerous local climates on different continents, and local climates are produced by a complex interplay between land, oceanic, and atmospheric phenomena. A rise in global temperature will make many localities warmer, but it will also make some cooler, as winds and ocean currents readjust to the changing conditions. Monitoring temperature changes in the middle and deep layers of the ocean is likely to be a particularly useful way of assessing global warming because the temperatures of these water layers fluctuate relatively little but have a profound effect on the global climate system (page 48).

The major cause for concern is that so-called greenhouse gases, most notably carbon dioxide, are increasing in concentration in the atmosphere. Since the 1960s, there has been a growing majority among scientists who believe these gases will have a warming effect on Earth, the repercussions of which are difficult to predict but are likely to be profound.

The Greenhouse Effect

On a sunny day, the inside of a greenhouse is much warmer than its surroundings. Sunlight enters the greenhouse through the glass panels and is absorbed by the ground, plants, and other objects inside. They, in turn, radiate heat in the form of infrared radiation. This radiation is of a longer wavelength than visible light and cannot readily pass through glass. The infrared rays are trapped, and the air inside the greenhouse becomes warmer.

In the atmosphere, carbon dioxide molecules—and other so-called greenhouse gases—act similarly to the greenhouse's glass. Sunlight reaches Earth's surface warming it, and Earth radiates infrared rays. The infrared rays are trapped by greenhouse gas molecules, and a portion of the radiated heat is thus trapped in the atmosphere, hence the term *the greenhouse effect*. As a result of this effect, the atmosphere stays warmer than it would if the heat were radiated freely into space. Some estimates suggest that Earth would be 50°F (10°C) colder were it not for the greenhouse effect.

The industrial revolution of the late 18th century onward has relied, and continues to rely, on carbon-based fuels—wood, charcoal, coal, oil, and natural gas—as the main source of energy. All these fuels share carbon dioxide as a main combustion product. Ice cores from Antarctica show that, since the mid-19th century, carbon dioxide concentrations in the air have increased by a remarkable (and disturbing) 25 percent. The carbon dioxide concentration continues to climb.

The rising carbon dioxide concentration will almost certainly raise the heat-trapping potential of the atmosphere and so very likely raise Earth's surface temperature, by how much is extremely difficult to predict. Several other compounds are important greenhouse gases—first and foremost, water itself, but also methane (CH_4), nitrous oxide N_2O) and chlorofluorocarbons (CFCs).

If global temperatures rise, several feedback mechanisms are likely to kick in, but it is difficult if not impossible to predict what the result of the various checks and balances will be. For example, raised temperatures will increase evaporation of

The greenhouse effect

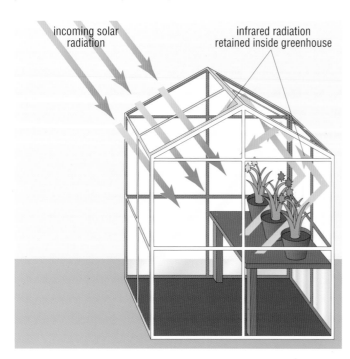

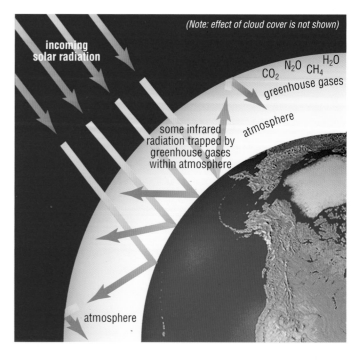

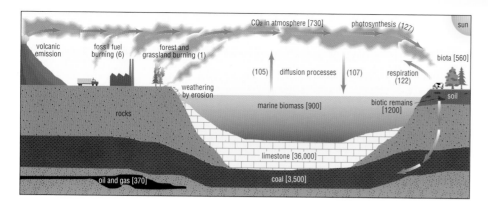

The carbon cycle. Reserves of carbon, in brackets, are shown in units of billions of metric tons. Fluxes of carbon, in parentheses, are shown in billions of metric tons per year. Notice the very large reserves of carbon in the deep ocean as sediments

water from the oceans. Increased moisture in the atmosphere will create more clouds. Clouds reflect sunlight back into space and therefore may be expected to limit further heating. On the other hand, water is also a greenhouse gas and traps heat energy in the atmosphere. The balance of these two effects—sunlight reflection or heat retention—is very much dependent on the nature of the cloud cover. Indeed, NASA has identified the nature and extent of cloud cover as being the greatest source of uncertainty in modeling the likely impact of greenhouse-effect heating. Added to this are the uncertainties about interactions between the oceans and the atmosphere (page 75).

The Carbon Cycle

While scientists debate the rate and magnitude of global warming, there is consensus that increased atmospheric carbon dioxide levels mean more heat energy trapped in the atmosphere. So how can the rising atmospheric carbon dioxide levels be moderated? This can be done by reducing the global rate of carbon dioxide production, by enhancing the rate at which carbon dioxide is extracted from the atmosphere, or, indeed, by a combination of the two.

Carbon dioxide emissions could be reduced by curbing the burning of fossil fuels. This may not happen in any significant way for another 25–50 years—rather too late to mitigate the present concerns about global warming. Attempts are being made to limit the production of other greenhouse gases, but the rhetoric and good intentions have not been met with equivalent action by world governments (see below).

As for raising the global ecosystem's biogeochemical ability to extract carbon dioxide from the atmosphere, recent trends have tended, if anything, to reduce rather than enhance this capacity. On

land, the removal of large tracts of tropical rain forest may well be lowering Earth's photosynthetic ability. Photosynthesis by trees and other plants removes carbon dioxide from the atmosphere and replaces it with oxygen. In the sea, marine pollution may have a detrimental effect on phytoplankton populations and therefore may be lowering the ocean's photosynthetic capacity. Oceanographers are now turning their attention to how phytoplankton productivity can be enhanced on a wide scale; recent iron-seeding experiments are a move in this direction (page 60).

The Effects of Global Warming

Not only is the very existence of global warning difficult to establish, but the likely effects of such warming are widespread and varied and sometimes seemingly contradictory. Some of the more generally accepted conclusions include:

- a reduction in agricultural productivity in many parts of the world. At present, farming in many locations is a marginal activity, limited by the very hot climate and lack of rainfall. In such areas, an upward temperature shift of only a few degrees would be sufficient to make agriculture impossible. This is likely to result in food shortages in many tropical and subtropical regions.

- climatic shifts requiring changes to domestic, commercial, industrial, and municipal infrastructures and major adjustments to farming practices

- flooding of low-lying areas and saltwater intrusion into inland soils as a result of a rise in global sea level (page 41).

The Way Ahead?

At the very least, action needs to be taken to

- greatly increase current knowledge of the role of clouds in transmitting, reflecting, and

absorbing heat and light energy under different scenarios; of interactions between the ocean and the atmosphere that influence the rate of global climate change and determine patterns of regional variation; of the quantification of the flux of greenhouse gases and their relative effects in a changing world climate; of the likely effects of global warming on the melting of polar-ice and sea-level rise

- extend the detail and magnitude of programs for monitoring atmospheric, land-based, and oceanic changes linked to climatic effects

- develop more sophisticated global climate models, with finer detailing, using the most powerful computer technology available

- reduce the increase in rate of consumption of fossil fuels, or, ideally, reverse the trend entirely so that global carbon-dioxide emissions are stabilized or, better still, lowered

- lower the rate of emission of other major greenhouse gases such as CFCs, methane, and dinitrogen oxide

- counter the continued destruction of tropical rain forests

- monitor marine phytoplankton populations to establish the key factors that are determining productivity and consider ways of enhancing productivity

In June 1992, at the United Nations Earth Summit in Rio de Janeiro, many countries supported the U.N. Framework Convention on Climate Change. This included a commitment to reduce the emissions of major greenhouse gases—carbon dioxide, methane, and dinitrogen oxide—to their 1990 levels by the year 2000. At the second Earth Summit in New York in June 1997, it was apparent that some countries—notably Germany, Holland, Switzerland, and the United Kingdom—were on-target to meet this pledge. But many of the richest countries were falling well short, including the United States, Canada, Italy, France, and Australia.

On the positive side, scientists in research programs such as the Global Ocean Observing System (GOOS) and in working groups such as the Intergovernmental Panel on Climate Change (IPCC) are gathering hard data and formulating closely reasoned rationale for future research programs and for mitigating the worst effects of global warming. Assuming that the specter of global warming is looming large, the findings—and arguments—of these professional groups and the pressure exerted by other agencies must convince politicians—and the public at large—to take sufficient action before it is too late.

The Evolution of Life

Evolution is the great unifying theory in biology. It refers to the gradual change in a species' genetic constitution over time. Since Charles Darwin placed arguments for evolution—and its possible mechanism—before public scrutiny in 1859, the theory in its broadest principles has been supported by a vast body of evidence. Darwin and Alfred Wallace proposed that the main mechanism by which evolution occurred was *natural selection*. Within a population of a single species, some individuals are better than others at coping with the demands of the environment. They may be better at obtaining food, more successful at avoiding predators, and more attractive to a potential mate. Such individuals are more likely to survive, and are more likely to mate and leave descendants, than other individuals. The characteristics of successful individuals—providing that they are genetic traits that can be passed on to offspring—are likely to accumulate in the population over generations. In this way, the population *adapts* to its environment; in other words, it evolves by the natural selection of its members.

Although biologists argue about the precise mechanisms of evolutionary change, the rapidity of change, and the relative importance of natural selection compared to other mechanisms, the general principle of evolution by natural selection is well established.

Various lines of evidence, ranging from examination of the fossil record to analysis of the chemical constituents of organisms, point to the fact that more complex life-forms have evolved from simpler ones.

History of Life

Remarkably, there has been life on this planet for more than three-quarters of Earth's 4.6-billion-year history. Whether life evolved from aggregations of complex chemicals on this planet or whether Earth was "seeded" by microbes of extraterrestrial origin is conjecture. Whatever the scenario, fossil remains dated as 3.5 billion years old indicate that simple life-forms were present at this time.

The earliest organisms we know and *all* major groups (phyla) of animals—both current and extinct—originated in the sea. Some groups have since exploited freshwater and terrestrial environments, but it still remains true that more phyla are found in the oceans than on land or in lakes and rivers. Until recently, biologists believed that many more animal species (perhaps 70 percent) were found on land rather than in water; this view is changing. Because of the great difficulties in exploring the ocean environment—sampling the ocean floor for animal life has been likened to towing a butterfly net behind an aircraft—the number of species in the oceans is probably grossly underestimated. Sampling the deep seafloor of the North Atlantic in recent years has yielded, on average, one new species in each sample taken. Admittedly, many of the new species are seemingly innocuous creatures such as sponges but it is nevertheless true that the current total of seafloor species—230,000 or so—is probably underestimated by a factor of at least three or four, and perhaps much more.

There are several very good reasons why life should evolve in the sea rather than on land. First, living organisms *are* mostly water: It is a fundamental constituent of their bodies. Whereas water is superabundant in oceans, it is scarce on land. Second, water is effective at absorbing harmful ultraviolet rays in sunlight. Ultraviolet rays cause mutations (changes in the genetic material of living cells). The atmosphere of early Earth absorbed much less ultraviolet radiation than the present atmosphere, and so ultraviolet radiation was present on Earth's surface at dangerously high lev-

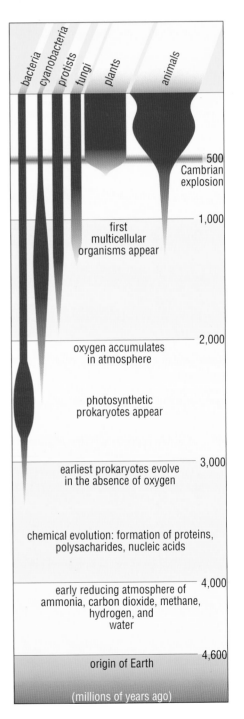

bacteria
cyanobacteria
protists
fungi
plants
animals

500
Cambrian
explosion

1,000

first
multicellular
organisms appear

2,000

oxygen accumulates
in atmosphere

photosynthetic
prokaryotes appear

3,000

earliest prokaryotes evolve
in the absence of oxygen

chemical evolution: formation of proteins,
polysacharides, nucleic acids

4,000

early reducing atmosphere of
ammonia, carbon dioxide, methane,
hydrogen, and
water

4,600

origin of Earth

(millions of years ago)

The evolution of life on Earth

els—too high to sustain life on land. In the sea, however, much ultraviolet radiation is absorbed within the top meter of water, so it poses little threat to organisms living below this depth. The chemical concentrations in freshwater environments are much less than those in the sea, and most simpler plants and animals have total chemical concentrations at levels quite similar to that of seawater, so it is reasonable to suppose that life evolved in the sea rather than in freshwater.

We can only speculate about the very earliest stages in the evolution of life on this planet. Some scientists suggest that comets containing microbes in suspended animation "seeded" the planet with life. Others suggest that meteors, comets, or cosmic dust might have delivered organic molecules such as amino acids—some of the chemical building blocks of life. But we do not have to invoke an extraterrestrial origin for such substances. In the early 1950s, Stanley Miller, at the time a graduate student, showed that by simulating the conditions on Earth during its early stages—by providing an appropriate chemical mix of water vapor, methane, ammonia, and hydrogen gas plus a source of energy in the form of an electrical spark (to simulate lightning)—he could produce a wide assortment of simple organic substances, including amino acids.

Today, ideas about Earth's early atmosphere have changed somewhat, and amino acids and other important biomolecules such as nucleotides (the building blocks of DNA, which comprises the genetic material of living organisms) are less readily formed under the atmosphere currently envisioned. Earlier theories saw life first evolving in shallow seashore pools where chemicals became concentrated. More recent ideas center on hydrothermal vents (page 43) or other tectonically active regions as possible locations, with organic molecules being attracted to sediments where they could accumulate at high concentration. Whatever the scenario, it is a big step from chemical building blocks to living organisms themselves.

What Characterizes Life?

A true living organism is enclosed by a membrane or other boundary layer that controls the entry and exit of substances and separates the organism from its surroundings. It is also able to grow and produce copies of itself. The organism actively maintains itself by taking in—or making—complex chemicals (the process of nutrition) and then breaking these down to release chemical energy that is harnessed to build complex useful substances such as proteins, fats, and nucleic acids. The process of harnessing usable energy by breaking down complex substances is called respiration; in some organisms, it does not require oxygen (it is an anaerobic process), but in most organisms it does (it is aerobic).

At its simplest, an organism consists of a single cell, but most organisms are constructed of hundreds, thousands, or even millions of cells. Whether a tiny single-celled organism or a giant creature such as a whale, all organisms share many similarities: they are responsive to their surroundings; they can reproduce; they make or obtain food supplies; and they respire. They are also constructed of similar chemical building blocks, notably carbohydrates, proteins, fats, and nucleic acids. Carbohydrates and fats meet most of the organisms's energy requirements and they act as energy stores. Proteins are constructed from chains of amino acids; they provide much of a cell's structure, as well as the enzymes that catalyze the vital chemical reactions in living cells. Deoxyribonucleic acid (DNA), a type of nucleic acid, provides the genetic material that encodes the instructions for building new cells and organisms. The DNA is passed from parents to offspring, and alterations in the sequence of chemicals within DNA provide the source of variation that ultimately gives rise to evolutionary change (page 80).

The Changing Atmosphere

Once living organisms evolved, they began to have a profound effect on their physical and chemical surroundings. They began to utilize certain types of chemicals and release (excrete) others. These chemical transformations would, in time, cause weathering effects on rocks and generate changes in the atmosphere. It is reasonable to suppose that the earliest living organisms were single-celled, bacterialike organisms, that they were anaerobic, and that they were chemosynthetic—they harnessed energy by oxidizing simple molecules and then used this energy in manufacturing their own food supplies. The bacteria in recently discovered hydrothermal vents (page 43) may offer suitable analogs for these primitive organisms. They, too, are chemosynthetic and utilize simple chemicals such as hydrogen sulfide or methane as their energy source, although in some cases they do so in the presence of oxygen.

Once these anaerobic microbes were well established, several landmark changes were to occur. Some organisms, instead of harnessing energy by degrading simple chemicals, instead trapped sunlight and used this energy to manufacture complex chemicals. This process—termed photosynthesis (literally, "manufacturing using light")—is efficient and utilizes an effectively inexhaustible energy source. These primitive microbes were established by 1.7 billion years ago and were probably similar to present-day cyanobacteria. They would have released oxygen gas as a by-product of photosynthesis. The atmosphere of early Earth was oxygen-free, and at the time of its appearance oxygen was probably treated by most organisms as a poisonous threat. In time, however, many organisms would evolve to capitalize on this new chemical resource.

By 1.2 billion years ago, more complex single-celled forms had evolved, related to present-day protists. These had a more complex cellular arrangement that included a distinct membrane-bound structure, the nucleus, in which was situated the cell's genetic material. Sexual reproduction (with genetic material being passed onto offspring from more than one source) was established by 900 million years ago and provided an abundant source of genetic variation as a font of evolutionary material. By 600 million years ago, the oxygen concentration of the atmosphere was probably only about 1 percent of its current value. This was nevertheless a crucial turning point: organisms that could utilize oxygen could gain energy more efficiently than those that could not. More efficient utilization of energy set the stage for an evolutionary explosion of lifeforms. At around this time, larger life-forms began to emerge. The simplest were simple aggregations of cells, similar to present-day colonial protozoa, with others more like sponges. Soon, true multicellular organisms appeared, and by 570 million years ago, the beginning of the Cambrian period, most major groups of marine organisms were evident. This sudden diversification in lifeforms has been dubbed the Cambrian explosion. Sponges, corals, jellyfish, and worms were abundant, as were the more complex animals and plants that were the immediate ancestors of those that would begin to colonize the land.

Biogeography of the Oceans

Water temperature is one of the most important physical parameters affecting marine life. An organism's body temperature, often influenced by its external environment, determines the rate of many of its chemical and biological processes. As a general rule, and within limits, an organism's rate of metabolism (and therefore activity) increases as its body temperature rises and decreases as its body temperature falls. At upper and lower extremes of temperature, enzymes fail to work properly or are even destroyed, causing the organism's death. For many marine organisms, temperature is the single most important factor influencing their biogeographical distribution.

Animals that cannot regulate their body temperature are known as poikilothermic, or less accurately, "cold-blooded": this includes invertebrates and most fish and reptiles. Their body temperature follows that of their surroundings. Homeothermic, or "warm-blooded," animals, on the other hand, can regulate their body temperatures and maintain them at a relatively constant level, largely independent of their surroundings. Marine birds and mammals are homeothermic and can often migrate across steep temperature gradients with relative ease. Most marine organisms, however, are adapted to live in particular temperature ranges. Many tropical species, for example, have enzymes that work best at high temperatures, and they cannot tolerate cold water. The reverse is true of many polar species. So to describe global animal and plant distribution, it is often useful to designate biogeographi-cal zones based on mean surface seawater temperatures.

In reality, biogeographic distributions tend to be much more complex than this. Why? Because the temperature of surface water is not necessarily a good indicator of water temperature at depths of 100 meters, 200 meters (330 feet, 660 feet) or more, where many organisms are found. Currents at different depths complicate matters.

In mid-water communities, the distribution of characteristic communities of animals is associated with particular water masses—often defined by a combination of water temperature and salinity. Each of these bodies of water forms

---

Biogeographic regions of the Atlantic Ocean

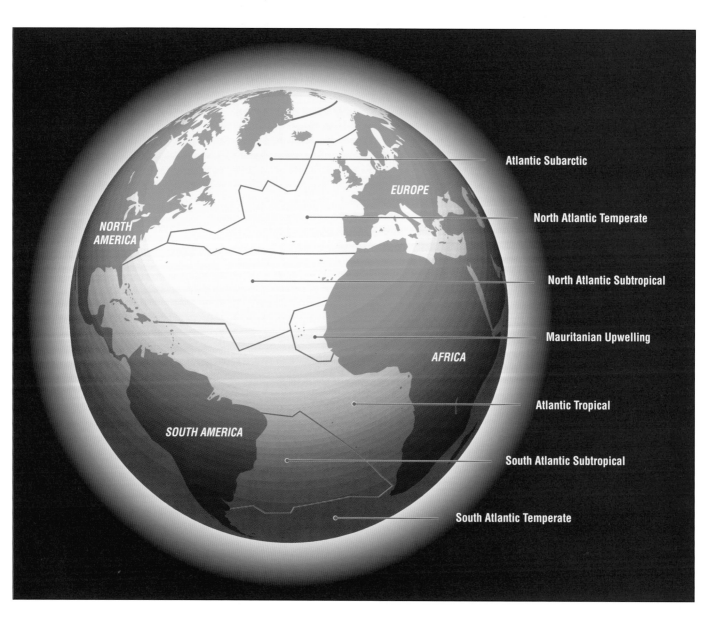

Atlantic Subarctic

EUROPE

North Atlantic Temperate

NORTH AMERICA

North Atlantic Subtropical

Mauritanian Upwelling

AFRICA

Atlantic Tropical

SOUTH AMERICA

South Atlantic Subtropical

South Atlantic Temperate

a different type of environment, and each commonly supports a distinctive community of organisms.

In the 1980s, R. H. Backus and colleagues from the Woods Hole Oceanographic Institution established eight regions for the Atlantic Ocean, delineated by their characteristic mid-water fish communities and the properties of the associated water masses, in particular temperature. Although these regions broadly corresponded with well-established biogeographic zones based on temperature, there were conspicuous exceptions. Two regions did not fit the overall pattern. For example, the Mauritanian Upwelling off the coast of northwestern Africa occurs where cold nutrient-rich water from Antarctic and sub-Antarctic regions wells up to the surface. It is extremely productive, in contrast to adjacent subtropical and tropical regions. The upwelling also has one species of mid-water fish, *Lamadena pontifex,* that is unique to it. The Gulf of Mexico, on the opposite side of the ocean, has no unique mid-water species: Its animal community is a mixture of species associated with adjacent regions—temperate, subtropical, and tropical.

The barriers to free movement of organisms from one place to another are much less obvious in the sea than they are on land, but they nevertheless exist. Some zooplankton (animal plankton) species have wide distributions that encompass a broad spectrum of environmental factors. Others are restricted to narrow limits of temperature, salinity, and other determinants and in such cases, they may be used as biological indicators of the particular water-mass types they inhabit. For example, in the Pacific Ocean are eight major plankton communities, each comprising a particular assemblage of zooplankton (in particular, foraminiferans, chaetognaths, and copepods, page 89) and each associated with a particular current system. These current systems appear to have been in existence for more than 26 million years, and these communities are constant in composition over thousands of kilometers of ocean; they probably represent some of the oldest species assemblages on the planet.

Human intervention inadvertently affects biogeographical distributions; for example, since the Suez Canal was opened in 1869 linking the Mediterranean with the Red Sea, some 140 species of zooplankton have colonized the Mediterranean from the south. Accidental transport of marine organisms in the ballast water of oceangoing vessels may also be having an as yet undetermined effect on the distribution of marine organisms. One of the few well-documented examples has drastically affected one fishery. The ctenophore or comb jelly, *Mnemiopsis leidyi,* a small jellyfishlike member of the zooplankton, is believed to have been transported from North America to the Black Sea in ballast water. By 1990, this species, previously unknown in the Black Sea, had increased its biomass enormously. As a voracious predator, it has probably had a drastic effect on fish-fry stocks and is believed to have had a greater impact on the heavily polluted Black Sea than any other human factor. The collapse of the Sea of Azov anchovy fishery is attributed to this predator.

Biogeographical distributions are complex, not only because of present-day physical and chemical phenomena, human interventions, and interactions between species, but also because of historical events over geological time. For instance, the Atlantic Ocean is probably about 40 million years old, much younger than the Pacific Ocean. The bottom-living (benthic) animals in the Atlantic are descended from arrivals from other oceans and seas; the diversity of the bottom-living animals in the Atlantic is therefore not as great as it is in the Pacific. For example, the Caribbean Sea off the Central Atlantic is without several genera of reef-building corals than are present in the Pacific.

Ecological Concepts

The combination of one or more biological communities in a geographic area and the habitats in which they live is called an ecosystem. Thus, an ecosystem is the term used to describe a stable, self-supporting system of living and nonliving components in a particular locality. Normally, an ecosystem has a more or less recognizable boundary: the Mediterranean Sea, a stretch of seashore, a tidal pool, and the seafloor around a hydrothermal vent, are all examples of ecosystems.

There is terminology used to describe the organisms that live in different parts of the ocean environment. Those that live on the seafloor (epifauna) or in the sediment (infauna) are termed benthic organisms and comprise the benthos. The terms *benthic* and *benthos* are sometimes extended to include those fish and other swimming animals closely associated with seafloor, although *demersal* is perhaps a better term for these. The benthic environment encompasses the entire seafloor, from the deepest depths to coastal waters, and includes that part of the seashore that is intermittently covered in water by the tides.

The water column, as distinct from the seafloor, is called the pelagic environment (meaning "open sea"). Actively swimming marine animals that live in the water column are called nekton, while plants, animals, and microscopic forms that float there form the plankton.

Competition

An important concept in ecology is the idea of an ecological niche. This refers to an organism's way of life within an ecosystem. It encompasses all or virtually all aspects of an organism's lifestyle: how precisely it obtains food, where exactly it lives, how it reproduces, and so on. Individuals within the same species occupy the same ecological niche, although there may be some variation (e.g., some individuals exploiting slightly different food resources). As a general rule, a particular niche within an ecosystem is occupied by only one species. When two species occupy a very similar niche within the same community, they compete intensely with each other because they both require similar resources. In such cases, one species almost always out-competes the other, the less successful species dying out within the locality while the other survives. This elimination of one species by the other is called the competitive-exclusion principle.

Sometimes, a shifting balance is struck between two competing species, particularly where local conditions are highly variable. In some cases, two or more species can avoid excluding one another if they each exploit just part of the resource. This sharing of a resource by specialization is called by some ecologists resource partitioning. The range of shorebirds that coexist on muddy shores (page 87) probably do so by exploiting different organisms at different levels in the mud.

Feeding Relationships

Most ecosystems are powered, directly or indirectly, by energy from the Sun (solar radiation). Energy and matter are exchanged between ecosystems and their surroundings. Energy flows through an ecosystem, while matter is recycled through an ecosystem.

The phytoplankton and, in coastal ecosystems, seaweeds and seagrasses are called producers; they *produce* the organic matter on which the other organisms in the community depend for their food supplies. Animals are the main consumers in an ecosystem; they *consume* producers and other animals to obtain organic matter. Decomposers are the third main category of organism in the community; in the sea, they make up mostly bacteria and animallike protists. They also break down microbial, plant, and animal wastes and convert them into simple inorganic substances, thereby recycling essential elements that will provide nutrients for producers (see nutrient cycles below). Decomposers and the dead organic matter on which they feed form detritus. Detrital feeders (detritivores) create another route for circulating organic matter back into the food web. In the oceans, the decomposers and the microscopic detritivores that feed on them are sometimes referred to as the microbial loop, an addition to conventional food webs and food chains.

Food Chains and Food Webs

The feeding relationships in a community are commonly depicted in the form of a food web. Because of the great complexity of feeding relationships within a community—hundreds of different species may be present, species change their diet at different stages in the life cycle, and individuals have parasites—the food web is invariably a great simplification. The web is nevertheless a useful means of focusing attention on the major biotic elements and their trophic (feeding) interactions. A food chain represents the flow of food (or energy) along a particular route through the food web. Each step in a food chain is called a trophic level. Often, decomposers are omitted from food webs and food chains even though they are a significant, indeed vital, part of the community.

Evidence is building that food webs that have many interconnections may be more resilient to environmental perturbation than those with few interconnections. For example, the Newfoundland herring restricts its diet to copepods, whereas its North Sea cousin has a much more diverse diet. Were there to be a catastrophic decline in copepod populations, the North Sea herring would appear to have other food options, whereas the Newfoundland herring would not. However, the general rule that complexity equals resilience is an oversimplification because one or a few species may play a disproportionate role in maintaining the integrity of an ecosystem; coral reefs have some of the most complex food webs and yet are relatively fragile ecosystems (page 113).

Energy Flow

When energy flows through an ecosystem, entering as solar radiation and then passing from producers to primary consumers, secondary consumers, and so on, a considerable amount of energy is lost at each stage. Photosynthesizing plankton and benthic plants utilize less than 1 percent of the solar radiation available at the sea surface. Once a producer manufactures organic compounds utilizing sunlight, energy is lost in respiration in simply maintaining the integrity of the organism, wastes are excreted, and chemical reactions fall far short of 100 percent efficiency. When a producer is then consumed, some of its body parts cannot be digested and utilized but are expelled as indigestible waste material. Only a fraction of the energy produced by photosynthesis is thus available to a consumer. Similar energy losses are experienced in passing from the second trophic level to the third and upward within a food chain.

Field and laboratory studies of marine food chains and food webs place the efficiency of energy transfer from one trophic level to the next at 6 percent to 15 percent. Put another way, only 6 percent to 15 percent of the energy available to any trophic level is passed on to the next. The average efficiency is about 10 percent, but a few benthic communities and some commercially exploited fish populations offer examples of energetic efficiencies of 20 percent or more. The true

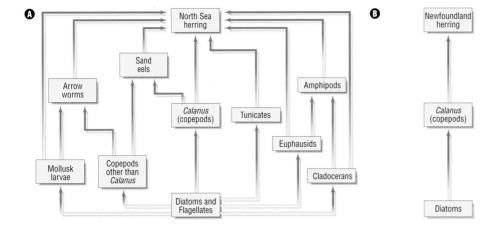

(A) A marine food web depicting the trophic interactions for the North Atlantic herring. (B) A food chain showing the much simpler trophic interactions for the Newfoundland herring

value of this efficiency is of real importance: it helps biologists estimate the sustainable fish harvest from an ecosystem and enables them to make comparisons between one ecosystem and another.

The progressive loss of available energy from one trophic level to the next limits the number of trophic levels to six or less. As a general rule, the biomass (mass of living material) of organisms at a low trophic level is greater than in the one above. However, there are exceptions. Measuring biomass represents a snapshot in time and is not necessarily a good indicator of the productivity (see below) of a particular trophic level. So, in the North Atlantic in winter, the biomass of phytoplankton may be somewhat lower than that of the zooplankton that normally feed on them. In spring, however, the phytoplankton multiply, and the expected biomass relationship—phytoplankton greater than zooplankton—is established.

Nutrient Cycles

Energy passes through an ecosystem and is eventually lost as heat energy. Taking the planet as a whole, the heat energy that enters the planetary ecosystem balances that lost. Currently, there may well be a slight imbalance that is resulting in global warming (page 78).

Chemical elements are cycled through the planetary ecosystem, although they may accumulate in one part and be scarce in another. Small-

and large-scale experiments such as Biosphere 1 and 2 show that an enclosed ecosystem, providing it receives a source of energy in the form of solar radiation, can recycle its chemical elements and maintain itself.

The cycling of a particular chemical element can be depicted in a flow diagram that attempts to summarize the major chemical transformations. Carbon, the key constituent in organic molecules and of major importance in determining atmospheric composition and global climate (page 79), is a prime candidate for such an analysis. Nitrogen is another important chemical element in the marine environment. Sufficient levels of nitrate are necessary for phytoplankton and other producers to manufacture organic chemicals by photosynthesis. In the pelagic environment of the open ocean, a single nitrogen atom may be cycled biogeochemically as many as 10 times in a single year. Each turn of the cycle involves, on average, three steps of bacterial decomposition, highlighting the vital role of these organisms in helping to maintain marine productivity.

Primary Productivity

Primary production—the conversion of inorganic carbon into organic carbon by photosynthetic or chemosynthetic organisms—is the source of food on which the rest of the biological community ultimately depends. Thus, measuring primary productivity gives an indication of the energy available to the rest of the community. The rate of primary production, or productivity, is expressed as the amount of carbon in grams fixed under a square meter of sea surface in a day ($gC/m^2/day$) or in a year ($gC/m^2/year$). In com-

munities where photosynthetic producers predominate (almost all marine communities), it refers to the production of both phytoplankton in the water column and plants that live on the sunlit seafloor.

Rates of primary production vary enormously in different parts of the ocean system, depending largely on availability of nutrients, sunlight, and suitable temperatures. Coral reefs (page 112), with their stable structures exposed to sunlight, are the most highly productive ecosystems, with productivities in the range 1,500–3,500 $gC/m^2/year$—more than double that of tropical rain forests and temperate agricultural fields on land. However, the most productive oceanic regions in terms of the marine produce that humans can directly exploit are the upwelling regions and estuarine areas that have high nutrient levels. Here primary productivity is typically in the range 110–370 $gC/m^2/year$. Food chains are short and plankton-eating fish and shellfish can be harvested from the second and third trophic levels.

Secondary Productivity

Within an ecosystem, the total amount of animal biomass produced in all higher trophic levels, per unit area per unit time, is called secondary production. Aspects of secondary production can be inferred from levels of primary production, at the bottom end of the food chain, and from catch statistics for commercially fished species, at the top end of the chain. However, that still leaves many aspects of secondary productivity unassessed. Noncommercial fish, jellyfish, ctenophores (comb jellies) and so on are not included in the assessment. Also, primary production may not be a good indicator of production in higher trophic levels; for example, the dominant phytoplankton species may not be one accessible to many of the zooplankton species. In such cases, much of the utilization of primary productivity may bypass the traditional pelagic food web and instead enter the microbial loop. Reliable estimates of secondary production—though difficult and time-consuming to gather—are important in helping us understand how the ecosystem operates and how the harvesting of commercial species may be sustained alongside noncommercial species that are competing for the same or similar resources (page 198).

Life on the Shore

The Intertidal Zone

The intertidal (or littoral) zone is that part of the shore that is intermittently covered and then exposed by rising and falling tides. This zone is the true meeting place between land and sea. Life in the intertidal zone is not easy. Two major physical factors—exposure to the air and wave action—shape the lives of inhabitants. In many parts of the world, tides rise and fall in a predictable cycle that repeats itself every 24 hours 50 minutes (page 70). In each tidal cycle, marine plants and animals as the top of the intertidal zone are exposed to the air for a relatively long period before being submerged again. If they are to survive, they must withstand drying out (desiccation), perhaps a temporary lack of food, and possibly a drastic change in ambient temperature. Organisms lower in the intertidal zone have to withstand only short periods out of water before their seawater surroundings are reestablished.

As for wave action, the force of impacting waves takes its toll of animals and plants. On the more exposed shores, only seaweeds with flexible fronds and strong holdfasts can withstand the onslaught of storm waves, and even then, some plants are commonly washed away and create spaces for new forms to colonize. On these wave-battered shores, animals have to be strongly attached to stable rocks and suitably shaped to shrug off the pounding by waves. Barnacles and limpets are among such forms.

The combination of tides and wave action creates a highly dynamic environment. The intertidal zone is constantly being shaped as animals and plants are swept away or holdfasts are disrupted, creating opportunities for colonizers to invade any newly created spaces.

Rocky Shores

Rocky shores can be smooth or boulder-strewn, and flat, sloping, or near vertical. The variety of shore profiles creates a wide diversity in the detailed structure of shore communities. Many rocky shores, however, show similar patterns if the informed observer knows where and what to look for.

A striking feature of rocky shores, particularly those that are vertical or steeply sloping, is that they exhibit clear bands or "zones" of plants and animals, with different species living at different levels in the intertidal zone. This vertical zonation is largely, but not entirely, based on sessile forms, such as marine algae, barnacles, and mussels. In general, physical factors in the environment,

together with biological factors such as competition, determine the upper limit of distribution of a species on the shore. Biotic factors such as competition, grazing, and predation determine a species's lower limit of distribution.

Splash (Supralittoral) Zone

This, the highest part of the intertidal zone, is rarely covered by seawater, although this region is quite frequently drenched in spray from crashing waves, hence its name the splash, or spray, zone. Organisms that live here need to be highly resistant to desiccation, and in this marginal zone between land and sea only a few species are successful; some are terrestrial, others marine. In temperate regions, lichens of various colors, from white and yellow through to black, are commonly associated with this zone.

The most common animal inhabitants of the splash zone are small snails, the periwinkles (*Littorina* species) that graze on microscopic algae and retreat to cracks and crevices in very hot conditions. They can seal themselves into their shells and remain attached to rock by a ring of dried mucus or slime. Limpets (e.g., *Colisella*) and sea lice, roaches, or slaters (*Ligia*) also graze on the algae. Relatively few marine predators venture into this zone; however, terrestrial predators such as birds or even humans may frequent this zone to feed on the mollusks.

The Middle Intertidal Zone

The middle intertidal zone forms the largest vertical extent on the rocky shore and is regularly submerged and uncovered by the tides. In temperate climates worldwide and on most rocky shores of the Pacific and Atlantic coasts of North America, this part of the shore often comprises distinct vertical zones of animals and plants: a clearly marked upper band of barnacles, below which is found a wide zone of mussels and seaweeds.

The location and species composition of the barnacle zone (commonly two or more species of barnacles compete for space here) is determined by a variety of factors. Experiments indicate that several factors—larval settlement patterns, how well the barnacles tolerate desiccation, competition for space, and predation—all influence which barnacles are found where. The barnacles are filter-feeding crustaceans, sieving the water for plankton and particulate matter by, in effect, standing on their heads and kicking their legs.

A region with dominant forms that include mussels (*Mytilus*) and brown seaweeds (*Fucus, Ascophyllum,* and *Pelvetia*) is commonly found below the barnacle zone. Often scattered among these are sessile forms, such as barnacles and sea anemones, and roaming over the terrain at high tide but disappearing under seaweed into crevices or in rock pools at low tide are a range of predators, such as crabs, sea stars, and dog whelks.

The Lower Intertidal Zone

This part of the intertidal is submerged for most of the time and is dominated by seaweeds. Marine predators, among them sea stars and dog whelks, have easy access to any growing barnacles and mussels, and so the abundance of these prey species is kept in check. Red, green, and brown algae compete for available light and are grazed by a variety of herbivores, including sea urchins (*Arbacia, Echinometra*). Carnivores include sea anemones (*Anthopleura, Metridium*), dogwhelks (*Nucella*), and various small fish that are well adapted to intertidal life, such as gobies (*Gobius*).

Sublittoral Zone

The lower boundary of the intertidal zone gradually merges with the sublittoral zone—the shallow waters next to the shore that are rarely if ever

Tidal rise and fall and its influence on the duration that intertidal animals and plants are exposed to the air. An organism at level A on the shore is exposed to the air for about two-thirds of this tidal cycle. An organism at B is uncovered for about one-third of the time.

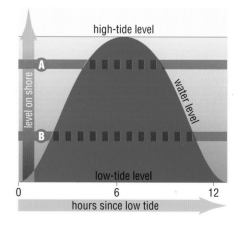

exposed by tides and storm waves. In tropical regions, various small species of brown algae (*Fucus*), sea grasses (page 114), or densely encrusting corals (page 112) may dominate the sublittoral, depending on the precise characteristics of the locality. In temperate latitudes, encrusting red algae (*Lithothamnion*) and large sea squirts (ascidians) may cover much of the sublittoral zone. In cold temperate and in polar regions, kelp (*Laminaria*) often dominate the rougher, shallow waters, producing so-called kelp forests (page 115) that may extend to depths of about 130 feet (40 m).

Sandy and Muddy Shores

Sandy and muddy shores, as distinct from rocky shores, do not have a stable foothold for seaweed or sessile animals to attach. Mudflats and sandy beaches are distinguished on the basis of particle size. Muddy shores tend to be flat or nearly flat and occur where the water is sufficiently slow moving for fine particles to settle out. Sandy beaches are composed of larger grains and are steeper and less stable than muddy shores. Sand shifts constantly and when exposed to the air dries out faster than mud.

Life in or on a sandy beach seems surprisingly sparse except, perhaps, for the scuttling crabs that are prevalent on some shores and the amphipods (beach hoppers or beach fleas) that are commonly found on the strandline. In reality, however, there is much activity below the sand's surface. Many of the larger representatives of the sandy shore community are burrowing creatures. Within moist sand they are protected from desiccation and temperature fluctuations and avoid those predators that patrol the surface of the sand.

There is a vertical zonation of animal life on sandy shores, but this is much less obvious than that found on rocky shores. As on rocky shores, the number of species and total biomass increases with distance down the intertidal zone, being greatest in the lower shore that is covered by seawater most of the time.

The macrofauna (larger animals) on sandy shores are usually well represented by five groups: bivalve mollusks, gastropod mollusks, annelid worms, crustaceans, and echinoderms. Many of these animals filter water to obtain food (suspension feeders) or feed on particles in or lying on the sediment (deposit feeders); a few are predatory.

Sandy-shore echinoderms tend to be found in the lower intertidal and remain below the surface of the sand. They include both deposit feeders and predatory forms. Heart urchins (*Echinocardium*) and sand dollars (*Mellita*) scrape off and ingest the organic matter from the surface of sand grains. Sand stars (e.g., *Astropecten*) use their five arms to burrow into the sand. They are voracious predators that consume crustaceans, mollusks, and other echinoderms. They pull open bivalve shells to reach the mollusk inside and then extend their stomach into the shell cavity to digest the unfortunate mollusk *in situ*.

The sand particles themselves and the spaces between them are the home for small or microscopic animals that comprise the meiofauna (from the Greek *meio* meaning "lesser" or "smaller"). Only 0.004–0.08 inches (0.1–2 mm) long, these animals represent a great diversity of animal groups: In some cases they are miniature forms of normally quite large animals such as polychaete worms, nematodes, and mollusks; in other cases, the forms are quite bizarre—hydroids with snakelike tentacles, protozoa that constantly change shape, or wormlike forms with strange vacuum-cleaning devices. The meiofauna form a diverse community in miniature, with a range of herbivores, omnivores, and carnivores. The meiofauna, in turn, are consumed by macrofauna (larger animals), particularly the deposit feeders and small predators such as shrimp and young fish.

The surface layers of the sand do contain photosynthesizing diatoms, dinoflagellates, and blue-green algae. But the bulk of the intertidal zone's food supply comes from seaweed brought in by the tides, the phytoplankton suspended in seawater, insects and organic material blown off the land, or the dead carcasses of terrestrial and marine animals.

Muddy Shores

Muddy shores are characterized by particle sizes of less than 0.002 inches (0.06 mm). They have little or no gradient, and they are commonly referred to as mudflats. Vertical zonation is almost absent on mudflats because of the lack of vertical gradients.

Because of their small particle size and low vertical gradients, muddy shores retain water much more readily than sandy beaches. Also, the lack of abrasion by sharp sandy particles and the relative absence of water movement mean that the environment is more stable. On the other hand, oxygen penetrates a shorter distance in mud than in sand. In mud, the respiration of microorganisms and the oxidation of chemicals within the sand effectively remove the available oxygen within a few centimeters—even within a few millimeters—of the surface. Below this depth, the mud is black and evil smelling; anaerobic chemosynthetic bacteria thrive here, and animals burrowing at this depth must obtain their oxygen supply from water that is drawn from above the surface of the mud.

Species diversity is low on muddy shores. However, what the burrowing macrofauna lack in diversity, they often make up for in terms of simple abundance. Pockmarks and holes in the moist surface of the mud give some indication of the vast population of bivalve mollusks, annelid worms, and other invertebrates below the surface. More than 5,000 burrowing clams have been counted in a square meter area of some lower muddy shores.

Photosynthesis occurs in the top few millimeters of the mud where sunlight penetrates and diatoms or dinoflagellates live, but detritus forms the bulk of the nutrient input on muddy shores. Organic material is readily trapped in the small spaces between mud particles, and a rich meiofauna is associated with the oxygenated parts of mud. Decomposition of organic material is slower in the deeper, anaerobic reaches but nevertheless still occurs under the action of bacteria, protists, and fungi.

Plankton

Food chains in the oceans are very different from those on land. In many terrestrial environments, producers are large (for example, trees) and dominate the landscape. In the sea, the main producers are microscopic, but their combined photosynthetic activity is greater than that of all trees. Most of Earth's biomass is not found within tropical rain forests or in vast fields of agricultural crops or anywhere else on land; it is found floating in the sunlit waters of the oceans as plankton.

Plankton refers to all those organisms—bacteria, protists, plants, and animals—that float in the surface waters and drift at the mercy of ocean currents. Some are able to swim and can adjust their buoyancy to move up or down within the water column, but they can only make significant progress horizontally by "hitching a ride" on currents at different levels in the water column.

Among plankton, the tiniest are bacteria and cyanobacteria, which together comprise the bacterioplankton, all less than 2 microns (two millionths of a meter) across. They include autotrophic forms (those that make their own organic food supplies by photosynthesis) and heterotrophic members (those that require their organic food ready made). The second major category of plankton is the phytoplankton—protists that photosynthesize. These are all quite small, ranging in size from individuals about 2 microns across to cells connected in chains that are barely 1–2 millimeters (0.04–0.08 inches) long. Floating seaweeds such as *Sargassum* are an occasional, much larger photosynthetic addition to the photosynthetic plankton. The animal plankton are called zooplankton. They range enormously in size from heterotrophic protists only 2 microns long to jellyfish that can reach 1 meter (39 inches) or more in diameter.

Within the last two decades, technological breakthroughs in analyzing the presence and role of microscopic plankton have revolutionized our understanding of the community of organisms living in the surface waters of the sea. Forty years ago, marine biologists felt that they had a reasonable grasp as to how plankton were distributed and how oceanic food webs operated; it is now clear that these phenomena are much more complex than originally thought. Plankton are not distributed uniformly across the oceans—their abundance is notoriously patchy—and many of the most significant plankton, in terms of productivity, are among the smallest in size.

Bacteria and Cyanobacteria

The role of bacteria and cyanobacteria in the marine planktonic community has, until recently,

Size category	Size range	Examples
Megaplankton	20–200 cm	Floating seaweeds, larger jellyfish, and siphonophores
Macroplankton	2–20 cm	Krill and other euphausiids, arrow worms, and smaller jellyfish
Mesoplankton	0.2–20 mm	Copepods, salps, ctenophores (comb jellies)
Microplankton	20–200 μm (microns)	Diatoms, dinoflagellates, colonial cyanobacteria
Nanoplankton	2–20 μm	Coccolithophorids, cryptomonads, and silicoflagellates
Picoplankton	0.2–2 μm	Unicellular cyanobacteria and bacteria
Femtoplankton	0.02–0.2 μm	Unicellular bacteria

CATEGORIES OF PLANKTON BASED ON SIZE

been vastly underestimated. Using finer filters to sieve ocean water has revealed that much of the planktonic community had simply been slipping through traditional nets and filters. These previously elusive smaller forms are called picoplankton (0.2–2 microns across). Most are bacteria or cyanobacteria. Actual numbers of these organisms and their productivity can now be estimated using sophisticated microscopic and biochemical techniques.

In the open ocean, the planktonic bacteria—bacterioplankton—are small and unattached. In estuarine regions, the bacterioplankton tend to be larger and are commonly attached to particles suspended in the water column. Some of the floating bacteria are heterotrophic: they rely on dissolved organic substances as their food source to provide both their energetic and material needs. Much of the organic material they absorb originates from phytoplankton that "leak" these chemical compounds. Cyanobacteria and some bacteria are autotrophic—they are photosynthetic—and supplement the primary productivity of the larger phytoplankton. A group of photosynthetic bacteria called the prochlorophytes are, in fact, the most abundant photosynthetic organisms in the sea. Together with cyanobacteria, these two forms can account for more than 80 percent of primary productivity in some localities, despite their small size. Cyanobacteria are particularly successful in some nutrient-deficient waters because they are able to fix atmospheric nitrogen gas rather than rely on nitrate as their main source of nitrogen. In some instances, cyanobacteria are responsible for so-called red tides (page 89).

Phytoplankton

The phytoplankton comprise protists—unicellular forms larger than bacteria—that photosynthesize. They are found singly or in simple chains or conglomerations. Together with photosynthetic bacteria and cyanobacteria, they perform almost all the photosynthesis occurring in the open ocean and account for about half of the planet's entire primary productivity (and hence half of the planet's oxygen production).

The net plankton—those forms trapped in traditional nets with 64-μm mesh—comprise microplankton and larger-size categories. Diatoms and dinoflagellates are the major phytoplankton component of the net plankton. Diatoms comprise a frustule, or external skeleton, containing silica. As nonmotile protists, they are commonly abundant in the nutrient-rich waters of temperate and polar regions where upwelllings occur.

Their skeletal remains accumulate on the seafloor to form diatomaceous ooze (page 36). Dinoflagellates, characterized by two flagella (whiplike structures) that enable locomotion, are more common in warmer waters. In the tropics and subtropics, they commonly replace diatoms as the main component of the microplankton.

Among the nanoplankton (smaller than net plankton), coccolithophorids are often the dominant component. More common in oceanic than coastal waters, they are named after the calcium-carbonate plates—coccoliths—that form their exoskeleton. These exoskeletons settle on the seafloor when the protists die and form very extensive chalky deposits—the world's largest stores of carbon extracted from the carbon dioxide of the atmosphere (page 79).

The phytoplankton are photosynthetically active only within the depth of substantial light penetration—the top 650 feet (200 m) of the ocean at most. Their productivity is limited primarily by the availability of nitrates, to a lesser extent phosphates, and sometimes iron. Phytoplankton are the main source of organic food for oceanic food chains. All the animals of the open ocean, from zooplankton to the largest creatures, depend directly or indirectly on phytoplankton for their food supplies. Humans, too, in harvesting the oceans, are dependent on phytoplankton productivity.

Zooplankton

Where upwellings bring water from the ocean depths, nutrient levels are high and, if sunlight is available, sustain rapid phytoplankton growth and multiplication. Herbivorous zooplankton feed on the phytoplankton and themselves form the food supply for larger zooplankton. These, in turn, sustain a food chain comprising predators of increasing size: fish and squid, seabirds, and marine mammals. Feces and animal remains, often forming small diffuse clumps evocatively called marine snow, sink to the ocean floor and provide food for bottom-dwelling animals and for a range of midwater creatures (page 94).

Zooplankton are grouped into two main categories: the holoplankton are those forms that spend their entire lives in the plankton community; meroplankton, on the other hand, spend only part of their life cycle as plankton, commonly as

larvae. Familiar animals such as barnacles, crabs, lobsters, and sea urchins have meroplanktonic larvae that bear little or no resemblance to their adult forms. Shallow waters may be dominated by these larval forms at certain times of the year. The planktonic larvae enable otherwise sessile forms, such as mussels and barnacles, to spread their offspring far and wide to colonize new habitats.

Microscopic phyto- and zooplankton are consumed by moderate-size zooplankton (mesoplankton) such as copepods, larvaceans, and salps. Larger predatory zooplankton that form part of the macroplankton include krill and other euphausids, arrow worms (chaetognaths), and the smaller jellyfish. These predators can markedly affect the composition of the rest of the plankton community. High densities of jellyfish, for example, are implicated in removing fish larvae and affecting stock recruitment in certain years (page 198).

The zooplankton community exploits a diverse range of feeding mechanisms to sift, sort, or grasp a meal from the floating soup of plankton. The abundant copepods—small crustaceans—use hairy limbs to sweep phytoplankton toward their mouthparts, but they can also selectively target small, slow-moving zooplankton. Salps and larvaceans filter seawater through gelatinous structures to extract phytoplankton. Jellyfish and siphonophores immobilize and capture prey using their stinging tentacles. Arrow worms are small nondiscriminating predators that usually use a wait-and-dart policy to grasp passing prey. Anchoveta and herring strain seawater through their gill arches to sieve out phytoplankton and zooplankton, respectively. The very largest creatures in the sea—basking sharks, whale sharks, and baleen whales—strain the water to extract zooplankton.

Red Tides

The term *red tide* refers to the astonishing phytoplankton blooms that accumulate on or near the sea surface under exceptional conditions. They are usually reddish brown, but they can be any color from blue to yellow depending on the main species responsible. They are usually caused by a meteoric rise in the population density of certain dinoflagellates. Red tides are of real concern for two reasons. First, when nutrient supplies are exhausted or the bloom dies for other reasons, the dead organisms decay and cause an explosion in bacterial numbers. The bacteria deplete the water of available oxygen and cause the death of other life-forms, notably fish and shellfish. A red tide off New Jersey in 1977 decimated clam and mussel beds because the shellfish were unable to escape the anaerobic conditions when the bloom subsided.

Second, the dinoflagellates associated with some red tides accumulate chemicals that are highly toxic. The most harmful of these chemicals is saxitoxin. It affects the nervous system of vertebrates but is noninjurious to most invertebrates. When zooplankton and filter-feeding shellfish such as clams, mussels, and oysters feed on the toxic dinoflagellates, they accumulate the toxin but are unharmed themselves. However, fish, birds, marine mammals, and even humans that feed on these zooplankton or shellfish are affected by saxitoxin and in some cases are killed by it. Amount for amount, the chemical is reputedly many times more deadly than strychnine or cyanide. Within the recorded medical history of the United States, saxitoxin has accounted for more than 1,000 cases of paralytic shellfish poisoning (PSP), including about 250 deaths. Blooms of toxic dinoflagellates are responsible for the closure of shellfish, crab, and lobster fisheries on the Canadian east coast at certain times of the year.

The factors that trigger red tides are not known precisely. Downwellings, where currents converge, can create accumulations of dinoflagellates as they swim upward against the current and toward the light. Organic pollution has been implicated in at least some red-tide cases. In Northwest Europe, when chemical fertilizer is used indiscriminately, excess nutrients, notably nitrates and phosphates, find their way through water courses into the North Sea, where they promote excessive phytoplankton growth. Why one species should dramatically increase in numbers—and not other species—is not understood.

Crab zoea
(Roger Steene/ENP Images)

Life in the Water Column

Between the warm, sunlit waters of the surface and the cold, lightless depths of the ocean basins, oceanographers divide the water column into somewhat arbitrary, but still useful, depth zones: the epipelagic zone, of sunlight penetration able to sustain photosynthesis; the mesopelagic zone, where sunlight still penetrates but at levels insufficient for photosynthesis; the bathypelagic zone, from 3,300 to 13,000 feet (1,000 to 4,000 m); and the abyssopelagic zone, from 13,000 feet to the deep ocean floor. Light, temperature, and water pressure all change with increasing depth, and creatures have adapted to conditions in a particular zone. Descending through the water column is a continual "light drizzle" of food in the form of fecal material and dead bodies sinking from the layers above. This flow is supplemented by vertical migrations of organisms in the column; they can be likened to a series of escalators, linking animals in one depth zone with those in another.

Features of Life in the Water Column

Light. The relative presence or absence of light is an overriding feature controlling the abundance and nature of life in the open ocean; almost all animal life depends, either directly or indirectly, on plant production in the epipelagic zone. Within the water column, animals are adapted to the presence or absence of light and to the quality of light where present. For example, many of the creatures of the epipelagic and upper mesopelagic zones are transparent or counter-shaded (paler on the bottom than on top), so they are camouflaged against the sunlight streaming through the surface waters above. In the lower mesopelagic and the bathy- and abyssopelagic zones, the eyes of most organisms are adapted for detecting blue-green wavelengths of light—characteristic of the biologically generated light of marine creatures.

Pressure. In the open sea, for each 33 feet (10 m) of depth, the pressure increases by another atmosphere. In the deepest parts of the ocean, at over 33,000 feet (10,000 m)—where sea slugs, worms, and shrimp have been found—the pressure is more than 1,000 atmospheres, or about 1 metric ton per square centimeter (14,700 pounds per square inch). Bone, muscle, and fluids of deep-sea creatures are virtually incompressible even under such high pressure, but gas-filled spaces are not. Most deep-sea animals have no air spaces, but those that do, including sperm whales that dive to 10,000 feet, have developed strategies

for regulating the size and composition of their air spaces. Those deep-living fish that have a gaseous swim bladder are able to control its internal pressure, unless they change depth rapidly: sudden and massive pressure changes, such as when animals are brought quickly to the surface, can cause fragile deep-sea creatures to be badly damaged.

Temperature. Wind and waves produce turbulent mixing that transfers heat downward from the sea's surface. In temperate and tropical latitudes, this creates a surface layer of nearly uniform temperature, extending 660–990 feet (200–300 m) deep in the open ocean. Below this, the temperature declines rapidly down to about 2,600–3,000 feet (800–1000 m) roughly corresponding to the bottom of the mesopelagic zone. Down through this temperature gradient, or thermocline, there is a marked density change at the boundary between warm surface waters and cold, deep-sea waters. This region of rapid density change forms an effective barrier to vertical water circulation, impedes the circulation of nutrients, and may also restrict the vertical movement of

Depth zones in the oceans

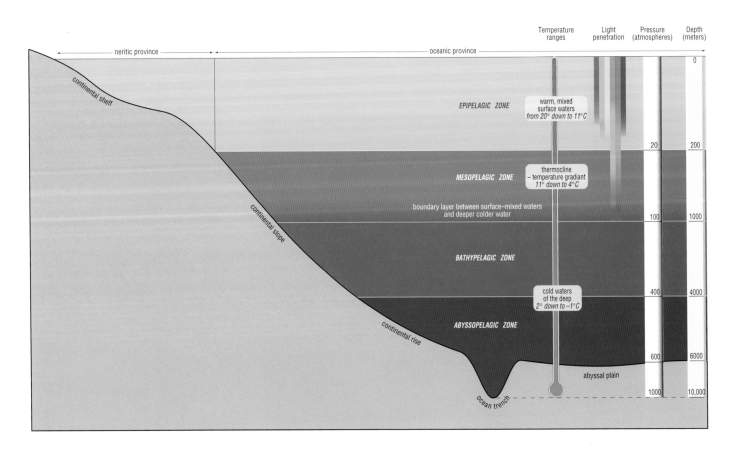

animals. Below this level, temperatures range from 30 to 39°F (-1 to 4°C). The deep sea barely gets any warmer from the poles to the equator, and it has relatively homogeneous temperatures throughout.

Vertical Migrations. Vertical migrations of animals and plants in the water column occur in many epipelagic and mesopelagic species. The organisms with diel vertical migrations (mig0rations with a 24-hour rhythm) are often responsible for the production of deep scattering layers (DSLs). DSLs, often caused by congregations of crustaceans or small fish, reflect sound and can be picked up by sonar (page 46).

These migrations may enable species to exploit favorable physical conditions and available food. Many herbivorous zooplankton ascend to the epipelagic zone near sunset and descend to the meso- or bathypelagic zone near sunrise as a means of harvesting the abundant plankton in the surface waters under cover of darkness, minimizing the chances of being eaten themselves. But these are not the only explanations for this behavior (page 98) and indeed other vertical migration patterns are common.

The Epipelagic Zone

650 FEET (0–200 m)

Also called the euphotic or sunlit zone, the epipelagic zone is the upper region of the water column in which sunlight penetration is sufficient to sustain photosynthesis. The phytoplankton community is the main source of productivity on which, directly or indirectly, almost all other oceanic species depend. The phytoplankton comprise two main single-celled forms: flagellates and diatoms (page 88). Grazing on the phytoplankton is a diverse collection of zooplankton, some of the most abundant being small crustacea. Also part of the zooplankton are the free-swimming larvae of shore- or bottom-dwelling animals such as crabs, starfish, and polychaete worms. Many zooplankton are transparent, which lessens their visibility in the sunlit waters. Some remain in the epipelagic zone; others move in and out of the zone in daily or seasonal migrations. The zooplankton sustain a surprisingly diverse range of larger creatures: from small fish such as anchovies to giant sieve-feeders such as basking sharks. Fish, squid, crustacea, and other creatures associated with the thin layer of epipelagic zone account for 90 percent of the world fisheries catch.

The Mesopelagic Zone

650–3,300 FEET (200–1,000 m)

The mesopelagic, sometimes called the twilight zone, begins where diffuse sunlight still penetrates but is insufficient for photosynthesis and extends to the limit of sunlight penetration, at about 3,300 feet (1,000 m). The light is predominantly of blue or blue-green wavelengths; many of the creatures that remain in the lower part of this zone are red or black, so they are effectively camouflaged by reflecting little or none of the ambient light. In some fish species, bioluminescence serves as a form of camouflage: when the fish is viewed from below by a potential predator, patches of light on its belly and flanks disrupt its outline against the bright background of light from above. Many zooplankton and fish living in the mesopelagic zone make daily vertical migrations, moving upward to the epipelagic zone at night to feed on phytoplankton. Many of the inhabitants of this zone, however, are carnivores or detritus feeders, feeding on dead bodies or fecal matter that sinks from the epipelagic zone.

Bathypelagic Zone

3,300–13,000 FEET (1,000–4,000 m)

Below 3,300 feet (1,000 m), there is no sunlight penetration. In the inky darkness, the only light is that produced by the animals themselves. Bioluminescence serves different functions in different species. Anglerfish have a luminous lure extending from the snout that is useful to attract prey. Lantern fishes (of the mesopelagic) intermittently cover and then reveal their bioluminescent patches, producing flashes of light, apparently to communicate between members of the species. Some deep-sea squid release clouds of luminescent fluid that may serve to distract would-be predators. Adapting to the demands of living in the deep ocean has yielded some bizarre, almost nightmarish, forms—but on a miniature scale. Most bathypelagic fish are relatively small and have puny bodies with relatively large heads, jaws, and teeth. Because of low population densities at this depth, finding a mate can be problematic: some species, such as anglerfish, solve the problem by the male, after a short, free-living phase, becoming permanently attached to the female as a miniature parasite. In the absence of sunlight, bright body coloration and bold patterning is largely redundant, and most species are uniformly red, brown, or black.

This basking shark is a sieve feeder, cruising for zooplankton in the epipelagic zone off the Isle of Man. (Jeremy Stafford-Deitsch/ENP Images)

Abyssopelagic Zone

BELOW 13,000 FEET (4,000 m)

This zone extends from about 13,000 feet (4,000 m) downward and is, in many respects, an extension of the bathypelagic zone but with even sparser fauna. The high pressure and cold temperatures limit enzyme activity and reduce the activity of fish. Within 33 feet (100 m), or so of the seafloor, there is an increase in the biomass, sustained at least in part by food creatures on the seafloor. This pelagic community is found on the continental rise as well as the abyssal seafloor and includes rattail fishes, which have been the subject of exploratory fishing in the 1980s and 1990s. Below about 19,700 feet (6,000 m) in the deep ocean trenches, pelagic forms are almost entirely absent, although there are a variety of fish, mollusks, crustacea, and worms living on or associated with the seafloor.

Life on the Seafloor

The seafloor forms the largest surface habitat on Earth. Like the water column itself, it is divided for descriptive convenience into a number of depth zones. The littoral or intertidal zone, as already described (page 86), refers to the seafloor at the edge of the sea that is intermittently covered and then exposed by the rising and falling tides. Below this, the shallow water from the edge of the littoral zone to the outer edge of the continental shelf is called the sublittoral or subtidal zone. Where the outer edge of the continental shelf breaks to become the continental slope is the start of the bathyal zone, which extends between a depth of about 650 feet (200 m) to 13,000 feet (4,000 m). Below this is the abyssal zone, from 13,000 feet (4,000 m) to the deepest depths. The abyssal zone includes more than 80 percent of the world's seafloor; it extends over the continental rise, the abyssal plain, and any ocean trenches (page 34).

The Sublittoral Zone: 0–650 Feet (200 m)

This is divided into the inner sublittoral zone—that part where there is sufficient sunlight penetration for plants to grow on the seafloor—and beyond this and extending to the edge of the continental shelf, the outer sublittoral zone that is devoid of attached plants because of lack of solar radiation.

The inner sublittoral, with the possibility of attached plants, is commonly among the most biologically productive part of the ocean. Tides, currents, and wave action stir the entire water column and thereby ensure that nutrients at the bottom are distributed to all levels. In addition, nutrients are added from runoff from land.

The type of substrate is a key factor in determining the nature of the inshore seafloor community. Sand or mud are the most common seafloor coverings on the world's continental shelves. As in the intertidal zone (page 86) the size of particles in the sediment determines the precise nature of the community. Sandy substrates in moving water tend to lack growth of seaweeds or seagrasses. In such areas, the subtidal community is quite similar to that found on adjacent sandy shores, with bivalve mollusks, annelid worms, crustaceans, and echinoderms predominating because there is little or no stable surface on which to attach. Because physical conditions are less demanding than on the seashore itself, species diversity tends to be higher in the subtidal than in the intertidal zone.

Seagrass communities (page 114) are scattered throughout the world, from tropical to temperate regions, in sheltered, shallow waters where there is a muddy or sandy floor. Kelp forest communities (page 115) are found on rocky seafloors in the colder subtidal regions of the Pacific and Atlantic Oceans. Coral reefs (page 112) flourish on shallow, rocky seafloors in those tropical and subtropical regions where waters are clear and pollution minimal.

As on a sandy or muddy shore (page 87), soft-bottomed shallow waters support a rich meiofauna (microscopic animals living within the sediment). Among the macrofauna (larger animals), feeding on fine particulate material is conducted primarily in one of two ways: deposit feeding or suspension feeding.

Deposit feeders consume organic matter that has settled in or on the sediment. Among those living within the sediment (infauna) are a range of

A coral reef on the floor of the Red Sea (Jeremy Stafford-Deitsch/ENP Images)

polychaete worms that obtain detritus and other particulate organic material by swallowing the sediment; other polychaetes use tentacles to obtain food particles from the surface of the sediment. Heart urchins, sand dollars, and sea cucumbers—all members of the echinoderms (spiny-skinned animals)—are burrowing deposit feeders.

Some deposit feeders seek food by actively moving about on the surface of the sediment; they form part of the epifauna. Among these are many forms of amphipod crustacean, plus small crabs and shrimps and a few species of brittle star. The larger shrimps and crabs are scavengers, feeding on any dead carcasses that settle on the seafloor.

Whereas deposit feeders tend to predominate in muddy seafloor communities, suspension feeders are more prevalent in sandy environments. They consume plankton and drifting detritus obtained from the water column itself. Many are filter feeders that create small-scale currents of water from which they filter suspended particles. Infaunal filter feeders include many types of clams and some amphipod crustaceans and polychaete worms. Members of the epifauna include sea pens and sea pansies—colonies formed from tens or hundreds of cnidarian polyps that together give the superficial appearance of a pale, delicate plant.

Preying on the brittle stars, clams, smaller crustaceans, polychaetes, and other suspension and deposit feeders are a range of active predators—sea stars, snails, crabs, lobsters, octopuses, and fish.

Because most parts of the continental shelf become covered with sediment, hard-bottomed shallow waters comprise a comparatively small area of inshore waters. Where they do occur, they often support a dense growth of seaweeds that compete with one another for space and light. Grazing on these seaweeds are a range of sea urchins and mollusks such as abalones, chitons, and limpets. In tropical waters, grazing fish—damselfishes, parrot fishes and surgeonfishes—are often the major grazing component of the community. Because there is little or no sediment, infauna are sparse or absent. However, a few bivalve mollusks—the rock-boring clam (*Pholas*), for example—can bore into softer rocks such as limestone and live embedded within the rock.

To combat the heavy grazing pressure, some seaweeds have developed defensive strategies. Upright brown seaweeds tend to be tough and leathery, while red and green coralline algae contain chalky deposits to deter grazers, and some species contain noxious chemicals. Living among the seaweeds, various creatures—barnacles, hydroids, sea squirts, soft corals, sponges, and tube-dwelling polychaetes—ply their trade as suspension feeders. A variety of predators feed on these and on each other. Sea anemones are sessile carnivores, whereas active predators include sea stars, some gastropod mollusks (notably snails and nudibranchs), crustaceans (particularly crabs and lobsters) and a variety of fish, octopuses, and even squids. Among the fish feeding on the seafloor inhabitants are skates, rays, and flatfish, though these tend to be more abundant on soft bottoms.

Marine biologists are coming to the view that the precise nature of a local inshore community is, at least in part, a function of serendipity. Which organisms predominate may simply be due to chance occurrences that cause one population to be wiped out—perhaps by a severe storm or a pollution incident—with larval settlement by another species occurring soon after to exploit the vacated space. Larvae settle on a "first come, first served" basis, and the component organisms of a community may simply be those lucky enough to be present at the right time.

The Bathyal Zone: 650–13,000 Feet (200–4,000 m)

Beyond the edge of the continental shelf, the soft sediment usually becomes softer still. Bottom currents are gentler, and any storm- or tidal-driven turbulence is negligible. Larger benthic animals are low in abundance, but tracks, openings, and mounds in the sediment are telltale signs of animal life. Suspension feeders—sea pens, soft corals, and sponges—can be locally abundant on the continental slope, their presence in local aggregations probably resulting from a particular combination of seafloor topography and bottom currents. Often, these aggregations harbor their own mini-community of tiny crabs and lobsters that live in and on the sessile suspension feeders. Burrowing sea cucumbers and sea stars are important deposit feeders in this part of the ocean floor.

Where the continental slope is rocky and bottom currents are faster moving, the benthic community may comprise a quite spectacular assemblage of small, colorful suspension feeders: colonial cnidarians, crinoids, sponges, and unusual, feathery-armed sea stars.

The continental slope lies within the bathyal zone; so too does the mid-ocean ridge—the tectonically active region where new seafloor is being created (page 30). On this ridge, barren rocks rise up from the surrounding seafloor sediments. In the median valley of the ridge system are found the extraordinary hydrothermal vent communities (page 116)—oases of life in the dark, barren mountain ranges that run lengthwise through the oceans.

The Abyssal Zone: Below 13,000 Feet (4,000 m)

As recently as the early 1980s, the abyssal zone was regarded as being a monotonous, unchanging expanse of sediment. In some parts of the world; however, the abyssal seafloor undergoes surprising seasonal changes. In the North Atlantic, for example, a late spring or early summer "rainfall" of detrital material sinks from the surface layers to the abyssal seafloor. This material—called phytodetritus—comprises the remnants of the spring phytoplankton bloom. It includes dead phytoplankton plus the carcasses, molted exoskeletons, and fecal material of small zooplankton. This loose, greeny brown sludge descends to the ocean floor and is carried along by bottom currents to gather in low-lying depressions and on the lee side of slopes.

Despite seasonal changes in the abundance of food supply, the abyssal zone is a place of sparse food resources. All the food matter finding its way here has had to run the gauntlet of hundreds of creatures in the surface-water and mid-water communities. The abyssal seafloor is an environment with long periods of food paucity interspersed by very occasional banquets when a large carcass—a whale or a giant squid perhaps—descends to the seafloor. Animal life is much sparser on the abyssal plain than it is on the continental shelf, and deposit feeders predominate here. The occasional sea cucumber—often with bizarre extensions of the body such as tentacles or sails—trundles over the seafloor and hoovers up the surface sediment to extract its paltry organic content. Burrow-dwelling echiuran worms sample the sediment in a circle around their burrows. Ghostly white galatheid crabs and vivid red giant prawns 12 inches (30 cm) long make occasional appearances as scavengers. The scavenging efficiency of the amphipods, crabs, prawns, and fishes is such that any large carcass is likely to be stripped to the bone within a matter of hours, with slower-moving echinoderms, crustaceans, and mollusks coming in later to finish the remaining scraps. The waste-disposal community of animals in the deep ocean is nothing if not efficient.

The Microscopic Infauna of Benthic Zones

In the sediments of the sublittoral, bathyal, and abyssal zones, the meiofauna, which are barely visible to the naked eye, and the microfauna, the animal-like protists, are just as important as they are in the littoral zone. These tiny animals, together with bacteria, have a significant role to play, not least in recycling nutrients and acting as food items for larger creatures. Their small size and relative inaccessibility (and therefore high costs to investigate) has meant that only recently have they been receiving scientific attention. An entirely new major taxonomic group—the phylum *Loricifera*—was established as late as 1983, based on tiny animals found in sediment from various parts of the North Atlantic, and from the Coral Sea in the Southwest Pacific.

Life in Mid-Water

The mid-water or mesopelagic zone at 660–3,300 feet (200–1,000 m) depth is the twilight world of the oceans, where there is a hint of sunlight, but it is not sufficient to sustain the photosynthesis of phytoplankton or seaweeds. In this dimly lit environment lives a shifting community of animals that hunt and are hunted. Many mesopelagic fish and zooplankton enter and leave this zone during their daily vertical migrations (page 98), spending part of their time in the surface waters where they feed on phytoplankton or on each other. Others remain in the mesopelagic zone and wait for dead bodies or fecal material to fall to their depth through the water column; others lie in wait for prey to come within reach. This eat-and-be-eaten world has produced many creatures that are subtly camouflaged in the flickering back-cloth of light that penetrates from the surface.

It is in the mesopelagic zone that both the thermocline (the major vertical temperature gradient) and the oxygen minimum layer are found. Organisms that undergo vertical migrations here commonly experience dramatic changes in temperature with depth. Particulate material, especially fecal pellets, tend to accumulate at depths in the range 1,300–2,650 feet (400–800 m), where this material is neutrally buoyant at ambient temperatures and pressures. This rich food source is broken down by bacteria but is also consumed by zooplankton that tend to congregate there. High levels of decomposition and animal respiration deplete the available oxygen, creating measurable layers in the water column where oxygen levels are minimal.

The Zooplankton Community

As in the sunlit surface waters, major components of the mid-water zooplankton community include crustaceans—euphausids, copepods, and shrimps, many of which are herbivorous or omnivorous—and also detritus feeders. However, unlike their epipelagic cousins, the mesopelagic species often have light-emitting organs (photophores). Other invertebrate members of the zooplankton community include predators—notably arrow worms, jellyfishes, and ctenophores (comb jellies).

Squid

Squid are a prominent feature of the mesopelagic community. Some are poor swimmers and are regarded as part of the plankton; others are quite

mobile and form part of the truly pelagic community, the nekton. Like other denizens of this depth zone, they often have photophores. These are arranged in patterns according to species and are used to break up the surface outline of the individual; they are probably used for communication between individuals of the same species as well.

The Fish Community

The mesopelagic zones of the world's oceans harbor 1,000 or so species of fish in total, and many of the species are very widely distributed. The largest fish that frequent this depth zone are only about 6.6 feet (2 m) in length. Remarkably, most of the fish are only 1–10 inches (2–25 cm) long. These include many of the stomiatoids, such as bristlemouths, and the myctophids, or lantern fish. Bristlemouths—with their serried rows of sharp teeth—are found in all oceans, and one species (*Cyclothone signata*) is arguably the most abundant fish in the world, outnumbering even the sardine or anchovy. Lantern fishes (*Myctophum*) and bristlemouths together make up 90 percent or more of the mid-water fish catch taken by some research trawlers.

Stomiatoid fish such as *Cyclothone* typically have elongate bodies, photophores arranged in horizontal rows, and large jaws armed with numerous needlelike teeth. Like many other mesopelagic forms, they are opportunist feeders, taking whatever comes their way, and so they rarely let a prey item escape, however large. Some of the deeper-living stomiatoids have the capacity to unhinge their jaws, which, combined with a distensible gut, is able to accommodate prey that is larger than the fish itself. Stomiatoid fish generally feed on zooplankton, squid, and other fish.

Lantern fish, so-called because of the arrangement of photophores on flanks and underside, undergo diel vertical migrations, sometimes even reaching the surface waters, where they feed on planktonic crustaceans and arrow worms. In turn, they become prey items for fast-moving squid, tuna, and even porpoises. Some lantern fish have light organs mounted in the head region that they appear to use as headlights for illuminating prey. In some species, the males have light organs mounted on the dorsal surface, whereas the females do not, suggesting that the differences may be important in sex recognition at mating time.

Hatchet fish (*Argyropelecus*)—another common group—show some of the most striking

adaptations of mid-water fish. Compressed in the vertical plane, seen from below they present a very narrow silhouette to a potential predator. Their remarkable light organs are half-silvered and not only break up the outline of the fish, but also help the fish to match the background light levels when it is viewed from different angles. The fish's silvered sides and dark dorsal surface add to this effect by providing countershading against the light from above. Finally, hatchet fish have large upwardly directed eyes and cavernous jaws to locate and then capture prey items floating or swimming above the fish. Their eyes have yellow filters enabling them to distinguish, to some extent, between background light and bioluminescence, thus partially overcoming the defensive camouflage of some bioluminescent prey.

Mesopelagic Adaptations

Common adaptations among hunters in the mesopelagic zone are sensitive eyes and other light-detecting organs that perceive outlines and movement at low light levels. Typically, such devices are a hundred times more sensitive to light than human eyes. Predators and prey tend to adopt camouflage strategies that involve body transparency, or color patterns and photophores that break up the body outline, or, as in the case of hatchet fish, a body flattened from side to side to yield only a narrow silhouette when viewed from below.

Creatures living in the upper part of the mesopelagic, where light intensities are higher, are more likely to be transparent. Zooplankton that penetrate the deeper levels of the mesopelagic are commonly orange, red, or purple, but in the blue-green background light are perceived as black or inconspicuous gray. Some mesopelagic fish have elongate bodies, which may be a means of extending the length of the lateral line—a vibration-detecting organ—thereby raising sensitivity for detecting predators or prey.

Most mid-water animals are bioluminescent. This ability has evolved many times by different mechanisms. Some organisms, such as the lantern fishes and bristlemouths, produce their own light utilizing specialized tissue adapted for this purpose. Others, such as certain species of cod, harbor light-producing symbiotic bacteria that are cultivated inside special light organs. Whatever the precise mechanism, biologically generated light is produced within living cells by the oxidation of organic compounds called luciferins under the action of the enzyme luciferase. Energy is released in the form of light rather than heat: bioluminescence is cold light. In some creatures, particularly jellylike zooplankton such as jellyfish and ctenophores, the reactions occur in scattered cells called photocytes. In others—particularly fish and squids—light-producing photophores are employed. Blue or green and, less commonly, yellow are the customary colors of bioluminescent light.

Bioluminescence serves a variety of functions. As described earlier, photophores can be used by fish and squid as a form of camouflage to break up the body outline and as counterillumination to match background light levels. Some lantern fish probably used light organs to improve visibility when seeking prey. In at least some fish, the location and pattern of light flashes is most likely used to communicate between individuals within a species and to distinguish between sexes and aid in selecting a mate. Many creatures use bioluminescence for defensive purposes: large gelatinous animals such as jellyfish, ctenophores, and salps produce an

explosive burst of bioluminescence across the body when disturbed. This presumably serves to blind or distract the predator temporarily. Some jellyfish, ctenophores, and squid shed luminescing tentacles when attacked. A few squid and octopuses produce bioluminescent ink to dazzle and confuse attackers while they escape under cover. Some zooplankton—particularly copepods, ostracods, and shrimps—squirt a bioluminescent fluid as defense.

In many parts of the ocean where bacteria and krill congregate in high numbers to feed on suspended particulate material, their metabolic activities deplete the water of available oxygen, thereby creating the oxygen-minimum layer. Those organisms that exploit the detritus in this layer or feed on other organisms found there must cope with low oxygen levels. The fish, krill, and shrimp associated with this layer characteristically have large gills and blood that is highly efficient at absorbing any available oxygen. Typically, such animals are also sluggish and adopt a wait-and-dart policy rather than actively hunting for prey. This way, they conserve energy and

reduce their oxygen requirements. Their skeleton and musculature is reduced, and they lack any streamlining. Body shape and form is subordinated to the need to remain floating in the water column with the minimum of muscular effort. Fish inhabiting this layer have often lost the swim bladder normally used to regulate buoyancy when changing depth.

Many of the creatures that remain in the oxygen-minimum layer for any length of time are nonmigrators—they do not form part of the daily vertical migrations. Many mesopelagic forms do, however, make these daily migrations and have suitable adaptations to enable them to do so. They must withstand considerable temperature and pressure changes. Some hatchet fish experience a 50°F (10°C) temperature change and a pressure differential of 50 atmospheres in a single 1,650-foot (500-m) ascent or descent within the space of an hour or so. In the case of migrating fish, they have well-developed bones and muscles for swimming, plus a functional swim bladder that is used to regulate buoyancy during ascent and descent.

Life in the Deep Sea

The bathypelagic zone, that part of the water column that is between 3,300 and 13,000 feet (1,000 and 4,000 m) deep, and the abyssopelagic zone below 13,000 feet form the inky depths beyond the reach of sunlight that comprise more than three-quarters of the total volume of seawater. Some of the animals that inhabit this region are, to us, truly alien creatures—the stuff of nightmares. It is difficult for us to imagine what this world is really like. The water pressure is almost beyond comprehension—sufficient to crush any surface-living creature into oblivion.

The bathy- and abyssopelagic zones form the largest near-uniform biological environment on the planet. Throughout much of these zones, the chemical and physical environment barely changes, except for rises in pressure and oxygen concentration with depth, and subtle differences in temperature. Temperatures lie within the range 30–39°F (-1–+4°C), except for higher values in the vicinity of hydrothermal vents. The abyssopelagic bottom water originates from polar regions of downwelling (page 69) and typically moves in the opposite direction to the slightly warmer overlying water of the bathypelagic zone.

Few creatures from the epi- or mesopelagic zones choose to enter the lightless deeper zones. If they do, they are likely to encounter one or more of the hideous, diminutive carnivorous fish that live there.

In the deeper oceanic zones, biomass is much reduced compared to the more shallow zones. However, biodiversity is surprisingly great: 2,000 species of fish have been identified so far from the bathy- and abyssopelagic zones. Bioluminescence is less ubiquitous than in the mesopelagic zone (page 94), and the production of light is used less as a defensive strategy or camouflage and more as a lure or a means of communication. The creatures here sport fewer photophores than midwater species, and where present, they tend to be on the head and flanks rather than the underside. Few animals migrate vertically.

Most animals are black, gray, or red—colors that are relatively inconspicuous against dark background when illuminated by blue or green biologically generated light. Shrimps at these depths tend to be predatory, rather than the detrital feeders of the mesopelagic. Particularly characteristic of the bathypelagic zone are the hundred or so species of anglerfish, so named because the females dangle a bioluminescent lure in front of their mouths to attract prey. The lure is on the end of a rod—a modified dorsal spine—and contains light-producing symbiotic bacteria. Other groups of fish also use bioluminescent lures, but these are usually on fleshy outgrowths (barbels) below the mouth. The trend for large mouths and reduced body muscle is taken to the extreme in some fish, which appear to be little more than giant mouths with a diminutive body trailing behind. Gulper eels, for example, have massive jaws with an almost pelicanlike throat that can expand to accommodate captured prey. Bristlemouths, widespread in the mesopelagic, are also common at these greater depths. Feeding on or near the seabed are found rat-tail fishes, some of which have light organs containing cultured bioluminescent bacteria. The emitted light shines through scaleless "windows" on the flanks or underside.

In the darkness, senses other than sight come to the fore. Eyes, in many cases, have degenerated completely or, where present, are very small. Many bathypelagic fish have highly developed lateral lines (a row of tiny, jelly-filled canals running along each flank) and other sense organs, such as sensory hairs, that detect vibrations in the water. Some deep-sea shrimps have evolved enormously long antennae—several times their own length—that are touch-sensitive and detect any prey item venturing near. Most deep-sea creatures are highly sensitive to smells in the water—whether the scent of a succulent prey item, the fragrance of a mate, or the odor of detrital material.

Waiting for a Meal

The food shortage experienced in the mesopelagic zone is exacerbated further in the deeper oceanic zones. Only about 5 percent of the production in epi- and mesopelagic zones reaches the inky darkness of the bathypelagic and below. Energy-saving adaptations, important in the mesopelagic, are even more important here. Most creatures adopt a wait-and-dart policy for capturing prey or cruise slowly at a relatively constant depth. In fish, the skeleton is much reduced, with cartilage commonly replacing bone. Many bathypelagic fish lack swim bladders, and to maintain neutral buoyancy they retain ammonium (NH_4^+) and chloride (Cl^-) ions in place of heavier magnesium (Mg^{2+}) and sulfate (SO_4^{2-}) ions and pack body tissues with larger-than-normal amounts of fat or water. Most resident fish are diminutive carnivores with cavernous mouths and capacious stomachs, in some cases able to take in a prey item larger than the fish itself. A meal—large and occasional—is digested slowly at the low temperatures experienced here.

Finding a Mate

If finding prey in the deep ocean is problematic, finding a mate is potentially harder still. With individuals widely dispersed, finding a partner of the same species in darkness is tough going. Most species probably accomplish this through the use of pheromones—chemical attractants that are released in tiny quantities and are detected by individuals of the same species. Bioluminescent light patterns are also used as displays to attract potential mates. It is possible that male anglerfish find females of the same species by both smell and by recognizing the female's bioluminescent lure—each species has a characteristic configuration for its structure. How most invertebrates might accomplish mate location is not known; it is possible that a combination of biochemical, visual, and vibrational signals are used. In some cases, individuals probably aggregate in large breeding groups.

Two extreme strategies have been adopted by deep-water fish to ensure reproductive success. In some species of anglerfish the male, having found a female, bites and attaches to her body near the vent and becomes parasitic. He obtains nutrients and oxygen from her through a placentalike structure that forms around his mouth. The two individuals function as a reproductive unit and ensure that the male is always available to fertilize any eggs the female produces. Most female anglerfish are small, only 6 inches (15 cm) or so in length, with males less than a quarter this size; but females of some species reach over 3 feet (1 m).

In a very few crustacean and fish species, adults are hermaphroditic—they have both male and female sex organs. This has the great advantage that *any* mature adult of the species is a potential mate for any other mature adult. Also, during coupling, *both* members of the union can become fertilized.

Living under Pressure

Relatively little is known about the behavior of deep sea creatures, other than what can be inferred from their appearance and structure and from occasional sightings from submersibles and remote operated vehicles (ROVs). Exploring the deep ocean is highly expensive—suitable research

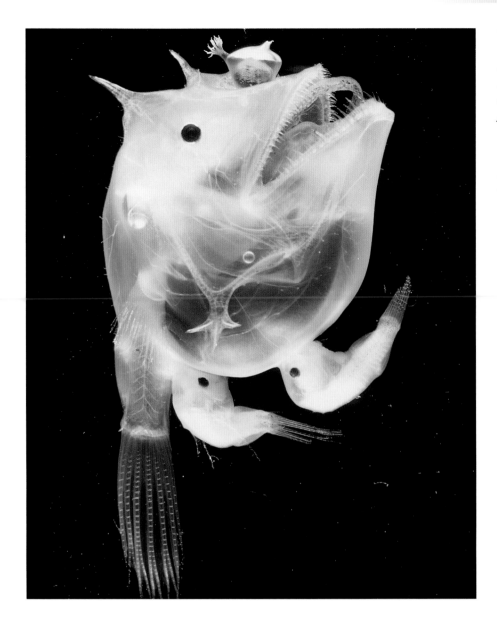

The diminutive but fearsome-looking female anglerfish. The males are much smaller and in some species, as here, they attach to the female and become parasitic, gaining their nourishment from her.
(Peter David/Planet Earth Pictures)

vessels typically cost $20,000 a day to operate. When creatures are raised from the depths, they suffer irreparable damage as a result of the pressure change. Much more will be known when the technology exists to raise these creatures from the depths relatively unharmed. It appears that the biochemistry and physiology of deep-sea organisms is probably fine-tuned to the specific depth (and therefore pressure) within the water column and this is probably a key factor in determining the vertical distribution of deep-sea organisms.

Interestingly, many of the fish inhabiting the very deepest waters and living on or close to the seafloor belong to some of the most ancient groups of fish—among them hagfishes, sharks, and rat-tail fishes. It is as though these forms have survived in only the most extreme conditions—high pressure, low temperatures, and poor food supply—and have lost out in competition with more advanced forms elsewhere.

Vertical Migrations

Since the *Challenger* expedition of the 1870s took net samples from different levels of the water column (page 53), marine scientists have recognized that many organisms in the upper levels of the sea do not remain at one level of the water column for long. They migrate up and down over a 24-hour period, most commonly descending during the day and ascending at night. This diel vertical migration (DVM) is still the subject of considerable interest and speculation. Many questions as to how and why marine creatures engage in this behavior have yet to be answered convincingly.

Daily Migration Patterns

Many epipelagic and mesopelagic creatures rise and fall within the water column in a daily rhythm that defies the simple depth boundaries imposed by scientists. Among the zooplankton community, euphausids and pelagic shrimps can migrate vertically over distances as great as 3,300 feet (1,000 m)—a truly marathon journey for organisms of such small size. Length for length, this daily return journey for a krill-like crustacean only about 1 inch (2–3 cm) long is equivalent to a 60-mile (100-km) swim for a human. Along the way, the creatures must experience a

wide range of physical differences: changes in light intensity, pressure, and temperature among them. Within the mesopelagic community, some fish and larger crustacea make daily vertical migrations at depths much greater than that of zooplankton.

Oceanographers recognize three general patterns of diel vertical migration. Nocturnal migrations are the most common type shown by zooplankton: many creatures move toward the surface near sunset and descend to deeper water near sunrise. Reverse migration is found occasionally among phytoplankton communities: individuals move toward the surface in the day and descend at night. The third pattern—twilight migration—is a double migration over a 24-hour period. Organisms rise upward at dusk, descend during the night, and then rise again at dawn to descend later to their daytime position.

Diel vertical migrations help explain the change in depth of deep scattering layers (DSLs) commonly observed on sonar traces at mesopelagic depths. Sonar traces show firm echoes (now interpreted as DSLs) appearing as a horizontal band caused by the scattering and reflection of sound waves. Although DSLs are in mid-water, they give the appearance of a false sea bottom. They were initially ascribed to physical phenom-

ena but are now believed to be commonly associated with fish and crustacea—particularly lantern fishes, euphausids, and shrimps—congregating at various depths. The DSLs often rise and fall with the vertical migration of the animals. Sometimes as many as five DSLs at different depths are apparent during the daytime, which then dissipate or merge as they rise in the water column at night. Jellyfish, squid, and smaller copepods are also found within net tows of DSLs but do not themselves show up on sonars.

The changing quality and intensity of light appears to be an obvious environmental cue in triggering the migrations at or around dawn and dusk. DSLs rise and fall in the water column with light intensity; they are deeper when there is a full Moon and a clear sky. They even respond by rising slightly when a cloud obscures the Moon or, in daytime, the sun. In darkness, ambient pressure and gravitational attraction provide depth and orientation cues. Fish can adjust their position in the water column by regulating the amount of gas in their swim bladder—removing some during

The life cycle of the copepod Neocalanus plumchrus *as it relates to water depth and season of the year off the coast of British Columbia, Canada*

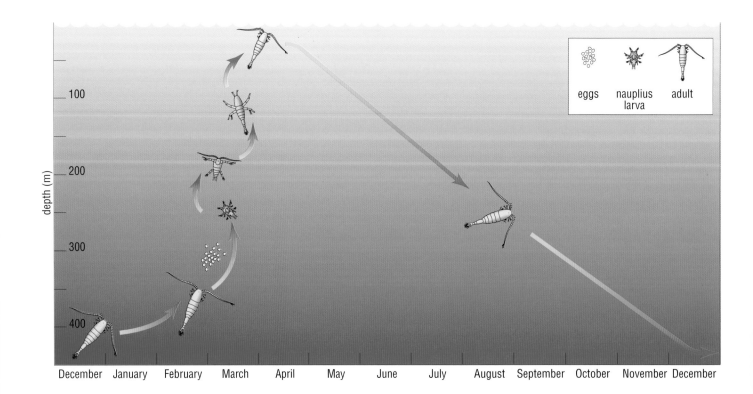

eggs   nauplius larva   adult

depth (m)

100

200

300

400

December   January   February   March   April   May   June   July   August   September   October   November   December

ascent when pressure on the bladder is decreased or adding more during descent when the external pressure rises. Phytoplankton and the smaller zooplankton alter their buoyancy—and their depth within the water column—by altering the trapped quantities of oil, gas, or certain salts. Producing trapped oil or gas will, in many cases, cause the organism to rise. Absorbing stored gas or chemically converting oil deposits will, conversely, induce the individual to sink.

Why Migrate Vertically?

Several explanations have been proposed to explain why marine animals exhibit DVMs. The different hypotheses are not mutually exclusive. It is quite possible that more than one explanation applies to the migrations of a particular species; the explanation's relative weighting varies from one species to another.

Zooplankton rise to the surface waters at night to feed on the phytoplankton that have been growing and multiplying during the day. An obvious explanation for zooplankton descending from the surface waters during the daytime is to avoid high light levels that would otherwise make them conspicuous to potential predators. However, this explanation is far from complete: many zooplankton migrate to daylight depths that are still dimly illuminated. In any case, certain zooplankton (crustacea, salps, larvaceans, and fish) that enter the surface waters at night are bioluminescent and may be visible by the light they generate themselves.

A second hypothesis is that zooplankton sink to cooler, deeper water during daytime in order to conserve energy. Metabolism (the sum total of chemical reactions within the body) is slower at cooler temperatures. Although zooplankton expend energy in swimming from one level to another, this energy consumption is probably much less than the energy conserved by remaining in cool water for a substantial part of the day.

A third possibility is that zooplankton alter their height in the water column to access horizontal water currents traveling in different directions. Zooplankton may deplete stocks of phytoplankton in a particular locality, so sinking within the water column is a means of reaching currents that can take the animals below new feeding areas, which they enter when they next ascend.

The Biological and Ecological Significance of Vertical Migration

Whatever the reasons for vertical migration, the existence of this phenomenon has biological and ecological repercussions. Such migrations and the horizontal movements that accompany them encourage the mixing of adjacent populations of the same species. This promotes genetic exchange between populations and enhances the genetic variability on which natural selection can act.

Vertical migrations also encourage the meeting of creatures from widely separated parts of the water column. The water column can be envisioned as a series of ladders or escalators, with species from one level rising and falling to meet those from other levels. Individuals may change level to seek prey or avoid predators, and in so doing their biomass is made available to different parts of the water column. When herbivorous zooplankton harvest phytoplankton in the epipelagic zone, their subsequent downward migration makes food available to lower levels of the ocean. The zooplankton may be eaten themselves or, at the very least, may release feces and excrete other materials that are potential food items. Carnivores and scavengers also undertake vertical migrations; the net effect is to encourage the descent of living biomass or of decaying material at rates far faster than would occur through passive descent. Fecal material is consumed, egested, and reconsumed several times in its descent from the surface waters to the seafloor. Vertical migrations hasten the delivery of food items to the depths and to the creatures living on the seafloor.

Seasonal Migration Patterns

Though daily vertical migration patterns are the most widespread, seasonal vertical migration patterns are also found, particularly in polar and temperate waters.

In polar regions, phytoplankton production is highly seasonal, and zooplankton are only found in the surface waters during spring and summer. They remain at depth during the polar winter and conserve their energy until food supplies are available the following year. In many parts of the world, a species's depth distribution changes with the season and corresponds with the developmental stage of the population.

So, for example, Canadian west-coast populations of a North Pacific copepod, *Neocalanus plumchrus,* lay their eggs at 980–1,300 feet (300–400 m) depth in winter and early spring. The eggs gradually rise toward the sea surface and hatch en route. Between spring and early summer, the larvae develop through several stages in the near-surface waters, their growth coinciding with the season of maximum primary productivity. In summer, the final-stage larvae descend to deeper waters, mature into adults, mate, and will later lay eggs to begin the annual cycle again. Similar migration patterns, but with different timings and through different depths, are found in copepods across the oceans.

When these seasonal migration patterns are considered together with diel migration patterns—and copepods show both—it is clear that the precise composition of the community at a given depth in temperate or polar waters changes considerably from place to place and season to season. It even differs from population to population for the same or similar species in different locations. As a general rule, the seasonal appearance of zooplankton in surface waters—either as larvae or adults—coincides with abundant food availability.

When productivity declines, zooplankton descend to deeper, cooler waters and their metabolism slows, thereby conserving energy reserves. It is also possible that changing depth with season coincides with the existence of specific currents at that time of the year. Because currents move in different directions at various depths (page 66), changing depth at a specific time may help ensure that a zooplankton population stays within a locality to crop a particular harvest. It is likely, for example, that some of the herbivorous zooplankton populations that exploit phytoplankton in the Peruvian upwelling have seasonal vertical migration patterns that are closely attuned to changing current patterns. These vertical migrations enable the zooplankton to remain within a favorable locality at the productive time of year.

The vertical migration patterns across the oceans thus present a complex picture; different species—and even different populations of the same species—express disparate patterns that may be local adaptations.

Marine Fishes I

In the shallow oceanic waters of late Cambrian times, some 500 or so million years ago, a strange, armor-plated, barely fishlike creature is clumsily swimming along the seafloor. It comes to a halt occasionally to suck up loose particles from the sediment with its oval, jawless mouth. This exotic creature, with two eyes but no fins, is covered in a flattened bony casing from head to the base of its scaly, flexible tail. This is a heterostracan, an early form of ostracoderm fish. The ostracoderms, primitive fish with bony coverings, are known only from their fossil remains. The heterostracan—clumsy, slow-moving, heavily armored—is a forerunner of all present-day fishes.

Jawless Fishes

The ostracoderms were jawless fishes. Today, the group of jawless fishes is represented by forms very different from their Cambrian ancestors. The 60 or so modern relatives are cyclostomes ("round mouths"), lampreys, and hagfishes. Adult lampreys and hagfishes are elongate, eel-like creatures that lack scales and paired fins. The cyclostomes have, to our eyes, rather unpleasant feeding habits. The adult lamprey is parasitic. It attaches by its sucking mouth to the surface of a host fish and uses its rasping tongue to cut into the flesh. It then sucks out body fluids and soft tissues and may severely weaken the fish, leaving a wound that can be fatal. Hagfishes are scavengers that burrow into dead or dying prey and consume the internal body parts.

All hagfishes are marine. Lampreys include both marine and freshwater species, but all spawn in freshwater and yield eggs that hatch into larvae that become filter-feeders, which inhabit small burrows in streams. The larvae of marine species metamorphose (undergo rapid, radical change) in freshwater but then migrate to the sea to complete their development. The sea lamprey, *Petromyzon marinus,* became landlocked in the Great Lakes above Ontario in the 1910s following deepening of a freshwater connection to the

Epaulette shark (Hemiscyllium freycineti)
Papua New Guinea
(Jeremy Stafford-Deitsch / ENP Images)

sea. Overfishing coupled with lamprey infestation caused a collapse of many trout fisheries by the 1950s and 1960s. A trout restocking program combined with control measures to reduce lamprey numbers is gradually reestablishing many of the fisheries.

Jawed Fishes

From the jawless fish of Cambrian times evolved two lines of descent of presently much more successful fish: the Chondrichthyes (cartilaginous fishes) and the Osteichthyes (the bony fishes). These exhibited two major evolutionary advances that heralded their success as fast-moving predators in the ocean realm. The first, unsurprisingly as their names imply, was the development of true jaws. The cartilaginous and bony fish have jaws that have evolved from part of the skeletal framework that supports the gills. Jaws enable fish to bite and chew rather than simply to suck or filter. The second major advance was the development of paired fins, found as a single pair in some later ostracoderms. Modern fish usually have two pairs of lateral fins: pectoral fins at the shoulder and pelvic fins near the vent that expels solid waste. These fins have enabled jawed fishes, particularly modern bony fish, to adopt a wider range of body shapes while still retaining good maneuverability and balance. These paired fins were, in time, to evolve to become the paired limbs that amphibians and, later, reptiles and mammals used and still use to walk about on land.

Cartilaginous Fish

Sharks, dogfish, skates, rays, and chimaeras belong to the vertebrate class Chondrichthyes (the cartilaginous fishes), which has about 800 living members. The members of this group have skeletons composed entirely of cartilage, rather than of bone, a curious feature, as their ancestors were bony. Unlike modern bony fish (see page 102), which have advanced osmoregulatory capacities (the ability to control the body's salt/water balance), cartilaginous fish have been much less successful at invading freshwater; almost all are marine. Sharks, dogfish, skates, and rays belong to the subgroup Elasmobranchii (the elasmobranchs). The 30 or so chimaeras or ratfishes (subgroup Holocephali) are an assemblage of rather bizarre-looking, often deep-water fish whose features bear resemblances to both elasmobranchs and present-day bony fish.

Most sharks are elegant fast-moving swimmers. They progress by sinuous waves of the body and, being denser than water, they must swim forward to counteract sinking. Their tail has a larger upper (dorsal) lobe that drives the tail downward and the head upward when swimming. The wedge-shaped head and flattened pectoral fins act similarly to airfoils to provide lift.

The elasmobranchs are covered in a tough, sandpapery skin embedded with numerous, toothlike placoid scales. The scales are, in fact, similar in structure to teeth and are highly abrasive.

Sharks have a formidable array of sensory equipment. Sharks' sense of smell is legendary—and justifiably so: they can detect chemicals at concentrations of one in a billion or less—equivalent to less than a single drop of blood in a bathful of water. They have a well-developed lateral line system that detects vibrations in the water, such as those generated by distressed fish. On the head are located ampullae of Lorenzini—sensors that detect bioelectric fields. With these they can, for example, detect the perfectly normal bioelectrical activity of prey fish buried in sand. The eyesight of sharks is poor to moderately good (depending on species) and is employed at medium to close distances.

The sharks have a notorious reputation as aggressive predators, but many are more scavengers and rather less active hunters. Of the nearly 250 species of sharks, about 25 have been strongly implicated in shark attacks of humans. Statistically, the chances of being attacked by a shark—unless you go out of your way to frequent dangerous, shark-infested waters—are much less than being struck by lightning. Many larger sharks feed almost exclusively on fish, although some species, notably the great white shark, *Carcharodon carcharias,* will also take marine mammals, such as seals. Those sharks that choose to live on or close to the seafloor feed on mollusks and crustaceans as well as fish. The two largest sharks—the basking shark, *Cetorhinus maximus,* and the whale shark, *Rhincodon typhus*—are not predatory but are gentle filter feeders, straining plankton from the water by using modified gill structures. The whale shark, at 49 feet (15 m) long, filters more than 260,000 gallons (1 million l) of water in an hour.

Most skates and rays live on the seafloor, and their shape is an adaptation to their bottom-living habit. They have greatly enlarged pectoral fins that act almost like underwater wings. Water is taken in through spiracles on the top of the head to prevent fouling of the gills by sediment. The majority have crushing teeth that are adapted to pulverize the benthic crustaceans, mollusks, and echinoderms, which are their main food source. The large manta rays (*Manta*), however, are plankton feeders. In stingrays (Dasyatidae and Urolophidae), poisonous spines on the tail are used as a defensive weapon. Electric rays (*Torpedo*) have modified dorsal muscle blocks that can generate a high-amperage electric current with a power output of several kilowatts; sufficient to deter predators and to stun small prey fish.

Sharks, skates, and rays have adopted a strategy of producing low numbers of offspring and investing reasonably large amounts of energy in each. In all species, coupling occurs and eggs are fertilized internally, sperm being delivered via the male's modified pelvic fins, called claspers. In some species, a few relatively large eggs are laid; in others, the young complete their development within the uterus of the female and are born live.

The diversity of species of cartilaginous fish has declined since the Permian period 250–300 million years ago, but they nevertheless represent a group that is supremely well-adapted to a predatory or scavenging life in the sea. Sharks, long feared by humans, are now under threat of overexploitation for their skin, fins, and meat. They are also caught inadvertently in large driftnets laid out to harvest squid. The preservation of shark stocks is fast becoming a major conservation issue. Because they mature slowly and produce few young, they are particularly vulnerable to overharvesting.

The head of a great white shark, south Australia (Jeremy Stafford-Deitsch)

Marine Fishes II

Bony Fish

Cartilaginous fish (page 100) are successful; bony fish are supersuccessful. Thanks to their versatile anatomy and physiology, bony fish have diversified to exploit almost every aquatic environment on the planet from frozen seas to hot springs and from sun-baked rock pools to the deepest ocean trenches and lightless caves. The largest group of bony fish, the ray-finned fishes (Actinopterygii), have been particularly successful with some 21,000 species. Their fins are supported by thin bony rays. Almost all of these are modern bony fish, the teleosts (Teleostei), that have lightweight, flexible scales. The lobe-finned fishes (Sarcopterygii) have fleshy fins supported by limb structures and are today represented by only seven species: six lungfish and the coelocanth (*Latimeria*). Modern lobe finned fish are of particular interest because they provide insight as to how amphibians—the first terrestrial vertebrates—probably evolved from lobe-finned ancestors that first set "fin" on land during Devonian times (some 355–410 million years ago).

The diversity of teleosts in the sea is almost comparable with the staggering range of insect life on land. The range of feeding mechanisms, body forms, and reproductive strategies among teleosts is astonishing. Herring are filter feeders, parrot fish bite off chunks of coral, and barracuda are active predators; moray eels are snakelike, stonefish look like lumps of rock, and puffer fish can inflate themselves to an almost spherical shape. Whereas cartilaginous fish lay few eggs or bear live young, teleosts produce numerous eggs at a single spawning and in almost all species they are fertilized externally.

Several evolutionary innovations lie at the heart of the bony fish success story. The swim bladder, an outfolding of the pharynx or throat region, probably evolved from a lunglike structure. It is a gas-filled space whose pressure can be altered, thereby affecting the overall buoyancy of the fish. Changing the gas pressure within this structure enables the fish to be neutrally buoyant at a given level in the water, thereby avoiding the need to swim actively to maintain position. This has great energy-saving benefits. A remarkable system of blood vessels— the *rête mirabile* (French for "marvelous net")—is able to concentrate gas in the swim bladder while minimizing the gas concentration in the bloodstream. As a result, a fish at 8,000 feet (2,400 m) depth has a swim bladder gas pressure of 240 atmospheres, while the partial pressure of oxygen in the fish's blood remains at only 20 percent of atmospheric pressure—in other words, 0.2 atmospheres. In some forms, the swim bladder has been retained as a lung to breathe atmospheric air rather

Comparison of the features of cartilaginous fish and bony fish

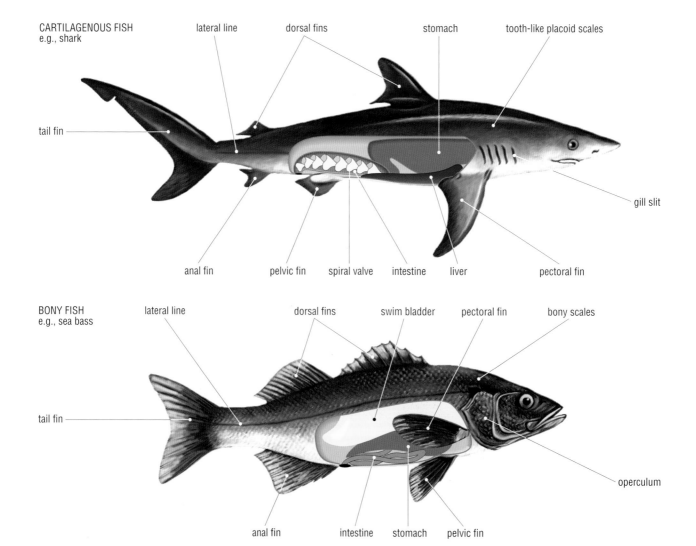

CARTILAGENOUS FISH
e.g., shark

lateral line · dorsal fins · stomach · tooth-like placoid scales

tail fin

gill slit

anal fin · pelvic fin · spiral valve · intestine · liver · pectoral fin

BONY FISH
e.g., sea bass

lateral line · dorsal fins · swim bladder · pectoral fin · bony scales

tail fin

operculum

anal fin · intestine · stomach · pelvic fin

KEY DIFFERENCES BETWEEN CARTILAGINOUS AND BONY FISH

	Cartilaginous fish e.g., shark or ray	A teleost bony fish e.g., herring or sea bass
Skeleton	composed entirely of cartilage	composed partly of bone and partly of cartilage
Paired fins	have limited range of movement	have greater range of movement, and can usually be rotated to act as brakes
Gill system	five gill slits visible at either side in the pectoral region	single gill flap (operculum) visible at either side
	parallel flow system (blood and water flowing in *same* direction)— *less* efficient at exchanging gases	countercurrent flow system (blood and water flowing in *opposite* directions)— *more* efficient at exchanging gases
Tail (caudal)	usually asymmetrical with upper lobe larger than lower lobe	usually roughly symmetrical with upper and lower lobes of equal size
Swim bladder	absent. Other methods must be employed to maintain buoyancy. The fish must keep swimming to maintain lift	customarily present. Used to regulate buoyancy when altering depth in water column
Skin	covered in toothlike placoid scales	usually covered in bony scales
Intestine	short, but with spiral valve to increase surface area for absorption	long to provide large absorptive surface. No spiral valve

The high potency of the salt-pumping mechanisms in gills coupled with the excretion of regulated quantities of water or salt through kidneys has meant that bony fish have been able to colonize freshwater—a medium with a much lower salt concentration than seawater (page 54). A few fish, including salmon and eels (page 108), migrate between the seawater and freshwater environment as part of their life cycle.

Some fish, most notably the freshwater lung fishes, have retained functional lungs or other arrangements for obtaining oxygen from the air. It is not hard to imagine that some air-breathing, lobe-finned fishes, using their pelvic and pectoral fins to crawl about on land, became the forerunners of the first terrestrial vertebrates. In fact, even some modern fish that are not closely related to lobe-finned fishes—mudskippers (*Periophthalmadon*) and eels (*Anguilla*) among them—do leave the water and hop, crawl, or slither about on land for periods of hours or days.

Unlike cartilaginous fish, which tend to produce relatively few eggs, most bony fish produce eggs in vast quantities. In most cases, these are fertilized outside the female. Individuals of oceanic species may produce many thousands or even millions of eggs at a single spawning, and these float up to the surface waters, where they form part of the plankton. Coastal species tend to be less profligate and release fewer eggs, which are usually quite large, may be buried in sediment or attached to weed, and, in the case of some inshore species, are guarded by an adult male. The astonishing diversity of fish life on coral reefs is mirrored by the range of their reproductive behaviors; some fish can even change sex when the need arises (page 113).

Bioluminescence (page 94), the production of highly dangerous toxins, the existence of fish that can travel widely between different depths and salinities, and even the ability of so-called flying fishes (Exocoetidae) to glide above the sea surface are some of the evolutionary responses that testify to the extraordinary adaptiveness of the bony fish design.

than relying solely on the gills to extract oxygen from water.

Unlike the moderately flexible paired fins of cartilaginous fish, teleost fins are highly maneuverable for fine control of body movement. In relatively slow-swimming teleosts, the bulk of the body flexes during swimming movements, but this induces side-to-side movements of the head that would generate considerable drag at higher speeds. Thus, fast-swimming predatory fish such as tuna, marlin, and swordfish generate the bulk of their propulsive thrust from the caudal (tail) fin with relatively little body movement.

The gills of teleost fish form a highly efficient gas exchange surface for absorbing oxygen for respiration and excreting waste carbon dioxide. In bony fish, the gills are protected by a movable flap called the operculum. In some fish, the exhalent current of water from beneath the operculum has had 85 percent of its oxygen removed, a testament to efficiency of these gills as a gas-exchange system.

Marine Reptiles and Seabirds

Marine Reptiles

Reptiles evolved on land and are fairly ill-suited to marine life. Nevertheless, straddling Jurassic and Cretaceous periods, between about 90–180 million years ago, reptiles such as plesiosaurs and ichyosaurs were dominant predators in the oceans. Today, of the 6,000 species of living reptile, only about 80 live in the sea or in brackish waters. More than 70 of these are snakes. Of the remainder, the seven species of marine turtle are perhaps the best known. Two species of crocodile—the American crocodile, *Crocodylus acutus,* and the Indo-Pacific crocodile, *Crocodylus porosus*—have wide distributions in brackish water. One species of marine lizard exists—the seaweed-eating iguana, *Amblyrhynchus cristatus,* of the Galápagos Islands.

The kidneys of reptiles are unable to excrete large quantities of salt, and marine reptiles have evolved special salt-excreting glands in the head region to cope with excess salt swallowed during feeding. Such glands, located next to the eyes, account for the turtle's salty tears.

Male marine turtles spend their whole adult lives at sea and mate with females offshore. Females return to land at night to lay their eggs and are particularly vulnerable to humans and other predators at this time. Typically, about 100 leathery eggs are laid in a hole scraped in the sand, which is then covered over. The eggs hatch in about two months, and the hatchlings immediately scramble into the sea, instinctively attracted by a combination of factors associated with the sea—the quality of light, noise, and air humidity. Recent research shows that turtles navigate using an internal magnetic compass, the establishment of which can be disrupted if hatchlings are subjected to unnatural light sources when they hatch. Human communities close to nesting beaches are encouraged to shield any artificial lights that might disorient the hatchlings. Sea turtles are renowned for their marathon migrations (page 109). Several species have been hunted close to extinction for their meat and shell products, and all species are considered more or less endangered and are protected by international legislation.

Turtlehead sea snakes courting, Cartier Island, Timor Sea (Gerald Allen/ENP IMages)

Most sea snakes are truly marine reptiles and bear their young live at sea. Some species are less well adapted and come ashore to lay eggs. All marine snakes are confined to the warm waters of the Indian and Pacific Oceans and are believed to have evolved from cobralike forms from the Indian subcontinent. Some marine species are among the most venomous of all snakes, producing a toxin that is potentially lethal to humans and rapidly subdues their normal prey—small fish. Attacks on humans are relatively uncommon because most species are timid and have small mouths. The majority of fatalities are among Southeast Asian fishermen, who receive multiple finger bites from snakes entangled in their nets. Some of the more colorful species are hunted for their skins and have become rare as a result.

Seabirds

Birds, like reptiles and mammals, evolved on land. Some have adapted to life at sea, and the best adapted are now regarded as seabirds: those that depend wholly or largely on the marine environment and have suitable adaptations for aquatic life such as webbed feet for swimming or paddling, and salt glands that empty into the nostrils to expel excess salt. Nevertheless, these seabirds are still constrained by the need to breathe atmospheric oxygen. In addition, seabirds require a land base on which to nest and lay their eggs.

Of the four major orders of marine-adapted birds, the penguins (17 species) are Southern Hemisphere species and the so-called tubenoses (the petrels and albatrosses) are predominantly so. The order of birds (Charadriiformes) that includes the auks, gulls, puffins, and terns is dominant in the Northern Hemisphere. The order Pelecaniformes that contains the cormorants, frigate birds, gannets, and pelicans is the only one that is particularly successful in the Tropics.

Of the 9,000 living species of birds, less than 350 (about 4 percent) are true seabirds, despite the fact that the planet is more than two-thirds covered in seawater. However, the seabirds play a greater role than their species diversity suggests. All seabirds are, to a greater or lesser extent, predators, and most catch fish, squid, or larger zooplankton. Some seabirds are extremely abundant and as active marine predators play a significant role in certain ecosystems, particularly the most productive ones that are close to shore. Penguins, for example, are major tertiary consumers in Antarctica, feeding on fish, squid, and krill (page 202). The Adélie penguins can form breeding colonies of more than 1 million birds and can have a substantial impact on local stocks of krill and other zooplankton. One study estimated that the 5 million Adélie penguins on Lawrie Island in the Antarctic Ocean were consuming 9,918 tons, (9,000 t) of fish larvae and krill every day.

Shorebirds are important predators in estuarine and muddy-shore ecosystems. In studies of surface waters, the effects of predation by seabirds are not always taken into account; yet their impact may be considerable. Studies indicate that more than 15 million seabirds—mostly cormorants—breed along the Peruvian coastline and typically consume 2.8 million tons (2.5 mil t) of fish annually. Almost all the fish prey are anchovies, and the harvest by seabirds has been equivalent to nearly one-third of the anchovy catch taken by fishermen in recent years. Certainly, when the Peruvian anchovy fishery suffered a devastating collapse in 1972 (page 190), humans were not the only ones to suffer.

Seabirds have descended from several distinct groups, and they vary considerably in their flying ability, feeding strategies, and ability to survive in the open ocean. Among the best marine-adapted species are the albatrosses. They can spend months or years away from land, gliding on air currents, only settling occasionally on the sea surface to catch small fish.

Penguins are the seabirds best adapted to swimming and diving. Having foregone the use of wings for flight, they use them to seemingly fly underwater. The emperor penguin, *Aptenodytes forsteri*, is the deepest diving of all birds and is able to capture prey at the remarkable depth of 820 feet (250 m).

Seabirds have adopted a quite startling range of specialized hunting techniques to exploit the animal communities of surface waters and to reduce competition with one another.

Some seabirds have an uncanny navigational ability and can seek out nesting sites on tiny islands in the middle of vast ocean expanses. They probably utilize a range of navigational cues—deciphering the combination of wave patterns, winds, and currents over long distances—and use a sense of smell at shorter range. The Arctic tern, *Sterna paradisaea*, is a transglobal migrator, circumnavigating the world in its journeys between its Arctic breeding sites and its Antarctic feeding areas. By following the Sun from one hemisphere to the other, it is able to live in almost perpetual daylight.

Seabird populations are both positively and negatively impacted upon by human activities. Scavenging birds, such as gulls and terns, benefit from offal and discarded small fish dumped at sea by factory trawlers. Gulls are able to live successfully alongside humans and are supreme opportunists, traveling inland to gather food. Most seabirds, however, have on balance suffered from human activities. Where there is localized overfishing, resident bird populations may suffer. Puffin numbers, for example, have declined along North Sea coasts following intensive industrialized fishing for sand eels in the 1980s. Oil spills have a catastrophic impact on local bird populations. In the *Exxon Valdez* spill in Prince William Sound, Alaska, in 1989, an estimated 100,000–300,000 seabirds perished. Long-term pollution has a more insidious effect, and the few documented examples may be just the tip of the iceberg. The decline in brown pelican numbers on Anacapa Island, off southern California, in the 1960s was attributed to accumulation of the pesticide residue DDT in the tissues of the birds. It is likely that DDT accumulated in fish, was consumed by pelicans, and concentrated in their tissues. The DDT appeared to effect the thickness of the eggshells the pelicans produced: The eggs had thinner shells and this probably reduced the percentage of birds that were successfully hatched. In the 1970s, a rise in the egg-hatching rate was correlated with both an increase in eggshell thickness and a reduction in DDT levels (page 182). Discarded plastic waste—from fish netting to packing straps—takes a relentless toll on seabirds that become entangled or strangled.

Those birds that depend on predator-free nesting sites on remote islands are among the worst affected by human activities. In former times, they were not only hunted by humans but introduced cats and dogs were also new and devastating predators. The great auk, *Pinguinus impennis*, reminiscent of a cross between a giant puffin and a penguin, was a nonflying inhabitant of remote North Atlantic islands. By the mid-19th century, seafarers hunted it to extinction for its feathers, meat, and eggs. The entire breeding population of the short-tailed albatross, *Diomedea albatrus*, was decimated by hunting in 1922–23. Since its protection in 1957, the population has only recovered to about 200–300 birds.

Whereas some species of seabirds are among the most abundant birds in the world—Wilson's storm petrel, *Oceanites oceanicus*, being perhaps *the* most abundant—some seabirds are among the most endangered of all birds. Several tropical and subtropical species of petrel are probably represented by less than 100 individuals. Worldwide, many wildlife organizations are striving to protect breeding sanctuaries on islands and remote coastlines (page 199).

A double-breasted cormorant, found in North America, northern Mexico, and the West Indies (Gerry Ellis/ENP Images)

Marine Mammals

Marine mammals first appeared in the fossil record some 65 million years ago. Small in number but diverse in range, relatively few mammals have made the difficult but rewarding transition from land to sea. They have done so on several different occasions and from very different ancestral stocks. Cetaceans (whales, dolphins, and porpoises) are most closely related to the terrestrial hoofed mammals; sirenians (dugongs and manatees) are related to modern-day proboscideans, the group that includes elephants; while pinnipeds (seals, sea lions, and walruses) are most closely related to carnivores—the group of carnivorous mammals that includes bears, cats, and dogs. Marine mammals, like their terrestrial relatives, are warm-blooded, breathe air, and suckle their young with milk from the mother's teats. In general, those mammals that have made the land-sea transition most recently—sea otters, for example—show the fewest structural differences compared to their freshwater or land-based relatives. Those that have made the transition in more remote times—the cetaceans, sirenians, and true seals—show the most highly developed marine adaptations.

Sea Otters

Sea otters are the smallest marine mammals. They inhabit kelp beds in the North Pacific from the Siberian coast to central California, feeding on bivalve mollusks, sea urchins, crabs, and fish. They are one of the few tool-using animals: they use their forelegs to smash a hard-shelled prey against a stone. Once hunted by humans for their fur, sea otters have been protected by international agreement since 1911, and their depleted numbers have revived somewhat. Where they occur, they may play an important role in controlling populations of sea urchins that might otherwise decimate kelp forests (page 115). Sea otters, though having adapted behaviorally to a marine existence, show relatively few structural and physiological adaptations to sea life when compared to their freshwater cousins. Nevertheless, they can spend their entire lives at sea, only coming ashore in emergencies, such as during heavy storms, or to bear their young.

Manatees and Dugongs

The sirenians or sea cows (order Sirenia) are a placid group of herbivorous sea mammals; elephants are their closest land-living relatives. Sirenians are reputedly the progenitors of the mermaid myth—they are the creatures that sailors mistook for semiaquatic women.

Today, the sirenians are represented by only four species: three manatees and the dugong. All inhabit estuaries and shallow offshore areas in tropical and subtropical latitudes and are well adapted to an aquatic existence. Their skin lacks hair, except for bristles within and around the mouth. A conspicuous tail has either horizontal flukes like those of whales (in the dugong) or is a beaverlike paddle (in manatees). Sirenians graze on seagrasses and live in social groups called herds. Along with the cetaceans, they are the only marine mammals that

Breaching orca
(Gerry Ellis/ENP Images)

give birth to young at sea, but they are less adapted to diving than whales and dolphins, and they can remain submerged for only 10 minutes or so.

Sirenians reach large sizes—up to 15 feet (4.5 m) and 1,320 pounds (600 kg) in the case of manatees and 10 feet (3 m) and 925 pounds (420 kg) for dugongs—and their slowness and bulk has attracted the attention of hunters: They have been heavily exploited for their meat, skin, and oil-rich blubber. The largest sirenian, Steller's sea cow, was driven to extinction by hunters within 21 years of its discovery by Europeans in 1741. The surviving species are now protected from hunting in parts of their range, but their numbers probably remain at low levels. The three manatee species are found in localized parts of the Atlantic Ocean and associated estuaries and rivers, whereas the dugong is associated with the Indian and western Pacific Oceans. All four species are susceptible to near-shore pollution hazards, such as oil spills, and each year many manatees off the Florida coasts are injured or killed by collisions with powerboats.

Seals, Sea Lions, and Walruses

The pinnipeds (order Pinnipedia)—seals, sea lions, and walruses—comprise a group of marine carnivores that are closely related to the land carnivores (order Carnivora), from which they evolved. Like other advanced marine-adapted mammals, most pinnipeds retain only vestiges of hair: a good insulator on land, hair is much less effective in water. Highly adapted marine mammals replace hair with a thick layer of insulating blubber—subcutaneous (below skin) fat. Blubber also serves as a high-energy food reserve and provides buoyancy. Although fur seals do have a short, dense fur coat, they also possess a thick insulating layer of blubber.

The true or earless seals include some 19 species, ranging from harbor seals (Phoca vitulina) of Atlantic and Pacific Oceans to elephant seals (Mirounga) of Southern and Northern Hemispheres, the males of which can reach 20 feet (6 m) in length and 7,900 pounds (3,600 kg) in weight. In contrast to the eared seals (see below), true seals cannot rotate their hind limbs forward for movement on land. Instead, they must propel their bodies along, using their front flippers. In the water, true seals use their hind limbs in a similar manner to a fish's tail, moving them from side to side in powerful strokes.

Seals come ashore to breed and to bear their young. In most species of true seal, the young are born at an advanced stage of development, and in some species they can swim within a few hours of birth. In contrast, sea lions and eared seals are born at an earlier stage of development and spend a longer time on land before taking to the water. The greater reliance and mobility of eared seals on land suggest that they adopted a marine existence more recently than their earless relatives, the true seals.

The walrus is second only to the elephant seals in size, with males reaching a length of 13 feet (4 m) and weighing more than 3,300 pounds (1,500 kg). Walruses are associated with the shallow coastal waters of the Arctic, where they feed on bottom-living invertebrates, particularly clams, crabs, and sea urchins, which they scoop up with their lips. Adults have two large downward-pointing tusks—modified incisor teeth—that in the males are particularly large and are used for display purposes and in gladiatorial contests with rival males.

Whales, Dolphins, and Porpoises

Whales and dolphins have captured the imagination of the general public more than any other marine creatures. Their often massive size coupled with their apparent intelligence, sociable behavior, and sometime affinity for human contact inspire a mixed response of awe and kinship.

Whales, dolphins, and porpoises are cetaceans (order Cetacea: from the Latin cetus meaning "a large sea creature"). There are 79 or so species divided among two major groups: the toothed whales (Odontoceti) and the baleen whales (Mysticeti). Technically, all cetaceans are whales, but small cetaceans with conical-shaped teeth can be correctly called dolphins, and those with spade-shaped teeth are referred to as porpoises, with the name whale being reserved for larger cetaceans.

Cetacean adaptation to life in the sea is so complete that superficially they resemble fish. The body is streamlined and lacks hair, and below the skin is a thick layer of insulating blubber. The skin flexes in response to subtle changes in pressure and so reduces turbulence. This results in a highly hydrodynamic body shape that generates minimal drag during swimming. The forelimbs serve as flippers for steering, and the hindlimbs are entirely absent, although in some species tiny vestiges of the hindlimbs are still present but not visible on the body surface. The long tapering tail with its two horizontal flukes is moved up and down in the water to propel the animal forward. The skull is highly modified, with nostrils located on the top of the head to form one or two blowholes (toothed whales have one blowhole; baleen whales have two) through which the whale breathes when on the surface. Whales are often identified by the shape of the water spout when they exhale. The spout is largely condensed water from the lungs. Except for the sirenians, cetaceans are the only mammals to give birth below the surface of the water.

Most cetaceans show a remarkably gentle disposition toward humans, a fact that has often led to their undoing at the hands of hunters. Some authorities consider them to have signs of intelligence equal to those of apes. This assertion may well be overrated, and although dolphins and some other cetaceans have large brains in comparison to their body size, experiments suggest that they are no more intelligent than marine mammals such as seals and sea lions. On the other hand, the world of a cetacean is one of sounds rather than sight, and our preconceived ideas of intelligence may belittle the wide and highly adaptive behavioral repertoire of dolphins and other toothed whales. Many whale species undoubtedly exhibit strong social ties. Killer whales (orcas) show sophisticated cooperative behavior in hunting and live together in close groups—or pods—the members of which commonly stay together for life.

The 68 or so species of odontocetes, the toothed whales, include dolphins, porpoises, most of the smaller whales, and a few of the larger whales, notably the sperm whale, Physeter catodon. As their name implies (odontos is the Greek for "tooth"), odontocetes possess teeth. However, the dentition varies considerably from species to species: Some have only a single tooth, others as many as 200. Most toothed whales catch fish, squid, or larger crustaceans, although some of the larger forms, such as orcas, will take other marine mammals. Toothed whales emit high-frequency clicking sounds. They detect the echoes from these clicks and use them to build up a "sound picture" of their surroundings and to echolocate their prey.

The 11 species of baleen whales include most of the larger whales. They probably diverged from the earlier toothed whales some 30 million years ago. Baleen refers to the structure that hangs from the upper jaw in place of teeth and that characterizes these whales. The baleen is constructed of a series of comblike filtering devices called baleen or whalebone plates that are formed from coalesced hairs. The baleen plates are used to strain the water for small marine crustaceans such as krill or, in some cases, for small fish or squid.

Of the baleen whale species, six are rorquals—characterized by the presence of conspicuous grooves, or pleats, on their throats and bellies. When the whale is feeding, these allow the mouth cavity to expand enormously to take in a large volume of water. The water is then strained through the baleen to extract food items. Most rorquals have a very streamlined body form. A conspicuous exception is the humpback whale, Megaptera novaengliae, notable for its knobby head, its regular migrations (page 109), and the extraordinarily complex songs of courting males.

Many factors have variously conspired to reduce massively the numbers of most cetaceans since the 1850s (page 188). Both the smallest cetacean, the vaquita, Phocoena sinus, a porpoise that reaches only 5 feet (1.5 m) long, and the largest, the blue whale, Balaenoptera musculus, at more than 99 feet (30 m) long and the largest animal on Earth, have been driven close to extinction.

Marine Migrations

Many marine creatures migrate: they make mass movements from one locality to another on a regular basis. In some cases, these migrations are truly extraordinary feats of direction finding and endurance.

Why do animals migrate? Migration is a way of optimizing feeding to ensure reproductive success and the survival of young. It helps ensure that adults and young are in the right place at the right time to capitalize on particular food resources. This often results in different stages of a life cycle being found in different localities. For example, fish larvae need to feed on small plankton of the right size if they are to survive. The adults, however, may well need to feed at a different depth and in an entirely different geographic location. Migrations tend to be more common in temperate and polar waters because here there is strong seasonality to the pattern of productivity: in tropical and subtropical waters, seasonality is much less evident, except where there are localized upwellings.

To migrate successfully, animals must be able to orient themselves in space and time—they must "know" when to set on their migration, where to go, and how to get there. Some animals—particularly birds—show a true ability to navigate, not just to orient themselves—it is as though they have an internal map so that if they are displaced from a location, they can find their way back to a home site. But the nature of this map is not known.

How animals find their way during migration and how they know when to set out is something of a mystery *and* a marvel. Migrations often coincide with regular climatic or celestial events—the seasons of the year or the phases of the Moon, Most migratory birds, for example, put on weight and show restless behavior prior to the normal time of migration. In birds—and probably in mammals—changes prior to migration are most likely triggered by the pineal body, a region within the brain that appears to measure day length and controls annual rhythms of reproduction. This gland works in concert with the pituitary gland at the base of the brain. Environmental triggers such as changes in temperature or in the hours of daylight or a decline in food supply may precipitate the precise timing of departure. Some animals appear to have an internal biological clock that triggers migration at the appropriate time, and in many animals this clock seems to provide a time base during migration.

As to how animals know where they are, numerous environmental factors are possible cues, and not all of these will be detected by the five senses with which humans are familiar. Within the water column, cues such as the speed, direction, depth, and smell of an underwater current may be used, which to us appear quite subtle but which may be very obvious to marine animals. Creatures that live on or above the surface or that regularly rise to it to breathe can use landmarks if they are near to shore. In some cases, animals can orient using the relative positions of the Sun, the Moon, and stars, particularly where these are correlated against a time base provided by the animal's internal clock. Many creatures have been shown to contain small amounts of a magnetized iron ore—magnetite—and some at least appear to orient themselves with respect to magnetic north and can probably detect the magnetic "signature" of a locality. By cross-referencing several environmental cues, many migratory animals can pinpoint their location in ways that we can only speculate about.

The migration routes and timings of animals that live on or above the sea surface—or must rise to the surface to breathe—are usually well documented. But the migrations of creatures that spend their whole lives below the water surface are less well known. By catching, tagging, releasing, and then recapturing animals, scientists can plot migration patterns. Microchip technology coupled with satellite communicate is enabling scientists to implant small electronic transmitters in larger creatures—whales, turtles, and some birds and fish, for example—and monitor their movements by satellite.

Fish Migrations

Several commercially important fish in Northern latitudes make significant migrations across the Atlantic Ocean. One stock of Atlantic cod, *Gadus morhua*, spawns just south of Iceland. After spawning, adults return to their feeding grounds off the west coast of Iceland and off the east coast and southern tip of Greenland. Meanwhile, the released eggs—up to 15 million per female—float in the westward surface currents and hatch after two weeks. The larvae then feed in midwater, traveling on currents that will take them to adult feeding grounds. They later join their parent stock, and return with them to the spawning grounds when adult.

A few species of fish do not just migrate across the oceans: They traverse the environmental barrier between freshwater and salt water. Anadramous fish spawn in freshwater, but they grow to adulthood in the sea; they include sturgeons (*Acipenser*) and smelts (*Osmerus*). But the best-known anadramous fish are the salmon of the North Atlantic and North Pacific. The salmon grow and mature in the sea, and they return to spawn in the very same well-oxygenated rivers or streams where they began life. The journey that spawning adults make from the sea to freshwater is something akin to an assault course: They leap up waterfalls, wriggle through rapids, and do their best to overcome any human-imposed obstacles, including dams, fishing nets, and pollution. After the exhausting journey, during which the potential parents do not feed, the eggs are laid in scooped-out hollows in gravel beds, which are then loosely covered by gravel. Atlantic salmon, *Salmo salar*, may make two or three such trips in a lifetime; the seven species of Pacific salmon, *Oncorhynchus*, almost invariably make but a single journey and die after spawning.

How do salmon find their way to their spawning grounds? Circumstantial evidence suggests that the salmon navigate at sea by using an internal compass and responding to geomagnetic clues. Alternatively, or additionally, they may recognize factors such as ocean currents, which have characteristic temperature gradients and food items, and use these to steer their way to coastal waters near the river of the salmon's origin. On reaching these waters, salmon recognize the subtle chemical cues of the waters in which they were hatched, and they follow these back to the source tributary and then to their spawning grounds.

Catadramous fish make the reverse journey: They spawn at sea and mature in freshwater. Much fewer in number of species, the 16 or so species of freshwater eels (*Anguilla*) are the best-known catadramous fish. The American and European freshwater eels (*A. rostrata* and *A. anguilla*) represent two different stocks that migrate to the Sargasso Sea, southeast of Bermuda, to spawn at slightly differing, but overlapping, seasons and locations. The North American stock of larval eels drift on the Gulf Stream east and then north from the Sargasso to reach North American coastal waters within a year or so. The European larval stock travel north and then west to reach the coasts of Western Europe after about three years. On arrival in coastal waters, the American or European larvae metamorphose into young eels, called elvers. The elvers enter rivers and move upstream to spend ten years or more feeding and growing in freshwater, only to return to the Sargasso Sea to spawn and die. Experimental evidence suggests that the adults use geomagnetic clues to guide their way.

A female green sea turtle, South Pacific (Gerry Ellis/ENP Images)

Turtle Migrations

Marine turtles lay their eggs on remote sandy beaches. It is not unusual for males and females to travel over long distances between feeding and nesting sites and to return with unerring accuracy to the beaches on which they themselves were hatched. Green turtles, *Chelonia mydas,* for example, make a 1,370-mile (2,200-km) journey from the coastal waters of Brazil to the beaches of Ascenscion Island—a tiny speck in the Atlantic Ocean just a few miles wide. Here they dig a hole in the sand above the highwater mark and lay their eggs. How do the turtles find their way across the ocean with unerring accuracy? Evidence suggests that it is by sensing a combination of environmental cues—smell, detecting ocean currents, and probably sensing local geomagnetic fields.

Recent studies at the University of North Carolina provide interesting clues as to how loggerhead turtle hatchlings establish a geomagnetic sense on their journey across the beach to the sea when they leave their sandy nest. On hatching, the young turtles move towards the surf guided by the light from the Moon and stars reflected off the sea surface. Once in the surf zone, they travel out to sea guided by the direction of incoming waves. In the absence of wave motion, the turtles appear to move away from the shore guided by a geomagnetic sense. In laboratory studies, changing the direction of an artificial magnetic field caused the turtle hatchlings to alter their direction of swimming. It seems likely that, in the wild, the hatchlings' first glimpses of the sea establish their internal magnetic compass. This compass will aid them in their subsequent navigations. Artificial lights near the beach may not only cause hatchlings to move away from the sea, but also cause them to wrongly "set" their internal magnetic compasses. In such cases, even if the hatchlings are caught and taken to the sea and released, their likelihood of returning to breed later in life is probably reduced by the inaccurate setting of the internal compass. On the other hand, if the magnetic compass is so important in turtle navigation, knowing how the mechanism works may one day enable scientists to adjust the turtle's internal compass purposely and "fool" turtles into returning to different—but safer—beaches when it is their turn to nest.

Bird Migrations

The migrations of birds are perhaps the most remarkable of all. The Arctic tern, *Sterna paradisaea,* arguably the world's greatest migrator, travels through both hemispheres and back again each year—a 16,000-kilometer (10,000-mile) round trip. Chasing the summer sun as it does so, it probably experiences more hours of daylight each year than any other creature on Earth. In autumn, it leaves its nesting sites along the northern coasts of America and Europe to travel to its winter feeding grounds in the extreme southern Atlantic and Pacific Oceans. After enjoying the brief but prolific southern summer, it sets off on the mammoth return journey in the following spring. Shearwaters and storm petrels migrate long distances but in almost the opposite direction to the Arctic tern—they breed in the Southern Hemisphere and then migrate northward as the days shorten.

How do birds find their way? Experimental evidence confirms that visual cues are important. Birds recognize topographic features and over long distances follow familiar migratory routes, often using prevailing winds to assist them. It seems that the experienced migrators in a flock pool their navigational resources—their "memories" and their innate abilities—for the benefit of the entire flock. It is becoming increasingly apparent that at least some species can detect and navigate by Earth's magnetic field. Work with starlings shows that these birds can navigate by "reading" celestial cues. During the day they migrate in a particular direction relative to the sun and then adjust this position as the sun moves across the sky. They are using the sun as a compass and are modifying their response to it according to their biological clock. At night, some bird species navigate by taking into account the positions of stars in the night sky. The ability of birds to navigate, rather than just orientate—coupled with their ability to fly at speed—makes them migrators par excellence. A Manx shearwater, *Puffinus puffinus,* was recovered in Brazil only 16 days after being banded in the United Kingdom. The bird had been covering an average straight-line distance of more than 360 miles (580 km) per day.

Whale Migrations

Among the baleen whales, two species, the gray whale, *Eschrichtius robustus,* and the humpback whale, *Megaptera novaeangliae,* have truly predictable migration routes that are repeated year after year. They, and almost all other baleen whales, migrate between tropical and subtropical breeding grounds—where calves can be born in warm water away from the attentions of killer whales—and polar or subpolar feeding grounds—where there are abundant food supplies in the short but highly productive summer season. Of the baleen whales, only the bowhead whale, *Balaena mysticetus,* calves in polar seas. The migration patterns of most baleen whales ensure that, when food resources are scarce (in the polar winter), they move to warmer waters where heat loss will be much reduced and energy expenditure that much lower.

Humpback whale populations are found in both hemispheres. Those in the Northern Hemisphere feed in subarctic waters in the northern summer and then winter in subtropical waters. Those in the Southern Hemisphere feed in Antarctic waters in the southern summer and winter in tropical and subtropical waters. DNA analysis of humpbacks in Hawaiian waters—a method that enables researchers to determine the parental relationships of different generations of whales—shows that the latest generation migrates to the same feeding grounds as their mothers.

The North Atlantic gray whale population was wiped out in the 19th century. The surviving populations elsewhere are making a comeback, and the species was taken off the endangered species list in 1994. Eastern Pacific gray whales are conceived in the waters off Baja, California, and are born in these same waters some 13 months later. In between, the males and females migrate northward along the Alaska coast to their feeding grounds in the Bering Sea. The whales are unusual in feeding on amphipod crustaceans, which they dislodge from the seafloor, rather than feeding on pelagic crustacea or fish as do other baleen whales. The whales return to Baja along a similar route the following year. When a newborn whale calf accompanies its mother on the northward migration, she takes a different route—longer, slower, farther from land, and probably safer. It is an exhausting journey for her, suckling the young as she travels, and not all mothers survive the journey. For adults, unaccompanied by whale calves, the migration cycle between breeding ground and feeding ground is an eight-month, 18,000-km (11,200-mile) round-trip.

Mangrove Swamp Communities

Mangrove swamps are, in many ways, the tropical and subtropical equivalents of the temperate and subarctic salt marshes. They develop on shores where muddy sediments accumulate, and they too are often associated with estuaries.

Mangrove bushes and trees are flowering plants—land plants—that have long since adapted to living in the intertidal zone in warm water habitats. The mangroves form dense forests that are sometimes referred to as mangals. The plants have shallow roots as well as aerial (aboveground) roots that form a tangled network for anchorage, nutrient absorption, and gas exchange—the aerial roots absorb oxygen directly from the atmosphere. Perhaps one-half of all tropical shores are lined with mangroves, such is their importance. Many tropical shores are lined with mangroves that are protected from strong currents and wave action by coral reefs lying offshore. Many of the plants of the mangrove community flourish in a wide range of salinities from full salt water to the barely saline water found deep within estuaries. Mangroves have physiological mechanisms for

excluding salt from their cells or for actively excreting excess salt. In some cases, salt is excreted out of small pores in the leaves; in others, it is collected in specific locations, such as old leaves that are soon to be shed. Some mangrove plants produce seeds that germinate while still on the parent tree; when they are released, they can immediately start to grow in the close vicinity where the substrate suits their specific requirements. Other mangroves produce seeds that float; these are carried some distance away from the parent plant before they sink to the bottom and germinate.

Mangrove stands show a distinctive zonation, with species that can best tolerate immersion in seawater—such as the red mangrove, *Rhizophora mangle*—on the seaward edge, and the more terrestrial species—such as the white mangrove, *Laguncularia racemosa*—on the landward side. The muddy sediment in which the seaward mangroves grow is oxygen poor and makes a difficult environment for oxygen-requiring organisms. The mangrove trees and shrubs themselves cope by having extensive aerial roots that can absorb oxygen directly from the

Birdsong mudskippers, northern coastal Australia (Jeremy Stafford-Deitsch)

atmosphere when they are exposed at low tide. Red mangroves, *Rhizophora*, produce "stilt-roots" that grow out sideways from the tree trunk and angle down into the mud to help support the tree. Black mangroves, *Avicennia*, produce "pencil-roots" or "peg-roots" that grow upward from shallow roots and appear above the surface of the mud like a small forest of spikes, each 6–12 inches (15–30 cm) long.

As sediment and detritus—leaves and other dead plant material—gradually accumulate around the mangrove roots, so the substrate in which the mangrove grows becomes, in time, gradually more soil-like. Meanwhile more sediment accumulates of the seaward side of the mangrove community, and—unless disrupted by catastrophic weather conditions or human intervention—the mangroves gradually extend the coastline seaward, effectively creating new land. On the landward side, the mangroves may, in time, be replaced by terrestrial plants. Thus mangroves swamps often represent a stage in the ecological succession between a truly marine and a truly terrestrial community.

The Animal Community

The maze of above-water roots and shoots provides a fascinating three-dimensional world at the interface between land and sea—a unique environment. Occupying the branches of the mangrove trees is an elaborate community of terrestrial and semiterrestrial animals—spiders, frogs, lizards, snakes, bats, and birds—that consume each other, feed on the animal life in the water below, and prey on insects living in the mangrove canopy. Tropical birds, such as egrets, nest in the mangrove canopy, and fruit bats roost there. Some strange visitors to this world also emerge from the waters below. Mudskippers (*Periophthalamus*) are fish that are well adapted to intermittent life out of water. They burrow in the mud, but they also climb up mangrove roots, using their pectoral fins for support. They spend hours out of water hunting insects and crabs and breathe by taking air into their mouths, from which the gills extract oxygen. A relatively small proportion of mangrove-tree productivity appears to be consumed by herbivores above the water. The majority enters the aquatics system as plant debris in the form of detritus, which is consumed by fish and a range of invertebrates.

Barnacles, oysters, sponges, and tunicates are often abundant and find attachment to the large surface area provided by the mangrove root system above the surface of the mud. In some localities, oysters are the major contributor to the animal community's biomass. Some isopod crustaceans are able to bore into the woody prop roots that provide additional support to the tree trunk. Some polychaete worms build their tubes on the hard surfaces offered by the root system, and marine snails—the periwinkles—graze on the algal film that grows on the damp root surfaces.

In the intertidal mud around the mangrove roots are found deposit and suspension feeders—clams, polychaete worms, shrimps, and so on—similar to those inhabiting mudflats and salt marshes in temperate regions. Fiddler crabs (*Uca*) and sea cucumbers move about on the surface of the mud, the former as scavengers and the latter as deposit feeders. Other species of crabs, together with amphipod crustaceans, feed on the red and green algae—unicellular and multicellular—that grow on the mud and on any hard, stable surfaces.

As the tide rises and falls, alternately immersing and exposing bottom mud and the aerial roots of mangroves, fish and crustacea enter and leave on the tide. Stands of mangroves are often crisscrossed by water channels that provide ideal nurseries for a host of commercially important animals—shrimps, spiny lobsters, crabs, and fishes.

The subtidal community on the seaward side of mangrove swamps is a rich and diverse one. In these waters, mangrove productivity is supplemented by phytoplankton and a surface covering of algae on the muddy bottom and on mangrove roots. In some localities, turtle grass (page 114) forms a dense covering on the subtidal mud. Nearshore fish, shellfish, and various crustacea—crabs, lobsters, and shrimps—are commonly abundant and often support local fisheries. Where the mangrove roots are free of mud but are continuously submerged in water, they support a dense growth of animals and plants—algae, sponges, sea anemones, hydroids, bryozoans, and tunicates. In the mud itself, a variety of burrowing creatures—polychaete worms, shrimps, and crabs among them—disturb the surface and provide access for oxygen to penetrate the otherwise largely anoxic substrate.

The Threatened Mangroves

Mangrove communities are threatened in many parts of their wide distribution. Like other coastal wetlands, they are commonly cleared and drained for urban or industrial development. Such clearance has been particularly prevalent in Southeast Asia, such as in and around Singapore. In the Indian Ocean–West Pacific region, strips of mangrove swamp are cleared for mariculture ponds, which, though locally productive, no longer provide the nursery waters for many commercially important crustacean and fish species over the wider area. In the Persian Gulf, mangrove stands have been severely affected by oil pollution, while in parts of the Indian Ocean, pesticides washed from the land accumulate in mangrove-swamp muds and may have a deleterious effect on the local animal community. During the Vietnam War, perhaps 247,000 acres (100,000 ha) of mangrove cover was defoliated and destroyed using Agent Orange sprayed from U.S. aircraft.

Efforts are being made by several countries and international agencies to introduce mangroves into suitable areas or to reintroduce them into areas where they have been previously cleared. On a worldwide basis, however, mangroves are being removed at a much greater rate than they are being replaced. Programs to manage the exploitation of mangrove forests—on a renewable basis, with replanting—are necessary. Ultimately, stemming the tide of mangrove loss depends on raising public awareness of the economic, cultural, and environmental importance of this unique resource, particularly in those areas where the short-term gain of a few outstrips the perceived greater need of the many to maintain this underrated habitat.

Coral-Reef Communities

Coral reefs are the marine equivalent of tropical rain forests on land. They are luxuriant, complex, biodiverse—and threatened.

Coral reefs are formed by a partnership between coral polyps—individual cnidarians (animals that belong to the phylum as jellyfish and sea anemones)—and symbiotic dinoflagellates, called zooxanthellae. Each reef-building polyp secretes a limestone (calcium carbonate) skeleton, and when the animal dies, its chalky construct remains. New generations of coral grow on top, thereby gradually building massive structures—coral reefs—over hundreds and thousands of years. The living coral thus forms a veneer on the chalky foundations of once-living coral.

Growing in water that is consistently at or above 70°F (21°C), coral reefs are restricted to the tropical and subtropical regions of the world. Moreover, coral—and the zooxanthellae they contain—require high levels of solar radiation and saline waters. Corals are absent from brackish waters near estuaries and are easily smothered by sediments. Thus, breaks in coral reefs are commonly associated with estuaries. Human activities that increase the sediment load in a locality are likely to disrupt the formation and survival of coral reefs.

Coral Polyps

The partnership between coral polyps and their resident zooxanthellae is a remarkable one. Corals are able to grow in clear, low-nutrient water because the zooxanthellae provide the coral host with oxygen and nutrients as a result of their photosynthetic activities. In return, the coral pro-

vides the zooxanthellae with a home and protection, and the coral's waste products—especially ammonia and carbon dioxide—provide nutrients for the zooxanthellae. The corals obtain food by using their stinging tentacles to capture passing plankton, but zooxanthellae provide much of the coral's nutrient supplies, in some cases as much as 90 percent. In fact, when corals lose their zooxanthellae partners, as they do in some circumstances, the coral polyps die leaving dead white patches—coral bleaching—amid the living colors of the coral reef.

Some corals—the soft corals—are not adapted to coexist with zooxanthellae, and they must rely solely on filter feeding for their food supplies. They do not require sunlight for their photosynthetic partners; they also tend to be slower growing than reef-building forms and are found much lower down in the reef formation. Here they can survive in the absence of competition from their faster-growing hard-coral cousins. Soft corals, unlike the reef-building hard corals, are widely distributed throughout the world, in cold waters as well as warm.

The reef-building corals are colonies of many thousands or millions of individuals. The corals grow in size by component individuals that reproduce asexually. Individuals simply bud to produce genetically identical copies of themselves. Some colonies on Australia's Great Barrier Reef are arguably the oldest living animals in the sea: each colony has descended from a single individual, and the colony has been growing for more than a thousand years. Corals also reproduce sexually. The Great Barrier Reef coral community engages in a synchronized burst of orgiastic

spawning near full Moon during the breeding season. The nighttime waters are filled with countless tiny pink spheres—the eggs and egg-sperm bundles released by corals. Successful fertilization in the surface waters results in the formation of larvae that can survive for weeks and drift hundreds of kilometers before settling. Successful larval polyps attach themselves to a suitable, hard substrate and then can grow and start to divide asexually to form a new colony.

Reef Formations

Coral reefs are recognized by their shape and mode of formation and fall into three main categories. Fringing reefs form along a coastline and gradually extend seaward; they are common in the Red Sea and around Caribbean islands. Barrier reefs, on the other hand, are separated from the shore by a lagoon of open water and occur where the coastline next to a fringing reef is gradually sinking. As the landmass is gradually inundated, so the nearby coral grows upward towards the light to form a dense, thick barrier reef. The Great Barrier Reef off the eastern coast of Australia is the largest example of this reef form and is the biggest biologically constructed structure on the planet. At more than 1,250 miles (2,000 km) in length, with a lagoon that averages 90 miles (150 km) across, it is visible from outer space.

Atolls represent a final stage in coral-reef development on volcanic islands. Where such islands are gradually sinking, the initial fringing reef becomes a barrier reef and, finally, a coral atoll. The atoll is the ring of living coral reef at the sea surface surrounding the now-submerged island. If the rate of subsidence is greater than the rate of coral growth, the coral too will submerge beneath the waves and eventually dies at sun-starved depths. The submerged atoll becomes a seamount.

Reef Zones

In a similar manner to intertidal rocky shores (page 86), the outer edge of a coral reef typically exhibits a characteristic vertical zonation pattern. The highest part is the reef crest, also called the algal ridge, and is often marked by a line of breaking surf. The turbulence here is too great for most

Exposed live hard corals on the Great Barrier Reef, north Queensland, Australia (Roger Steene/ENP Images)

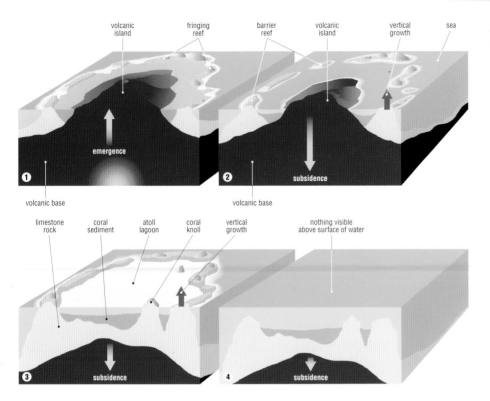

volcanic island · fringing reef · barrier reef · volcanic island · vertical growth · sea

1 emergence

2 subsidence

volcanic base · volcanic base

limestone rock · coral sediment · atoll lagoon · coral knoll · vertical growth · nothing visible above surface of water

3 subsidence

4 subsidence

The formation of a coral atoll

corals, and the zone is inhabited largely by encrusting coralline algae. Below this, the reef face or front is dominated by corals. Strong corals that can withstand surge conditions are more prevalent toward the upper part of the face, while finer, more delicate forms are more common lower down, typically extending as far as 160 feet (50 m) or so. Below these depths, the reef face often falls away near vertically as a reef cliff—the plunging "drop off" familiar to scuba divers—that is often constructed of long dead coral. Here sponges and sea whips replace the living coral surface layer.

On barrier reefs, the inner or landward edge of a coral reef commonly comprises an extensive reef flat that, being relatively protected and close to the surface, contains a rich diversity of corals. The reef may gradually give way to a coral-sand lagoon, perhaps harboring seagrass meadows (page 114). Mangrove swamps (page 110) or palm trees are commonly found on the nearby shore.

Reef Biodiversity

The myriad forms of coral and the sessile animals and plants associated with them provide a multitude of microhabitats, refuges, and food sources for animals that crawl and swim. A recent estimate suggests that about 93,000 species of organism—perhaps a third of all species identified in the oceans so far—come from coral reefs. Some animals, such as the crown-of-thorns starfish (*Acanthaster planci*) and the parrot fishes (*Scarus* species)

feed on corals directly, but many do not; instead, they use the reef as a place of attachment or refuge, perhaps feeding on the plankton and suspended matter in passing water or consuming plants and animals associated with the coral reef system.

A turf of fine algae grows on every available surface of the reef and is grazed by sea urchins and many mollusks, together with small fishes. The herbivores form the base level of a food web of carnivores of increasing size, culminating in predators such as moray eels, barracudas, sharks, and venomous sea snakes. To avoid predation, many reef animals are brightly patterned, broadcasting the fact that they are unpalatable or poisonous. The bright colors of many active reef animals serve another purpose: they enable individuals to recognize members of their own species of the same or opposite sex for the purposes of mate selection. Reproductive behavior among coral reef fish is diverse. One species of blenny lives in territorial shoals of females protected by a few males. When males are in short supply, one or more females will change sex to make up the shortfall!

Since the 1960s, the crown-of-thorns starfish, a coral predator, has devastated a number of reefs in the Pacific and Indian Oceans, although usually it is present in relatively low numbers. Parrot fish are also major coral predators but apparently are not prone to such destructive population explosions: they use their beak-shaped jaws to bite off chunks of coral, which are then crushed by plate-like teeth. The coral polyps are digested, and the remains of the skeletons are voided as sand particles, which often accumulate near reefs to form sandy sea bottoms.

An Abundance of Riches

The symbiotic relationship between corals and their dinoflagellate companions makes coral reefs the most productive parts of the ocean, despite the fact that the surrounding waters are so nutrient-deficient. Within the coral polyps, nutrients are cycled between the zooxanthellae and the polyp host with great efficiency. The result is that the primary productivity of the reef system is tens or even hundreds of times as great as that of the open ocean. Coral reefs may produce 1.5–5 kilograms of carbon per square meter per year, making them the most biologically productive ecosystems in the ocean.

Coral reefs, in conjunction with nearby seagrass meadows and mangrove swamps, create vital feeding, breeding, and nursery grounds for a wide range of marine creatures, many of which are exploited commercially. Millions of people depend, directly and indirectly, on reefs for their livelihood, and much of the potential harvest from coral reefs has yet to be realized. For example, the pharmaceutical potential of the coral-reef community is only just beginning to be tapped (page 119).

Threats to Coral Reefs

According to the World Conservation Union (IUCN), significant damage to reef systems has occurred in 93 countries out of the 109 where coral reefs occur. The threats to these often delicate communities are many and varied. Fishing using dynamite is quick and easy but wipes out several square meters of reef with each blast. Using sodium cyanide to stun fish for the aquarium trade is a relatively unselective method and may cause fish and other creatures permanent damage. Food fishing for the Nassau grouper on spawning grounds has made this once abundant fish one of the first coral species to be listed as threatened on the IUCN Red List.

Building construction and development of towns and cities has claimed many coral reefs, or parts of them. In some cases, the reefs are built on directly; in others, the corals, and their nearby coral sands, are used as building materials. Being on or close to coastlines, many coral reefs live with the actual or potential threat of coastal pollution by oil, agrochemical runoff, heavy-metal contamination, or sewage discharges, and changing land use has altered sedimentation patterns, making smothering of reefs more likely. Tourism in coral reef areas is a very mixed blessing and usually results in degradation of nearby coral reefs, except where great care is taken in managing a responsible "green" tourist industry.

Seagrass Meadows and Kelp Forests

Seagrass Meadows

Seagrasses are descended from flowering plants—true land plants—and are the only such plants to have adopted a truly underwater marine lifestyle. Seagrasses flower underwater and release their pollen, which is carried on water currents to reach and pollinate the flowers of other individuals of the same species. The seeds are dispersed by being shed into water and floating on the water currents, although in some cases the seeds are encased in fruits and are consumed by fish and other browsing animals, which then eject the seeds as part of their feces. Unlike seaweeds, which use a holdfast to secure themselves to a solid substrate, mature seagrasses have true roots that they use to anchor themselves in the sandy or muddy seafloor. They are thus much more successful than seaweeds in exploiting inshore soft-bottom areas. They can also spread outward by vegetative growth that uses specialized branching stems—rhizomes—that run under the sand and give rise to new shoots.

Seagrasses have elongated leaves similar to those of grasses on land, but seagrasses are not descended from terrestrial grasses; they are more closely related to lilies. Although seagrasses are found in the lower intertidal zone in suitable locations, the most extensive areas—appropriately called meadows—occupy the sandy subtidal zone in areas protected from ocean swell. Seagrasses are widely distributed from tropical to temperate latitudes, commonly in sheltered bays and on the lee side of islands. In temperate waters, they are often found on the seaward side of salt marshes. In the Tropics, they are commonly found in coastal lagoons or in quiet water behind coral reefs (page 112) and are associated with the subtidal regions close to mangrove swamps (page 110). There are nearly 50 species of seagrasses, most of which are restricted to tropical waters. The dominant seagrasses in temperate latitudes are the eelgrasses (*Zostera*). In tropical regions, these are replaced by turtle grasses (*Thalassia*), manatee grasses (*Syringodium*), and other varieties.

Giant kelp forest, east Pacific coast, North America
(Brandon D. Cole/ENP Images)

Seagrass beds are among the most productive shallow-water communities on soft-bottom seafloors. This high productivity—the standing biomass of turtle grass, for example, can reach 1 kilogram dry weight per square meter (about 0.2 pounds per square foot)—is partly due to the high light penetration in shallow, clear water, but the main factor is the availability of nutrients in the sediments that are accessed directly by the seagrass-root system. Seaweeds and most phytoplankton, by contrast, must rely on the relatively meager nutrient supply dissolved in seawater.

On the surface of seagrass leaves grow microscopic photosynthetic forms—particularly diatoms and cyanobacteria—together with green algae. These epiphytes supplement the primary productivity of the seagrasses themselves. Additionally, the cyanobacteria can fix dissolved nitrogen gas and convert it into valuable nitrogenous nutrients, which are then made available to the rest of the community when the microbes die. The combined productivity of seagrasses and their epiphytes can reach 650 grams of carbon per square meter per year, in the tropics this figure is as high as 1 kilogram of carbon per square meter per year.

Relatively few animals consume seagrass leaves, although a larger number graze on the epiphytes growing on the leaves. Nevertheless, many creatures do indirectly exploit the high productivity of seagrass beds: they feed on the detritus produced by the decomposing leaves and other plant debris. Fungi and bacteria decompose this material and are consumed by larger microbes. These, in turn, form the part of the diet of deposit feeders—polychaete worms, clams, and sea cucumbers.

A variety of miniature, attached (sessile) animals also live on the surface of seagrass leaves. These include hydroids, sea squirts, bryozoans, and tube-dwelling polychaetes—all these forms tend to be suspension feeders. Bivalves, snails, and polychaete worms live in the muddy or sandy substrate around the seagrass roots. Crabs and lobsters graze or scavenge on and around the seagrasses.

Seagrass beds provide nursery grounds—a relatively safe haven for young fish, crustacea, and bivalve mollusks. Around the coasts of North America, commercial fish species such as menhaden and salmon spend their early subadult lives in seagrass communities. The value of seagrass meadows is much more than that offered by the community of organisms associated with them. The meadows, by causing sedimentation and acting as a break to waves and currents, serve to protect many coastlines from erosion.

Kelp Forests

Kelp is the general term that refers to various large brown algae. Two genera of kelps—*Macrocystis* and *Nereocystis*—are the largest of all forms of seaweed, and it is these that commonly grow to reach the surface and in so doing may form dense "forests." Smaller kelps—*Ecklonia* and *Laminaria*—do not form a surface canopy, but where they grow in abundance they form kelp "beds" rather than forests.

Kelp dominates many subtidal rocky communities in temperate and polar regions, preferring moderately exposed areas where there is reasonable water circulation but not where there are very fast currents and heavy surf. They require water temperature below about 68°F (20°C) and occupy the types of habitats that are occupied by coral reefs in tropical or subtropical waters. The largest variety, the giant kelp, *Macrocystis pyrifera,* can reach a height of 165 feet (50 m) and therefore is visible above the surface when growing in 130 feet (40 m) of water. It also has a prodigious rate of growth, some 12 inches (30 cm) or more per day at its peak—among the fastest growth rates for any plant on land or in water. In clear waters with moderately high nutrient loads, productivity of kelp forests may reach more than 2 kilograms of carbon per square meter per year—higher than that of seagrass communities and nearly comparable to that of coral reefs.

A kelp plant typically has a long flexible stipe (stalk), also called a trunk (thallus), to which are attached many fronds (blades), which are the equivalent of leaves. The stalk is attached to a hard substrate on the seafloor by a structure called a holdfast. The location of the fronds on the stalk varies from species to species. Some kelps, such as *Nereocystis* and *Laminaria,* have one or more fronds emerging from the end of the stalk; others, like the giant kelp, *Macrocystis,* have fronds emerging along the length of the stalk. Some kelps, including *Macrocystis* and *Nereocystis,* have a gas-filled float or floats (pneumatocysts) at the base of the fronds that buoy up the plant and ensure that the fronds are held up toward the light.

Kelps, like most other seaweeds, have a complex life cycle that involves two different forms—an asexual phase of the life cycle that alternates with a sexual phase. The quick-growing, robust plant—the kelp with its frond—is technically called the sporophyte and is the asexual phase. It produces many spores that can disperse, settle, and grow to colonize suitable spaces that are available. The second phase of the life cycle, the sexual one, involves spores growing to form tiny gametophytes—plants that will produce sex cells (gametes). Some of the spores will grow into female gametophytes (that will produce egg cells), and others will develop into male gametophytes (that will produce sperm cells). Fertilization of released egg cells by sperm cells is a hit-and-miss affair, but where it succeeds, it gives rise to a sporophyte generation that is genetically different from the contributing parents. Generating variation in this manner, though costly, has evolutionary advantages for the species by producing new genetic combinations among descendants on which natural selection can act.

Where kelps form dense forests, their effects are not dissimilar to those of forests on land. They form a canopy that traps much of the available sunlight, thereby forming an understory with relatively little light where only selected plants can survive—some smaller kelps and red algae. The understory with its associated seafloor is usually inhabited by sponges and seasquirts, lobsters, crabs, sea stars, various bivalve mollusks (particularly abalones), and octopuses. The fronds of the kelp plants form a surface on which many microscopic forms can grow—particularly plantlike protists such as diatoms—as well as slightly larger forms such as bryozoans and hydroids. Snails and small crustacea graze or hunt on the fronds, and filter-feeding polychaetes live there safe within their constructed tubes. The kelp fronds provide food for a few forms, particularly sea urchins and some snails and sea slugs. The kelp provides shelter for many more animals—fish, crabs, and sea otters among them—that find protection from larger carnivores such as seals and sharks. A range of suspension-feeding invertebrates live on and around the holdfasts—polychaete worms, brittlestars, and a variety of crustacea. Fishes are common at all levels of the kelp forest.

The sea otter, *Enhydra lutris,* is a keystone species in at least some North Pacific kelp forests. In some North American localities where sea otters have been exterminated by hunting, the kelp forests have succumbed to the ravages of a dominant population of sea urchins (*Stronglocentrotus*). Once the kelp have been largely consumed, the sea urchin population dies back through starvation and disease, allowing the kelp to recover gradually. Where sea otters are present, these boom-and-bust cycles rarely seem to occur. The otters, by feeding on sea urchins as part of their varied animal diet, keep sea urchin numbers in check, and they do not reach the high population densities that would otherwise decimate the kelp forests. Maintaining the sea otters seems to help maintain the kelp forests. However, the absence of sea otters is certainly not the only explanation for sea-urchin population explosions. In California waters, sea otters have been absent since the mid-19th century, but decimation of kelp forests by sea urchins has only been witnessed since the 1950s. Other factors—the absence of other sea-urchin predators, the removal of sea-urchin competitors such as abalones, and changes in water temperature and nutrient loading that adversely affect the growth of kelp—may be implicated. The direct and indirect effects of human activities on kelp forests are many and subtle.

On the positive side, many kelps are harvested or cultivated on a sustainable basis. Kelps provide numerous consumables: they can be used directly as a human food delicacy or as cattle feed; they contain alginates, which are used extensively in the cosmetics, foods, and medical industries (page 119); and they are used as a local source of fertilizer by some agricultural communities. The annual commercial harvest of giant kelp in North America typically amounts to about 22,000 tons (20,000 t) dry weight.

Hydrothermal Vents and Cold-Water Seeps

Deep-Sea Hydrothermal Vents

In 1977 marine scientists from the Woods Hole Oceanographic Institution were working off the Galápagos Islands at a depth of about 8,200 feet (2,500 m). Safe within the submersible *Alvin,* they were exploring a region where new seafloor was being created. They had little or no idea that they were about to encounter, not sea monsters, but something almost as surprising—hundreds of giant worms in densities and sizes never before seen. Apart from these 3-foot (1-m) long worms, there were large mussels and giant clams up to 10 inches (25 cm) long. These creatures were at a size and abundance rarely if ever before seen, and these were just some of the animals they found in a flourishing community around a system of hot-water vents. What was the energy source supplying food to these animal populations? In the absence of seaweeds or phytoplankton at this depth and with only a trickle of detritus falling through the water column, what was fueling such prolific communities? The groundbreaking discovery was that, in the absence of sunlight, the primary producers of the vent communities are bacteria, and their energy source is the range of chemicals released through the hydrothermal (hot-water) vents.

The Vent Bacteria

Along mid-ocean ridges (page 34), seawater trickles into fissures and cracks in Earth's crust. Some of the water that reemerges through hydrothermal vents has been heated to temperatures in the range 86–660°F (30–350°C), the exact temperature depending on the nature of the vent. Diffuse vents, such as some of those along the Galápagos Ridge, release warm water, whereas so-called white smokers and black smokers discharge superheated water (page 43). This water is laden with chemicals, one of the most important of which is hydrogen sulfide (H_2S). Science teachers and schoolchildren know this substance as "bad-egg gas," and it is highly toxic to most life-forms, but many of the bacteria in the vicinity of hydrothermal vents are adapted to exploit this substance. They use it in a process dubbed chemosynthesis in much the same manner that photosynthetic plants utilize light energy. These chemosynthetic bacteria are the primary producers of hydrothermal vent communities. These sulfur-oxidizing bacteria are believed to comprise most of the bacterial biomass in vent areas. But they are not the only chemosynthetic bacteria found there: others utilize different inorganic materials, such as methane and ammonia, and they too contribute to primary productivity.

The Vent Animal Community

Around the vents themselves, a thick bacterial soup provides food for filter feeders. In Galápagos vent communities, large pale-shelled clams (*Calyptogena*) and giant mussels (*Bathymodiolus*) strain bacteria from the water. In some vent communities along the mid-Atlantic Ridge, a shrimp (*Rimicaris*) is the dominant animal. It consumes the thick carpet of filamentous bacteria—up to 1.17 inches (3 cm) thick—covering the surface of mineral deposits around the vents. These shrimps are remarkable in that having lost the use of normal crustacean eyes—of little use in the inky depths around these vents—they have evolved an entirely new light-detecting apparatus: two patches on top of the crustacean's head detect infrared frequencies of light undetectable to most other animals. The crustacea probably detect the infrared radiation released by the superheated water emerging from the vents. Biologists hypothesize that the shrimps detect active vents by using their infrared-detecting devices. They also take care not to approach too close and so avoid becoming cooked in the superheated water.

From the animal community's viewpoint, the most important bacteria at hydrothermal vents are not free-living, but are symbiotic—many live within the animals themselves. Preeminent among the animals adapted to harbor symbiotic bacteria are the giant tube worms (*Riftia*)—the animals that first startled the *Alvin* explorers. The tube worms no longer have a functional gut but have a "feeding body," the trophosome, that is packed with symbiotic bacteria. The dry weight of bacteria is greater than that of the worm's body that surrounds them. The trophosome provides the bacteria with an ideal living environment, in return, the chemosynthesizing bacteria supply the worms with organic matter. The worms have a bright red gill-like structure, the plume, that they use to absorb oxygen and hydrogen sulfide and to excrete carbon dioxide. The bacteria chemosynthesize by using hydrogen sulfide delivered through the worm's blood system. The worm protects itself from the harmful effect of hydrogen sulfide by using modified hemoglobin—the blood pigment that usually carries oxygen—to carry the poisonous gas. The hemoglobin has two binding sites—one for oxygen and one for hydrogen sulfide—so that it can carry both substances at one and the same time.

Vent clams have not adopted this biochemical strategy but instead use a new molecule whose sole function is to transport hydrogen sulfide in an innocuous form. The large clams, *Calyptogena,* have abundant hemoglobin in their blood, giving their gills a bright red color. In both clams and worms, the hemoglobin is an adaptation to absorb and transport oxygen in a low-oxygen environment.

Since the 1977 discoveries at the Galápagos Rift, deep-sea hydrothermal vents have been recorded at various sites in the eastern and western Pacific, and since 1985, along the mid-oceanic ridge in the Atlantic. There is variety among vent communities, with sediment-covered vents harboring different fauna compared to sediment-free vents in rocky areas such as those along the Galápagos Ridge. The species composition of Atlantic communities differs, in greater part, from those in the Pacific.

Vent-Community Biodiversity and Productivity

More than 90 percent of the animals discovered at hydrothermal vents are of previously unknown species, and, indeed, several new taxonomic families have been established to accommodate them. The productivity of these submarine sites is startling. At the original Galápagos site, the combined biomass of giant tube worms and clams is of the order of 20–30 kilograms wet weight per square meter (4–6 pounds per square foot)—a surprisingly high figure—and densities of *Riftia* reach more than 150 per square meter (14 per square foot). At these hydrothermal vents, primary production by bacteria is estimated to be two to three times that of photosynthetic production in the water of the surface layers.

In the Galápagos vent communities, pale crabs and shrimps clamber over the tube worms, mussels, and clams, and the nearby rocks are carpeted with sea anemones. At the edge of the vent field, where bacterial concentrations are lower, spaghettilike acorn worms and gelatinous "dandelions" (siphonophores) harvest the suspended bacteria. Other hydrothermal vents at rocky sites in the Pacific harbor similar forms, with some variations on the theme from one site to the next. Vent communities in the Atlantic have rather different dominant animals forms. In general, biodiversity at vent sites is not high: it appears that relatively few animals have successfully exploited this demanding environment.

Vent Colonization

While hydrothermal vents are remarkable systems, they are also highly ephemeral ones. Hydrothermal vents commonly last only a matter of decades before the superheated water ceases to flow, and the local animals die unless they are able to migrate to other vents.

Active vents are few and far between, and once one system dies there is no guarantee that there will be another one in the locality. Some scientists speculate that the bacterial and animal components of the vent community can "island-hop" from one vent to another by taking advantage of occasional giant carcasses, such as dead whales, that descend to the ocean floor. After the scavengers have left, the remains of the carcass decay, producing hydrogen sulfide and other energy-rich chemicals associated with low-oxygen conditions. It is possible that chemosynthetic bacteria can colonize such carcasses and temporarily support an animal community such as those found at vents. However, these food supplies are even more ephemeral than the vents themselves.

It is apparent that most of the animal species at vent communities are either attached and immobile, or they are unable to walk or swim very far. It is the larvae—rather than the adults—that must spearhead colonization of new vents. The prolific inhabitants of vent communities presumably adopt an opportunistic, boom-and-bust ecological strategy. Current research has identified the larvae of more than 30 species of vent-associated bivalve mollusks. Most of these larvae utilize a stored-yolk food supply and under normal conditions would be expected to remain in the plankton and disperse during periods ranging from a few hours to a few days. Only a few species have larvae capable of feeding while in the plankton community and that are capable of dispersing during extended periods. How the larvae seek out and find new vents—or whether the process is much more random than that—has yet to be determined. Colonization of vent areas by larvae is a very active area of current research.

Shallow Vents

Hydrothermal vents are occasionally found in shallow water and in intertidal zones. Off southern California, sulfides are released by geothermal activity on some rocky shores, and here mats of sulfur-oxidizing bacteria supplement the more conventional primary production by phytoplankton and seaweeds. Limpets in such localities graze on bacterial mats, rather than the surface film of photosynthetic protists that is their normal fare.

Cold-Water Seeps

In 1984 seafloor communities based on chemosynthetic bacteria were discovered in the Gulf of Mexico, but these were not associated with hot vents. Rather, those communities were found where chemical-rich cold water was seeping out of rocks or sediments at moderate depths—so-called cold-water seeps. Such seeps are found at specific locations on continental margins, continental slopes, and also subduction zones, regions where oceanic crust is being returned to the mantle. Here, hydrogen sulfide and organic chemicals such as methane seep out from the seafloor. In such localities, bacterial and animal communities similar to deep-sea hot springs have been found. Therefore, high temperatures are not the overriding factor in sustaining these productive systems based on chemosynthetic bacteria, but the plentiful supply of chemical-rich water is.

The discovery of biological communities associated with hot vents and cold-water seeps has shaken earlier ideas about the nature of early life on this planet and has overturned the previous assumption that all animal communities ultimately obtain their organic supplies from photosynthetic plants. Less than 1 percent of the worldwide mid-oceanic ridge system has been explored; who knows what new species and new forms of vent community have yet to be discovered? About 300 new species of animals have been identified at deep-sea vents; by the mid-1990s, vents had been identified at 11 places worldwide and seeps at eight locations. How many more wait to be found elsewhere?

New Developments in Marine Biology

As marine scientists develop new instrumentation to study marine life and devise pioneering vehicles to explore the ocean depths, so new lifeforms are being discovered at a surprisingly high pace. Only about 275,000 marine species have been described so far; conservative estimates suggest that there are at least three or four times this number still to be identified, and liberal estimates suggest 30 to 40 times this number.

With improved sampling and culture techniques, microbes of progressively smaller size are being discovered and their activities studied. We are beginning to appreciate the true importance of the ultramicroscopic plankton—those too small to be retained by conventional nets and filters. In the sediment deposits that stretch across the expanses of the ocean from the shore to the greatest depths, many hundreds of thousands of new animal species are waiting to be discovered. When we consider the number of protists and other microbes that live within these seafloor deposits, then we really have just scratched the surface.

Submersibles and ROVs are taking scientists—whether literally or figuratively—to ocean depths with mathematical precision. Cameras and mechanical sampling equipment are enabling detailed and systematic investigation of deep-sea phenomena such as hydrothermal vents and cold-water seeps. As in other aspects of ocean science, such as meteorology and geology, international cooperation in marine biological studies is absolutely vital to understand large-scale oceanographic processes. The workings of the ocean system respect no political or economic boundaries.

New Experiments

The vast size of the oceans, the fact that their waters are continually in motion, and the dynamic nature of the oceanic community, particularly in the surface waters, means that sampling a body of water for a period of time is absolutely no guarantee that the physical and chemical conditions—and the organisms found there—will remain the same for very long. Experimental approaches are needed to help isolate the factors being studied. Two main approaches are being used to supplement field studies: laboratory-scale investigations and enclosed ecosystem experiments.

Laboratory experiments are particularly useful for studying aspects of the biology of a single species on a small scale—for example, the feeding preferences of a particular species of copepod—or for studying interactions between populations of small-sized organisms, such as different species of zooplankton or zooplankton that feed on phytoplankton. In the laboratory, biologists can obtain precise measurements for nutrient uptake by a particular species, they can calculate the organism's efficiency at converting consumed food matter into biomass, and so on enabling productivities and energy transfer efficiencies to be calculated. This information can then be extrapolated and applied back to the natural situation, with, of course, some major provisos. The laboratory situation is an artificial one, and whereas environmental conditions can be simplified and controlled in the laboratory, the natural situation is bound to be far more complex and variable. Also, only some organisms are amenable to laboratory investigation—try studying a large whale or a school of barracuda in an artificial enclosure. Nevertheless, many of the most important organisms in the sea are small, and laboratory investigations are a valid—and invaluable—approach to supplementing results collected in the field.

Enclosed ecosystem studies involve surrounding a body of seawater under otherwise natural conditions and then conducting experiments within such enclosures. If a large enough volume of water can be enclosed, then many components of the pelagic community can be included, and the conditions inside the enclosure can approximate oceanic food webs in the surface waters, albeit with larger and rarer components excluded. In practice, enclosures must accommodate at least 130–1,300 cubic yards (100 to 1,000 m³) of water if they are to fulfill such criteria. Transparent containers made of nontoxic material are usually used to provide the seawater containers. Enclosed ecosystem experiments have now been conducted in many parts of the world, with notable contributions from studies in Loch Ewe, Scotland; the CEPEX experiments off British Columbia, Canada; the Marine Ecosystem Research Laboratory in Rhode Island; and Xiamen in the People's Republic of China. Some of these experiments have examined the effects of natural variations in physical parameters, such as vertical mixing and light intensity, and their effects on the composition of the plankton community.

Others have explored the effects of chemical changes—particularly the effects of chemical pollutants. The Controlled Ecosystem Pollution Experiments (CEPEX) conducted off British Columbia utilized 99-foot (30-m) deep containers each enclosing about 1,700 cubic yards (1,300 m³) of seawater. The investigations examined the effects of trace amounts of chemical pollutants on the composition of the plankton community and on fish larvae. Several containers were used, with pollutants at different concentrations in each. One enclosure was used as a control to compare conditions within enclosures with those in nearby unenclosed waters. A range of pollutants were studied, including the metals copper and mercury and various petroleum hydrocarbons, all of which are commonly found contaminating coastal waters close to industrial conurbations and ports or harbors. The experiments convincingly demonstrated that some of these pollutants dramatically change the composition of the plankton community. In the presence of copper, for example, long-chain diatoms such as *Chaetoceros* die off and are replaced by much smaller phytoplankton, most notably flagellates that are less than 20 microns (0.02 millimeters). This change has repercussions throughout the zooplankton community, and the ecology of the experimental and control enclosures became very different within a matter of weeks. Such clear-cut findings are difficult or impossible to obtain using much smaller laboratory-scale experiments or by field studies or field experiments where enclosures are not used.

Using enclosures does have some drawbacks: for example, they tend to reduce turbulence, and the water circulation in such containers may be very different to that outside. Nevertheless, enclosed ecosystem experiments, properly conducted and evaluated, provide a very useful weapon in the experimental armory needed to investigate the pressing problems we face in understanding and protecting oceanic ecosystems.

Making Connections: Viewing Earth from Space

Satellite technology coupled with remote sensing is enabling scientists to monitor some crucial physical, chemical, and biological parameters—particularly surface temperatures and chlorophyll concentrations—over large areas of the ocean on a day-by-day basis. The satellite-borne Coastal Zone Color Scanner (CZCS), for example, records the color changes in surface waters produced by the photosynthetic pigments in phytoplankton. By taking into account the weather at the time and relating results to on-the-spot measurements of chlorophyll concentration made by oceangoing vessels, an estimate of primary productivity (the amount of carbon fixed by photosynthesis per unit time) can be made for vast areas

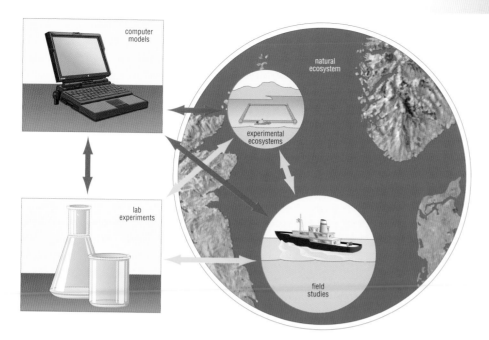

The interaction between field studies, experimental approaches, and computer modeling in studying the workings of natural ecosystems

of surface water. When sufficient data is available, false-color images can be computed showing the relative amounts of primary productivity in different parts of the ocean. Although they carry an error of ± 50 percent, these productivity estimates are a major advance in helping marine scientists' understanding of the dynamic nature of marine productivity. Similar images compiled with data from thermal imaging cameras enable scientists to monitor the progress of ocean-surface currents, and this data can be correlated with productivity distributions. Remote sensing as a biological research tool is likely to become increasingly important as international cooperation continues to flourish.

New Products

For thousands of years, humans have been exploiting the sea's flora and fauna as a treasure trove of useful substances. The many uses of seaweed extracts were documented in the *Pen Tsao* Chinese pharmacopoeia dating from 2800 B.C.E. Since that time, seaweeds have yielded substances with an astonishing range of medical uses—from killing parasitic worms to dilating women's cervixes. Agar—the gel-like support medium on which scientists grow bacterial and fungal cultures—is obtained from red algae. When Alexander Fleming stumbled across the *Penicilium* fungus—the source of penicillin, the first antibiotic—it was growing on an agar plate.

Today, the search for pharmaceutically active substances continues. Within the last 20 years, marine sponges have yielded Ara-A and Ara-C—the former an antiviral substance, the latter a chemical that helps combat certain forms of leukemia. Research on one aspect of marine physiology sometimes yields wholly unexpected payoffs elsewhere. In 1955, researchers discovered the factor that causes the blood of horseshoe crabs, *Limulus polyphemus,* to clot. Today, this discovery forms the basis for a routine diagnostic test that determines whether a person's blood is contaminated with endotoxins—chemicals released during bacterial infection.

Many everyday items—foods, cosmetics, and household products—contain substances that originate from marine organisms. Alginates from seaweeds are used as emulsifiers, thickeners, and stabilizers in a surprising range of items: they thicken instant soups, replace oil and eggs in low-fat mayonnaise, and even help maintain the foamy head on freshly poured beer.

Coral reefs, like tropical rain forests, are increasingly perceived as an invaluable biochemical resource. In the prolific community of the coral reef, space is at a premium. Sessile animals defend their space and launch attacks using chemical warfare. The search is on to establish which of these chemicals might be usefully harnessed for medical use (page 173).

Computer Power and Information Technology

Computer models provide a means of simulating natural events and/or offering predictions about possible future events under given scenarios. These mathematical models use data gathered from many sources—satellite imagery, field studies, and laboratory and enclosed ecosystem experiments. The computer models normally incorporate algebraic expressions that define nonlinear relationships between variables (where variables are not related to one another in a linear or proportional manner). With so many interacting factors—physical, chemical, and biological—many assumptions need to be made in constructing such models, and even if the assumptions are valid, the models are only as good as the accuracy and completeness of the data on which they are based. The construction of computer models needs to go hand in hand with gathering data in the field and with constructing and testing hypotheses with real data if such models are to have practical validity and not simply to be elegant, but theoretical, constructs. For example, many of the fisheries models developed in the 1940s and 1950s—though sophisticated at the time—did not take key variables into account (page 198). Thus, their predictions were, in some cases, extremely misleading and inadvertently led to the premature demise of some fisheries.

International networks of scientists—such as those involved in the Global Ocean Observing System (GOOS)—are striving to collect data and develop predictive models of ocean ecosystems that will incorporate physical, chemical, and biological interactions. The task is a formidable one.

Ships: From Dugouts to Steamships

Seafarers make a clear distinction between a *boat* and a *ship;* for many people without nautical experience, this difference is anything but distinct. Most mariners regard a ship as a large vessel that is substantially decked—its hull contains one or more horizontal platforms on which people can walk. A boat is a smaller vessel, with little or no decking, and can be carried on board a ship. However, there are many exceptions to this general rule. Some fairly large vessels are called boats: fishing boats, tug boats, and ferryboats, for example.

It is likely that seagoing vessels have been part of humankind's history for at least 40,000 years. We know that people migrated southward from Southeast Asia into New Guinea and Australia at around this time, and to do so they must have traversed stretches of sea at least 25 miles (40 km) across. The aboriginal people of Australia are only "aboriginal" from our modern perspective: 40,000 years ago they were explorers entering a vast continent for the first time.

The first seagoing vessels were probably inshore vessels—dugout canoes, reed boats, skin canoes, or log rafts—adapted to withstand the more demanding conditions of the open ocean. The earliest, well-documented seagoing craft are recorded in Egyptian wall paintings from the third millennium B.C.E. A remarkably intact funeral ship was quite recently excavated from the vicinity of the Cheops pyramid at Giza in Egypt. Dating from about 2530 B.C.E., this vessel was more than 133 feet (40 m) in length, and although it was ceremonial rather than practical, similar seagoing vessels are depicted in Egyptian artwork of the time. Circumstantial evidence suggests that Egyptian sailors voyaged as far as Crete and Lebanon. It is likely that several other societies in the Mediterranean area and spanning the Pacific, from South and Central America to eastern Asia, had developed seaworthy vessels by this time, but little evidence has survived.

By the third millennium B.C.E., Egyptian vessels were powered by rowers—perhaps 13 or more on either side—and supplemented by wind power, which was harnessed by a simple rectangular sail hoisted on a mast. Steering was accomplished using an extralarge oar slung over one side near the stern. This oar was called the steerboard and probably gave rise to the term *starboard,* referring to the right side of the vessel.

Phoenicians, Greeks, and Romans

The Phoenicians (who originated in what is now a coastal region of Syria) were the preeminent sailors and traders of the Mediterranean between about 1000 and 250 B.C.E. They ventured out into the Atlantic and as far north as the Scilly Isles and—if the writings of Herodotus are to be believed—also turned southward, rounded the Cape of Good Hope, and entered the Indian Ocean. Phoenician vessels were more refined versions of Egyptian designs; some were primarily warships (page 126), and others were cargo vessels.

By the start of the first millennium B.C.E., the principles of wooden-hull design were well established and remained essentially unchanged, in Europe at least, until steel replaced wood in the 19th century C.E. The hull frame consisted of a central spine or keel attached to ribs on either side and a

A Chinese junk. Similar vessels probably originate from the first millennium B.C.E. and were far in advance of European designs

stempost and sternpost fore (front) and aft (back), respectively. Additional structural support was provided by cross-bracing members or by longitudinal members (stringers). The wooden components were held together by wooden pegs—later, iron nails—and the planking was waterproofed by using pitch.

Greek and Roman vessels c. 500 B.C.E. were either sleek warships—the triremes—or deep-hulled cargo ships with sometimes surprisingly large storage capacity—275 tons (250 t) in some cases.

Chinese and Middle-Eastern Vessels

The sailing vessels developed by those communities bordering the Indian Ocean and the western Pacific were supremely adapted to the local maritime conditions. These vessels were rather different in design from those being devised in Europe, and they included innovations that were far in advance of European designs of the time. The Chinese design, the junk, was in evidence by the beginning of the first millennium B.C.E. The flat-bottomed hull was without a keel and was raised at bow and stern. A stern rudder was in use by 500 B.C.E., and by 250 B.C.E. fore-and-aft sails were commonplace. The sails, supported by full-length battens, could be rapidly shortened, rather like Venetian blinds. Later developments included decking and transverse bulkheads that separated the hull space into compartments. All in all, in terms of sailing ability and general seaworthiness, junks were far superior to European vessels and remained that way right up until the 16th century C.E.

The steady winds associated with the monsoons of the northwest Indian Ocean gave rise to the characteristic lateen-rigged (triangular-sail) vessels of the Arab, Persian, and Indian nations. On Arab dhows and feluccas (more properly called *markeb*), the triangular sail is slung from a long yard (crosswood) attached to a short mast. The lateen design seems inefficient because the sail must be lowered and raised again with each major change in direction, but, in practice, this a rare occurrence in a monsoon region, where steady winds tend to blow from one direction day after day.

Early European Vessels

By the seventh century C.E. the Vikings of Scandinavia were carrying out raids across Northeast Europe using characteristic wooden longboats propelled by oars and a single sail. These double-ended vessels were about 80 feet (25 m) long and held perhaps 40–50 mariners. Leif Eriksson in about 1000 C.E. made landing on the North American continent, nearly 500 years before Columbus was to do so. William the Conqueror's vessels that he used in the invasion of England in 1066 were—as depicted in the Bayeux Tapestry—of essentially similar design to the Viking longboat but with partial decking and castlelike turrets at bow and stern to accommodate archers.

The Western Age of Sail

In the 12th and 13th centuries B.C.E., innovations in the design of European vessels followed similar lines to those of Far Eastern boats many centuries earlier. The sail replaced the oar as the primary means of propulsion, and a rudder at the stern replaced the steerboard at the side. In 13th-century northern Europe, the cog—a deep-hulled vessel with decking, fore and stern castles, a single rectangular sail, and a rudder—was, with its large cargo hold, the most common seagoing merchant ship. The caravel design, originating from technologically advanced Mediterranean countries, spread rapidly through northern Europe. The caravel began as an elegant, sleek-hulled, two-decked, two-masted vessel with lateen rig (triangular sails slung from a yard). Utilizing the combination of multiple sails and a rudder, vessels could now sail close-hauled—that is, as close to the wind as possible—in practice, up to about 45° of the wind's direction. The great voyages of exploration of Bartholomeu Dias, Ferdinand Magellan, Vasco da Gama, and Christopher Columbus (page 147) were all made in vessels of this type. To our eyes, it is remarkable that open-ocean voyages of several thousand miles into the unknown were made in such small and frail craft. Columbus's *Santa Maria,* for example, was a 110-ton (100-t) vessel with a crew of 40.

With the development of open-ocean sea routes between Europe and the Far East via the Cape of Good Hope, and from Europe to the New World across the Atlantic, trade links were established and larger vessels were required to transport the high volumes of goods. By the 16th century, Spain had built cargo vessels of 1,760 tons (1,600 t)—the forerunners of the heavily armed galleons that were to become engaged in sea battles with England (page 128).

By the 17th and 18th centuries, the elite European sailing vessels were caravel types, most notable of which were those of the British and Dutch East India Companies. These remarkable sailing vessels, developed for European trade with the East Indies (present-day Indonesia), represented the peak of the shipbuilder's art. Reaching to as much as 200 feet (60 m) in length and more than 50 feet (15 m) in breadth, they sported a single or double row of cannon for protection and large holds for cargo and were commonly fitted with luxurious cabins for passengers. Typically three masted and square rigged (rectangular sailed), the largest could carry 0.5 acres (0.2 ha) of sail.

The 19th century saw the development of even larger merchant vessels—four to seven masted—that traveled from Europe to Australia, North and South America, and the Far East. The demand for haste and distance—in Europe, for example, the Chinese tea crop that arrived on the first ships of the season commanded the highest prices—saw the development of sleek, high-speed vessels. These clipper ships—so-called because they clipped days off the normal journey—reached speeds in excess of 18 knots (20 miles per hour or 32 kilometers per hour) and were faster than many 20th-century steam vessels.

Today, sailing ships have been almost entirely superseded by engine-powered vessels, although junks are still widely used in the Far East, and some vessels supplement their engine power with wind power.

Steam-Powered Vessels and Ironclad Ships

The age of the steamship was slow in coming. James Watt started to manufacture steam engines in 1774, and some were experimentally incorporated in boats and small ships from the late 1770s, but it was not until 1807 that the first moderate-size vessel incorporated a coal-fired steam engine in its design. The 150-feet (45-m) ship, the *Clermont,* was powered by paddle wheels connected to a steam engine via cranks and connecting rods. On her maiden voyage, she traveled up the Hudson River from New York to Albany and back in a little more than two and a half days—a return trip of 150 miles (240 km). Such medium-size paddle ships were suitable on inland waters but were unsuitable in the rougher waters of the open sea.

It was not until 1819 that a steamship crossed the Atlantic Ocean. Even then, this U.S. vessel—the *Savannah*—carried a full complement of masts and sails, and the steam engine was operating for only about one-eighth of the crossing time. In 1838, Isambard Kingdom Brunel's massive wooden-paddle steamer, the *Great Western,* made its maiden voyage; within a few years, this vessel was completing the Atlantic crossing—Bristol to New York—under steam in 15 days.

The period 1850–1900 was to see great improvements in steam-engine and screw-propeller design. By the turn of the 20th century, steam turbines were replacing steam engines, and oil was becoming an alternative fuel source to coal, giving rise to the first diesel-powered vessels by 1910. Today, merchant ships are propelled by multicylinder diesel engines or by older-style steam turbines driven by oil-fired boilers. Many warships are powered by diesel engines, but some of the largest are nuclear powered, and some of the smallest use gas turbines.

Ports

Ports are the meeting points between transportation on sea and on land. Ports as communities produce ambivalent responses among those who live and work there. The lives of seafarers, spending months at sea, set themselves apart from those who habitually stay on land. The behavior of seafarers is often one of extremes: rampant enthusiasm for life when they return from a long voyage and boredom once they have been ashore for weeks or months.

In terms of volume, about 90 percent of world trade is funneled through ports. Today, these handling centers are highly mechanized to enable goods to pass through with the maximum of speed and efficiency and with the minimum of storage time. Some ports now specialize in a single type of cargo; others carry raw materials in bulk to serve large industries located alongside or nearby. But many ports continue to handle a diverse range of goods and serve a wide hinterland. Rotterdam, for example, is a through port for goods supplied to more than 250 million people in continental Europe. Many of the world's greatest cities—including Hong Kong, London, New York, and Tokyo—are ports themselves or have major ports closely associated with them.

Many modern ports have grown up in hundreds of years, but their continued success depends on a variety of factors—geographic, economic, and technological. Today's vessels are much larger than those of even 20 or 30 years ago, and natural or artificial deep-water channels must be maintained to allow them access to ports. Where this is not feasible, it is a major restriction to that port's development. In most cases, the port also requires good land transport links—road, rail, and possibly inland waterways—to deliver goods to or from hinterlands. Physical barriers such as mountain ranges can act as a major brake to port development, as has happened along the western coast of South America where the Andes restrict transport inland. Ports are also more likely to flourish and grow where they are close to major shipping routes. To reduce overheads, shipowners minimize fuel-consumption and cargo-handling costs by ensuring that large vessels make the fewest number of stops for unloading and take the fastest sea routes commensurate with safety. Goods unloaded at major ports can then be transshipped to smaller ports by feeder vessels.

Europe

The European coastline is heavily dotted with seaports, reflecting the European Community's (EC's) industrial and commercial importance and its dependence on international seaborne trade. There is intense competition between ports, both nationally and internationally, and so inland-transport networks tend to be extensive and efficient. The largest European port is Rotterdam, situated on the Rhine delta, not an ideal location perhaps, but Dutch ingenuity in molding and shaping the coastline and in providing technological developments in cargo handling has ensured Rotterdam's continued success.

Despite the deposition of silt within the locality, the Rotterdam port authorities ensure that deepwater channels are created and maintained by intensive dredging operations. Substantial areas of shallow water have been reclaimed for siting new facilities—handling, storage, and processing buildings and other structures associated

The locations of the world's 20 top container ports

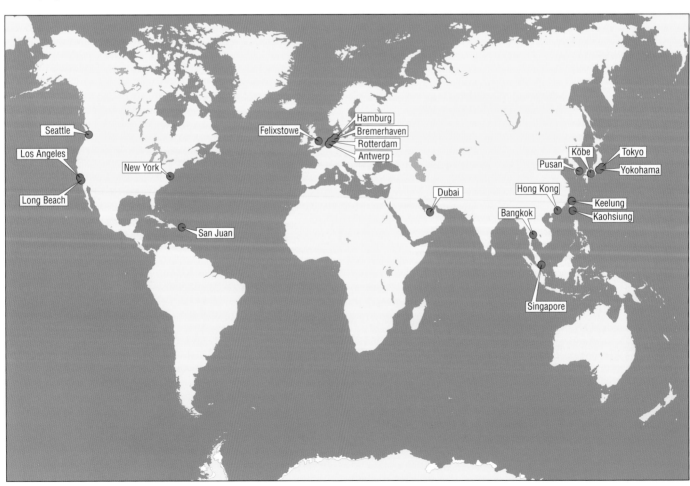

THE 20 TOP CONTAINER PORTS IN 1994

	Container Throughput in 1994 (in million TEUs*)
1. Hong Kong	11.1
2. Singapore	10.4
3. Kaohsiung, Taiwan	4.9
4. Rotterdam, Netherlands	4.5
5. Pusan, South Korea	3.8
6. Kōbe, Japan	2.8
7. Hamburg, Germany	2.7
8. Long Beach, United States	2.6
9. Los Angeles, United States	2.5
10. Yokohama, Japan	2.3
11. Antwerp, Belgium	2.2
12. Keelung, Taiwan	2.0
13. New York, United States	2.0
14. Dubai, United Arab Emirates	1.7
15. Felixstowe, United Kingdom	1.6
16. San Juan, Puerto Rico	1.6
17. Tokyo, Japan	1.5
18. Bremerhaven, Germany	1.5
19. Seattle, United States	1.4
20. Bangkok, Thailand	1.3

*A TEU is a 20-foot equivalent, a measure used to describe the carrying capacity of container ships. A TEU is typically 20 × 8 × 8 feet (6 × 2.5 × 2.5 m)

with the port. Although the port facility handles many types of cargo—Rotterdam handles Europe's largest volume of container traffic—the growth of the port since World War II has been particularly associated with the importation of oil. Petrochemical- and oil-refining complexes now occupy large areas of the port. Any expansion of the complex of facilities at Rotterdam must now meet increasingly stringent environmental constraints.

North and South America

Much of the west coast of North America, like that of South America, has unfavorable topography for port development. There are relatively few bays or inlets that offer natural harbors, and broad mountain ranges limit inland access. However, major ports are found in and around the superb natural harbors of San Francisco and Vancouver.

The east coast offers many more opportunities for safe harborage, with several drowned river valleys (rias) that offer suitable sites for ports that serve the highest population densities in North America.

The Great Lakes region on the United States–Canada border, with its associated ports of Chicago, Cleveland, Detroit, Montreal, and Toronto, serves the farming communities and industrial regions of the Midwest.

Bulk commodities—especially petroleum products, iron ore, coal, and grain—dominate much of U.S. shipborne trade. The Gulf of Mexico and the Florida peninsula, though offering relatively few good port locations and beset by potentially damaging storms, have flourished to serve oil extraction and related industries. The lack of mainland facilities with sufficient depth to accommodate large tankers has meant that suitable facilities are often developed on offshore islands.

In South America, the problems besetting port location on the west coast—the Andes running close to and parallel to the coast, the scarcity of suitable natural harbors, the relative absence of navigable rivers, and the risk of earthquakes—has meant that most ports here are created from artificial harbors, with moles and breakwaters (barriers perpendicular to the shore and extending out to sea) that offer protection from winds and waves. The east coast, by contrast, offers many opportunities for port development: Rio de Janeiro, located on one of the world's finest natural harbors, has grown into a flourishing port, metropolitan area, and capital city of Brazil as a result. Other major east-coast ports have also become the capital cities of their respective countries.

India, the Middle East, and Far East

In Asia, the convoluted coastlines and preponderance of offshore islands and archipelagos have ensured that sea transport has played a major role in local, regional, and international trade. India and Japan are at or near two ends of the spectrum of economic development, but both are provided with large seaports. In the case of Japan, these ports are among the most technologically advanced in the world. Elsewhere in the West Pacific region and in the South China Sea, the rapid industrialization of some countries has resulted in international trade in goods, from clothes to high-tech, electronic products. By the mid-1990s, Hong Kong, Japan, Singapore, and Taiwan were hosting the world's busiest ports in terms of container traffic.

The Philippines and Indonesia, with their numerous islands, are served by a network of ports, with the larger ports catering to international trade and then transshipping goods to regional and local ports.

The Persian Gulf is now a central hub for the world oil trade. Many offshore terminals have been constructed to provide access for some of the world's largest oil tankers. Since 1973, increased oil revenues to Middle East states have encouraged increasing traffic of other goods associated with burgeoning economic development. Existing harbors have been expanded, and new cargo handling technology has been incorporated to cope with the increased demand.

Africa and Australasia

The ports of Australia developed for the exporting of wool and grain and importing of goods and settlers from the United Kingdom. Many Pacific islands are coral fringed, and ports are established behind natural breaks in the reef system. Often, these breaks have had to be enlarged and channels dredged to provide access to larger ships. Once constructed, these ports offer effective safe harbors.

The densely populated central west coast of Africa, with its fairly flat hinterland and navigable rivers, has numerous ports, although in many cases the shelter is provided by artificial constructions rather than natural features. The northwest, southwest, and east coasts of Africa have relatively few ports, reflecting low population densities and relatively sparse natural resources. Dar es Salaam and Mombasa on the east coast are major ports supplying a vast hinterland, including the landlocked countries of Burundi, Rwanda, Uganda, and Zambia.

Shipping Routes and Modern Cargo Ships

Despite the occasional major tragedy, such as the sinking of the *Titanic* (page 137), the first half of the 20th century was the era of the passenger liner. For most migrants and tourists, these ships were the only available means of transoceanic travel. The great expansion of air travel in the 1950s ended the reign of the passenger liners almost overnight, just when these ships were at their fastest and most luxurious.

Cargo Ships

Until the 1950s, passenger liners shared the busy ocean routes with several types of cargo vessel. Mixed cargoes were usually carried by three-island freighters, so-called because when they emerged above the horizon, three parts were first visible—the forecastle at the bow, the bridge superstructure midships, and the poop at the stern—giving the appearance of three islands. Cargo was stored below deck in a hold accessed via hatches. Hold compartments were loaded and unloaded by derricks (lifting devices) that were carried on deck. In the 1940s, three-island ships were gradually supplanted by one-island ships. The mass-produced Liberty and Victory ships built by the United States during World War II, which played a vital supply and troop-carrying role in the conflict, were of the one-island type. With larger hatches and holds, they were easier to load and unload, and similar, though technologically more advanced, vessels were built until recently. The high cost of loading and unloading such vessels—a cranes-and-derricks operation that tends to be slow and rather inefficient—has resulted in these ships being largely usurped by other types of general cargo freighter.

Since the 1960s, many cargo ships and cargo-handling ports have undergone a revolutionary change with the advent of containerization. A cargo container is essentially a sealable metal box with dimensions 20 ft × 8 ft × 8 feet (6 × 2.5 × 2.5 meters) or some simple multiple of this size. Carrying goods in such boxes has many advantages. The conditions inside the box can be controlled to preserve the goods it contains; the box keeps out seawater and other potentially damaging agents, including potential thieves; containers can be stacked close together in ships or on the quayside; and on board they are much more stable, and thus safer, than carrying loose cargo. Loading large, standard boxes on and off ships and then onto rail or road transport has developed into a production-line process that is quick,

| THE TOP 10 MERCHANT FLEETS IN JANUARY 1995 |||
Countries	No. Ships	Gross Tonnage in Thousands of Long Tons (1 long ton = 1.016 metric tons)
Panama	3,488	62,185
Liberia	1,534	57,703
Greece	981	29,386
Cyprus	1,436	23,222
Bahamas	910	22,121
Norway	678	19,662
Japan	812	17,839
Malta	925	15,225
China	1,387	14,590
United States	543	14,126

cheap, and efficient. Lift-on lift-off (LoLo) container ships, loaded by crane, have evolved as specialized vessels for handling containers. The sealed boxes are carried in the hold and on deck. As many as 4,000 TEUs (20-foot equivalent units) can be carried on a single vessel, and ships are on the drawing board that will have twice this capacity—equivalent to that of 30 or more standard World War II freighters.

Roll-on roll-off (RoRo) supercarriers have evolved from smaller vessels originally used as ferries or for trade over short distances. Goods on wheels are loaded via ramps in the stern or sides of the ship. These vessels carry cars, trucks, and other vehicles. Today, RoRo supercarriers carry containers, either preloaded onto trucks, rolled into the hold, or loaded by crane onto the deck.

Lighter-aboard-ship (LASH) vessels are essentially barge-carrying ships (*lighter* is an alternative name for a barge). The preloaded lighters are towed by tugs to a seaport, where they meet a LASH vessel. They are lifted aboard by crane and are stowed above and below deck for transport across the ocean. At the destination seaport, they are unloaded and towed by tugboats to their final destination, usually some distance from the port.

Supertankers and Bulk Carriers

Tankers for transporting crude oil first made their appearance in the late 1880s. They required many new technological features to carry the valuable but potentially hazardous cargo. Tanks in the holds were separated one from another by coffer-dams that prevent leakage. To cope with increased evaporation with rising temperature, and

increased viscosity (reduced flow) with falling temperature, expansion chambers, venting machinery, and heating devices were incorporated. By filling empty tanks with seawater, the ship's trim fore-and-aft could be maintained. The spinoff of this development was that the bulk of the ship's superstructure (the above-deck parts of the ship) and the ship's engines no longer needed to be positioned near the middle of the vessel. They could be sited at the stern, so shortening the propeller shafts, steering linkages, and so on. On tankers, the bridge and funnel are aft (at the rear) not in the middle. As other types of vessel resolved the problems of maintaining fore-and-aft trim, so they too have tended toward the machinery and superstructure aft design, and many of today's vessels—from bulk cargo carriers to ferries—have the familiar modern silhouette with bridge and funnel aft.

During the 1950s and 1960s, tanker sizes doubled, then quadrupled, and then rapidly broke through the 100,000-ton (90,000 t) barrier, ushering in the era of the supertanker. This development was spurred on by the closure of the Suez Canal in 1956 and then again in 1967. With the usual short route between the Middle East and Europe blocked, oil tankers had to make the trip around the Cape of Good Hope. To make this voyage financially viable, economies of scale dictated a larger vessel, and the supertanker was the response to this need.

Today, very large crude carriers (VLCCs) are oil tankers that have a capacity in the region of 275,000 tons (250,000 t) but ultra large crude carriers (ULCCs) have an astonishing capacity of 495,000 tons (450,000 t). Such giant supertankers are only used for long hauls and can only be

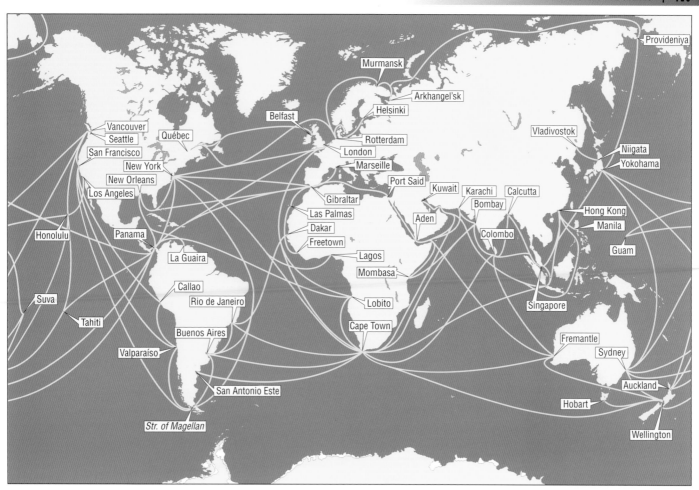

Some major shipping routes and ports

accommodated in deep ports—those approaching 100 feet (30 m) depth. There are major safety and environmental considerations. Because of their size, supertankers are difficult to maneuver and require many miles to come to a halt. When routed through busy seaways, they pose a potential hazard to other shipping, particularly when sea conditions are treacherous. When a tanker runs aground or collides with another vessel—worldwide, such incidents happen once every few years—apart from the obvious danger to human life, the short-term environmental consequences can be devastating. Such an event occurred when the *Exxon Valdez* grounded in Prince William Sound, Alaska, in 1989, spilling 35,200 tons (32,000 t) of crude oil (page 184).

Bulk carriers carry dry, loose material—grain, sugar, wood chips, mineral ores, and so on—in bulk. Modern bulk carriers vary in size from those with a capacity of about 22,000–77,000 tons (20,000–70,000 t) usually dry-food carriers and small enough to pass through the Panama Canal to larger oceangoing vessels that carry mineral ores and have capacities in excess of 132,000 tons (120,000 t).

Many variations on the major designs of freighter exist; for example, most tankers carry liquid petroleum products, but some are specialized for refrigeration and carry liquefied natural gas or petroleum gas, and others are partitioned to enable them to carry oil, mineral ores, or a combination of the two.

Merchant Fleets

In January 1995, there were about 25,000 cargo vessels in excess of 1,100 tons (1,000 t) registered in the world's merchant fleets. The top 10 fleets, in terms of registered gross tonnages and in decreasing order were: Panama, Liberia, Greece, Cyprus, Bahamas, Norway, Japan, Malta, China, and the United States (see box, page 124). There is little or no correspondence between a country's size and the size of its registered merchant fleet.

Some of the greatest seafaring nations—France, Italy, the Netherlands, and the United Kingdom—do not appear on this list, and the United States, with the greatest international trade of any nation, ranks only 10th. The reason for this apparent anomaly is that many of the world's largest cargo vessels are operated by one country, constructed in another, and registered in yet a third. What are the advantages in doing so? The obvious answer is cost. Vessels operated by U.S. shipping lines are commonly ordered from other countries where build quality is relatively high but construction costs are much lower. These ships are then registered under the flag of another nation, such as Panama or Liberia. Registering with a small, developing country under so-called flags of convenience means that shipping operators pay lower taxes, pay smaller wages to crews, do not have to train crews to the same level of expertise, and have to comply with fewer safety regulations. It is a chastening thought that much of the food, oil, and other basic commodities we need are carried in these cost-saving but far-from-ideal circumstances.

Ancient Maritime Conflicts

The earliest documented warships that were specifically adapted for fighting at sea date from the seventh century B.C.E. These Greek and Phoenician fighting ships were galleys, that is, long, slender vessels powered by oarsmen. A rectangular sail was hoisted when the vessel was cruising; in battle, the sail was lowered and oarsmen alone provided the ship's necessary speed and maneuverability. The earliest-known fighting vessels were biremes—galleys with two banks of oarsmen staggered one above the other.

The three chief strategies in ancient maritime warfare were to sink the opposition, to board their vessels, or to set fire to them. The galleys had a bow extended into a ram and during engagement would commonly seek to drive the ram into the enemy's warship, making a hole in the vessel at or below the waterline and so sinking it.

By the fifth century B.C.E., the bireme had evolved into the trireme—literally a "three row"—that incorporated three banks of oarsmen, one rower to each oar. Increasing the numbers of oarsmen increased the speed and power of the warship, and because it was not feasible to increase the length of the ship without substantially weakening it, additional rowers were accommodated by adding another bank or by increasing the number of rowers to each oar. Versions of the trireme were operational within Roman fleets, as well as in Phoenician and Greek navies. Three banks of oars does seem to be the maximum used in warships. When faithful reconstructions of Greek triremes were built in the 1970s and 1980s, the speed and sophistication of these vessels surprised modern sailors and scholars. In the ancient Mediterranean at the height of Greek power, such vessels must have struck terror in the hearts of their slower and poorer-armed naval opponents.

Techniques of warfare became increasingly sophisticated, and the Greeks devised a surprisingly diverse range of strategies. Ramming and boarding techniques were supplemented by dropping heavy weights onto enemy ships from poles, shooting burning arrows, and discharging "Greek fire"—a burning liquid—from metal containers. The recipe for Greek fire has been lost through time, but the mix probably included naptha, quicklime, and sulfur. Its special property was the capacity to burn underwater.

Naval supremacy was of paramount importance in the expansion and maintenance of most military empires from the first millennium B.C.E. right up until the present day. The crucial role of

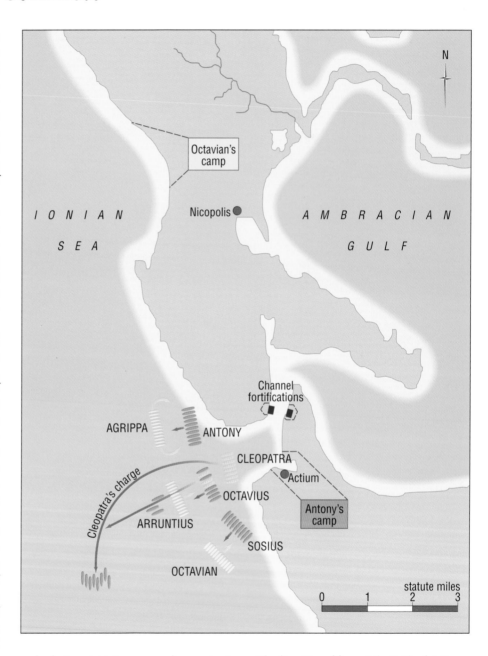

The disposition of forces at the Battle of Actium

sea battles in maintaining or expanding empires is well illustrated by two examples, one from classical Greece the other from ancient Rome.

The Battle of Salamis, 480 B.C.E.

Salamis is an island just off the Greek mainland and within 37 miles (60 km) of Athens. By 480 B.C.E., the Greeks and the Persians had been engaged in a war for several years, with the Persians making considerable inroads into the Greek Empire. The Greek defeat at Thermopylae in the summer of 480 B.C.E. exposed the Greek mainland to attack. Xerxes, the Persian king, before pressing home an attack on land, wished to help

guarantee successful conquest by smashing the Greek fleet.

It was September 480 B.C.E. The Greek fleet under the leadership of the Athenian commander Themistocles was at anchor in the Bay of Eleusis between Salamis and the Greek mainland. Themistocles' strategy was to entice the Persian fleet to do battle in waters that gave an advantage to the Greeks and so help counter the Persian superiority in numbers.

Xerxes gathered most of his fleet on the east side of Salamis and sent a contingent of ships from Egypt—their allies—to seal off the Greeks' exit route on the west side of the island. The Greek vessels came under attack by the Persian fleet when the Persian commander made the fatal error of precipitating conflict in the fairly narrow straits between island and mainland. In these confined waters, the Persians were at a disadvantage and could not exploit their advantage in size. In addition, Themistocles waited until the Persian vessels were well within the confines of the narrow channel. A wind sprung up that made the high-sided Persian vessels more difficult to maneuver than the sleeker Greek vessels. Cimon, second-in-command to Themistocles, launched an attack when the Persian vessels were well within the channel. In the restricted waters and the subsequent confusion of battle, 200 Persian vessels were lost—either sunk or burned—in about eight hours, while Greek losses were about 40 ships. Aeschylus, an eyewitness to the battle, recorded these impressions: "They [the Athenians] smashed at men like tunny fish, with broken oars and pieces of timber," and "I saw the Aegean Sea blossoming with corpses." The Persian king—watching from a nearby vantage point—was reputedly so incensed at the loss of about one-third of his fleet that he ordered put to death any sailors that were washed ashore on the nearby mainland—whether Persian or Greek. The remains of the Persian fleet withdrew to nearby Phalerum. This sea battle was the turning point in the Greek-Persian war and ultimately compelled Xerxes to withdraw his forces from Mediterranean Europe. The 50 years following the Battle of Salamis represented the zenith of ancient Greek political and cultural achievement.

The Battle of Actium, 31 B.C.E.

Octavian—the future Emperor Augustus—was a rival with his famous brother-in-law Mark Antony for the leadership of the Roman Empire. Antony had established an alliance with Queen Cleopatra of Egypt. The enmity between Octavian and Antony was based on Octavian's need for riches with which to reward his supporters; these resources were to be found in the East—including Egypt—a region under the control of Antony. Antony's support of Egypt as a state independent of Rome was another source of discord. Sea forces under the command of the brothers came into conflict on a number of occasions between 32 and 31 B.C.E., culminating in the Battle of Actium on September 2, 31 B.C.E.

In the summer of 31 B.C.E., a fleet under the command of Agrippa, an admiral serving Octavian, amassed in the Ionian Sea and threatened to entirely cut off supplies to Antony's fleet and to his stronghold on the mainland promontory of Actium. This peninsula is located at the southern side of a strait that leads into the present-day Gulf of Arta. Antony's forces were low in provisions and manpower, and he had reduced his initially very large fleet to about 200 vessels, including 60 vessels under the command of Cleopatra. Antony's ships were larger than Octavian's but slower and more cumbersome; Antony's vessels also were equipped with artillery towers and grappling irons, whereas Octavian's ships carried large numbers of soldiers and were fitted with devices for propelling burning charcoal and pitch. Both sides were fairly equally matched in terms of numbers of vessels. Antony's intention was to return to Egypt and, if necessary, defeat Octavian's fleet on the way.

By late morning on September 2, the opposing fleets were facing each other just off the Ambracian Gulf (today, the Gulf of Arta). At around midday, Antony's forward squadrons advanced to do battle, but soon after, Cleopatra's squadron, with sails hoisted, shot through the facing squadrons of Antony's and Octavian's vessels. Opinions are very divided as to whether this move was an ill-advised attempt to divert the opposition and force the issue or simply a wish to flee. In either case, once her squadron was downwind of the battle lines, Cleopatra was unable to rejoin the battle even had she wished to. Seeing Cleopatra's squadron leave, Antony and some of his vessels followed her, while the bulk of his fleet stayed behind and was subjected to a fierce attack from Octavian's fleet, with many vessels being sunk by ramming or being burnt. By the late afternoon, the remnants of Antony's fleet fled.

Antony had lost the battle and with it his reputation. Antony and Cleopatra returned to Egypt, where Antony's remaining ships and men soon deserted him. In Alexandria the following year, Antony committed suicide. Octavian's power was established, and he went on to become Emperor Augustus. The victory at Actium was to mark the beginning of Rome's naval supremacy that helped underpin the might of the Roman Empire throughout its period of dominance until 284 C.E.

Maritime Conflict in the Western Age of Sail

The Battle of Lepanto

The last major sea battle involving a clash of vessels driven by oarsmen occurred just off the Greek mainland at the entrance to the Gulf of Patras on October 7, 1571. An alliance of Christian states bordering the Mediterranean eventually overcame a large Turkish force—the Ottoman fleet—in what was to be regarded as the last crusade against the Turks. About 200 larger Christian galleys faced the 273 smaller Turkish vessels in long lines abreast. Both fleets probably had about 75,000 warriors. The battle was long and bloody with those on one side using grappling hooks to restrain and then board vessels of the opposition. The Turkish forces were renowned for their devastating use of rapid-fire archers, while the Christian vessels were larger and had greater firepower overall. The loss of life was considerable—and much greater than in later sea battles such as the loss of the Spanish Armada and the Battle of Trafalgar. An estimated 20,000 lives were lost on the Turkish side and 8,000 from the Christian fleet. The outcome of the battle had great political impact, stemming, as it did, the very real threat of Turkish domination of the Mediterranean. The alliance forces on the Christian side were said to contain representatives from every noble house in Italy and Spain and volunteers from many European countries, including England. Among the Christian forces was the Spaniard Don Miguel de Cervantes Saavendra (c. 1547–1616). Author of the famous novel *Don Quixote*, he lost an arm during the battle.

The Defeat of the Spanish Armada

By the late 16th century, European warships had become quite sophisticated, and in the case of some Spanish galleons, large and elaborate. Warships were typically three masted with fore- and aftcastles and carried guns that fired cannonballs at opposing ships. Frigates of the English fleet were about 100 feet (30 m) in length, weighed about 110 tons (100 t), typically carried 18–30 cannon, and were crewed by some 60–80 seafarers. The greatest Spanish galleons of the time were much larger, up to 1,100 tons (1,000 t). The major European seapowers were the Dutch, the French, the Spaniards, and the English. Given the political and religious climate of the time—much of southern and northwestern Europe was Catholic, while England was stridently Protestant—an attempted invasion of England by one of the other major naval powers was simply a

matter of time. Time ran out in the summer of 1588 when King Philip II of Spain made a bid to overthrow Queen Elizabeth I and establish himself on the throne of England.

Philip of Spain amassed a fleet of some 130 vessels, ranging in size from 1,100-ton (1,000-t) galleons to 110-ton (100-t) frigates and supply vessels. The fleet was manned by about 8,000 sailors, 2,000 galley slaves, 19,000 soldiers, and about 1,500 others, ranging from camp followers to leading clergy members of the Spanish Inquisition. The defending English force was to comprise only 80 vessels, but strategy, as well as unusually turbulent summer weather, were to turn the outcome of the battle in England's favor.

Philip's intention was for the Spanish fleet—dubbed before it sailed "the most fortunate and invincible," later to be called the Armada—to force its way through the English Channel, pick up the army of the Prince of Parma at Calais, and then transport the combined force across the English Channel to England. It was not Philip's intention for the fleet to engage in a sea battle if this could be avoided.

The Spanish fleet left Lisbon, Portugal, at the end of May, but bad weather impeded progress; after berthing at Coruña, Spain, the fleet did not leave this port until mid-July. The Armada was spotted off Cornwall, England, on July 19. The English fleet of about 130 vessels had a large western squadron based at Plymouth, Devon, and a smaller eastern squadron at Dover, Kent. The western squadron set sail as soon as the Armada was sighted, while the eastern squadron waited until events at Calais began to develop.

The first shots were fired on July 21 when England's western force—under the leadership of Lord Howard of Effingham, with Sir Francis Drake second-in-command—began to engage the Spanish. Meanwhile the Spanish fleet continued sailing eastward along the English Channel in a majestic, crescent-shaped formation. The smaller, faster, and more maneuverable English ships harried the Armada for the next two days, causing more annoyance than serious damage, although two Spanish vessels were lost. By July 27, some straggling Spanish vessels were lost to English attacks, but the bulk of the Spanish fleet remained in formation and successfully reached anchor off Calais. The English ships were, by this time, running low on ammunition and other provisions but were resupplied from shore and were also joined by the eastern squadron from Dover.

Effingham and Drake realized that drastic action was necessary to prevent Parma's army

being picked up by the Spanish fleet. That evening, several small English vessels—estimates vary between six and eight—were allowed to drift on the wind toward the Spanish fleet at anchor. The impending arrival of fireships amid the tightly packed Spanish force caused panic, and to save themselves from the likely conflagration, the Spanish cut their moorings and sailed before the wind, closely pursued by the English. Fighting took place just off the Netherlands, where three Spanish galleons were lost. The Spanish vessels were in danger of running aground in shallow water—the Dutch shoals—but a sudden change in wind direction enabled them to sail northward.

Over the ensuing weeks, the Spanish fleet had a disastrous time. Invasion was now impossible. The Armada—without Parma's army and low on ammunition and provisions—could not fight its way back through the channel and instead was forced to take the long route around the north of Scotland and west of Ireland. Harried by English ships on the journey up the North Sea, many Spanish vessels that escaped northward later became shipwrecked on the rocky coasts of Scotland and Ireland; these vessels were pillaged and the crews slaughtered by local inhabitants. The remnants of the Spanish fleet arrived home beginning in September. Of the 130 ships that started out, only 67 returned.

The invasion of England had been averted and England's naval reputation enhanced. The Spanish fleet was reequipped, and in close alliance with the Netherlands, the Spanish fleet remained a potent naval force for another century. The Spanish did not, however, make another attempt to invade England.

The Battle of Trafalgar

The Battle of Trafalgar on the October 21, 1805, was the last but one major sea battle of the classic days of sail. The Battle of Trafalgar—and the destruction of the bulk of the Franco-Spanish fleet as the outcome—removed any realistic possibility of Napoleon controlling the waters of the English Channel, the Atlantic, and the Mediterranean during the last decade of the Napoleonic Wars (1803–1815).

The battle between the Franco-Spanish and English fleets occurred off Cape Trafalgar on the southwestern coast of Spain. Admiral Villeneuve, commander of the Franco-Spanish fleet, left the safe harbor of Cádiz on October 19 under the

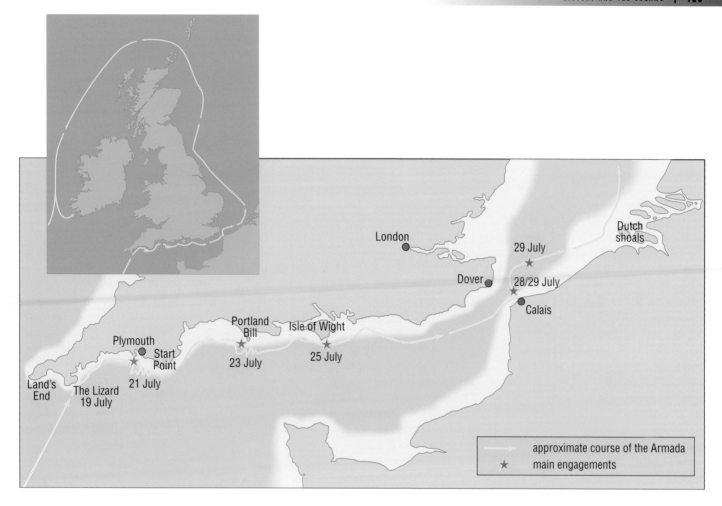

London

Dutch shoals

29 July
★

Dover ●
28/29 July
★
Calais ●

Portland Bill
Isle of Wight
★
23 July
★
25 July

Plymouth ●
Start Point
★
21 July

Land's End
The Lizard
19 July

→ approximate course of the Armada
★ main engagements

*The route of the Spanish Armada
between July and fall 1588*

orders of Napoleon, who wished him to bring the fleet to the Mediterranean. Villeneuve was due to be replaced by Admiral Rosily en route. Against Villeneuve's better judgment, the fleet left harbor and sailed southward for the Straits of Gibraltar. Opposing the Franco-Spanish force was a fleet under the command of the distinguished admiral Horatio Nelson (1758–1805). For the next two days, frigates of Nelson's fleet kept watch on Villeneuve's force while Nelson kept the bulk of his fleet just over the horizon. He had no wish to scare the Franco-Spanish fleet into returning back to Cádiz: His intention all along was to annihilate the opposing fleet. The opportunity came on the morning of October 21. At daybreak, the two fleets were in sight of one another. Villeneuve decided to return to Cádiz, but by then it was too late to avoid battle.

Nelson's battle plan was daring, unconventional, and—as events proved—devastatingly effective. It was also the classic example of the sea commander truly leading from the front—a risk that led to Nelson making the ultimate sacrifice.

The opposing forces were fairly evenly matched, the English fleet with 26 vessels and the combined Franco-Spanish fleet with 33 (18 French and 15 Spanish). Nelson made the unorthodox decision to split his force into two columns that would attack two clearly defined points near the center of the opponent's fleet. Nelson in the *Victory* would lead one column, and Vice-Admiral Collingwood in the *Royal Sovereign* the other. The lead ships would be subjected to raking broadsides well before they would be in a position to make an effective reply. However, were they to break through the Franco-Spanish lines, great confusion and a great advantage would result. This is exactly what occurred: the lead ships suffered considerable damage and casualties but did break

through the enemy line, and they and the following column were able to exert heavy firepower on the center of the enemy fleet. Collingwood's *Royal Sovereign* broke the enemy line first, while about a half-hour later Nelson's *Victory* broke through the French line. But in close fighting with the French ship *Redoubtable*, Nelson was mortally wounded: he died at about 4.30 P.M. shortly after being informed of the English victory. Eventually, 18 French and Spanish vessels were captured or destroyed, whereas no English ships were sunk, although many were severely damaged.

The victory at Trafalgar confirmed that England was the foremost naval power and was to remain so until the beginning of the 20th century. The Royal Navy, effectively unchallenged, was able to provide the seapower necessary to consolidate the expanding British Empire.

The Battle of Navarino in 1827 between Turkish and Greek-alliance forces was to be the last major battle between sailing warships.

Maritime Conflict in the Modern Era

The modern era of naval warfare was heralded by several major scientific and technological developments of the 19th century. Sail propulsion gradually gave way to steam power, wooden hulls were replaced by those of iron and later steel, and ball-firing cannons were superseded by shell-firing devices—cannons that fired explosive projectiles.

The transition period from sailing ship to steamship was grudgingly slow. Paddle wheels and their enclosures were particularly vulnerable to gunfire; therefore, the use of naval steamships did not really get under way until the 1840s and 1850s when the newly invented steam-driven propeller was available. Nevertheless, for the next 40 years, many naval ships retained masts and sails alongside the steam engine and propeller, such was the distrust in the new technology and the establishment's resistance to change. The British Navy, for example, clung to its sailing traditions in the belief that knowledge of sail was essential in the making of a true seafarer.

The development of shell-firing cannon soon made wooden vessels obsolete. During the Russo-Turkish War in 1853, the Turkish fleet of wooden vessels was almost entirely annihilated by Russian shell-firing vessels in an engagement at Sinope (later Sinop). British and U.S. experiments with covering wooden hulls with iron plate were successful, and these so-called ironclads were to supersede wooden-hulled vessels temporarily.

The Clash of Ironclads

The first engagement between armored vessels was one of history's most famous sea battles and also the first major naval engagement of the American Civil War. In 1861, Confederate forces resurrected the scuttled Union vessel, the frigate *Merrimac,* and converted it into an ironclad ship and renamed it the *Virginia.* This heavy vessel, with its armour plating and 10 heavy guns, sailed into Hampton Roads on March 8, 1862, and quickly destroyed two wooden warships of the Union fleet. When the Union fleet responded with gunfire, the cannonballs simply bounced off *Virginia*'s armored decks. The Union's only ironclad naval vessel of the time, the *Monitor,* was hurriedly sent for and arrived by sea the following morning. The *Monitor* was much smaller than the *Virginia* but was faster, more maneuverable, and of greater sophistication. Its two large guns were mounted on a rotating gun turret—an innovation that was developed independently in the United States and in England. This device enabled fewer but larger guns to be carried. Each gun could be rotated to fire at different angles.

The two ironclad ships engaged in a four-hour gun battle with neither being able to penetrate the armor plating of the other. From that day on, the need for armored naval vessels, and the necessity for greater firepower if such armor was to be penetrated, was clearly understood.

In the decade 1860–70, Britain took the lead in building naval vessels with hulls of iron, and this trend was rapidly followed by navies throughout the world. Steel—lighter and with a higher tensile strength—replaced iron as the material of choice during the period 1875–80. Improvements in steam-engine design continued until the beginning of the 20th century, when steam turbines supplanted steam engines.

Alongside developments in ship propulsion and hull design, ships' armaments were increasing in variety and effectiveness. Improvements in gun mechanisms—for example, breech-loading—and better explosive propellants—such as nitrocellulose—resulted in naval guns with greater range, firepower, and speed of operation. Instead of cannons in serried rows, ships were now armed with fewer but more-powerful cannons mounted on rotating turrets.

By the 1880s, warships were beginning to diversify. With the invention of the self-propelled torpedo, small, swift vessels could now be effective in sinking large ships. The response to this development was the fast-moving destroyer that was designed to attack torpedo boats and, later, to destroy submarines.

The symbol of naval power from the beginning of the 20th century until the early 1940s was the dreadnought battleship—a general term for a large vessel that carried very large guns and relatively little secondary armament. The HMS *Dreadnought* of the British Navy, launched in 1906, was the first vessel of this type. During World War I and the early years of World War II, a battleship fleet would comprise one or more battleships screened by several cruisers and destroyers. Cruisers are essentially small, fast versions of battleships with lighter guns and armor. Torpedo-carrying destroyers tended to rely on their speed and maneuverability to avoid direct hits and so carried little armor.

By the early 1940s, the increased sophistication of submarines and the superior flexibility of the aircraft carrier with its strike force of dive bombers, torpedo bombers, and fighters caused battleships to become increasingly outmoded. The effectiveness of aircraft carriers was established beyond all doubt at the Battle of Midway in 1942.

Midway

The June 4, 1942, Battle of Midway between the Japanese and United States fleets was a conflict that neither side could afford to lose. The outcome was to change the tide of World War II and would redefine naval combat.

Between 1939 and spring 1942, Japanese expansion in the Pacific Ocean had been a remarkable success story: Japanese land forces spearheaded by their navy had swept across Manchuria, Burma, the Philippines, the Dutch East Indies (now Indonesia), and Malaya.

By spring 1942, the Japanese fleet under the command of Admiral Yamamoto had yet to experience defeat. The U.S. Pacific fleet under the leadership of Admiral Chester Nimitz had yet to taste victory. The U.S. naval forces were still licking their wounds after the ignominious destruction of much of the Pacific fleet at Pearl Harbor on December 7, 1941. The Japanese strike demonstrated the remarkable effectiveness of aircraft carriers: 350 planes launched from six Japanese carriers sank six U.S. vessels and badly damaged 10 others in a matter of hours. (U.S. aircraft carriers were on maneuvers that day and were left untouched by the Japanese attack.) Throughout the engagement, the Japanese fleet remained 275 miles away from Pearl Harbor; these ships did not fire a single shot.

In spring 1942, Admiral Nimitz orchestrated hit-and-run raids on Japanese forces and territories using aircraft flying from carriers. One of these nuisance attacks was a bombing raid on Tokyo to coincide with the emperor's birthday. This brought home the vulnerability of the Japanese mainland to attack from carriers and spurred the Japanese into prioritizing the destruction of U.S. carriers in the Pacific. To this end, Yamamoto planned to draw U.S. forces into the defense of Midway Island, in the course of which he sought to destroy the carriers. This plan might have worked, but the U.S. was able to decode Japanese naval communications and in doing so were forewarned of Yamamoto's intentions. Admiral Nimitz planned to spring his own surprise.

Although Nimitz knew that the Japanese planned to attack Midway on June 4, he did not know the precise locations of the four Japanese carriers—*Akagi, Kaga, Soryu,* and *Hiryu*—from which the attack would be launched. U.S. reconnaissance aircraft sited the Japanese fleet only 20 hours before the intended attack on Midway, giving insufficient time for the U.S. carriers to protect Midway before the fighting started. The Japanese launched their attack on the early morning of June 4, sending 200 planes against Midway. The island's defenses were soon overwhelmed, but unknown to the Japanese, the U.S. carrier forces were to be within strike range by mid-morning. The four Japanese carriers were to be pitted against the three U.S. carriers—*Hornet, Enterprise,* and *Yorktown* (the latter still not fully operational from damage sustained in engagements in the Coral Sea the month before). The U.S. forces, however, had the element of surprise: the Japanese were not expecting their arrival for another two days.

Despite the element of surprise, the waves of dive bombers, torpedo bombers, and fighters launched from U.S. carriers met great resistance from Japanese fighters, and more than 100 U.S. aircraft were shot down before they could press home their attack on the Japanese carriers. Those that did break through the aerial defenses demonstrated one other feature of carriers—their vulnerability. With a flight deck covered with aircraft, fuel, and ammunition, any bombs landing on target were likely to set off a chain of explosions, and this is exactly what happened. Within a 10-minute period in mid-morning, three of the four Japanese carriers were hit, and in a matter of minutes the outcome of the Pacific War—and arguably World War II itself—was changed. The Japanese fleet had lost three of four vital ships and could no longer press home its conquest of the Pacific.

The remaining Japanese carrier, the *Hiryu,* retaliated, and knocked out the *Yorktown,* but was soon attacked and destroyed herself. Of the seven carriers that engaged in the battle, five were sunk. The U.S. vessels *Hornet* and *Enterprise* were the only carriers to survive the battle. The victory at Midway was one of the most decisive in naval history and at the time was all the more remarkable for taking place without either fleet actually seeing the other. Aircraft carriers had established a strategic significance far beyond their numbers, and this remains so to this day.

After World War II

Today, carrier-centered task forces remain a major component of U.S. and other naval forces. The development of nuclear weapons, nuclear propulsion, and missile-guidance systems has revolutionized the structure of naval forces. The largest surface vessels are nuclear-powered aircraft carriers, but during the cold war, nuclear-powered ballistic-missile submarines took on a major strategic role that to some extent still remains. Guided missiles can be launched from ships or submarines against aircraft, land forces, or seacraft and have rendered shipborne guns almost entirely obsolete. The traditional classification—corvette, destroyer, cruiser, carrier, and so on—is becoming redundant as the roles of these different craft come to overlap.

In major naval engagements since the 1980s—notably the Falklands conflict and the Gulf War—the dominant role of carrier-launched aircraft, the devastating effectiveness of guided missiles, and the coordination between sea, air, and land actions have been well established. During the Falklands War, the Argentine cruiser *General Belgrano* was torpedoed and sunk by a British submarine and two British destroyers, and two frigates were attacked and sunk by Argentinian air attacks. The British task force that retook the Falkland Islands after the Argentinian invasion was made up of two carriers, plus destroyers, frigates, troop carriers, landing ships, and supply vessels, many of which sailed a distance of some 8,000 miles (12,500 km) between Britain and the battle zone.

Today's naval conflicts are increasingly technologically sophisticated. In the Gulf War, cruise missiles launched from U.S. warships and laser-guided bombs and TV-guided missiles released from carrier-launched aircraft were used to attack Iraqi targets with clinical precision. A panoply of electronic jamming devices, antiradar aircraft, and antimissile missiles are now part of the hardware of modern naval warfare.

The Strategic Use of the Sea

All oceans and seas have strategic significance. Coastal waters are a—perhaps *the*—main route of access into a country or a continent. Most of a country's bulk trade, at one stage or another, is transported by sea. The very term *gunboat diplomacy*—diplomatic negotiations stimulated by the threat of military action—reflects the historical importance of the power wielded by navies in settling disputes. Though military strategists tended to downplay the importance of surface naval power during the cold war, several incidents in the last 20 years have confirmed gunboat diplomacy as an important reality in world political affairs.

Sea Power

Seas as avenues of transport provide an unrivaled capacity for delivering a flexible military force to distant locations en masse. The major maritime powers—currently, the United States, the United Kingdom, Russia, France, and China—demand freedom of the open ocean to deploy their navies at long distances from home waters. These and other naval forces monitor one another and protect their national interests. They offer security to their merchant and fishing fleets and occasionally are called upon to threaten or to intervene in disputes over perceived rights, whether on the high seas or in territorial waters. Naval forces have great strength in their flexibility. Movement of a large fleet of warships to a particular region of the world is a very powerful threat but can occur without any territory actually being invaded. Such movements spur governments into action when diplomatic moves are floundering.

Since World War II, more countries have invested in establishing navies, and naval activities have become much more diverse, as nations have come to recognize the benefits of having a navy—even a small one. Exercising sea power is a means of staking—or defending—a claim to marine territory and with it marine resources (page 194).

Attack and Defense

The balance of power throughout much of the world is achieved by the policy of deterrence—dissuading an enemy from attacking because of the dire retaliation that may result; deterrence is generally regarded as the best means of defense. The navies of the major maritime powers under-

pin two main approaches to deterrence: the first is the ability to launch a precision counterattack using nonnuclear weapons; the second is a nuclear second-strike capability—the threatened response to a nuclear first strike—and also an implied counterthreat to the use of chemical or biological weapons by an enemy force. It is the nuclear second-strike capability that has arguably kept the cold war peace for nearly 40 years. It is also, some military experts argue, the threat of nuclear response by the United States that dissuaded Iraq from using chemical weaponry on a widespread basis in the Gulf War of 1991. The ability to conduct precision counterattacks with nonnuclear weaponry was amply demonstrated in the Gulf War of 1991 and in the Falklands conflict of 1982.

Today, sea-launched thermonuclear bombs are still the first-choice deterrent weapon of the major powers, and the percentage of nuclear strategic weapons launched from sea is gradually increasing as land- and air-launched weapons decline in numbers. The submarines that deliver these weapons do so via ballistic missiles that are normally launched from under water. The submarines that have this strike capacity tend to be nuclear powered and are called nuclear-powered ballistic submarines (SSBNs). Currently, the United States has 17 such submarines, the United Kingdom 4, Russia about 36, France 5, and China 1. The situation is less clear-cut than it seems because the Russian submarines, though more numerous and with greater firepower than U.S. submarines, have lower technical sophistication and missile accuracy.

Below the surface of the sea, modern nuclear submarines monitor the world's shipping. They can operate for months at sea without surfacing and can utilize natural underwater features—undersea ridges and the SOFAR layer, for example—so that they are virtually undetectable.

As well as their ballistic-missile submarine (SSBN) capability, the five major maritime powers also operate nuclear attack submarines (SSNs). At least three other nation-states—India, Brazil, and Japan—have intentions or long-term aspirations to build such submarines. These attack submarines have a remarkable reach. They operate with cunning stealth, are able to keep surface forces under constant surveillance, and have the capacity to attack surface ships with a high probability of success. In the Falklands campaign, the cruiser *General Belgrano* was sunk by a nuclear-powered attack submarine.

More than 40 states have diesel-electric submarines, although some of the major sea powers have taken theirs out of service. Though smaller, less heavily armed, and with a range much less than that of nuclear-powered submarines, they nevertheless play an important role in patroling home waters.

The larger naval fleets rely substantially on aircraft carriers, often nuclear-powered, that deploy war planes and helicopters and are accompanied by a range of smaller craft—destroyers, corvettes, and so on. Both submarines and surface ships are sometimes utilized for mine laying. Sea mines, like their land counterparts, are disruptive physical and psychological weapons. Lying silently in wait, tethered below the water surface, they have the power to deter a marine invasion or prevent ships from entering or leaving port. They are a powerful means of engaging the enemy at a distance and at low cost.

Trouble Spots

Gunboat diplomacy is still very much alive. In March 1996, the Chinese navy's annual maneuvers in the Straits of Taiwan took on a much more sinister and threatening aspect. Whether designed to influence the Taiwanese electorate (presidential elections were taking place later in the month), or whether actual acts of aggression were intended, the Chinese military maneuvers were a clear manifestation of China's long-standing intention to reannex Taiwan. At the time, the U.S. military response to the threat involved moving the carrier *Independence* and its entourage of warships to the locality, thereby emphasizing the United States's unconditional support for Taiwanese independence. The incident also served to illustrate the cooperation between North Atlantic Treaty Organization (NATO) forces. As *Independence* sailed from the Persian Gulf to the trouble zone, so its Gulf role was replaced by another U.S. force from the Mediterranean, and the Mediterranean gap was then filled by NATO allies.

Other potential trouble spots include the South China Sea (where China is making extensive territorial claims) and the Persian Gulf (where Iran continues to adopt a confrontational military posture to pressure neighboring states). In the eastern Aegean Sea, lack of progress over the partition of Cyprus and the absence of any diplomatic settlement over disputed islands near the Turkish coast means that problems can flare up at any time. In early 1996, sizable Greek and

THE BAY OF PIGS AND THE CUBAN MISSILE CRISIS

In April 1961, President John F. Kennedy sanctioned U.S. backing for an invasion of Cuba by exiles attempting to overthrow Fidel Castro's communist government. On April 17 more than 1,000 Cuban exiles landed at the Bay of Pigs, Cuba, aided by Cuban-exiled pilots flying U.S.-procured planes. Soviet leader Nikita Khrushchev threatened to defend Cuba should the United States have any further plans for supporting the attack. The attempt to oust Castro was ill-conceived, and the attacking force was overpowered within 48 hours. The débâcle was to be called the Bay of Pigs fiasco.

The following year, Cuba, the Soviet Union, and the United States were to become embroiled in an encounter that was to take the world to the brink of a nuclear war. On August 29 a U.S. spy plane flying over Cuba photographed launchpads for surface-to-air missiles being assembled. On October 14 further photographs showed that not only defensive missile bases were being constructed but offensive missile sites too. These would be capable of firing nuclear warheads to reach the U.S. mainland. In the political climate of the time—and at the height of the cold war with the Bay of Pigs fiasco only a recent memory—Kennedy, and indeed the U.S. Congress, could not be seen to allow this extension of Soviet power. U.S. intelligence agencies knew that nuclear warheads could be brought in and prepared for launching within as little as 14 days (Soviet records later showed that some nuclear warheads were already in Cuba). There was little time to maneuver. On October 22 President Kennedy announced his decision to impose a naval blockade around Cuba. He also insisted that the missiles and their bases be removed, saying they (the Soviet nuclear missiles and bombers based on Cuba) were an "explicit threat to the peace and security of all the Ameri-

cas." On October 24, two missile-carrying Soviet merchant vessels and their Soviet submarine escort were halted by the U.S. naval blockade some 500 miles from Cuba. Meanwhile, on Cuba, the missile bases were still being assembled. Khrushchev was trying to call Kennedy's bluff and was attempting to argue to the world's governments and media that the missile sites were not offensive but purely defensive and nonnuclear. On October 25 the U.S. delegate to the United Nations showed the photographic proof that confirmed the true nature of the missile bases. Khrushchev's lie was exposed but he too was under political pressure at home to gain the most mileage from the by now frighteningly risky imbroglio. A U.S. spy plane flying over Cuba was shot down and the crisis reached its climax on October 27 when U.S. forces were on the point of attacking Cuba. Khrushchev, at this point, had probably decided that he would withdraw the missiles if he could gain some political advantage—such as the U.S.'s agreement to allow the Soviets to continue to defend Cuba's communist interests but without the presence of nuclear weaponry. In the days that followed the two sides reached agreement, although nothing was formally committed to paper and signed by the parties involved. The missiles were removed, and the status quo over Cuba has remained since then. Washington military sources at the time attributed the United States's success in handling the crisis to two key advantages: first, the U.S.'s capacity to take detailed reconnaissance photographs that could prove the nature of the missile sites; and second, the U.S. Navy's ability to successfully enforce a naval blockade of Cuba. The strength of the world's biggest navy was pivotal in bringing an event of world-threatening proportions to a nonviolent conclusion.

Turkish naval forces were deployed to where a Turkish coaster had run aground on an island claimed by both Greece and Turkey. The captain of the Turkish vessel had refused assistance from a Greek tug on the grounds that his vessel was in Turkish waters, not Greek. Media coverage inflamed the incident.

North and South Korea did not sign a peace treaty after the 1950—53 Korean War, and North Korean forces have intruded on South Korean territory on a number of occasions since. Recent negotiations, international diplomatic intervention, and provision of aid—North Korea has experienced catastrophic crop failures between 1995 and 1997—may be the start of moves towards a lasting peace.

Current and Future Exercise of Sea Power

Many Western countries are now dependent on Middle East oil and on products from the tiger economies of East Asia (Hong Kong, Singapore, South Korea, and Taiwan). Major industrial nations have little alternative but to continue to exercise naval power to help ensure the "peaceful passage of vital seaborne trade" to their shores. The U.S. navy is by and large the most powerful in this regard, and many other countries are more or less shielded by the umbrella of U.S. naval power—a situation that many nations take for granted. In the absence of this power, govern-

ments that flout the generally accepted rules of international behavior would have greater influence on seaborne activities.

The United States and the United Kingdom continue to see a balanced fleet as essential to ensure their very survival in time of war, and in peacetime, to uphold their interests at sea, sometimes many thousands of miles from home. A balanced fleet has both nonnuclear and nuclear armament capability. It comprises surface and subsurface vessels, and it has the flexibility to conduct aerial and amphibious operations to support and implement actions on land. Balanced naval fleets continue to act as major deterrent forces that maintain a peace—albeit sometimes shaky—over much of the developed and developing world.

The Sea in Literature

For as long as humans have encountered the sea, this most changeable of environments must have engendered complex, contradictory emotions—fear and wonder, anger and delight. The sea is contrary. Its tides are more or less predictable, the harvest is bounteous, and when calm, its beauty is serene. Yet it can change in an hour—strong winds, fast currents, and giant waves whipping and stirring the calm waters into a life-threatening turmoil. The contrary nature of the sea as life giver and destroyer, always worthy of respect, has played a major role in countless works of art and literature, for example, Ernest Hemingway's Pulitzer Prize–winning novella *The Old Man and the Sea.*

The sea is inherently mysterious. As we stand on a headland looking out to sea, far more remains hidden than is revealed. It remains an enigma, a backcloth onto which our deepest fears and wishes are projected. In writing about the sea, the imaginative author is afforded a large canvas and a many-colored palette, an abundance of riches. The literature of the sea over place and time is, like its subject, vast. The following account, with its strong Western bias, cannot attempt to do justice to the rich tradition of sea literature across the world's cultures.

Nature

From the sensory detail of the seashore captured in Gerard Manley Hopkins's notes and poetry to Richard Henry Dana's dramatic account of a storm in the Pacific in *Two Years Before the Mast,* the sea—whether in microcosm or macrocosm—has an easy capacity to fascinate and inspire. The sea is at once a creator of weather, a restless color-changing surface, a mirror that reflects that certain quality of light, and a setting for events on land. The urgent warnings in Rachel Carson's *The Sea Around Us* and Michael Weber and Judith Gradwohl's *The Wealth of Oceans* remind us that the lives of all beings on planet Earth and the very nature of land and air as places in which to live and breathe are inextricably linked with the oceans. The rhythm and pulse of ocean currents; the cycling of energy and matter between sea, land, and air; the living and nonliving resources we gather and consume from within and below the oceans—all influence terrestrial life in general and help establish the success or otherwise of human life in particular.

Adventure

Many facets of the sea's particular capacity to fascinate are woven into one of the oldest and most famous sea stories—Homer's epic poem, the *Odyssey.* Where Homer's earlier *Iliad* describes the Trojan War, culminating in Odysseus's successful wooden-horse stratagem, the *Odyssey* details the story of Odysseus's voyage from Troy to his homeland of Ithaca and the slaying of his wife's suitors on his return. Drama abounds: Unfavorable

---

Sunset at Woodlands Beach,
Montserrat, Caribbean.
(Gerry Ellis/ENP Images)

winds carry his vessel out of the Aegean and into the Mediterranean, where he finds himself in a fabulous world. Here, he braves all manner of temptations and dangers, including amorous liaisons with the goddess Calypso and the witch Circe and encounters with monsters such as the one-eyed Polyphemus, the legendary Scylla—a beast with a beguiling woman's voice—and Charybdis—a dangerous whirlpool (today, Scylla and Charybdis are identified as two navigational hazards in the Straits of Messina).

The words of the *Iliad* and the *Odyssey* are attributed to Homer (c. 810–730 B.C.E.), but the stories on which they are based derive from historical events, legends, and folktales passed down through several centuries by word of mouth and song. Homer's works contain haunting phrases that resound through the millennia to describe the many moods of the sea: "belching in terrible wise," "wine dark," and "with many voices," and these epic poems are rightly regarded as some of the world's greatest sea literature.

The stories of marine adventure in the last few hundred years are as full of dramatic contradiction as are the characters themselves. In real life and in fictional stories, the motivations for exploration are both noble and base: curiosity and greed, a quest for knowledge and the pursuit of power, an opportunity to test endurance and the tacit permission to exploit others.

War

Whenever events are set down in works of literature, they reflect a particular viewpoint, whether intentioned or not. Often driven by a certain political or religious view, whether we are conscious of it or not, our words reflect the social circumstance of our times, and this, of course, is part of their fascination. So, Sir Walter Raleigh's *The Last Fight of the Revenge*, a remarkably factual account, is imbued with the bold spirit of its author, and Robert Southey's *The Life of Nelson* and its description of the Battle of Trafalgar (pages 128–129) provide heroic figures of their time who, because of their pivotal roles in history, become the role models for courage and decisive action for generations of schoolchildren in Britain.

Within the last 50 years, at least three stunning works of fiction—based more or less on fact—have emerged to describe naval activities in World War II. Nicholas Monserrat's *The Cruel Sea* depicts, with chilling authenticity, the adventures of young naval conscripts who in the space of two years graduated from landlubbers to seasoned crews fighting in corvettes on the North Atlantic. In Herman Wouk's *The Caine Mutiny*, a real life event—an advancing typhoon that threatened Task Force 38 in December 1944—forms the setting for the fictional revolt of a life-threatened ship's crew against their irrational and seemingly paranoid captain. The experiences of German war correspondent Lothar-Gunthar Buchheim aboard one of Doenitz's U-boats at the height of the Battle of the Atlantic provided the raw material for the dark, claustrophobic novel *U-Boat*, which inspired the critically acclaimed film *Das Boot*. Buchheim's life expectancy, along with that of the captain and crew of the U-boat in which he sailed, would have been less than two war patrols. After three patrols, his time had not yet run out, but during the U-boat war, that of 27,000 German submariners did. More than two-thirds of German submariners did not survive their sorties.

Myth and Mystery

The very size of the oceans and their relative inaccessibility to all but the few who dare to venture over them has meant that the claims of seafarers cannot be substantiated—or denied—except by a select few. A rich tapestry of folklore, legend, and myth has thus grown up around the sea and its inhabitants. Giant monsters attack sailing vessels, a ship's crew disappears in mysterious circumstances, and parts of the ocean—the so-called Bermuda Triangle for one—become imbued with mystical power. Most of these phenomena are explicable when subjected to the intense light of rational inquiry, but the resulting explanations are nonetheless fascinating.

With much of the ocean world unknown—and unknowable—until the 20th century, some authors have been able to mine a rich vein of fantasy from below the sea's surface, as in Jules Verne's novel of 1869, *Twenty Thousand Leagues Under the Sea* which, in its depiction of diving apparatus and submarines, was surprisingly prophetic.

The ocean and its creatures provide archetypal images and symbols for cultures across the world, from classical Greece to ancient Polynesia. In many cultures, the sea, not surprisingly, plays a lead role in creation myths. Across Oceania, some cultures implicate giant clams in the creation of Heaven and Earth; in other communities, a mythical great spotted octopus holds Heaven and Earth together.

Spirit

A ship with its crew becomes a microcosm of human society, where, under testing conditions, struggles occur within the psyche of men, conflicts arise between disparate personalities on board, and there are epic clashes between the ship's members and the forces of nature outside. Captain Ahab's pursuit of an albino whale in Herman Melville's *Moby Dick*—an account so rich in meaning and so open to interpretation—is as much a story about a man's attempts to conquer the beast within as it is his pursuit of the beast without.

Journeys across the sea—whether real or imagined—mirror our life story: from leaving port, traversing storm-tossed seas, to final anchorage in safe harbor. Putting out to sea is also a metaphor for the beginning of our journey in the afterlife.

CROSSING THE BAR

Sunset and evening star,
And one clear call for me!
And may there be no moaning of the bar,
When I put out to sea.

But such a tide as moving seems asleep,
Too full for sound and foam,
When that which drew from out the boundless deep
Turns again home.

Twilight and evening bell,
After that the dark!
And may there be no sadness of farewell
When I embark. . . .

—ALFRED, LORD TENNYSON (1809–1892)

Underwater Archaeology

Marine archaeology—interpreting humankind's cultural heritage from recovered underwater remains and artifacts—has a much more recent history than its counterpart on land. The difficulties in locating features such as shipwrecks and submerged buildings—and once found, the problems in uncovering and bringing artifacts to the surface—has meant that marine archaeology only began to get under way in earnest in the 1940s with the invention of scuba-diving gear (page 153); modern techniques of underwater mapping, recording, and recovery only emerged in the 1960s. Even then, the operating constraints of underwater archaeology are considerable: winds, waves, and currents impede progress both before and after locating the archaeological site; additional hazards not experienced on land include the high pressure under water, low temperatures, and poor visibility.

Although recovering valuable objects from shipwrecks has a history as old as the shipwrecks themselves, many of the earlier explorers were primarily treasure hunters, seeking financial gain rather than understanding. This conflict between the motives of the archaeologist and those of the treasure hunter is still with us today.

In the 17th century, expeditions to recover underwater objects were carried out by divers using wooden diving bells to provide the oxygen to breathe underwater. Such methods were hazardous, to say the least. By the 19th century, the familiar spherical metal diving helmet was in use, with pumped air being supplied via a pipeline from a surface ship. Today, at depths of up to 165 feet (50 m) or so, more or less standard scuba-diving equipment is suitable, but at depths of 197–1,970 feet (60–600 m), much more sophisticated diving equipment is needed: diving suits that are cold resistant and pressure resistant, supplies of special gas mixtures for breathing, and chambers for underwater living and/or decompression. At a depth of more than 1,970 feet (600 m), submersibles—whether manned or remote control—are really the only option.

Underwater Expeditions

Finding a shipwreck or a submerged settlement is usually a detective story. Old documents and sea charts are sought and analyzed, and once a probable location has been suggested and there is a strong likelihood of a successful find, an expedition can be raised.

A modern archaeological team uses a vast array of equipment to locate and then map an archaeological site. Initial investigations commonly involve the use of sophisticated sonars. Side-scan sonars can determine the three-dimensional conformation of the seabed, whereas sub-bottom sonars reveal objects buried below the bottom sediment.

Once located, a shallow-water site is mapped in detail and excavated in a rather different manner to a deep-water site. To try to ensure that the site is protected from pillaging—some form of legal protection is sought and gained at an early stage. The international legislation for protecting marine archaeological sites is still far from satisfactory, although there are moves to improve this situation. Even where legal protection exists, it is difficult to enforce. An offshore wreck is prohibitively expensive to keep under constant surveillance, and a wreck site can be damaged inadvertently by the normal activities of a fishing boat or a dredging vessel.

In shallow water, a grid-work and photographic record of the area is commonly established at an early stage. The grid is set out using anchored scaffolding or tape, and each square within the grid is examined in a systematic fashion. A diver may record the appearance of any finds in situ, making drawings and notes using wax crayons and pencils on plastic paper. Fine layers of sediment are removed by brush or fan or by using water-jets. Larger volumes of sediment are cleared using a device that is rather like a giant underwater vacuum cleaner. Powered by compressed air, the device draws up water and sediment, which is filtered to recover any small objects or fragments of archaeological interest. As excavation proceeds, all revealed objects of reasonable size are tagged and numbered. Small to medium-size heavy finds are delicately released from their surroundings and are raised to the surface in a net or a crate below an air-filled lift bag—an air lift. Heavier objects such as cannon and parts of a ship's hull are winched to the surface by rope, sometimes cradled in a sling or customized frame. As excavation proceeds, a three-dimensional map of the site is assembled on computer using data from sonar surveys, the photographic record, and the records of individual finds. All are mapped and located within the established grid system.

Once items have been recovered, the archaeologist is confronted with a new set of problems—how to clean and preserve the recovered artifacts and how to collate and analyze the information to draw conclusions.

Seawater preserves some organic objects quite well, particularly when they are buried in sediment from which oxygen-respiring organisms are excluded. Thus, wooden-hull fragments and leather items may be remarkably intact, but once they are brought to the surface, degradation will occur very rapidly if they are simply allowed to dry out. A variety of preservation techniques are used. When timbers from King Henry VIII of England's flagship the *Mary Rose* were raised to the surface in 1982, the timbers were preserved by spraying or soaking with chemicals such as polyethylene glycol. Sometimes items are freeze-dried to preserve them. Iron can be prevented from rusting by roasting in a furnace with pure hydrogen. Once objects have been suitably treated, they usually need to be kept within strictly defined environmental parameters—at particular temperatures and humidities and in a specified gaseous environment from which potentially harmful organisms are excluded. Only this way will the objects survive for posterity. Commonly, the recovered relics are placed on display to the general public.

The *Vasa*—A Shallow Water Wreck

The *Vasa (Wasa)*, a large Swedish warship, sank in Stockholm harbor in 1628 during a squall. Attempts were made to raise her soon after, but these failed and there she remained until located in 1956 and major salvage operations began in 1959. The low salinity of Baltic waters had ensured that teredo worms—destructive wood-borers in waters of near-normal salinity—did not affect the *Vasa* and the hull—both above and below the bottom sediment—had remained remarkably intact. In 1961 the hull of the warship was raised to the surface from a depth of 108 feet (33 m). Now preserved and on display in Stockholm, some 25,000 listed artifacts have been assembled from the site, including wooden sculptures and complete skeletons with leather items such as belts, shoes, and purses intact. They form a remarkable time capsule of life at sea in the early 17th century.

The Fate of an Ancient Greek Merchant Vessel

Applying the techniques of modern marine archaeology can reveal fascinating insights into maritime life in a very remote era. In the 1960s, a cluster of ancient amphorae (vases for transporting liquids) was found on a seaweed-covered seabed about 1.2 miles (2 km) from the ancient harbor of Kyrenia in what is now Cyprus. When the sandy sediment was removed by divers using a suction airlift, the cargo of a Greek merchant ship from the fourth century B.C.E. was revealed. The vessel had settled on her port (left) side, which over time had become covered in sediment. The starboard side had deteriorated, and some of the amphorae had spilled out of the hull. When the excavation was complete, a startling 400 intact, or largely intact, amphorae were recovered, most originating from the Greek island Rhodes but with a few from Samos, further north. A cargo of almonds was also revealed, with grinding stones on the floor of the hull serving as ballast. Crockery from fore and aft cabins suggested a crew of four, and remnants of garlic, olives, grapes, and figs hinted at the nature of their diets. Lead weights used on fishing lines or nets were also found. The vessel's hull—though riddled with holes made by teredo worms—was nevertheless more than two-thirds complete. Its preservation had been aided by being buried in sediment, and the hull and keel had been encased in lead sheeting to protect against worm damage when the vessel was operational.

Titanic–A Deep-Water Wreck

On April 10, 1912, the Cunard line's premier passenger liner, the RMS *Titanic,* left Southampton, England, on its maiden voyage. Dubbed the ship "God himself could not sink," the massive liner—longer than a football field and with a displacement of more than 50,700 tons (46,000 t)—was the state-of-the-art liner of its time. Fitted with a swimming pool, squash court, "sidewalk cafes," elevators, and other luxurious features, the ship was reputedly safeguarded against sinking by having watertight bulkheads that could localize any

flooding. Tragically, these bulkheads did not extend the full height of the hull, and were one bulkhead to be completely flooded, the water would spill over into the next. This would continue in a cascade effect. If five of the ship's 16 bulkheads became flooded, the ship would be in danger of sinking.

During the Atlantic crossing, *Titanic* Captain E. J. Smith received repeated radio warnings of icebergs of the vicinity. Spurred on by the need to meet an exacting schedule, and probably overconfident in the invincibility of his vessel, the voyage continued at high speed—25 miles an hour (just less than 41 kilometers an hour). At 11.40 P.M. on April 14, the *Titanic* hit an iceberg with a glancing blow that damaged the ship's starboard (right) bow. By 2.20 A.M. the *Titanic* had sunk, taking with it more than 1,500 people. Under ideal conditions, there would have been lifeboats and other small craft available to rescue just more than half of the passengers and crew. As it turned out, of the 2,207 on board, there were only 705 survivors. Following the tragedy, much more stringent international safety regulations were instituted on passenger liners. In the future, sufficient lifeboats would be required for all passengers and crew, lifeboat drills would be compulsory, and wireless operating procedures would be tightened. The U.S. Navy began an ice patrol to monitor iceberg movements in the North Atlantic. This surveillance program became international from 1914 and continues to this day.

On September 1, 1985, a joint French-American expedition using sophisticated sonars located the *Titanic* at 41°46' N latitude and 50°14' W longitude near the Grand Banks, where it had sunk in more than 2.5 miles (4 km) of water. The Woods Hole Oceanographic Institution's remotely operated vehicle *Argo,* equipped with scanning sonar and video cameras, took the first pictures of the wreck. The following year, Robert

Ballard returned to the site and, using the manned submersible *Alvin,* obtained a detailed video record of the *Titanic.* But he decided to leave the wreck undisturbed, wishing it to be regarded with the status accorded to a mass grave site. Controversially, a French salvage expedition returned to the site shortly afterward and retrieved some crockery, jewels, and money, which were exhibited in Paris in 1987. Since then, others have considered the possibility of raising the vessel. By March 1998 about 4,000 items had been recovered from the wreck and were being prepared for display at more than eight locations across North America and Europe.

Titanic Fever

The United States—and with it, much of the movie-watching world—was gripped by *Titanic* fever in the late summer of 1997 and the spring of 1998. James Cameron's movie was not only the most expensive made to date—reputedly costing $200 million—but within six months of launching, it had broken all box-office records by taking in over $1 billion worldwide. In March 1998, the movie scooped 11 Oscars, including Best Film and Best Director, a record equalled only by the movie *Ben Hur* nearly four decades earlier. From the opening minutes of the movie—with two French submersibles exploring the hull and decking of the stricken vessel—the film attempts to re-create both the ship's fateful journey and present-day efforts to explore and recover objects from the remains. One thing seems sure: *Titanic* has captured the public imagination, and the wreck—and its contents—will not be readily laid to rest. Expensive day-trips to view the wreck by submersible are expected to begin operation by the year 2000.

The Art and Science of Navigation

The first marine explorers setting out to find new lands and fishing opportunities would have stayed within the comparative safety of coastal waters. We cannot know when the first oceanic explorers lost sight of land or whether this was by design or accident, but by 1500 B.C.E. the more adventurous seafarers of the Southwest Pacific were used to traveling for days seeing little but sea and sky. They must have mastered the ability to "read" the sea and sky for clues about wind, current, and landfall.

Early Navigators

To progress from one place to another by design—in other words, to navigate—it helps to know three things: where you are located, the locale of the place you intend to reach, and the route or direction to take between the two.

One of the key indicators of orientation is the movement of the Sun. The Sun rises in the east, sets in the west, and during the day its movement describes an arc across the sky. In the Northern Hemisphere, the arc is tilted towards the south; in the Southern Hemisphere it is to the north. So, the Sun's movement over the space of a few hours can provide a clear indication of east-west orientation: away from the equator, the tilt of the Sun's arc in the sky helps establish the north-south orientation.

At night in the Northern Hemisphere, the North Star (*Polaris*)—a seemingly stationary star around which the constellations rotate—indicates north. Two stars of the Great Bear, or Big Dipper, constellation, *Ursa Major,* act as a signpost always pointing to the North Star. In the Southern Hemisphere, the bright constellation, the Southern Cross, or *Crux Australis,* provides an indication of south. Of course, such polar indicators can only be used on a clear night, and the polar constellations are not visible close to the equator. These drawbacks aside, the stars are invaluable signposts, and the greater the astronomical knowledge of a navigator, the greater the number of celestial clues that can be utilized in direction finding. So the Sun during the day and the stars at night will have helped ancient mariners navigate when out of sight of land, but together these would not have provided sufficient information to guarantee safe passage from one location to another. What other indicators would have been used?

Long before classical antiquity, some sailors demonstrated remarkably high standards of seamanship. Pacific islanders—the Polynesians and Micronesians, for example—must have been supreme mariners, but historical evidence for their long-standing navigational traditions is sparse. In coastal waters and within sight of land, they no doubt orientated with respect to known landmarks. Whether close to land or in the open sea, navigational clues above and below the waterline are numerous to those able to appreciate them. Winds and cloud patterns provided—and still provide—clues about location.

The sea's color and clarity can be deciphered to reveal water depth and the presence of cold or warm currents. Productive cold currents are often associated with upwellings and high levels of biological activity and are often colored green, red, or brown, while clear, blue waters tend to be associated with less productive warm-water currents. The presence of sediment from rivers often turns water brown. Even seawater's taste and smell can provide clues to its origins.

Dead reckoning is a useful adjunct to these approaches and is a necessity when other clues are lacking. Dead reckoning is based on plotting direction—and time and speed as distance—onto a physical or mental map, making due allowance for the effects of winds, currents, and tides. In this way, the ship's progress can be estimated and any corrections made when the next sighting of an established feature is made. As recently as the 19th century, European seafarers checked the speed of their vessel using a piece of wood—a "log"—thrown overboard and attached to a length of rope knotted at intervals. As the rope was paid out, so the number of knots passing through the hand, in a given time, measured the speed of the boat. This activity has given rise to two terms still in use today: the *logbook* in which a ship's captain or other staff records daily readings and observations at sea, and the *knot* as a measure of speed—equivalent to 1 nautical mile an hour (1.15 miles an hour or 1.85 kilometers an hour).

The Magnetic Compass

The first recognizable navigational instrument was probably the magnetic compass. We now know that Earth behaves, in essence, like a bar magnet, and a magnetized needle or bar will orient itself along this axis. However, true north and magnetic north generally do not coincide. Earth's axis and the magnetic alignment only correspond approximately, and Earth's magnetic field fluctuates with changing flows of magnetic material in Earth's core. In North America or Europe, magnetic north can deviate as much as 20–30° from true north, depending on date and location. Nevertheless, a magnetic compass can be a useful navigational aid, enabling mariners to orient themselves out of sight of land and at times when celestial cues are obscured by clouds.

Eleventh-century China offers the first convincing record of a magnetic compass being used for navigation at sea. When the compass arrived in Europe about a century later, it revolutionized navigation and encouraged mariners to sail beyond sight of land. By the late 13th century, compasses were graduated: they displayed a scale, a circle divided into 32 "quarters" or points, for measuring direction precisely. A graduated compass provides a reference from which a particular bearing could be steered. On its own, however, a compass measurement does not define a location. To establish location, a measurement of bearing from two or more known locations is needed, or a measurement of bearing and distance from a single known location.

Latitude

In 14th-century Europe, the notion of the classical Greeks that Earth was a sphere was reestablished. By the end of that century European navigators could calculate latitude—north–south location on Earth—a facility that the Greeks had originally developed in the first millennium B.C.E.

A line of latitude is an imaginary line that encircles the globe from east to west and indicates distance from the equator. Latitude is measured as the angular distance from the equator—0° latitude at the equator and 90° latitude at the pole. Angular distance can be estimated by measuring the altitude of the sun above the horizon at midday. If the sun is nearly directly overhead at midday, other things being equal, then the ship is near the equator; if the sun is low at midday, the vessel is near the pole. By the end of the 15th century, devices such as the cross staff and backstaff were being used to measure the altitude of celestial objects—and hence latitude. Reliable measurement of longitude—east–west location on Earth—was still a long way off.

Longitude

Establishing longitude was a technologically more demanding exercise. In 1530 Flemish astronomer Gemma Frisius concluded that since Earth rotates on its axis at a constant speed and that at noon in a given location the Sun is at its highest point in the sky—either directly overhead or due south or north—the time that elapses between noon at one point on Earth and noon at another point can be used to determine the longitudinal distance between the two. In practice, this involves using a magnetic compass or an elevation-measuring device such as a sextant to determine when the Sun is at its highest point in the sky and therefore it is noon locally. Alterna-

tively, lunar methods can be used. The local noon is compared with the time given by a clock that has been set for a known longitude. The deviation from local noon and the time on the clock is read off on a set of nautical tables to give the angular distance (longitudinal distance) between the present location and the known longitude, thereby giving the vessel's precise longitude position.

All this is well and good, but it depends on the ship's clock being very accurate. A second of time represents 15 seconds of longitude; close to the equator, this translates into a distance of about 0.9 miles (nearly 1.4 km). Other things being equal, a clock that is fast or slow by only one minute will give a location that is about 50 miles (80 km) from the true one. The significance of time accuracy was amply demonstrated in 1707 when four British ships under the command of Sir Cloudesley Shovell ran aground on the Isles of Scilly in the North Atlantic with the loss of 2,000 mariners. The fleet had lost track of its longitude.

In 1714 the British government offered a £20,000 prize (in excess of $2 million today) to the inventor of a ship's clock that would determine longitude to within 0.5° (2 minutes of time) after a voyage to the West Indies. Yorkshire cabinetmaker John Harrison took up the challenge and in 1728 began to work on such a timepiece. His chronometer was driven by a balance spring, rather than a pendulum, and it remained horizontal regardless of the movement of the ship. It was a delicate, costly, and complicated device, but it worked. Though Harrison's chronometer was well within the limits set by the government, there was little political will to pay the prize money. It was argued that Harrison's chronometer could not be produced readily in large numbers—the government had shifted goal posts to avoid paying out the money. In 1773, King George III interceded on Harrison's behalf, and at the age of 80 he finally received the prize money.

As timekeeping technology advanced, altitude measuring instruments were improved to keep step. By the late 18th century, the sextant (a device with a 60° arc but able to measure angles

of up to 120°) was devised to determine precise altitudes at sea. Even today, using a sextant and chronometer and referring to nautical tables is a means of fixing a ship's position with reasonable accuracy.

In 1884, the zero line of longitude, or Greenwich Meridian, used by the British was adopted worldwide and international time (Greenwich Mean Time, or GMT) was henceforth calculated relative to this line (see APPENDIX).

Modern Navigation

Although latitude and longitude still form the gridwork by which position on the planet's surface is defined, the methods to do this today are highly sophisticated. RADAR (Radio Detection And Ranging) has revolutionized surface travel at sea. All large vessels use an onboard radar scanner to detect landforms and avoid other vessels. Along busy shipping routes, vessels are restricted to shipping lanes, and the traffic flow is carefully controlled. In places like the English Channel and in the St. Lawrence Seaway, Canada, radar stations on shore monitor traffic flow and are in radio contact with vessels.

Both out at sea and close to shore, there are now a wide range of methods to establish location, ranging from traditional visual methods such as the sextant to those using the latest satellite systems. Fast becoming the most widely used all-weather system is the satellite-based Global Positioning System (GPS). As GPS satellites pass overhead, they emit a continuous stream of radio data about their positions. This information is received on board ship. As the satellites progress, their positions relative to the ship change, and this is detected. The shipboard computer calculates changes in time and satellite location and computes the ship's position to within an accuracy of about 328 feet (100 m) or, with further decoding, to an accuracy of about 49 feet (15 m). Determining position is an easy matter for today's navigator: navigation has progressed from art to exact science.

Charting the Oceans

The idea of Earth as a globe or sphere rather than flat was fairly well established by the fourth century B.C.E., although a zealous Christian monk of the sixth century C.E. was later to overturn this idea, reestablishing the notion of a flat Earth. The concept of a spherical Earth began to reemerge in the 12th and 13th centuries under the influence of scholars such as German monk Albertus Magnus and English friar Roger Bacon.

Many classical historians consider that Anaximander, a philosopher living in the Miletus (a region of present-day Turkey) of the sixth century B.C.E. was the first person to draw a map of the world based on widely gathered evidence. Later that century, and during the time of Anaximander's famous pupil, Pythagoras, Earth was being considered as a sphere or possibly a cylinder. The first maps of the oceans—or at least those seas and oceans known by Mediterranean seafarers—date from the third century B.C.E. Even at that early time, the Phoenicians and the Greeks used stars to navigate by (page 138), and Greek mathematicians and astronomers employed the detailed observations of navigators such as Pytheas (page 142) to compile their maps. Eratosthenes (276–c. 194 B.C.E.), a Greek living in Alexandria, drew a map of the then-known world that employed longitudinal and latitudinal lines with distances marked in *stadia* (1 Roman mile = 8 stadia = 4,840 feet) from zero lines in the Atlantic or Indian Oceans. Eratosthenes' great claim to fame is his calculation of Earth's circumference about the poles—most scholars agree his figure lies within 200 miles (322 km) of today's estimate of 24,862 miles (40,010 km).

It was a geographer, Marinus of Tyre, in the first century C.E. who probably produced the first charts for seafarers. He, like Eratosthenes before him, employed longitudinal meridians and latitudinal parallels. But the best-known Greek cartographer of all was Ptolemy (Claudius Ptolemaeus) who worked in Alexandria in the second century C.E. He is well known because his works have survived, whereas the works of earlier cartographers have not. Nevertheless, Ptolemy was probably the first to devise a map projection that attempted to translate accurately the curved surface of the planet onto the flat surface of a map—Ptolemy's attempt was a conic projection.

Although Romans mapped the world as a means of administering their conquests, they showed little interest in pushing back the frontiers of maritime chart making. After the fall of Rome in 476 C.E. Ptolemy's maps were missing, only to reappear nearly a millennium later. It fell to the Arabs to take up the legacy of Greek science, and when maritime mapping reemerged as a serious enterprise in the 15th century, it was principally Arab cartographers and Jewish astronomers who had retained the necessary expertise.

With the development of the graduated magnetic compass by the late 13th century, navigators could begin to take bearings relative to known landmarks and the cardinal points of the compass. European seafarers' voyages of exploration in the 13th and 14th century employed the magnetic compass, the sandglass, and log and line as standard navigational equipment. The compass provided directional guidance, while the sandglass and log and line were used to measure speed and therefore distance traveled. Navigators began to plot courses; such information was summarized on a new form of chart—a portulan (harbor-finding chart)—a map of a sea area based on compass readings. These charts showed constructions—lighthouses, harbors, and so on—as well as natural features such as sandbars, shoals, and currents. The early portulans were produced at the end of the 13th century and probably originated from Venice and Genoa. The first ones depicted regions of the Mediterranean Sea and its environs and were drawn on vellum (sheepskin or goatskin). In time, charts were produced for more remote areas—the coasts of northern Europe, for example. By the 16th century, portulans reached the peak of their perfection in the hands of cartographers from Portugal and Spain.

About 1400, Portuguese navigators who visited Constantinople discovered Ptolemy's long-forgotten maps and realized their significance. These discoveries, combined with contemporary improvements in Portuguese ship design and fueled by Prince Henry of Portugal's passionate interest in navigation, resulted in a new breed of merchant adventurer. Henry established a school of navigation and became—to history—Henry the Navigator. His school trained hundreds of seafarers who extended the reach of Portugal's power and influence. Indeed, the rise and fall of Portugal's maritime dominance between 1400 and 1600 closely parallels the activities of its mapmakers and navigators. The excellence and exclusivity of Portuguese navigational skills faded over time as the efforts of the pioneers became less valued, and maps and navigational skills were sold or traded to other nations.

By the 15th century, instruments such as the cross staff and back staff were being employed to measure latitude (page 139), and such measurements were added to charts. This additional information was particularly necessary in the wider reaches of the Atlantic Ocean. Here distances were more variable and tidal changes larger than those in the Mediterranean. The inaccuracies of portulans became evident, and the limitations of poor latitude measurement—and even poorer or nonexistent longitude measurement—began to tell on longer journeys.

By the end of the 15th century, new navigational instruments were being developed, such as the sea astrolabe, which measured the precise altitudes of stars and planets. Ship's pilots were able to establish latitude with greater accuracy. All such findings gradually found their way onto ship's charts and encouraged merchant adventurers to travel more widely. During the period 1519–22 Magellan circumnavigated the globe (page 147) and established the true extent of the Pacific Ocean, hitherto considered to be much smaller. A solution to the problem of translating the curved surface of the planet onto a flat piece of paper was published by the cartographer Gerardus Mercator in 1569—the famous Mercator projection still in use today. Mercator's solution enabled distances to be depicted with greater accuracy so that courses could be plotted with higher reliability. His approach, in effect, was to plot Earth's surface features onto a cylinder of paper. This paper encircled the globe at the equator and was oriented parallel to Earth's axis. The parallels of latitude and meridians of longitude emerged as straight lines, and any distortion was minimal at the equator and maximal at the poles. Most navigation did—and still does—take place from temperate to tropical zones, and so any distortion introduced by the plotting method was of little consequence over most routes and, in any case, was a great improvement over previous charts.

Between the 16th and 19th centuries, sea charts increased in accuracy and reliability as better technology was developed for measuring latitude and longitude and for establishing speed and distance traveled. English navigator Captain James Cook (page 148), in three exploratory voyages from 1768 to 1779, established much more systematic approaches to measuring location and sea depth. Transferring these records to maps, the charts that resulted from his travels were the most accurate of their time.

By the 18th century, charts were devised that showed local magnetic variation, and compasses became available that could compensate for local magnetic anomalies. There was general agreement

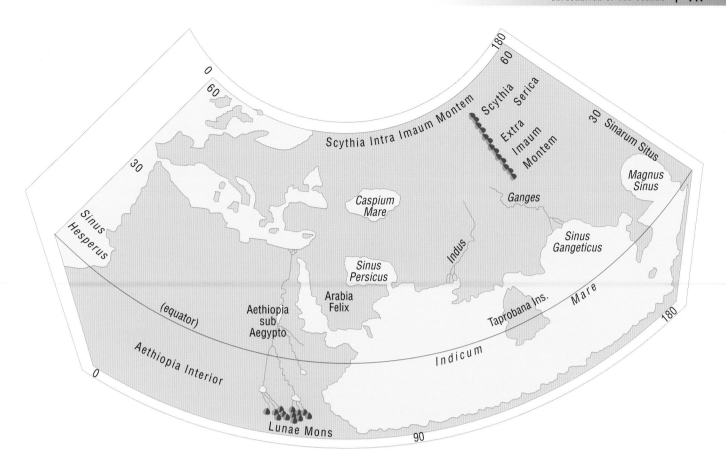

Ptolemy's view of the world 140 C.E. He used a conic projection to depict the curved surface of the planet on a flat sheet of paper. His maps were rediscovered in the early 15th century and showed no sea route between the Atlantic and Indian Oceans. Such maps helped dissuade many 15th-century explorers from attempting to circumnavigate Africa.

among European chartmakers that the equator established the line of zero latitude, but the zero line from which longitude was measured was not agreed internationally until 1884, when the Greenwich Meridian was adopted worldwide.

Matthew Fontaine Maury (1806–1873), a U.S. naval officer, took a serious interest in gathering information about the physical features of oceans and transferred this data to sea charts for the benefit of navigators. Amongst his achievements, he published the first ocean-basin chart in 1855. Depicting the North Atlantic ocean floor, the chart was based on a systematic series of soundings made with lead and line.

In the 20th century, the harnessing of electricity enabled the creation of navigational instruments with accuracies previously unheard of. The gyroscopic compass, for example, developed in the early 1900s, always aligns itself with true north and does not depend on Earth's magnetic field. From the 1940s to the 1960s, first radar and then satellite communication were developed as ways of plotting position with great accuracy. Since the 1960s, the technological revolution in satellite-based remote sensing (page 156) has resulted in real-time maps of a region being available at the touch of a button. Sea charts are increasingly likely to be electronic data stored temporarily in computer memories, perhaps updated daily, rather than the more or less permanent lines committed to maps on paper. Not only are modern electronic charts dynamic—often color-coded and animated—but they can tell us much more about what is happening above and below the sea.

Ancient Voyages of Discovery

By 1500 B.C.E., seafarers of the Southwest Pacific had long since broken the psychological barrier of sailing beyond sight of land. These early seafarers are, to us, anonymous: their names have not been recorded in history like those of their later counterparts in and around the Mediterranean Sea. The Pacific seafarers, expanding eastward from Indonesia (formerly the East Indies) to New Guinea and then on to the Solomon Islands, must have faced numerous hazards. From the 15th century onward, European explorers came upon the widely scattered Polynesian islands—from Hawaii in the north, to Easter Island in the east, and New Zealand to the south—islands that had already been colonized hundreds of years earlier by seafarers from the West Pacific.

The Old World

At about the time that Pacific colonizers were moving westward into Polynesia, the voyages of maritime explorers from the great civilizations of the Mediterranean and Mesopotamia were being driven by the desire to trade rather than to colonize. As early as 2500 B.C.E. Egyptian expeditions were traveling down the Red Sea to Punt (modern Somalia) and bringing back spices, aromatic herbs, and other goods. In the 15th century B.C.E. Hatshepsut is recorded to have sent five ships to

Punt for, among other goods: "fragrant woods . . . myrrh . . . ebony and pure ivory . . . apes, monkeys, dogs . . . skins of the southern panther . . . and natives and their children."

The Old World explorers were much less inclined to sail beyond sight of land than their Pacific counterparts, but though remaining in coastal waters, Egyptian, Phoenician, and Greek merchants and adventurers nevertheless undertook very long voyages. According to the Greek historian Herodotus, about 600 B.C.E. the Egyptian pharaoh Necho II organized a Phoenician expedition to find the sea passage from the Red Sea to the Mediterranean—so confirming a sea connection between the two seas that bordered Egypt. To achieve this, the expedition sailed down the east coast of Africa, around the Cape, up the west coast of Africa, and then through the Straits of Gibraltar (the Pillars of Hercules) and into the Mediterranean. As luck would have it, choosing to sail from the Red Sea to the Mediterranean (rather than the reverse route) meant that favorable winds and currents helped them for most of the way, no doubt contributing greatly to the success of the mission. Expeditions of the fifth century B.C.E. that left the Mediterranean and attempted to circumnavigate Africa were greatly hindered by adverse winds and currents and reached only as far as the West Africa coast.

As for explorations north of the Straits of Gibraltar, by 700 B.C.E. Cádiz was an established Phoenician port handling tin and amber from barely known lands in northern Europe. About 460 B.C.E. Herodotus described such commodities as "coming from the ends of the Earth." The first well-documented sea trip from the Mediterranean to these little-known lands was described by Pytheas, a Greek citizen from Massilia (now Marseilles). About 330 B.C.E., Pytheas sailed northward via the west coast of Spain, visited the tin mines of Cornwall, England, sailed up the Irish Sea, visited Ireland, and then circumnavigated the British mainland before returning to Marseilles via a North European coastal route. On a subsequent voyage it is quite likely that Pytheas entered the Baltic Sea.

After Alexander the Great's campaign in India ended in 325 B.C.E. Nearchus, one of Alexander's generals, commanded a fleet that sailed from the mouth of the Indus River to the Persian Gulf. This coastal voyage was not simply an organized withdrawal; it was truly a voyage of discovery. En route, Nearchus reconnoitered the layout of the coast and the disposition of any cities he encoun-

The voyages of Pytheas (c 330 B.C.E.) and Nearchus (c. 325 B.C.E.)

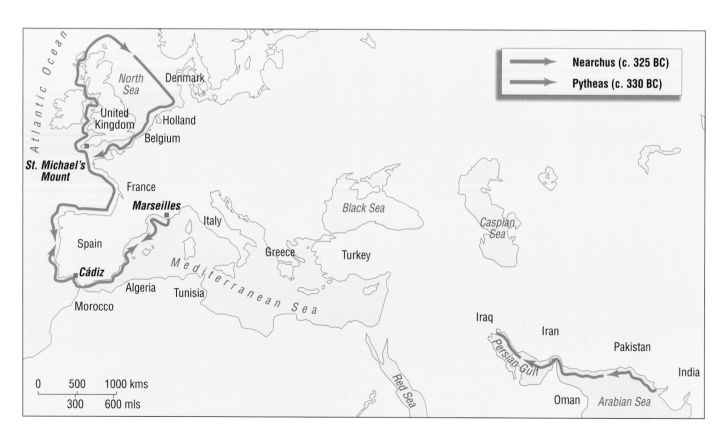

tered. It was also the first voyage across the Indian Ocean by Europeans.

Less well documented or researched by Western scholars are the voyages of Southeast Asian seafarers into the Indian Ocean. By the third millennium B.C.E., trade between the Persian Gulf and the Indus was very well established. The Indian subcontinent, as the natural link between oriental cultures to the east and African and Middle Eastern cultures to the west, received all manner of cargo in its seaports. These trade links were well extended by the first century B.C.E., and Greco-Roman objects have been found at settlements encircling much of the Indian Ocean, from East Africa to Indochina.

By the third century C.E., at least two-thirds of the world's oceanic expanse had been traversed by one culture or another, even if many of these voyages had remained within sight of land.

The Pacific

How people first colonized the Pacific Islands is one of the more incomplete chapters of world history. Most geographers divide the Pacific islands into three groupings: Micronesia ("small islands"), Melanesia ("black islands"), and Polynesia ("many islands"). Archaeological evidence suggests that colonizers from New Guinea may have ventured eastward onto nearby islands of Melanesia by 4000–5000 B.C.E. and then reached the Polynesian islands of Tonga and Samoa, via Fiji, by 1500 B.C.E. Polynesian culture developed over the next millennium, and by 500 B.C.E., a Polynesian seafaring tradition might have become established. But the first evidence of human settlement on the eastern Polynesian islands, dating from 300 C.E., is found on the Marquesas Islands. Within Polynesia, strong cultural and biological similarities are found among the Maori of New Zealand to the south, the people of Hawaii to the north, and the Easter Islanders of the 16th century; yet these communities are separated by many thousands of miles of island-dotted ocean. How were these islands colonized? The available evidence does not tell us, but one adventurous anthropologist has sought the answer in a rather direct fashion.

Reconstructing the Past

Question: How can you decide whether a particular sea voyage was feasible in ancient times? Answer: Attempt to reenact the voyage.

In the 1940s, Thor Heyerdahl, a Norwegian biologist-turned-anthropologist, suggested that the Inca of Peru had reached the South Pacific prior to the arrival of the Polynesians and that this accounted for some similarities between South Pacific and South American cultures. Heyerdahl decided that the best way to lend credence to his idea was to demonstrate that such a voyage was possible. In 1947, Heyerdahl finished constructing a balsa-wood raft to the design of 15th-century rafts seen by Europeans when they first entered Peru. Heyerdahl called the craft Kon-Tiki after a legendary Inca sun king. Leaving Callao, Peru, Heyerdahl sailed on the South Equatorial Current and after 101 days and traveling about 5,000 miles (8,000 km), he and his crew reached the Tuamotou Islands. Heyerdahl had shown that such a trip was possible, although he could not prove that a similar trip had actually taken place in historical times. Nevertheless, it did offer support to the notion that some of the Polynesian Islands might have been colonized from the east before they received the influx of people from New Guinea to the west.

In 1969, Thor Heyerdahl left Morocco in a papyrus boat constructed according to designs used by ancient Egyptian seafarers and using boat-building methods imported from present-day Lake Chad. This time, Heyerdahl's experiment was designed to show that Egyptians could have crossed the Atlantic in ancient times and that it is these colonizers who might have given rise to the Mayan and Incan civilizations of South America. He believed that the New World and Old World cultures bore resemblances that were more than merely coincidental. His craft, named Ra after the ancient Egyptian sun god, experienced a series of disasters—including a broken mast—and eventually became badly damaged after a storm; the trip had to be abandoned about 600 miles (about 1,000 km) from landfall in the West Indies. The following year, Heyerdahl repeated the voyage in Ra II—a craft of improved design and built by Bolivian Indians from Lake Titicaca who were well used to constructing reed boats. The second mission was a success, and Heyerdahl and his crew made the crossing from Morocco to Bridgetown, Barbados, in 57 days. Again, Heyerdahl had shown that it was perfectly feasible to cross an ocean on a simple craft—certainly in trade-wind regions where winds and currents are fairly constant and favorable.

Others have performed similar reconstruction experiments. Tim Severin, in the 1970s, sailed from Ireland to Labrador by way of the Hebrides, the Faroes, Iceland, and Greenland in a leather curragh—a banana-shaped boat—based on a design thought to have been used by St. Brendan in the sixth century C.E. Accounts suggest that St. Brendan visited Iceland and Greenland. Whether he reached North America is unknown, but Severin's voyage at least confirmed that it was possible. In the early 1980s, Severin sailed from Oman to China—across the Indian Ocean—in an Arab dhow of traditional design. Such modern voyages serve to demonstrate the capabilities of ancient seafarers and their craft. They demonstrate the possibility, if not the certainty, that some remarkable ancient sea voyages have taken place for which little or no record exists.

The Dark and Middle Ages

In Western history, the so-called Dark Ages refer to the period of political, religious, and cultural fragmentation between the fall of the Roman Empire and the height of the Middle Ages, spanning c. 500–1110 C.E. The European Middle Ages are generally regarded as encompassing the period c. 1000–1400 C.E., corresponding to the rise of Catholicism and the emergence of the papacy as an international religious and political power. Some authors regard the Middle Ages in a broader context as the period between the fall of the Roman Empire and the beginning of the Renaissance (c. 500–1500). However defined, this period of Western history saw exploratory sea voyages from Europe to North America and to the Middle and Far East. At this time, a long-established Eastern seafaring tradition supported trade throughout much of the Indian Ocean and the western Pacific, but records of these activities are relatively poorly researched by Western scholars.

The Vikings

By the eighth century the Vikings—fishing and farming inhabitants of Norway, Denmark, and Sweden—were beginning to strike out from their overpopulated lands. With a justified historical reputation for piracy, rape, and pillage, they were nevertheless also traders and settlers. The Vikings were the consummate adventurers and sailors of northern Europe.

Traveling under oar and sail in their longboats, they attacked coastal communities in Britain, Ireland, and France, looting and burning as they went, but occasionally they settled as farmers. The feat of exploration for which they are most acknowledged was the European discovery of North America nearly five centuries before Columbus.

Vikings began their migrations across the North Atlantic in the eighth century, first settling in the Orkneys and Shetlands near Scotland and then traveling further west to the Hebrides, then Ireland, the Faroes, and by the late ninth century, as far as Iceland. In 982, Erik the Red, a formidable Viking who had been exiled first from Norway and then from Iceland for various killings, traveled westward from Iceland to serve a three-year banishment. Encouraged by stories of sailors who had been blown off course and sighted unknown lands to the west, his longboat braved gales and dense fog to arrive, some 450 miles later, on the east coast of what is now Greenland. He explored Greenland's southwest before returning to Iceland after his period of exile. He recruited many others who joined him in 25 ships to accompany him back to Greenland to settle. Only 14 vessels completed the journey, such were the dangers encountered along the way. Erik, leader of his settlers, established himself near Greenland's southern tip. The remains of Erik's farm have recently been investigated by archaeologists.

About 1000, Leif Eriksson, one of Erik's son, sailed westward from Iceland, like his father in search of new lands seen from afar by sailors. Leif encountered a rocky coastline, probably part of present-day Baffin Island, which he called Helluland, or "land of stone slabs." Sailing south, he came to Markland, or "land of woods," today recognized as probably being southern Labrador. As the climate became milder and the coastal landscape more lush, he and his crew settled and wintered in an area of rich grassland and salmon-filled rivers that he called Vinland, "land of the vine," because of the abundance of berry-bearing bushes and trees. Today, this location is widely regarded as being near present-day L'Anse-aux-Meadows in Newfoundland. In the 1960s, a Viking settlement was excavated here, the probable remains of Leif Eriksson's base. As far as we know, Eriksson and his followers were the first Europeans to set foot on North America.

Leif returned to Iceland, and other members of Erik's family formed later expeditions to Vinland; they traveled farther south and encountered Native Americans, whom they summarily killed. Further expeditions were met with an understandably hostile response from indigenous peoples. Some Vikings did settle there, however, although by the 15th century these communities had died out, eventually succumbing to the combined ravages of cold, disease, malnutrition, and attacks from hostile Native Americans. Later that century, 2,000 miles to the south, Columbus and other Europeans were to "rediscover" the Americas.

Marco Polo

The medieval crusades (1096–1271) saw European forces fighting Muslims in Syria and Palestine for control of the disputed Holy Land. Only a few European merchants ventured far into Asia, but of those who did, by far the most famous was the Venetian explorer and adventurer Marco Polo, son of Niccolò Polo, himself a merchant adventurer.

During the years 1260–1269 Niccolò Polo and Marco's uncle, Maffeo Polo, traveled across the dangerous central region of Asia while Marco was still a child in Venice. Niccolò and Maffeo were the first Europeans to cross the entire continent of Asia, and they were well received in Khanbalik, or as the Polos called it, Cambaluc (now Beijing), where Kublai Khan, the Mongol emperor of China, treated them with respect and honor and asked them to deliver messages to the pope. On their return, Niccolò and Maffeo discovered that the pope had died and a successor had yet to be appointed, so the khan's letters remained undelivered. Two years later, in 1271, a new pope was appointed, the requests from the khan were delivered, and the pope instructed the Polos to pass on messages and gifts to him. The Polos were more than happy to comply, and this time the young Marco accompanied them on their journey. The Polos toyed with the idea of breaking up the land journey by sailing from the Persian Gulf to India, but unaccustomed to the eastern design of vessels, they felt the craft were too flimsy for comfort. As it happened, the overland journey was slow and difficult, and it took them three and one-half years to reach Cambaluc and then Shangtu, a former province of East China, where Kublai Khan was in summer residence.

Marco Polo was soon employed by Kublai Khan as a high-ranking civil servant. Reputedly mastering four languages, he was employed, in effect, as an official reporter, traveling widely throughout the Mongol Empire and reporting to the khan about customs and events while acting as his personal envoy. Polo retained this role for 17 years, loyally serving Kublai Khan and reporting on lands as far away as Mongolia and Siberia in the north, Armenia to the west, Korea to the east, and Burma and India to the south.

Having acclimatized to the cultures and customs of the East, the Polos were more predisposed to sea journeys when they decided to return to Venice in 1292. Kublai Khan only reluctantly agreed to them leaving court, and then only on condition that they escort a Tartar princess and deliver her to her betrothed in Persia (modern Iran). The two-year journey from China to the Persian Gulf via Sumatra, the Andaman Islands, Sri Lanka, and India was eventful. The fleet of 14 four-masted ships encountered many dangers, and some 600 men are said to have died in the early stages of the journey. From Persia, the Polos returned to Venice in 1295, and the following year Marco Polo commanded his own vessel in an action against the Genoese, with

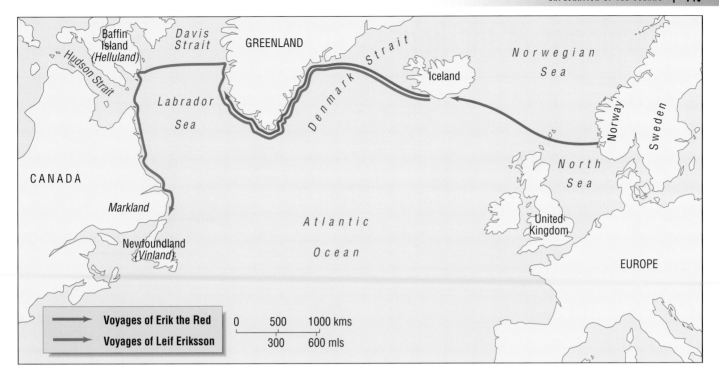

The Viking migration across the North Atlantic and the European discovery of North America by Leif Eriksson

whom the Venetians were at war. Marco Polo was captured and held as a prisoner of war in Genoa (Genova) for some three years. Fortuitously, he was imprisoned with a writer, Rustichello (or Rusticiano) of Pisa, and together they worked on recording Marco's adventures in a book entitled *Book of Ser Marco Polo Concerning the Kingdoms and Marvels of the East*. While some of the events it depicts—such as magicians changing the weather—were somewhat fanciful, the book is an invaluable European record of Eastern cultures at the time. The book met with a very mixed response when it was published in the 1300s. Many Europeans thought themselves highly cultured and were reluctant to believe that Eastern technology and hygiene might be in advance of their own. Marco Polo's interests in architecture and in ship design, and in religious and current affairs and natural history, are well reflected in the book. Marco was released in 1299 and died in 1324 having seen more of the world than any other person of his time.

Ibn Battutah

Ibn Battutah (the name has various transliterations) was a devout Muslim who in 1325, at the age of 21, set out on his first pilgrimage to Mecca (Makkah). Traveling overland from his home city of Tangier, Morocco, his trek began as a more or less straightforward journey of religious observance—the *hajj*. He started out as an official within one of the smaller caravans, but soon after arriving in Egypt he left the main caravan to take a more adventurous route to Mecca. He had developed a taste for travel that was to lead to a series of journeys over a period of nearly 30 years and a distance of 75,000 miles (120,000 km), encompassing almost the entire geographic spread of the Islamic world.

Ibn Battutah's religion was both his motivation for travel and his passport. As a learned legal and Islamic scholar, his status and religion guaranteed him practical and financial help as he journeyed from one Islamic country to another. In 1326 in Alexandria he recorded meeting a religious elder of the Sufi sect who informed Ibn Battutah that he would be traveling widely to meet specific Sufi holy men in China and India. This prophesy, while not entirely fulfilled, was apparently the major spur to Ibn Battutah's wanderings far and wide. He committed himself to traveling throughout the Islamic world, meeting these holy men, and where possible, avoiding traveling along the same route twice.

After reaching Mecca in October 1326 and staying to undertake the prescribed religious rituals, he traveled on to Persia (Iran) and Iraq, where he met the sultan of Baghdad, and then returned to Mecca in 1327. Between 1327–1333 Ibn Battutah crisscrossed the Red Sea and Persian Gulf and traveled northward to cross the Black Sea before making his way back to Mecca and then on to India. Here his fortunes were incredibly varied. He was made a judge by Muhammad ibn Tughluq, the sultan of Delhi, and spent eight years in this post before being imprisoned on suspicion of treachery. He was soon released, spent several months in religious retreat, and emerged to become in 1342 the sultan's ambassador to the emperor of China. In 1345 he traveled to Canton (Guangzhou), China, via Bengal, Burma, and Sumatra, but though impressed by the culture, he was ill at ease in a community where the Islamic influence was small.

In 1346, he returned to India and then traveled overland through the by now plague-ravaged countries of Persia, Iraq, and Syria before returning once more to Mecca. By early 1349, he was back in Tangier, nearly 24 years after leaving. In two rounds of travel between 1349 and 1354, he visited Spain and then Northeast Africa and on his return to Morocco, enlisted the help of Ibn Juzayy to write a strongly Islamic-influenced and historically valuable account—the *Rihlah*—describing the numerous cultures Ibn Battutah had visited on his travels.

Ibn Battutah was not an explorer in the generally accepted sense—that he was discovering lands previously unknown to his culture—but he had a unique overview of Eastern cultures greater than anyone else of his time. By the early 1990s, a full English translation of the *Rihlah* had yet to be completed, and Ibn Battutah's work is, as yet, poorly appreciated in the West.

The Explorers of the Renaissance

The Renaissance is generally regarded as the period of classical revival and intellectual and cultural development that began in Italy in the mid-14th century and spread to northern Europe, where it flourished until the mid-16th century. The 30-year time span, 1492–1522, was later to acquire the title The Western Age of Discovery. During that brief period, Europeans were, for the first time, to appreciate the full breadth of the world and its oceans. By 1522, the geographic world had been found to be larger than anticipated, but its easterly and westerly limits had been established on paper and in the human mind.

One of the major events that triggered the European interest in exploration was the closure of the major overland trade route to the East with the capture of Constantinople in 1453 by the Ottoman sultan Mehmed II. Mediterranean ports were now isolated from trade with India, East Asia, and the East Indies (modern Indonesia), so Western navigators began to search for a new seaborne trade route through to the East via the Horn of Africa. The maps Europe had inherited from Ptolemy (page 140) suggested that a sea route around Africa did not exist; however, as Portuguese vessels began to explore further and further down the west coast of Africa, it was only a matter of time before they reached the southern tip.

The Portuguese Explorers

Prince Henry of Portugal (1394–1460) and his school of navigation, founded in 1416, was to establish a new generation of highly skilled Portuguese navigators and explorers. These seafarers were quickly pressed into service to forge trade links across the world. New colonies and trade routes were sought to meet urgent social and economic demands at home. The fertile Atlantic islands of Madeira and the Azores were acquired by the 1480s, and in 1486 Bartholomeu Dias extended Portuguese exploration along the west coast of Africa. As far as we know, he was the first European to sail round the tip of Africa and enter the Indian Ocean. Just over a decade later, in 1498, Vasco de Gama sailed around the tip of Africa and northward through the Indian Ocean to reach Calicut port in India, thus opening up a sea route for trade between Europe and the East.

Admiral Zheng Ho

When Portuguese seafarers first arrived in the Indian Ocean at the end of the 15th century, they discovered themselves in waters busy with trading craft from Middle and Far Eastern countries. Indeed, decades before the Portuguese arrival, a Chinese admiral, Zheng Ho, had explored much of the Indian Ocean. Zheng Ho, chief eunuch in Chinese emperor Yongle's court, was commanded to seek out a deposed emperor to ensure that he was no longer a threat. Zheng was also asked to establish diplomatic and trade links across the Indian Ocean. A supremely able commander, Zheng Ho fulfilled these obligations in various

Voyages of Zheng Ho (1405–33), Christopher Columbus (1492–93), and Ferdinand Magellan's expedition (1519–22)

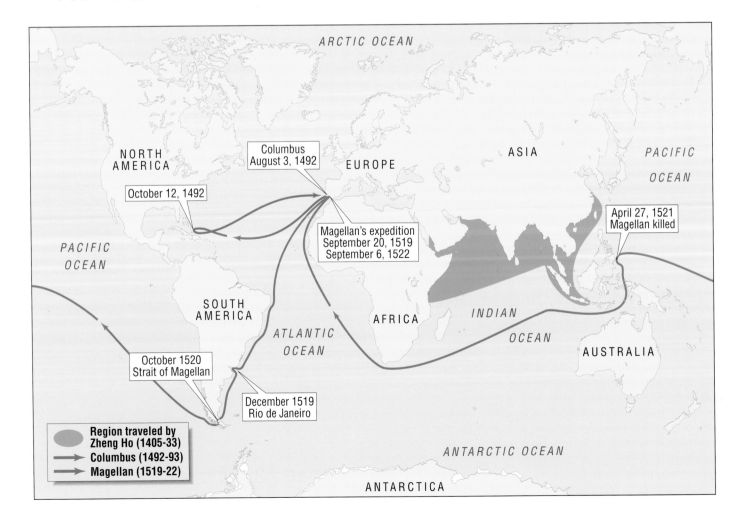

voyages during the period 1405–33. Sometimes commanding a fleet of 60 or more large Chinese junks, he visited Indochina, the Malay Peninsula, Indonesia, Sri Lanka and southern India, the Persian Gulf, Arabia, and the eastern coast of Africa as far south as Kilwa, just short of Madagascar.

Christopher Columbus

The clear-cut, textbook descriptions of the voyages of Christopher Columbus and his "discovery" of the American continent in 1492 belie the complex nature of this man and his eventful life. Many generally accepted notions about his origins and achievements are now disputed.

Born in 1451 or 1452 in the Italian city-state of Genoa, little is known about Columbus's early life. He was the son of a weaver (his father's national origins are disputed). Columbus's name is rendered Cristoforo Colombo in Italian, Christavão Colombo in Portuguese, or Cristóbal Colón in Spanish: Spanish was the language he most often used during adult life. Columbus attached great significance to his first name (*Christopher* means "Christ-bearer") and was driven by a Christian zeal to achieve great things in the name of God. Apparently, a man of remarkable presence, he was also perceived as arrogant, ruthless, and despotic.

By his early 20s, Columbus had committed his working life to sea travel; between 1476 and 1484 he had traveled to Iceland and the west coast of Africa and been shipwrecked at least once. Most of his time on shore was spent in Portugal or Madeira. Columbus nurtured an obsession to find a westward route to the Indies—what was then Southeast Asia, the East Indies (Indonesia), China, and Japan. He contrived to calculate the distance across the Atlantic Ocean to Japan on the assumption that there was no landmass in between. His calculations vastly underestimated the true distance (indeed, calculations of the ancient Greeks were far more respectable than those of Columbus). As it happened, Columbus's calculation of distance was to be sufficient to bring him as far as the Americas but was less than a quarter of the true distance to Japan.

Columbus spent much of his free time between 1484 and 1492 trying to persuade first King John II of Portugal and then Queen Isabella and King Ferdinand of Spain to support an expedition—his "enterprise of the Indies." After two years of persistent lobbying, he obtained the Spanish backing he needed, and his historic expedition was hastily assembled. His three ships, the *Niña,* the *Pinta,* and the *Santa Maria,* embarked on August 3, 1492, from the Spanish port of Palos de la Frontera. After stopping off at the Canary Islands, the ships sailed westward on September 6, and after five weeks without sight of land (an unheard of occurrence in those days), they came within sight of what later turned out to be an island in the Bahamas group. Columbus was convinced they had arrived at the East Indies, and he called the inhabitants "Indians." Columbus's story from that point is full of twist and turns. Suffice it to say that he was feted on his return to Spain, and between 1493 and 1504 was to make three more voyages to the Caribbean region. His irascibility eventually led to him falling from favor with the Spanish throne, and he died in 1506 an embittered man.

The repercussions of Columbus's first voyage to the Americas were staggering. On his heels followed many colonizing expeditions: the Spanish consolidated the Caribbean and Central America, and the Portuguese the east coast of South America. In 1497 John Cabot sailed across the North Atlantic from Bristol, England, and landed at Newfoundland—the first European to land on North American soil since the Vikings (page XX). Waves of European colonization—particularly by the Dutch and English—saw the east coast of North America gradually settled. The final outcome of such incursions for hundreds of years was the European and Christian conquest of the Americas and the eventual subjugation of its native peoples. For the colonizers, the discovery of the "New World" was a success story that led to the establishment of the world's most powerful democratic nation. For the indigenous peoples, the history of colonization (as is so often the case) was largely a catalog of genocide, oppression, and coercion into a foreign religion and way of life.

Ferdinand Magellan

The ultimate achievement in the Western age of exploration was the circumnavigation of the globe. Ferdinand Magellan, a Portuguese nobleman born c. 1480, served in the Indian Ocean in his early adult life. Later, he was wounded in a battle in Morocco that left him lame. Disenchanted by lack of recognition in Portugal, he sought Spanish sponsorship for an expedition that was to be like no other before or since. The justification for the voyage was to establish Spanish ownership of the lucrative Spice Islands (today, the Moluccas in Indonesia). In the late 15th century the Spanish and the Portuguese had agreed on a line of demarcation in the Atlantic Ocean as a means of settling disputes about claims to new colonies. By 1514, a papal agreement had established Spanish rights to new colonies west of this line, while the Portuguese were given rights to land to the east (the power of the Catholic church at this time is clearly evident). By sailing west around the world and reaching the East Indies, Magellan could claim the Spice Islands for Spain on the assumption that they were located in the "Spanish hemisphere" of the world. In fact, the journey was much longer and more hazardous than Magellan anticipated and, as history was later to establish, the Spice Islands were, in fact, situated in the "Portuguese hemisphere."

In September 1519, Magellan left Sanlúcar de Barrameda, Spain, with a fleet of five small and rather ramshackle ships. At the end of March 1520, having sailed southward along the South American coast without finding a passage through to the Pacific, he decided to winter on Argentina's coast, a decision that prompted three of the ship's captains and crew to mutiny. Magellan regained control, and in October 1520 the four remaining ships (one was shipwrecked) sought and found a passage between the South American mainland and Tierra del Fuego, a feature now called the Strait of Magellan. Soon after reaching the Pacific Ocean, the captain and crew of the largest of the four vessels deserted, and the three remaining ships had to make the Pacific crossing with reduced supplies. Magellan had vastly underestimated the time it would take to cross the Pacific (no European had done so before), and it took a devastating 100 days for the ships to reach landfall—on March 6, 1521, in Guam in the Mariana Islands. By this time, the crew was reduced to eating rats and mice, chewing leather, and drinking a soup made from wood shavings; many had succumbed to scurvy. The reception they received in the Marianas was an inhospitable one; they left the islands and dubbed them the *Islas de Landrones* ("Isles of Thieves").

They sailed on to the Philippines where, disastrously, in April 1521 Magellan was killed on the island of Mactan in a skirmish between warring islanders. At this late stage in the voyage, one of the three remaining ships was torched. The last two vessels struggled on to reach the Spice Islands in November 1521. They loaded up with spices and embarked on the return journey; one vessel, the *Trinidad,* attempted to retrace the steps of the voyage; the other, the *Victoria,* continued to sail westward. The *Trinidad* was eventually captured by the Portuguese and its beleaguered crew, after all their tribulations, were imprisoned. The *Victoria,* under the command of Juan Sebastián de Elcano, crossed the Indian Ocean and arrived back in Spain in September 1522. Once people recognized the full significance of the expedition's achievement, the crew was accorded a hero's welcome. Only 18 of the original 237 had completed the circumnavigation. During the three-year voyage, they had sailed more than 43,500 miles (70,000 km)—an incomparable achievement bearing in mind the size of their craft, their lack of provisions, and the fact that about half of the voyage was across unknown waters. No other maritime journey in history can come close to matching this achievement.

Exploration after the Renaissance

Marine exploration from the mid-16th to the late 18th century was characterized by the consolidation of trade routes to lands already discovered. The outline of the Americas was mapped as navigators sought to find westward routes around it. Gradually, commercial routes were established across the major oceans; these tended to follow the path of those wind systems that provided a reliable motive force for sailing ships (page 65). Meanwhile, as new sea areas were discovered, so fisherman and hunters moved into these areas to exploit the untapped marine harvest. The unsustainable exploitation of marine stocks had begun (page 188).

Atlantic Ocean

Magellan (page 147) had found a southerly route past the Americas, but it would not be until the mid-19th century that a northerly route—the so-called Northwest Passage—would be pioneered. Finding this route was a particular fascination of British and Dutch explorers from the 16th century onward. They well knew that finding a sea route around North America would almost halve the distance to Japan, compared to the route around South America. So began a British and Dutch tradition that is recorded in northern sea and land features that bear the names of those who pioneered, and in some cases perished, in the search for the Northwest Passage, including Frobisher, Barents, Hudson, Baffin, and Ross. It was Englishman Robert McClure, in an expedition from 1850 to 1854, who finally completed the passage while searching for the ill-fated Franklin expedition (page 149). McClure traversed from west to east and for the last part without his ship, *Investigator*, which had become locked in ice.

After Columbus's successful passage from Europe to the Americas in 1492–93 (page 147), a spate of expeditions followed, and soon major trade routes were established from Europe to North America (arriving close to Newfoundland and progressing along the eastern seaboard) and from Europe to the north coast of South America and to the Caribbean. In the North Atlantic, the abundant fish and whale populations off the Newfoundland coast began to be exploited by European seafarers.

Pacific Ocean

After Magellan's initially successful voyage across the Pacific in 1520–21 (page 147), his sponsors, the Spanish, soon sought other trans-Pacific routes that linked the Americas with the Far East. By 1527 the fast route from Mexico to the Philippines was revealed, riding on the east trade winds and the North Equatorial Current. The return journey, against the prevailing winds, was much less favorable, but by 1565 the Spanish had pioneered a west-east route that made use of the North Pacific Drift, a major ocean current, and then picked up the California Current flowing southward near the American mainland. This path was to become the famous Manila-Acapulco route that Spanish galleons took from the Philippines to Mexico each year starting in 1574. On the slow, seven-month return journey from the East, they carried Oriental silks and porcelain. On the fast, outward-bound leg from the West, they took American silver.

Toward the end of the 16th century, any exploration of the Pacific Ocean tended to yield a relatively poor economic return, bearing in mind the vast size of this ocean and the small, scattered landfalls. Even during Francis Drake's global circumnavigation in 1577–80, although he explored the Pacific coast of North America and sought the Northwest Passage from the Pacific side, the major gains he made in the area were from plundering any Spanish galleons he found there.

The European discovery of Australia probably occurred later on the Pacific side than it did on the edge bordering the Indian Ocean. Reputedly, the Portuguese began to map the Pacific coast of Australia in the 1530s, and the Spanish explorer Luis Vaez de Torres sailed around Australia's northern tip in 1606.

The preeminent European explorer of the Pacific—and one who was genuinely motivated by geographic and scientific interest rather than primarily economic gain—was Englishman Captain James Cook (1728–79). In his first Pacific voyage (1768–71) he sought to find the "great southern continent" hinted at by earlier French navigators (what we now recognize as Antarctica). Instead, Cook discovered and mapped much of the coastline of New Zealand, New Guinea, and the Pacific coast of Australia. On his second voyage (1772–75) he sailed close to the 60° line of southern latitude and circumnavigated the southern oceans, still seeking the southern continent. At one point, he did enter what we now recognize as the Antarctic Circle and did encounter plenty of ice, but he did not find the southern continent (it lay at a latitude farther south than he ventured). Nevertheless, Cook did find and accurately chart many of the southern islands in the Pacific, including South Georgia and the South Sandwich Islands. On his third and final voyage (1776–79) he sailed into the North Pacific and encountered the Hawaiian Islands and progressed northward in an effort to find a western entrance to the Northwest Passage. After entering the Bering Sea the expedition was turned back by pack ice. He was the first navigator to have sailed in both Arctic and Antarctic seas. On his return via the Hawaiian Islands in 1779, he was killed (like Magellan before him) in a dispute with indigenous peoples.

Cook left a remarkable legacy: numerous maps and charts detailing the coastlines of Pacific islands and bordering continents. The naturalists he had taken on his voyages returned with detailed records of the indigenous peoples, flora, fauna, and geology they had encountered. Cook's reports largely demystified the southern extent of the Pacific Ocean. Within 10 years of Cook's discovery of the sub-Antarctic islands, hunters returned to exploit the seal populations there (page 202).

Indian Ocean

At the end of the 15th century, Vasco da Gama opened up the trans-Indian Ocean route from Europe to the East, and within 50 years, Portuguese seafarers were making the regular six- to eight-month voyage to the Indian subcontinent and its vicinity. On their heels, other nations followed to exploit the new-found opportunities in Africa, India, and the Far East. England and the Netherlands were to prove the major competitors intent on breaking the Spanish-Portuguese monopoly on European trade with the East.

The massively powerful and influential East India Companies—the British company incorporated in 1600 and the Dutch in 1602—pioneered the use of sleek, fast vessels (clippers) on new routes to the East Indies. Henrik Brouwer of the Dutch East India Company initiated a novel route in 1611 that took vessels along a temperate route in the south Indian Ocean from the Horn of Africa to a longitude almost as far as Java before turning northward. This route avoided the slow crossing through tropical waters that sailors had had to endure previously and that caused cargoes to perish in hot, humid conditions.

Brouwer's route brought vessels to within 800 kilometers (500 miles) of the coast of Western Australia. When vessels overshot the planned route, sailors would catch a glimpse of the unexplored continent of Australia.

Polar Exploration

Although the polar regions were uninviting, some explorers sought to find new lands there (as in the case of Cook) or discover new sea routes (as in that of those explorers seeking the Northwest Passage between the Atlantic and Pacific). Once subpolar seas were navigated, hunters and fishermen soon followed. By the 17th century, seasonal industries were based on fishing off Newfoundland and whaling off Labrador and Spitzbergen. These commercial operations became highly intensive, and there was fierce rivalry between competing nations—most notably between the English and the Dutch.

The search for the Northwest Passage was an ongoing saga of bravery and tragedy. In 1728, the Bering Strait—the stretch of water that separates America from Asia—was discovered by the Russian-sponsored Dane, Vitus Bering. In 1818, John Ross sailed up the west coast of Greenland and entered Baffin Bay and just over a decade later, he navigated the islands and sea passages of the Canadian Arctic.

Other explorers were not so fortunate as to enter Arctic waters and escape with their lives. In 1846, Sir John Franklin's expedition to find the Northwest Passage was prematurely ended when their two vessels became icebound when trying to find passage between Baffin Bay and the Beaufort Sea. The entire expedition of 134 men perished from cold, disease, and malnutrition after enduring an Arctic winter and attempting to find a route of escape on foot.

In 1903, Norwegian Roald Amundsen's expedition was the first to find a Northwest Passage traversable by boat, so ending a 300-year search for this elusive route.

As for exploration of the polar region in the Southern Hemisphere, during James Cook's second voyage in 1773 his expedition was the first to enter the Antarctic Circle. They came within 100 miles (160 km) of the southern continent, only to be turned back by pack ice. Later that year, Cook sailed even farther south—to latitude 71°10' S— but finding nothing but ice, felt entitled to claim that as he had not seen the "great southern continent," it was a myth. It was left to the Russian navigator Fabian von Bellingshausen, between 1819 and 1821, to discover the Antarctic Peninsula and confirm the existence of the mythical continent, which he circumnavigated. In the two decades that followed, expeditions such as those of Englishman James Weddell in 1823 and James Clark Ross in 1840–43 helped chart the fringes of the Antarctic continent. The last unexplored edges of the ocean world had begun to be mapped.

The History of Oceanography

Oceanography, the scientific study of the oceans, had a long and protracted birth. The coming together of the various strands of oceanography—the physical, chemical, biological, and geological—was a process that took the best part of 250 years, and only in the 20th century could oceanography truly begin to call itself an integrated science.

Key factors in the slow progress of early oceanography were the difficulties inherent in studying an environment as vast and complex as an ocean—problems that are still with us today. Also, it was not until the 1760s, with the development of accurate and affordable chronometers (page 139), that a ship's location in the ocean could be correctly fixed in terms of both latitude *and* longitude. British explorer Captain James Cook (1728–79) was perhaps the first to exploit the new scientific opportunities provided by accurate position finding. His expeditions between 1768 and 1779 not only penetrated previously unknown waters and accurately plotted coastlines, but they also pioneered the systematic measurement of winds, sea currents, surface temperatures, and seafloor depth.

Until the mid-19th century, ocean science was fragmentary, with little drive to coordinate research between different countries or to link physical, chemical, and biological data. This was to change in the latter half of the 19th century, and a leading light in this regard was Matthew Fontaine Maury (1806–73), Superintendent of the U.S. Navy's Depot of Charts and Instruments. Maury was eager that ships of different nationalities record details of wind and weather and a system be devised so that these results could be pooled. To this effect, Maury helped organize the first International Meteorological Conference, held in Brussels in 1853. One outcome was a standardized approach to observation and record keeping. The conference was a milestone in establishing international cooperation in scientific research—an approach that was vital to the development of oceanography. Maury's pioneering 1855 book, *The Physical Geography of the Sea,* contained the first bathymetric (depth) chart of an ocean basin. His contribution to ocean science has led some to dub him the father of oceanography.

In the first half of the 19th century, some marine biological investigations were carried out at sea. Englishman John Ross designed a special seafloor sampling device that he used, in 1817 and 1818, to obtain bottom samples in Baffin Bay, Canada, an Arctic region. At a depth of about 6,300 feet (1,920 m), the sediment still contained obvious signs of life—worms and starfish. John

Ross's nephew, James Clark Ross, extended the deep-sampling work and during 1839–43, in a series of voyages to Antarctica, he sampled the seafloor at a depth of nearly 23,000 feet (about 7,000 m). The starfish and worms he found at this depth were essentially the same species as those John Ross had found more than 20 years earlier in Arctic waters. James Ross concluded that waters of the deep ocean must be at a uniform cold temperature over much, or all, of the world.

Englishman Charles Darwin (1809–82), like many naturalists of his time, had joined a ship on a surveying expedition. The *Beagle* was to undertake a survey the coast of Patagonia (Argentina) and Tierra del Fuego. As naturalist on the expedition, Darwin's discoveries on the voyage were to lead him to develop theories that would overturn conventional views as to how complex life developed on the planet. These ideas have withstood the test of time and have, by and large, received overwhelming evidential support. But Darwin also made important contributions to the narrower field of marine biology. His monograph on barnacles is still referred to by specialists today and his proposition that coral atolls (page 122) are formed by submersion of the island around which they form is still considered by many the most likely explanation for atoll formation.

British naturalist Edward Forbes (1815–54) pioneered the investigation of the vertical distribution of life in the sea, describing depth zones that supported their own particular communities of organisms (page 90). He also surmised that the concentration of animal life decreased with increasing depth, perhaps to the point in the deep ocean depths at which no life would be found. The notion that the deep oceans were lifeless—supposedly because of the high pressures and absence of light and air—was well established by the mid-19th century, even though the Rosses had earlier found evidence that contradicted this idea. But in 1860, a submarine cable was brought up from the bottom at a depth of about 6,000 feet (1,830 m). It was encrusted with animals. This finding was widely reported and provided just the encouragement needed by would-be deep-sea investigators. By the 1870s, the first large-scale scientific exploration of the sea, the *Challenger* expedition, marked oceanography's true birth.

The *Challenger* Expedition

The *Challenger* expedition was, to 19th-century marine science, the equivalent of the *Apollo* mis-

sions to space exploration. One writer, Ray Lancaster, commenting on the *Challenger* expedition, claimed with some justification that "Never did an expedition cost so little and produce such momentous results for human knowledge." When the expedition's findings were analyzed, they yielded more information about the world beneath the surface of the ocean than had been previously gathered throughout human history.

In 1868, two influential British scientists, William Benjamin Carpenter and Sir Charles Wyville Thomson, won backing to use British Navy survey ships to dredge in deep water. During three voyages, they amassed incontrovertible evidence for the presence of abundant life in deep water. Spurred on by these developments, the two scientists garnered support from political and scientific communities to fund a major expedition. Though hurriedly prepared, the three-and-a-half-year expedition that resulted was to become a remarkable success story.

The *Challenger* expedition of 1872–76 was a round-the-world voyage that covered about 79,220 miles (127,500 km). During the expedition, a staggering tally of readings was taken: 133 bottom dredges, 151 open-water trawls, 263 serial water-temperature observations, and 492 deep-water soundings. The scientists made many unexpected discoveries. Biological samples revealed a total of 4,417 new species. The deepest sounding measured a depth of 26,850 feet (8,185 m) and came from the Mariana Trench in the western North Pacific. A prodigious number of samples and data were collected. It took at least 76 scientists more than 20 years to analyze the material. Fifty thick volumes of scientific reports based on the *Challenger* expedition were published during a period of 19 years.

Polar Exploration

The inhospitable polar regions were to be the last surface areas of the oceans to be investigated scientifically. In 1879 a U.S. expedition headed by George Washington DeLong (1844–81) attempted to sail through the Bering Strait between Alaska and Russia in a vessel, the *Jeanette*. The plan was to reach Wrangell Island and establish whether or not this island was a peninsula of a polar continent. The *Jeanette* became stuck fast in ice and drifted north of Wrangell Island, and after traveling several hundred miles locked in the ice, the ship was crushed. Five years later, the remains of *Jeanette* were found in ice on the opposite side of the North Pole.

HMS Challenger, *the vessel used on the* Challenger *expedition, 1872–76*

The implication was that these articles had drifted in the pack ice, taking a route over or close to the North Pole. Norwegian explorer and scientist Fridtjof Nansen (1861–1930) decided to test this idea and sought funding to construct a strong vessel that would drift with the Arctic pack ice without being crushed. In June 1893, this vessel, the *Fram,* sailed from Oslo, Norway, with a crew of 13 and provisions for five years. Within three months, the *Fram* became locked in sea ice north of Siberia and remained trapped for nearly three years, during which time it drifted 1,028 miles (1,658 km) with the pack ice. Averaging a speed of 1.2 miles (2 km) a day, at one point the *Fram* came to within 248 miles (400 km) of the North Pole. In August 1896, the *Fram* was released from the ice near Spitsbergen—an island about midway between Norway and Greenland.

The drift of the *Fram* established that the Arctic, unlike Antarctica, was a frozen polar sea, not an ice-covered continent. During the *Fram*'s drift, oceanographic readings showed that the depth of the Arctic Ocean sometimes exceeded 9,840 feet (3,000 m) and that a body of relatively warm water, as high as 35°F (1.5°C), was found at depths of between 490 and 950 feet (150 and 900 m) sandwiched between colder water. Nansen correctly concluded that this feature was caused by Atlantic water penetrating below the less-saline Arctic water.

Marine Laboratories

In 1872, the year *Challenger* embarked on its historic expedition, the world's first marine laboratory opened. Funded by the German government and headed by German biologist Anton Dohrn (1840–1909), the Stazione Zoologica was sited in Naples, Italy. It was the first of many laboratories throughout the world to undertake observations and experiments on living marine organisms. Until then, most investigations of open-ocean species were observations made on board ship or examinations of dead specimens preserved in jars. Few investigations had been carried out on marine organisms from the open ocean.

Meanwhile, in the United States, the status of marine science had declined somewhat after the death of Matthew Maury in 1873 (the fact that he sided with the Confederates in the Civil War had not helped his subsequent reputation). The U.S. government was reluctant to fund marine research, and several marine biological laboratories set up in the early 1870s failed to flourish—with one exception. In 1873, Swiss zoologist Louis Agassiz (1807–73) established a marine laboratory on the East Coast. This moved to Woods Hole, Massachusetts, in 1888. By 1930 it had become the world-famous Woods Hole Oceanographic Institution.

Gradually, other marine stations and laboratories were established in the United States, among them the Scripps Institution of Oceanography in La Jolla, California. In the 1930s, the institution's director completed a world survey that established that there were more than 250 institutions dedicated to marine research. Today, almost all countries that border an ocean have at least one oceanographic or fisheries research center; several have a dozen or more.

20th-Century Oceanography

The 20th century has seen oceanographic sampling technologies become highly automated. Instead of scattered on-the-spot sampling, there has been a trend toward continuous sampling along a vessel's path. Today, a plethora of new technologies scan the oceans from above and below. They include research vessels with sophisticated sonars, submersibles with cameras (page 154), and satellites with sensors (page 156).

Another development is the increasingly international nature of oceanographic research. With some issues of territoriality still to be resolved (page 194), there is nevertheless considerable international cooperation in studying oceanographic and meteorological processes (page 75). Understanding how the oceans work and finding solutions to some of our most pressing environmental problems require coordinated international effort.

Diving

Free diving—staying submerged without any mechanical assistance—has been conducted on a commercial basis since ancient times and is still practiced in some tropical locations. Free diving is limited by the volume of the individual's lungs and their capacity to deliver oxygen around the body and the body's ability to cope with the absence of oxygen when breath is held during a dive. Pressure change during a dive is also a limiting factor. Ambient pressure increases by 1 atmosphere for each 33 feet (10 m) of depth, and during a dive, the increased pressure exerted on the swimmer's lungs and eardrums can be hazardous. As a result, for most trained divers, free dives are limited to a time of about two minutes and a maximum depth of about 33–36 feet (10–11 m). Greater depths and durations have been recorded, but such attempts are extremely hazardous and are only successful after considerable training and when special techniques are employed.

Assisted Diving

Just prior to the Battle of Salamis in 480 B.C.E. (page 126), a Greek diver, Seyllis, and his daughter, Cyane, are reported to have cut the anchor ropes of the Persian fleet, thereby creating havoc among enemy ships. To remain undetected, they employed snorkels made of hollow reeds to breath while under water. Aristotle, in the fourth century B.C.E., describes metal tubing being used for snorkels; he also describes a form of diving bell—a large container of air that is lowered underwater—although the details of how this device worked in practice are unclear.

The first well-documented practical device for assisting a diver is attributed to esteemed English scientist Edmond Halley (1656–1742) near the turn of the 18th century. His "diving bell" was an inverted, weighted, cone-shaped wooden vessel, open at the bottom. To allow light to enter, a glass lens was set into the top. As the bell was lowered into the sea and descended through the water column, the air inside it became compressed. This air was topped up by a barrel of air that was lowered to below the level of the diving bell. The barrel had an opening at the bottom, and the high water pressure forced air out of the barrel through a connecting tube and into the bell. A single diver could sit inside the bell, leave through the bottom to explore the vicinity, and then return for more air. As the air inside the bell became stale, it was replenished by air from a fresh barrel. Though using the diving bell was fraught with hazards, it was nevertheless used with success to recover objects from wrecks.

Various refinements were added to Halley's basic design. Toward the end of the 18th century, diving bells were being cast in metal and supplied with air pumped from the surface. Two-person bells were used to assist divers when building or repairing underwater constructions such as harbors, canal works, and bridge supports.

Early Diving Suits and Helmets

Diving bells of improved design were used right up until the 20th century; indeed, some submersibles and underwater platforms, though far

Divers with a green sea turtle, equatorial Pacific Ocean (Andy Caulfield/ENP Images)

more sophisticated than diving bells, still work on the principle of allowing divers access through an open port on the underside.

Diving bells were a solution to the provision of air under water, but the effects of pressure, poor visibility, and coldness were still major limitations for divers. By wearing a protective suit and a metal helmet with viewing window, many of these problems could be countered. At the same time, the helmets and diving suits provided an opportunity to deliver air directly to the diver rather than via a bell. By the 1830s, the English brothers John and Charles Deane had developed a metal diving helmet supplied by air pump and connected to a watertight rubber suit. By 1837, the German inventor Augustus Siebe had developed a more elegant helmet-and-suit combination that remained full of air and was watertight. The Siebe "closed" suit, the classic design used for the rest of the 19th century and into the 20th century, incorporates the familiar metal helmet design seen in old Hollywood adventure movies. Using this kit, divers could descend to about 200 feet (60 m). The suit offered a mobility far greater than that provided by a diving bell.

Deep Diving

While the Siebe diving suit was the 19th-century answer to shallow-water diving, another solution was needed for diving beyond 200 feet (60 m). A major impetus for the design of deep-diving equipment came with the sinking of the British liner *Egypt* off Ushant in 1922. It lay on the bottom in 390 feet (119 m) of water and held a cargo that included 11 tons (10 t) of gold and 22 tons (20 t) of silver. The salvage operation was organized by an Italian firm, Sorima, using German suits produced by Neufeldt and Kuhnke. Highly innovative at the time, the suits were armored to resist pressure. The air inside the suit was reused many times; chemicals were provided to absorb the carbon dioxide breathed out, and oxygen bottles within the suit were discharged periodically to top up the air with oxygen. Breathing air at normal pressure avoids the dangers of decompression sickness on ascent. The drawback of the suit is the relative lack of mobility: the suit is jointed at arms and legs, but hands cannot be used to manipulate objects, other than via pincers. Despite these limitations, the Italian divers did succeed in recovering the bullion from the sunken *Egypt*.

Deep-diving suits of today work on essentially the same principles. The diver is enclosed in air at atmospheric pressure and the suit is robotlike and articulated with sophisticated manipulators to grasp objects. Modern materials such as carbon fiber, aluminum alloy, and reinforced plastic are used in their construction. Being weight-for-weight much stronger than traditional materials, modern suits can be worn to depth of 1,500 feet (450 meters) or more. Even though submersibles are increasingly used in deep-sea exploration (page 154), they cannot yet equal the mobility and dexterity of a suited diver. Deep-sea divers still play a vital role in maintaining and repairing underwater structures such as the supports of drilling platforms used in the oil industry.

Scuba Diving

The Siebe diving suit was supplied with air from the surface and weighted boots to ensure that the diver was properly oriented in the water. The diver was unable to swim in the water, only hang suspended, or stand or walk on the seafloor. A radical improvement would be a self-contained diving apparatus that would enable the diver to swim and be independent of the surface vessel. In the 1870s, Frenchman H. A. Fleuss developed the first self-contained breathing apparatus for divers. It relied on the diver carrying an air supply in a pressurized cylinder on his back. The diver rebreathed air from which carbon dioxide was removed and extra oxygen gradually added. The apparatus was still coupled, however, with a traditional, heavy-booted diving suit.

The invention of the "self-contained underwater breathing apparatus" (scuba) or aqualung is attributed to Frenchmen Jacques Cousteau and Émile Gagnan in 1943. Their radical advance was the development of the demand valve, or regulator—a device that ensured that the diver breathed in air at the same pressure as that of the surrounding water. The diver could now breathe underwater with much greater ease, and the air supply kept in pressurized tanks on the diver's back could last for an hour or more. When coupled with a rubber diving suit, mask, and fins, the equipment gave a freedom of movement and level of safety previously unobtainable.

Today, scuba gear is the equipment of choice for shallow-water diving, whether by amateurs or professionals. Even so, scuba gear does have its limitations and dangers. Ordinary air is breathable down to the pressures found at a depth of about 200 feet (60 m). At greater depth, the nitrogen in normal air dissolves in the blood at dangerously high levels. This produces a narcotic effect—superficially similar to drunkenness—that Cousteau called "rapture of the deep." Professional scuba divers who go beyond these depths use an expensive mixture of helium and oxygen in place of normal air.

Another problem in scuba diving is decompression. As a diver ascends through the water column, the pressure exerted on the lungs and bloodstream is reduced. If the ascent is made swiftly (and if the diver has been at depth for a long period), there is a real danger that nitrogen gas will bubble out of the bloodstream and form gas bubbles that can block small blood vessels. This can cause excruciating pain in muscles and joints and may even cause more serious damage to vital organs such as the kidneys or brain. This effect is decompression sickness, or "the bends"; it can be alleviated by slowly reducing the pressure on ascent so that the nitrogen gas can dissipate without any danger of bubbling. This is achieved in one of two ways. The diver can slow the ascent, pausing at intervals according to a prescribed regime (diving tables and electronic devices can be used to compute this—the longer and deeper the dive, the greater the time required for the ascent). An alternative approach, and one normally only available to professional divers, is to enter a decompression chamber (essentially a form of pressurized diving bell) during the ascent. The decompression chamber can be brought back to the surface quickly, but the pressure inside is reduced only gradually according to a regime similar to that used for open-water ascent.

Decompression is a major limiting factor in scuba diving, even where oxygen-helium mixtures are used. For example, a diver who spends five minutes at a depth of about 610 feet (185 m) must allow for nearly six hours' decompression time. Only by providing pressurized artificial environments at depth—artificial underwater communities such as the French *Conshelf* project and the U.S. *Sealab* and *Tektite* ventures of the 1960s and 1970s—can scuba divers remain at depth for long periods without increasing their decompression time. Once a diver's blood is saturated with inert gas—either nitrogen or helium—then the required decompression time is at its maximum, no matter how much longer the diver stays at depth.

The world's only remaining underwater laboratory, Aquarius–2000, owned by the U.S. National Oceanic and Atmospheric Administration (NOAA), is continuing and expanding the tradition of providing scuba divers with both a temporary underwater home and a productive research facility.

Submarines, Satellites, and Future Exploration

Submarines, Submersibles, and AUVS

Currently, the deepest recorded open-ocean dive by a suited individual is about 1,500 feet (457 m). The theoretical limit for deep-water diving is about 1,970 feet (600 m). To go beyond this depth, an explorer needs to be protected from the high pressure by being enclosed in a vessel of some kind.

A submersible is essentially a chamber in which air pressure remains the same as or close to that at the ocean surface. Submersibles are used for exploratory purposes or for maintenance and repair of underwater constructions, although they can have military uses; in general, they can stay submerged only for relatively short periods of time. Submarines, on the other hand, are first and foremost naval vessels; they have the capacity to remain submerged for extended periods of time and even, in some cases, many months. A third type of underwater craft has come to prominence since the 1960s—the remotely operated vehicle (ROV). ROVs are unpiloted, and because they do not carry an air supply for the operator, they can be small and stay submerged for long periods. They are usually controlled via an umbilical cord that links the ROV with a surface craft or a submersible. The autonomous underwater vehicle (AUV) represents the latest stage in underwater vehicle development. Such devices are untethered and are self-contained units that can operate on their own. Several such vehicles are currently undergoing tests, and the intention is that such devices will be able to gather data by operating independently for several months at a time.

EARLY SUBMERSIBLES AND SUBMARINES

The early impetus for developing underwater craft was essentially a military one. By approaching the enemy from under water, a submersible could place an explosive charge against an enemy vessel unobserved. During the American Revolutionary War, colonist David Bushnell built a wooden submersible that was used in an attack on a British warship. The submersible operator did place an explosive charge against the warship's hull, but because he was unable to place the device inside the hull—he tried boring a hole with a drill device but was unsuccessful—the charge exploded harmlessly. However, the unexpected explosion was sufficient to make the British pull up anchor and leave the vicinity.

In the first half of the 19th century, various fish-shaped submersibles were developed with varying degrees of success. The first that claimed a military target was a craft used by the Confederates against a Federal vessel in the U.S. Civil War. In 1863, the *H.L. Hunley,* one of a fleet of submersibles that operated just below the surface of the water, torpedoed and sank the federal sloop, *Housatonic.* The *Hunley* was also sunk in the resulting explosion.

MODERN SUBMARINES

Today, two types of submarine are used by navies. Conventional submarines are deployed by most maritime nations. They are powered by diesel engine when on or near the surface and use battery power when submerged. Their range and performance are more restricted than that of the second type, nuclear-powered submarines, but they are much less costly. The conventional submarine's time submerged is limited by the need to surface (or to cruise just below the surface) so as to run diesel engines to recharge the batteries. The use of such engines requires direct contact with the atmosphere to take on air and to vent waste gases. Conventional submarines nevertheless remain a potent adversary.

Nuclear-powered submarines—expensive and highly sophisticated—are driven by nuclear reactors; some of these submarines carry nuclear weapons, but many do not. A nuclear reactor does not require atmospheric air or need to vent waste gases, so a nuclear-powered submarine could, theoretically, stay submerged for years on end. In practice, human constraints mean that submarine patrols are limited to a few months. When submerged, electrolysis of water provides oxygen to replenish that breathed in and consumed by the crew.

Nuclear-powered submarines armed with ballistic nuclear missiles are a major component of the defense strategy of Western and Eastern alliances. Nuclear-powered attack submarines, on the other hand, carry nonnuclear armory but have tremendous reach. They are a potent force: they are able to attack surface ships, land forces, and other submarines, while remaining virtually undetectable. Some nuclear-powered submarines can cruise at the astonishingly high speed of 50 miles an hour (about 80 km an hour). The depths at which submarines operate is, not surprisingly, classified information; their advertised maximum operating depths, typically several hundred meters, are underestimates. Nevertheless, operating depth is one area where today's specialized submersibles and other underwater craft score highly over submarines.

MODERN SUBMERSIBLES

A major breakthrough in deep-sea exploration came in 1934 in the waters off Bermuda. Zoologist William Beebe and engineer Otis Barton descended to a depth of 3,028 feet (923 m) in Barton's revolutionary submersible, the bathysphere. This craft—essentially a steel sphere with viewing ports—was lowered by cable from a surface ship. Swiss engineer Auguste Piccard adopted the steel-sphere principle in his 1948 bathyscaphe ("deep boat"), but the major advance was in suspending the sphere below a submarinelike chamber that was filled with gasoline. The bathyscaphe's buoyancy could be regulated and it was maneuverable, unlike the bathysphere. In 1954, the bathyscaphe dived to 10,392 feet (3,170 m) off the Italian coast. Piccard then sold the design to the U.S. Navy and in 1960, Piccard's son, Jacques, led a record-breaking dive in the bathyscaphe *Trieste*. The vessel touched bottom in the southwest Pacific's Mariana Trench at a depth of 35,800 feet (10,900 m). This depth record has yet to be equaled, although the Japanese came to within 2 feet (0.6 m) of doing so in March 1995 using a tethered unmanned craft, *Kaiko*.

There were rapid advances in submersible technology in the 1960s and 1970s, although very few have survived through various incarnations since then to form part of today's repertoire of underwater vehicles. Limited funding, technical deficiencies, and the lack of suitable applications to justify the expense have all taken their toll. Perhaps the most successful of the 1960s submersibles was the three-person *Alvin*, operated by the Woods Hole Oceanographic Institution. Modified and refitted, this workhorse is still in use today. It was in *Alvin* that Woods Hole scientists explored the Galápagos Rift in 1977 and discovered the remarkable hydrothermal vent communities (page 116). In 1986, it was in *Alvin* that Robert Ballard's team photographed the *Titanic,* using remotely operated vehicles (see page 155) that were tethered to it. Since the 1970s, France, Japan, and the former Soviet Union have been building submersibles for scientific and sometimes military purposes; even *Alvin* has been involved in military operations. In 1966, for example, it played a major role in locating and recovering an atomic bomb. However, most submersibles for most of the time are used for scientific purposes: they offer almost unrivaled opportunities for gathering samples and observing deep-sea life and seafloor structures firsthand. The upgraded *Alvin* can dive to 2.5 miles (more than 4 km), while France's *Nautile,* Russia's *Mir I* and

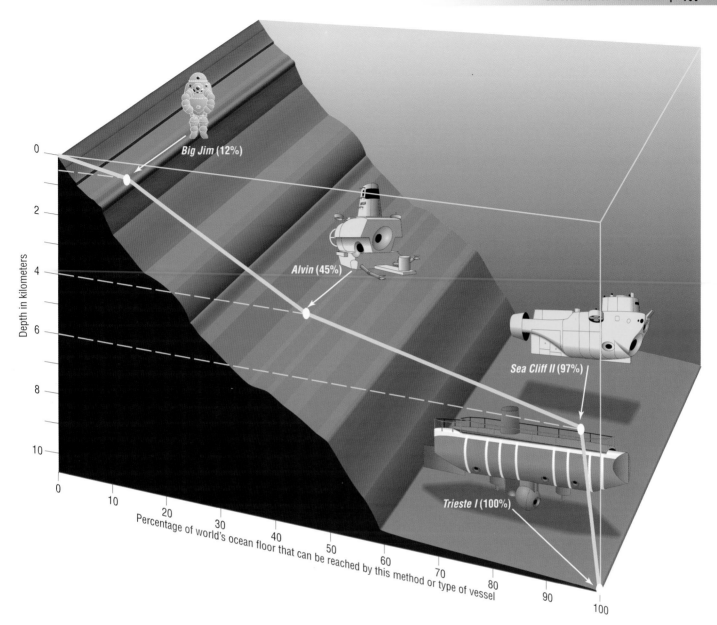

The depths (and percentages of the world's ocean floor) that different diving methods and vehicles can reach

Mir II, the Japanese *Shinkai 6500,* and the U.S. *Sea Cliff* can all dive to 3.7 miles (6 km) or beyond—a depth that encompasses 97 percent of the ocean floor and includes all but the deepest trenches.

Carrying people on board severely limits the time a vessel can stay submerged. In many cases, a dive is limited to 12 hours, of which perhaps eight hours may be spent in traveling to and from the operating depth. For this reason, many scientists believe that other options—ROVs and AUVs—are likely to be the deep-water craft of the future. Others argue that scientists will always wish to observe firsthand, and despite the limitations, manned submersibles will continue to play a major role in deep-sea exploration. A new gen-

eration of manned submersibles is currently being developed (page 157).

ROVS AND AUVS

Compared to piloted submersibles, remotely operated vehicles (ROVs) are cheaper and safer to operate and can stay submerged for much longer periods. Since the 1960s, ROV technology has advanced alongside that of submersibles, and some ROVs are, in fact, launched from submersibles. ROVs are normally controlled via an umbilical linkage that connects them to a surface vessel or submersible. In the exploration of the *Titanic* in 1985 and 1986, for example, the ROV *Argo* was towed behind the surface vessel, and from it was launched a tethered smaller vehicle, *Jason Jr.* The following year, *Jason Jr.* was launched from the manned submersible *Alvin.* ROVs could explore the *Titanic* more intimately and with much greater safety than a piloted craft. Many ROVs are in almost weekly use throughout the

world but receive little publicity. These are the ROVs associated with the offshore oil industry that are used for inspections and maintenance procedures. In the early 1990s, there were more than 190 of these craft operating worldwide.

The Japanese are now at the leading edge of ROV technology. In March 1995, the tethered ROV *Kaiko* almost equaled *Trieste's* long-held depth record, and unlike the *Trieste,* which did not have cameras on board, the *Kaiko* was able to establish that there was life at this depth. Japan's interest in deep-sea exploration is primarily motivated by two factors: commercial exploitation of the possible riches that lie at the bottom of the sea, and attempts to predict natural threats to the nation's landmasses. Japan is one of the most tectonically active parts of the world and is subject to catastrophic earthquakes, such as the Kobe tremors in 1995 in which 5,500 people perished. These quakes often originate from fissures deep on the ocean floor. The prospects for commercial exploitation of seafloor mineral resources are currently in a state of flux (page 194), but the need for seismic and tectonic investigations is as urgent as ever.

Perhaps the ultimate development in underwater craft is the autonomous underwater vehicle (AUV). Such devices have been used by the military since the 1960s, but for scientific surveying, they are very much a phenomenon of the 1990s. Such craft are designed to operate independently, without external control, for months on end if necessary. Among the U.S. vehicles undergoing trials are Woods Hole's Autonomous Benthic Explorer (*ABE*) and the Massachusetts Institute of Technology's partly government-funded craft, the *Odyssey*. These AUVs can gather and store data, periodically resurfacing to download their information to researchers. Ultimately, rather than following preprogrammed routes, such vehicles may have "artificial intelligence" that enables them to adapt their responses according to prevailing conditions. The future is likely to see underwater vehicles of several types—submersibles. ROVs, and AUVs—communicating with one another and providing a flexible response to the problems of gathering data and performing technical operations in the depths of the sea.

Satellites

Satellites in today's world fulfill many roles: they relay communications of many kinds, they provide the network for today's state-of-the-art navigational systems (page 139), and they gather information about weather systems, enabling meteorological predictions to be made (page 75). Migrating animals that have been electronically tagged relay their position via satellites (page 108). Fishermen can obtain real-time views of sea areas that reveal features such as surface temperature and color; from these, they can locate surface schools of fish by noting temperature features and plankton congregations where fish are likely to gather. In many ways, satellites are today's explorers: they provide us with a view of the world—and the oceans within that world—that we cannot obtain in other ways.

The oceans are so large that taking an on-the-spot reading or sample from a particular location is, literally as well as metaphorically, a drop in the ocean. To make sense of these readings, many need to be taken for a short period of time from a large number of different locations, and this is costly. In 1997, the running costs for a research vessel at sea were of the order of $20,000–$30,000 a day. The capital costs for a research vessel—essentially a floating laboratory—can reach $75 million. There is also the problem that in moving from one location to another, you are not really taking a "snap-shot" of the larger area at a single moment in time. The ocean is a very dynamic environment, and water does not stay in one place for long, so the patterns that emerge from such sampling may have as much to do with temporal as well as spatial change.

Satellites can overcome some of these sampling problems. A satellite can monitor a large area of Earth's surface at any one time, and by orbiting Earth in a prescribed manner, a satellite can cover most of the planet's surface in a day or two. But satellites do have their limitations, and the readings obtained from satellite sensory methods can only be interpreted when calibrated against on-the-spot readings. So the two methods—conventional sampling and satellite imaging—are complementary and will remain so for the foreseeable future.

THE EARLY SATELLITES

Astronauts orbiting Earth in the 1960s noticed some large-scale oceanic features—such as the dispersal of sediment from a river or the location of a front (a natural boundary between two bodies of water of different temperatures and densities)—that were difficult and time consuming to locate from sea level but obvious from space. Specialized satellites were flown for the first time in 1978 with the specific intention of gathering information about the oceans. In that year, the three satellites—*Seasat–A, Tiros–N,* and *Nimbus–7*—all carried sensors capable of measuring oceanographic features. It was *Seasat–A* that established, above all, the value of taking such measurements. In its three-month life, the satellite beamed down data that were used to determine sea-surface topography, wind speed and direction, surface temperature, ice cover and its characteristics, wave patterns and ocean currents, and near-surface coloration caused by biological phenomena, sediment, or oil pollution. The mission came to an abrupt halt due to a short circuit, although some journalists at the time speculated that the mission was abandoned prematurely because it was *too* successful and was making available data that could be used for military purposes by other nations.

CURRENT TECHNOLOGY

Satellite remote sensing, as it is called, utilizes electromagnetic radiation. Within the electromagnetic spectrum, there are three "windows"—three regions of wavelengths—where electromagnetic waves can pass through the atmosphere relatively unaffected. In terms of wavelength, these regions are the visible spectrum (400–700 nanometers), the infrared region (specific locations within the range 3–13 micrometers), and microwaves such as radar and radio transmission (wavelengths longer than about 10 millimeters [0.39 inches]). The atmosphere markedly absorbs or scatters other regions of the electromagnetic spectrum.

There are two kinds of sensors that are carried by satellites to record features of the planet's surface. Active sensors probe the planet with pulses of radio waves; the returns from these pulses provide data about distance from, and texture of, Earth's surface. Active sensors have a key advantage: they can operate all the time, irrespective of weather conditions. Passive sensors, on the other hand, detect the longer wavelengths of electromagnetic radiation that are reflected or emitted from Earth's surface. These wavelengths—the visible and infrared regions of the spectrum—are absorbed or scattered by clouds, so the use of passive sensors is affected by weather conditions.

Whether active or passive sensors are used, none of the usable wavelengths can penetrate far into seawater, so the data gathered relates to conditions at or near the surface of the water, with one major exception: the topography of the sea surface is influenced by gravitational attraction. To some extent, the topography of the seabed can be inferred from the topography of the sea surface (see below). But in other respects, if oceanographers want to find out what is happening far below the surface of the water, they need to use subsurface acoustic or radio methods, or direct sampling, not satellite remote sensing.

Currently, active satellite remote sensing is used to measure the surface topography of the sea by measuring the time taken for a radio wave pulse to leave and return to the satellite. This measures the altitude of the satellite and therefore indirectly establishes the surface level of the sea at that point. From many such readings, two kinds of parameter can be derived: the roughness of the surface waters (at scales down to a few centimeters), and the slope of the sea surface (at scales of the order of tens of kilometers). Passive satellite remote sensing establishes two kinds of parameter: the temperature of the ocean's surface and the color of the near-surface waters. From these parameters other properties can be inferred. For example, the color of the near-surface waters can be used to estimate chlorophyll content and, in turn, the primary productivity of the upper waters. The surface slope can be used to infer seafloor topography or ocean currents (wind-driven water builds up slightly in the direction in which it is flowing). Surface roughness provides a measure of the size, abundance, and orientation of ripples that, in turn, can be related to wind speed and direction.

The great gains to be achieved by refining satellite data using data obtained in other ways are confirmed by recent work carried out by Walter Smith and David Sandwell of the National Oceanic and Atmospheric Administration. The topography of the ocean surface as determined by satellite radar altimetry (measuring altitude using radio waves) has great precision, but the readings obtained are not always reliable. The surface of the ocean is sculpted by the influence of gravity from the seafloor below, but if the seafloor varies substantially in composition, this will influence the gravitational effect on the sea level above and will produce false depth readings. By correcting satellite data using depth soundings obtained from ships, the research team is producing a bathymetric chart for the world's oceans. This chart attempts to merge the best characteristics of both types of approach—soundings and satellite data—to produce a composite that is more comprehensive than soundings data alone but more reliable than satellite data. It has been estimated that it would take a state-of-the-art research vessel more than one century to map fully the oceans from soundings, and the enterprise would cost more than $1 billion at today's prices. Walter Smith has estimated that to map the world's oceans by correcting satellite data using existing sounding measurements will not produce a chart as reliable, but the cost will be in the region of $60 million and it will have taken a year.

The oceanographic data that is gathered daily by satellites and relayed around the world is truly phenomenal, and this will only increase. North American, European, and Japanese space agencies are all committed to continuing their Earth Observation Satellite programs, and at least some of these craft will have sensors dedicated for oceanographic applications.

The Future of Marine Exploration

Historical trends in ocean exploration have seen direct observation of the ocean's surface and its land boundaries giving way to indirect observation of the ocean world from both above and below the sea surface. Nowadays, satellites, research vessels, and various kinds of underwater vehicle monitor the ocean world, and their data are mathematical in nature. Computers manipulate this data and display it in a visual form that summarizes useful information about the ocean world. So, for example, satellite images are color coded to show the average temperatures of different parts of the ocean surface. This trend is likely to continue so that as new sensing devices are developed and as computers become faster and more sophisticated, more facets of the ocean world can be identified and displayed. Much of future marine exploration is likely to focus on exploring the ocean world we already know, but in new ways.

But what about direct observation of the underwater world? The following analogy can be drawn. If this double-page spread represents the total area of the world's ocean floors, then the period at the end of this sentence represents the area that has been seen directly through the eyes of divers, those piloting submersibles, or via video cameras attached to ROVs and AUVs. There is a massive expanse of the ocean floor still to explore. Scientists and explorers have diverse views about the best ways of progressing with deep-sea exploration.

Robert Ballard, a pioneering figure whose remarkable track record includes being leader of the first expeditions to the Galápagos hydrothermal vents and to the wreck of the *Titanic*, sees ROVs and AUVs, not piloted submersibles, as the workhorses of future deep-sea exploration. Interviewed by *Time* magazine in 1995, he was also dubious about the value in spending time and money exploring the very deepest parts of the ocean—the 3 percent that is below about 21,300 feet (6,500 m)—the limit of today's piloted submersibles. He believes that, scientifically and commercially, the shallow and medium depths have much more to offer and was quoted in *Time* as saying "I believe that the deep sea has very little to offer. I've been there, I've spent a career there, I don't see the future there." Others feel differently. Greg Stone of the New England Aquarium in Boston, Massachusetts, says "We won't know what [the deep sea below 6,500 meters] holds until we've been there. There will certainly be new creatures. We'll be able to learn where gases from the atmosphere go into the ocean. We'll be able to get closest to where the geological action is. We know very little about the details of these processes. And once we're there, I'm sure studies will open up whole sets of new questions."

Reaching the deep sea might be very, very expensive. A new version of the Japanese craft *Shinkai 6500*—the deepest-diving piloted submersible—would probably cost $100 million. However, a new generation of highly maneuverable and relatively cheap submersibles is being tested. Deep Ocean Engineering—a firm that designs and builds undersea vehicles—was founded by engineer Graham Hawkes and former chief scientist for the National Oceanic and Atmospheric Administration Sylvia Earle. Today, this company builds vehicles for a range of clients: the oil and gas industry, television companies, universities, and navies.

Graham Hawkes's latest venture, and independent of the company he cofounded, is a submersible that "flies" underwater. *Deep Flight I,* costing in the region of $5 million, has stubby wings, flaps, and tail fins that enable it to fly underwater. It is designed to reach a depth of about 3,300 feet (1 km), and were the craft to "stall" underwater, it should simply float to the surface. *Deep Flight I* is currently undergoing trials. Hawkes is planning *Deep Flight II,* a one- or two-seater submersible that will be able to reach the deepest 3 percent of the ocean floor.

Meanwhile, Robert Ballard is pursuing the idea of bringing "real-time" underwater exploration to the televisions and computer screens of people in their own homes. Using remote-controlled video cameras placed on the seafloor or mounted on ROVs, he is planning to relay live pictures from future explorations to anyone linked to the Internet. He has his immediate sights set on expeditions to the sites of naval battles in the Pacific and the ancient graveyards of Black Sea ships.

The Value of Water

Water, water, everywhere
And all the boards did shrink
Water, water everywhere
Nor any drop to drink

—SAMUEL TAYLOR COLERIDGE
The Rime of the Ancient Mariner

This extract underlines the unpleasant irony that a sailor at sea, surrounded by a seemingly inexhaustible supply of ocean water, cannot use this abundance as an immediate source of drinking water. Indeed, because of the high salinity of ocean water, drinking seawater (if the person can keep it down) will only dehydrate the body further. Far from quenching a thirst, seawater will exacerbate it.

An adult typically needs to drink at least 1 liter (1.75 pints) of water a day to maintain the salt/water balance in the body. In a hot, dry environment where water loss from sweat and exhaled air is that much greater, the individual will need a substantially larger daily quota of water. The water—if drunk as freshwater—also needs to be uncontaminated and low in mineral salts. In practice, many of us obtain most or all of our water supply in the foods we eat and the beverages we drink rather than by drinking clean, clear water itself.

Most animals are 70 percent water; most plants are 90 percent water. Water is thus a basic requirement for life. As humans, we also use water for cleaning purposes and in waste disposal. For these purposes, the water quality need not be as high as that required for drinking water. When you take into account the water used in agricultural, industrial, and commercial processes to provide the food, services, and consumer goods that we demand, the per capita consumption of water rises to surprisingly high levels.

The demand for water even for basic activities varies by an extraordinary amount from one part of the world to the other. Estimates for daily water consumption per person in 1990 (for drinking, cleaning, and waste disposal) give the United States average at about 580 liters (613 quarts), the United Kingdom at 136 liters (144 quarts), Uganda about 5 liters (5 quarts), and Equatorial Guinea, about 3 liters (3 quarts)—nearly a 200-fold difference between the highest and the lowest consumers.

The regions of the planet where water is in short supply are not always in developing countries, although in these regions the need is clearly most pressing because human survival depends on it. Southeast Africa and equatorial regions of East Africa are among the worst affected, but in developed countries, there also are regions—southeastern Australia, California in the United States, and southern Spain—where water shortages can be severe.

The water-supply solution that is appropriate for a particular geographic locality is determined by a range of factors, including the use to which the water will be put (is it for drinking or for irrigation, for example?), the availability of funds (is it an affluent part of North America or an unprosperous region of Africa?), and the geographic location relative to potential water supplies. Different solutions apply in different places. Most of Earth's surface water is found in the oceans (but not in an immediately usable form) or frozen at Earth's poles (in a usable form but in the wrong place).

A quick examination of the statistics for natural water supplies on the planet's surface reveals the huge abundance of water in the oceans. The frozen ice at the poles represents much more than double the freshwater in circulation elsewhere in the world. So, seawater and polar ice would be potential sources of valuable water if they could be harnessed and transported to those regions on the planet that most require it. How feasible is this?

Iceberg in Bransfield Strait, Antarctic Peninsula
(Gerry Ellis/ENP Images)

THE PARTITION OF WATER ON EARTH'S SURFACE

	% of freshwater	% of total water
Oceans	—	97.54
Ice	73.9	1.81
Groundwater	25.7	0.63
Lakes and streams		
Freshwater	0.36	0.009
Salt water	—	0.007
Atmosphere	0.04	0.001

Note: The figures above do not include the small total amount of water held within living organisms.

Desalination

Seawater could provide an abundant source of freshwater if only the salt could be separated out. In practice, doing this requires a high input of energy. In those countries where there are the worst water shortages, desalination (removing the salt from water) is currently only conducted on a relatively small scale. It is available on a larger scale in those countries where the demand is sufficiently strong and there are financial resources to support such schemes. Whether desalination is used in a developed or a developing country, or on a small or large scale, the high costs and technicalities of the method usually restrict its use to providing drinking water only. It is not a viable method for providing, say, irrigation water or water for industrial processes unless the benefits from the location of these processes in water-scarce regions are exceptionally high.

Desalination most commonly involves distillation: seawater or saline water from other sources is heated or boiled to drive off water vapor. The vapor is condensed to yield water of high purity; the residue contains a little water together with high concentrations of salts. The condensed water has to be collected and the residue safely disposed of, both being costly operations. The heat required to speed the distillation process, if provided by burning a conventional carbon-based fuel, is also costly, and there are environmental implications because carbon dioxide is a by-product (page 78). A good alternative energy source is solar radiation—heat from the Sun—but this is relatively low-level heat. To produce a large volume of desalinated water using solar radiation requires water to be spread over a wide area. This requires very large facilities—a large city would require a solar-powered desalination plant of many thousands of square kilometers to provide even its drinking-water supplies. Thus, desalination facilities work where need is greatest and the overall demand is not very high. They tend to operate in affluent countries or regions that are blessed with a warm climate. Thus, of the 2,500 or so desalination plants operating in the mid-1990s, many more than half were located in the Middle East. Among the world's largest desalination plants, two operate in California.

Towing Icebergs

At first glance, the notion of transporting large volumes of ice from one place to another sounds like a rather crazy idea, but it has many historical precedents. The Romans cut ice from alpine lakes and, after wrapping it in straw, transported it several hundred miles to Rome. Before refrigeration units were invented in the late 19th century, Great Britain imported ice taken from Norwegian glaciers or as ice chunks calved into Norwegian lakes. By 1898, Britain was importing more than a half-million metric tons of Norwegian ice, much of it being used to preserve the British fish catch. At about this time, ice was being transported by ship from Alaska to supply California. There is at least one record of a small iceberg being towed behind a vessel (rather than the ice being stored within the ship's hold) on a journey from southern to northern Chile. With the development of commercial refrigeration plants, the "natural ice" trade declined.

The idea of towing icebergs was resurrected in the 1950s by researcher John D. Isaacs at the Scripps Institution of Oceanography. The aim was not to provide ice as such, but to transport much-needed water from regions of water abundance to those of water scarcity. Isaacs suggested towing icebergs southward from Alaska or northward from Antarctica to meet the water shortfall in California. Northwest Atlantic tugs were already used to tow icebergs out of the way of drilling rigs. The idea of iceberg towing to supply water was explored theoretically during the 1960s and 1970s, and by 1973 the possibility of towing icebergs from Antarctica to Southern Hemisphere destinations seemed to be an idea worth pursuing. Calculations suggested that iceberg water could be delivered to sites in South America or western Australia for a few thousandths of a cent per cubic meter—substantially less than the cost of desalination. Exactly how the ice would be thawed and the water recovered at the destination was a problem still to be addressed.

The Antarctic ice sheet contains about 70 percent of the available stock of freshwater on Earth's surface. Only a small fraction of this is calved off each year to form icebergs—some 5,000–10,000 icebergs a year with a total volume equivalent to about half that of the annual output of the Amazon River. So the total amount of iceberg water that is realistically harvestable is not huge, but in a water-depleted world, it is a potentially invaluable source of high-grade water.

Current thoughts on iceberg towing run along these lines. Tugs could capture an Antarctic iceberg of suitable size and shape and surround the berg with a bridle; then several tugs could tow the iceberg at low speed to a suitable water-scarce location. The three sites under consideration are: the Atacama Desert in northern Chile; the Namib Desert of southeastern Africa; and Western Australia and the Great Australian Bight. All three sites have cold surface water and favorable currents along a route from Antarctica, all have deep water close inshore, and all have a serious local need for water, whether for drinking or for irrigation.

There are obvious difficulties inherent in towing ice long distances. At least half of the mass of the iceberg will melt en route unless the iceberg is protected and insulated in some way. Enclosing the iceberg in an insulating jacket is a possible solution, but the technology for this has still to be explored. Once the iceberg has reached its destination, extracting the water is no easy matter. Current ideas center on harnessing the iceberg offshore and then breaking it into manageable chunks that will be brought inshore to a lagoon. The most cost-effective solution is to combine iceberg processing with an ocean thermal-energy conversion (OTEC) scheme (page 172). As the iceberg fragments melt, the heat released (ice has a high latent heat of fusion) would be used to vaporize ammonia and so drive a turbine to generate electricity.

Using efficient heat-exchange technology, the electrical energy obtained would be of similar economic value to the water itself. The combined operation—the so-called "Icetec" concept—could provide sufficient water and power for an agricultural complex with some associated settlement and industry. Before promoters are likely to invest in a pilot project, they would need to be convinced that the raw material—icebergs—could be delivered to the site reliably and economically. The first step toward this end will be to undertake an experimental iceberg tow from, say, Antarctica to Australia and in so doing identify the practical constraints and economic potential of the idea. Sooner or later, iceberg towing for water supply is likely to become a reality.

The Diversity of Marine Resources

Seawater itself is a valuable resource, but so too are some of the minerals dissolved in it, the creatures than swim in it, and the minerals and fossil fuels that lie in the rock strata beneath it. The oceans also have a vast capacity for storing, transporting, and releasing energy that, if properly harnessed, could go some way to meeting our future energy needs.

Living Resources

Although oceans provide less than 10 percent of the world's food by weight, this contribution is much more important than mere weight suggests. Most of the marine animals we exploit for food are rich in protein. In protein-scarce regions of tropical developing countries, marine produce can and does provide much-needed protein, vitamins, and minerals. Recent research suggests that oil-rich fish—salmon and mackerel, for example—are rich in essential fatty acids that can help reduce levels of cholesterol and other fatty constituents in the blood. Other things being equal, lowered cholesterol levels reduce the risk of heart and circulatory disease, the greatest life-takers in most Westernized countries—so fish may have an important role to play in the diet of affluent countries as well as in developing countries.

Unfortunately, marine produce today is rarely harvested on a sustainable basis. Most marine stocks are overexploited to the point at which returns become gradually smaller, and fishermen move on to new stocks to maintain an economic return. Various factors contribute to this situation. Fishing has the historical legacy of a hunting culture—a "free-for-all" attitude in the pursuit of fish stocks. Until ownership of living resources can be firmly established and enforced (page 194) and fishery stocks properly managed (page 198), the decimation of fish populations will continue. Mariculture—the farming of marine produce—will undoubtedly become more important in the future (page 175). Currently, it accounts for about 20 percent or so of the value of marine food stocks; this is likely to increase, and maricultural produce, currently a major provider of luxury seafood, will provide more protein for the many.

Aside from food, marine plants and animals provide many other products of commercial

Pleasure cruising in the Caribbean
(Gerry Ellis/ENP Images)

importance. Several useful substances are extracted from seaweeds: algin, a widely used emulsifier, stabilizer, binder, and texture enhancer, is used in a range of products from pharmaceuticals and cosmetics to convenience foods; potash (potassium chloride) from seaweeds is used in agricultural fertilizers. Increasingly, pharmacologically active substances are being sought and found in marine organisms. Coral reefs, in many respects the marine equivalent of tropical rain forests on land, are a repository of as yet untapped medicines and other biologically active substances such as "natural" pesticides (page 173).

Chemical Resources

Although seawater contains numerous chemical elements that are dissolved or suspended in it, only a very few are present in sufficient quantities to make their extraction commercially viable. Sodium chloride (NaCl), or common salt, is by far the most abundant chemical species dissolved in seawater. It is an important mineral component and flavor enhancer in many foods and is used as an additive. Table salt is produced in many warmer countries by the evaporation of seawater in natural or artificial ponds and lagoons. India, Mexico, and southern European countries are the world's largest producers of sea salt and together contribute nearly one-third of the world's salt supply from all sources. Evaporated sea salt contains other mineral elements—iron, calcium, magnesium, and the like—which, if present as salts in moderate concentrations, can introduce a bitter taste. To obtain pure salt, several stages of crystallization may be needed.

The only two other chemical elements extracted commercially from seawater are magnesium and bromine. Nearly 20 percent of world magnesium production comes from seawater, much of it from the United States. The metal is extracted by chemical reaction with dolomite, a calcium-magnesium carbonate rock that precipitates the magnesium as a hydroxide. This is converted to magnesium chloride by chemical reaction, and the magnesium and chlorine are then liberated by electrolysis (passing an electric current through the solution). Magnesium is an exceptionally light metal that is used in making specialist alloys. Bromine is obtained as an early by-product of magnesium production, but it is also obtained as a by-product from purifying seawater by crystallization.

Minerals

Sand and gravel of various sizes and compositions are important raw materials used as components in building materials. Together, they comprise by far the greatest bulk—and also have the greatest value—of the minerals extracted from the bottom of the sea. As onshore and shallow offshore deposits become exhausted, so the search will extend to slightly deeper continental shelf reserves (page 168).

Much less abundant but high in value are the precious minerals—gold and diamond—and the industrially important metals—tin and chromium. These and other moderately high-value minerals are obtained from placer deposits—concentrations of minerals produced by the sorting action of water movement—particularly those on shores or in shallow water. Of enormous potential but yet to be extracted commercially are manganese nodules. These tennis ball–size accumulations of manganese, copper, nickel, and other useful metals form on regions of the deep ocean floor well away from land. Hydrothermal deposits (these form where superheated water percolates through the crust and then discharges on the ocean floor) are localized sources of high-value metals. These reserves will shortly begin to be utilized, but they are much less abundant than manganese nodule deposits (page 37).

Nonrenewable Energy Resources

Oil and gas (page 170) and to a lesser extent coal are vitally important energy sources that fuel our industrialized societies. Offshore oil and gas together account for about 40 percent of total worldwide production, and this percentage is gradually increasing as land-based deposits become exhausted. As shallow-water fields become depleted, so the search for new reserves moves into deeper water. Based on current estimates, supplies of oil and gas will fail to meet predicted demand by the latter half of the 21st century, by which time other energy sources will have to replace or supplement them. Large deposits of gas hydrates (natural gas combined with water in a crystalline structure) do exist in cold, pressurized conditions beneath the seabed in moderately deep water, but even if a way can be found to harness this abundance, this will only delay the inevitable exhaustion of natural-gas deposits by a decade or two. By that time, renewable energy sources such as those from marine sources (see below) will probably need to play a much larger role to help bridge the shortfall.

Renewable Energy Resources

Wind power, tidal power, wave power, ocean currents, and the vast heat-storage capacity of seawa-ter are all potential sources of renewable energy that could be harnessed (page 172). The technology to utilize these sometimes novel energy sources is, in many cases, still in its infancy. But renewable energy provided by natural oceanic processes is likely to become of much greater significance in the 21st century. For one thing, these sources tend to be environmentally "cleaner" than conventional energy stores.

Transport and Communication

With the advent of air travel and electronic communication, the role of shipping routes as avenues of communication and cultural exchange has lessened. Nevertheless, sea travel remains the most important means of transporting heavy goods for long distances. In terms of volume, about 90 percent of world trade travels by ship at some stage. Submarine telephone cables still provide a crucial communication link across the oceans, although their importance is gradually being eroded by satellite telecommunication.

Recreation

The oceans and their shores provide all manner of recreational amenities: places to swim, to surf, to dive, to sail, to fish, to sunbathe, and to relax and be invigorated. In the United States alone, marine recreational activities probably account for 25–30 percent of all public expenditure on recreational and leisure pursuits. Increasing numbers of people across the world now have the opportunity to travel to seaside resorts as tourists. Much of the amenity value of the oceans—opportunities for contemplation perhaps—is difficult if not impossible to quantify.

Real Estate

Experimental underwater habitations were constructed in the 1960s and 1970s (page 153), but relatively little progress has been made since. Nevertheless, in the 21st century, the first underwater cities are likely to house some of our grandchildren. In the meantime, artificial islands, offshore structures, and floating platforms will no doubt be constructed in localities most densely populated—Hong Kong and coastal cities of Japan, for example. In the next century it is quite possible that floating cities—with full infrastructure and residential and commercial facilities—that are towed from one locality to another to enjoy the best of the seasons will house some of the world's most desirable residences.

Hunting and Fishing in the Sea

*Subsistence fishing by local anglers
in Bahía de Banderas, Puerto Vallarta, Mexico
(Michael Willhelm/ENP Images)*

*Give a man a fish and you feed him for a day.
Teach him how to fish, and you feed him and his
family for a lifetime.*

—ATTRIBUTED TO CONFUCIUS
(C.551-479 B.C.E.)

Throughout human history, communities have been using marine animals and plants as a source of food. Early maritime communities gathered seaweed and shellfish from shores, and some hunted seals. Later, many communities took to boats and used nets to capture fish from farther afield. Such communities might have depleted wildlife stocks locally, but they had little impact on the vast biological wealth of the oceans. With the increased mechanization of hunting and fishing in the last 300 years, we now have the capacity—as demonstrated on several occasions—to entirely wipe out a species or population by overexploitation.

Artisanal Fishing

Commercial fishing and aquaculture (pages 166) together yield about 10 percent of the world's food supplies. Artisanal fishing (fishing on a small scale) yields an amount that is only a fraction of the large-scale commercial catch, but it is vitally important in developing countries. It is a rich source of protein in many parts of the world where other sources are scarce, and probably 8 million or more local fishermen catch marine produce that are not included in official catch statistics. Artisanal techniques are particularly abundant in tropical, coastal regions where the range of species caught is diverse. In temperate waters, fishing tends to be more intensive and mechanized, with single species as the target.

The diversity of artisanal fishing techniques is truly astonishing—there are probably many more than 100 distinct methods employed worldwide—and even in a single locality, a half-dozen or so are typically used. Often, these techniques are local adaptations to the prevailing conditions and species found there. For example, in Lake Manzala, a brackish water lagoon in northern Egypt, fishing methods include seine nets, circular cast nets, gill nets, and several types of fish traps. In addition, there is the truly novel method of "foot-trapping," which employs one fish species's predilection for inhabiting small hollows on the lake floor. The fishermen wade through the shallow lake margins and a half-hour or so later return to retrace their steps. In their absence, fish colonize their footprints, so it is simply a case of treading on a fish every now and then and hauling it out of the water and into a floating plastic container.

Hook-and-line methods are employed in many parts of the world. The crudest form of this approach is a gorge—a splint of wood or bone that is tied in the middle to a line and then embedded in a bait. When the bait is swallowed by a fish, the splint rotates and lodges in the gullet, and the catch is readily hauled in. Traditional hooks were commonly made of shaped wood or shell, and lines were often of twine from vegetables fibers. Today, such tackle is usually replaced by its modern counterparts—metal hooks and monofilament nylon. Sometimes, an artificial lure is used in place of a natural bait. Traditional lures, designed to resemble prey items, were cut and shaped from bone or shell. Sometimes feathers were used, but increasingly plastic or metal lures and steel hooks are employed.

Fish traps are often cunningly designed and indicate that the designer has a detailed knowledge of the target animal's behavior. Some Congolese traps employ a triggering device that closes a trapdoor when a fish pulls on the bait. In temperate waters, lobster pots are constructed of strong netting or basketwork on a wooden frame. Baited with fish scraps, the lobster enters it and cannot escape through the neck of the pot. Many traps employ the tendency of fish to move inshore with the tide; several designs trap the fish behind netting, wooden, or stone constructions as the water level falls with the ebbing tide. Many larger traps are intricate contraptions based on netting fences or channels that direct fish into a collecting area from which they cannot escape.

Several kinds of fishing net—both active and passive—are used by artisanal communities. Various kinds of scoop net or dragnet can be used in shallow water by one or more fishermen. Seine nets and gill nets are essentially smaller versions of the ones employed in large-scale commercial fishing (page 164). One of the most widespread artisanal nets used in tropical waters is the circular cast net. Up to 30 feet (9 m) across and handled by a single fisherman, this device is thrown outspread onto the water surface. As it is hauled in, its weighted edges bring the sides of the net together to enclose any fish encircled by the net. As with other kinds of artisanal fishing technology, traditional materials have been superseded by cheaper, harder-wearing, and more-efficient synthetic replacements. Most nets today are made of nylon monofilament or twine mesh.

Hunting

Fishing is really a form of hunting, but the term *hunting* is normally restricted to the targeting of large, individual creatures. In the context of the ocean world, it is marine mammals in particular that are—and have been—hunted.

The hunting of marine mammals has a tradition of particularly aggressive commercialism. Steller's sea cow, a syrenian, was encountered by Western sailors entering the Bering Sea early in the 18th century. A particularly large and slow-moving animal, it weighed an estimated 11 tons (10 t), and its flesh was reputedly "as good as the best cuts of beef." It was hunted to extinction within three decades.

In whale hunting, or whaling, there is a fairly clear historical continuum between artisanal activities and wider-scale commercial operations. Whaling can be conducted by traditional communities operating in coastal waters, and Native Americans undoubtedly hunted gray whales in prehistoric times. In Europe, whaling had developed into a larger-scale activity by the 12th cen-

tury, and by the 17th century, having exhausted local whale stocks, the Basques of northern Spain were traveling widely across the North Atlantic to Newfoundland and Spitzbergen in search of whales. There, they competed with whalers from Holland, England, France, and Germany. The history of whaling from this point onward is a catalog of finding, overexploiting, and then exhausting one stock after another. American whalers from New England joined the hunt in the late 1600s. Whaling at this time was still quite primitive and highly dangerous, with sailors throwing hand-held harpoons from small open boats launched from larger sailing vessels.

A range of valuable products was obtained from whales. Blubber was boiled down to yield a relatively thin oil that was used to fuel lamps and as a major ingredient in soap. Baleen (whalebone) from the whale's mouthparts was used as supports in women's corsets and other underwear. The meat—regarded as a delicacy by some Eastern cultures but considered a low-grade meat by many other nations—was recoverable in very large amounts. Spermaceti—a waxy substance extracted from the heads of sperm whales—was used as a fixative in the perfume and cosmetic industry.

The slower-swimming whales that floated when dead were the first to be hunted to commercial extinction. The North Atlantic right-whale population was heavily depleted as early as 1700, with the bowhead following suit by 1840. Primitive harpooning methods were still being

A harpooned sperm whale, Iceland
(Tony Martin/ENP Images)

employed right up until the mid-19th century, when a variety of technological developments revolutionized whaling. By the 1860s, long-distance oceangoing vessels were increasingly steel hulled and steam driven, and later that decade the Norwegians introduced the explosive harpoon, a device fired from a cannon mounted on board a steamship. Whaling was now much safer (from the whaler's point of view at least) and much more efficient. Ships could travel further, could pursue faster-swimming whales, and could subdue even the largest whales in a relatively short time. The stage was set for an unchecked exploitation of the world's whale stocks that was to last about a century.

By the 1910s, the Norwegian pioneers of the new technology had exhausted the North Atlantic whale stocks and they had turned their attention to the Antarctic Ocean and the rich feeding grounds of Antarctica; the United States, Great Britain, and other nations also embarked on the Antarctic bonanza. By the 1930s, factory ships—large vessels serviced by a fleet of smaller hunting vessels—processed whale carcasses at sea, so freeing the smaller vessels to continue hunting. The ruthlessly efficient harvesting of whales continued until the 1970s, by which time all the larger species had been hunted to commercial extinction, and some species, notably the blue whale and certain stocks of humpback whales, appeared to be dangerously close to actual extinction. Many whalers could no longer make a living, and those who remained turned their attention to smaller species such as the sei and minke. A moratorium on commercial whaling came into force in 1986; most nations abide by this (page 189).

Commercial Fisheries

Commercial fisheries—in contrast to artisanal activities—operate using large, mechanized vessels that often travel long distances from home ports to target specific fish stocks. The catch is sorted, processed, and preserved on board so that the vessels can stay at sea for extended periods. In the Northern Hemisphere, demersal (bottom-dwelling) fish such as cod and plaice are the main prize. These are caught by trawlers that work the continental shelves in temperate and subpolar waters. Elsewhere in the world, most commercial operations target pelagic fish, ranging from sardines and anchovies to the much larger tunas. Of the 20,000 or so species of fish in the sea, less than half are caught for food, and only 22 species are caught in quantities of more than 110,200 tons (100,000 m t) a year. Five kinds of fish—herring, cod, jack, redfish, and mackerel—comprise half of the annual world catch.

The Development of Commercial Fisheries

Large-scale fishing operations in northern Europe began in the 15th and 16th centuries. Fishermen ventured beyond inshore waters to harvest the abundant herring populations in the North Sea. By the 17th century, English fishermen were crossing the North Atlantic to Newfoundland to exploit virtually untapped stocks of cod. On board ship, the fish were preserved by salting.

With the development of steam-driven ships in the mid-19th century and of diesel-driven vessels in the early 20th century, fishing fleets could travel farther and faster. Ice (often imported from Norway) was used to preserve the catch on board ship. Vessels now ranged freely across the North Atlantic and later penetrated the Arctic Circle in the search for cod and haddock.

The development of sonar during World War II revolutionized the ability to locate underwater

Two fishing methods that account for the bulk of the world's fish catch: (1) the purse seine, used for encircling and capturing shoals of pelagic fish, such as tuna, anchovies, and sardines, and (2) the otter trawl, which is hauled along the seabed to capture demersal fish, such as cod, haddock, and various flatfish

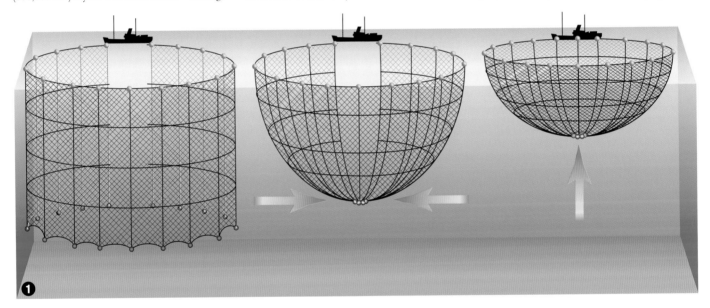

❶

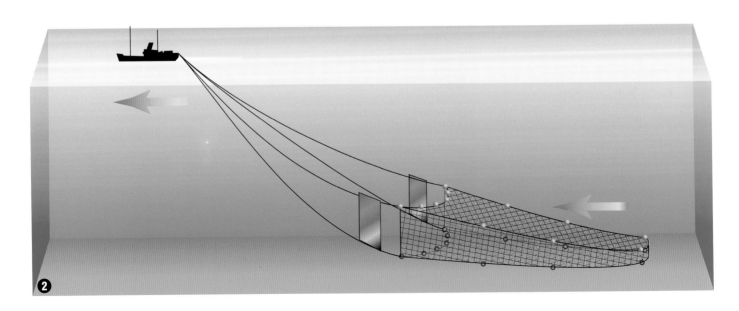

❷

features where fish might congregate. As the equipment improved, it was able to visualize the fish shoals themselves. Fishing vessels were now equipped with refrigeration facilities and so could remain at sea until their holds were full.

Commercial Fishing Vessels

In the mid-20th century, three new types of vessel were being developed for long-distance fishing fleets. Giant purse seiners—evolved from the northern European nets used for catching herring and mackerel—were designed to encircle a large school of pelagic fish with a curtain of netting. This was then drawn together into a "purse" to capture the enclosed fish. Whole schools of tuna, sardines, or anchovy can be caught using this method. U.S. vessels of this type are capable of holding 2,200 tons (2,000 t) of tuna before returning to port.

A second type of vessel—oceanic long-liners—were developed to fish for deeper-swimming tunas and other large, fast-swimming, pelagic predators such as marlin and billfish. These vessels pull longlines—up to 20 miles (30 km) long—that carry numerous baited hooks. A recent development is the use of massively long drift nets that are set and recovered by essentially the same machinery as that used for longlines. These nets—called curtains of death by some environmentalists—do not discriminate between targeted fish and nontarget animals such as dolphins and turtles. Their use in the South Pacific is banned by a regional convention.

Factory trawlers are designed to range long distances well away from home waters and often to trawl just outside the Exclusive Economic Zones (EEZs) of other nations (page 194). Such vessels may fish even closer to shore where a nation has yet to clearly establish or control its EEZ or where the country has granted specific licenses to fleets of other nationalities. Factory trawlers can stay at sea for many months, only returning to base or to other ports to sell their catch when their massive holds are full. Most of these vessels belong to the former Soviet Union or to Asian states; by the early 1990s, they were vigorously exploiting the penaeid prawn and spiny lobster fisheries of tropical waters. In temperate and subpolar waters, they are often involved in what used to be called klondyking—waiting just outside an EEZ to buy the catch from a local nation's fleet of smaller fishing vessels.

By-Catch

An issue of continuing concern to environmentalists and development economists is the wasteful catching and dumping of unwanted species—the so-called by-catch. The by-catch is usually returned to the sea—dead. It provides food for seagulls and scavenging fish, but otherwise it represents the squandering of a valuable resource. Ideally, the catching of unwanted species should be minimized, but failing that, a use should be found for this precious protein source. In tropical waters, factory trawling operations decimate large swathes of seabed offshore in the pursuit of high-value penaeid prawns and spiny lobsters. In such circumstances, the by-catch can be as high as 80 percent of the total and often comprises the juveniles of other high-value species. The by-catch could be processed into animal feed or sold to local ports to help alleviate protein shortages. Currently, the factory ships simply dump the by-catch at sea to ensure room in the hold for the high-value catch.

New Fish Stocks

Consumers in many developed parts of the world are notoriously fickle when it comes to buying and eating fish. In the United States, for example, some restaurant-goers are suspicious of squid and monkfish, though these products are held in high esteem elsewhere. One way in which the current catch could be better utilized is through better marketing of squid and other species that are currently regarded as a by-catch or are exported. By-catch fish can also be processed into textured fish meal that can be reconstituted into crab sticks and other products, and this approach is gradually gaining acceptance.

There are a few fish stocks that appear to be unexploited or underexploited. Either a suitable means of harvesting them has yet to be developed or the fish have yet to be considered acceptable, high-value food. Krill—the shrimplike crustacean present in great abundance in Antarctic waters—was once considered a future savior of the world fishing industry, but after a record catch of a half-million metric tons (about 550,000 tons) in 1982, the large-scale development of the krill fishing industry never materialized. A variety of factors were responsible: Though krill are rich in protein, vitamins, and minerals, their taste—even when fresh—is bland, and after canning or freezing, their taste is even less appetizing. The long trip to the inhospitable waters of the Antarctic, the high cost of maintaining vessels to withstand such conditions, and the poor consumer response to krill as a product have simply made krill exploitation uneconomic. There is also another concern: krill are the staple food of baleen whales (page 107), and harvesting krill in large quantities may impede the recovery of baleen-whale populations following many years of intensive hunting (page 188).

For the future, the utilization of unexploited fish stocks is likely to rest with bathypelagic species such as lantern fishes (page 94)—for which fishing methods and suitable markets have yet to be created. Currently, about 30 percent of the world's catch of fish is converted into fish oil, fish meal as feed for cattle and poultry, or bonemeal for use as a fertilizer. This proportion may well increase as fishing efforts turn to less-valued species.

Farming the Sea

An alternative to exploiting natural marine stocks is to rear marine species in a manner similar to farming on land. This idea is not new: the Chinese have been rearing freshwater, brackish-water, and marine fish species for more than 3,000 years, and the oldest existing "textbook" on this subject dates from about 475 B.C.E.

Applying farming techniques to the growth of marine species is called mariculture; the rearing of aquatic forms generally, including freshwater, brackish-water, and marine, is termed aquaculture. In the mid-1990s, world aquaculture production reached about 23 million metric tons (about 25 million tons) (based on U.N. Food and Agriculture Organization estimates), of which mariculture accounted for about 10 million metric tons (11 million tons). With the current aquatic catch (from all sources) at about 100 million metric tons (about 110 million tons), the mariculture component lies at about 10 percent. The economic value of this component is nearer 20 percent of the whole and is thus significant. By the year 2000, mariculture is likely to provide about 25 percent by weight of all seafood consumed in the United States.

Most mariculture aims to rear organisms for food, but nonfood commodities are also cultivated. In parts of Asia, cultured pearls have been grown using farming methods for at least 2,000 years. High-value fishes are reared throughout the world for the aquarium trade, particularly now that some species—diverse coral-reef fishes, for example—are endangered.

Traditional (Open) Mariculture

Traditional mariculture is still practiced in many parts of Southeast Asia. Fish farmers seed ponds or enclosures with fish eggs or fish fry (or in some cases, the eggs or larvae of high-value crustaceans, such as shrimps). As the juvenile forms grow, they are transferred to larger ponds, where they are fed by natural productivity—plankton, algae, and seaweed—or with ground-up agricultural by-products that are scattered over the water. In Southeast Asia, the milkfish, *Chanos chanos,* is extensively cultivated in brackish-water ponds using traditional methods. These operations provide much-needed employment and convert agricultural waste to high-value protein.

Such operations—where organisms are reared under more or less "natural" conditions—are deemed open mariculture. This approach has been applied for hundreds of years by communities around the world. In Europe, the United States, Southeast Asia (especially Japan and Tai-wan), Australia, and New Zealand, bivalve mollusks, including abalone, clams, mussels, oysters, and scallops, are grown on structures suspended in the water column. Sometimes baskets, wooden fences, or float-supported ropes are used, and these are seeded with spat—larvae—that are allowed to grow to juveniles or adults in sheltered waters. In scattered parts of the world—from Norway and Scotland in the north to Chile and Southeast Asia in the south—fish such as salmon, mullet, and sea bream are reared in large floating pens or cages. In many cases, these practices have relatively little environmental impact, but this is not always the case. The construction of ponds for shrimp fisheries in Thailand and Ecuador has resulted in the destruction of large areas of mangrove forest, with the effective removal of nursery grounds for many fish and crustacea. In some Scottish lochs, there is concern that the feces, urine, and uneaten food from salmon rearing is causing localized pollution and the depletion of dissolved oxygen levels and is thereby affecting other species. Where antibiotics are added to food pellets for the fish, there is understandable concern that these chemicals are entering local food chains. Developments in the near future are likely to see fish pens being located in the open sea rather than in lochs or other enclosed bodies of water, thereby minimizing problems of pollution buildup.

Intensive (Closed) Mariculture

In some industrialized nations, there are moves to establish much more intensive maricultural operations. As in intensive agriculture on land, selected strains are bred under conditions where environmental factors are tightly controlled; in practice, this means in tanks, pools, or other holding facilities where high-quality, oxygenated water of specified salinity and temperature is supplied. This requires an abundant supply of suitable water or else costly facilities for recycling the water (the holding water must be replaced or recycled on a continuous or near-continuous basis).

Under intensive conditions, where animals are reared at high densities, the likelihood of disease epidemics is that much greater, and monitoring for parasites and other disease organisms is routine. Applying preventative or treatment regimes is an ongoing aspect of this type of operation. When the feeding requirements of different stages in the life cycle and the social behavior of the farmed species are also taken into account, intensively rearing marine species soon becomes a sophisticated operation. To make it cost-effective, only the highest-value fish and crustacea are farmed. Interest in rearing flatfish—particularly sole, turbot, and halibut—is developing in Europe. In the United States and elsewhere, salmon and high-value shrimp species are already cultivated under intensive conditions, and pilot lobster-farming projects are under way.

Genetic manipulation of farmed stock is becoming increasingly important. In some cases, individuals that contain three sets of chromosomes as genetic material (triploid) instead of the normal two sets (diploid) are cultivated. Moral objections aside, this genetic alteration has at least two advantages to the mariculturalist: the individuals are sterile and cannot interbreed to give rise to unwanted offspring; also, the energy that would otherwise be diverted to reproduction is used in growth of flesh. In the case of oysters, triploid animals taste better than diploid individuals that carry eggs.

One way or another, because of the high-tech equipment and specialized operating personnel involved, intensive maricultural operations are unlikely to be a major source of protein for the poorest developing countries in the short term. For some time to come intensive mariculture is likely to remain the province of the more affluent communities seeking variety and high quality in their seafood. Nevertheless, some researchers are optimistic that the intensive farming of fast-growing strains will soon become more viable for developing countries.

Ocean Ranching

Ocean ranching is as open as mariculture can become before we are back in the realm of open fishing. In ocean ranching, juvenile fish are reared to a suitable size, or transported from other locations, and released at sites where a high survival rate is anticipated. The fish stay in the locality and grow or, as in the case of salmon, migrate but return in later life. If the organizations that fund such schemes can guarantee that they will be the ones who will be able to benefit from their efforts in the years to come, then ocean ranching can be a worthwhile venture.

Investigations in the 1970s suggested that plaice hatchlings from the Dutch coast grew more rapidly and with greater survival rates when they were transplanted to the Dogger Bank in the center of the North Sea. Unfortunately, no one has pursued this idea as a commercial ocean-

*Queen conch aqua farm, Provo Island
(Gerry Ellis/ENP Image)*

ranching project, presumably because, under present legislation and practice, there is no guarantee that the investors will be the ones who gain when the fish grow to harvestable size. Salmon ranching, on the other hand, is successful in many parts of the world. In some operations—such as those in Japan and Alaska—it is primarily the operators themselves who benefit. In European operations, the benefits tend to be spread wider amongst sports anglers and other commercial operators as well as the ranchers themselves. In salmon ranch-

ing, it is the ability of the adult fish to seek out and return to the freshwaters from which they originated that makes the enterprise a viable proposition. (page 108)

New Developments

The manipulation of the genetic constitution of species represents one of the areas in which the greatest breakthroughs in mariculture are likely to be made. With genetic engineering, faster-growing and disease-resistant forms are likely to be developed. Genetic manipulation is also being applied to improve the taste of the final product.

Another initiative is in the use of water derived from other commercial or industrial processes. The warmed water from power stations or other plants can be used to speed growth rates of cultured species. Ocean thermal energy conversion (OTEC) schemes (page 172) could bring nutrient-rich water from the deep ocean to the surface to be utilized not just in harnessing energy but also in providing productive waters for growing phytoplankton as food for larval fish, mollusks, and crustacea. It is not inconceivable that pumping deep, cold, nutrient-rich water to the surface might become a means of increasing productivity offshore that could be harnessed by rearing food species in cages or pens.

Mining for Minerals

Nine chemical elements, oxygen, iron, silicon, magnesium, sulfur, nickel, aluminum, sodium, and calcium, account for more than 98 percent of Earth's crust. Some of these chemical constituents, notably iron and silicon (in sand, for example), are both abundant and of particular usefulness. But many of the elements that are scarce are also extremely useful and therefore have acquired high value. Among these are precious metals, such as gold, platinum, and silver, but also uranium (as a nuclear energy source) and many metals that have industrial and commercial uses, such as copper, tin, and chromium.

Seawater contains almost all the known chemical elements dissolved or suspended in it. However, with the conspicuous exception of sodium chloride (common salt), other components are present in relatively small quantities. Vast quantities of seawater would need to be processed to extract its more valuable constituents—platinum, gold, silver, and the like. The technology does not yet exist to remove such metals selectively and certainly not without very high cost. Harvesting the shores or the bottom of the oceans for minerals is a much more lucrative enterprise.

Aggregates

Of surprising importance to the world's economy is the sand and gravel extracted from beneath the sea. Indeed, the present value of these offshore mineral deposits is second only to offshore oil and gas.

Until the mid-20th century, sand and gravel for the building industry were commonly removed from beaches. With growing awareness of the value of beaches as attractive amenities in themselves, and realization of the wider-scale implications of removing natural seashore defenses, removal of aggregates from such coastal sites has declined substantially. Instead, prospectors now seek these aggregates offshore. They tap deposits that were laid down during the ice ages—former beaches, dunes, and river channels—that are now inundated and lie on continental shelves. Most of the exploited deposits lie at depths of about 150 feet (less than 45 m), though deeper deposits will probably be sought within the next decade or so.

Japan is by far the largest extractor of offshore aggregates and provides about 50 percent of the world market in this commodity. The United States has substantial offshore deposits of sand and gravel but has been far more cautious in exploiting them. There is widely held concern that removal of such deposits will influence coastal deposition and thus will affect the maintenance of beaches and other coastal landforms. In the North Sea near the United Kingdom, extraction of sand is regulated, and concessions tend to be granted in those areas where impact on coastal deposition is likely to be minimal.

The sand found on coral-fringed tropical islands is chalky, not quartz-based like the sand found elsewhere. Coral sands are formed from the calcium carbonate skeletons and shells of long-dead animals—particularly corals, mollusks, and some forms of plankton, notably foraminifera. Rich in chalk, these sands are used to manufacture cement, and in many tropical regions, they provide the main source of building material. Indiscriminate removal of such sands not only markedly alters current patterns, which can result in unwanted coastal erosion, but the suspended sediment can swamp nearby coral reefs. The environmental impact of sand removal needs to be assessed if short-term gains are not to be outweighed by long-term problems.

Placer Deposits

The action of waves and tides, both on beaches and off the shore, sifts and sorts sediments and concentrates certain minerals in one place. Hard and heavy minerals are commonly deposited in depressions: these concentrations of minerals, arising from the mechanical action of water movement, are called placer deposits. Such deposits are also formed in rivers and streams, and many such deposits formed during the ice ages have since become inundated and are now found on continental shelves. Commonly, those placer deposits worth exploiting are found in a locality where high-value minerals have been weathered from nearby rocks. The action of water is providing a natural means of sifting, sorting, and concentrating valuable minerals. The old-fashioned prospector panning for gold in a river or stream also uses water motion to separate gold grains from other materials.

Currently, placer deposits are being excavated on shores and in shallow seabeds in many parts of the world. Gold is mined from beaches in Alaska and Nova Scotia, and chromite (for chromium) from Oregon. In Namibia, diamond is mined from beaches and offshore. Elsewhere, cassiterite (for tin) is mined off Indonesia, Malaysia, and Thailand, and together these marine placers account for about 10 percent of world tin trade.

Other minerals, such as chromite and zircon (for zirconium), are being dredged from offshore deposits, and the range of other minerals extracted from marine placers will increase once the potential return on investment swings in favor of their recovery. Currently, most extractions are from depths of less than 165 feet (50 m), but the technical know-how exists to extract from 2.5 miles (4 km) deep if the commercial rewards warrant it.

Manganese Nodules

Manganese nodules—potato-size chunks of manganese and other metals—form gradually in deep water in many parts of the world's oceans (page 37). The largest accumulations of high-grade metal-rich nodules are in the Pacific basin, away from land-derived sediments and at depths of more than 2.5 miles (4 km). They represent huge reserves of valuable metals, but the costs of extraction from deep water are, at present, higher than mining for such minerals on land. Also, the mechanics of recovering minerals from deep water has yet to be devised. Current suggestions center on using various devices (AUVs, for example) to "sweep" the nodules into high-density collections that can be dredged or "vacuumed" from the seabed. The possibility of processing the nodules underwater at or near the collection site is also being considered.

Once obtained, separating the metals within the nodule could be complicated—copper and nickel occur in association with manganese oxide, rather than as separate minerals. Nevertheless, the potential importance of manganese nodules for the future is widely known, and they are one of the reserves of special concern when international Law of the Sea conferences are convened (page 194). Manganese nodules contain a range of valuable metals—platinum as well as manganese, copper, and nickel.

Phosphorite

Phosphorite—a rock rich in calcium carbonate-fluorapatite—forms in phosphate-rich waters, particularly where upwellings occur on the west sides of continents. These deposits vary markedly in the size of their constituent particles—tiny grains in some case, boulders in others. The accumulations are usually found at depths of 330–3,300 feet (100–1,000 m) and so are reasonably accessible. Currently, phosphorite deposits on land provide much of the world's phosphate fertilizer. It is quite likely that this situation will change within the next 50 years when offshore phosphorite deposits begin to make a significant impact on the world phosphate market.

Hydrothermal Deposits

Hydrothermal deposits associated with the precipitation of metals at deep-sea vents (page 43) are another potentially rich source of minerals. In most parts of the ocean, these deposits are at much too great a depth—and in insufficient quantities—to make extraction viable. However, in some localities concentrations are sufficiently high, and the seafloor shallow enough, to make extraction feasible in the near future. Metal-rich muds in the Red Sea contain sufficient concentrations of metals such as copper, lead, manganese, and zinc to arouse much current interest. The deposits are 6–80 feet (2–25 m) thick and are at a depth of some 6,000 feet (1,800 m). Exploratory dredging is under way, and several companies are exploring the possibility of mining these deposits. Meanwhile, off the coast of Papua New Guinea, large hydrothermal vent fields at depths of 1 mile (1.6 km) are being considered for exploration. In January 1998 an Australian mining company was granted rights to explore them. It hopes to mine the sulfurous hydrothermal vent chimneys for a variety of precious metals, including gold, silver, arsenic, and mercury.

Up for Grabs

Exploitation of the deep-sea mineral deposits of the world is to some extent held in abeyance until various legal, technological, and environmental issues have been more clearly resolved. Under Part XI of the United Nations Convention on the Law of the Sea (UNCLOS), the mineral resources of the seabed beyond the continental shelf are considered as "the common heritage of mankind." UNCLOS holds the International Seabed Mining Authority to be the organization responsible for licensing and controlling deep-sea mining. A few large national and multinational companies have developed the expensive technology to exploit deep-sea resources. They would much prefer to operate under national law rather than international direction, and they have lobbied governments of industrialized nations who, in turn, have been reluctant to ratify certain provisions of UNCLOS. Environmental pressure groups have argued that deep-sea dredging operations will release sediment that will swamp deep-water animal communities. Mining companies are concerned that if their deep-sea activities are to come under international jurisdiction, then their commercial operations will be tightly constrained.

Oil and Gas

Oil is the life-blood of industrialized societies—a source of much of the energy and synthetic materials on which we have come to rely. But the cost of finding, extracting, and then consuming oil can be high, in both economic and environmental terms. Oil is often extracted from the most inhospitable parts of our world—from parched deserts on land and from seabeds more than half a mile below gale-lashed waters. As land-based oil reserves become depleted, exploiting offshore oil and gas deposits becomes increasingly attractive. In 1969, offshore oil accounted for about 13 percent of total world oil production; in 1985, the proportion was 28 percent; by the mid-1990s, the figure was approaching 40 percent.

How Gas and Oil Form

Oil and gas are formed in sedimentary rocks 1.3–2.5 miles (2–4 km) down in Earth's crust. These fossil fuels are derived from the very slow breakdown of dead plant and animal material when subjected to high pressure and warm conditions for long periods of time. Dead biological material is quickly decomposed under normal conditions where free-living bacteria are present and there is abundant oxygen. So for large deposits of organic material to accumulate underground, the dead material needs to be covered quickly so that air is excluded. Productive shallow waters at the margins of oceans are ideal places

The Glomar Beaufort Sea Station, an offshore oil-drilling platform, Prudhoe Bay, Alaska (Gary Braasch / ENP Images)

for this to occur. When phytoplankton and zooplankton die, they may settle on the seabed and soon be covered in sediments discharged by rivers or eroded from land nearby. As the sediments accumulate for many thousands of years and more material is added on top, the buried organic remains become subjected to intense pressure and raised temperatures. The carbon-rich remains are gradually converted to hydrocarbons (molecules rich in hydrogen and carbon).

The larger hydrocarbon molecules tend to be liquid while the smaller ones are gaseous, so that cocktails of heavy hydrocarbons form oil while mixtures of the lighter hydrocarbons form natural gas. Even these conditions, on their own, are insufficient to result in oil and gas deposits that are worth exploiting. To make extraction economically viable, the fossil fuels need to migrate to locations where they are trapped below impermeable rock. The particular combination of conditions that favor the accumulation of oil and gas in this manner are not that common, hence the intensive hunt to find the locations where these combinations of features do occur.

Oil Exploration

Early offshore oil exploration was targeted at those regions where oil seeped onto nearby shores: off California, for example, where trial drilling from wooden wharves began as early as 1894. Extraction of oil offshore was, and is, costly when compared to oil recovered from land-based oil fields. Nevertheless, as demand for oil has increased and land-based deposits have become exhausted, offshore exploration has become worthwhile. Commercial drilling operations began in the Gulf of Mexico in 1936 and rapidly expanded so that by 1948 the first offshore platform beyond sight of land was established off the Louisiana coast. This was linked to the mainland by the world's first offshore pipeline. The basic components enabling offshore extraction on a large scale were now in place.

Today, oil exploration is normally conducted in the first instance by survey ships utilizing seismic soundings. A "shot"—an explosive charge or high-pressure air gun—is set off at the water surface. As the seismic waves move outwards, they are reflected off the seabed and from the underlying strata. The reflected waves are detected by an array of hydrophones towed behind the survey ship, and the decoded "sonic picture" is analyzed to determine whether the underlying strata are composed of likely oil- or gas-bearing sedimentary rocks. Likely formations produce characteristic seismic profiles. Once a promising geological structure is detected, test drilling can proceed. The majority of such features contain water-bearing sedimentary rock or sparse or difficult oil and gas deposits that are unsuitable or uneconomic to exploit.

Exploratory drilling is carried out by a drill ship or one of several forms of semimobile rig. Whichever type of exploratory platform is used, once an exploitable oil or gas deposit is found, some form of surface platform or subsea system needs to be erected and secured in position on the seabed before extraction can begin. Undersea pipelines carry the oil or gas to terminals on land, where the resource can often be processed into a wide range of fractions. Some crude oils, for example, can be separated into the following components: petroleum gas, gasoline, kerosene, diesel, fuel oil, chemical feedstock, refinery fuel, and bitumen. Some of these fractions can, in turn, be separated into more components, so the final range of products obtained from the single resource is truly staggering. Apart from fuels, some components are used in the manufacture of plastics and synthetic fabrics—materials we take for granted in today's world.

In extracting, transporting, and processing oil and gas, safety is paramount, and environmental considerations have a high priority. In 1979, when the IXTOC–1 rig blew out in the Bahía de Campeche, Gulf of Mexico, in the region of 1.1 million tons (1 million t) of oil were released into the sea—the biggest single oil pollution incident so far. Today, the restrictions on exploiting oil in coastal areas have been considerably tightened.

Offshore Drilling

As shallow-water oil deposits become exhausted, so the search extends into deeper and deeper water. In the Gulf of Mexico, operating depths of about 700 feet (213 m) were reached in 1978, and about 3,000 feet (914 m) in 1994. Drilling and production platforms are of several designs, each adapted to specific sea conditions and depth of water. Shallow- to medium-water rigs have rigid legs and support structures that extend to the seabed. Deeper-water rigs are tethered to the seabed by cables, and some have platforms that are semisubmersible and are thus more stable and less affected by wave and wind action. The deepest rigs are "subsurface systems" where the wellhead is on the seafloor and is attached directly to a pipeline.

During the last two decades or so, regular forecasts have predicted that the world's exploitable oil reserves would run out in about 40 years from the date when each prediction is made. As technology advances, so more reserves are found or methods are developed to extract more oil from existing reserves. This situation cannot continue indefinitely, however, and it is likely that oil reserves will not meet existing demands by the latter half of the 21st century. By this time, other sources of readily transportable energy will need to have been developed to meet the shortfall.

Gas Hydrates

Oil is formed when organic remains decompose at high pressure and warm temperatures under specific conditions. Such conditions are not found in the deep ocean. Here the overlying sediment is too shallow and the temperatures are too cold. But natural gas is liberated from decomposing remains, and under these cool, high-pressure conditions, novel molecules—gases combined with water—are formed. These gas hydrates (also called cathrates) mostly comprise methane combined with water to form crystals, but other hydrocarbon gases—ethane and propane, for example—may also be incorporated along with gases such as carbon dioxide and hydrogen sulfide. The upshot of all this is that lying in strata below the seabed in the deeper parts of the ocean are huge deposits of natural gas trapped in a crystalline form. Perhaps they could be exploited as an energy source.

Estimates suggest that about 10 percent of the total ocean area could yield gas hydrates; the molecules seem to be concentrated on continental slopes and rises below about 1,000 feet (300 m). If a means could be found to extract and utilize this natural-gas source, then the existing gas deposits would be greatly extended and greater leeway in finding alternatives to oil and gas as fuels would be provided. There is, perhaps, another motivation in finding a use for these deep-sea methane deposits. Although burning the gas derived from this source does produce combustion products that are greenhouse gases, methane in itself is a notorious greenhouse gas. If these vast reserves of methane were released into the atmosphere by some unforeseen circumstance—the likelihood of this happening is being investigated—then the effect on global climate could be significant.

New Developments in Exploiting Ocean Resources

The ebb and flow of tides, the progression of winds and currents, the movement of waves, even temperature variations in the water column, these are all vast sources of potential and kinetic energy—*if* they can be harnessed. As nonrenewable sources of energy become depleted, and as the polluting effects of their combustion become increasingly acknowledged, so the idea of utilizing clean, renewable sources of energy becomes increasingly attractive. Compared to the more-conventional electricity-generating power stations that yield acid rain, greenhouse gases, or radioactive wastes, the less-conventional sources of marine energy are positively wholesome.

WIND POWER

For thousands of years, winds have been used as a source of power by vessels at sea. This use has declined dramatically since the introduction of steamships in the mid-19th century. Some new ships are readopting wind as an energy source, using aluminum sails rather than the cloth sails of old.

Wind-driven turbines to generate electricity are an energy option in maritime regions subject to plentiful onshore and offshore winds. However, the visual intrusiveness of large wind-driven sails or airfoils is, to some, its own form of pollution. That aside, wind-power generation is a viable option for coastal communities and small island nations where power requirements are fairly limited. A wind turbine is currently operating on the coast of Hawaii, and Sweden has plans to install devices on its coasts.

TIDAL POWER

The rise and fall of tides or the ebb and flow of tidal currents have been harnessed in Europe as a small-scale source of power for hundreds of years; the Dutch took paddle-driven tidal mills to America in the 17th century. Modern approaches to utilizing tidal power tend to be on a much grander scale. The Rance barrage near Saint-Malo in Brittany, northern France, is about 1 kilometer in length. Equipped with turbines that are driven on both the ebb and the flood tides, it typically generates a half-million kilowatts of power on each tide. Built in 1966 at a cost of $100 million, its operating costs are lower than that of any conventional power station in France.

A tidal range of about 33 feet (10 m) or more seems to be a prerequisite for siting a large-scale electricity-generating system driven by tidal power. Such ranges exist in many parts of the world, and power-generating barrages have been built in Canada, China, and the former Soviet Union. In the United Kingdom, a large 9.9-mile-long (16-k-long) tidal barrage was being considered for the Severn estuary. This scheme could potentially generate 8,000 megawatts (MW) and could supply 7 percent of the electrical demand of England and Wales. The scheme would carry a public highway (as the French Rance scheme does), and it would incorporate two locks: one for shipping and one for smaller craft. Environmental impact studies are necessary to establish the less obvious ramifications of all such schemes. In the case of the Severn project, beneficial effects are likely to be clearer water above the barrage, thereby increasing light penetration and raising the productivity of photosynthetic organisms located there. A reduction in the severity of water currents is likely to establish a more stable mud-flat fauna both above and below the barrier. So, it is quite likely that the estuary will be able to support more fish and birds after such a scheme than before, although the nature of the biological community may well change. Possible negative effects might be an increased risk of flooding inland and the greater accumulation of pollutants above the barrage as normal tidal flushing is restricted.

WAVE POWER

In those coastal regions where tidal variation is substantially less than 33 feet (10 m), harnessing wave energy may be a viable energy alternative. It could also be used as an adjunct to tidal-based power schemes during neap tides. Current developments in wave-power technology are small scale, but results are most encouraging and much larger-scale projects are likely in the next decade or so.

Devices for harnessing wave power fall into two categories: fixed or floating. In fixed devices, a column of air is compressed or expands as waves rise and fall. The moving air produced in this way is used to rotate an electricity-generating turbine. Among floating devices, Professor Stephen Salter of the University of Edinburgh, Scotland, has designed a series of hollow concrete floats—appropriately called "ducks" because of the way they bob up and down under the action of waves. The ducks are attached in a long series to a central spine or axle. Each float makes a small arc as it bobs up and down with the waves, and this movement is harnessed by a cleverly designed gyroscope assembly that is used to drive a high-pressure hydraulic system. Flowing oil moved by this system powers an electricity-generating turbine. The "Salter duck" system of floats is perhaps the most efficient means of harnessing the vertical motion of ocean waves to generate electricity. Trials are currently under way in the United Kingdom.

OCEAN CURRENTS

The major ocean currents—the "rivers in the sea"—offer a massive source of energy that is virtually untapped. The Gulf Stream, which transports a volume of water several times greater than that of all the world's rivers, is a vast but diffuse flow of water that is difficult to tap as an energy source. If the technical problems of harnessing this power can be overcome and start-up costs can be met by investors, the long-term rewards are potentially great. In the 1970s, scientists at Woods Hole Oceanographic Institution calculated that an array of turbines stretched across the current in the Florida Straits could generate 1,000 megawatts (MW)—an output equivalent to that of two conventional nuclear-power stations.

THERMAL ENERGY

The temperature differential between warm surface water and cold deep water in warm parts of the world (the temperature differential needs to be at least 36°F or 20°C) is sufficient to power heat-exchange systems that can generate electricity. Ocean thermal-energy conversion systems (OTECs) use cold deep water to condense ammonia or to liquefy other gases of similar condensation temperature. The liquefied gas is then warmed by warm surface water and becomes gaseous. The cycling of the gas between liquid and gaseous states is used to drive a turbine. Such systems also provide nutrient-rich seawater of moderate temperature as a valuable by-product. This water can be utilized to provide an excellent medium for phytoplankton growth which, in turn, can support intensive mariculture operations to grow high-value, protein-rich fish, mollusks or crustacea (page 167).

Alternatively, the cool water can be used for air-conditioning or for chilling soil to grow temperate crops in tropical climates. By desalination or through condensation of moist air, the cool water can also provide a source of freshwater for drinking or irrigation. The way ahead seems to lie in coupling OTEC schemes with aquacultural and agricultural operations. Such options are being explored at the Natural Energy Laboratory in Hawaii.

The temperature differentials in OTEC schemes are much lower than those in conventional power stations. As a result, the thermal efficiency (the efficiency of heat-energy transfer) in OTEC schemes is only 3–4 percent, whereas in oil- or coal-fired steam plants it is 30–35 percent. Although marine water is an abundant, locally available resource, it needs to be pumped in large volumes to make OTEC schemes viable, and seawater is corrosive to most metals. However, if the polluting effects of conventional fossil fuels are actually costed—in effect, a "green tax" on atmospheric pollution—schemes such as OTEC or tidal barriers become much more attractive.

Pharmaceutical Resources

Drug companies that scour the terrestrial rain forests for novel chemicals are now turning their attention to the living resources of the oceans. In recent years, at least four species of sea creature—a sea squirt, a bryozoan, a sponge, and a sea hare—have yielded exciting new pharmaceutical compounds. Several other compounds are in advanced stages of development for pharmaceutical use, and many others await discovery in equally innocuous marine animals.

About half of the drugs in use today are derived from natural products, most of which were extracted originally from land plants. Because the oceans are so different chemically from terrestrial environments—elements such as chlorine (Cl) and bromine (Br) are much more abundant in the sea than they are on land—marine creatures have sometimes exploited biochemical pathways that are quite different from those used by terrestrial creatures. Also, many marine creatures stay attached to a rock or other feature on the seafloor; thus, they would be very susceptible to predation if they could not protect themselves in some way. Often, they defend themselves by producing toxins—poisons—that ward off a potential attacker. In the dog-eat-dog world of the coral reef, where life is luxuriant and space is limited, many creatures produce substances that keep neighbors at bay. Some of these chemicals, often harmful to other creatures, including ourselves, can nevertheless be harnessed by drug companies and converted into a substance that has specific pharmaceutical actions. The new generations of drugs emerging from studies of sea creatures are providing a range of possibilities, from local anesthetics to cancer treatments.

DRUG TESTING AND DEVELOPMENT

The discovery and development of a potentially useful drug is a long, laborious, and expensive process. Four main approaches are used in the search for a medically useful drug, and three of the four have been used with drugs extracted from marine organisms. The first method is to isolate or imitate a natural substance that is known to be beneficial medically. For example, a food-supplement extract from marine mussels appeared to be effective in relieving signs and symptoms of arthritis, and the active ingredient has since been isolated for development as a drug (see below). A second approach is to mimic an existing drug, but to modify its design slightly in the hope of making it more effective. The third approach—and one that is being used systematically with marine organisms—is simply to screen millions of organic (carbon-containing) substances, whether natural or artificial, in the hope of finding ones that are pharmaceutically active. The fourth approach attempts to design drugs, working from principles as to how the body works at a biochemical or physiological level.

When marine organisms are screened for their pharmaceutical potential, the organism is typically collected, frozen, and sent to laboratories for analysis. Crude extracts are tested for their capacity to kill or otherwise inhibit the growth of bacteria, fungi, and viruses. Currently, extracts are also tested for their impact on cancerous cells, for their possible use as antiinflammatory agents, and potentially for their usefulness against HIV, the virus that causes AIDS.

To find out whether a drug is useful—and if so, how—its effect is first tested on animals or, increasingly, on tissue cultures grown in glassware. Testing on tissue samples, rather than whole live animals, is preferable for ethical reasons but is often not possible. A drug commonly works rather differently on isolated tissues than it does inside a whole, living organism. If initial results are encouraging, more-refined tests are carried out. If the drug passes these early trials—and most do not—then the drug is tested for its effects on a trial group of healthy human volunteers. The drug is administered under strictly controlled conditions, and its activity and side effects are carefully monitored. A drug that makes it beyond this stage is then tested on 5,000–15,000 volunteers before a report is sent to the licensing authority (in the United States, the Food and Drug Administration) and a request is made for a clinical trial. If the application is successful, the new drug is then tested on patients most commonly using a "double-blind" protocol: half the patients are given an identical-looking placebo (a substance without effect), and the other half are given the drug. The trial is constructed in such a way that neither the patients nor the researchers know which patient is taking the drug and which is receiving the placebo. It is only later that the results are decoded and the effectiveness of the drug becomes apparent. If the drug passes clinical trials and is later marketed, then testing will still continue, and medical practitioners will be encouraged to report any side effects.

For every 10,000 chemical compounds screened, perhaps only 20 will be tested on human volunteers and only one will be found safe and effective and have potential for marketing. Even when a promising chemical compound has been identified, it takes, on average, in excess of 10 years and a $200-million investment before it makes its appearance as a prescribed drug in the hospital or drugstore.

AN ANTI-ARTHRITIC DRUG

An extract from green-lipped mussels, *Perna canaliculus,* native to New Zealand, has been sold in more than 60 countries since the 1970s under the brand name Seatone. Marketed as a food supplement, in the 1990s it was established that the extract contains an active ingredient, a glycoprotein, that appears to relieve symptoms of arthritis. This chemical blocks the settlement of neutrophils, certain types of white blood cells that are part of the body's own chemical defense system. Neutrophils normally work by attaching themselves to blood vessels at sites of injury or infection; in so doing, they increase the "leakiness" of blood vessels and cause local swelling or inflammation that serves to bring other useful white blood cells to the region and encourages the removal of harmful substances. However, in rheumatoid arthritis, such inflammatin occurs at otherwise healthy joints and causes the joints to break down gradually. Using the mussel extract to block neutrophil settlement thus relieves the symptoms of arthritis. Green-lipped mussels are being reared by the hundreds of tons in marine farms in New Zealand. It is hoped that the active ingredient will be marketed as a drug before the end of the 1990s.

ANTI-CANCER DRUGS

By the late 1980s, an innocuous Caribbean sea squirt, *Ecteinascidia turbinata,* had come up trumps as containing a chemical of potential use in treating cancer. The chemical, dubbed ecteinascidin–743, was in 1996 undergoing the first phase of clinical trials in several European countries. If ecteinascidin–743 makes it all the way through testing to become an approved drug, there is certain to be controversy around its availability to meet likely demand.

Currently, the sea squirt seems to be harvestable on a sustainable basis, provided that its habitat is not damaged and that the sessile, jelly-like animals are cropped in a manner that leaves their rootlike stolons behind so that they can grow back. With increased demand, natural supplies will be insufficient, and other ways will need to be found to harvest the chemical. There are at least three possibilities. One way is to farm the organism, as in the case of the green-lipped mussel in New Zealand. However, many invertebrate animals—among them sea squirts—require quite

specific conditions to grow well. If sea squirts can be reared artificially, there is still the danger of the cultured population suffering a catastrophe, such as a failure to breed or a disease epidemic. Also, very large quantities of material are required to harvest even small quantities of useful chemical. In the case of *Ecteinascidia*, it takes about 1 metric ton (about 1.1 tons) of sea-squirt tissue to yield 1 gram (0.035 ounce) of ecteinascidin–743!

While advanced aquaculture techniques can be used to isolate strains of the organism that might yield higher concentrations of the drug, there would still be considerable wastage. A better approach would be to culture just those tissues that were responsible for manufacturing the wanted chemical and to grow these in glassware under precisely controlled conditions. Even better, but less likely, is the possibility of artificially manufacturing an equivalent drug. Unfortunately, the biochemistry that has enabled creation of ecteinascidin–743 in the bodies of sea squirts is sufficiently unusual as to make laboratory synthesis unlikely in the short term. Researchers have had better success, however, with substances extracted from other marine organisms.

Sponges—small, primitive, sessile animals—have had to withstand the predatory onslaught of all manner of animals for millions of years. They have done so using an impressive armory of chemical weapons. Now some of these chemicals are about to be utilized by humans for surprisingly beneficial uses.

Discodermalide, a substance extracted from the mid-water Caribbean sponge *Discodermia dissoluta*, has recently been found to be a possible treatment for breast cancer and, more potently, for certain types of leukemia. The chemical stops cancerous cells from dividing. When discodermalide was discovered in the mid-1980s, researchers immediately began to seek ways of artificially synthesizing it. They now have at least three alternative methods of doing so. Discodermalide is undergoing clinical trials, and early results are encouraging. The advantage of determining a drug's structure and then being able to synthesize the chemical artificially is that variants of the drug can be developed should the drug itself fail any of the preregistration tests.

The Future Exploitation of the Oceans

It is a brave, if not a foolish, person who can predict with confidence how the oceans will be utilized in 50 years' time. A highly complex, inter-

Orcas (killer whales) and ecotourists (Brandon D. Cole/ENP Images)

dependent system, any one of numerous factors could change to profoundly influence all or most of the others; for example, if some of the worst fears about global warming come to fruition (page 79), then coastlines will alter, circulation patterns will change, and any detailed attempt at predicting developments in fisheries and mariculture will be difficult to say the least. But there are a number of statements we can make if current trends are extrapolated into the future.

Perhaps the overriding factor is human population increase. Population projections compiled by the World Resources Institute suggest that (taking values in the middle range of likely possibilities) the world population will have reached about 10 billion by the year 2050—approaching double the early 1990s population size. Many pressures on natural resources will result. Water will become an even more valuable resource than at present, and alternative methods of water provision—be it more desalination plants, iceberg towing, or whatever—will need to be sought. Mariculture is likely to make a bigger contribution to world food resources than at present while the yield from fishing may well stabilize or make a smaller contribution than at present. Imaginative schemes that involve pumping nutrient-rich water from the depths might boost primary productivity and, in so doing, boost fish yields in the open ocean or in confined areas. However, current problems with the combined effects of overfishing, pollution, and coastal habitat destruction suggest that we will be doing well to keep fisheries productivity at today's levels, particularly as more and more coastline is likely to be demarcated for mariculture and other developments. Oil and gas reserves will have become more or less depleted by the second half of the 21st century, and renewable energy sources—winds, currents, tides, and temperature differentials—will be used as much cleaner sources of power. Transportation methods will changes as conventional fuel-burning engines are phased out. It is in the arena of transport and communications that some of the most dramatic changes are likely, but in ways that are difficult for us to predict.

Within a century, many companies will have developed new ways of finding and extracting mineral resources from the bottom of the sea and, in doing so, are likely to make available new kinds of alloys containing metals that were formerly scarce. Assuming that we have not polluted the oceans on such a wide scale that there are few safe refuges for larger marine organisms, we can expect that there will be many more parts of the sea where access is controlled to enable at least some biological communities to thrive. These are likely to be popular places for tourists—as ecotourists.

The sections below consider three burgeoning areas for future development.

BIOTECHNOLOGY AND PHARMACEUTICALS
By the early 1990s, products from biotechnology—most notably those related to food production, pharmaceuticals, and the chemical industries—accounted for an annual U.S. income of $4 billion. This will increase substantially, and the exploitation of living marine biotechnological resources will probably play an important part. At present, annual U.S. income from marine biotechnology is on the order of $75–100 million per year, but, bearing in mind the diversity of marine life and the very early stage in their utilization as biotechnological resources, this is likely to expand enormously, particularly in the fields of pharmacology and diagnostics.

Currently, we obtain at least two dozen or so drugs from the sea, among them: anti-inflammatory agents, antiviral drugs, worming agents, muscle relaxants, local anesthetics, and anticancer drugs. Clotting agents extracted from horseshoe-crab blood (page 119) and phosphorescent (light-emitting) chemicals that are extracted from several planktonic marine organisms are proving invaluable in diagnosing infection and tracking the course of biochemical reactions. Many other useful chemicals of biological origin are being isolated and put to good use: "natural" insecticides from annelid worms, antifouling agents from bryozoans that prevent the settlement and growth of marine organisms, and even coral skeletons that are being cut and shaped for use as splints and bone replacements in medical procedures. The exploitation of biochemical resources is one of the strongest commercial arguments for maintaining the rich biodiversity of the oceans (page 178).

MARICULTURE
All but two of the 15 major fishing regions across the world are in decline (page 186). The total tonnage of fish caught commercially (from both marine and freshwater environments) seems to have stabilized at a level in the region of 85–90 million metric tons (94–99 million tons). If the global supply of fish and shellfish is to increase substantially to meet rising human population numbers, it is from aquaculture (of which mariculture forms a significant part) that this increase will come. Between 1984 and 1993, the contribution of aquaculture to world fish and shellfish supplies increased from 12 percent to 22 percent. A recent FAO (Food and Agricultural Organization of the United Nations) report suggests that this contribution could be increased to 40 percent in 30–50 years. The biggest hurdles lie in how to achieve this without disrupting natural ecosystems. Maricultural practices often involve the removal of coastal habitats and the discharge of high levels of pollution. Another fear concerns the escape of genetically engineered fish that could oust natural populations or hybridize with them and in so doing reduce the genetic diversity of natural communities.

THE OCEANS AS A RECREATIONAL RESOURCE
Sandy beaches and clear waters have always attracted tourists and, as long as these features exist, they will continue to do so. There is a trend toward protecting specific areas of sea in order to maintain the rich diversity of creatures there and to preserve types of biological community that are under threat elsewhere (page 200). It is easy to see how these conservation projects could be partly financed by environmentally friendly tourist activities as, indeed, is happening in some marine protected areas (MPAs) at the moment. Easier access to distant locations coupled with greater media coverage of marine issues has increased public awareness about the extraordinary beauty and fascinating behavior of sea life. This trend is likely to grow, and whale-watching trips, diving expeditions, and excursions in submersibles are likely to flourish unless environmental disturbances on a major scale—global warming or other effects of pollution—threaten marine habitats.

How Healthy Are the Oceans?

How healthy are the oceans? Not very, is the short answer, and matters are likely to get worse before they get better. Governments across the world are gradually waking up to the idea that the oceans are not endless providers of food and that they cannot be used as dumping grounds for wastes on the assumption that the tides and currents will take pollution away and dilute it out of existence. The coasts—meeting points between land and sea—are worst affected. Coastal waters receive the brunt of marine pollution, and they are encroached upon by activities on land that seek to tame or develop the fringes of the oceans. The inshore waters are both the most productive waters and the most threatened.

Loss of Biodiversity

Biodiversity, short for biological diversity—the richness and variety of life—has, in the 1990s, risen to the forefront of public awareness. At the 1992 Earth Summit Conference in Rio de Janeiro, biodiversity was high on the agenda. The loss of marine biodiversity is now becoming an issue of serious concern. Until the 1960s, conventional wisdom assumed that the oceans were simply too vast—and marine populations too large and scattered—for an entire species to be fished or hunted to extinction or forced into a premature demise by pollution or habitat loss. Such assumptions are now being reevaluated. Stocks of marine species—particularly noncommercial ones—are rarely monitored on a systematic basis, and the truth is that we simply do not have reliable measures of the rate of marine extinctions in the last century or so. Only the more obvious losses—such as the Steller's sea cow and four species of marine mollusk—are well documented. Many more extinctions may have occurred about which marine biologists are unaware.

It is apparent that commercially exploited populations can be driven seemingly close to extinction by overhunting or overfishing, as has happened in the case of some whales, reptiles, fish, crustaceans, and mollusks. It will be decades before we will know whether some species will recover or whether their numbers are too depleted for reproduction and natural selection to replace the losses (page 80). Meanwhile, pollution, habitat loss, or compensatory changes in the biological community may have prevented their recovery.

As far as we know, all species eventually become extinct, but estimates by international agencies suggest that global extinction rates have increased several hundredfold as a result of human activities within the last 10,000 years, and rates of extinction are increasing.

Pollution

The oceans may be vast but they are finite: they cannot be treated as a garbage dump on the proviso "out of sight, out of mind." Volume for volume, oil pollution—though highly visible—probably accounts for less than 1 percent of total offshore pollution. Most marine pollution originates directly from land-based activities, with pollutants entering the sea in river water in direct runoff from land and via sewage outfalls. Also, gases of combustion discharged by power stations, motor vehicles, and other activities on land enter the oceans via the atmosphere. Comparatively little marine pollution is the result of dumping at sea, although that which does occur often involves the most harmful substances. Apart from oil, common contaminants of the marine environment include untreated sewage, heavy metals, and synthetic carbon-based compounds such as chlorinated hydrocarbons (including DDT and polychlorinated biphenyls, or PCBs). Although such pollutants are usually at highest concentration in coastal waters, trace amounts of lubricating oil, industrially derived heavy metals, and other toxic chemicals are sampled even in the deep ocean hundreds of miles from coasts. PCBs are among the most pervasive and highly toxic substances and have been implicated in the deaths of dolphins, seals, and sea lions in recent years.

Overhunting

Some marine mammals—particularly fur seals and some of the larger whales—have been hunted to the verge of extinction. The blue whale—the largest animal on Earth—probably numbered in excess of 200,000 before it was hunted commercially. By the mid-1960s, its numbers had fallen to below 10,000; many whale experts believe the number to be less than 2,000. The humpback whale, probably numbering 125,000 in preindustrial times, has been reduced to about 10,000 individuals. The Juan Fernandez fur seal has dropped from 4 million to less than 1,000 within several decades as a result of overhunting, habitat loss, loss of food supply, and possibly the effects of pollution.

The protection of species that have been worst affected by commercial hunting does show that some populations can rebound when given the opportunity to do so. The North American gray whale, reduced to about 10,000 individuals in the North Pacific by the 1950s, has doubled its numbers since it was classified as an endangered species by the International Union for the Conservation of Nature (IUCN). The Antarctic fur seal, hunted almost to oblivion by the turn of the 20th century, numbered about 1.5 million by the early-1990s. The situation is still far from rosy, however: some species may have dropped to numbers that are insufficient to support a recovery. Time will tell.

Globally, most whale and porpoise populations are declining. Smaller whales, dolphins, and porpoises are still being entrapped by fishing gear set for fish and squid. Coastal marine mammals must bear the onslaught of a generous mixture of different pollutants, and overfishing (page 177) is

*The heavily developed coastline
of Honolulu, Hawaii
(Gerry Ellis/ENP Images)*

taking away the very food items on which many marine mammals depend. In the face of all this, the 1986-enacted ban on the commercial hunting of larger whales is holding (page 189) but is regularly under siege from countries such as Norway and Iceland who claim that their economies depend on commercial whaling being resumed as soon as possible.

Overfishing

A scientific paper published in the prestigious journal *Nature* in 1995 suggested that about 8 percent of the ocean's primary productivity (the amount of carbon trapped and incorporated into producers, page 85) was diverted for human use. Overall, this percentage of the ocean's biological productivity was fished, hunted, or farmed. This percentage is higher in upwelling areas (25 percent) and is higher still on the continental shelves of temperate waters (35 percent) where the most intense fishing occurs.

So humans are very intensive predators in the marine environment, and they are very selective predators. It is often animals at or near the top of marine food chains that have the highest value and tend to be fished commercially—cod and tuna, for example. Their removal alters biological communities out of proportion to their abundance. When fish lower down in the food chain are removed—anchovies, sardines, herring, and the like—food supplies that would otherwise be available to other predators, such as whales and larger fish, are taken out. But fishermen are not so selective that they do not catch fish that the marketplace decides have little or no economic value. Between a quarter and a third of all fish and shellfish caught are simply returned to the sea, often dead, an extremely wasteful and destructive policy (page 165).

Many fish stocks are being overfished. A 1995 estimate by the U.N. Food and Agricultural Organization (FAO) gave 22 percent of the world's fisheries as overexploited or already depleted, with a further 44 percent regarded as being at the limit of their exploitation. Two-thirds of the world's fisheries cannot withstand an increase in fishing effort. Overfishing threatens the genetic diversity of fish populations (page 178) and threatens the fishermen's jobs as well (page 187).

Habitat Loss

The loss or degradation of marine habitats ranks alongside pollution and overexploitation (overhunting and overfishing) as being the factors most destructive of the health of the oceans (page 192). About 60 percent of the world's population is concentrated within 62 miles (100 km) of the nearest coast. Human activities seek to tame coastlines; in so doing they destroy ecologically important wetlands and create changes in currents and sedimentation patterns that have detrimental effects on marine communities many miles away. The creation or expansion of coastal towns, cities, and industrial areas alters runoff patterns and often profoundly changes the seawater quality in the vicinity, altering its salinity, sediment load, temperature, and other physical and chemical factors, including its overall pollution load. Even the seafloor many miles from the coast is not exempt from damage of one sort or another: the dredges and trawls used in some fisheries (page 164) cause widespread damage to nontarget species and their habitats as these devices are dragged along the seafloor.

Biodiversity

Biological diversity, or biodiversity—the richness and variety of life—can be defined in many ways depending on what we decide "richness" to be; in fact, our ability to understand and evaluate biodiversity is in its very early stages. Scientists still have a long way to go before they understand why biodiversity is so important, how it is best measured, and (assuming that biodiversity *is* important) how it is best conserved.

At its simplest, biodiversity refers to the number of different species living together in an area—be it a beach, an ocean, or the entire biosphere. However, scientists studying biodiversity often use more complex measures: the relative abundances of different species in an area, the diversity of habitats in an area, or the genetic diversity within a population of a single species.

Why Is Biodiversity Important?

There are many reasons—philosophical and practical—why we should be concerned about loss of biodiversity. One of the strongest arguments is essentially a moral one. Evidence suggests that human activities are eliminating animal and plant species, biological communities, and perhaps whole ecosystems. This diminishes the richness of life on our planet; whether we regard ourselves as guardians of nature or simply cohabitants on planet Earth, we have no moral right to wipe out other species and destroy habitats simply to fuel our greed.

Even if we take a more self-centered view, reducing the richness of life on the planet diminishes our enjoyment of nature and the legacy our children will inherit. If certain coral reefs are destroyed, our grandchildren will be denied the opportunity to see them. On a practical level, the huge variety of animals, plants, and microbes represent a biochemical treasure trove (page 173)—many thousands of useful chemicals await to be discovered in the bodies of marine organisms. If we lose species, what invaluable drugs or new structural materials might we be losing as well?

Evidence is gradually accumulating that biodiversity is important—in and of itself—in maintaining healthy ecosystems and, indeed, in maintaining the health of planet Earth. Diverse communities appear to be more efficient at utilizing environmental resources and transferring energy; they are also more resilient at withstanding environmental change. A community that is impoverished in terms of its number of species is less efficient at utilizing

natural resources; it is also more likely to be affected detrimentally by environmental change. If this argument is carried through to its ultimate conclusion, the very survival of Earth's biosphere depends on maintaining a diverse global community of organisms.

Estimates of Biodiversity

In 1995 the United Nations Environment Program (UNEP) published its *Global Biodiversity Assessment*. The report concluded that about 1.7 million species had been identified so far, although in all likelihood at least 12 million more have yet to be described. Of the 1.7 million species cataloged, only about 250,000 or so come from marine environments. Taken as a simple proportion of the whole, there are probably at least 1.5 million species of marine organisms yet to be identified. However, for reasons of inaccessibility, marine organisms are harder to sample than terrestrial ones, and the marine component is therefore probably underestimated. Many marine biologists believe there are at least 2–3 million species of marine organism, perhaps many more. We are only just beginning to explore deep-sea environments, and the diversity of marine habitats may be greater than we anticipate (page 118).

Although, in all likelihood, there are considerably fewer species in marine environments than there are in terrestrial ones, the diversity of body form is greater in the sea than on land. Using membership of a phylum (major group of organisms) as indication of similarity of "body design," there is considerably more diversity in marine animals than in terrestrial ones. Of the 40 or so animal phyla commonly recognized, all but one are found in the sea, and about half of the phyla are exclusively marine.

We tend to focus our attention on those organisms that are the largest and the most obvious, but in the biological economy of the planet, microbes are the most important agents in biogeochemical cycles, in maintaining atmospheric composition, and so on. We do not know the extent to which the diversity of microbes is threatened.

Biodiversity Loss

One of the major problems in determining biodiversity loss is that relatively few long-term stud-

ies of marine communities have been carried out, and even fewer have attempted to take *all* the component species of the community into account. Often, only the largest and the most obvious organisms are subjected to systematic analysis of their numbers and species composition, and just when biodiversity is becoming a hot topic, fewer taxonomists (biologists who specialize in the identification and classification of organisms) are being trained than ever before.

Despite this shortage of specialists, marine biologists have studied habitats in sufficient detail to know that significant changes are taking place in many communities. Even if species are not dying out entirely, the numbers of many species have certainly experienced catastrophic declines. Many stocks of whales, dolphins, and commercial fish species have declined dramatically in the last century. It is less clear what is happening to noncommercial marine species: true extinctions may seem comparatively rare, but one species of limpet, formerly abundant along the North Atlantic coast of the United States, has become extinct since the 1930s; this disappearance took place under the noses of thousands of trained biologists in the prestigious marine laboratories of New England. The disappearance was not noticed until the 1980s and was not formally documented until 1991. What other creatures have disappeared surreptitiously in areas where marine biologists are less diligent?

For a species to be formally recognized as extinct, there needs to be an absence of recorded sightings for a period of 50 years. Some species—particularly long-lived ones such as sea turtles or marine mammals—may be hovering on the edge of extinction, their population numbers too low to support recovery, but we will not know the outcome for many decades.

Even if a species does not become extinct in the short term but simply disappears from certain localities or forms populations of smaller size, this too can have important ramifications in the longer term. Other things being equal, fewer populations or smaller populations are both likely to reduce the genetic variability of a species. This may well make the species less able to adapt to changing environmental conditions (genetic diversity is the raw material on which natural selection acts, page 80). A significant drop in genetic variability increases the likelihood of the species becoming extinct sooner rather than later. The loss of a species in a particular locality can also have effects for other species, particularly where the absent species is a "keystone" component of the community. Sea otters, for example, seem to play a leading role in maintaining some kelp-forest communities (page 114). On some Caribbean coral reefs, the removal of key predators by overfishing is implicated in causing population outbursts among prey species of sea urchin.

Maintaining Marine Biodiversity

If we agree that biodiversity is important, how can we maintain it? A starting point is to improve the monitoring of marine populations. Without baseline data from which we can seek to measure biodiversity, how can we determine whether biodiversity is changing and in what ways? Governments and international agencies are gradually realizing the importance of conducting this baseline research. To do this, more scientists need to be trained to undertake field studies, and more biologists need to be encouraged—and funded— to become specialists in taxonomy.

Global programs to monitor the health of the oceans—several under the auspices of the United Nations Environment Program (UNEP)—have already been established. The 1992 Earth Summit Conference in Rio de Janeiro led to agreement among participants that protecting biodiversity requires developing countries to be assisted by developed countries in growing economically while at the same time minimizing disruption to natural ecosystems. This concept, economic growth in tandem with conservation of the environment—so-called sustainable development—is one that developed countries themselves failed to practice earlier when *they* were growing economically and environmental issues had a much lower profile.

Protecting marine biodiversity must stem from an awareness that events hundreds or thousands of miles away may profoundly affect the survival of marine organisms in a given locality. Spawning grounds may be very localized and widely separated from the adult feeding grounds. Larval stages of both vertebrate and invertebrate species often travel long distances between spawning grounds and their final destinations. Also, human activities on land or sea some distance away may result in physical and chemical changes that are transported to the region under consideration. Thus, deforesting a river valley may increase sediment discharge from the estuary downstream that will detrimentally affect a coral reef many miles away. So providing protection for a particular locality must take into account the physical, chemical, and biological inputs from elsewhere that may impact on that locality. Bearing in mind that the activities of several countries may profoundly affect a single stretch of water, the need for international cooperation is clear.

There are moves in this direction. About 1,300 marine protected areas (MPAs) were established between the 1950s and the mid-1990s. These vary greatly in size (page 200), and to be adequately protected from effects at a distance, they need to be incorporated into regional management schemes (page 201). International treaties provide a vehicle for controlling wider-scale human activities that might be detrimental to the maintenance of biodiversity. Among such treaties are the 1973 Convention on International Trade in Endangered Species (CITES) and the 1978 International Convention on the Prevention of Pollution from Ships (MARPOL). Of course, such treaties only work to the extent that their provisions are enforceable. The Convention on Biological Diversity (CBD) that was agreed on at the Rio de Janeiro Earth Summit Conference in 1992 and ratified in December 1993 is a comprehensive and binding agreement that commits countries to the protection and sustainable use of biodiversity. Annual meetings of the convention provide an international forum for continuing dialogue about biodiversity-related issues. The 1995 meeting focused on marine biodiversity.

Convention on Biological Diversity

Various estimates suggest that 40 percent of the world's economy and perhaps 80 percent of the needs of the poor are derived from biological resources—whether wood for building, wool for clothing, or fish for food. The CBD recognizes the importance of biological resources, directs attention at the need to conserve them in their rich variety, and seeks to ensure—as in the provisions of the United Nations Convention on the Law of the Sea (page 194)—that developing countries have access to such resources and that the more industrialized nations cannot simply dictate how these resources will be utilized worldwide. CBD is recognized not simply as a legal instrument that seeks to protect threatened genetic resources, species, and ecosystems. It also underpins the move toward "sustainable development"—the belief that development that improves the lives of people today should not deplete natural resources nor increase environmental problems for future generations (page 204).

In November 1988, at a time of growing awareness in international circles of the threats to biological diversity and the need to conserve this diversity, the UNEP convened a working party of experts. By May 1992, this group had devised an agreed text for a CBD. The convention was opened for signature on June 5, 1992, at the United Nations Conference on Environment and Development, also called the Rio Conference or Earth Summit (page 197). One year later there were 168 signatories, of which 135 have since ratified the convention. It came into force on December 29, 1993.

The convention's two main objectives are

- the conservation of biological diversity and the sustainable use of its components

- fair and equitable sharing of the benefits arising out of the utilization of genetic resources (including the transfer of technology to developing countries under favorable terms)

Marine Pollution

What is pollution? The meaning of the word *pollution* seems straightforward enough, but is it? Most people, when asked what they consider pollution to be, answer with something like "damage to the environment caused by chemicals released by humans." This begs many questions. How do you assess damage to the environment? When power plants discharge heat energy, they raise local water temperatures and influence nearby biological communities; in this case, it is heat energy, not a chemical, that is affecting the environment. Is this pollution? When oil and gas seep naturally from the bottom of the sea and affect nearby organisms, is this pollution? Does pollution refer to the damage done to the environment, the agents responsible for the damage, or any agent that might potentially harm the environment? It soon becomes clear that we need to be more precise in forming our definition.

Today, scientists who study pollution in the sea commonly make a distinction between the polluting agents themselves (calling them inputs), their demonstrable occurrence in the sea (contamination), and their damaging effects on the environment (pollution). These distinctions are recommended by international advisory bodies such as ICES (the International Commission for the Exploration of the Sea) and GESAMP (the United Nations Group of Experts on the Scientific Aspects of Marine Pollution). In more general use, inputs that are shown to be harmful are commonly referred to as pollutants.

Pollutants

It is dramatic incidents such as major oil spills that grab the headlines, but only 10–20 percent of marine pollution is the result of polluting agents that are dumped or discharged at sea; the other 80–90 percent derive from discharge directly from the land or are chemicals that are carried from the land and through the atmosphere before they reach the sea. Dumping or spillage by vessels at sea is an important source of pollution—and some of the most damaging chemical or physical agents enter the sea in this way—but volume for volume, considerably more is carried into the sea from discharge pipes, from land runoff, or from gases or particles carried through the air from the land.

Contamination

One of the many problems in assessing marine pollution is in disentangling natural inputs from those arising from human activities. For example, oil seeps naturally into the sea in the Gulf of Mexico and in the Pacific Ocean off the California coast. Some naturally occurring radioactive material is eroded continually from the coasts of southwest India and Brazil. Finding measurable levels of a contaminant does not necessarily mean that the substance entered the sea by human means. Levels of "natural" pollutants vary considerably depending on location, and natural occurrences of substances need to be taken into account. Occasionally, these natural discharges produce much higher levels of "pollution" than human activities.

However, many pollutants of concern are not naturally occurring substances. Their existence in the sea can be attributed fairly and squarely to human activity. Questions then arise, such as: What concentration of a pollutant is harmful? Harmful to what, and in what circumstances? Undoubtedly, some chemical pollutants interact with one another, and whereas a chemical on its own might be relatively harmless, in combination with other chemicals it may be converted to a substance that is lethal to at least some organisms. In any case, the sea is not a neutral or chemical-free environment. Substances often interact with ions (charged atoms and molecules) in seawater. Substances may be selectively adsorbed onto particles and therefore may accumulate in sediment on the seafloor. Here, they are much more likely to encounter living organisms than if the substance were simply dissolved and floating free in the water column. Measuring the concentration of a substance in, say, water at the sea surface may tell you little about where the substance has actually accumulated and the likely effect of this pollutant on organisms in the vicinity.

Pollution: A Question of Priorities

GESAMP defines *contamination* as "the introduction of substances into the marine environment which alters the concentration and distribution of substances within the ocean." The organization goes on to define *marine pollution* as the human introduction of substances or energy into the marine environment that result in "such deleterious effects as harm to living resources, hazards to human health, hindrance to human activities including fisheries, impairment of quality for use of seawater, and reduction of amenities." The emphasis is largely, but not entirely, on the effect of agents that reduce the quality of the marine environment or its products as experienced by humans. Contamination becomes pollution when humans release contaminants that harm organisms, damage or remove amenities, or in other

A common scoter covered in oil,
after the Sea Empress *disaster*
on the Pembrokeshire Coast, South Wales
(David Woodfall / ENP Images)

ways create changes so that humans cannot benefit from the sea in ways they could previously.

Pollution is obvious when it is at its most severe: beaches are covered with oil, hundreds or thousands of sea birds and mammals die, and the evidence is there for all to see. Most pollution is not like this at all. Most pollution is, instead, insidious. Much of it is goes unnoticed.

In an ideal world, it would be helpful not to discharge any wastes at all that might enter the sea. After all, we do not know what effect they might have. This is impractical and unrealistic. In reality, we need to consider that pollution occurs because one set of human interests (the need or desire for services and products) conflicts with another set of interests (such as the provision of healthy seawater, amenities, and food from the sea). Putting aside wider issues, such as maintaining biodiversity and the importance of maintaining a "healthy" biosphere, decisions about pollution are often about balancing one set of interests against the other. When human health is threatened, as in the case of mercury poisoning in Japan (page 184), decisions about pollution may well override all other considerations. But this is rarely the case. In reality, the pollution issue is much more complex, and some of the greatest environmental time bombs—global warming for example (page 78)—are caused by the release of pollutants for which large sections of the global human population are ultimately responsible.

In his dispassionate book *Marine Pollution,* British pollution expert Professor R. B. Clark summarized a set of questions that help clarify thinking about specific pollution incidences:

- What is the level of contamination in the area we are interested in?

- What form does it take?

- Where does it come from?

- What happens to it?

- What does it do to the plants and animals there?

- If plants and animals are affected, does it matter?

- To whom does it matter? What other interest is affected?

- How much does it matter to them?

- If it does matter, what can we do about it?

- What do we do with the polluting material if it is not put in the sea?

- Would the alternative be better or worse than putting it in the sea?

- How much would it cost?

When we consider such questions, it soon becomes clear how complex pollution issues really are. To answer all these questions for a specific pollution incident would be both time consuming and extremely costly. Who will pay for this work? It is not so surprising that only the worst pollution incidents result in prosecutions.

The American Chemical Society has registered many more than 10 million new chemicals since 1957. A recent report by the U.S. National Research Council noted that of 66,000 chemicals selected for consideration (drugs, pesticides, and other industrial chemicals), toxicity data was completely lacking for 70 percent of them, and for only 2 percent was there sufficient data to enable a complete health-hazard evaluation. Of the numerous substances released into the environment, only a small fraction can be tracked systematically and assessed for their effects on living organisms.

The diversity of potentially hazardous agents that enter the sea from human activities is staggering; the range includes oils of various kinds, human sewage, heavy metals, synthetic chemicals such as chlorinated hydrocarbons (organochlorines) and numerous kinds of plastic, particulate matter from mining operations, thermal (heat) pollution, and radioactive waste.

Oil

Crude oil is a thick, dark, greenish-brown liquid—a mixture of many different kind of hydrocarbon (page 171). When refined, crude oil yields a wide range of useful substances: chemicals that can be used directly for fuel, or as lubricants, or in the manufacture of plastics, synthetic fibers, rubber, fertilizers, and numerous other products upon which industrialized societies have come to depend. In short, crude oil is a very valuable commodity: despite occasional serious incidents and continuing background oil pollution, oil extraction and transport will continue. For the time being at least, we have to live with the problems of oil discharge—whether intentional or not—and minimize its occurrence and environmental impact.

Oil is widespread in the sea. A small amount arises from natural discharge, but the bulk is released by human activities. Much of the world's oil, whether extracted from below the sea or from land, is transported across the oceans by tankers, and it is tanker operations that probably account for the highest proportion of marine oil pollution. Tankers discharge oil when they are unloading the oil by pipeline, when they illegally clean their tanks at sea, when they empty their ballast tanks, and when there is the occasional and highly publicized shipwreck. Legislation in the form of MARPOL (the International Conven-

tion for the Prevention of Pollution from Ships) aims to curtail oil-polluting activities at sea, but this is easier said than done (page 196). In fact, the technology does exist for identifying offenders. Vessels discharging oil often show up clearly on satellite images, and freshly discharged oil carries its own specific "fingerprint": crude oil extracted from a specific location has a unique mixture of hydrocarbon that can be identified. The problem lies in successfully prosecuting oil polluters—a difficult and protracted business. In practice, only the worst offenders are prosecuted.

Another important source of oil pollution is the runoff and discharges from cities. A rich cocktail of different types of oil find its way into storm drains and sewers, which may discharge directly into the sea or via rivers. Some oil finds its way into the sea from coastal refineries. Ranking alongside tanker collisions in the severity of local spillage are the occasional but dramatic blowouts of offshore rigs. The largest single oil-pollution incident to date was the blowout of an exploration well in the Bahía de Campeche of the Gulf of Mexico, which released nearly a half-million metric tons (550,000 tons) of oil.

Sewage

Sewage, or general waste water, has been and continues to be a major source of pollution along many of the world's coasts. Sewage from urban communities is mostly organic (carbon-containing) matter, but it is usually mixed with all manner of other substances—oils, heavy metals, plastics, and so on (see sections following)—because sewers often receive discharges from commercial and industrial premises as well as households.

Aside from the problems of chemicals introduced by industrial processes, there are four main kinds of problem created by the discharge of raw (untreated) sewage. Organic matter in sewage is broken down by bacteria in the water column; this activity typically requires oxygen, and if organic matter is present in very high concentrations, the water becomes depleted of oxygen. Many life-forms, particularly fish and most invertebrates, are unable to survive. Sewage water often contains high levels of nutrients such as phosphates and nitrates, and these cause enrichment of seawater, resulting in increased photosynthetic activity. Blooms of phytoplankton are sometimes produced, clouding the water and preventing light penetration to seaweeds on the seafloor. When the phytoplankton die and bacteria decompose them, this causes oxygen depletion that kills other organisms in the bottom waters. Some blooms involve phytoplankton that release toxic substances, giving rise to harmful "red tides" (page 89). Finally, disease-causing viruses, bacteria, and protists, together with the eggs and larvae of parasitic flatworms, are commonly found in raw sewage. Although many are killed or immobilized in contact with seawater, others are not, and people can become infected when they swallow fouled seawater or eat contaminated shellfish.

Raw sewage can be treated to minimize one or more of the above problems. In primary treatment (this involves physical and sometimes chemical processing), sewage is screened to remove all large items, and it is allowed to settle so that the larger suspended solids separate out. Oil or grease may be skimmed off the water surface. Secondary treatment involves mainly biological processing. The partially treated sewage passes through a filter bed where various microbes—protists, bacteria, and fungi—remove and break down much of the dissolved or suspended organic matter. Typically, after primary and secondary treatment, about 90 percent of suspended solids are removed, along with about one-half and one-third respectively of the wastewater's nitrogen and phosphorus content. The levels of most pathogens are markedly reduced, too.

The main by-product of primary and secondary treatment is sewage sludge that is rich in organic matter. This can produce its own disposal problems, but sludge can be recycled in various ways: as compost, fertilizer, or landfill, or dried and compressed into building blocks. Unfortunately, in some parts of the United States sewage sludge is dumped out at sea, although this practice is gradually being phased out.

According to the U.S. Environmental Protection Agency, in 1986 about three-quarters of urban sewage received at least secondary treatment. Unfortunately, in many coastal regions of the United States, towns and cities rely on the simple expedient of discharging raw sewage or, at best, primary-treated sewage, through outfall pipes that empty into estuaries or discharge several hundred meters offshore. The assumption is that currents and tides will distribute and dilute the waste over a wide area; this does not necessarily happen, and accumulations have occurred, for example, in the waters of Chesapeake Bay and Long Island Sound. Furthermore, in many countries of the world, safe means of sewage disposal are considered to be even less of a priority than they are in the United States.

Heavy Metals

Heavy metals are a group of high-density metals that include mercury, lead, cadmium, and others. One feature they share is the tendency to accumulate in the bodies of organisms that ingest them, and as a result, their concentration tends to rise with increasing height in a food chain (page 84). This phenomenon is termed *biological magnification*. Some seaweeds, for example, concentrate heavy metals at levels a hundred times greater than in the surrounding water. Herbivorous fish that graze upon the seaweed concentrate the metals further, and when these fish, in turn, are eaten by predatory fish, the metals are concentrated yet again. Eventually, birds and mammals at the top of local food chains contain the highest levels of heavy metals, and in these animals the metals occasionally cause debilitating conditions or even death.

Many industrial processes produce heavy-metals or heavy-metal compounds as by-products, and these substances—along with oil-related products and synthetic organic substances—are routinely monitored in marine pollution studies. The classic case of heavy-metal marine pollution that resulted in human deaths is considered on page 184.

Synthetic Organic Compounds

Synthetic, organic (carbon-containing) compounds are widespread in marine environments. Some are nonbiodegradable, and so they persist in the environment, remaining trapped in sediment or being circulated through biogeochemical cycles for hundreds or thousands of years. Notable among these are the chlorinated hydrocarbons. Many of these—DDT (dichlorodiphenyltrichloroethane), aldrin, dieldrin, and chlordane, for example—were widely used as pesticides between the 1950s and 1970s. Their indiscriminate usage was then massively curtailed in most countries. These chemicals suffer from the disadvantage that they undergo biological magnification in food chains (see above). The top carnivores in a food chain may have concentrations several hundred or thousand times greater than that found in their surroundings. Levels of DDT and other chlorinated hydrocarbons have, on occasion, reached harmful levels in birds, fish, and marine mammals (page 184).

Polychlorinated biphenyls (PCBs)—really a specific type of chlorinated hydrocarbon—also exhibit biological magnification. PCBs as industrial chemicals have been used in a wide range of products from plastics to paints. Used in vast quantities between the 1930s and 1970s, high levels of PCBs have been implicated in disrupting the normal reproductive behavior of seabirds and marine mammals because some PCBs are converted to sex-hormonelike substances. High levels of PCBs have been found in the tissues of seals, sea lions, and dolphins following unexpected die-offs (page 184). PCB use has long since been phased out in most developed countries: the United States banned them in 1979.

However, we have inherited a considerable legacy of waste items—plastics, electrical equipment, and so on—that contain PCBs and have to be disposed of somewhere.

Particulates

Discharged sediments, though perhaps nontoxic, are nevertheless important pollutants. They cloud the water and reduce light penetration, starving photosynthetic organisms of sunlight. When the sediments settle, they further disrupt the community by smothering organisms on the seafloor and clogging the feeding apparatus of filter feeders. In 1990, United Nations pollution experts estimated that the world's rivers now discharge three times more sediment than they did in preagricultural, preindustrial times.

Larger Solid Wastes

A wide range of solid materials—from styrofoam cups and packaging, through plastic bottles and bags, to discarded nylon netting and heavier objects such as metal sheets and glass fragments—settle on the seafloor or bob up and down on the ocean waves for months or years on end. Many of these items are biodegradable, but many are not, and although they may be broken into smaller fragments, they will form unsightly and dangerous debris that will be with us for hundreds or thousands of years. Weathered styrofoam and plastic bags, line, and netting are particularly harmful to marine animals. Fragments of plastic or styrofoam are often confused for prey items and are swallowed but, being indigestible, can clog the digestive tract. Sea turtles, seabirds, and smaller marine mammals—particularly seals and dolphins—are susceptible to entanglement in line or netting and suffer a lingering, painful death as a result. In the early 1990s, an estimated 165,000 tons (150,000 t) of nylon lines and netting were being lost or discarded by sea fishermen every year.

Radioactive Waste

Radioactive substances differ from other chemical pollutants in that they can exert their effect "at a distance" because they release high-energy waves and particles that can damage living tissues. The substance's harmful effects have a reach of up to several meters or more. Radioactive material can retain this potency for thousands of years. The high level of concern about radioactive contamination and the fact that radioactive emissions are easily detectable using the right equipment mean

However, low-level radioactive effluent is still discharged into coastal waters from nuclear-reprocessing plants such as Cap de la Hague in France and Sellafield in the United Kingdom. Constant vigilance is necessary because there are several potentially new sources of high-level radiation in the sea: from sunken nuclear-powered submarines, leaking (pre-1982) containment vessels, and possibly crashed planes and satellites.

Thermal Pollution

Thermal (heat) pollution occurs locally where coastally situated power plants, oil refineries, and other industrial processes discharge warm water into the marine environment. This warm water originates from seawater or river water that is used as a coolant. Raising seawater's temperature by a few degrees locally may not appear to be much of a problem, but in reality it can markedly change the nature of nearby biological communities. Higher temperatures also lower the oxygen-carrying capacity of seawater by an amount that can be detrimental to much marine life.

On a wider scale, global warming (page 78) is probably exerting profound influences on marine populations. Coral bleaching (page 112) and other temperature-related changes are occurring in marine communities. One survey conducted off the coast of southern California between 1951 and 1993 appears to show an 80 percent decline in zooplankton density correlated with 1.2–1.6°C rises in surface temperatures.

Sound Pollution

It may not be immediately obvious that sound pollution is an issue of importance in the sea. However, whales communicate by sound (page 107), and some scientists believe that noise from ships and other machinery might be highly disruptive to whales and other marine life. In 1994, scientists had planned to begin a series of experiments using very loud, low-frequency sound transmitted through the Pacific Ocean. Measuring the speed of transmission of such sound waves would enable scientists to determine the temperature of ocean water accurately over large areas. These experiments were part of an international program to help determine the extent to which global warming is taking place. The experiments were postponed because of concerns by animal-rights groups that whales might be harmed by the experiments.

Chemical runoff into the Irish Sea,
Whitehaven, England
(David Woodfall/ENP Images)

that systematic monitoring of radiation levels is carried out on a routine basis across all oceans. Natural radiation arises from localized deposits of uranium and other heavy metals, radon gas released by certain rocks, and cosmic radiation from space, but much of Earth's background radiation is produced by human activities: the nuclear energy industry, medical and industrial applications, and nuclear weapons testing aboveground until phased out in 1980.

Concern about pollution by radioactive substances continues, but in reality, radiation levels tend to be much higher on land than in aquatic environments. Dumping of radioactive waste in containment drums and tanks at sea began in 1946 and was being phased out internationally by 1982.

Pollution—Case Studies

The *Exxon Valdez* Oil Spill

Crude oils—those involved in most of the major marine incidents—contain a diverse mix of different hydrocarbons. Most of these chemical components float on the water surface, but after the lighter, more-volatile constituents have evaporated, a thick tarry residue remains that may float for months or years on end, may sink to the bottom of the sea, or may be washed ashore. The oil can clog the feathers of birds, the gills of fish, or the skin and lungs of seals and other mammals, resulting in a slow lingering death for the affected animals. The more soluble oil components are toxic to many animals and plants: they may inhibit the growth of phytoplankton, make fish more susceptible to disease, and disrupt the growth and maturation of larvae within the zooplankton. The saving grace is that oil is biodegradable; given enough time, the oil is broken down by the activity of bacteria and other biological agents.

The southern end of the Trans-Alaska Pipeline lies in the port of Valdez in Prince William Sound, Alaska. In this rugged coastal region, wildlife abounds, but the sound is also a major thoroughfare for tankers that ply to and from Valdez to refinery facilities elsewhere. On the morning of the March 23, 1989 the tanker *Exxon Valdez* ran aground on rocks in Prince William Sound and spilled 38,500 tons (35,000 t) of crude oil—the largest and most destructive spillage to date in U.S. waters.

By the time an organized response to the spillage was under way, oil had been discharged that was to spread through more than 900 square miles (2,300 sq km) of water. Skimmers (devices operated from vessels to remove oil from the surface) were able to recover only a small proportion of the oil. Within four days, the discharged oil had mixed with water to form a frothy, mousselike emulsion that could not be skimmed or broken up or burned. Exxon scientists sprayed oil-soluble fertilizers on polluted beaches in an effort to encourage the proliferation of oil-digesting bacteria; this $10 million experiment proved to be partially successful. Another technique, hot-water washing of beaches, though superficially effective, probably caused more longer-term damage than simply allowing nature to run its course. The hot water kills microbes, including those that might, in time, degrade the oil; blasting the oil with hot water forces the oil deep into crevices and other oxygen-deficient locations where the oil degrades more slowly. Three weeks after the spill, only about 4 percent of the discharged oil had actually been recovered, leaving more than 95 percent to be degraded mainly by natural processes.

An estimated 100,000–300,000 birds were killed by the spillage, among them bald eagles and cormorants. Sea mammals were also badly affected: 3,500–5,500 sea otters were killed along with 200 harbor seals. Commercial fishing was disrupted, and both local herring and salmon fisheries were temporarily closed. The economic costs of the spill have been high: Exxon Corporation has been ordered to pay $5 billion in damages, plus $287 million to local fishermen, and Exxon claims to have paid $3.5 billion for cleanup operations. Ongoing litigation has meant that many of the lessons we could learn from the spillage and its subsequent cleanup are being delayed because the gathered data form part of the evidence being used in lawsuits. Much of this invaluable information is thus unavailable to the public and the scientific community at large.

One of the lessons learned from the *Exxon Valdez* incident is that bacteria and fungi in the natural environment can degrade oil fairly rapidly and can probably be encouraged to do so. Research under way at several U.S. scientific institutions is testing the effectiveness of various strains of "customized" oil-digesting bacteria, one of the most encouraging developments for improving the efficiency of cleanup operations on beaches.

Minamata Disease

Heavy metals and synthetic organic compounds such as DDT and PCBs, far from being broken down in the natural marine environment, are concentrated in living tissues. Some, as in the case of the bacterial conversion of mercury to methyl mercury, are converted to substances that are more toxic than the original pollutant.

The classic, and tragic, example of heavy-metal poisoning occurred in Minamata Bay, Japan, in the 1950s and 1960s. This was to be the first well-documented example of human deaths arising from heavy-metal pollution in the marine environment.

In 1938, a chemical factory that manufactured acetaldehyde and other organic substances was established on the shores of Minamata Bay. Mercury compounds were being used in the manufacturing process, and these were being discharged into the bay as a constituent of the factory's wastewater. In 1950, the first major changes in the bay's biological community were noted, and by 1953 unusual signs and symptoms were being detected among the local human population. The full story only gradually emerged: methyl mercury discharged into the bay was accumulating in those organisms higher up in the food chains (page 84). Fish and shellfish, in particular, concentrated the metal, and levels as high as 50 parts per million (p.p.m)—several hundred times today's recommended safe concentration based on the seafood consumption rates of the local population—were found in the flesh of local fish. The fish and shellfish were a major part of the diet of local people, and the mercury was accumulating inside their bodies. The signs and symptoms of mercury poisoning were extremely distressing—muscular spasms, paralysis, and in many cases, severe brain damage leading to death. By 1960, 43 people had died of the condition—later dubbed Minamata Disease—and a further 116 had been permanently disabled by it. It was not, however, until 1968 that the Japanese declared that mercury was, indeed, the cause of the condition and shut down the plant. By that time, about 1,000 local inhabitants were showing signs and symptoms of mercury poisoning.

DDT and Eggshells

The pesticide DDT (dichlorodiphenyltrichloroethane), the best known of the persistent chlorinated hydrocarbons, was, by the late 1960s, identified as a pollutant with adverse effects on marine wildlife. Between the 1940s and 1960s, DDT was widely used as a cheap and effective insecticide. Unfortunately, some of the very properties that made DDT so successful—for example its persistence—were also to prove the chemical's major problem as a pollutant.

The most noticeable effect of DDT in U.S. waters was on the reproductive success of the brown pelican, *Pelecanus occidentalis,* along the West, Southeast, and Gulf coasts. Here, by the early 1970s, many pelican populations had declined drastically. DDT was concentrated in food chains, and pelicans, being fish-eaters, were at the top of some food chains and the final recipients of elevated levels of DDT. Tissue samples taken from nesting pelicans in the Gulf of Mexico, southern California, and elsewhere showed high levels of DDT and related chemicals, particularly in body fat. These chemicals appeared to effect the pelicans' capacity to produce normal eggshells: instead, the eggshells were too thin and cracked before chicks completed their incubation. The effect on the pelicans' reproductive success was catastrophic (although the scarcity of sardines, their staple food, was also implicated). In the entire colony of the Channel Islands off southern California, only one chick was recorded in 1970. In this locality, a major coastal input of DDT was traced to a chemical plant—at this time, the world's largest producer of DDT. U.S. legislation introduced by 1972 greatly restricted the use of DDT and related chemicals as pesticides. In many other industrialized countries similar legislation was introduced. With the decline of DDT use, so the levels of DDT dropped in the tissues of pelicans and other marine creatures, and gradually the brown pelican populations recovered. Brown pelicans, scarce over much of the United States in the early 1970s, became common once again by the late 1980s.

The DDT pollution problem has subsided but not disappeared entirely. Chlorinated hydrocarbons, being cheap and effective, are still the insecticides of choice in developing countries where environmental concerns may have a lower priority. DDT still continues to be released into the global ocean, and DDT residues have been recorded in the tissues of Antarctic penguins, indicating that these chemicals are truly persistent and can be transported long distances from sources of input. However, the issue of DDT pollution needs to be set within the broader context. DDT is a cheap and effective insecticide that is safe for humans to use providing guidelines are followed. In the fight against malaria (responsible for more human fatalities than any other transmittable disease), DDT is highly effective in killing the mosquitoes that transmit the disease. In Sri Lanka in 1960, following a 14-year mosquito control program using DDT, cases of malaria had dropped to 110 cases per year. When the program was stopped—because of fears about DDT use—cases of malaria rose to 2.5 million by 1968. No human deaths from DDT usage have yet to be recorded, yet when DDT use was phased out in North Carolina in 1970, the insecticide that replaced it, parathion—a hazardous nerve toxin requiring strict control in use—was responsible for the death of 40 people.

PCBs and Marine Mammal Deaths

PCBs have been implicated in the deaths of seals, sea lions, and dolphins and may interfere with the reproductive behavior and physiology of marine mammals.

Various seal populations in the Baltic Sea have shown reduced reproductive capacities since the early 1970s. The tissues of sampled animals showed high levels of PCBs, and when their reproductive systems were examined, females showed reproductive abnormalities that reduced their fertility. However, other populations of seals, including several in the North Sea, showed even higher levels of PCBs in their tissues, yet they showed no reproductive disturbances. Other evidence does suggest that very high levels of PCBs cause infertility in male mammals by sharply reducing the production of healthy sperm. In marine mammals, such infertility has been recorded in individuals with PCB levels of 50 p.p.m. in their blubber. High rates of spontaneous abortion were found among California sea lions; PCBs (along with DDT) were implicated, but it is very difficult to assign PCBs as the cause of the reproductive failure, other than by association. In such circumstances, it is often only by performing experiments on live animals that the effect of PCBs can be proved. Nevertheless, the circumstantial evidence is building.

Very high levels of PCBs have been found in dead dolphins and porpoises from European waters. In 1988, an epidemic of viral distemper struck colonies of common seals in the North Sea. Mortalities were high, and it was suggested that PCBs—in combination with other pollutants—had weakened the seals' immune systems and made them more vulnerable to infection.

Kaneohe Bay

The devastating effects of uncontrolled sewage discharge on a coral reef system are illustrated by the case of Kaneohe Bay on Oahu Island in Hawaii. In the 1960s, the once luxuriant coral reefs of Kaneohe Bay were dying, many areas smothered by the growth of green algae. The algal growth was attributed to the buildup of nutrients in the bay. Between the 1930s and 1950s, the Kaneohe Bay area had been first militarized and then developed for residential use. Sewage from the growing population was discharged directly into the bay, and as the bay became nutrient-enriched, so algal mats began to grow and smother the coral. The sewage, acting as a fertilizer, caused phytoplankton to multiply as well and soon the crystal clear waters of the bay became cloudy. By 1978 more than 5 million gallons (more than 20,000 cubic m) of sewage was being discharged into Kaneohe Bay each day. At that time, a long overdue response to public pressure resulted in the construction of a new outfall so that much of the sewage was discharged offshore. As a result nutrient levels in the bay soon dropped dramatically. The coral ecosystem's response was surprisingly rapid. By the early 1980s, the green algae was dying back and the dead coral patches were beginning to be recolonized.

The sewage pollution, however, had left its legacy. When Hurricane Iwa struck Kaneohe Bay in 1982, damage to the coral system was much greater than expected because the coral had not yet entirely recovered from the pollution damage. The weakened coral structure had collapsed in many placed under the onslaught of the hurricane-driven seas. Nevertheless, despite structural damage, the reef system continued its recovery during the 1980s until, in 1990, its revival seemed to grind to a halt.

In the early 1990s, some parts of the reef system began to decline again, and dense coverings of green algae began to reappear. A combination of factors was blamed: the buildup of sewage levels in the bay as aging sewer systems began to overflow; additional sewage finding its way into the bay from private residences and boats; dredging operations, construction, land clearing, and flood-control schemes combining to raise the levels of suspended sediments in the bay; and possibly, the discharge of toxic chemicals from various sources—a result of increased population levels and the growth in commercial and leisure activities in the vicinity.

The coral gardens in Kaneohe Bay took thousands of years to form but only a decade or two to spoil.

Hunting and Fishing—When Enough Is Too Much

Many kinds of marine organisms are harvested, from seaweed to marine mammals, but fish comprise at least 85 percent by weight of marine life extracted from the oceans. In international fisheries terminology, fish are referred to as *finfish*. The term *shellfish* refers to mollusks (squids, octopuses, and bivalves such as clams and mussels) and crustaceans (crabs, lobsters, shrimp, prawns, and so on).

Marine finfish and shellfish together provide, on average, about 10 percent of the protein in human diets. Marine food products are luxury commodities in some Western countries, whereas in the coastal communities of many developing countries they are a staple part of the diet and provide up to 95 percent of the dietary intake of protein. So, in both industrialized and developing nations, seafood plays an important dietary and economic role. As the global human population continues to rise, so the demand for food from the sea increases.

Between the 1950s and 1980s, there was reasonable optimism that the marine catch would simply continue to rise as fishing effort increased. Harvesting more from the oceans was simply a case of increasing the efficiency of catch methods, where necessary managing stocks, and if existing stocks were becoming depleted, turning attention to new, unexploited fish populations. Between 1950 and 1989 the global catch increased nearly fivefold. Then reality hit home. In 1989, the total recorded marine catch of finfish and shellfish was 95.2 million tons (86.4 million t)—a record high. Between 1990 and 1992,

despite increasing fishing pressure, the recorded weight of catch fell, bottoming out at 90.9 million tons (82.5 million t) in 1992, although it has edged upward slightly since. Any substantial increases in fish and shellfish yield since 1989 have come from mariculture (fish and shellfish farming), not from fishing.

That the oceans cannot provide an inexhaustible supply of food was, in reality, clear from the 1950s. Like the overexploitation of whale populations (page 188), fish stocks cannot withstand uncontrolled harvesting. In the late 1950s, California's sardine fishery collapsed, followed in the 1970s by the Peruvian anchovy fishery and in the 1990s, the Canadian cod fishery. In 1995, a report by the U.N. Food and Agricultural Organization concluded that 22 percent of the world's major fisheries were overexploited if not severely depleted, and a further 44 percent were being exploited to their sustainable limit. By 2010, the fish catch per person on Earth is estimated to drop to the late 1950s level. Far from fish helping to meet the shortfall in world food supplies as the human population increases in size, fish supplies will fall further and further behind demand.

If current fishing practices continue unabated, the outlook for the future is not good. Despite the best efforts of fisheries scientists, the harvesting of natural populations of finfish and shellfish in anything like a sustainable manner is highly problematic for a variety of reasons (page 187). Economic and political pressures that are invariably short sighted encourage fishermen to wipe out fish stocks. National subsidies encourage

commercial fisheries to purchase more sophisticated fishing gear in an effort to remain competitive in the international "gold rush" for remaining fish stocks on the open ocean. Fish stocks, like many other products from the sea, do not respect national boundaries. Although the adults of a fish population may lie within one country's Exclusive Economic Zone (EEZ), earlier life-cycle stages may lie outside this zone and may be influenced by pollution or harvesting elsewhere.

Fish Stocks

Fish populations, like those of any other living creature, thrive under suitable conditions, and reproductively active adults produce far more offspring than the environment is capable of sustaining. Fish populations do not simply expand unchecked because both natural and human-related factors curb the increase in population size. Although a single adult cod produces millions of eggs—many of which are successfully fertilized—there is enormous wastage. Many eggs and the larvae into which they hatch are consumed by other animals. Larvae may be swept along by ocean currents into locations where they die because of unfavorable physical or chemical conditions or because of lack of food. The young fish may encounter lethal pollution.

It is not just physical, chemical, and biological factors in the environment that limit the population size: when there is crowding within a population, various factors operate to slow down further increase in population size. Under crowded conditions, there will be greater competition for the available food, and disease epidemics are more likely. Some species of fish even release chemicals that inhibit reproduction when the population density is high.

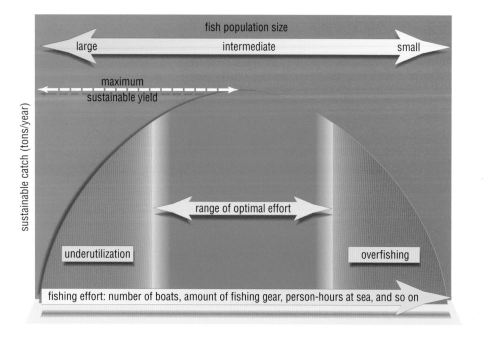

A catch-effort curve for an idealized fishery. When fishing effort is low and the fishery is underutilized, increasing the effort will increase the catch up to a certain point—the optimal yield. After this point, increased effort will result in a decreased overall catch, and the fishery is being overexploited. The range of optimal effort extends slightly above and below the maximum sustainable yield. In practice, the fishery's response to fishing pressure is much more complex than this, and natural environmental factors need to be taken into account

Overfishing

Properly treated fish stocks are renewable resources. Through natural reproduction and growth, fish populations can replenish their numbers and biomass. Problems arise when fishermen remove more fish than the population can sustain. Instead of replenishing itself, the population strives to "catch up" but falls short. There are fewer reproductive adults available to replenish the stock, and there are fewer fish to catch. The fishermen have to work harder to catch the same weight of fish as they could in previous years, and often the size of fish declines because most or all of the larger fish have been removed in previous years. By this time, the fishery is overexploited and is on a downward spiral. How can this be avoided? To begin to find an answer, we need to consider some simple population biology.

The absolute reproductive rate of a population—the overall number of offspring produced per year—depends at least in part on that population's size. If the population size is relatively small, there are comparatively few reproductively active adults available to produce young, so the absolute reproductive rate is small. If the population size is relatively large and the population density is high, there is overcrowding and intense competition for food; this, together with other factors, is likely to lower the reproductive rate. Larval survival and growth to adulthood is likely to be depressed. Other things being equal, population growth rate and hence the population's capacity to replenish itself is highest when the population is neither too large nor too small but is of some intermediate size or density.

To harvest a natural population of fish in a sustainable way (in other words, without the population declining significantly in the long term), the number and weight of fish caught need to be replaced by a similar number and weight of new fish. These new fish are "recruited" by reproduction and the subsequent growth and survival of offspring. The sustainable yield of a population is the weight that can be caught annually and can be replaced by recruitment year after year. The sustainable yield will depend on the size of the fish population (remember: reproductive rate is highest at intermediate population densities). Therefore, ignoring other factors for the moment, the highest sustainable yield will be obtainable from a population of intermediate size. Theoretically, the maximum sustainable yield—the highest annual catch that can be repeated year after year without threatening the stock—will be obtainable from a fish population of intermediate size. How is this achieved? Therein lies the problem.

Imagine this scenario. Some enterprising fishermen discover a new population of fish, a stock that is as yet completely untapped. The discoverers have rich pickings for a while; in fact, in the early stages of the exploitation of a fishery, the fish population is often exploited well below its maximum sustainable level. Only a small fraction of the stock is removed, and the removed fish can be replenished well within the limits of the population's capacity to do so. But whether this population is found in international waters or in waters under a single nation's jurisdiction, the resource is available to other fishermen and not just those who discovered it. The new population does not remain a secret for long.

Soon other fishermen learn about the new-found resource and start to fish it. Fishing effort (the number of fishing boats, amount of fishing gear, person-hours at sea, and so on) increases. Soon the fishery is being harvested at its maximum sustainable level, but this situation does not become stabilized. Fishing effort continues to increase, the population declines in size, and as fishing effort rises further, so catch rates fall. The maximum sustainable yield has been exceeded, and the fish population is in decline. So why don't the fishermen limit themselves before it is too late? The simple answer is that in an open, unregulated fishery where market forces operate, fishermen and the governments that support them will choose short-term gain over longer-term conservation. After all, they argue if we do not catch the fish, someone else will. The answer, of course, is to regulate the fishing to maintain the fish stock at sustainable levels. But this is nowhere near as easy as it sounds.

To convince politicians, administrators, and the fishermen themselves that fishing should be regulated and of the manner in which it should be done, scientific data and convincing arguments are needed. The maximum sustainable yield for a fishery is difficult to estimate. To make this calculation, fisheries biologists need, first, to know the size and composition of the fish population, how quickly the fish grow and reproduce, what they eat (which often is quite different at different parts of the life cycle), and the life expectancy of the fish; second, to know the major environmental factors that influence reproduction and mortality and how these vary from year to year; and third, to predict how the fish population will respond to certain types of fishing effort (for example, nets with larger mesh sizes will select only larger fish, and this will affect the composition of the fish population in a different manner to nets of smaller mesh size). The catching of target species may alter the size of other animal populations that compete with the fish for food, and so the harvested fish stock may decrease in size because of competition from other species. These are just some of the biological factors to consider.

At the end of the day, it is preferable to manage fish stocks on a sustainable basis rather than hunt them to economic extinction (page 190). Providing agreement can be reached on catch quotas and fishermen (and nations) can be relied on to meet imposed restrictions—or policed into doing so—then various strategies can be used to manage the fishery (page 198).

Overhunting and Overfishing—Case Studies

Overhunting

The Inuit of North America have been hunting seals and whales for thousands of years, but the earliest documentary evidence of whaling comes from northern Europe between the 9th and 11th centuries. Whaling became a commercial enterprise in the 18th century (page 148), but it was not until the early 1900s that it became highly mechanized. Technological advances, such as motorized, long-haul vessels that carried cannons to fire explosive harpoons, provided the means to ruthlessly exploit whale populations across all oceans. By the late 1920s, factory ships could process carcasses at sea, enabling the hunting vessels that served them to be active for much longer periods each year.

Hunting whale populations was certainly an efficient means of harvesting the oceans' abundance. Most of the larger whales are baleen whales; they sieve the water for herbivorous plankton or fish, and so the marine food chains with these whales as the top predator are very short. The transfer of energy from phytoplankton to whales (and then to whalers) is efficient because there are few links in the food chain (page 84). In effect, the whales are acting as giant gatherers, consuming small but abundant creatures and converting this energy to whale biomass, which is made available to human hunters. This conversion may be efficient, but since the 1960s, public awareness has been raised about the catastrophic depletion of whale stocks and the apparent cruelty of the methods used to subdue and then kill whales. As early as 1900, it was apparent that many whale stocks in the Northern Hemisphere had been hunted to economic extinction. Whalers were having to travel much farther distances to find their quarry. By the late 1920s, the Antarctic Ocean was becoming established as the world's most prolific whaling ground.

In 1946 the International Whaling Commission (IWC) was established, ostensibly to regulate whale hunting and prevent overfishing. The IWC gathered data, mostly from the whalers' reported catches, and attempted to set annual quotas for the numbers of different species that could be taken. In its early years, the IWC was more concerned about saving the whaling industry rather than saving whale species themselves, and it is only since the 1960s, under mounting pressure from conservationists, that the IWC's role has included the need to protect whale stocks from actual extinction. In general, IWC bans on the taking of particular whale species have come into force very late. The blue whale received protected status only in 1965–66, long after the stock was so reduced that the whale was rarely encountered. Even then, non-IWC nations continued hunting them until 1971. In 1972, the U.S. Congress passed the Marine Mammal Protection Act to ban all hunting of marine mammals (except for specified activities by indigenous peoples) in territories within its jurisdiction and to ban all imports of marine mammal products.

BALEEN WHALES OF THE ANTARCTIC OCEAN

In 1904, the British established a shore whaling operation on South Georgia, one of the Falkland Islands, and within a few years had established

Inuit hunter with head of a narwhal, Baffin Island, Canada (Tony Martin/ENP Images)

GLOBAL POPULATIONS OF FIVE BALEEN-WHALE SPECIES BEFORE AND AFTER INTENSIVE EXPLOITATION

Species	Population estimates		Status
	1900	Early 1990s	
Blue whale	>200,00	<10,000	Endangered
Fin whale	>500,00	120,000	Endangered
Humpback whale	115,00	10,000	Endangered
Sei whale	250,00	50,000	Endangered
Minke whale	140,000	700,000	Hunted

Estimates are those of the International Whaling Commission. The status of a species is assigned by the International Union for the Conservation of Nature

ESTIMATED CHANGES IN ANTARCTIC KRILL CONSUMPTION BEFORE AND AFTER INTENSIVE EXPLOITATION OF THE LARGER BALEEN-WHALE SPECIES.

Predator	Annual krill consumption (in millions of metric tons)	
	1900	Mid-1980s
Baleen whales	190	40
Seals	50	130
Penguins	50	130
Squid	80	100
Fish	100	70
Total	470	470

whaling stations elsewhere in British territories. During these early years, humpback whales—large, slow moving, and often coastal—were a dominant part of the catch. By the 1920s, blue whales and fin whales—larger and faster moving than humpbacks—dominated the catch. Total annual catches increased during the 1930s as more nations became involved and as factory ships that were used to process whale carcasses at sea were introduced. During World War II, whaling activity declined enormously, but after the war whaling resumed. As early as the mid-1930s, the catch of blue whales had been declining despite rising effort. The fin whale catch was later to follow suit. By the early 1960s, the two largest-size whales—the blue and fin whales—were being caught in much reduced numbers, and average whale size had plummeted. More than 80 percent of blue whales that were captured at this time were sexually immature. Whalers were having to turn their attention to much smaller-size whales—first sei whales and then, in the early 1970s, to minke whales—a species that, until then, was considered far too small to be worthy of consideration.

Since 1970, four out of the five exploited baleen whale species of the Antarctic Ocean have been placed on the endangered species list by the International Union for the Conservation of Nature (IUCN). Interestingly, since the dramatic decline of Antarctic whale stocks, there has probably been considerable change in the population sizes of competing species. Krill (page 165) is the main food item of Antarctic Ocean baleen whales and several species of seal, penguin, fish, and squid. Some scientists calculate that prior to intensive whaling, Antarctic Ocean baleen whales probably consumed about 209 million tons (190 million t) of krill each year—equivalent to about twice the annual global fish catch of today's fishermen. By the mid-1980s, consumption of krill by baleen whales had dropped to less than a quarter of this (although, as the table shows, as the larger baleen whale species have declined in numbers, so one of the smaller species—the minke—has increased substantially). The shortfall in krill consumption by whales has been met by increased consumption by other predators. As a result, Antarctic seal, penguin, fish, and squid populations have probably grown larger since 1900.

Most larger whales reach adulthood within five to 10 years, but mature females produce typically only one young every two or three years. Given the low reproductive rate of whales, depleted populations are likely to take decades to recover. In 1986, the IWC voted to establish a five-year ban on commercial whaling in the hope of reestablishing endangered stocks; the ban has been continued in further rounds of voting since then. A few whaling nations—notably Norway and Japan—have refused to comply with the moratorium, claiming that they take only a few whales for scientific purposes. The products from these whales are nevertheless sold commercially.

In 1979, a whale sanctuary was established in the Indian Ocean and in 1994 one in the Antarctic Ocean. These sanctuaries serve to promote the recovery of open-ocean whale stocks, and commercial whaling within them is banned. However, the Japanese still catch minke whales in Antarctica in defiance of this prohibition. For many smaller whale species, coastal pollution and accidental entanglement in fishing gear are still important sources of human-induced mortality.

DOLPHINS AND PORPOISES

Dolphin populations face an onslaught from many quarters. Drift nets, purse seines, and other fishing gear inadvertently capture tens of thousands of dolphins and porpoises each year. Many dolphin-unfriendly fishing practices continue, and dolphin populations have declined noticeably in the eastern Pacific, particularly among stocks of coastal spotted dolphins and eastern spinner dolphins. Environmental legislation that is properly enforced can have a powerful effect. Between 1972 (when the U.S. Marine Mammal Protection Act was introduced) and 1990, annual dolphin deaths at the hands of U.S. fishing fleets declined from an estimated 200,000 to effectively zero. Special dolphin-friendly nets were gradually introduced, and observers on fishing fleets were employed to ensure that fishermen complied with the provisions of the act.

Drift nets—the so-called walls of death—are up to 200 feet (60 m) long and 50 feet (15 m) deep. They are set to catch squid and pelagic fish, notably tuna. Such nets are indiscriminate takers of small marine mammals and other threatened forms of wildlife such as turtles. In the early 1990s international pressure persuaded Japan and Taiwan to discontinue drift-net fishing in the Pacific and instead to use dolphin-friendly long-lines and other methods. In 1990, three of the biggest tuna-packing operations in the United States refused to deal in tuna that were caught using methods that might kill or injure dolphins; later, the sale of tuna in the United States was restricted to include only those products caught using dolphin-safe methods. The use of drift nets has declined in many parts of the world, but they are still operated by some nations.

Dolphins, porpoises, and other small whales that inhabit or enter coastal waters are increasingly affected by broad-spectrum pollution and the alteration and destruction of coastal habitats. There is little doubt that the beluga whale populations in the St. Lawrence Estuary of eastern Canada are threatened by high levels of DDT and PCBs (page 184) that have accumulated in their tissues. Some species of river dolphin in tropical-estuarine regions are at critically low levels. Also, the rarest porpoise, the diminutive vaquita, *Phocoena sinus,* is found only in the northern Gulf of California, where there are an estimated 200–500 individuals remaining.

Overfishing

Although global fish yield rose until the mid-1990s, this has been the result of rising production from mariculture (fish and shellfish farming), not higher yields from open-water fisheries. In fact, many stocks of high-value species have been systematically overfished for many years, and stocks are heavily depleted. Anglers have had to switch their attention to lower-value species.

CALIFORNIAN SARDINES AND PERUVIAN ANCHOVY

The California sardine fishery is probably the first well-documented example of the boom-and-bust cycle that seems to characterize intensive marine fisheries. In the 1920s and 1930s, the period of severe economic depression, the sardine fishery appeared to represent an unlimited supply of freely available food and a potential provider of much-needed employment. Money was poured into the fishery with the result that it became overcapitalized. In the 1930s, annual catches peaked at more than 1 million metric tons (1.1 million tons). By the 1940s, 80 purse seiners were operating from the Monterey Bay area, and along Cannery Row there were more than 30 facilities for canning or processing the fish. By this time, too many vessels were chasing too few fish. The crash finally came in 1950: the annual catch plummeted, and the canneries and the sardine fishing fleet that supplied them were forced to shut down by the early 1950s.

Overfishing was seen as the prime cause of the demise of the sardine fishery, but long-term temperature shifts were also implicated. Studies of fish-scale preserving sediments from the Santa Barbara Basin indicate fluctuations in the sizes of sardine and anchovy populations that extend back 1,700 years and appear to be climate related rather than determined by fishing effort. In other words, fish populations fluctuate in size because of natural changes. Fishing effort can exacerbate such changes and result in a catastrophic decline in the fishery.

By the 1970s and 1980s, the Californian sardine fishery was showing some signs of recovery, and sardine fishing began again but with annual catches far below those of the heydays of the 1930s.

With the collapse of the Californian sardine fishery in the early 1950s, the stage was set for the rise of the Peruvian anchovy fishery. By this time, there was a worldwide demand for fish meal and oil. During the 1950s and 1960s, the Peruvian fishery became highly capitalized. After the demise of the Californian sardine fishery, the intention was for the Peruvian anchovy fishery to be the model of successful fishery management. Although these plans took account of fishing effort, they failed to incorporate natural environmental factors that might affect the fish population, a common failing in fishery management programs until recently. The Peruvian anchovy fishery, even more so than the sardine fishery, is dramatically influenced by recurring climatic changes, most notably the El Niño phenomenon (page 69).

When an El Niño event occurs, cold nutrient-rich water no longer wells to the surface off the Peruvian coast, and the anchovy stock stays away from the surface, out of reach of the fishermen. Following the strong El Niño event of 1972–73 and the record catch of 13 million metric tons (about 14 million tons) in 1970, the fishery failed to recover. Intensive fishing continued despite the relatively poor return, and by the early 1980s, catches had plummeted to less than 10 percent of catches from the late 1960s. Fishing effort aside, the species composition of the pelagic fish catch along the South American Pacific coast had also changed, from 90 percent anchovy in the late 1960s to less than 10 percent in the 1980s before rising to about 50 percent in the mid-1990s. Climatic changes are strongly implicated in the speed and strength of the anchovy fishery recovery since the massive decline in the 1970s. In 1992, the Peruvian anchovy catch—at 5.5 million metric tons (about 6 million tons)—represented the biggest single contributor to the world's fish catch.

NORTH SEA HERRING

The North Sea herring has been fished by the Dutch since the 16th century, but British, Norwegian, Icelandic, and German fishermen only turned their attention to this food fish in the 19th and 20th centuries. Although herring fishing became intensive and internationally competitive, fishing methods were relatively inefficient, and sufficient herring escaped capture to ensure recruitment to stocks in later years. In the 1960s, however, drift nets were replaced by more efficient purse-seine nets. A single net could now scoop out an entire shoal of herring. Overfishing

inevitably ensued, and bans on North Sea fishing were introduced. Fishermen now turned their attention to sand eels—the food of many birds and predatory fish. Previously regarded only as bait fish, sand eels were processed into fish meal and fertilizer. Overfishing of sand eels may well have led to reductions in the size of bird and fish populations that depend on them for food.

Rising surface temperatures coupled with lowered nutrient levels (and hence lowered phytoplankton productivity) have also been implicated in the decline and recovery of herring stocks between the 1930s and the present day, but overfishing was certainly responsible for the stock collapse in the 1960s.

NORTHWEST ATLANTIC COD

The Atlantic cod, *Gadus morhua,* and related species—haddock, hake, pollock, and whiting—are groundfish (fish that live near the ocean floor) that have formed an important part of the North Atlantic fish catch for hundreds of years. These fish are caught by trawling a large net on or near the seafloor. Even before the European colonization of the United States, fishermen from western Europe were harvesting the fish populations of the Grand Banks off Newfoundland. Cod formed an important part of the diet for European settlers of Atlantic Canada, Massachusetts, and New England. Before the 19th century, when ice began to be used for preservation, most fish caught far from land were salted and dried to preserve them. They were then soaked in water prior to cooking.

Concerns about the overfishing of Northwest Atlantic groundfish stocks have come and gone since the mid-19th century. In 1964, the International Commission for the Northwest Atlantic Fisheries (ICNAF) concluded that fishing effort was probably exceeding the maximum sustainable level for the fisheries. By the late 1970s, the United States and Canada had gained control of their fisheries within 200 nautical miles (370 km) of their coastline, but despite the exclusion of fishing vessels of other nations, fishing effort was to increase. Governments were encouraging investment in local fishing fleets. Fisheries scientists, on the other hand, were hoping that the fish stocks would be given a reprieve. This did not happen.

By the late 1980s, the cod fisheries of the Northwest Atlantic were showing all the classic symptoms of heavily overfished stocks—increased effort resulting in a decreased catch of smaller fish. By 1992, cod stocks were estimated to be at only 10 percent of their long-term average. In 1992, Canada imposed a moratorium on the Grand Banks fishery although the small portion of the fishery that lies outside Canada's Exclusive Economic Zone (EEZ) is still heavily fished. In 1994 the Georges Bank cod fishery off New

England was also closed. Such closures have created widespread unemployment in the Canadian and U.S. fishing industry and its associated food-processing concerns. In eastern Canada alone, 40,000 fishermen and other workers have been laid off as a result of the fishery closures.

Even with a reduction or cessation in fishing effort, there is no absolute guarantee that the fish stocks will recover because changes in competing fish populations have occurred. In the Northwest Atlantic, groundfish such as cod, haddock, and flounder once formed the dominant stocks. Now, as a result of overfishing, squid, dogfish, and skate have largely replaced them.

Although long-term temperature shifts probably do affect the distribution and successful recruitment of cod stocks in the Northwest Atlantic, it is overfishing that is leveled as being the prime cause of the catastrophic decline in cod numbers on the Grand Banks, Georges Banks, and elsewhere.

Slaughter of pilot whales, Faroe Islands, Denmark (Tony Martin/ENP Images)

TUNA

Tuna is a popular, high-value fish consumed in many parts of the world. Of the six major market species widely distributed in tropical and subtropical waters, skipjack tuna is the most important commercially, and northern bluefin is the least important. However, the west Atlantic population of northern bluefin tuna serves to illustrate many of the problems that beset an open-ocean fishery.

The northern bluefin tuna is a remarkable fish. It weighs up to 1,540 pounds (700 kg) and can swim at up to 56 miles an hour (90 km per hour). It is such a valuable item—a single 496-pound (225 kg) fish was sold for $67,500 in 1992—that it is being heavily overfished, and the West Atlantic stock dropped by an estimated 80 percent between 1970 and 1993. The breeding stock itself (fish of eight years and more) is believed to have declined by 90 percent during that period.

The International Commission for the Conservation of Atlantic Tuna (ICCAT) is responsible for monitoring the fishery and setting limits. It seeks to manage the fishery by a combination of minimum size limits, catch restrictions, and closed areas. Like other international commissions formed by treaty, ICCAT has no enforcement power but must rely on the signatory states themselves to enforce provisions. Herein lies the problem because the treaty states do not agree among themselves on the state of the fishery, what the maximum sustainable yield is, and how this should be allocated. About 20 nations are members of ICCAT, and most of these have citizens that fish for Atlantic tuna in international waters, and not all treaty nations are honest in stating their catch returns. ICCAT claims that if catch rates and size limits set for the mid-1990s were honestly maintained, then the fishery would undergo a recovery within 30 years.

The U.S. National Audubon Society, on the other hand, in 1992 pressed to have the West Atlantic bluefin tuna assigned as an endangered species under the Convention on International Trade in Endangered Species (CITES). If the fishery decline continues, some member-nation governments and environmental groups will undoubtedly press for ICCAT to take a more strident stance.

Fragile Ecosystems in Retreat

Coastal ecosystems and their associated continental shelves comprise less than 10 percent of the total area of the oceans, but they have an importance disproportionate to their size. About one-third of the ocean's productivity occurs on continental shelves: the bulk of the world's marine catch is taken there, and coral reefs, the ocean's most biodiverse communities, are congregated there. At the same time, of marine ecosystems, it is coastal environments and inshore waters that are most threatened by human activities. On a global scale, among the most threatened of these environments are estuaries in general (page 22) and salt marshes (page 24), sea grass meadows, and kelp forests (page 114) in particular. In warmer waters, mangroves (page 110) and coral reefs (page 112) are witnessing some of the most devastating losses, and these two habitats have been surveyed on a wide scale in recent years. Satellite imagery has helped in assessing the extent and health of these two coastal ecosystems.

Mangroves

Mangrove communities were once found to cover more than half of tropical and subtropical coastlines. Current estimates suggest that about 50 percent of the world's mangrove cover has been lost in the last few centuries. Mangrove removal is widespread across the world, and 70 percent or more of the original mangrove cover has been removed in extensive regions of Southeast Asia, Africa, and the Caribbean. A wide variety of human activities contribute to the removal of mangroves or cause damage to their habitat. Mangroves are cleared to provide land for agriculture, industry, and urban communities. The trees are sometimes overharvested simply to provide timber or fuel. In parts of Asia and in South and Central America, mangroves have been removed to create coastal ponds for mariculture. Pollution from heavy metals, chlorinated hydrocarbons, PCBs, and untreated sewage is widespread, particularly in developing regions of Africa, the Caribbean, and the Indian subcontinent and bordering coastal regions. Oil pollution severely affects mangroves in parts of the Middle East and the Caribbean. Damming of rivers alters the flow regime of coastal waters and changes salinities, thereby affecting those mangrove communities that are adapted to brackish water.

Mangrove communities are important because—growing partly above and partly below the water—they support a terrestrial (land-based) biological community as well as an aquatic one. Their aquatic communities are not among the most diverse in the marine world (globally, an estimated 400 fish species depend on mangrove communities). Nevertheless, in terms of their turnover per unit area, mangrove communities are among the world's most productive ecosystems. They also form the nursery grounds for many commercially important species—fish, shellfish, shrimp, and prawn. Networks of mangrove roots help trap and bind coastal sediments. Where mangroves are removed, coasts are more liable to erosion.

International environmental agencies have long realized the economic, cultural, and environmental importance of mangrove communities. Many developing countries are also realizing this. Unfortunately, despite the implementation of programs to encourage the sustainable harvesting of mangroves and their replanting in areas from which they have been removed, the loss of mangroves still outstrips their replacement.

Snappers in mangroves at high tide, the Bahamas (Jeremy Stafford-Deitsch)

*A native fish trap on coral reef,
Lesser Antilles, Caribbean
(Brandon D. Cole/ENP Images)*

Coral Reefs

Coral reefs thrive only in warm, clear, shallow, saline water. As such, coral reefs are particularly susceptible to disturbance by human activities. An assessment made in 1992 estimated that 5 to 10 percent of the world's coral reefs had been destroyed within the last century.

Coral reefs are the most biodiverse marine communities humans have studied: perhaps one-quarter of all marine species and one-fifth of sea fish species live there. Coral reefs are also important economically. Roughly 20 to 25 percent of the fish catch from developing countries is taken from coral reefs and their immediate surroundings. Coral reefs are ranked—by most people who have seen them—as the most stunning underwater creations the sea has to offer and as such attract millions of tourists each year.

The human activities that degrade coral reef systems are, like those affecting mangrove communities, many and varied. Overfishing has severely depleted stocks of commercially important reef fish in an estimated 80 countries. Sometimes very destructive fishing methods are used: dynamiting (which also provides coral fragments that can be sold as ornaments or used for building materials) and cyanide poisoning (used to stun fish for the aquarium market). Coastal building developments, whether industrial, urban, or those catering to tourists, are all potential threats to local or even distant coral reefs. Land-use changes affect the water runoff from coastal lands in terms of its nature, amount, and quality. Coral reefs are very susceptible to smothering by sediments and to die-off caused by exposure to water of low salinity. Coral reefs are also very sensitive to many forms of pollution, ranging from persistent chemicals to sewage (page 181) and even thermal pollution. Reef-building corals thrive in those waters that are near the upper limit of the coral's temperature tolerance. Slight rises in water temperature (of the order of 1–2°C) can be sufficient to cause coral die-off. Between 1983 and 1991, incidences of coral bleaching (where corals eject their symbiotic green algae and die as a result) were recorded across all oceans during 1983, 1987, and 1991. These incidences were correlated with water temperature rises of 1°C or more. Global warming, in concert with other factors, may be one of the greatest short- to medium-term threats to our coral reefs.

As part of a campaign to generate interest and raise support for a global reef-monitoring program, 1997 was designated International Year of the Reef. A global survey called Reef Check—conducted by 750 volunteer divers and 100 marine biologists in the summer of 1997—estimated that more than 90 percent of the world's coral reefs had been visually damaged by local activities: overfishing, poisoning, dynamiting, pollution, or ships' anchors. Many of the world's marine protected areas (MPAs) contain coral reef systems (page 200).

Seafloor Communities

Arguably, we know less about the deep ocean floor than any other habitat on Earth. Even the seafloor communities on continental shelves are rarely sampled systematically and monitored over long periods of time. We know little about the effect that commercial trawling (involving a large, bag-shaped fishing net being dragged along or near the seafloor) has on the community of bottom-living organisms, other than that it can be highly disruptive. Undoubtedly, the delicate burrows of many worms and mollusks are damaged, many organisms are probably crushed or dislodged by the passing net, and sediments will be raised that might smother organisms. Which creatures are worst affected and how quickly the community recovers are the subjects of ongoing research.

Who Owns the Sea and Its Resources?

The oceans have, for thousands of years, represented a huge environment open to any nation with the might, money, and expertise to exploit it. The oceans also form an avenue for transport and communication: indeed, for many nations, waging war involves the extension of military power over stretches of ocean. The oceans are also, of course, vast reservoirs of living and non-living resources. In the last hundred years or so, developed nations have become much more expert at exploiting these resources, although often in a manner that is unsustainable and damaging to the natural environment.

In the early 17th century, the Portuguese and later the Spanish proclaimed vast areas of the high seas as part of their territorial domain. In response to these developments, Huigh de Groot (Hugo Grotius), a Dutch statesman, established the concept of freedom of the seas in his work, *Mare Liberum,* published in 1609: in effect, the oceans were to be deemed an open resource, with free access to all, and could not be appropriated by any one nation. This view suited the purposes of many European states at the time because they wanted free access to explore and expand trade with other parts of the globe, in particular the Far East. During the 17th century, another principle developed alongside the notion of freedom of the seas: a narrow strip of sea alongside the coast was considered as part of the bordering state. In practice, this coastal zone of territorial water was about 3 nautical miles wide—a width that could be protected by cannonfire from land.

These two traditions—freedom of the high seas combined with national jurisdiction over territorial water—remained more or less unchanged until the 20th century. By the middle of this century, various fishing agreements and national claims had begun to erode the freedom-of-the-seas principle. There was a trend toward nation-states attempting to claim wider and wider stretches of territorial water in order to control the exploitation of resources in offshore waters.

The United Nations Conference on the Law of the Sea

In both 1958 and 1960, conferences were convened in an attempt to develop a comprehensive formula for access to, and management of, the world's oceans. These First and Second U.N. Conferences on the Law of the Sea (UNCLOS I and II) failed to resolve many of the problems and disputes of the time. By the 1960s, it was becoming clear that some of the more developed nations were using their economic and technological superiority to exploit open-ocean resources in a way that poorer nations could not possibly match or prevent. Indeed, factory ships from larger nations could fish within a few miles of smaller nations' coasts with impunity. Stronger nations with open coastlines could extend their territorial waters to 12 or even 200 nautical miles from land, but weaker nations in congested parts of the world were left with the traditional 3-mile zone. With the realization that the deep seafloor contained considerable wealth in the form of oil and gas deposits and manganese nodules, less-developed countries were concerned that they might be denied any access to these resources.

By the mid-1960s, a groundswell of opinion in international circles began to see the open oceans (and certainly their deep seabeds) as the common heritage of humankind. The oceans, it was argued, should be managed by an international body such as the United Nations. A more equitable means of establishing the extent of territorial water was also needed. Between 1973 and 1982 the many meetings and protracted negotiations of UNCLOS III finally led to the signing of the United Nations Convention of the Law of the Sea (UNCLOS). Of the 151 delegations attending, 130 supported the new treaty, 4 voted against, and 17 abstained. This was a great achievement, marred by the fact that some of the more developed nation-states were among both those who opposed the treaty (Israel, Turkey, the

United States, and Venezuela) and those who abstained (including Belgium, Italy, the Netherlands, the former Soviet Union, the United Kingdom, and West Germany). The primary objection of many of these parties concerned the exploitation of resources on deep seabeds—designated by UNCLOS as The Area.

The treaty was ratified by the 60th nation in November 1994 and became international law in 1995. Several of the objecting or abstaining nations have since signed, following further negotiations on exploitation of deep-water sites. Even those who have yet to sign or ratify the treaty have been guided by it in making territorial claims and in the way they are conducting themselves on the international scene.

The convention includes these provisions:

1. *Coastal states jurisdiction.* Coastal nations are entitled to claim up to four main zones:

- A **territorial sea** that extends up to 12 nautical miles from the shore. The coastal state has complete authority over this zone, including the air space above it and the seabed below it, although foreign vessels are entitled to right of innocent passage through this zone. Innocent passage is deemed to be that which is not prejudicial to "the peace, good order, and security of the coastal state."

- A **contiguous zone** that lies beyond the territorial sea and extends up to 24 nautical miles from the shore. The coastal state may exercise control over this zone to prevent infringement of its customs and excise, fiscal, immigration, and sanitary laws.

- An **exclusive economic zone** that extends up to 200 nautical miles from the shore (see below)

- A **continental-shelf zone** where the continental shelf extends beyond the 200-nautical-mile zone. This zone may extend along the seabed (but *not* the overlying water) up to a further 150 nautical miles (see following)

2. *Free passage.* Unimpeded free passage—on and below the water—is guaranteed on the high seas, within territorial seas (with the provisos above), and through straits used for international navigation. These provisions have great significance for international trade and the strategic maintenance of peace.

3. *Deep seabeds designated The Area.* The waters of 60 percent of the oceans area are the traditional commons with freedom of access and exploitation. But 42 percent of the seafloor in this area is designated "the common heritage of (hu)mankind," and its use will be controlled by the International Seabed Authority (ISA) under the auspices of the United Nations. This provision, which caused many industrialized nations to oppose ratification, has been modified following recent negotiations. This change has encouraged some of the nations with deep-sea mining capability to sign the treaty.

4. *Arbitration of disputes.* A recently formed United Nations Law of the Sea tribunal will carry out this function.

Exclusive Economic Zones and Continental-Shelf Zones

The exclusive economic zone (EEZ) was a concept seized upon by many countries at an early stage in UNCLOS III negotiations. It allows

Maritime claims that can be considered under UNCLOS

maritime nations to control all commercial activity—including the exploitation of living and nonliving resources of the waters and seabed—extending to a distance of 200 nautical miles from the coast (notionally taken to be to the edge of the continental shelf). Within the EEZ, the coastal nation has the right to generate power from waves or tides, can establish artificial islands, and has functional control over scientific research and environmental protection. Nations, in fact, are expected to legislate and act to prevent and control pollution in these waters.

Interestingly, there is provision for an extension of a coastal state's claim in cases where the continental shelf extends beyond 200 nautical miles from the coast. The coastal state may claim the continental shelf up to 150 nautical miles beyond the 200-mile limit, but only in terms of the seabed, *not* the overlying water. On the shelf beyond 200 nautical miles, the state has the sole right to control resources on the seabed, whether living ones, such as crabs, or nonliving ones, such as oil reserves. Nations with continental shelves extending beyond 200 nautical miles include Australia, Brazil, Canada, and the United States.

Boundary Agreements

There are clearly many situations where claims from neighboring states overlap, such as when two countries face one another across a narrow sea and so have to share an EEZ. In practice, a boundary line midway between the two coasts is usually agreed. In cases of difficulty, the International Court of Justice or another arbitrating body may decide the boundary. Many important

boundaries such as that between France and the United Kingdom in the English Channel and between Canada and the United States in the Gulf of Maine have been agreed.

Consequences and Exceptions

One consequence of the treaty is that nations owning tiny islands can now claim large areas of the surrounding waters and seabed, together with the living and nonliving resources found there. The Republic of Kiribati—a group of tiny Pacific islands with a total area of just 280 square miles (725 km^2)—has an EEZ of 1.3 million square miles (3.4 million km^2) and grants fishing licenses to other countries to use its waters. The United States can claim an EEZ around the Hawaiian Islands, and Britain around the Falkland Islands. In some cases, this has led to a heightening of international disagreement. For example, several nations claim the Paracel Islands and Spratly Islands in the South China Sea—a general area that contains extensive oil and gas deposits. Special arrangements have also been made for some nations that comprise archipelagos or widely scattered islands. Claims are measured from straight lines drawn between their outermost islands. This has been advantageous for archipelagic countries such as Indonesia and Fiji.

One continent lies outside the territorial provisions of UNCLOS. Antarctica comes under the jurisdiction of the Antarctic Treaty (page 203).

UNCLOS is certainly not an ideal solution to the problems of managing the oceans, but despite the treaty's flaws, our oceans are much better off with it than without it.

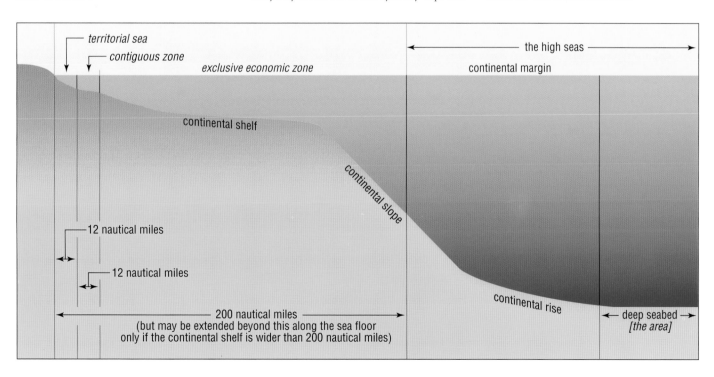

territorial sea
contiguous zone
exclusive economic zone
the high seas
continental margin
continental shelf
continental slope
12 nautical miles
12 nautical miles
continental rise
deep seabed
[the area]
200 nautical miles
(but may be extended beyond this along the sea floor only if the continental shelf is wider than 200 nautical miles)

Managing Marine Pollution

Marine pollution cannot be neatly separated from land-based, freshwater, or air pollution because pollutants from all these environments can and do find their way into the sea. Marine pollution issues do not have clear-cut boundaries. In fact, one way or another, it is activities on land that largely determine the quality of seawater nearby (page 176).

Assuming that the global human population will continue to increase and that it will probably double by about the year 2100, where will all the waste produced by people be put? In the developed world, each person currently generates, on average, about 2.2 tons (about 2 t) of domestic waste every year. This is waste of all kinds, not just sewage, but paper, card, plastic packaging, glass jars, tin cans, and so on. Added to this are the products of industrial and agricultural processes: the tailings from mining, the fly ash from coal-burning power stations, the pesticides, and the fertilizers from farming. Then there are gaseous pollutants that enter the air from all kinds of activities: fumes from motor vehicles, chimney discharges from power stations, even methane from cows! Some of these gaseous wastes are threatening the biosphere by being greenhouse gases that are implicated in global warming (page 78). Among the pollutants that find their way into aquatic systems are heavy metals and synthetic chemicals such as PCBs that are not just persistent, but become concentrated in food chains (page 84).

If we take domestic waste alone, then production per person will increase massively as developing countries become more developed. At present, there is an eightfold disparity in the amount of waste per person produced by those in developing and those in developed countries. We need to do something if, as populations increase and standards of living in the developing world rise, the world is not to become swamped in domestic and industrial waste.

The most obvious answer is to reduce the amount of waste we produce. We can do this to some extent by recycling materials and being much less indulgent in the amount of packaging we require. We can adopt a greener lifestyle if we readjust our priorities. There is, however, a limit to this: on a per-person basis, we will still produce a similar amount of sewage, and the total amount will inevitably increase as populations grow. Sewage sludge (the solid material from sewage processing) will need to be disposed of or recycled somewhere, and in many developed

countries today, about two-thirds of domestic refuse is simply buried in the ground in landfill sites. This poses risks of contamination of groundwater and the buildup of gases such as methane from decomposition belowground. Solutions may be found to these problems, but land is expensive and in demand for other purposes. At the end of the day, the choice to use the deep oceans as a dumping ground for all manner of waste may well prove irresistible (see below).

International Legislation

International law is moving toward banning almost all forms of waste disposal in the ocean. Various conventions create rules of international law that are binding on the states who ratify them once the law comes into force. In practice, these conventions set out an international code of conduct, but it is left to the nations themselves to enforce its terms through national legislation backed up by regulatory and enforcement agencies. There is considerable variation in the degree of rigor with which the terms of a treaty are enforced. Intergovernmental organizations such as the International Maritime Organization (IMO)—in this case armed with responsibility for overseeing marine pollution from vessels—promotes codes of practice and makes recommendations for member states to use as a basis for national legislation.

There are several international treaties that regulate the dumping of wastes at sea, the most important of which is the 1972 Convention on the Prevention of Marine Pollution by Dumping of Wastes and Other Matter (more conveniently known as the London Dumping Convention). In 1995, 69 countries were contracting states to this agreement, and these states agree to control waste dumping principally through national legislation and regulation, being guided by international standards.

Another important treaty, in this case focused largely on oil pollution, is the 1973 International Convention for the Prevention of Pollution from Ships (commonly abbreviated to MARPOL). This treaty and its amendments came into force in 1983 and has since been supplemented by provisions against the dumping of plastic at sea.

How well do these treaties work? Not very well as yet. An assessment by the U.S. General Accounting Office in 1991 determined that only

about 60 percent of the states that were party to the 1972 London Dumping Convention conformed with reporting regulations, while only 30 percent of the members of the MARPOL convention complied. There are signs of improvement since that time, and further legislation such as UNCLOS (page 194) seeks to reaffirm the international commitment to pollution control.

The United Nations Environment Program (UNEP) has, since the early 1970s, taken a lead in tackling marine pollution. Through its Regional Seas Program, it is highlighting the worst-affected areas and is seeking to bring states together to promote measures to protect the marine environment.

Closed Seas

In general, it is coastal waters that are the worst-affected by pollution, and away from the coast, it is in enclosed seas where the impact is the most heightened. The classic example of a heavily polluted, nearly enclosed sea is the Mediterranean (page 16).

In fact, the Mediterranean is not one sea but a complex of several seas. To the west, they are linked to the Atlantic by the Straits of Gibraltar, and to the east they connect to the Black Sea via the Sea of Marmara and the Bosphorus and the Dardanelles. To the south, the 19th-century construction, the Suez Canal, connects the Mediterranean to the Red Sea. More water enters the Mediterranean (from the Atlantic through the Straits of Gibraltar) than leaves. So, the turnover of ocean water within the Mediterranean is low; any contaminants that enter tend to remain there. Pollutants of all kinds—untreated sewage, agricultural fertilizers, heavy metals, pesticides, and so on—enter via rivers or, in some cases, are discharged directly into the sea. Also, at least 24 countries have territories bordering the sea, and they reflect many shades of political opinion and levels of economic development, including industrialized European nations to the north, developing countries of North Africa to the south, and socialist or former socialist countries to the east.

Representatives from 17th countries met at the Barcelona Convention in 1976 and began to address the Mediterranean's pollution problems. By 1985, a Mediterranean Action Plan (MAP) had been decided that aimed to reduce pollution from land, sea, and air; protect endangered

INTERGOVERNMENTAL ORGANIZATIONS

Intergovernmental organizations (IGOs) are set up and funded by governments across the world. They include the International Council for the Exploration of the Sea (ICES), the International Whaling Commission (IWC), and United Nations agencies, such as the International Maritime Organization (IMO) and the United Nations Development Program (UNDP). One of the most important functions of IGOs is in fostering and coordinating environmental monitoring activities.

The ozone hole over Antarctica was discovered by luck, not by design. Scientists studying atmospheric circulation by satellite and from the ground stumbled across CFC-driven ozone thinning, a phenomenon that had nevertheless been predicted. What other important environmental changes are taking place for which we do not have adequate records?

Programs to monitor the environment are not glamorous: they are long-term studies that do not offer a quick return on investment and are, at present, unlikely to offer scientists a quick route up the academic hierarchy. Nevertheless, such studies are vital. IGOs have the funding and the long-term commitment to coordinate such programs. Only by studying the environment for long periods can natural fluctuations be distinguished from human-induced changes.

International cooperation in questions of methods and standards is imperative if findings from one study are to be compared directly with those from another. Much progress is needed in agreeing and instituting common standards of practice. Organizations such as the United Nations Environment Program (UNEP) are spearheading such moves.

The work of IGOs is brought to a focus at international conferences. Perhaps the most important—certainly the largest—in recent years was the United Nations Conference on Environment and Development (UNCED) held in Rio de Janeiro in 1992. Two treaties—binding on ratifying parties—were finalized at the conference and have since entered into force. The Framework Convention on Climate Change (FCCC) seeks to stabilize atmospheric levels of greenhouse gases. This is to be done within a time frame that will prevent "dangerous anthropogenic [human-induced] interferences with the climate system." It also requires industrialized countries to devise and submit their plans to bring emissions of these gases to "earlier levels" by the year 2000. The Convention on Biological Diversity obliges states to develop plans for protecting habitats and their resident species. Together, these treaties seek to tackle two of the most important environmental issues that face us today—habitat loss and global warming.

---

species; establish marine protected areas; and require environmental impact reports on all major new developments. Progress to translate words into action has been relatively slow since then. Fred Pearce, a science journalist, writing in the *New Scientist*, concluded that 10 of the major objectives for MAP that were set for achievement by 1995 had not been achieved. In 1994, more than 1,000 Mediterranean dolphins were reportedly killed by a distemperlike virus; also, red tides are a repeated occurrence in the Aegean (page 89). Pollution is considered as one of the causative factors in these outbreaks. In the summer tourist season, 230 million people are found on or close to Mediterranean coasts, and each year 440 million tons (more than 400 million metric tons) of raw sewage are discharged into the sea. Coordinated action is needed, but too often, seaside resorts only take steps to reduce sewage discharge when there is an obvious visual impact or a public-health problem that disrupts local tourism.

The Deep Ocean

About half of the world's ocean area is water with a depth of 10,000 feet (3,000 m) or more. In comparison to almost any other habitat on Earth, this deep water is barely utilized by humans for any purpose. We do not catch fish commercially from these depths, nor do we use it as a supply of other resources—at least not yet. This deep water is part of a slow vertical circulation that rises and descends in polar or subpolar regions and at other upwellings and downwellings at specific locations in the world's oceans (page 66). Typically, this water takes 200 or 300 years to travel from the center of a deep ocean to an upwelling, and so any contaminants have plenty of time of disperse, be degraded, or otherwise be removed from the water column. Could this deep water be used as a dumping ground for some of our waste? The answer is probably yes *and* no.

Yes, in theory, the deep ocean seems like a good repository for various kinds of waste. There is a very active scavenging community on the deep seafloor (page 93), so sewage waste—if it could be delivered to the ocean floor somehow and in moderation—would probably be degraded by the larger detritus feeders and bacteria. Heavy metals deposited on the ocean floor in some temperate regions would be rapidly covered or chemically scavenged by a continuous rainfall of sediment that would then incorporate the metals in buried seafloor deposits. Arguably, even certain kinds of radioactive waste could be disposed of on the deep ocean floor if sufficient care is given to their placement and incarceration: They should not be placed near tectonically active areas such as active trenches or seafloor-spreading zones. In any case, the conservation of networks of hydrothermal vent and cold seep communities is an important consideration.

However, all these ideas are subject to testing. It is vital that these options are subjected to proper scientific evaluation and experimental testing *before* socioeconomic pressures to use the deep oceans for waste disposal become overwhelming.

Managing Fisheries

The global yield of fish and shellfish may well have stabilized (page 186), but if so, this is because the yield from mariculture (page 166) is increasing. Many marine fisheries—particularly those in the North Atlantic—are declining or are already heavily depleted as a result of overfishing (page 187). What can be done to prevent this from happening in the future, and what can be done to enable depleted stocks to recover?

We have already seen that, left to their own devices, fishermen will almost invariably overfish a resource unless they are regulated in some way. At the end of the day, short-term economic arguments seem to win over long-term biological ones. This short-sighted view is certainly not in the best long-term interests of the fishery or its fishermen—but market-place economics invariably press for the exploitation of an open-access natural resource until it is exhausted and a sound economic return is no longer achievable.

There are four main reasons why today's fish stocks have become overexploited: first, the fishery may be open access, without any restrictions to prevent overfishing; second, restrictions may be in force, but fishermen—at least some of them—ignore restrictions, and because the fishery is not properly policed, the fishermen get away with breaking the rules; third, there may be lack of scientific information on which to base a sound fishery-management policy, or else the fishery-management model being used may be based on incorrect assumptions; fourth, even if there is good scientific data to form the basis for a sound fishery policy, data or recommendations may be ignored or "interpreted" by regulatory authorities in such a way as to threaten the long-term survival of the fishery. In practice, two or three of the above problems often apply at one and the same time.

Traditional Fisheries Models

Traditional management of fisheries was based on so-called stock/recruitment models. *Stock* refers to the number of adult fish in the population; *recruitment* refers to the number of young fish entering the adult population in a year. According to traditional stock/recruitment theories, the recruitment to a population is dependent on the number of eggs produced and the subsequent survival of hatchlings to adulthood. The total number of eggs produced is proportional to the size of the adult population, and rates of survival to adulthood are regarded as more or less con-

stant. Seen in this way, the volume and nature of fishing effort is regarded as the main way in which the size of the adult population can be regulated. More fishing will decrease the size of the adult population (and so reduce recruitment), while reducing fishing pressure will enable the adult population to increase in size and so encourage recruitment. In turn, fishing pressure can be regulated by controlling factors such as the total number of boats or fishermen, the size and type of fishing gear, and the total allowable catch from the fishery.

These traditional approaches (used for the best part of a century) beg many questions. In a moderately exploited fish population, is fishing pressure the prime factor affecting adult population size and, in turn, recruitment? Is mortality (from factors other than fishing) constant from year to year? We now know that many environmental factors *do* cause the reproductive success, survival, and growth of members of a fish population to vary from year to year. For example, herring populations in the North Atlantic and sardine and anchovy populations in the eastern Pacific undergo natural fluctuations in population size that result from long-term climatic changes (page 190). Also, changes among populations of competitors or prey may alter the exploited population's reproductive success, larval survival, and hence productivity.

Management Methods

Bearing in mind that factors other than fishing pressure may strongly influence a fish population's productivity, it makes sense in calculating sustainable yields to err on the side of caution, but, as we have seen, because of short-term economic pressures, what is desirable is not necessarily what actually occurs.

Assuming a sound fishery-management policy (based on scientific data and fishery models that take into account environmental fluctuations and competing species), then there are many ways to manage a fishery.

With the implementation of UNCLOS (page 194), nations now have the legal right to manage their own fisheries within their 200-mile (370-km) Exclusive Economic Zone (EEZ). In fact, more than 90 percent of the world's marine fish catch comes from within EEZs. A nation can control access to its EEZ, keeping out foreign vessels or allowing them access under a license system. Vessels fishing without permission or

using illegal gear can be impounded—providing they can be caught.

Once agreement is reached on the type and amount of catch that is sustainable, then limits of various kinds can be set. The size and number of vessels can be restricted, the length of the fishing season shortened, types of gear specified, and catch limits set for each boat. Limits can be set on the size of fish (to prevent undersize fish being retained) and even, in some cases, to prevent females being taken (providing sexes can be readily distinguished).

Two innovative approaches to fisheries management are gaining ground in some parts of the world. New Zealand has pioneered the use of the individual transferable quota (ITQ) system. The size of a fish stock is assessed annually by fisheries scientists, and a total allowable catch (TAC) is determined for the season for that species. Fishermen can purchase or trade an ITQ—a percentage of that year's TAC—and this quota of fish is then regarded as their private property. They are then left to catch this quota in the most cost-effective way they can (providing they do not contravene other regulations).

This system has several benefits. The fishermen can plan ahead for the season, knowing what their allowable catch will be. The system is much less competitive than the free-for-all, winner-take-all system of traditional fisheries management. Because the fishermen have paid for their quota in advance, they have a vested interest in ensuring that other fishermen do not undermine the system and that they themselves are not caught doing so. Lastly, the system is closely tied to biological assessments of stock levels; this approach has proved a means of gradually reducing the fishing effort on a stock.

Unfortunately, fishermen do not just catch the fish for which they have a quota, but they also have an incidental catch of other fish. The problem is that they ditch these fish at sea or they dump the smaller, less-valuable fish of their allowable catch. They concentrate on returning to port with only the larger fish within their quota. This dumping of by-catch (most of which dies) is wasteful, and means are being sought to regulate it. But overall the system is sufficiently successful as to encourage Australia, Canada, Iceland, and the United States to begin to adopt similar schemes.

Another pioneering approach is the "no-take" zone. Researchers in various parts of the world—Florida and the Caribbean, the Philippines, New Zealand, and East Africa—have been experimenting with no-take marine areas. The argument is this: by banning *all* fishing within a particular zone, the area becomes a refuge in which fish can grow to a large size. Larger fish produce many more eggs than smaller individuals, and so they provide a source of fish fry for recruitment to the wider population. Assuming fish of commercially important species do breed in the no-take zone, at least some of the larvae that hatch from their eggs will leave the zone and supplement populations in adjacent areas where fishing is allowed. Does this idea work in practice? It seems to, although much further research work is required. Evidence from southern Kenya shows that when no-take zones were established in an overexploited fishery, although the fishermen now had a reduced area in which to catch fish, their catches improved. It remains to see how well this experience will export to other parts of the world. However, the notion of keeping some areas unfished is a highly attractive one, even if just to provide a safeguard against the total collapse of a nearby fishery or to allow a fishery to recover (page 190). The broader conservation issues (page 200) and the maintenance of genetic diversity are also important arguments in favor of the no-take-zone approach (page 178).

The Future

Schools of fish are often associated with fronts (near-vertical boundaries between two water masses), localized regions of high productivity or specific temperature regimes. Such oceanographic features are detectable by satellite sensory arrays (page 156). The use of sensitive sonar equipment, real-time oceanographic data from satellite remote sensing, and high-tech navigational methods such as the Global Positioning System (GPS) have enabled fishermen to locate fish populations precisely and then use sophisticated fishing gear to remove them with almost surgical precision. On the other hand, new technology also provides ways of monitoring a fishing boat's activities and is a means of enforcing fishery regulations. A boat's position and speed can be monitored by a combination of GPS records and satellite remote sensing. Some kinds of violation, such as fishing at the wrong time or in the wrong place (vessels travel much slower when pulling a net) can be ascertained. Fishing effort can be more precisely regulated, and such methods would provide an invaluable adjunct to traditional methods of inspection. The European Union, for one, has agreed to use satellites to monitor illegal fishing from June 1998 onward.

NONGOVERNMENTAL ORGANIZATIONS

Nongovernmental organizations (NGOs) are organizations—often of a charitable, research, or educational nature—that, as their name implies, do not represent governments, nor are they normally funded directly by governments, although they may receive funding via research agencies or education-funding bodies, which themselves receive government-allocated monies. However, with a few exceptions, they operate independent of governments. Most NGOs raise much of their money from public sources.

Strictly speaking, to be called an NGO, the organization needs to be accorded official status by the United Nations (U.N.). This enables the organization to attend certain meetings of U.N. bodies and act as observers or participate in a consultative capacity. Increasingly, NGOs channel information and views to U.N. committees.

Currently, there are many more than 5,000 international NGOs. Among those NGOs concerned with marine environmental issues are the Cousteau Society, Friends of the Earth, Greenpeace, the Sierra Club, the World Conservation Union (IUCN), and the World Wide Fund for Nature (WWF). They vary enormously in size and in the breadth of their activities. Some have close working relationships with governments and international agencies; the IUCN, for example, is unusual among NGOs in that it coordinates contributions from numerous other NGOs and numbers more than 70 states and nearly 100 government agencies among its members. Both the IUCN and the WWF receive some funding from governments and aid agencies for specified projects. In many cases, the work of NGOs is nonconfrontational and seeks to inform the wider debate on environmental and development issues. On the other hand, some NGOs, such as Greenpeace, are extremely independent and are prepared to take a strong, confrontational stance in their dealings with governments and multinational companies.

The recent activities of two rather different environmental groups serve to give a flavor of how NGOs operate.

One of WWF's greatest successes has been in its efforts to halt the trade in endangered species by working with the IUCN to foster national and international legislation and through TRAFFIC (the wildlife trade monitoring program of WWF and IUCN).

At the beginning of 1998, the WWF raised public awareness about 1998 as the United Nations Year of the Oceans. The fund worked to establish marine protected areas off Kenya, Mozambique, and Tanzania to offer greater security to the remaining but depleted populations of dugongs. The WWF was one of several organizations that called for no-fishing areas to be set aside in the North Sea, promoted the use of food labels that indicated whether fish products were obtained from sustainable stocks, and campaigned for the introduction of international legislation to conserve depleted stocks of sharks.

Greenpeace campaigns are often uncompromising, and their nonviolent, direct-action protests have claimed a number of spectacular successes over the years. In June 1995, Shell UK towed its defunct oil platform, *Brent Spa*, around the north coast of Scotland with the intention of scuttling the structure just off the continental shelf. Greenpeace intervened, boarded the oil platform, and publicized to the world what Shell UK was planning to do. Had Shell UK succeeded with the dumping, it would have set a historic precedent and encouraged others to follow suit, using deep water as a suitable dump site for other giant scrap objects.

Greenpeace's publicity campaign, though marred by some statements containing scientific inaccuracies, was nevertheless highly successful. It resulted in Shell UK abandoning the dumping attempt and then asking for proposals from industry as to how to dispose of the structure. The platform, meanwhile, was towed to Erfjord, Norway. Shell received a range of imaginative proposals, from converting the platform to a wind- and wave-driven power plant to using it as a harbor gate. All but one idea involved either keeping the bulk of the structure but using it for another purpose, or cutting up the oil platform and recycling its parts. These options are considerably more expensive than the original dumping plan but are probably less harmful to the environment. They certainly make use of an otherwise wasted resource.

Marine Conservation

Marine conservation does not necessarily mean the maintenance of habitats in a pristine state, apparently untouched by human existence. It does mean making the maintenance of habitats and their communities of organisms a high priority alongside other activities such as tourism and fishing. Worldwide, initiatives are under way to help conserve the marine environment.

Marine Protected Areas

About 1,300 marine and estuarine sites around the world have been designated as marine protected areas (MPAs). Many of these are very small, and the degree of protection sought—and actually achieved—varies considerably from one MPA to another. Specific MPAs usually have titles that incorporate the term *park, sanctuary,* or

reserve plus a place or habitat name. A site may be protected for a variety of reasons: as a site of outstanding natural beauty; because of historic or cultural associations, perhaps because it houses a shipwreck; because it encompasses a habitat especially worthy of protection as it is an outstanding example of its type or endangered species are to be found there. Some MPAs are created with the intention of improving local fisheries (page 198). Many MPAs are actively employed for educational and scientific purposes. Shiprock Aquatic Reserve, near Sydney, Australia, at 7.5 acres (3 ha) is probably the world's smallest MPA; the Great Barrier Reef Park, also in Australia, at 87 million acres (35 million ha) is undoubtedly the largest.

The designation *marine protected area* suggests that a site is safeguarded against a wide range of activities that might be prejudicial to the habitat and its wildlife. In fact, many MPAs receive very

An aerial view of Heron Island, Great Barrier Reef Marine Park, Queensland, Australia (Gerry Ellis/ENP Images)

little protection, and even among those that do, the protection may be very selective and ban only heavy industrial activities such as mining and oil exploration while still allowing many commercial and recreational activities that could be harmful. Some of the MPAs associated with the Florida Keys have, since the 1970s, been severely affected by increased sediments and sewage discharges from nearby land-based residential developments. These have degraded the quality of some of the previously lush coral reefs.

Increased leisure and commercial fishing has also depleted the stocks of fish and lobster. There are moves throughout the United States to tighten controls on its MPAs and to designate new ones. For example, an MPA much larger than about 3 million acres (1 million ha) in size was established in 1992, incorporating Monterey Bay and the adjacent central California coast.

The Great Barrier Reef Marine Park stands as one of the better managed and longer-standing models of MPA. Even here, however, some areas of coral and its associated animal community have been badly damaged or depleted by tourism and fishing.

Within its boundaries, 75–85 percent of the park is designated for "general use" (including many leisure activities, regulated fishing, but very restricted industrial usage); 14–24 percent of the area is for "nonexploitative activities" (underwater observation, photography, and the like); and about 1 percent is for "reference and research purposes" from which the general public is excluded. Other areas are closed seasonally to protect turtle- and seabird-breeding areas, and some locations are periodically closed, sometimes on a rotational basis, for "appreciation" or "replenishment." The park hosts a staggering variety of reef habitats, including fringe reefs, inshore and offshore sandy areas, as well as the expected barrier-reef assemblages. The park joined the World Heritage List in 1981.

In the United Nations International Year of the Oceans in 1998, the establishment of a coordinated network of MPAs was one of the outcomes the U.N. and other agencies pressed for. Many MPAs are too small (about half are less than 2,470 acres [1,000 ha] in area) to incorporate the feeding, breeding, and nursery areas of many of the species they contain. Either the MPAs need to be larger, or they need to form an interconnected network of smaller MPAs that encompass specific areas crucial for different stages of life cycles.

Bioregional Management

There is growing recognition that many of the problems besetting the conservation of marine ecosystems cannot be tackled on a purely local level but require management on a much wider scale. By the 1980s, UNEP Regional Seas agreements such as the Mediterranean Action Plan (pages 17) and the Caribbean Environment Program (page 15) sought to coordinate the activities of many countries in tackling pollution, coastal development, and other environmental issues within a region. The fact that these initiatives have achieved only moderate success shows how difficult progress can be using this approach.

However, such initiatives are vital if the quality of the marine environment within semienclosed seas is to improve, not worsen. But progress is slow. The encouraging news is that implacable political enemies can and do meet, discuss, and work together toward solutions for shared environmental problems.

Environmental Treaties

International agreements provide a means of limiting those activities that might have a detrimental effect on the marine environment; whether by pollution, habitat loss, or direct exploitation of living resources. Dozens of environmental treaties directly concern the marine environment, and of the nearly 200 environmental treaties to date, many affect the marine environment indirectly.

Environmental treaties may not actually achieve anything tangible, unless such treaties give rise to regulatory frameworks that can be enforced. There needs to be more than just a commitment from those parties who sign the treaty to comply with the directives. Member organizations may pay lip service to treaty directives and not implement them in practice. There needs to be a means of exposing those who break the rules and, ideally, a mechanism for applying sanctions if necessary.

Poor compliance with pollution agreements such as the 1972 London Dumping Convention and the 1973 MARPOL convention on pollution from ships does not lend credibility to the effectiveness of international legislation. Also, developing countries sometimes cannot comply with international accords because promised financial and technological support from industrialized countries does not materialize. Nevertheless, we would be in an even worse state of affairs without international agreements, and there are success stories. The 1987 Montreal Protocol on the Depletion of the Ozone Layer has resulted in a decline in ozone-destructive chlorofluorocarbon (CFC) emissions. Although the ozone hole over the Antarctic is still expanding, if further reductions in ozone-depleting emissions are instituted within the next decade, we should be turning the corner on the destruction of the ozone layer. By halting increases in UV-light penetration, international cooperation will have prevented many millions of potential cases of skin cancer and will have helped to protect land-based and aquatic ecosystems from rising mutation rates.

Another success is the 1991 accord for Antarctica (page 203) that has banned mining exploration and development for 50 years. Perhaps most important for the marine environment, apart from the 1992 U.N. Framework Convention on Climate Change, is the 1982 U.N. Convention on the Law of the Sea (UNCLOS). This entered into force in November 1994 (page 194). Since then, other provisions such as the Conservation and Management of Straddling Fish Stocks and Highly Migratory Fish Stocks have been negotiated within its framework. UNCLOS has the potential to be the landmark achievement, making possible the conservation of life across the global marine ecosystem.

Existing agreements and those in negotiation have the potential to protect the marine environment for the foreseeable future, providing that there is the political will to see that they are properly implemented and are translated into action. At the time of this writing, the global marine environment, however, continues to deteriorate and the specter of global warming looms large.

Antarctica: Exploitation, Conservation, and Management

Antarctica comprises a vast open ocean—the Antarctic Ocean—surrounding an ice-covered continent larger than the United States and Mexico put together. In winter, the seas freeze and the size of the continent effectively doubles. The Antarctic continent is the last unspoiled landmass of any great size remaining on Earth.

The Antarctic Ocean Ecosystem

Terrestrial plant and animal life on the continent is sparse. In contrast, the Antarctic Ocean is one of the most productive regions on Earth. It generates massive summer outbursts of marine phytoplankton, nurtured by nutrient-rich upwellings associated with the Antarctic convergence zone (page 13). This vast community of phytoplankton is, in turn, eaten by zooplankton, about half of which is krill. The shrimplike krill provide the basic food for five species of whale, three species of seal, 20 fish species, and the main support of 40 bird species, from penguins to albatrosses. The various predators feed on krill at different stages in the prey's life cycle, at different places, depths, and times of year so that competition between the predators is minimized, and exploitation of the resource is maximized.

Sensitivity to Pollution

The potential for environmental damage in Antarctica is high. In the cold environment, the processes of biological degradation operate slowly: crude oil,

if spilled, is likely to take years to degrade, rather than the few months it would take in warmer waters. The extraction and transportation of oil in the cold and violent waters of the Antarctic Ocean is hazardous at the best of times. An oil spill on ice would increase its capacity to absorb solar radiation, causing the ice to melt with potentially disastrous results. An oil spill in water would threaten many of the resident marine birds and mammals.

If the ozone hole in the atmosphere above Antarctica were to get substantially worse (page 197), this would cause damaging levels of ultraviolet radiation to penetrate the surface waters and harm the phytoplankton at the base of the Antarctic food web.

Scientific Importance

Antarctica holds special interest for scientists studying Earth's history and atmosphere. It was in the 1980s that British scientists working in Antarctica found the now infamous "ozone hole" in the atmosphere. The Antarctic ice itself provides a frozen record of Earth's recent history. Layers of Antarctic pack ice 2 miles (3.2 km) deep, compacted over the millennia, have provided scientists with a history of Earth's climate stretching back 160,000 years. By studying cores drilled out of the ice, scientists can detect temperature and chemical changes for the centuries and millenia. Trapped air bubbles record changes in the concentration of carbon dioxide in the atmosphere and show how levels have

fluctuated during millennia but have increased steadily within the last two centuries (page 78). Ice cores also reveal how radioactive fallout and atmospheric lead pollution have increased since 1945.

The reflected solar radiation from the Antarctic ice sheet and the descending cold waters of the Antarctic Ocean power the circulation of air and water across the world and thereby control the world's climate. With global warming (page 78), many scientists fear that the polar regions will warm up faster than tropical regions and that the driving forces that power the world's climate will shift, resulting in worldwide, unpredictable climatic change. The importance of Antarctica's role in monitoring and giving early warning of global change is now generally recognized.

Antarctica, as a preserve of unusual objects retained in pristine state, was the source of a meteorite of Martian origin. In the summer of 1996, some NASA scientists claimed that this rock might hold the first signs of extraterrestrial life in the shape of fossilized, microscopic life-forms.

Exploitation of Antarctic Resources

Since the British explorer James Cook reached Antarctica in the 1770s and reported the existence of its vast seal colonies, humans have returned as hunters. Sealers almost totally destroyed the Antarctic fur-seal colonies in the 1820s and then again in the 1870s. It has taken 80 years for the species to recover.

Whalers have killed an estimated 98 percent of the region's blue whales: the population has fallen from an estimated 250,000 at the beginning of the 20th century to about 500 in the early 1990s. Similarly, the populations of humpbacks and fin whales have fallen by 95 percent and 80 percent respectively. In 1972, the U.N. declared a total moratorium on the catching of all the larger whale species, and in 1994, the International Whaling Commission agreed to establish a whale sanctuary around Antarctica in which all commercial whaling is banned for 10 years.

The substantial reduction in the numbers of filter-feeding baleen whales (page 189) must have had a huge impact on the population of krill on which they fed. It has been estimated that before the whales were exploited, they alone consumed about 210 million tons (190 million t) of krill

An Adélie penguin is visited by ecotourists, Antarctic Peninsula, Antarctica (Gerry Ellis/ENP Images)

ANTARCTIC TREATY: SUMMARY OF MAIN PROVISIONS

Article I. Antarctica shall be used for peaceful purposes only. It is prohibited to establish military bases, carry out maneuvers, or test weapons within the area.

Article II. Freedom of scientific investigation and cooperation toward that end shall continue.

Article III. Scientific information and personnel shall be freely exchanged between the signatory states.

Article IV. The treaty does not recognize, dispute, or establish territorial claims. No new claim to territorial sovereignty may be asserted while the treaty is in force.

Article V. Nuclear explosions and the disposal of radioactive wastes are prohibited within Antarctica.

Article VI. The provisions of the treaty apply to the land area and ice shelves below 60°S latitude. The high seas are not included but are covered under international law.

Article VII. Each treaty state has the right to send observers to carry out inspections in Antarctica. Other treaty states must be notified of all expeditions and stations.

Article VIII. Observers under Article VII and scientific personnel under Article III are subject to the jurisdiction of their own state.

Article IX. The treaty states shall take measures to further the principles and objectives of the treaty, including the preservation and conservation of living resources.

Argentina, Australia, Belgium, Chile, France, Japan, New Zealand, Norway, South Africa, the United Kingdom, the United States and the USSR were the 12 original signatories to the 1959 treaty; it has since been signed by a further 28 states.

each year. With the absence of many baleen whales, there must now be a surplus of krill potentially available for exploitation. (This surplus may be more apparent than real because other predators have increased in numbers to take advantage of the krill abundance.) Krill fishing is being carried out by several nations, in particular Russia and Japan, and processing krill to produce animal feed is now an emerging Antarctic industry. Although the tonnage caught is relatively small—several hundred thousand metric tons a year—the effects of harvesting will need to be monitored carefully. Krill play such a central role in the Antarctic food web that uncontrolled exploitation could have disastrous repercussions for the entire Antarctic Ocean ecosystem.

Attention is also turning to Antarctic squid and fish stocks. At present, our knowledge of their biology and ecology is too partial to determine whether or not they could sustain long-term harvesting, but the history of arctic and subarctic fisheries suggests that fish stocks could support only moderate levels of exploitation. At present, just a few fish species are being caught, with Poland and Russia as the main operators. Some scientists estimate that the combined catch of krill, squid, and fish from Antarctic waters could be sustained at a level equal to the present annual world fish catch.

Iron ore and coal deposits have been found in the mountain ranges of the Antarctic continent, and in 1972, the deep-drilling ship, *Glomar Challenger,* found deposits of natural gas in the sediments beneath the Ross Sea. Offshore oil also exists around the narrow continental shelf. At present, the huge economic costs of extracting minerals, oil, or gas in such an inhospitable and icebound environment prevent their commercial exploitation, but with innovations in technology, coupled with the increasing scarcity and rising price of mineral and fossil-fuel reserves, the situation may not remain that way for too long.

Future of Antarctica

By the early 1950s, seven countries had claimed various parts of Antarctica, with some of these areas overlapping and thus subject to border disputes. Recognition of Antarctica's global importance and of the need for greater understanding of its role reached a turning point in 1957–58, International Geophysical Year. Twelve nations, among them the seven territory-claiming ones, set up scientific research stations on the continent. The cooperative scientific effort proved so fruitful that it gave rise to the Antarctic Treaty that the 12 nations signed on

Research refuse on Danco Island,
Antarctic Peninsula
(Gerry Ellis/ENP Images)

December 1, 1959. The treaty nations have agreed to keep the Antarctic continent demilitarized, nuclear free, and devoted to research. By the early 1990s, the treaty was being supported by 26 voting member nations. The Convention on the Conservation of Antarctic Marine Living Resources (CCAMLR) came into force in April 1982 and established a decision-making commission and an advisory scientific body. It is primarily concerned with controlling Antarctic fisheries, particularly krill, to ensure that catch levels do not threaten krill populations or impede the recovery of the baleen whale populations. In October 1991, the Environmental Protocol was signed, a treaty that bans mining and drilling for the subsequent 50 years; any move to lift the ban would now require approval by 75 percent of the consultative nations of the Antarctic Treaty Body. The protocol, supplemented by later annexes, imposes strict environmental controls on research bases and expeditions. Essentially, all waste is required to be taken off-continent, and expeditions are to leave the environment, as far as possible, in the same state as when they arrived.

There is little room for complacency. Treaty violations do occur—illegal whaling, for example—and some of the treaty signatories have been responsible for serious pollution incidents. In the past, abandoned research camps have been left as giant garbage dumps, and active camps have polluted their surroundings. New airstrips have destroyed bird nesting sites, while noise pollution from planes and helicopters continues to disturb breeding populations of seal and birds. Many nongovernmental bodies are pressing for the Antarctic continent and ocean to be designated as a "world park" protected by stronger environmental legislation and tougher means of enforcement. There is still much work to be done to ensure that the treaty signatories clean up their act.

Oceans—Their Future?

Arguably, the biggest problem facing humanity as we enter the 21st century is how we can reconcile human population increase with economic growth and yet still maintain a healthy global environment. If current trends continue, then something will have to give—and sooner rather than later. Even the most optimistic population forecasts suggest that the world's human population will have almost doubled (to about 10 billion) by the year 2100. The greatest successes in reducing birthrates seem to occur where educational provision is increased, particularly for women.

Some leading marine biologists, speaking off the record, strongly believe that one or more catastrophic environmental events—most likely involving millions of people—would happen by the end of the 21st century and probably before 2050 if we simply sat back and failed to act *before* these events occurred. High on the list were dramatic climatic changes and rises in sea level as a result of global warming.

Unfortunately, experts have a poor track record at predicting the major events that affect our lives. Who predicted the fall of the Berlin Wall, the collapse of the Soviet Union, or the recent crash in Asian economies? But when hundreds of well-respected scientists from many different disciplines say that we should beware of global warming, then we should sit up, listen and, if necessary, act.

What can we do? As individuals we do have power. As consumers, we can demand that products are obtained in ways that minimize destructive effects on the environment. In industrialized countries, there are many examples of successful campaigns that have altered consumers' buying habits and have forced companies to change their commodities or the way they produce them. As voters, we can elect politicians who take environmental issues seriously, who are willing to educate themselves about the most serious social and environmental problems facing us today, and who will act with integrity and resolve. At home and when traveling, we can make choices that minimize energy consumption, reduce waste, and cut down on pollution. In our workplace, we can encourage practices that do the same. We can set an example. We can join organizations that have a commitment to social development and environmental protection on an international as well as a local scale. Above all, we can keep ourselves informed.

Many multinational companies involved in the energy and transport industries are quietly kicking and screaming as they enter the 21st century, doing all they can to slow the introduction of far-reaching legislation to reduce greenhouse-gas emissions.

Beachcomber at sunset, southern California (Gerry Ellis/ENP Images)

Even these organizations are gradually, grudgingly, realizing that our environment cannot continue to absorb emissions from the burning of fossil fuels at the rate it has. Current means of energy production and consumption may need to be phased out *well before* fossil-fuel reserves reach low levels.

In international political circles, there is a growing commitment to the concept of sustainable development—the notion that development that improves the lives of people today must not deplete natural resources nor increase environmental problems for future generations. However, this idea, while being enshrined in much international legislation, has barely begun to be put into practice in a practical, grass-roots way over much of the world. But change is happening.

Above all, what is needed is a change of heart and mind. In the industrialized world and now in the developing world, most people are conditioned to expect economic growth, which is translated into being able to buy more, better, and newer products. Indeed, most countries are committed to this form of economic growth. If we are to con-

tinue living on an increasingly overcrowded planet, then we will have to change our expectations and understanding of what we mean by development. Increase in the quality of our lives will need to occur alongside a decrease in the amount we need to buy, consume, and waste. Indeed, this will need to happen if we are to maintain the quality of our environment. Our creative efforts would be better channeled into finding ways of living in harmony with our surroundings, in a sustainable way, rather than pillaging the environment for short-term, short-sighted gain.

Many people in the world—particularly the industrialized world—have lost their emotional connection with nature. Perhaps this is the greatest challenge for the 21st century: how we can use new technologies to increase, not decrease, our connection with the natural world, to bring us closer to nature, not alienate us from it.

Appendixes

METRIC UNITS OF MEASUREMENT

Length
1 micron (μ) = 0.001 millimeter (mm)
1 millimeter = 1,000 microns =
   0.001 meter (m)
1 centimeter = 10 millimeters =
   0.01 meter
1 meter = 100 centimeters =
   0.001 kilometer (km)
1 kilometer = 1,000 meters

Area
1 square meter (sq m) =
   10,000 square centimeters (sq cm)
1 hectare (ha) =
   10,000 square meters
1 square kilometer (sq km) =
   100 hectares =
   1,000,000 square meters

Volume
1 milliliter (ml) =
   1 cubic centimeter (cc) =
   0.001 liter
1 liter (l) = 1,000 milliliters =
   1,000 cubic centimeters
1 cubic meter = 1,000 liters

Weight/Mass
1 milligram (mg) = 0.001 gram
1 gram = 1,000 milligrams =
   0.001 kilogram
1 kilogram (kg) = 1,000 grams
1 metric ton = 1,000 kilograms

Temperature
Freezing point of water =
   0 degrees Celsius (°C)
Boiling point of water =
   100 degrees Celsius

Speed/Velocity
1 kilometer per hour =
   27.8 centimeters per second

CONVERSIONS

Length
1 centimeter = 0.394 inches
1 meter = 39.37 inches = 3.28 feet
1 kilometer = 0.62 mile = 3,280 feet
1 inch = 2.54 centimeters
1 foot = 0.3048 meter
1 fathom = 6 feet = 1.83 meters
1 mile = 5,280 feet = 1.61 kilometers
1 mile = 0.87 nautical miles
1 nautical mile = 6,075 feet = 1.85 kilometers
1 nautical mile = 1.15 miles

Area
1 square meter = 10.8 square feet
1 hectare = 2.47 acres
1 square kilometer = 0.386 square miles = 247.1 acres
1 square foot = 0.279 square meter
1 square mile = 2.59 square kilometers
1 acre = 43,560 square feet = 4,047 square meters = 0.40 hectares

Volume
1 cubic meter = 35.31 cubic feet
1 cubic kilometer = 0.240 cubic mile
1 cubic foot = 0.028 cubic meter = 28.32 liters
1 cubic mile = 4.17 cubic kilometers

Liquid Volume
1 liter = 0.264 U.S. gallon = 0.220 imperial gallon
1 cubic meter = 264 U.S. gallons = 220 imperial gallons
1 U.S. gallon = 3.78 liters
1 imperial gallon = 4.54 liters

Weight/Mass
1 kilogram = 2.20 pounds
1 metric ton = 2.205 pounds
1 lb = 0.454 kilogram
1 ton (US) = 2,000 pounds = 909 kilograms
1 ton (imperial) = 2,240 pounds = 1,016 kilograms

Temperature
From degrees Celsius (°C) to degrees Fahrenheit (°F):
°F = (1.8 x °C) + 32
From degrees Fahrenheit (°F) to degrees Celsius (°C):
°C = (°F − 32)/1.8

Speed/Velocity
1 mile per hour = 0.87 nautical mile per hour = 1.61 kilometers per hour
1 knot (kn) = 1 nautical mile per hour = 1.15 miles per hour = 1.85 kilometers per hour

Latitude and Longitude

LATITUDE

Latitude is the distance north or south of the equator and is measured in degrees and minutes. The vertical distance from the equator to the North or South Pole is 90°. The equator thus lies at 0° N or 0° S, while the North Pole occupies 90° N and the South Pole 90° S. Each degree of latitude is subdivided into 60 minutes (60').

A series of notional grid lines encircles Earth and connects all the points that are equidistant from the nearest pole. These grid lines are parallels of latitude. The tropic of Capricorn is depicted by a parallel of latitude at 23°28' S, and the tropic of Cancer at 23°28' N. Between the two are the tropical latitudes.

LONGITUDE

Longitude is the distance east or west of the Prime Meridian, taken to be the Greenwich Meridian. Meridians of longitude are lines running north-south from pole to pole that depict points of equal angular distance from the Prime Meridian. Going westward from the Prime Meridian (0°), longitude increases until, at the opposite side of the globe and in the Pacific Ocean, the 180° meridian is reached. Going westward in this manner, from the 0° to 180°, the Western Hemisphere is traversed. Similarly, going eastward from the Prime Meridian (0°) to the 180° meridian, the observer is traversing the Eastern Hemisphere.

Longitude and time are directly related since Earth rotates once on its axis every 24 hours. Earth spins through 360° in 24 hours, or 15° in one hour. At sea, longitude can be determined by measuring the difference between local time (as measured by local noon when the sun is highest in the sky) and Greenwich mean time (time at the Prime Meridian). For the purposes of establishing longitude, if measured local time is found to be two hours ahead of Greenwich mean time, then the current location lies on the 30° E meridian. If local time is two hours behind Greenwich mean time, the observer is located on the 30° W meridian.

Following the longitude-time relationship through to its logical conclusion, there must be a place on Earth where the "new day" begins. For convenience, this is taken to be the 180° meridian (or a line near it), which lies in the Pacific Ocean. Adopting this as the International Date Line is no accident. Being located in the Pacific, it circumvents the problem of adjacent cities being one day apart in time. This remedy also explains, in part, why the Greenwich Meridian (on the opposite side of the globe) has been adopted as the Prime Meridian.

The precise position of any place on Earth can be denoted by its latitude and longitude. New York City in the United States, for example, lies at 40°43' N 74°00' W and Luanda, Angola, at 8°45' S 13°18' E.

Selected Reading

General

Couper, Alastair, ed. *Atlas and Encyclopedia of the Sea.* 2nd ed. London: Times Books Ltd., 1989. A tour de force. As a comprehensive compendium of marine matters, this award-winning atlas has never been equaled.

Doubilet, David. *Light in the Sea.* Köln, Germany: Evergreen, 1995. A stunning collection of photographs that show just how magical the undersea world can be.

Earle, Sylvia A. *Sea Change: A Message of the Oceans.* New York: G.P. Putnam's & Sons, 1995. A passionate and authoritative plea for the defense of our oceans. A highly readable blend of science and adventure.

Jackson, Jack. *Top Dive Sites of the World.* London: New Holland, 1997. Highly illustrated. The title says it all.

Kennish, Michael J. *Practical Handbook of Marine Science.* Grand Rapids, Mich.: CRC Publications, 1994. A technical compendium of facts and figures about most aspects of marine science.

Pirie, R. Gordon, ed. *Oceanography: Contemporary Readings in Ocean Sciences.* 3rd ed. New York: Oxford University Press, 1996. A broad-ranging U.S. anthology, from great white sharks to oil pollution.

Sear, Douglas A. *An Introduction to Ocean Sciences.* Belmont, Calif.: Wadsworth, 1998. An up-to-date and accessible guide.

Summerhayes, C. P., and S. A. Thorpe, eds. *Oceanography: An Illustrated Guide.* London: Manson, 1996. A superb, highly illustrated compilation with individual chapters by specialists in the field.

Part 1. Geography of the Oceans

Couper, Alastair, ed. *Atlas and Encyclopedia of the Sea.* 2nd ed. London: Times Books Ltd, 1989. The definitive work, although now rather dated.

Pernetta, John, ed. *Philip's Atlas of the Oceans.* London: Reed Consumer Books Ltd, 1994. Good coverage—in text, maps, and illustrations—of the oceans and major seas of the world.

Part 2. Geology of the Oceans

Libes, Susan M. *An Introduction to Marine Biogeochemistry.* New York: John Wiley & Sons, 1992. An authoritative yet very readable guide to chemical and geological interactions in the sea.

Montgomery, Carla W. *Environmental Geology.* 4th ed. Dubuque, Iowa: Wm. C. Brown, 1995. Geology considered within the wider context of social, industrial, and environmental issues.

Thurman, Harold V. *Essentials of Oceanography.* 5th ed. Englewood Cliffs, N.J.: Prentice-Hall, 1996. Includes sections which cover key aspects of marine geology.

Part 3. Chemistry of the Oceans

Andrews, J. E., P. Brimblecombe, T. D. Jickells, and P. S. Liss. *An Introduction to Environmental Chemistry.* Oxford: Blackwell, 1996. Contains useful sections on marine chemistry set within the context of environmental chemistry as a whole.

Libes, Susan M. *An Introduction to Marine Biogeochemistry.* New York: John Wiley & Sons, 1992. An authoritative yet very readable guide to marine chemistry set within the wider context of geological and biological phenomena.

Part 4. Atmosphere and the Oceans

Intergovernmental Panel on Climate Change. *Climate Change 1995: The Science of Climate Change, and Impacts, Adaptations and Mitigation of Climate Change.* London: Cambridge University Press, 1996. Two volumes containing the findings and predictions of hundreds of scientists from around the world. Authoritative yet remarkably clear reading, even for nonspecialists. Highly recommended for the mid-1990s state-of-the-art on climate change.

Thurman, Harold V. *Essentials of Oceanography.* 5th ed. Englewood Cliffs, N.J.: Prentice-Hall, 1996. Strong on ocean-atmosphere interactions, particularly ocean currents.

Part 5. Biology of the Oceans

Castro, Peter, and Michael E. Huber. *Marine Biology.* Dubuque, Iowa: Wm. C. Brown Publishers, 1997. An accessible introduction to marine biology with a broad overview and plenty of study exercises for student use.

Köhler, Annemarie, and Danja Köhler. *The Underwater Explorer.* London: New Holland, 1997. Highly illustrated. Explains what you can expect to see if you dive underwater.

Lalli, Carol M., and Timothy R. Parsons. *Biological Oceanography.* 2nd ed. Oxford: Butterworth-Heinemann, 1997. One of the few texts that explains biological phenomena within the context of physical and chemical oceanographic processes in a clear manner, with the minimum of mathematics.

Paxton, John R., and William N. Eschmeyer. *Encyclopedia of Fishes.* San Diego, Calif.: Academic Press, 1994. Comprehensive and beautifully illustrated with fascinating accounts by experts.

Sumich, James L. *An Introduction to the Biology of Marine Life.* 6th ed. Dubuque, Iowa: Wm. C. Brown Publishers, 1996. An accessible guide.

Part 6. History and the Oceans

Coote, John, ed. *The Faber Book of the Sea.* London: Faber & Faber, 1989. A compilation of extracts from all kinds of stories about the sea, both fiction and nonfiction, with strong emphasis on Western authors.

Kemp, Peter, ed. *The Oxford Companion to Ships and the Sea.* Oxford: Oxford University Press, 1976. A treasure trove of information about nautical matters through history.

Sanderson, Michael. *Sea Battles.* London: David & Charles, London, 1975. Fascinating accounts of sea battles, from ancient times to World War II.

Stanford, Michael. *A Companion to the Study of History.* Oxford: Blackwell, 1994. A clear overview of the methods and interpretative approaches and ideas used in the study of history.

Sharpe, Richard, ed. *Jane's Fighting Ships 1996–7.* Surrey, England: Jane's Information Group, 1996. Look for the latest edition for everything you wanted to know about modern fighting ships.

Part 7. Exploration of the Oceans

Burton, Rosemary, Richard Cavendish, and Bernard Stonehouse. *Journeys of the Great Explorers.* New York: Facts On File, 1992. Illustrated accounts of the journeys of explorers—both famous and obscure—from ancient times to the 1980s.

Sobel, Dava. *Longitude.* London: Fourth Estate, 1996. History, science, and technology come to life. An award-winning account of John Harrison's trials and tribulations in designing and constructing the world's first chronometer.

Van Dover, Cindy Lee. *The Octopus's Garden.* Reading, Mass.: Addison Wesley, 1997. A vivid, lyrical account of recent explorations to the ocean floor.

Part 8. Economic Resources of the Oceans

Pirie, R. Gordon, ed. *Oceanography: Contemporary Readings in Ocean Sciences.* 3rd ed. New York: Oxford University Press, 1996. Contains several chapters on the U.S. perspective.

Summerhayes, C. P., and S. A. Thorpe, eds. *Oceanography: An Illustrated Guide.* London: Manson, 1996. Contains several chapters with a broad international overview.

Weber, Michael L., and Judith A. Gradwohl. *The Wealth of Oceans.* New York: W.W. Norton & Co, 1995. Potent essays on what we should be doing to manage the oceans to preserve our marine heritage.

Chapter 9. How Healthy Are the Oceans?

Clark, R. B. *Marine Pollution.* 4th ed. Oxford: Clarendon Press, 1997. A classic in its field.

Pickering, Kevin T., and Lewis A. Owen. *Global Environmental Issues.* 2nd ed. London: Routledge, 1997. A textbook with a wide-ranging compilation of data and discussion on environmental issues.

World Resources Institute. *World Resources 1996–97: A Guide to the Global Environment.* Oxford: Oxford University Press, 1996. Includes a section on marine biodiversity.

Part 10. Management of the Oceans

Agardy, Tundy Spring. *Marine Protected Areas and Ocean Conservation.* Austin, Texas: R.G. Landes, 1997. The state of the art on MPAs.

Bergsen, Helge Ole, et al., eds. *Green Globe Yearbook 1996.* Oxford: Oxford University Press, 1996. A who's who of IGOs and NGOs, plus scholarly essays on environmental matters.

Gibbons, Whit. *Keeping All the Pieces.* Washington, D. C.: Smithsonian Institution Press, 1993. A scholar and naturalist argues persuasively why we should be concerned about our environment and outlines the action that we can take.

Myers, Norman, ed. *The Gaia Atlas of Planet Management.* London: Gaia Books Ltd, 1994. A highly accessible, illustrated overview of Earth management.

Wakeford, Tom, and Martin Walters, eds. *Science for the Earth.* Sussex, England: John Wiley, 1995. The contributors assert why science must reform itself if it is to contribute to solving the social and environmental problems of the 21st century.

World Resources Institute. *World Resources 1994–95: A Guide to the Global Environment.* Oxford: Oxford University Press, 1994. Includes sections on marine fisheries and their management.

Journals and Magazines That Feature Articles on Marine Matters

Discover
National Geographic
National Wildlife
Natural History
New Scientist
Oceanus
Science
Scientific American
Sea Frontiers
Smithsonian

Web Sites

Web sites come and go. Here are some of the most useful ones as of September 1998:

American Association for the Advancement of Science (AAAS) www.aaas.org
Food and Agricultural Organization (FAO) . . . . www.fao.org
International Council for the Exploration of the Sea (ICES) .www.ices.inst.dk
IUCN—The World Conservation Union . . . . .www.iucn.org
NASA . . . . .www.nasa.gov
New Scientist magazine . . . . .www.newscientist.com
Science magazine . . . . .www.sciencemag.org
United Nations Development Program (UNDP) . . . . .www.undp.org
United Nations Environment Program (UNEP) . . . . .www.unep.org
World Metereological Organization (WMO) . . . . .www.wmo.ch
World-Wide Web Virtual Library: Oceans . . . . .www.mth.uea.ac.uk/ocean